The Encyclopedia of the Jewish Diaspora, Poland Series: Lwów Volume
(Lviv, Ukraine)

Translation of
Encyclopedia Shel Galuyot: Lwów

Original Book Edited by: Dr. N.M. Gelber

Originally published in Tel Aviv 1956

JewishGen
מרכז עולמי לגנאלוגיה יהודית
The Global Home for Jewish Genealogy

A Publication of JewishGen, INC
Edmond J. Safra Plaza, 36 Battery Place, New York, NY 10280
646.494.2972 | info@JewishGen.org | www.jewishgen.org

MUSEUM OF
JEWISH HERITAGE
A LIVING MEMORIAL
TO THE HOLOCAUST

The Encyclopedia of the Jewish Diaspora, Poland Series: Lwów Volume (Lviv, Ukraine)
Translation of *Encyclopedia Shel Galuyot: Lwów*

Copyright © 2025 by JewishGen, INC All rights reserved.
First Printing: march 2025, Adar 5785
Editor of Original Yizkor Book: Dr. N.M. Gelber
Translator and Project Coordinator: Myra Yael Ecker, PhD.
Cover Design: Irv Osterer
Layout: Jonathan Wind
Name Indexing: Stefanie Holzman

JewishGen INC. is not responsible for inaccuracies or omissions in the original work and makes no representations regarding the accuracy of this translation. Digital images of the original book's contents can be seen online at the New York Public Library website or the Yiddish Book Center website.

Printed in the United States of America by Lightning Source, Inc.

Library of Congress Control Number (LCCN): 2023931443

ISBN: 978-1-954176-71-3 (hard cover: 454 pages, alk. paper)

About JewishGen.org

JewishGen, is a Genealogical Research Division of the Museum of Jewish Heritage - A Living Memorial to the Holocaust, serves as the global home for Jewish genealogy.

Featuring unparalleled access to 30+ million records, it offers unique search tools, along with opportunities for researchers to connect with others who share similar interests. Award winning resources such as the Family Finder, Discussion Groups, and ViewMate, are relied upon by thousands each day.

In addition, JewishGen's extensive informational, educational and historical offerings, such as the Jewish Communities Database, Yizkor Book translations, InfoFiles, Family Tree of the Jewish People, and KehilaLinks, provide critical insights, first-hand accounts, and context about Jewish communal and familial life throughout the world.

Offered as a free resource, JewishGen.org has facilitated thousands of family connections and success stories, and is currently engaged in an intensive expansion effort that will bring many more records, tools, and resources to its collections.

Please visit https://www.jewishgen.org/ to learn more.

Vice President for JewishGen: Avraham Groll

About the JewishGen Yizkor Book Project

Yizkor Books (Memorial Books) were traditionally written to memorialize the names of departed family and martyrs during holiday services in the synagogue (a practice that still exists in many synagogues today).

Over the centuries, as a result of countless persecutions and horrific atrocities committed against the Jews, Yizkor Books (Sefer Zikaron in Hebrew) were expanded to include more historical information, such as biographical sketches of famous personalities and descriptions of daily town life.

Following the Holocaust, the idea of remembrance and learning took on an urgent and crucial importance. Survivors of the Holocaust sought out other surviving residents of their former towns to memorialize and document the names and way of life of those who were ruthlessly murdered by the Nazis. These remembrances were documented in Yizkor Books, hundreds of which were published in the first decades after the Holocaust.

Most of these books were published privately, or through *Landsmanshaftn* (social organizations comprised of members originating from the same European town or region) that still existed, and were often distributed free of charge. The languages used to document these crucial histories and links to our past were mostly Yiddish and Hebrew. JewishGen has undertaken the sacred responsibility of translating these books into English so that the culture and way of life of these communities will be preserved and transmitted to future generations.

In 1986, a group of farsighted JewishGenners started a project to pool their efforts together in groups based upon their ancestors' towns and donate funds to translate the Yizkor books of their ancestral towns into English. As the translated material became available, it was made accessible for free at https://www.JewishGen.org/Yizkor . Hardcover copies can be purchased by visiting https://www.jewishgen.org/Yizkor/ybip.html (see section below).

It is our hope that the translation of these books into English (and other languages) will assist the countless Jewish family researchers who are so desperately seeking to forge a connection with their heritage.

Director of JewishGen Yizkor Book Project: Lance Ackerfeld

About JewishGen Press

JewishGen Press (formerly the Yizkor Books-in-Print Project) is the publishing division of JewishGen.org, and provides a venue for the publication of non-fiction books pertaining to Jewish genealogy, history, culture, and heritage.

In addition to the Yizkor Book category, publications in the Other Non-Fiction category include Shoah memoirs and research, genealogical research, collections of genealogical and historical materials, biographies, diaries and letters, studies of Jewish experience and cultural life in the past, academic theses, and other books of interest to the Jewish community.

Please visit https://www.jewishgen.org/Yizkor/ybip.html to learn more.

Director of JewishGen Press: Joel Alpert
Managing Editor – Peter Harris
Publications Manager - Susan Rosin

Notes to the Reader

The images in the original book were reproduced from photographs from the time of the first edition. These reproductions were already of poor quality, being pre-war and at least 60 or more years old. As a result, the images in the book are the best achievable.
A reader can view the original scans of the book on the websites listed below.

The original book can be seen online at the Yiddish Book Center website:

https://www.yiddishbookcenter.org/collections/yizkor-books/yzk-nybc313875/gelber-n-m-levov

OR

at the New York Public Library Digital Collections website:

https://digitalcollections.nypl.org/items/615cf960-6561-0133-95a3-00505686d14e#/?uuid=61eb1e40-6561-0133-d0c4-00505686d14e

To obtain a list of Shoah victims from **Lwów** (Lviv, Ukraine), the reader should access the Yad Vashem web site listed below; one can also search for specific family names using family name option. These lists are continually updated by Yad Vashem, so it is worthwhile to search these lists periodically.
There is more valuable information (including the Pages of Testimony, etc.) available on this website: https://yvng.yadvashem.org/

For additional information, please visit: https://kehilalinks.jewishgen.org/Lviv/Home.html

A list of all books available from JewishGen Press along with prices is available at:
https://www.jewishgen.org/Yizkor/ybip.html

Photo Credits

Cover Design by: Irv Osterer

Front Cover:

Postcard of the Temple Synagogue in Lwów, Poland c.1917

Back Cover:

Lithograph— Interior of the Tempel Synagogue in Lviv, Poland. Piotr Piller Publishing House, Lemberg, 1846.
https://commons.wikimedia.org/wiki/File:Lemberg,Temple_Synagogue.jpg

Geopolitical Information

Lviv, Ukraine is located at 49°50' N 24°00' E 292 miles W of Kyyiv

	Town	District	Province	Country
Before WWI (c. 1900):	Lemberg	Lwów	Galicia	Austrian Empire
Between the wars (c. 1930):	Lwów	Lwów	Lwów	Poland
After WWII (c. 1950):	L'vov			Soviet Union
Today (c. 2000):	L'viv			Ukraine

Alternate Names for the Town:

L'viv [Ukr], Lwów [Pol], Lemberg [Ger], Lemberik [Yid], L'vov [Rus], Leopol [Lat]

Nearby Jewish Communities:

Znesinnya 3 miles ENE

Vynnyky 5 miles ESE

Navariya 6 miles SSW

Pidbirtsi 7 miles E

Kamianopil 8 miles ENE

Podliski Malyye 9 miles NE

Pykulovychi 10 miles ENE

Kulykiv 11 miles NNE

Borshchovychi 12 miles E

Zvenyhorod 13 miles ESE

Ivano-Frankove 13 miles WNW

Kukeziv 14 miles ENE

Velikiy Lyuben 14 miles WSW

Artasiv 14 miles NNE

Shchyrets 14 miles SSW

Novyy Yarychiv 15 miles ENE

Zhovtantsi 15 miles NE

Horodok 16 miles WSW

Zhovkva 16 miles N

Mykolayiv 16 miles ESE

Hlynsk 17 miles NNW

Didyliv 18 miles ENE

Bobrka 19 miles SE

Komarno 19 miles SW

Vybranivka 22 miles SSE

Mykolayiv 22 miles S

Batyatychi 22 miles NNE

Hlyniany 23 miles E

Svirzh 23 miles ESE

Maheriv 23 miles NNW

Kamyanka Buzka 24 miles NE

Lyubelya 25 miles N

Rozdil 26 miles S

Rudky 26 miles WSW

Peremyshlyany 27 miles ESE

Berezdivtsi 27 miles SSE

Sokolya 27 miles NE

Novi Strilyshcha 28 miles SE

Yavoriv 28 miles WNW

Velyki Mosty 28 miles NNE

Sudova Vyshnya 28 miles W

Vul'ka-Mazovetskaya 29 miles NNW

Busk 30 miles ENE

Medenychi 30 miles SSW

Jewish Population: 44,000 in 1900

Table of Contents

IV. The Destruction and the Holocaust

The Encyclopaedia of the Jewish Diaspora, Poland Series: Lwów Volume (Lviv, Ukraine)

49°50' / 24°00'

Translation of
Encycolpedia Shel Galuyot: Lwów

Edited by Dr. N.M. Gelber

Published in Tel Aviv: 1956

This is a translation from: *Encycolpedia Shel Galuyot: Lwów*; Encyclopaedia of the Jewish Diaspora, A memorial library of countries and communities, Poland Series: Lwów Volume: Part I, Edited by Dr. N.M. Gelber, Published by the Encyclopaedia of the Jewish Diaspora, Jerusalem - Tel Aviv: 1956

Note: The original book can be seen online at the NY Public Library site: Lviv

אנציקלופדיה
של גלויות

כרך רביעי

ל ב ו ב

(חלק א')

העורך: ד"ר נ. מ. גלבר

הוצאת חברת "אנציקלופדיה של גלויות" בע"מ
ירושלים - תל אביב

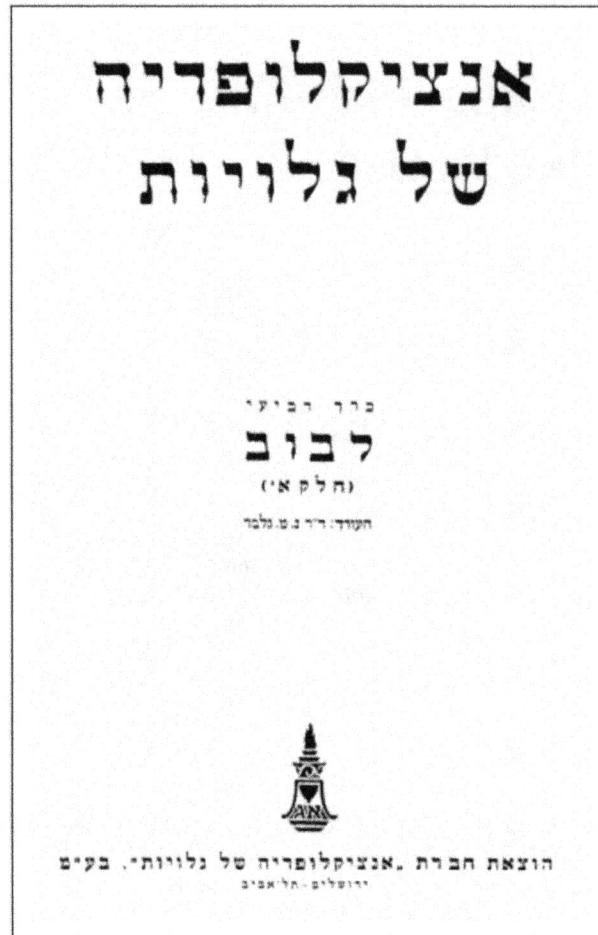

Translator's Note*:*

When I undertook the translation of this volume of Yizkor Book, I did so both in order to find out about the history of the Jews of Lwów and in memory of Lwów's Jews who found their end at the hands of the barbaric German Nazis and their indigenous sympathisers during WWII. In memory of generations of Jews whose past existence in the place was wiped out by destroying historical records and flattening historic Jewish cemeteries. In memory of those members of my paternal family who remained in Lwów when the Nazis invaded, in particular in memory of my grandmother, Antonina Ecker *bat* Nuchim Reiss.

Ever since the Molotov-Ribbentrop, German-Soviet Nonaggression Pact of the 23rd August 1939, Lwów, or Lemberg, the capital of Galicia which had been part of Poland, became part of the Soviet Union, but today, as part of western Ukraine, it is known as Lviv. Nevertheless, throughout this translation I tried to keep the name of towns, districts and individuals as they were known and spelt during the period when Polish was the spoken language, a language in which the major historical research into the history of the Jews in the area was published.

During my translation of this work I received assistance in clarifying some names and expressions, and I should like to extend my thanks to:

    Wojciech Janik, librarian at the School of Slavonic and East European Studies, London.
    Erla Zimmer, librarian at the London School of Jewish Studies, London.
    Librarians at the Biblioteka Narodowa, Warsaw.

The anomalies which occur regarding some footnotes were transferred from the original text.

Throughout this translation the comments in square brackets were added by myself.

Myra Yael Ecker PhD.
Feb. 2023

[Pages 21-22]

I

History of the Jews of Lwów

By Dr. N. M. Gelber [Nathan Michael Gelber (1891–1966)]
Chapter 1: The Jewish Settlement – its Beginnings
Translated by Myra Yael Ecker
Edited by Yocheved Klausner

Condition of the Jews in the days of Casimir the Great [Kazimierz III Wielki].The legal status of the community, in town and in its surroundings. Role of the Jews in transit trade, in the days of Jagiełło [Władysław Jagiełło]. Wolczko and his business. The lessee Natko. Jewish occupations: Leases. Trade. Finance. Crusaders' attack on the Jews of Lwów. The struggle with the townspeople in the years 1488–1528. The accord between the Jews and the townspeople. The role of Josef ben–Schachna. Trade relations with Turkey.

When and whence came the Jews to Lwów? This is one of the most interesting problems in the history of the Jews in Lesser Poland which was formerly known as "Red–Reissen" [or "Red–Ruthenia"].

By the tenth century Jews had already arrived from the Byzantine Empire and Khazaria — they were the trade intermediaries between the East and West on the route: Halicz [Halych]—Kiev—the Black Sea. In the towns of Reissen,[1] Jews had lived long before the arrival of the German and Polish settlers. At the time, apart from the Ruthenians and the Tatars in Lwów, Jews also enjoyed some rights under the rule of the Reissen Princes. Together with the Jews, Karaites also settled in Lwów, and their synagogue stood close to where later the town's synagogue (*Städtische Schul*) was built. The Karaite cemetery was located not far from the Krakówite Quarter.[2] The Jews lived at the south–western edge of the city wall, in the direction of Żółkiewska–Rynek Street, in a number of small houses with adjacent stores, stables and silos. After the new town was constructed in the middle of the 14th century, the old town turned into a suburb. In the new town – apart from the Jewish community of the old town and the Karaite community – a third Jewish community was also established. So that in the early period there were two Jewish settlements in Lwów: within the town lived Jews from western countries; and in the Krakówite Quarter (Krakówer Vorstadt) Jews who originated in Khazaria, in eastern countries, and Karaites. These two communities were distinct from one another in their customs and in the way of life of their inhabitants.

The Jews within the town were subject to the authority and jurisdiction of *Palatinus Russ* [Russian palatine], and acting as his deputies and representatives were the Prince's clerk together with the elected Jewish leaders.

The Jews in the borough adjacent to the prince's palace were subject to the jurisdiction of the Palace's judge. According to Reissen Law, they could appeal against the Palace–judge's decision before the deputy–Starosta, or the castellan of the castle.

The princes,[3] keen to see the town of Lwów and its trade develop, made great effort to attract Jewish residents who willingly settled there because they enjoyed there rights which improved their living conditions. The renown of Lwów as a trade centre had reached the communities of Western Europe, and even Spain, such that the author of the Catalan Atlas (*Carta Catalana*), Jehuda [or Jefudà] Cresques, entered Lwów on the map as "Ciutat de Leo," and noted that it was the intersection station on the trade route to the East.

With the development of settlements by Venetian and Genoese expatriates on the shores of the Black Sea, a new trade route, the Tatar route, was established to connect the settlements with the mother towns. That route carried goods to Lwów and from there, via Torun to the Baltic States, and via Kraków to Germany. Along a separate route which started in Transylvania, goods were transported via Lwów to the Black Sea and to Asia Minor.

[Pages 23-24]

Although the Jews were a decisive factor in that transit trade, they were faced with difficulty from the stiff competition of the Armenian and Greek traders who spared no means to concentrate all trade in their own hands. But their connections with the diaspora helped Jews to withstand their economic struggle.

In April 1340, after the death of the Ruthenian Prince Boleslaw "Mazow" [Masovia], internal riots broke out in the country and Reissen was conquered by the king of Poland, Casimir the Great (1333–1370).

There was hardly any change in the situation of the Jews. The Jews received a privilege from the King which did not diminish any of their rights. The sole change was the composition of the Jewish population. As is well known, during the reign of Casimir the stream of Jewish immigration from Germany, to whom the king offered greater privileges, increased. The wave of refugees reached also Lwów. By and by the new immigrants displaced the Khazar–Karaite community from its standing. Instead of the Slavic language, the German–Yiddish language now prevailed and the customs of Ashkenazi Jews took priority.

The privilege granted by Casimir the Great on the 17th June 1356, which awarded Lwów the right to adopt the Magdeburg Law, set no restrictions on its Jewish population.[4] That privilege incorporated the rule that in case the Jews preferred to forgo the use of the Magdeburg Law, they could settle their internal affairs, autonomously, and they were allowed to adopt their particular jurisprudence. They were completely removed from the jurisdiction of the municipality, and remained under the jurisdiction of the castellan ("burgrave") with the right to appeal to the Starosta, the King's representative in Reissen.

In the Town Bylaws (*Wilkierz*) of 1360 which King Casimir the Great approved at Kraków, and which incorporated Criminal and Inheritance Law, there was also no mention of the Jews.

In 1364, the general privilege granted to the Lwów Jews by Boleslawthe Pious in 1264 (*Statuta Judaeorum*), was further expanded. From then on the culture of Western Jewry was integrated, and in time the tradition of Eastern Jewry disappeared and was replaced by Ashkenazi traditions in daily life, in prayer and in community life.

After the fire of 1350, the town was rebuilt. From then on the Jews lived in two separate areas: in the urban quarter – Blacharska–Serbska Street – Boimów – adjacent to the town market (*Rynek*), and termed "Jewish Street [Ulica Zydowska]", where the prosperous Jews lived; while in the Krakówite quarter lived the poorer members of the community.

On the 25th April 1367, at the request of the Jews of Lwów, Kraków and Samdomiez, Casimir confirmed to all the Jews in Lesser Poland, the extended and complete general privilege ratified in the Statute of 1264.

After the death of Casimir in 1370, his heir of Poland, Ludwik [Louis] of Anjou, King of Hungary, handed the rule over Reissen to his relative Władysław Opolczyk [Ladislaus of Opole], an efficient administrator who included in his special interest the development of trade with the East. The life of the Jews remained unaltered. Their rights were confirmed and even expanded, and they were granted special discounts on trade with Hungary.

At the end of the 14th century and during the 15th, Lwów became a major crossing station between West and East. With the growth of the colonies of Venice and Genoa on the shores of the Black Sea, the trade route which connected these colonies with their mother towns, known as the Tatar Road, was widened. Produce and merchandise from the East continued to travel along that route via Lwów and Torun to the Baltic States, and via Kraków to Nuremberg. Along the Moldova route, merchandise passed also through Lwów on its way to Transylvania and farther on to the Black Sea and Asia Minor.

Jews played no small part in the trading procedures. Unlike the Germans who established the town's organisational administration, and the Greeks who were very familiar with the East, the advantage of the Jews was their connections with the diaspora communities in those regions.

In the Responsa of Rabbi Israel ben Pethahiah (MaHaraI Isserlein) 1390–1460), as mentioned in the book *Leket Yosher* published by his pupil Yosef Ben Moshe, of Hoechstadt,[5] the trade route from Austria to Hungary via Przemyśl—Lwów is discussed.

The Jews of Reissen, engaged in wholesale trade with countries in the East, established also trade partnerships. The partnership of three Jews from Lwów: Szloma [Shloma], Czewja (Chewia=Tzvi?) and Jakob[6] supplied the town of Lwów, in 1383, with a large cargo of peppercorns, valued at 150 grzywny.[7] There were also Jews who were mortgage lenders, who in their contracts imposed the right to sell the mortgaged property if the borrower did not redeem the loan on the set date.

After the death of Ludwik in 1382, his daughter Jadwiga who was crowned Queen of Poland in 1384, continued with the economic policies of Władysław. In 1387, she made Lwów the centre ("Emporium") for all the goods arriving from the East. In the privilege which she issued were ratified all the rights and privileges of the Ruthenian, Armenian, Saracen and Jewish inhabitants of the town.[8]

[Pages 25-26]

The Jews benefitted in particular when Lwów turned "Emporium" (centre for storing goods). According to the regulation all traders, be they Hungarian or Polish, who set out with their merchandise towards the East or to the land of the Tatars, were obliged to pass through Lwów; to remain there a fortnight; and to offer their goods for sale or exchange, solely to the Lwów traders. The remainder of their merchandise the traders could take with them only after paying customs fees. The 1379 trade regulations issued to Lwów, introduced no adverse changes for the Jews.

A Polish Jew, 1766

The situation of the Jews, who handled a large portion of the trade, improved considerably after the Turks had captured Constantinople in 1453. Now that Christian merchants feared to travel to lands held by the Turks, all trade with the East passed into the hands of Jewish merchants, the majority of whom were in Lwów. They traded in perfume, English and Flemish fabrics, and silk fabrics; and from Lwów they brought their merchandise also to Kraków, and through their connections with Christian traders, to the other Polish towns too. In the 15th and the 16th centuries extensive trade was also conducted with Breslau [Wrocław]; Jewish merchants from Lwów travelled there in person, or sent their agents. As for example the Jewish trader Szlome Judaeus who did business with the merchant Spitzmar, and others. Jewish wholesalers from Constantinople had agencies in Lwów and held the monopoly on all Turkish–Polish trade. One of them, Dawid, kept his agent Józef in Lwów, and supplied via him alum ("alaun") and kaftan (Turkish silk fabric), wine, perfume, lemons – in exchange for English fabrics. Another Turkish Jew, Moses, was agent of his brother Zachariah, and supplied goods from Turkey to Wallachia and to Suczawa [Suceava] via Lwów. Abraham, another Jewish wholesaler from Constantinople who traded in medicaments, brought to Lwów products in the value of 2300 Florins,[9] in a single year.

As a merchant in Lwów trading in Turkish produce, we know also of Szachna [Schachna],[10] a wholesaler in Turkish silk fabric.

The ties with the East renewed even the slave–trade via Lwów. Among the Jews one knows of the trader Izak Sokolowicz.[11]

During the reign of Władysław Jagiełło (1386–1434), the heads of the [Jewish] community of Lwów tried several times – the first time when he was at Lwów on the 30th September 1387 – to have him reconfirm the privileges which Casimir the Great had granted them in 1367, but Jagiełło refused. After his Christian conversion, and influenced by the Church, he served it faithfully.[12]

A Polish Jew, 1766

Nevertheless, all his financial affairs in Reissen, especially in Lwów, were handled by a Jewish agent, Wolczko Czolner of Lwów. Wolczko Czolner was a banker and took care of the King's accounts with the town of Lwów (he was probably from Drohobycz [Drohobych]). Apart from his financial business with members of the nobility and with high ranking officers, he also leased salt–mines in Drohobych, and road taxes. He also lent the King moneys required for the King's expenses, which he deducted

[Pages 27-28]

from the sum he owed the King for the lease as customs officer. After the Jewish tax–collector Gut, the King leased to him the tax collection at Chelm. In 1410 he underwrote the war against the Crusaders, which ended with a Polish victory at Grunwald (1410). Another Jew, Jacob Slomkowicz of Lutsk, who had business association with the Jewish banker Levko [Leib] of Kraków, lent a substantial sum to the municipality of Lwów in order to pay the levy enforced on it by the King for that war.[13] Wolczko lent money to members of the nobility as well, and was also interested in agricultural economics. As known, Jagiełło allotted large areas of Reissen to his citizens and his knights, so they would settle and found villages and towns. By an ordinance of the 17th June 1423, Jagiełło also gave Wolczko a large tract of land between the Dniester and the river Szczerzec [Shchyrka], for the purpose of colonisation; granted him all the privileges and the jurisdiction over the settlers; and appointed him head of the village of Werbiz.[14] The general purpose for giving away that tract of land was to secure income for the King. The King referred to him as "agent" (*officialis noster*); his official title was – "customs–officer". The King liked Wolczko and wanted him to convert to Christianity, but when he refused to give up his faith, he was made to surrender his authority over several villages to a Christian, since the clergy objected that a Jew should impose his authority over his Christian population. By and by Wolczko was obliged to sell the villages and to give up his agricultural activities.[15] From then on he concentrated solely on commerce and tax collecting, be it state or municipal taxes, and became the greatest wholesaler. He kept also fish–farms in the vicinity of Sambor, and just at a time when Lwów was an international centre for the trade in fish and caviar (fish–roe), he endeavoured to introduce into its market fish from the output of Poland. The fish was imported from the banks of the Black Sea and sent on to the rest of Europe. That trade was also in the hands of the Jews of Lwów. Wolczko owned also a house in the Jewish Quarter of Lwów, and died childless, most probably in 1441.

The Pillar-of-Shame ("Pillory") in the Synagogue

At the same period we know of another Jewish royal tax–collector in Lwów, named Natko. He was a cattle merchant. In 1452 King Casimir Jagiellon leased to him the customs of Lwów. In the title deed of the lease dated the 2nd July 1452, the King states that the integrity, loyalty and aptitudes of the Jew Natko of Lwów, who excels in agility, reached the King's knowledge through numerous recommendations in his favour and praise, to give to him, to "our Jew" (*Judeus noster*) the customs for two years for a leasing fee of one thousand Greczybni (Greczyni = 48 Groszy), in four instalments. In 1452 Natko leased also the salt mines in Drohobych, and the customs in Grodek.[16]

Among the Jews of Lwów we know also of the wholesaler Szachna [Schachna] and his son Joseph. Schachna had trade relations with Jewish traders from Constantinople and Italy, who had settled in Caffa [Kefe] (Crimea) and from there conducted wide spread trade with Poland. One of them, Caleb, arrived in 1442 in Lwów where he opened a branch. In documents he was entered as Kalp Judaeus da Caffa Aliance da Liopoli (Caleb, a Jew of Caffa, as well as of Lwów).[17]

Schachna, who was at the time the tax–collector at Lwów, granted him important easements in order that goods from the East, in the value of 2000 Gulden, be transported via the customs station at Lwów. In 1440 their relationship deteriorated after Schachna refused to pay Christophorus Guardia a debt redemption of 100 Gulden according to the guarantee of Caleb. The matter ended in a protracted trial. Caleb found himself a protector and supporter in Piotr Odrowąż[18] the Voivode [Wojewode; governor, 'warlord'] of Lwów, who also vouched for him; a sponsorship which earned the Voivode substantial profits.[19] Schachna managed a variety of businesses, he lent moneys to King Władysław Warneńczyk, to the Voivode of Podolia, to the castellan of Chelm, against the mortgage of houses and estates. The extent of his business forced him to accept loans from the Archbishop of Lwów. His wife Dina, and son Joseph worked together with him.

Among the professional lenders known to us during that period are Szloma, who gave more than twenty loans to the municipality of Lwów during 5 years (1382–1387); Izak who mostly lent moneys to members of the nobility and to Jewish customs–lessees, as well as to Armenian and Ruthenian merchants. Some Jewish women were also engaged in the business

[Pages 29-30]

of credit. In particular one knows of: Lena, Hannah, Miriam (1483), the wife of Jurden (1483–1487); her financial business was mostly with Armenians. A well known woman banker was Gerszonowa, the wife of Tuvye who was killed by the Christian Krzysztof Kolar.

During the reign of King Jagiellon Casimir [Jagiellończyk] after the unification of Poland and Lithuania, many Jews left Lwów for Lithuania. In 1388, his brother Witold [Vytautas] the Grand Prince of Lithuania, granted a charter to the Jews of Brisk and Troki, which repeated word for word the charter Casimir the Great had granted the Jews of Lwów 'Prout in Lamburge a Judaeis Habentur'.

During this period the Jews of Lwów enlarged the cemetery[20] and strengthened the basis of their community. In contrast with the intolerance towards the Jews which was widespread throughout Poland at the time, the situation in Lwów was tolerable and the Jews did not suffer any discriminations or religious persecution.

But the situation changed under the influence of the Catholic Church, as well as due to the envy of the Christian merchants most of whom were Germans who took a dim view of the concentration of trade, wholesale and retail, in the hands of Jews.

In 1412 the municipal council passed[21] an anti–Jewish resolution according to which it was forbidden for all mead–brewers to purchase effervescent mead from Jews; anyone violating that prohibition would be charged a fine of 60 Groszy on every barrel. But the anti–Jewish incitement had not yet reached such a level as to worsen the condition of the Jews in Lwów, while the anti–Jewish atmosphere felt in the rest of Poland was not found there. The heir of Władysław Jagiełło, his younger son Władysław [Ladislaus] III of Varna (1434–1444) confirmed in 1435 the trade rights of Lwów and forbade noblemen to charge on their estates, customs–fees, road–tax or bridges–tax from any Lwów trader, irrespective of their religion or nationality.

Even the anti–Jewish policy which his brother and heir Casimir IV Jagiellon [Kazimierz IV Jagiellończyk] (1444–1492) was forced to adopt under pressure from the Catholic Church – which engaged the zealot monk [John of] Capistrano, and which incited the masses against the Jews as in German towns at the time – did not affect the Jews of Lwów. Cardinal Zbigniew Oleśnicki, aware that the King required the Church's help in his fight against the Teutonic Knights, compelled the King, in the Nieszawa Statutes[22] of November 1454 (in which he had conceded to the nobles a significant share in government), to annul the rights he had granted to the Jews of Greater Poland on the 13th August 1453; and to the Jews of Lesser Poland on the 24th August 1453.[23]

Indeed, in 1455, on the death of Oleśnicki, the Jews were given back part of the privileges. Due to the Jews a conflict then broke out between the Starosta of the Krakówski suburb, and the City Council. The craftsmen in the suburb paid their taxes to the Privy Purse. The Christian craftsmen in town considered them tough competitors and demanded that the town limit their numbers. In 1458 the chief Starosta of Reissen, Andrzej Odrowąż (*ze Sprowy* [of Sprowa]), brought about an accord accepted also by the council, according to which within the confines of the Castle's jurisdiction only a number of Jewish tradesmen were allowed to reside: one tailor, two blacksmiths, two shoemakers, apart from the craftsmen shoemakers who had plied their trades in the past. Other tradesmen were prohibited from being admitted, so as not to damage the Christian craftsmen's guilds.

It was decided that also in the future the Starosta would not permit the Jews in his jurisdiction to engage in the trade and the serving of spirits.

The accord granted the municipality jurisdiction over the Armenians and other nationals, be they in the town or the suburb, except for those who had ever since resided at the foot of the Castle, as well as foreign Christian traders or Pagans. Only the Jews in the suburb remained under the judgment and protection of the royal jurisdiction. The Jews in town and in the suburb were entitled to make use of the mills of the town or those of the Starosta, except for the brewers of beer and bakers who were obliged to mill solely in the king's mills.

That accord stated, to the disadvantage of the Jews, that it was forbidden to hold the annual trade fairs within the bounds of the Starosta.

During the governance of the chief Starosta Andrzej Odrowąż, small and large towns in Reissen saw the spread of crusader gangs on their way East; crusaders who had been recruited in 1463 by Pope Pius II to assist Hungary against the Turks.

A Pole named Szczęsny [Szczensny][24] gathered some 12,000 men, mostly bandits and adventurers, who invaded villages and towns, robbed, looted and killed. Those residing on the outskirts of town fled from them into the town. After destroying its environs, the knights stood before the walls of Lwów and threatened to demolish the town if the Jews were not handed over to them. Fear engulfed the Jewish population but the town council declared that it did not intend to hand over the Jews; and it decided to fight. The gangs, realising the difficulty of a siege due to the shortage of food, opened negotiations which ended with the municipality handing over moneys and food. From Lwów the robbers set out towards Kraków.

[Pages 31-32]

The Kraków municipality did not even consider the possibility of protecting its Jews, and did nothing. When the town's masses together with the gangs attacked the Jewish Quarter, they killed some 30 people. Because of this act King Casimir Jagiellon punished the town.

Just at that time the number of Jews in Lwów grew as a stream of refugees escaped from Germany. Amongst them were also Jewish scholars and affluent Jews who acquired houses in the Jewish Quarter of the town.

At the end of the 15th century the Jews of Lwów expanded the trade contacts with Nurernberg, Breslau, Danzig, especially the trade in crops which was carried on the Vistula [Wisla] river. The Lwów townspeople feared that the increased Jewish trade would undermine their general existence and made every effort to halt it.

The principle that only a Christian, a Roman–Catholic Christian, could be the town's citizen, determined the attitude of the townspeople towards the Jews.

In time the economic activity of the Jews increased, in investments and in their trade connections with Jews outside Poland. And just at that moment – 1488 – started the conflict between the townspeople and the Jews of Lwów, and the municipality began to restrict the economic transactions of the Jews.

A similar process was evident also in Kraków, where on the 6th June 1485 the municipality successfully came to an agreement with representatives of the Jewish community. Accordingly the Jews committed themselves "voluntarily and not under duress" to forego the rights to trade and handle work within the Kraków inner town. They were only permitted to trade in pawned objects whose repayment date had expired, or in clothes sawn by Jewish tailors and furriers. That agreement encouraged the Lwów townspeople to aim for a similar arrangement.

In March 1488, Crown Prince Jan Olbracht [John I Albert] following the King's instruction, invited[25] the Jewish traders and the Lwów town advisors to appear at his castle in Belz, with the privileges, in order to reach a final settlement over the disputes. After hearing out both sides he decided in favour of the townspeople, who demanded that the Jews of Lwów should not enjoy greater privileges than the Jews of Kraków, Poznan and Sandomierz. He also restricted the trade by Jews to wholesale, and to the sale of pawned objects.

However, the Jews of Lwów did not give in as the Jews of Kraków had done; they did not want to give up their privileges. On the contrary, they fought against the decision by the crown prince which would have led to the decline in the trade by Jews. In 1490–1492 trials were held between the two sides – the townspeople and the Jews – and then, due to its anger at "the Jewish stubbornness", the municipality demanded that all trade by Jews be stopped.[26] The Jews invested their money mostly in mortgages, to a greater extent than before 1488, and therefore they did not give up their fight. On the 15th February 1493 they were granted by Olbracht a temporary (interim) agreement[27] which indeed restricted their trade, except for two types: cattle and textile. They were entitled to bring each year to the fairs at Przemyśl and Jaroslaw 1000 bulls and to sell there also 500 bales of textile. In Lwów they were allowed to sell fabric, wholesale. The townspeople were keen to keep for themselves the retail trade which commanded great profits, and to leave to the Jews the wholesale trade which was bound with dangers and with difficulties of import from eastern countries.

A short time after the 1494 accord a great fire broke out in the Jewish Quarter. Their houses were burnt down, and the neighbouring areas suffered also heavy damage. As a result, Jan Olbracht released the entire town from paying royal taxes for ten years, and those whose houses had burnt down – for 15 years. Probably the hardship moved the Council to grant the Jews the right to trade in wholesale textiles with no restrictions, as well as to sell suits in fairs outside Lwów. The Christian traders who meanwhile had lost the Eastern market due to the Turkish invasions, wanted to draw their earnings from the loss of the Jews, and to seize their business. In 1497 they succeeded in prohibiting the Jews of the suburb from trading in certain goods. And yet, when in the same year they submitted the town's privileges to King Jan Olbracht for his approval, he acknowledged the rights of the Jews and the Ruthenians who resided in the suburbs, to enjoy all the free trade privileges and sale of goods, since they bore the burden of municipal taxes. In 1498, the Moldovan hospodar Stephan, attacked Reissen and reached Lwów. The town's suburbs were destroyed, the town defended itself and Stephan was forced to retreat in May 1498. But the peace did not last long. In June 1498 the Tatars invaded again, and in the autumn the Turks reached the town, and although they did not succeed in conquering the town, the suburbs suffered extensive damage. Within the town, houses in the Jewish Quarter which stood adjacent to the town wall were demolished, for security reasons. In 1498–1500 the Jews of Lwów suffered gravely by the hands of the crusaders who passed through Reissen. Only this time the municipality of Lwów did nothing to protect them, as it had done in 1463. The situation worsened to the extent that King Jan Olbracht ordered the municipality to protect the Jews from attacks by the crusaders, but the municipality did not comply with the order.

After the death of Jan Olbracht (1492–1501),

[Pages 33-34]

the Jews of Lwów lobbied his heir Alexander (1501–1506) to annul the 1493 restrictions on their trading. Thanks to their connections at the King's Court, their efforts succeeded. In the meanwhile they renewed their trade connections with Constantinople. At the *Sejm* of Radom in 1503, the King exempted the Jews of Lwów from customs payments as well as road and bridge tolls, just as the rest of the population, on the basis that they cleared taxes like the Christians.

In 1506 the Jews of Lwów complained to the King over the delays and restrictions they faced in trade and work. They secured from him an order stating that they were entitled to trade freely at fairs and markets,[28] and to the easing of customs, road and bridge taxes, like the rest of Lwów's residents. The King reduced also their taxes from 200 Gulden to 100 Gulden for a period of four years.[29] Indeed, the townspeople did not agree with that revised status.

Sigismund I (1506–1548) confirmed in 1507 the privileges granted to the Jews of Lwów by his predecessors. Meanwhile the Christian merchants of Lwów made every effort to eliminate the Jewish trade. In 1512, following their advice, Michał Lanckoroński wilfully confiscated 1673 bulls from Jewish merchants. The Jews complained to the King who protected them. In 1519, he ensured parity of the Jews in the suburb and their brethren in town, with regard to their privileges of ease of commerce, and the exemption from taxes.

In 1515, after the Jews were granted by King Sigismund I the right to trade in fabrics, including retail during the fairs, and to bring 2000 bulls for sale rather than 1000, the townspeople increased their fight. The municipality of Lwów decided to grasp at any means to limit competition from the Jews; that led to efforts to create a union of the major towns in Poland. Towards the *Sejm* of Piotrkow in 1521 the Lwów municipality approached the municipalities of Lublin and Poznan with the suggestion to submit a joint complaint to the *Sejm* "In the matter of the freedom of the Jews, and our hardship. We hope that a joint action against the Jews will result in the loss of their rights." In a joint action of the townspeople of Lwów, Lublin and Poznan, they sent their spokesmen to the *Sejm* and waited for its decision.[30] Since the King's advisors supported their demands to suppress the trade by Jews, the King issued a regulation which annulled all privileges, which meant the destruction of the Jews of Lwów's trade. According to that Regulation:

> A.   Their trade is limited to four types: 1. Textiles, wholesale with no restriction, and retail only during fairs; 2. The sale of bulls – no more than 2000; 3. Wax; 4. Leather. All goods, other than textiles, they are allowed to sell only outside the fairs.

> B.   Jewish women are prohibited from peddling goods or selling baskets containing fabrics in cloth and silk, peppercorn, saffron and perfume.

> C.   Jews are prohibited from storing any stocks in their houses.

This Regulation applied to the Jews in Lwów, be they in town or the suburbs, as well as to foreign Jewish merchants who came to Lwów. The King charged the Lwów Starosta with ensuring that the Jews did not transgress the limits set in the regulation. The authorities were instructed to confiscate the goods destined to be sold in contravention of the regulation, to the benefit of the treasury.

Despite the severity of the regulation the Jews of Lwów were not shaken. On the contrary, they increased their efforts to have it annulled. On the eve of 1527,[31] they succeeded in obtaining a new regulation which permitted them unrestricted commerce. As a result they built houses in the town suburbs, ordered large quantities of goods and greatly expanded their commerce.

The Christian merchants set up a storm. They petitioned the King that the regulation contravened their own privileges, according to which Jews and Armenians were prohibited from trading in the suburbs. The Christian merchants and town's advisors knew how to buy the hearts of the King's advisors, as well as of members of the *Sejm* and the Senate. Under that pressure the King annulled the last regulation on the 3rd April 1527. Nonetheless, he took into consideration the investment in goods which the Jews had made, and instructed that for the first year the Jews could trade with no restrictions, but from the second year the restriction of 1521 would apply to them. The merchants were satisfied with their victory,[32] but the Jews did not give up. They approached the King with memorandums and explained that the matter would lead to their bankruptcy – which would damage the King's treasury who was interested in maintaining their freedom of commerce. That argument hit the target and during 1527 the King issued a regulation to limit the commerce to four types as in 1521, only the number of bulls for sale was increased to 2500. To prevent Jewish retailers from selling textiles in Lwów, the King decided that the municipality's advisors be authorised to have their goods checked by a special officer appointed by the Starosta or his deputy; and the Jews would be forbidden to sell in Lwów any textiles they had left over from the fairs. Were they to contravene the prohibition, their entire stock would be seized, half to the benefit of the town and half to the King's treasury.[33] On the 3rd June 1527 a huge fire broke out and destroyed almost the entire town, and this led the townspeople, who needed money in order to rebuild their houses, to concessions. The King sent special commissars to bring the two parties to an agreement, and he wrote

[Pages 35-36]

to the municipality (1528) stating that it too had to make concessions to the Jews in the suburbs, but his counsel was in vain. The Jews claimed again that because of investments in stock and the expense of rebuilding houses and stores, they would have to plead bankruptcy which would greatly disadvantage the treasury. The King, keen to hinder it, informed the municipality of Lwów that he would not permit to bring destruction on the Jews and grave damage to the treasury. Therefore they were obliged to accept the situation and compromise. The letter convinced the municipality and it signed an accord with the Jews in the suburbs, giving them the same trade rights enjoyed by the Jews in town, in return for a special annual payment of 32 Gulden.

In 1543 the King exempted the Jews from the payment of tax in parity with the rest of the Christian population. Despite that improvement the town's municipality demonstrated its hatred of the Jews with its resolution of 1534, that any Christian acting as advocate for a Jew in a trial, would be boycotted. The same resolution determined that Catholics would take the oath in court, Armenians and Ruthenians in their churches, only the Jew, were he to commit perjury, would be sworn in, in accordance with Boleslaw's Statute of 1264, wrapped in a tallit [prayer shawl] and "kittel," and standing barefoot on a chair while being subjected to terrible curses.

The peace did not last long. The town's people continued to petition the King with complaints and demanded to check whether the Jewish cattle traders did not exceed their quota. In 1537 Sigismund I ordered all governors of the provinces, heads of towns and owners of villages, to detain any Jew of Lwów who exceeded the permitted quota, and to expropriate his merchandise. But the order remained unexecuted. Although according to the agreement of 1527 the Jews were permitted to sell 2000–2500 oxen, they did not keep meticulously to those numbers. It is known that in 1533/34 through the Krzepice customs office alone, the Jews of Lwów transported 2004 oxen out of the 20,057 which passed through that station; in 1548, at the customs–office of Grodek, 3023 oxen out of a total number of 18,056; in 1549, 3482 out of a total number of 16,803 oxen. Indeed in the years 1546–1547 the numbers went down so that there were in 1546 – 2294 oxen out of 20,083, and in 1547 only 1718 out of a total number of 15,122.[34] On the other hand, Jews brought from Podolia and Lithuania a large number of oxen to sell.

In 1546, the municipality of Lwów lobbied King Sigismund I for new privileges that would include restrictions regarding the Jews. In his statute the King restated the prohibition to keep taverns, shops and workshops at the foot of the palace, or to hold weekly fairs there. The following year (1547) the King affirmed the privilege of the Christian textile traders that they alone had the right to sell fabric by the cubit [yard] or by the piece.

A typical Galician Jewess

During that period many Jews who had been expelled from the Czech lands (1541) [lands which for long were under diverse rulers, including those of Bohemia, Moravia, Hungary and Austria],[35] streamed into Lwów, and the townspeople feared new competition which would further increase the existing Jewish trade and thus compromise their livelihood. The townspeople succeeded in having the King issue a command (1543) to the Starosta Odnowski, to extend to the municipality every help in the search and expulsion of the Jewish refugees. But the municipality's efforts were in vain. The number of foreign Jews and their trade grew, especially after Jewish merchants from Turkey arrived in Lwów. The trade from Lwów by Jews also increased despite the restrictions. They brought large quantities of goods: leather, Zuechten (<u>dyed</u> goats' leather), velvet, silk, textiles, furs, blankets, carpets, iron goods, milk, Turkish pitchers, perfumes, raisins, plums, mead, honey, fish, peppercorn, ginger, hops, and also wine from Hungary, Italy and from countries in the East. The Jewish trade comprised all branches of the economy, despite the prohibitions and restrictions of 1521 and 1527. The Jews of Lwów expanded their trade also to the other towns of Poland. In the period 1519–1531 many Jewish merchants from Lwów came to Poznan.[36]

Although the town's advisors made efforts to restrict the trade by Jews, they did not fail to safeguard the town's interests and its rights at trade centres. On the 18th March 1512 they gained an order from the King which was distributed to all the Voivodes,

[Pages 37-38]

Castellans and Starostas. It stated explicitly that all Jewish merchants, wagoners from Reissen and Podolia who transported goods to Kraków, Lublin and other towns, and who bypassed the trade centre of Lwów, had to respect its rights in the future.[37] In 1537 a similar dispute arose with Lublin, regarding the merchants who arrived from Turkey, merchants who were forbidden by the Lwów municipality from going to the Lublin fairs. This time King Sigismund ruled in Kraków on the 27th February 1538, that Lwów's townspeople were entitled to coerce Turkish, Tatar and Wallachian merchants to store their merchandise at the Lwów trade centre but without prejudicing the Lublin merchants.[38] All the restrictions remained unimplemented since the Jews were supported by Polish noblemen who then acquired for them citizenship of the city, so that they numbered among the patrician strata. Probably under their influence the relationship improved between the townspeople and the Jews. Despite any improvement the struggle continued for decades, with both sides engaging the authorities in appeals, objections and trials. That situation continued till 1578, when the sides agreed to postpone any legal actions till the *Sejm*'s Court convened.

But the matter was not brought to the agenda of the *Sejm*'s Court. When its turn for deliberation had arrived, the Jews had a chance of winning. The municipality hesitated as it well knew that even if it were to win in court the Jews would always find ways and means to hold on to the trade. It thus preferred to enter into direct negotiation with the Jews in order to arrive at a mutual agreement. The municipality's efforts resulted in a compromise which was signed on the 20th January 1580.

In that struggle with the municipality one Jewish wholesaler excelled in particular, Josef ben Schachna (Josko Szachnowicz), the son of the tax–collector Schachna. His father, who was from Hrubieszow, settled in Lwów in the middle of the 16th century, and occupied an important role in the life of the Jewish Community. Josef inherited from his father a large estate, and in the years 1484–1487 he himself leased the customs at Hrubieszow, Lublin and Belz,[39] and later also at Lobachev, Lwów and Chelm. His multiple incomes made him one of the money magnates who influenced the economies of Reissen and Wolyn [Volhynia]. The townspeople hated him and envied his status. In 1504 they plundered his mansions and houses, and on the 19th December 1504 he was released from his payments for 3 years.[40] At the same time the King gave him the leases on transit–goods payments, and bridge–tolls in Podolia, Halicz, Lwów, Sanok, Przemyśl, Belz and Chelm, against the payment of 400 Marks, and granted him all the rights awarded to a king's lessee. He was also exempted from the regular jurisdiction.[41] In 1505 the *Sejm* at Radom decided to forbid the Jews from leasing any public revenue, so Yosko gave up all leasing, moved to Lublin and turned instead to banking. He died in 1507. His wife, Golda Yoskova, maintained trade relations with King Sigismund's court, and remained in Lublin. Their son Pessach managed his father's affairs, and his younger brother Shalom Schachna went to Kraków to study at the Yeshiva of Rabbi Jacob Pollak. After completing his studies he returned to Lublin where he was elected rabbi and in 1541 he was appointed, together with Dr. Moshe Fischel, as chief rabbi of Lesser Poland. He died in Lublin, in 1559.

In 1548 King Sigismund I died and his successor Sigismund Augustus (1548–1572), a Renaissance man, was tolerant regarding religions, and a peace lover. He treated the Jews fairly and maintained amicable relations with Jewish doctors and bankers. He invited the renowned Jewish doctor, Amatus Lusitanus, a Portuguese Marrano, to be his physician; after the latter declined the invitation the King invited Dr. Salomon Askenazy [Aszkenazy] of Udine. Once Dr. Askenazy left for Turkey, Dr. Solomon Calahorra, another exile from Spain who had settled in Kraków, was appointed in his place.

Sigismund Augustus confirmed at the *Sejm* at Piotrkow (1548) the privileges which the Jews were granted by Casimir the Great.

In 1568 a fire broke out in Lwów which destroyed the documents detailing the Privileges granted to the Jews, and when the Jews approached the King to renew their privileges, he acceded to their request and on the 1st October 1568 he granted them in Warsaw "the Privilege of the Jews of Lwów" (*Privilegium Judaeorum Leopoliensium*). That Privilege entitled Jews to keep real–estate in perpetuity, a right of which they may not be denied, and even any future royal decree obtained against them, would be legally invalid. Any issues concerning the dividing up of plots of land, whether for sale or as real–estate gifts, had to be regulated by the Voivode [district governor] of Reissen, since the Jews were his subjects and had to be registered with him, in the Jews' book of certificates. Taxes, rents and all payments to the Palace and the town, the Jews would pay according to the regulations. At the end of the Privilege, an instruction was given to the authorities and the clerks in charge, and especially to the castellan of Przemyśl and the Starosta of Lwów, as well as to the town's authorities, to implement those rights.[42]

Sigismund Augustus maintained particularly the rights of those Jews whose services he required: Izaac Nachman (Nachmanowitz) wanted to build a house on the Street of the Jews, on a plot which bordered on Ruska Street which lay outside the Jewish Quarter. The plot on Ruska Street belonged to a Christian widow who did not wish to sell it even at a high price. In 1571, in a personal letter to the municipality of Lwów, the King ordered the appropriation of at least half the widow's plot, and in order to settle the matter he sent his clerk

[Pages 39-40]

Jacob Szabinski of Warsaw, and the Jew was given the plot for the building.

In 1571 a great fire broke out in the Jewish Quarter within the town, and destroyed almost all the houses in the Quarter as well as the neighbouring houses on Ruska–Blacharska Street, the Dominicans' Square with the old Ruthenian Church (Cerkiew Woloska). With no regard to the great disaster the municipality wanted to take advantage of the opportunity and end the struggle against the Jews by forcing them inside the city walls.

In their despair the Jews turned to King Sigismund Augustus, and on the 15th June 1571 he ordered the town's mayor not to abuse the Jews, and permit them to build their houses on the previous plots, be they wood or stone houses, according to their choice.

In a separate regulation he freed the Jews from paying taxes due to the damage they had suffered in that fire, and he appointed the Starosta Mikołaj Herburt of Felsztyn to implement his order with rigour.

The Jews rebuilt their Quarter and moved even closer to the city wall.

The struggle with the townspeople was not in vain. The Jews took advantage of the short period during which they benefitted from free trade, to renew their trade contacts with Constantinople, contacts which had come to a halt at the end of the 15th century.

Lwów turned again into one of the major stations on the trade routes to the East, where also Turkish Jews brought their goods to sell. Moshe, one of them, was accused of acts of espionage by the Lwów townspeople, whose jealous competition led to his incarceration in 1502. He died in jail. The matter led to the diplomatic intervention of Sultan Bayezid II, regarding the return of Moshe's goods which had been confiscated before his incarceration.

The citizens of Lwów spread rumours that the Jewish immigrants, from both Poland and Constantinople, were traitors and spies for Turkey.[43] But the townspeople's schemes bore no fruit. The Jews emerged innocent of those accusations and continued the Turkish–Polish trade in both directions. That trade circuit grew further, under the trade accords that the Jagiellonians reached with Turkey in 1519, 1523, 1553 and 1560, in which Jews played a decisive role.

In 1531 the Jews Nathan and Moshe managed a large volume of trade with Turkey via Suczawa. And in 1532, Moshe, together with Schlome of Lwów, were given by the King of Poland a protection missive to pursue free trade with Turkey.

Among the Turkish Jews who settled and established trade agencies in Lwów were the agents of Joseph Nasi, [Nassi] Duke of Naxos. The townspeople who worried about the new competitors began to persecute them, but King Sigismund Augustus curbed their opposition. Just then he was keen to maintain good relations with Turkey and with Joseph Nasi, Duke of Naxos, who was in charge of the admittance of foreign envoys into the Sultan's court. As a result, on the 22nd January 1567 the King permitted Joseph Nasi, "who has always helped us and our envoy and stood by him at every opportunity", to establish in Poland wine–storehouses, and to send his two agents Chaim Kohen and Abraham de–Mosso for that purpose. They were granted the right to trade everywhere and especially in Lwów, and to transfer their goods without payment of any tax. They were also not subject to the jurisdiction of the town or the Voivode. They had to report solely to the King or to his commissars. These agents, Jews from Portugal, arrived in Lwów in May 1567 and immediately started trading. The municipality did all it could to remove the undesired competitors, and did not recoil even from annulling the King's privilege. But the King stood fast and sent a severe warning to the town threatening a fine of 2000 Florins if they disregarded his rulings. In that instant the municipality was even assisted by the town's Jews who saw in the agents unwanted competitors to themselves, and for a reason.

In the years 1567–1569 Joseph Nasi's agents, Chaim Kohen and Abraham de–Mosso sold in Lwów proper 377 barrels of Malmsey wine, in the value of 30,000 Florins; 212 barrels of Muscat wine and goods in the value of 5,000 Florins; and during one year (25.5.1569–25.5.1570) 374 barrels of Malmsey wine and 70 barrels of Muscat wine. After the death of Abraham de–Mosso, his two sons Moses and Mordechai de–Mosso took over the management of his business. Don David Passis from Pera (a suburb of Constantinople) worked together with them. Jacob Sydis, another Portuguese Jew, also joined the partnership. The team of merchants, who took over the entire wine trade, worried not only the Christian merchants but also the Jews. All the attempts to be rid of those merchants were in vain since the "Franks" as they were termed by Jews, were protected by the chancellor [Kanclerz] Jan Zamojski. In 1570 that partnership sold 230 barrels of Malmsey wine for 6,900 Thalers, which arrived on two boats via the Black Sea. Apart from that partnership there was in Lwów another Portuguese Jew, Jacob Ben Raphael, and a group of Jews from Venice, who conducted wholesale trade.

In 1605, after the death of their protector, the chancellor Jan Zamojski, they all disappeared from the trading scene of Poland.

The extent of the money business by Jews increased also in exchange for promissory notes, mortgages and collaterals. The business was conducted principally

[Pages 41-42]

at the Lwów fair on Agnieszka [Agnes] Day celebrated on the 21st January, which was attended by traders from all over Poland, but especially from the eastern regions. Here loans were extended also by Jewish lenders who lent small sums to Christian traders, and to craftsmen against securities. In the main they added the interest to the capital; otherwise they deducted it right away.

One of the most interesting transactions was the loan extended by a Jew, Israel ben Jakób, to the Ruthenian printer Iwan Fedorowicz, against the mortgage of a printing house. In 1584, Israel demanded the ownership of the printing house and 140 printed books, since the debt had not been paid off. The Ruthenian Bishop of Lwów, Gedeon Bałaban, made every effort to extract the printing house from the hands of the Jew. Reb Israel demanded the capital with interest of 1500 Zloty. Since the bishop did not have the funds, he sent a friar to collect from his devotees the sum required to clear the debt.[44]

The authorities came out strongly against Jews who took gold and silver vessels, as mortgages from churches, and in 1641 the *Sejmik* at Wisznice demanded to expel the Jews from any town where such practice had taken place.

Apart from trade, the Jews engaged also in different crafts. A certificate from the year 1460 mentions that a number of Jews were tanners of red–dyed skins, a field which they had developed since.[45] In 1445, Jews are mentioned in Lwów as being engaged in working Kamcha (Chinese or Turkish silk fabrics for suits, introduced into Poland in the 15th century). Isaac ("Izack Kamcharez") is known in particular. There were also Jewish glaziers: in 1499–1500 one knows of the glaziers Yom–Tov and Jacob.[46] In the middle of the 16th century, there were also Jewish goldsmiths who owned workshops: best known in 1552, was the goldsmith Israel.

The condition of the Jewish craftsmen was not easy, faced as they were with Christian craftsmen who by the middle of the 15th century were already organised in 25 guilds. The Christian craftsmen, especially tailors and furriers, tried to limit the free actions of the Jews. In 1543 the Christian tailors and furriers of Lwów managed to obtain from King Sigismund a prohibition, stopping Jewish craftsmen from sewing suits, especially village garments, and to sell those at the fairs. The prohibition was ineffective and in 1548 the craftsmen's guilds asked again for the King's help against the Jewish competition.

Despite the efficient organisation and the rivalry from the Christian craftsmen, the Jews managed to endure due to the quality of their work and their inexpensive products.

The synagogue in "disfigurement"

In the middle of the 16th century (1557–9) King Sigismund Augustus (1572–1548) permitted spirits to be distilled and served, exclusively in the town of Lwów and its suburbs. A year later (1558), the municipality leased the privilege to Israel ben Jona for three years, at the cost of 80 Gulden a year. That trade remained in Jewish hands for many years.

Among other professions, we know in Lwów only of three Jewish doctors: Izak (Isack Medicus) who, apart from his medical activities (1496) was also involved in financial businesses – lending for mortgages which he sold off after their redemption date, and he was known also as a real–estate agent.[47] The second was Doctor Simeon, of whom little is known other than that he worked as a doctor in Lwów in 1468, and that he owned a house in the Jewish Quarter of Lwów.[48] The third was Aharon, a specialist doctor (known as "Ahron Doctor in Medicinis"). In 1570 he bought a house from the Christians Jan and Agnieszka Schultz, for 200 Polish Zlotys.

Till the 16th century there were no significant changes in the development of the Jewish economy, apart from trade and handcrafts. The population grew, especially that outside the town. In 1550 there were 52 houses and 559 persons. The synagogue built on Kraków Square (*Krakówskie Plac*) was burnt down together with the entire Quarter in 1623. The new Quarter built in 1632, a little farther north, together with the new synagogue which till the end of the 18th century served as fortress, existed till the outbreak of the Second World War (1939).

The community within the town increased also, especially after the great fires of 1527 and 1571. In 1550 there were 20 houses in the Jewish Quarter with 352 inhabitants, which indicates the congestion the Jews lived in, at the time. But in the years 1580–1582 the Jews succeeded in purchasing new plots and expanding the area of their settlement.

In the Jewish Quarter within the town stood the old synagogue, which was beautifully decorated. Opposite the synagogue were food shops and goods storages. The Jewish Quarter conjoined the Christian town via a gate at the corner of Ruska Street.

[Pages 343-344]

All notes in square brackets [ ] were made by the translator.

Notes: CHAPTER 1

1.   The Earliest information of a Jewish community in Reissen, is about Przemyśl from 1031, which was an important station along the trade route from East to the West, when the Russian Princes Yaroslav and Mstislav invaded Poland. (Dr. Y. Brutzkus: "Di Ershte Yedies Wegen Yiden in Poilen" in: *Historische Schriften,* YIVO Warsaw 1929. Vol. 1 pp. 67–78).

2.   Karaites were also known as Saraceens (Sarazani). Nahum Sokolov quotes in his book *Sin'at Olam* (Warsaw 1881, p. 82) a hand written manuscript from 1356, which talks of two types of Jews: "Yudai" and Karaites, who are known here as "Sarazani". The Polish writer Józef Bartłomiej Zimorowic [1597–1677], states, in his book *Pisma do dziejów Lwowa*, Ed. Heck, Lwów 1899; p.71., specifically, that Prince Leo Lev subdivided the town into four areas "for the Jews and other circumcised also from the South", i.e. Karaites.
The Karaite community existed already at the end of the 15th Century. Documents mention that in the Krakówite Quarter there was, next to the Rabbinic (Rabanowe) community, also a Karaite community. Already in 1570, the inheritance of a Karaite is mentioned in documents. At the beginning of the 16th Century, the Karaites moved to Davidov, near Lwów. (Bałaban, [Dr. Majer], Dzielnica żydowska we Lwowie ["Jewish Quarter in Lwów"; 1909] 6–7)

3.   After Prince Daniel (Danylo), his son Lev (Leo=Loewe) inherited Reissen, he transferred his capital from Halicz to Lwów. It is an historical mistake to assume that he had established the city of Lwów, and that it was named after him. The name "Lwów" suggests Lion, the symbol of the Slavic deity "Zernobocq" ["Chernobog"]. During the reign of Daniel, the Mongols and the Tatars invaded Reissen. In an attempt to overthrow their yoke, he set out, together with Prince Andrey of Vladimir, to fight them. In one of the battles he was killed. The throne then passed down to his sister's son, the Prince of Mazovia, Boleslaw, who was known as Mazur, after he converted to Eastern [Orthodox] Christianity and changed his name to Jerzy. Since his politics was leaning toward Poland, he faced opposition from his Boyars (noblemen) who subsequently poisoned him. After his death, his throne was claimed by the Lithuanian Prince Lubart, the Hungarian King Ludwik and by the Polish King Casimir who signed a treaty with the Hungarians that if Ludwik did not ascend the throne in Poland, he would hand over Red–Reissen to the Hungarians, in exchange for 100,00 Ducats. After the agreement, Casimir invaded Red–Reissen and after a short war he conquered Lwów and the entire country. The boyars joined the Tatars, but when they suffered a heavy defeat, they were forced to accept Casimir's rule

4.   The document is published in: Akta grodzkie, Lwów T. III. Nr. 5.

5.   Edition Dr. Freimann in "Mekitze Nirdamim", Berlin

6.   A. Czołowski: *Pomniki dziejowe Lwowa.* 1892 t. I. Nr. 241, 248, 714, Lwów, 1903–1904.
Dr. Ignacy Schipper: *Studja nad stosunkami gospodarczymi Zydow w Polsce podczas sredniowiecza.* Lwów, 1911, p. 173.

7.   "Grzywny" (Grzywna), from the 14th century, referred to the weight of 200 gm. silver.

8.   In 1386, Jadwiga confirmed the town's statutes (Jus Teutonicum), wherein it is said that they affect all residents "omnes mercatores et homines ab undecunque venientes." That means that the Law does not anticipate from Jews any civil service, yet

they were granted rights of permanent residents which included State protection.
Alexander Kraushar: *Historia Zydôw w Polsce*, Warzawa 1865 T. II, p. 56

9.   Dr. Schipper: Der Anteil der Juden am europaeischen Grosshandel mit dem Orient. Heimker Czernowitz 1912 p. 25–26. Extensive Archive material on the trade of Jews of Turkey with Poland in the years 1479–1467, in the Appendices in Dr. Yitzhak [Ignacy/Ignaz] Schiper's book: *Studja …* pp. 339–345

10.   He was sued by Grzegorz [Gregory] of Sanok, the trial was on the 1st March 1440. see: Helcel ; Starodawne Prawa Polskiego Pomniki, t. II. Nr. 2833;
J. Schipper: *Studja* pp. 134–135.

11.   Akta grodzkie i ziemskie t. XIV Nr. 263.

12.   In 1873, the Polish historian Dr. Wyshlowcki published in: Przewodnik Naukowy i literacki Lwów 1873, t. III., pp. 717–726, a research titled: "Przywilej Kazimierza w dany Zydom m. Lwowa i calej Rusi. Potwerdzony przez Wladyst, wa Jagielly we Lwowie d. 30 wrzesnia 1387" – the wording of the privilege which Jagiełło confirmed to the Jews of Lwów on the 30th September 1387; in manuscript form it is kept in the Ossolineum library. This document coincides with Jagiełło's stay at Lwów, and the names of the witnesses are those of his escorts. Also the officially published form is identical with other charters granted by the King. However, according to Dr. Meir Bałaban, as mentioned in his article: "Czy zatwierdzil Jagiello przywielje zydow Lwowskich. Kwartalnik hist. Lwów 1811 t. XXV pp. 228–239", the matter here is not one of an authentic Charter manuscript, but a version of a fair copy by a priest, which lacks any seal, and it is just a private copy

13.   Jaworski: *Lwów za Jagielly* p.27

14.   Akta grodzkie i ziemskie Lwów, t. II, Nr. 42, 45.

15.   Dr. J. Schipper in his article: "Agrarkolonisation der Juden in Polen." in the Collection: Juedische Fragen, Wien 1908, pp. 64–78, states that Wolczko settled Jews in his agricultural villages, but the conflicts he had with the farmers and with the transfer of his villages to the Catholic Church prove that there was no question of a Jewish settlement.

16.   On the 30th October 1453, a trial was held against him, brought by the Armenian plaintiff Piotr, in the matter of 48 oxen and calves. Natko did not come to the trial.
Akta grodzkie i ziemskie, Lwów, t. XIV Nr. 2954a.

[Pages 343-344]

17.   Printed in: Berschadski: Russko-Jewrejskij Archiw. t. III. Nr. 3, pp. 12–16; Nr. 4, pp. 16–19.

18.   Akta grodzkie Lwów, t. XIV Nr. 93, 119, 121, 130, §40, 141, 142, 160, 161.

19.   Dr. J. Schipper: *Studja*, pp. 177–178.

20.   The cemetery is first mentioned in municipal records in 1414. In the cemetery there is a gravestone from 1378 which says: "Here lies the honest modest Miriam Marisha, daughter of our teacher R'Samuel who died on Sunday 2nd Tamuz 140 of the sixth thousand. May her soul be bound in the bond of everlasting life.

21.   In the town of Lwów the influence of German was greater than in towns of Western Poland. In 1406 the members of the Council were: Piotr Eysinhutel, Jan Worst, Niklos Werner, Neco Reuse, Clugn Andris and Piotr Kusnierz [Jan] Ptasnik: *Miasta w Polsce*

22.   The sentence which rescinds the privileges:
"Listy jakiekolwiek zabezpieczajace rozmaite wolnosci ktoresmy Zydom mieszkajacym w Krolestwie Naszem dali w dniu Naszej Koronacyi, a ktore sa przeciwne Prawu i konstytucjom ziemskim odwolujemy. znosimy i odbieramy im wszelka wage i Moc. ktore to odwolane wszystkim do wiadomosci podajemy."
Published in: M Bersohn: Dyplomatarjusz dotyczacy Zydow w dawnej Polsce. Nr. 12, pp. 18–22.

23.   Berschadskij: Russko–Jewreis. Archiv III., t. III, Nr. 5, pp.23–28

24.   Zubrzycki: *Kronika miasta Lwowa* pp. 114–115.

25.   Akta grodzkie i zeimskie t. XV Nr. 89.

26.   Dr. Łucja Charewiczowa: *Ograniczenia gospodarcze nacyj schizmatyckich i Zydow we Lwowie XV i XVI w.* Kwartanik historyczny 1925 (t. 39) zeszyt 2.

27.   Berschadski: Archiw III Nr. 10. p.32.

28.   Bersohn: Dyplomatarjusz sz. Nr. 8. p. 24.

29.   Bersohn: Dyplomatarjusz Nr. 7. p. 23.

30.   Published among the appendices in the book of Dr. Yitzhak Schieffer: Studya Nr. VIII
Regarding the battle of the towns against the Jews, in 1539 appeared a pamphlet titled "ad querelam mercatorum Cracoviensium responsum Judaeorum de mercatura", which defended the trade by Jews that brings money to the treasury and stated that the

Christian merchants should live in greater austerity and be satisfied with smaller profits, like the Jews. According to the pamphlet there were, at the time in Poland, 3200 Jewish merchants compared with 500 Christian merchants.

31.   Dr. M. Bałaban Zydzi Lwowascy. Materjaly Nr. 4.

32.   Berschadskij: Russko–Jewrejs Archiw. III. Nr. 136, pp. 174–176.

33.   Berschadskij: Russko–Jewrejs Archiw. III. Nr. 141, pp. 184–185. "possint libere eiusdem civitatis leopoliensis consules adhibito ad se aliquo officiale seu revisore Castri illius Leopokiensis, quem Capitaneus vel eius vicegerens nemquam eis denegare debet, pannos omnes et singulos per Judeos reductos revidere."

34.   Roman Rybarski: Handel i polityka handlu Polski w 16 wieku t. I, p. 227 (Poznan 1928).

35.   The flow of Czech Jews into Poland started as early as 1516, and was encouraged by King Sigismund I, who saw them as a positive element since they brought in funds, and due to their high cultural level.

36.   Mgr. — Goldberg —Feldmann: Der Handel fun di Poisner Yidden, in *Bletter fir Geschichte* [Pages for history]. Warsaw, 1934, pp 51–52.

37.   Dr. O. Balcer Corpus iuris Polonici Cracovia 1906 Nr. 106.

38.   Jan Riabinin *Materjały do historji miasta Lublina* . 1317–1792 Lublin 1938, pp. 55–56.

39.   About his leases of the customs at Lwów and Belz: Berschadskij: Russko–Jewrejs Archiw. III. Nr. 30, pp. 50–53.

40.   Berschadskij: Russko–Jewrejs Archiw. III. Nr. 31, p. 54.

41.   Berschadskij: Russko–Jewrejs Archiw. III. Nr. 33, pp. 56–57. Nr. 34, 35, 43, 57

42.   Berschadskij: Russko–Jewrejs Archiw. III. Nr. 173, pp. 246–247.

43.   The townspeople did not shy away from accusing the Jews of slandering the Christian Faith. In that way, by order of the Municipality, Abraham, the Jewish merchant from Lwów was imprisoned for defaming the Christian Faith. Only after the community's representatives lobbied the King, was Abraham released on bail. In the course of the investigation and trial it became clear that all blame laid against him was influenced by Christian merchants and their hatred of the Jews.

44.   "Judeis rubricedonibus, qui ab antiquo ibi, labores suos exercebant". Akta grodzkie i ziemskie t. VI, p.62.

45.   Dr. M. Bałaban; Zydzi Lwowscy, pp. 378–379
Dr. M. Bałaban: Soncinoblaetter III, p. 14

46.   Akta grodzkie i ziemskie Lwów, t. XV. Nr. 2180, 3003

47.   Akta grodzkie i ziemskie Lwów, t. XV. Nr. 2507–2509, 2557.

48.   Akta grodzkie i ziemskie Lwów, t. XV. Nr. 638

[Pages 45-46]

Chapter 2: The Community

Translated by Myra Yael Ecker

Edited by Yocheved Klausner

The Jewish Quarter. The structure of the community and its organization. The types of Jurisdiction. Taxation of Jews. Spiritual life.

By the middle of the 16th century the community within the town had established itself and numbered no fewer citizens than the community outside the town. It extended between Blacharska Street (from the corner of Ruska Street) to the money-changers' Square, and the upper section of Boimów Street. The Jewish Quarter (Platea Judeaorum) was segregated from the town by a gate which was shut during the night hours, during Christian processions as well as in times of anti-Semitic rampages. The Jews within the town had a synagogue.

The Jews lived under difficult hygienic conditions which endangered their health while they were enclosed within narrow streets and houses in which the congestion is hard to imagine. Due to the expansion of trade, there was an increased number of Jews who came to settle in the town, and consequently the price of flats and shops rose. An average house which in 1474 was worth 159 Gulden, was sold in that very year for 190 Gulden, while in 1580 its value rose to 1500 Gulden. This illustrates the difficulties faced by a Jew who wished to settle in the town, or to acquire his own dwelling.

At that period the Jews had two independent communities: a community within the town, and a community outside town. Each community was headed by four community leaders (seniores [elders]), three town's dignitaries (bonis viri [good men]) and a council (quadra ginta verat). Vis-a-vis the authorities and in matters concerning external affairs, the community was represented by the monthly elected community-elder (titled in Polish: Burmistrz Kahalni [mayor of the Jewish community]). In important matters he was accompanied by two community-leaders and the beadle.

From the 17th century onwards his official title was lobbyist invested with full power (syndic; syndicus plenipotent). The first lobbyist we know of within the town, was Simon ben Schaul, a native of Lwów. We know the composition of the first community management of 1497, and the names of the community-leaders were: Schlome (Magnus), Schlome (Minor), Salomone (Claudus) and Izaak[1]. They assembled for their meetings in the old synagogue (termed by the authorities szkolka murowana [the brick school])

Maintaining two communities resulted in duplication in the management of Jewish affairs, as well as in matters of law and justice[2]. In criminal and financial matters they were under the jurisdiction of the Voivode (district governor), while in matters of plots of land, houses and building permissions, they were under the jurisdiction of the Starosta or his deputy. That division of the jurisdictions did not always follow the administrative outlines of the communities. For instance, Jews who resided on municipal land in the suburb (on the left bank of the Peltew), were subject to the jurisdiction of the municipality and not to that of the Starosta.

All trials between Jews were under the jurisdiction of the Jewish law-court [Beth-Din]. Trials between a Christian plaintiff and a Jewish accused, were under the jurisdiction of the Jewish judge (Iudex Judaeorum [judge of the Jews]). In 1440 we know of two Jewish judges: Iben Dzordz [George] (of Stopnica) who was Iudex Judaeorum specialiter, and Stefan Bydłowski known as Iudex id deputatos.

In 1445, we know that the judge of the Jews was the Italian, Krzysztof de Sancto Romulo [St. Romulus] of Genoa, who was also one of the greatest merchants in Poland. He resided in Lwów since 1443, and died in 1466. He leased the mines of Drohobych and the customs in Grodek, he was ennobled, and kept in close contact with other Jewish merchants[3]. Bystram of Lopiennik followed him in the post. In 1446, the Voivode's scribe Mikołaj Stradowski filled the role of judge, and from 1491 onwards the Starosta filled that role.

The Jewish jurisdiction was initially determined together with the regulation granted to the Jews of Lwów, in the 1364 directive of Casimir the Great, and in the article that set the Jews under the jurisdiction of the Voivode or his judge[4]. The issue was clarified in the directive (decree) of Sigismund Augustus of the 9th April 1551[5], in which he pointed out the misrepresentation of the Jews in the jurisdiction. This suggests that the Jews were subject to the Voivode's jurisdiction. The same directive also incorporated the interdiction to lock up Jews in the castle, and it settled the issue of appeals.

On the 10th April 1553, Sigismund Augustus granted the Jews of Lwów a special privilege regarding the pledge and responsibility for objects derived from theft. In the regulation of February 1569, the issues of jurisdiction over the Jews were arranged in 12 Clauses, according to which

[Pages 47-48]

the Voivode had to appoint the Jewish judge solely from among members of the nobility. Certificates and books of the Jewish law-court had to remain inside the synagogue; the Jewish judge was forbidden from inserting any inscription into the certificates without the knowledge of the Jewish community-elders. It was also forbidden to accept a scribe without the knowledge of the community-elders. The Jewish community-elders were selected solely by members of the Jewish community. Once selected, they would be presented to the Voivode for approval. It was further determined, that it was forbidden to sequester or expropriate the synagogue; that the community-elders were entitled to punish Jewish criminals and to impose on them bans in accordance with their religion; and that the Voivode was not allowed to appoint a Rabbi, unless he had been elected by the Jews.

The Jewish judge could only issue instructions in cooperation with the community leaders. That regulation, fundamental to the jurisdiction affecting the Jews, incorporated also a clause of an economic nature: that Shechita [ritual livestock slaughter] was free to Jews and that they were permitted to sell the meat to non-Jews too, in the custom of the Jews at Kraków, Poznan and Lublin[6]. In the 1571 regulation[7], the jurisdiction was again entered in the first Clause.

Based on these regulations, the authorities subsequently issued their statutes (Porządki Wojewódzki [provincial orders]).

On the 27th January 1604, the Voivode of Reissen, Stanislaw Golski, issued a statute regarding the Jews of Lwów, made up of 25 clauses which determined the composition, powers and payments of the Jewish law-court. Based on that regulation, the Voivode of Reissen, Stefan Czamiecki, issued on the 17th March 1660 the second statute, with no alteration[8].

The last franchise (ordinance) granted to the Jews of Lwów, was accorded by the Voivode Marek Matczynski in 1692 (21st March), wherein were determined the salaries due at the Jewish law-court. According to it, the two communities and the Rabbis were to provide the Voivode's Privy Purse with 4000 Polish Zlotys annually, submitted in four payments. After clearing the sum, the Voivode, his deputy and his officers had no further claim to receive foodstuffs such as fish, perfumes etc. from the communities. The deputy-voivode (*podwojewoda*) and the judge were forbidden from holding any other office.

It was reconfirmed that the law-court be situated next to the synagogue, and that without delay the community-elders be elected by the Jews, in accordance with their laws and customs. That was followed by details about the law-courts such as summons to trials, determination of dates, safekeeping of protocols.

A special clause (§9) emphasized that trials in which both parties were Jews, were not subject to the jurisdiction of the *podwojewoda*.

That regulation remained in force till 1732.

On the 31st January of the same year, Prince Augustus Czartoryski ratified the regulation in its entirety. He made a single change however, that the seat of the law-courts and the affairs of the two communities of Lwów be conducted in an appropriate place and not in a small room adjacent to the synagogue[9].

The Great Synagogue outside the town

In the suburb the Jews were under the jurisdiction of the castle in all matters which were subject to the jurisdiction of the Voivode, including plots of land and houses. And that, even though the regulation which King Sigismund Augustus granted to the Jews of the Lwów suburb, on the 1st of October 1586, stated that the purchase and sale of real-estate did not require to be registered with the Starosta. Nevertheless, in practice the purchases and sales were registered with the Starosta, and in many cases the Starosta even assumed the right to sit in judgement over Jews in civil and criminal cases. In time the Jews of the suburb were placed under the authority and jurisdiction of the Starosta. Trials between a Jewish plaintiff and a Christian defendant were under the judicial authority of the defendant. That is to say, if he were a nobleman – at a special law-court ([sad] grodzki [castle court]); a townsman – at a municipal court (Lawa, Rada [Bench, Council]); a farmer – under the jurisdiction of the landowner, and a priest – under the jurisdiction of the Church. Civil cases with an Armenian defendant were heard before the principal law-court of the Armenians. Appeals against judgements of these law-courts were considered at the assessors' courts. Special cases were judged by a mixed court (Judicium compositum) composed of members of the municipality and of community leaders. These law-courts had in fact the attributes of courts of arbitration.

Until 1520, the Jews were levied state taxes – payments to the King: szos królewski from Jewish houses at the rate of 2-4 Zloty per house; payments to the King's officials, to the Church, municipal taxes and payment for the right to dwell on private estates. In 1466-1506 the Jews of Lwów paid 200 Florins state tax (“*stacyjne*”), and in the years 1506-1510,

[Pages 49-50]

100 Florins; in 1510, 200 Florins[10]. Each community had its own incomes and expenses, as well as joint expenses of both. The incomes of the communities were made up of congregation-tax which each Jew paid in accordance with the actuaries' assessment; income from meat-tax (korobka); tenure fees for the right to dwell; the construction of houses; licenses to trade, work and lease; payments for chuppah [Jewish marriage ceremony]; payments for status “Member” and “Our Teacher”; burial fees; payments for the law-court, and levies on commodities: wine and similar. The revenues were needed by the community which kept at its expense a Rabbi, a cantor, beadles, lobbyists, as well as paying the costs of the synagogues, hospitals, the Jewish law-courts; provisions for Jewish prisoners; travel expenses for rabbis, community-elders and lobbyists to regional and national conferences; hosting of soldiers and payments

Keter-Torah Ornament

of bribes to officials and the authorities. The joint expenses of the two communities were: payments in cash, materials and supplies to the Voivode (the governor) and his officials; payments in cash and in supplies to the deputy priests, and leasing fees for the cemetery. The community within the town was also obliged to make payments: 1. to the Catholic clergy for the Catholic school, 2. to the municipality. Until 1506 the Jews of Lwów paid no municipal tax, but that changed with the King's order that instead of the 200 Florins the Jews had to pay him, they would now pay him just 100 Florins, but for the following four years they would have to participate in the municipal taxes: a. for trading rights; b. to the craftsmen's guilds (*cechy*); c. tax on each barrel of Kosher wine; d. an appropriate share of the expenses of a municipal police with 50 policemen (in 1573 these expenses amounted to 1585 Zloty, 14 Groszy, towards which the community contributed 297 Zloty 15 Groszy).

In 1475, the Jews in the Krakóẇite Quarter paid the Voivode or the Starosta 5 *grzywny* [fines]. Apart from that it was incumbent upon them to guard thieves and to bring them to the palace, as well as to arrange certain works: on the King's visit they had to provide a number of coaches, horses and supplies for the King's kitchen, and to pay the expenses for protecting the palace. The Jews exempted the Karaites who resided in the Krakóẇite Quarter, from contributing towards those expenses[11]. In time, the services were replaced by cash payments – for a limited trading right the Jews in the suburb paid the municipality a fixed fee.

Besides the taxes and payments made by each community individually, they also had joint expenses, such as: legal expenses for trading rights, repairs to synagogues, hospitals, bathhouses, building licenses after fires, etc.

Besides the payments by the community or through it, every Jew had to pay – as member of the community within the town – a leasing tax to the municipality (*emphyteusis*) for each house, a tax known as *straz wielka* of 6 Zloty, 6 Groszy per house, as well as payments for crossing bridges and roads, liquor tax (*czopowe*) and balances.

Every Jew of the community outside the town paid property tax to the Starosta in addition to indirect taxes, just like the Jews within the town.

The community leaders were responsible for collecting the taxes, and for payments. In 1499, the community leaders were incarcerated by the Starosta because of a late tax payment of 24 Florins for houses and real-estate property (*szos królewski*) from the Jewess Jacobowa, and they were released only after Isaac ben Mordechai, (Markowicz) the lobbyist for the Jews, had pawned the objects in the synagogue[12]. From the end of the 15th century special tax collectors were appointed. In 1498, one of the first tax collectors in Greater Poland was Fischel from Kraków. It is likely that the Lwów community leaders (dectores Judaeorum) also helped to fulfil the role. In one document of 1496, the wife of the community leader Joseph is mentioned, and in a document of the 19th July 1497, his name was entered: "Iudaea Joseph dectores iudaeici"[13]. Those who mediated between the government and the Jews on taxes, were not in fact the communities but rather the community-elders, to whom the King had handed the lists of taxes due from the Jews in their community.

In the days of Sigismund [Zygmunt] I, an institution was founded of the king's principal Jewish treasurers who were in direct contact with the exchequer's treasurer. In 1512, two wealthy Jews were appointed to the post: Avrahm from Bohemia, and Franczek (Ephraim, son of Moses Fischel)

[Pages 51-52]

from Kraków), whose influence stretched from Kraków to Greater-Poland and Mazovia [Mazowsze], to Lesser-Poland and Reissen. The communities of Kraków and Lwów objected to the treasurers' institution, with the rest of the communities following suit. They too refused to recognize it and its officers or to clear their taxes, despite the King's orders and threats. The situation had reached the point that Ephraim was unable to fulfil his obligations towards the King's exchequer, and only the Queen [dowager] Elizabeth saved him from bankruptcy. His role together with additional powers were transferred by the King to Avrahm from Bohemia who was banker to the Emperor Maximilian and to King Władysław Jagiellończyk [Vladislau II]. After being expelled from the Czech lands, he was among the Jewish refugees who arrived in Poland where he established trade agencies. On the 13th October 1517, after negotiations with Avrahm, the Lwów community-elders came to an agreement how to clear the *czasowa* [temporary] tax levied on it according to the treaty. From each walled-house a payment of 4 Zloty, and from each small house 2 Zloty a year, that is to say, 200 Florins in 1517, and a collective annual tax of 150 Florins from the community. Representing the community in the document were Israel ben Jona (Jonaszowicz), Isaac, Baruch, Jehuda, Ezriel, Samuel and Bocher[14].

In 1550, the Jews had 71 houses which housed close to 2000 persons, and in 1578 there were 2400 persons in Lwów.

The Harvester Square (Plac Zbozowy)

From earlier periods the names of Rabbis and scholars who taught the Torah in Lwów, are not known. The state of knowledge and education there was as poor as it was throughout Poland. "And due to their wretched livelihoods they were unable to study the Torah, but they hired a knowledgeable man to be their cantor, advisor on Jewish law, as well as Torah teacher for their sons. As not everyone in the community was able to contribute personally towards their wages, the community established the regulation that they would be the recipients of all the charity collections of Purim and of Simchat Torah, and also of the donations gathered from grooms and from those feasting at their weddings, without their knowledge, so as not to offend them, and so the pleasure of joy and food and drink would lead from one Mitzvah to another. And were that practice to be cancelled, their wages would not suffice for their living and they would abandon their services and leave the community with no Torah and with no prayer and with no advisor[15]." That was the 13th-century depiction by Rabbi Eliezer from Bohemia, of the spiritual state of Poland which was equally applicable to Lwów. Only with the arrival of exiles from Ashkenaz [Germany] to Lwów, did the situation improve. The exiles brought with them Talmudic scholars, rabbis and teachers. One of the first experienced scholars to train many others in Lwów, was Rabbi Levi ben Jacob Kikenes, who held in Lwów the posts of head of the rabbinic court, and head of the Yeshiva. He died on the first day of Pessach 1503.

The first rabbi known from accredited certificates was Rabbi Kalman of Worms [Vermeisa]. He reached Lwów from southern Germany around 1518, and was among those who moulded the spiritual life of his community. He served in the rabbinate of both communities. His renown as a Talmudic scholar spread outside Poland too, and he exchanged letters with the great scholars of his generation. He died in 1559. He was followed as head of the Rabbinate by Asher ben Isaac Kohen, who also headed the Jewish burial society [Chevra Kadisha] and was one of the community treasurers. He died in 1579. After him no rabbi served again both communities of Lwów. Instead, there were two rabbis, one within the town the other outside it. That situation lasted till 1680.

It is interesting to note that during the period when the archbishopric was moved from Halicz to Lwów, the archbishop was the renowned scholar Gregory of Sanok [Grzegorz z Sanok] (1406-1477), who was among the early poets and writers who founded Polish Humanism. He kept in contact with Jewish scholars in Lwów, but their names are not known. His friend, the renowned humanist Filip Kallimach Buonaccorsi [Filippo Buonaccorsi, known as Callimachus], who came to Poland from Italy, read the Bible in its original Hebrew and was a friend to the Jews, also lived for a period at Lwów and defended the town's Jews.

[Pages 347-348]

Notes: CHAPTER 2

1.   In one of King Sigismund Augustus's documents of the 9th April 1548, the lobbyist was also known as: synagogae praefectio(nem) skolnik dictum.

2.   Akta grodzkie i ziemskie t. XV Nr. 2538.

3.   "Judaei duplicia sua judicia habet in certis causes.".

4.   Kutrzeba: *Handel polski ze wschodem.* Przeglad polski 1903, t. 48; pp. 483-485.

5.   "Sed nos tantumodo aut noster Palatinus, sed eius iudex iudicium in eis (Judaeis exerceit).

6.   Dr. Z. Pazdro: *Organizacja i praktyka zydowskich sadow podwojewodzinskich w okresie 1740-1772* r. Lwów, 1903, Nr. 2.

7.   Published in: Pazdro Nr. 11.

8.   "To tylko wyjawszy, aby sady i sprawy kahalow lwowskich miejskich i przedmiejskich n przystojnem miejscu, a nie w izdebce przy szkole zydowskiej odprawowaly sie i sadzily. ex respectu powagi i jurysdykcyi mojej wojewodzkiej i oficyalistow moich". Pazdro Nr. 12 p. 180.

9.   Pazdro 1.c. Nr. 4, pp. 163-165.

10.   Pazdro 1.c. Nr. 10.

11.   Pazdro Nr. 11, pp. 176-179.
Also in Dr. Moshe Schorr's book: *Zydzi w Przemyślu* Nr. 9.

12.   The title *doctor Judaeorum* [learned Jews] was also given to Rabbis, court judges and principals of yeshivot. *See*: Wetzstein, "Kadmoniyot Kraków" [Early history of Kraków] in *Hamagid,* 1897, sheet 5.

13.   Dr. M. Schorr: *Organizacja Zydow w Polsce* p. 11. 2.(14).

14.   Published in the book of Dr. Ignacy Schipper: *Studja* p. 349 Nr. VII.

15.   The responsum of Rabbeinu Eliezer [Eliezer ben Joel Halevi (c.1160 - c.1225)] of Bohemia, pupil of Rabbeinu Tam [Jacob ben Meir; (c.1100 - c.1171)], published in the Responsa of MaHaRaM [Meir] bar Baruch, Part 3, Clause 112.

[Pages 53-54]

Chapter 3: The Trial against the Jesuits

Translated by Myra Yael Ecker

The Jews of Lwów in the days of Henryk Walezy and Stefan Batory. The Jesuits demand the synagogue within the town. The verdict of the royal tribunal. The nobles backed the Jews against the Jesuits. The compromise and return of the synagogue to the ownership of the Jews. The development of the community within the town. The fires in the years 1616, 1623. Towards the disaster of 1648.

After the death of Sigismund Augustus (1572), during the interregnum, the Jews of Lwów waited with worry and anxiety for the things to come under the new king, whose name and nature they did not yet know.

In the meantime they were obliged to contribute to the cost of keeping 50 soldiers whom the municipality had recruited due to the danger that threatened the town during that period of emergency. In 1573, these expenses amounted to 1586 Gulden 15

Groszy, of which the Jews paid 297 Gulden 15 Groszy. In 1574, these expenses were 264 Gulden, and in 1575, they were 1218 Gulden, with a quarter of the two sums paid for by the Jews.

King Henry III of France Henryk Walezy [Alexandre Édouard de Valois; later Henri III of France] (1573–1574), the son of Catherine de Medici instigator of the "St. Bartholomew's Day massacre," was chosen in 1573. Although his selection rested on the Jewish doctor Salomon Askenazy, who had acquired the Turkish Vizier Sokollu for his candidacy – he did not like Jews. According to the Jewish historian Hilary Nussbaum,[1] he did not want to ratify the general privilege of the Jews, nor the privileges of the Jews of Reissen. Nonetheless, in 1600, in the claims presented by the Lwów community leaders to the committee regarding the Jesuits, Nachman ben Izak stated explicitly that in 1574, Henryk Walezy had ratified the privileges of the Jews of Lwów.[2] He also granted to the Ruthenians at Lwów total freedom of trade, after they had sent a special delegation to the *Sejm* at Warsaw (1572), but that was not accepted by the municipality, which forcibly evicted the Ruthenian merchants from the fairs.

The King's Catholic fervour increased the hatred towards the Jewish people among the Catholic masses.[3] His rule did not last long. Once he heard that his brother had died leaving no male heir, he fled to France. Thirteen months after he had fled, Stefan Batory Prince of Transilvania was elected King of Poland (1576–1586). En route to his coronation at Kraków, he stayed at Lwów where he was received by the citizens with open arms. After he was crowned, he ratified the privileges of the different ethnic peoples of Lwów. He treated the Jews sympathetically. In a special order of the 5th July 1576, he protected them against blood libel allegations, emphasizing that false allegations had reached him. As a result even their detractors admitted that they had accused the Jews of murdering Christian children, or of taking the sacramental bread (*Hostia*) for cursing and blasphemy, and that in every case it was invariably proven that lies had been testified against them. Therefore, the King prohibited to impute such guilt on the Jews. Were a Jew to be punished by death in such a trial, the accuser would receive measure for measure. Apart from that the King determined that the municipalities be responsible for all damages caused to the synagogues and Jewish cemeteries, and that in such cases the municipalities could expect severe punishments. In 1578, the King spent the entire winter at Lwów. In the same year a Jew filed a lawsuit against the Starosta Mikołaj Herburt of Felsztyn [Fulsztyna], known also by his name Odnowski. The Starosta declined to attend, but the King did not accept his refusal, since both the Starosta and the Jews were subjects to his rule.

Considering the townspeople's complaints that the municipality's entire authority lay in the hands of advisors, Batory reorganized the composition of the municipality (the consuls), and he established that the town council be enlarged by additional 40 men. Also that it be composed of advisors, judges and another 40 men (*quadraginta viri*), half of whom were to be elected by merchants and half by craftsmen, and that without their consent it would be prohibited to create expenses, or to set taxes and financial levies.

Assigning such a team did not suit the Jews who found it easier to deal with the advisors than with the merchants and craftsmen, who considered the Jews their competitors. Thence forth the Jews required assets in order to settle their affairs with the advisors and members of the team, which always entailed special expenses.

Nevertheless, due to Stefan Batory's sympathy with the Jews, the council was swayed to sign an agreement with the Jews, bringing an end to the conflict between them and the town which had lasted since 1521.

In 1578, King Batory confirmed two of the privileges granted by his predecessors, according to which the Jews of Lwów were entitled to conduct any trade, just as other traders.

[Pages 55-56]

The Synagogue of Rabbi Izak Nachmanowicz

During his reign the community leaders Izak ben Nachman and his sons Nachman and Mardochaj [Marek] built a new synagogue named "The Synagogue of Turei Zahav [Golden Columns]." Five years later Izak and his wife bought a plot adjacent to the synagogue, which his son Mardochaj utilized for its enlargement.

The family of Rabbi Izak ben Nachman remained for several years at the head of the community, and established important public enterprises and institutions.

After the death of Stefan King Batory (1586), in order to protect the town from attacks by gangs during the interregnum, the Jews again participated in maintaining 250 soldiers. They contributed 104 Ducats toward the cost, only on that occasion they paid disproportionately more than other sections of the population. Consequently, the Jews who considered themselves wronged by such disproportionate demands, refused to pay the annual payment of 50 Gulden to the municipality, which was levied on them in the 1581 contract.

King Sigismund III, immediately after his coronation on the 25th March 1588, also issued at Kraków a regulation convenient to the Jews. Also, in the general privileges granted to the Jews of Poland in 1600, the Jews were taxed in all fields of trade throughout the country, equally as the Christians, so that the circumstances of the Jews of Lwów did not alter.

In the days of Sigismund a grave event befell the life of the community of Lwów:

On the 1st September 1591, against the wishes of the Church and the other religious sects, Archbishop Solikowski brought in a festive procession the first Jesuits (3 in number) to Lwów, gave them a small church and housed them in a private house.

The Jesuits sought in vain a place for their monastery and church. Archbishop Solikowski lobbied the municipality, but it refused to accommodate them, claiming that it had no space. The clergy at the cathedral did not view them favourably either, especially since they planned to establish a school at Lwów, which would have reduced the number of pupils at the Catholic school, and consequently their income. Despite those objections, the Jesuits who immediately after their arrival established the "Collegium Societatis Jesu Leopolisansis," had no intention to forgo Lwów. The Jesuits were not deterred, and decided to search a place for their buildings within the Jewish Quarter. Without prior warning they declared that the new synagogue which Izak ben Nachman (Nachmanowicz) had built, was constructed without a license from the king, even though all their claims were incorrect.

During the Piast dynasty in Poland, the construction of synagogues was unrestricted. The sole restriction was that the synagogue not be externally adorned, or differ in size from other houses. The Church and the synods strove to restrict the freedom to build, such that the synod of 1542 at Piotrków[4], led by the infamous enemy of the Jewish people, [Bishop] Piotr Gamrat, decreed that the King should not allow the building of new synagogues, but only the repair of existing ones.[5] That decree was further toughened by the synod at Gniezno in 1589, in a decision of protest against the magnificent synagogues which the Jews had constructed in the royal towns, asking that the King should forbid it in a severe regulation.

And in fact King Wladyslaw IV determined clearly that the Jews should not dare construct new synagogues, and Alexandre forbade even the repair of the old synagogues.

After the synagogue was burnt down in 1571, the Jews of Lwów faced great difficulties to rebuild it again. Izak ben Nachum, who stood at the head of the community, decided to purchase a plot for the synagogue which would be his private property.

In 1578 he began to negotiate the purchase of the plot "Olesko Square," on which stood only the ruins of the "horse treadmill"]młyn koński[as well as the adjacent vacant plot, for which he required a license from the town council, the commission of forty, the clergy and the King.

On the 24th September 1580, the town council decided to sell the plot to Izak ben Nachum, and within two days the purchase

[Pages 57-58]

was concluded at the cost of 1500 Gulden, and Izak was given the right to the property. On the 24th March 1581 he was granted a license from the King. During that period, the patricians and the well–to–do circles – such as: Kampian, Abrahamowicz, Boimów family, Lorencowicz – erected magnificent buildings in the Renaissance style, built by the Italian builders and architects Pietro di Barbone, Petrus Italus and Paulus Italus [Paolo Romano]. Paulus constructed the Ruthenian church (Cerkiew Woloska) on Ruska Street, distinguished by its Renaissance style, and Rabbi Izak invited him to construct the synagogue on the plot on which the "horse treadmill" had stood. Paulus erected the building in the Gothic style, and finished it in 1582. During the construction, Izak tried to obtain a license from Archbishop Solikowski too, in order to avoid disputes with the synod's decision. But despite all the efforts and recommendations the Archbishop refused to consent, so as not to oppose the synod's decision. Nevertheless, Izak finished the building. On the facade facing the square, Paulus built for him his residence (27 Blacharska Street), and the entrance to the synagogue was solely through his house. Naturally, at prayer times Rabbi Izak permitted the worshipers to enter the synagogue through his house. Outwardly, however, the building was the private synagogue of Rabbi Izak's family.

It was that synagogue on which the Jesuits focused their attention in 1600. The opposing municipal camp informed them that the municipality had sold to the Jews plots which had not belonged to it. Here the Jesuits found a suitable opportunity to reach their goal – to acquire a plot on which to construct a collegium and church. They began to research the legal basis by which the Jews had purchased the plot on which the synagogue stood, and according to what license had they erected it.

They relied on their connections at the royal court, and they also succeeded with the help of the royal court's preacher, the priest Piotr Skarga, to convince the King to send to Lwów a commission assigned to find for the Jesuits the site they required. The King ordered the Starosta of Lwów, Jerzy Mniszek, to support and assist them in all their endeavours. The Jesuits complained to the King about the municipality for its illegal sale of the plot, and about the Jews for their purchase and possession of property which was against the law. Both parties in the dispute insisted that they acted in the spirit of the law, and therefore their deal was valid. Apparently, the committee was unsuccessful in its efforts. After a new head of the Order (superior), Adrian Radzimski was elected new efforts were made for the King to appoint a new committee.

Interior of Rabbi Izak Nachmanowicz's Synagogue

In 1603, the King appointed a new committee to investigate the question of building plots at Lwów, and in his letter to the municipality he recommended that the municipality transfer to the Jesuits any plot selected by the committee. On the 24th November 1603, the King's letter to the municipality was read out at the Jewish synagogue, and the community leaders were invited to appear before the committee, with the warning not to dare interrupt. It was thus clear that the committee intended to proffer to the Jesuits the plot the synagogue stood on.

In the meantime the patron of the Jesuits, Archbishop Jan Dymitr Solikowski had died, and his appointed successor Jan Zamojski, student of the Kraków Academy, was not among the sympathisers of the Jesuits. On the 10th October 1603, two committee members arrived at Lwów: Adam Stadnicki (the Starosta of Przemyśl Stanislaw Stadnicki; the other members: Hieronim Gostmoski (Voivode of Poznań), Stanisław Garwawski and Jan Świętosławski did not come. Just at the time they arrived at Lwów, a controversy broke out among the townspeople: the committee for soldiers' wage payments coerced the traders to pay a large sum which greatly angered people. At the same time the *Sejmik* (the regional parliament) of Reissen assembled at Lwów; among its members were many opponents of the regime who hated the Jesuits and were also hostile towards the King. The regional Jewish committee of Reissen, Podolia, Volhynia and Podlasie [Podlachia], also met at the same time. The deliberations with the royal committee were set to be held at the offices of the municipality. Before these began, the three town's advisors approached the *Sejmik* and requested from Stanisław Żółkiewski, member of the committee for soldiers' wage payments, to protect the town's affairs, since

[Pages 59-60]

the traders had contributed large sums just a few days earlier. Żółkiewski went to the seat of the municipality, checked the committee members' certificates, and left the hall. Meanwhile, arguments broke out within the *Sejmik* about the plots that were sold to the Jews. 18 speakers spoke in favour of the Jews and only two delegates sided with the Jesuits. The debate at the municipality continued, the community representatives arrived, headed by Rabbi Izak ben Nachman, and expressed their objection to the debate as they did not recognize the authority of the commissaries, only two of whom attended, rather than the five members of the committee; the town of Lwów, governed by the Magdeburg Law, was not subject to the jurisdiction of commissaries. The deputy–Starosta Poradowski, counter claimed against them that the commissaries had the authority of the committee even if only two of them attended, and the town was subject to their jurisdiction as they were not a law–court of the nobles, but rather representatives of the King's law–court. Representatives of the Jews and of the town submitted their petition to the *Sejm* against such an interpretation, and demanded that the legal authority of the committee be verified. The Jesuits wanted to avoid the matter being submitted to the *Sejm*, since most of their objectors were found there. Therefore, they insisted that the deputy–Starosta who appeared as prosecutor (instigator), continue the debate and boycott the appeal which was not worthy of being submitted. On behalf of the Jews, Nachman ben Izak protested with the assertion that the Magdeburg Law excluded all committees, and that that Law applied also to the Jews in accordance with Sigismund Augustus I's regulation of 1538, and that all the privileges accorded to the Jews of Lwów and approved, starting with Casimir the Great, and ending with King Henryk Walezy in 1574, were valid. Regarding the matter itself, the Jews were prohibited from negotiating with the Jesuits due to the precedence right of the municipality to purchase plots. The municipality's representative stood his ground and rebuked the deputy–Starosta for appearing in the role of prosecutor, on his own account, while the King's letter had not assigned any member to the role.

The commissaries were astounded. Inside the hall angry voices on both sides were heard, while outside, a crowd incited by the cathedral's clergy, demonstrated against the Jesuits. In that confusion the commissaries adjourned the meeting, claiming that they were prevented from carrying out their duty.

Nevertheless, the Jesuits persevered. At the same time their representatives, commissaries and supporters from among the committee members convened, and it was agreed to transfer to the Jesuits the plots and houses belonging to the Jews, with no commitment to compensate their costs from the town's treasury. The legal aspect and coming to an agreement with the Jews, was assigned to the Jesuits.

After the meeting the commissaries invited the eight Jewish owners of plots and houses, and it was imposed on them to prove, within three days, how – despite the kings' prohibitions – they had become owners of plots and houses that had been acquired against the law, and that no permission for their sale had existed.

On the 13th October 1603 the town council convened, attended by the commissaries, Jesuits and the Jewish owners of plots and houses. The councillor Andrzej Dąbrowski stressed in his speech that the council welcomed the idea of establishing a Jesuit collegium at Lwów, and that it would do everything to carry it out, but precluding causing any damage to the town itself.

The Jews did not respond to the commissaries' demands, and declared that they recognized solely the town council, from whom they had acquired the plots, and that they had no intention of entering into negotiation with the Jesuits. And were their rights violated, they would submit claims against the town and against the Jesuits.

Serbska Street

When the town's advisors saw the steadfastness of the Jews, they began to favour them. The commissaries wished to bring the matter to an end, and ruled that the Quarter with the eight houses which belonged to the Jews together with the synagogue of Izak ben Nachman, be made available to the Jesuits. There and then the Jews appealed to the King. On the 15th October, two days after the commissaries' ruling, Nachman ben Izak in the name of the Jewish community, entered into the documents presented to the *Grod* [castle] (law–court), the issue of disagreement, and clarified the legal position of the Jews of Lwów: The Jews resided at Lwów in accordance with the Magdeburg Law and were subject to it in matters of real estate. They were themselves subject to the Voivode, they bore their share in all the town's burdens and were thus also entitled to have rights. To recover the ownership of purchased plots (evictio), was a right granted solely to the town itself, and therefore it was the sole authority with which they could negotiate. In a memorandum they entered in brief all the privileges of the Jews of Lwów up to 1603.[5]

[Pages 61-62]

The Jews began to prepare their claim even to the royal law–court. For that purpose they tried to obtain from the town's archive the privileges and the purchase contracts for the properties, but the proconsul refused to produce them, and that despite the protestation of the town's notary who was ready to extract them from the documents.

The Jews presented their claim without any documents. The court session was held at Kraków in November 1603. The town representatives, who were at Kraków at the time, did not attend, and the session was set for the 15th December 1603. But again they did not attend and the final date was set for the 15th January 1604.

In the meanwhile the town and the Jews sought support in recommendations. The town was interested to thwart the Jesuits' admittance. With its influence, Zamojski and Żółkiewski attempted at the *Sejm* to oppose the construction of a collegium for the Jesuits.

On the 15th January 1604 the court session took place, led by the King. The Jews proved that they had bought the plots and declared that they demanded new places of residence and compensation in the sum of 100,000 Marks. The town delegates found themselves in difficulty as they claimed that the need for protection and fortifications forced them to sell the plots which had stood empty for a long time, and since there was no other purchaser they had to sell them to the Jews. Finally they showed the King the privilege by Casimir the Great who had granted to all of the town's citizens, the Magdeburg Law, as well as the sale and purchase contracts and the statement of accounts which they had received from the Jewish purchasers.

When he saw this, the King realized that a great injustice had been done to the Jews, and he annulled the committee's decision. In order to settle the matter the King appointed new commissaries and instructed them to provide him with oral statements, at Kraków. Besides the two earlier commissaries, the Archbishop of Przemyśl and vice–chancellor Maciej Pstrokoński, the Voivode of Reissen Stanisław Golski, and Jan Łahodowski were also appointed. On the 3rd February 1604, the committee arrived at Lwów, its members surveyed the plots and houses, followed by a secret meeting. Two members of the committee, Golski and Łahodowski, declared that the plots were crowded and unsuited for erecting a collegium, but three opposed them.

The delegates of the community and of the municipality were invited to the committee, and the municipality was charged with suggesting a space where it could settle the evacuated Jews. The Jews were charged with stating what location they would have wanted, in case they had to vacate their houses. The following day the committee met with the delegates of the Jesuits, members of the town council and the delegates of the community. Straight away one of the committee members turned to the Jews with the warning that they should not resist the King's decision, and demanded their response.

Nachman ben Izak declared that under no circumstances would they relinquish their places. Nevertheless, they would be willing to contribute a few thousand Gulden, were the King to demand it. They were unwilling to negotiate with the committee, as it had no authority.

The town's delegate declared that he was unable to offer an area for the Jews and that it would need to be taken from the Christians. Secondly, the town was unable to repurchase the plots, as it had no funds and it saw no urgent reason for their purchase.[6]

The committee interrupted its deliberations since both sides refused to sign the property–transfer certificates. Consequently, the committee decided to propose to the King a decision that would blame both sides, and that would punish them. The matter was postponed with no settlement. The Jews could not concede and the Jesuits insisted and did not want to concede, even though they were advised to do so.[7]

On the 29th November 1604, the deliberation took place at the tribunal at Kraków. The town was represented by Mikołaj Witkowski, and the Jews by Przeworski.

The parties proved that the purchases were made legally. In respect of the synagogue, it was accepted that the action was illegal since the King's license had made no provision for it. The Jews responded to that objection with the information that the synagogue was not a public one, but rather a private, family prayer house.

In spite of it, on the 3rd January 1603 the tribunal arrived at the verdict that the town had to repurchase the plots from the Jews and compensate them for their investments in those. Regarding the synagogue, the plot would remain in the ownership of the Jews, but the building would have to be demolished or handed over to the King.

The town and the Jews appealed against the verdict, to the King in person. In the meantime, the Jesuits collected testimonies from Christians, who were familiar with the Jewish Quarter, that the synagogue was public and not private. On the other hand, they also tried to influence the King with the help of their supporters. At the end of 1605 the appeal was heard at Kraków. The town was represented by the advisor Stanislaw Anserinus; the Jews – by Nachman ben Izak, Moysa Doktorowicz of Lublin, and the lawyer Laurentius Zarębski.

Against the claims of the delegates representing the town, and the Jews, the prosecutor Stanisław Witkowski showed that the purchase contracts between the Jews and the municipality were totally illegal. Subsequently, the tribunal reached the verdict that the synagogue be confiscated and handed over to the Jesuits. With regard to the plots and houses, their owners had to be compensated, and the purchase prices and the investment expenses had to be reimbursed.

Nevertheless, the verdict was not validated as long as it had not been confirmed by the King.

[Pages 63-64]

The Jews took steps to defer it, while the Jesuits did everything to hasten it, and they succeeded. On the 8th January 1606, they obtained an order in which the King recommended to the town council, to address the repurchase of the plots and houses without delay.

The Jews still wanted to appeal to the crown–court (*trybunal koronny*) at the *Sejm* which was supposed to convene at Warsaw, that frightened the Jesuits since they knew that most of the nobles opposed them.

In February 1606, the legal representatives of the community Nachman ben Izak, Aron ben Rubin and the lobbyist Mendel went to Warsaw. However, only a small number of the nobles assembled there, so that the Jews could do little. For their part, the Jesuits pressed the town to implement the verdict. The municipality rejected, but eventually demanded from them "handout–certificates" and received the certificates.

On the 28th February 1606, they came to receive the synagogue. Mardochaj ben Izak, the brother of Nachman, stood at the entrance to his house when the Jesuits, the representatives of the municipality and clerks arrived. He let them into the synagogue and gave the Jesuits everything with no objection, in the spirit of the King's ruling.

Meanwhile a crowd of Christians arrived, jubilant of their victory over the Jews.

After the synagogue was handed over to the Jesuits, they and their escorts left the building. But the entrance to, and exit from it was solely via the corridor in Mardochaj's apartment, and here he blocked their passage and declared that the priests and worshippers would depend wholly on his permission to enter the "new church". Therefore, he proposed that the Jesuits sell him the building and build themselves their church elsewhere. When the Jesuits rejected his proposal, Mardochaj informed them that it was only on that occasion that he had let them pass; in the future he would not let anyone pass through his corridor, since that was not included in the King's ruling. There and then the Jesuits protested against his remark. Mardochaj let them out, then he locked the gate and took away the key.

The following day, the friar Gajowski arrived and found that the door to the corridor which had always stood open, was shut.

The Jesuits submitted an appeal to the town council. Mardochaj did not attend but declared through his counsel that he did not recognize its authority. He only appeared on the third date, and declared that the Jesuits were demanding something which was not theirs. The only option left to the town council was to recognize the truth of Mardochaj's pleading.

In the intervening period the political events in Poland had undergone changes. In 1606, Mikołaj Zebrzydowski, Janusz Radziwill and Herburt, who led the rebellion, assembled at Sandomir [Sadomierz] the confederation [commonwealth] which established among the 64 complaints against the King, also that he had been surrounded by Jesuits. The changes forced the Jesuits to compromise with the Jews, since they feared that the Jews would find support from the *Sejm*, and would win. Archbishop Zamojski, the superior of the Jesuits Decyusz Striver, the friar Gajowski and delegates of the Jews who were at the time at Warsaw, arrived at an agreement on the 16th April 1606, without the knowledge of the town council. According to the agreement, for the houses and the plots in the Jewish area – the old synagogue and the municipal baths – the Jews of Lwów were to provide other houses, which they would need to buy and transfer to the Jesuits, in exchange. They had to buy the houses by the 15th August 1606. And the Jesuits had to obtain the consent of the town council and the King's confirmation, and to waive all claims on the houses and plots of the Jews, which were handed over to them according to the verdict of the 3rd January 1606.

Interior of the Great Synagogue on Boimów Street

When, after their return to Lwów, the delegates of the Jews started to negotiate with the municipality about the sale of the old synagogue and the bathhouse, and offered 3000 Zloty as compensation, the municipality did not agree to their sale. The interest of the municipality lay in not letting the Jesuits into the town. It also did not recognize the agreement between the Jesuits and the Jews, and rejected the purchase of the plots of the Jews.

When the Jesuits realized the difficulties, they decided to wait. Meanwhile the rebel army of Zebrzydowski which was in part directed against the Jesuits had been defeated. That moment, the Jesuits considered

[Pages 65-66]

the right time to act. They started by gaining the support of those influential within the royal court. To the King who was in need of funds to pay army wages, they lent 10,000 Zloty, and gained his support in their issues. Under the influence of his wife, Żółkiewski also recommended them to the King, and Queen Constance [Konstanza] of Austria spoke in their favour too. The King established a new committee, headed by Żółkiewski, whose purpose was to transfer the old synagogue, the bathhouse and the adjacent plots, over to the Jesuits. Actually, the action was directed against the municipality due to its recalcitrant, negative attitude.

When in the middle of January 1607 the committee arrived at Lwów, it estimated the value of the buildings at 3,000 Zloty.[8] The Jews agreed to find the sum, but the town council did not accept the committee's decision. On the contrary, it immediately submitted its objection. Despite the appeal, the committee transferred the buildings to the Jesuits, and ordered to record the matter in the register of the *Grod* (law–court).

Presented with a fait accompli, the municipality decided to send to Kraków a delegation to the King. The delegation was received by the King with great anger, and it returned home with no actual results.

Then an opportunity arose which compelled the municipality to make concessions. At the same time the citizens of the suburbs suggested to incorporate their houses within the other side of the town–walls, and suggested to the King to extend the town–walls. The King accepted the suggestion. The municipality objected to that since it feared that those changes might also lead to extending the privileges, to the suburbs, something which was inconvenient for the municipality.

For that reason, they decided to concede to the Jesuits if in turn they would agree to support their cause, with the King. The superior of the Jesuits agreed to the municipality's suggestion. The municipality's delegate and the Jesuits went to Kraków, and on the 11th June 1608 the tribunal headed by King Sigismund III, determined that within six weeks the municipality had to transfer the old synagogue and the bathhouse, for the sum of 3000 Zloty. The order given to the Jews on the 3rd June 1606 was repealed, and their confiscated houses including the new synagogue, were returned to them. In order to settle all the issues a committee of three commissaries was appointed, which issued its report on the 13th June 1608, stating that the Jews had to pay the municipality the sum of 3,000 Zloty for the bathhouse and the old synagogue; for the repair of the town–wall till 1611, 4,000 Zloty in three instalments; compensation for the rent of the old synagogue till 1614, 100 Zloty per year, and in 1614, 2,000 Zloty. According to the committee's decision the new synagogue was returned to the Jews solely as a private house, and its use for prayers would henceforth depend on the wishes of the King and the archbishop of Lwów.

On the 23rd June 1608, a new agreement was signed between the Jews and the Jesuits, replacing the agreement of the 10th April 1606. The Jews undertook to find the moneys for the purchase of the houses, the Jesuits agreed to return to the Jews the plots and houses which had been confiscated from them and given to the Jesuits. On 25th June 1606, the Jews received from the Jesuits the certificates for the transfer of the property, and on that very day the King's confirmation was also obtained.

The tombstone on the grave of the author of "Turei Zahav

On the 23rd July the committee arrived at Lwów and immediately took care of all details of the agreements, and entered in the documents of the *Grod*, a protocol of its actions. That ended the conflict between the Jews and the Jesuits which had cost them the sum of 20,600 Zloty, out of which the municipality received 9,600 and the Jesuits 11,000 Żloty, and another sum for the purchase of an additional house. The Jews paid the moneys punctually, and completed the payments on the 15th January 1613. In the spring of 1609, the new synagogue was festively opened. To mark the occasion, Rabbi Izak ben Samuel Halevy,[9]the brother of David ben Samuel Halevy author of "Turei Zahav composed a special prayer song. With great joy they celebrated the return of the new synagogue. With that came to an end the difficult chapter in the history of the Jews within the town.

At that period, the development of the community saw great advancement.

[Pages 67-68]

The Great Synagogue within the Town

Apart from the synagogue, in the years 1571–1600 were constructed: a hospital, an almshouse, a yeshiva. Within the Quarter itself several houses were constructed, a road was paved from the house of Nachman ben Izak up to Ruska Street, the streets were repaired and improved. At the time, the first Hebrew printing house was established at Lwów.

After the trial with the Jesuits, peace and well–being reigned, but not for long. On the 26th May 1616, a great fire broke out which lasted two days and destroyed all the houses in the Jewish street. The condition of the casualties was so severe that the King issued a special order on the 28th December 1616, to release them from all taxes and payments for the following four years.

The community started to construct houses straight away. And on that occasion most of the rest of the houses and plots near the town–wall and within the Jewish Quarter, passed into Jewish ownership.

In 1623, another fire broke out in town, and hardly had they recovered when in 1624 the Tatars invaded Reissen, killing and robbing whole settlements on their way. At Lwów only the Jews outside the town suffered at their hands.

The heir of Sigismund, his eldest son Władisław IV (1632–1648) ratified the privileges, and during his reign both communities developed.

Under him, in 1639, the agreement was renewed with the municipality which made concessions in favour of Jewish trade, since it had to contribute 102,000 Gulden towards the army wages, and it required the support of the Jews. In 1645, the community suffered again from a great fire.

Three years had not yet passed before the disaster of 1648.

[Pages 347-348]

Notes: – CHAPTER 3

All notes in square brackets [ ] were made by the translator.

1. Hilary Nussbaum: *Historya Zydow* t. V. Warszawa 1890, p. 168.

2. Dr. M. Bałaban: *Zydzi lwowscy* p. 97, Nr. 49, p. 4–5.

3. The increased hatred towards the Jews can be read in the words of the writer Zimorowic, who terms the Jews: *hirudines* (leeches), *greges glirium* (flocks of dormice), *colluvies* (pollution). from: *Leopolis Triplex*, ed. K. Heck pp. 43, 63.

4. The content of that privilege appeared also in the decision of the *Sejm* of Piotrków.

5. "sinagogas novas unique etiam Cracovice muro extructas, destrui facere mandat, licet eium in memoriam passionis Salvatoris nostri. Judaei ab ecclesia tolerentur tamen numerrus forum auger debet menime qui iuxa sacrarium canoaum dispositionem veteres sinagogas reformare, novas autem praesertim ex muro minime construere possunt". (Ulanowski: Materialy do historyi ustawodawstwa synodalnego w Polsce XVI wieku t. IX, pp. 67–68).

6. Published in: Bałaban 1. c. materyaly Nr. 49.

7. One of the landowners in Lesser Poland, whose advice the Jesuits sought, told them clearly that:"Patres qui vobis suasit ut contra Judaeos causam moveretis, erat vester maximus hostis". ("Fathers, whoever advised you to start a dispute with the Jews was your greatest foe"). (Scriptores verum polonicarum t. II, p. 70 Nr. 62)

8. Bałaban: *Zydzi Lwowscy* p.134.

9. Born c.1589, at Vladimir Volhynia, was a pupil of Jozue [Joshua] Falk, known as a scholar and expert also in secular knowledge, his song was published in print with commentary. Dr. J. Caro: *Geschichte der Juden in Lemberg.* pp 152–158.
Rabbi Izak was rabbi at Chelm Volynskyi and in 1627 he became head of the Yeshiva at Poznań. He wrote a book on grammar which was, according to *SaDaL* [Samuel David Luzzatto], the first Hebrew grammar, as well as Responsa on Jewish Law. Rabbi Jozue [Joshua] Falk, and Rabbi Majer of Lublin determined that his song be read out at all the communities during the morning prayer on the Sabbath after Purim. He died in 1638.

[Pages 69-70]

Chapter 4: Misgivings over Jewish Trade and Craft

Translated by Myra Yael Ecker

The 1578 agreement. Trade of the "Franks". The townspeople demand the restriction of Jewish trade. Lobbying by the Jews. The commission of King Sigismunt III and its actions. The Jews file a court action against the municipality. Support of the nobles. Objection of the craftsmen and the municipality's policy. The 1592 agreement. The standpoint of the Councils of the Four Lands. The compromise of 1629. Annulment of the 1634 contract. The king's regulation of the 26th October 1634. Validity of the contract until 1642. The struggle of the Jewish furriers. The intervention of the *Sejmik* at Vyshnia. The compromise with the Christian furriers' guild in 1642. The municipality signs the agreement in 1664. The Jewish trade and its extent

In 1578, the dispute between the municipality and the Jews regarding Jewish trade, had reached its peak, and it was decided to defer the issue to the *Sejm*'s sitting. Once the municipality realized that they would face defeat at the *Sejm*, they settled for a compromise which extended over eight years, that is to say, till the 20th November 1589. In the preface to the compromise document was determined: that all the regulations and privileges were temporarily deferred; that the community within the town had to draw up, annually, a list of the permanent Jewish residents; and that the Jews within the town were forbidden from forming partnerships with Jews outside the town in order to ratify their business.

In the agreement, the Jews within the town were permitted four types of trade: trading in cattle (the number of bulls was restricted to 2000 at most), buying and selling merchandise solely at the fairs, and only if packaged and in bulk weight. In towns and small towns, on the other hand, trading was permitted by the Cubit and the Pound. The Jews within the town could, at the Lwów fairs, trade in any goods imported from Turkey apart from drink, medication and spices such as: pepper, ginger and turmeric. At each fair, every trader was permitted to purchase merchandise in the value of 1,500 Gulden, that is to say, 6,000 Gulden at the four annual fairs. To supervise the transactions the purchase would be made in the presence of an interpreter, and mostly the interpreter was an Armenian from Lwów.

Jewish women were only permitted to trade in home–made goods or in pawned objects whose pledged date had elapsed. The community was permitted to order annually just 20 barrels of Kosher wine, taxed at half a Gulden per barrel. The community was responsible for any transgressors of the contract. Anyone caught, purchasing without the presence of the interpreter, or trading in retail and in illicit merchandise, or if the cost of the merchandise were greater than the fixed price, would be fined 100 Gulden.

For the compromise franchise the community was charged 50 Gulden annually, and the compromise would be cancelled were the community to fail in submitting the payment or in handing over any transgressors.

According to the compromise franchise, the Jews obtained freedom to trade in merchandise from Turkey, retail outside Lwów, and they were permitted to trade in perfume. The women were also free to trade in home–made goods. Compared to the prohibition of 1521, there was little change. The Jews were not permitted to trade in any merchandise imported from the West, restriction was removed only from trade in merchandise from the East. Indeed, retail trade outside Lwów was permitted.

Although the compromise applied only to the Jews within the town of Lwów, the Jews outside the town also started to trade in large scale. The Starosta Herburt, without considering the municipality, permitted the Jewish craftsmen to work in the area near the castle, and leased them outlying areas and warehouses.

The municipality remonstrated with the King who ruled in their favour, but the municipality was unable to carry out the verdict.

That period saw extensive development in the trade of the "Franks" and growth in the Jewish settlement. The Jews banished from western countries and Vienna came to Lwów, the number of houses increased, and houses were built nearly on every vacant plot in the Jewish Quarter. The increased population again exacerbated the relations between the townspeople and the Jews.

The tension that time was spurred by the commission of forty which was in dispute with the oligarchic municipality. In 1576, headed by Jan Seidlitz, it undertook to introduce demands, one of which was to abolish the agreement signed with the Jews in 1581. A rumour spread also among the masses that the patricians had been bribed in order to grant the Jews their rights.[1] As the 20th January 1589 approached, both sides – the Jews and the municipality – considered the compromise of 1581, annulled. And again a new chapter opened in the relations between the municipality and the Jews. The townspeople continued with their previous policy using any means to restrict the freedom of the Jews to trade in town and in its surroundings.

[Pages 71-72]

Synagogue "The Golden Rose"

Those who had left the town for the fairs, were barred from returning, and Jews were also stopped from leaving the town to participate in the fair. Guards were placed at the town gates. Within the town, Jews were not permitted to use the town's balances, also the interpreter and his mediators were forbidden from negotiating between the Jews and the oriental merchants. The community itself also ensured that no foreign Jew settled at Lwów, to prevent escalating the competition between the Jewish traders and craftsmen. For that purpose, trustees were appointed from among the community–leaders and dignitaries – probably four as at Kraków, who supervised the balances, measures and standards, and ensured that no Jew from out of town settled within it. The trustees drew up lists of the Jewish citizens within the town, which were handed to the municipality. Only with a special license from the monthly community–leader was a foreign Jew permitted to rent himself accommodation within the Jewish Quarter in town. The authority of the monthly community–leader extended even to expelling a foreign Jew from the community boundaries.[2]

The townspeople had thus succeeded in undermining the Jewish trade in every way. The Jews were again in dire straits since they had amassed merchandise of which they were then unable to dispose, and were consequently unable to meet their business obligations which led them to the brink of bankruptcy. The Jews did not resign themselves to the situation. They sought assistance from the starosta, but in vain, they filed a suit with King Sigismund III (1587–1632) that the municipality interfered with their trade, in contravention of the privileges granted to them. In his ruling the King made the municipality wholly responsible for the results till the matter was resolved, and he recommended that they permit free trade to the Jews, but the townspeople did not obey even the King's instruction. On the 17th April 1589, Sigismund III appointed a special commission which included the Voivode of Reissen, Herburt of Felsztyn [Fulszryn], Mikołaj Herburt the Starosta of Lwów, Stanislaw

Podolecki, the deputy–judge Wiktoryn Kowalski, and the Starosta of Halicz & Kolomia, Stanisław Włodek of Hermanow. The purpose of the commission was to find out, on location, the privileges of the townspeople and of the Jews, and to submit their views to the tribunal which handled the appeals of the municipal law–court, and the granting of privileges.

At first the municipality evaded appearing in front of the commission with the excuse that the Magdeburg Law released the townspeople from such jurisdiction. Eventually the municipality agreed to submit the privileges. The Jews submitted the rulings of King Casimir Jagiellon from 1453, and of Sigismund I from 1515, according to which they were permitted to trade throughout the kingdom in accordance with the ancient customs. Their representatives claimed also that restricting their trading damaged the whole of Reissen and especially the nobles. The commission recognised that the claims of the Jews were right and submitted to the King four proposals that clarified the rights of the Jews. The decision of the commission was sent in November 1590, and the municipality submitted an appeal to the law–court of the *Sejm* questioning the authority of the commission.

The municipality was successful that time. On the 27th January 1591, the King dismissed the commission and its decision, and transferred the entire matter to the royal law–court. Meanwhile, the Jews submitted their protests. On the 6th July 1591, the King issued a ruling limiting the trade by Jews within the town, in the spirit of the 1521 rule, while the Jews outside the town were forbidden from undertaking any trade. The townspeople were pleased to have succeeded.

But despite everything the Jews continued to trade. The municipality issued strict instructions to rigorously maintain the ban, and matters reached conflicts, attacks and arrests.

The municipality and the Jews came to the conclusion that the situation could not continue as it had, and that the only resolve was a compromise. The townspeople objected, but the city council stood fast and on the 28th October 1592 the deputy judge Wiktoryn Kowalski, and the deputy starosta Pstrokoński signed on its behalf the new compromise, which was according to its wishes.

According to the compromise, which was also set for eight years – until the 28th September 1600 – Jews were not permitted to undertake retail sale. However, a new clause was introduced permitting

[Pages 73-74]

Jews to sell specific merchandise at all times, but solely to townspeople at Lwów. Merchandise in which Jews were not permitted to trade, if they had purchased those from townspeople of Lwów, they could resell them within the town and even at other fairs.

Regarding the import–trade from countries to the South and East, the permit was expanded to include silk merchandise from Italy, Turkey and Wallachia up to 1,500 Florins per quarter year. It was permitted to sell such merchandise to townspeople at Lwów, throughout the year, and to foreigners during the fairs at which it was permitted to trade in any merchandise except for that from Austria, lead, brass, steel and rivets. It was not determined whether the Jews were permitted to trade in foodstuffs.

The compromise included a further condition, that merchandise which Jews had purchased and which was not sold during the fair, had to be removed from Lwów immediately after the fair, to another fair, or be sold wholesale to the townspeople of Lwów. It was forbidden to set warehouses in small towns and to sell inside Lwów other than during the fairs. Trade in milk was permitted, and the trade in Kosher wine was increased to 30 barrels. Three further reservations were set: the Jews were not permitted to interfere while a townsperson made their purchase; goods put into storage could be purchased by Jews only a week later; any partnership with Jews outside the town was forbidden. For the compromise–right the community had to pay 50 Gulden annually. Any breach of contract would see the merchandise confiscated, and a serious breach carried a fine of up to 30 Gulden. That compromise turned the Jew into a fairs' trader and pedlar, and stripped him of his status of a serious resident–trader.

The Jew turned into a supplier of specific goods to the townspeople, while all competition in foreign trade was banned. The Jewish merchant faced dangers, damages and bankruptcy, which began to spread among the Jews of Lwów as well as at other towns as a result of limiting the commercial activities. According to the ruling of the Council of the Four Lands, in 1626,[3] and later in 1632, 1634, 1638 and 1642, the "acts of escapees" (label for bankrupts) – had reached such proportions that the committee was obliged to proclaim severe resolutions to stop acts of fraud and crime that slandered the Jews.

Once the period of the compromise had come to an end on the 28th September 1600, the Jews asked to have it extended. The municipality, however, was not eager to renew it since the commission of forty objected, the wealthy commission members, such as Marcin Kampian.

Once the period of the compromise had come to an end on the 28th September 1600, Pawel Boim, Andrzej Dąbrowski etc., who had lent funds to the municipality, had not suffered due to the Jewish trade. The middling traders, however, and especially the Armenians who had taken over the trade with the East, were hostile towards the Jewish merchants who, according to the compromise, were entitled to trade in eastern merchandise. Even in 1597, nearly two years after the compromise had been signed, all the craftsmen's guilds submitted a protest against the municipality which, of its own accord, had dared sign with the Jews a contract in which, to the detriment of the townspeople, it had granted them any trade not just at Lwów but in the whole of Reissen.[4] The nobles viewed the compromise from a different angle. They needed the Jewish mediator and so ignored the monopoly demanded by the townspeople. In addition, it was convenient for a squire to use a Jewish tradesman who was agile and sold cheaper than the non–Jewish trader in town.

The municipality did not give in to the opposition headed by Alembek, who numbered among the wealthy. On the contrary, on the 26th November 1601, the advisor Andrzej Dąbrowski informed the opposition that: "Today we shall sign an agreement with the Jews, as it is in our power, and we shall not continue to ask you."

The very same day a third contract was signed, which included no new clauses but instead extended the compromise of 1592. In 1604 however, the municipality and the commission of forty had reached an agreement, and the matter was removed from the agenda.

The situation of the Jews continued to worsen. Apart from that there were other events which hit the community, such as: the trial with the Jesuits,

"Eliyahu's Seat"

the fire in area of the community outside the town, destruction by the Tatars and Polish soldiers.

The distress had reached its peak on the 24th June 1627 when, in the name of the municipality, it was announced in the synagogue and the Jewish Quarter: "Take note that the advisors, with the permission

[Pages 75-76]

of the Lwów residents, inform and announce that all the contracts which were signed with the Jews are terminated and have definitely ceased. The trade in merchandise that was permitted on the basis of those contracts, will be forbidden in the future, and those who dare trade in them, after the publication of this announcement, will be arrested by the town gentlemen in accordance with the statutes and rights of this town".[5]

Salver of a Sandek [the man who holds the baby during the ritual circumcision ceremony]

That announcement ruined the Jewish trade, and in effect allowed the townspeople to treat the Jews as they wished, which started with attacks on the Jews. The Jews turned to the nobles, who preferred the Jewish to the Christian merchant, and they turned to the King with the grievance of the high cost of goods, and the difficulties of purchasing.

Under such pressure, on the 4th December 1627, King Sigismund III turned to the municipality with the recommendation to reach a compromise with the Jews taking into account, the demands of the nobles, and the fact that the Jews were obliged to participate, at the time, in the expenses of the realm. On the 29th August 1629, under the influence of the nobles and the King, the municipality had reached a compromise with the Jews and signed a third contract, valid for ten years. The clauses in that contract were no different from those in the contract of 1592, apart from quantities of the permitted goods which had increased. Thus the value of the goods from Turkey had increased from 1,000 to 2,000 Gulden; from Moldavia, from 1,500 to 2,000 Gulden, although the Jews were warned not to harm the retail trade at Lwów. Instead of the 50 Gulden, the community was charged 200 Gulden annually. The Jews were permitted to purchase merchandise from foreign traders already on the sixth day after their arrival at Lwów.

The trade in fur and leather was also restricted: the Jews were permitted to purchase those only in a raw state, and if already prepared, only from Christian furriers, and to sell them solely to townspeople and nobles. Since the fur trade was one of the most important of the Jewish trades, the Jews endeavoured to join the furriers' guild, but its management objected.

The Jews approached the municipality as well as the King, but in vain. On the 20th July 1629, King Sigismund III determined that due to religious grounds the Jews could not become members of craftsmen's guilds.

In 1634, the heir of Sigismund III, his son, young King Wladyslaw IV, spent time at Lwów and was interested in the state of the town. He was a lawyer and made efforts to learn the ropes.

The members of the commission of forty took advantage of the opportunity and obtained a decision from the King that the council was neither authorised nor qualified to sign contracts with the Jews without the consent of all the bodies which made up the municipality. With that decision, the contract of 1629 which, as said, was valid until 1636, was thus annulled.

That decision meant victory for the opposition in the municipality under the leadership of Wojciech Ostrogorski–Scharfenberg, and it was handed the controlling power. It then started to oppress the Jews and to conduct severe supervision over their trading, but it did not dare to fully abolish the 1636 contract.

But the Jews did not rest. They pursued every effort to obtain another King's regulation. Eventually, on the 26th October 1634, they succeeded and were granted a determination by the King which recommended that the municipality, in agreement with town's classes, sign a new contract within two years. Consequently, the 1629 contract could not be terminated. However, the inspection of merchandise which continued, led to conflicts between the Jews, the municipality and the craftsmen's guilds, especially the furriers'. Although in a special regulation of the 27th July 1635 the King had warned not to violate the rights of the Jews, it was to no avail. The Jews filed lawsuits and complaints without achieving any improvement in their condition. The townspeople again remonstrated with the King: "No trader or craftsman will be able to perform his trade due to the delays caused by the evil, heathen Jewish people. They already have control over almost 3/4 of the town of Lwów, and the Christians are left crowded in the fourth quarter of the town.[6]

As 1636 got nearer, the Jews demanded from the municipality to extend the contract. The council refused the request, as it did not want to act unilaterally.

Indeed, they accused the Jews, especially the wholesalers, of controlling the entire foreign trade through their connections with Jews in Wallachia and Turkey; and that they had depleted the town so far that its standing might have descended completely, were it not for the meagre income they could gain from restaurants and the armed forces.

[Pages 77-78]

The Jewish wholesalers did indeed manage a significant portion of the foreign trade which they exported to the fairs of Torun, Gdansk [Danzig], Königsberg. To Gdansk they sold wood products, potash and oxen, and from Gdansk they imported to Poland colonial products; from Germany they imported iron goods from Nürnberg [Nuremberg].

The scope of the Jewish trade was curbed by the municipality, which wavered from negotiating a new contract due to the objection of the commission of forty, the Armenians and the Ruthenians, who also claimed to suffer from competition by the Jews.

The attempts by the Jews were supported also by the Voivode and the Starosta, but in vain. By the end of 1636, the municipality sent a warning to the Jewish community not to dare trade or sell, and to act within the guidelines set in the rulings of previous kings, until the King's decision. Before submitting a legal claim the representative Mojzesz ben Abraham made another attempt – to request the municipality to sign a new contract. The municipality responded that it was agreeable, but the commission of forty did not permit it and hindered it.

Clothes worn by Jews in the 17th century

Since the agreement of 1629 had expired, the Jews had no alternative but to negotiate with the commission of forty, and the "nations" (the Armenians and the Ruthenians). The conditions they set were tough and included demands such as a new, ten years' contract solely for the Jews within the town; confiscation of all the forbidden merchandise to the benefit of the town; for that contract the Jews were expected to pay 4,000 Zloty, since the craftsmen and the "nations" were willing to pay 2,000 Zloty if the municipality did not sign a contract with the Jews. According to those conditions the Jewish traders had to make use of the "emporium" of Lwów; and lastly appeared the severest clause of all, that the Jews commit themselves that at the end of the ten years they would never again demand new contracts.

The Jews responded in the negative, and that they did not wish to enter into negotiation on that basis. They would continue trading to their hearts' content and would approach the King straightaway.

The King dispatched commissaries, but they too were unsuccessful in convincing the municipality. Then they began to confiscate the goods of the Jews, not only from shops and warehouses but also on the roads, which led to serious conflicts.

The Jews approached the municipality to enquire on what legal basis their merchandise had been confiscated, but in vain. Quite the reverse, at once the commission of forty organized an auction. They received 2,191 Florins for the goods, out of which the senator Walenty Stancel received 1,810 Gulden, and Doctor Jakob Gidzielczyk 300 Florins for travel expenses to Warsaw in order to represent the town. Jakob Gombrycht, Izak Markowicz, the lobbyists Zelik and Szymon ben Saul travelled on behalf of the Jews.

On the 13th February 1637, the King issued an order to return the goods to the Jews, it was too late however as those had been sold at auction. Negotiations began at Warsaw, and with his authority the King extended the contract of 1629 for another 15 years, that is to say until 1652, with a single change. Now, the Jews had to pay 2,000 Gulden rather than 1,000 Gulden annually, in two instalments. At the end of the period of 15 years both sides would have to sign a contract, and if they would not agree, the King would again renew the existing contract. The King imposed on the municipality to return the goods, and were that not possible – to reimburse the Jews in lieu.

For the first time the King issued a regulation regardless of the town's rights and statutes, and created a dangerous precedent for the town. On that occasion, the King's intervention settled the matter with a win for the Jews.

During that period the Jews took hold of a new branch, the fur trade. The Jews ordered their merchandise from Russia, and competed with the Christian furriers' guild, who were both craftsmen and traders. Apart from fur merchants Jews were also

[Pages 79-80]

furrier–craftsmen who worked to commissions from Jewish merchants as well as from nobles. The fur trade spread especially in the town's suburb, since the nobles who came to Lwów resided in hostelries in the suburbs, and preferred to buy from Jews who sold inexpensively. The Christian furriers' guild refused to tolerate the situation and began to chase Jews and confiscate the furs they had in their hands. The Jews claimed that they were permitted to sell furs which had not been produced at Lwów. On the other hand, the Christian furriers demanded to forbid the Jews from all trade in leather or furs. At the time there were 50 furriers at Lwów, according to whom the Jews undermined their trade and caused their economic impoverishment. The furriers were supported by the Armenians and the Greeks who blamed the Jews for their economic decline. In contrast with the townspeople who lived in austerity, the Jews wander about in "silk, costly furs of ermine (sable); they conduct sumptuous weddings and parties; in town they ride carriages drawn by six–horses in the manner of the nobles, accompanied by servants. Their parties are accompanied by orchestral music and great splendour, every trade and business is in their hands and the Christian are left only with poverty and depletion and they have to pay taxes."[7]

Regarding the confiscation of merchandise by the furriers, a certain Jew stood trial and was punished by an appeals court where the King's verdict stated that he should lose his merchandise. The verdict condemned Jews for transgressing the contract with the town.

That verdict encouraged the furriers' guild to supervise with rigour the Jewish trade which had already been so suppressed that the Jews could no longer sell neither at Lwów nor at fairs that remained empty, since the sole remaining furriers demanded too high prices. The nobles who had been used to get the merchandise from Jews at low prices, opposed it. As a result the *Sejmik* which convened at Vyshnia [Wisznia] in 1640, imposed on its delegates to lobby the *Sejm* to cancel all the restrictions on the Jewish trade.

In response to the nobles' demands, the King ordered in a ruling of the 28th January 1642, that the municipality should try and bring the furriers to an agreement with the Jews. The municipality made great effort to respond to the King's order but with no success. Eventually the King sent a special commission to formulate proposals, and on the 24th December 1642 he issued a regulation, valid for ten years, which obliged the Jews to pass all the sewing of furs to the Christian furriers' guild. The Jews were permitted to sell in town only fur from abroad, but not in the suburbs, except when a noble specifically invited the Jewish merchant there. Among that type of merchant would be included, in a restricted number, Jews solely from within the town, and in accordance to a special list edited by mutual agreement. The Jews were permitted to purchase merchandise from foreign traders, ten days after they had arrived at Lwów, and to sell the merchandise solely to nobles and townspeople. The Jews had to pay the Christian furriers' guild 300 Gulden annually, in two instalments.

In the first year the Jews made a profit of 150 Florins, however the furriers demanded alterations to two clauses in the King's regulation, which even resulted in clashes in the town square. And again, the court cases started.

On the 30th December 1643, the King sent a warning to the municipality and demanded that it resolve the matter. With help from the municipality an agreement was reached in which the guild approved of 50 Jewish furriers. When the Jews gave the municipality a list of 50 names, the guild demanded to meet them in person for fear that they were fur merchants. The Jews did not respond to the demand and continued their trade in fur, and even engaged Christians apprentices, and despite the prohibition they traded in wolf, fox, rabbit and sheep skins. Their agents and middlemen milled about in the suburbs. When the municipality realized that the struggle could not continue, it agreed to sign a contract with the Jews on the 21st March 1654, valid for 15 years.

That was the fourth contract and its content repeated that of the 1629 contract, with the single exception that it now included also a clause that promised free trade in fur, as it had been determined in the King's order.

According to the new contract the Jews were levied by the municipality an annual payment of 1450 Gulden, besides the payment of 300 Gulden to the Christian furriers' guild.

That brought to an end the conflict between the Jewish and the Christian merchants, which had lasted for over 150 years.

The Jewish trade expanded both in its type and the scope of merchandise: the majority of trade was in perfume, peppercorns, cinnamon, salt from the King's mines at Drohobych and Wieliczka, anise, fabrics, textiles, potash, dates and honey, grains, wood, leather, bulls – merchandise marketed not only at Lwów but dispatched also to Breslau, Königsberg, Danzig, Brunsberg [Braniewo]. In particular, the wholesale trade in grain, cattle and bulls at those towns, was concentrated in their hands. The transportation of the cargo was undertaken by Jewish coachmen who were also responsible for the cargo in their charge. The safety conditions en route were precarious and open to attacks by bandits, among whom were also Jews, and much of the cargo was robbed with many people killed and murdered on such occasions. The import of eastern goods from Turkey to Poland was in the hands of Jews

[Pages 81-82]

mostly of Turkish origin.[8] Around 12 wholesalers [9] are known, who at the time kept trade–agencies at Lwów. Many of them lived at Lwów or Zamosc, and most of them left Lwów after the death of the Kanzler Zamojski.

In the first half of the seventeenth century we know only of two Jewish wholesalers from Turkey who had agencies at Lwów, Samuel Czelebi who resided at Lwów in the years 1621–1635, and traded in merchandise from the East; and Szmaje Skampis, who bought a house at Lwów and lived in it during the seventeen forties.[10] Apart from them a Jewish wholesaler from Italy, Abraham Szkatulnik, also resided at Lwów. As they did not know Polish, they employed the municipal translator, Lukaszewicz.

The trade by the Jews of Lwów extended as far as Wallachia, Moldova, Hungary and reached even Moscow, from where they imported leather and furs. The trade in religious books, in Greek and Slav languages and published by the Ruthenian publisher (Stauropegion) of Lwów, was also in their hands. Within Poland the Jews of Lwów regularly traded with Poznan, Lublin, Kraków, Jaroslaw, Krotoszyn, and the Ruthenian towns where they purchased cattle, horses and timber which they sold to eastern countries or to Germany.

The Jews of Lwów leased whole estates for that purpose, where they cultivated crops, timber and cattle. During that period one knows of Israel Złoczowski, Abraham ben Mojzesz, who burnt potash in the forests and sold a large quantity of his produce abroad. On their estates, the Jews established also distilleries of wine and liquor.

To develop that large scale import–export trade the merchants required large sums of money. Such sums were offered to clients by special middlemen who found sources, raised the funds, arranged loans in promissory notes and took care of settling the loans. At Lwów, the lobbyist Mardochaj ben Israel, is known to have engaged in that trade.

Apart from trade Jews were also employed in handcrafts. In the seventeenth century almost all the handcrafts were in the hands of Jews: the butchers and the tailors were organized in craftsmen's guilds. Of course, the craftsmen faced great misgivings since the Christian craftsmen's guilds guarded their interests and did not hesitate, as mentioned above in the conflict of the furriers, from using any means to crush the Jewish competitor.

Unlike the Christian guilds, the Jewish craftsmen had no structured organizations except for the tailors and the butchers.

In 1627 the Jewish tailors' guild still existed, headed by Szymon, a Jew from the suburb. The Jewish tailors employed also Christian apprentices, and paid them better salaries than the Christian tailors did. The butchers too had their own guild. Most of them resided in the suburbs and were the sole protectors of the Jewish residents in the event of attacks and riots, and they cast fear in the Christian marauders.

Among the other craftsmen one needs to mention tanners, shoemakers, furriers, silversmiths [11] who were also traders, twiners, buttoners, who had been granted a privilege by King Wladislaw to engage in their trade, in 1634. There were also Jews engaged in casting metal and tin.

The Jewish craftsmen faced a permanent difficult struggle with the Christian craftsmen who missed no opportunity to undermine the

The Lane of the "Golden Columns" Synagogue

existence of their opponents whom they considered their toughest rivals. The Christian customers of all classes of society preferred the Jewish craftsmen due to their low wages and the price of their products.

The craftsmen maintained synagogues and specific societies: synagogue of tailors, of bakers ("Beth–Lechem" [house–of–bread]), porters (shoulder–bearers). The synagogues were managed by the head of the craftsmen's associations, where they prayed and studied.

Even in the large synagogues – within the town and in the suburb – there were specific rooms including prayer–houses for the craftsmen.

Within the Jewish Quarter there was also an orchestra, but its members were not professional musicians.

[Pages 83-84]

Most of them worked as craftsmen. At the beginning of the 17th century there was a 13–members orchestra at Lwów. They played at Jewish weddings. There was at Lwów a Christian musicians' guild with a religious character, which played in churches and was forbidden from playing at Jewish weddings. Conversely, they agreed that the Jewish orchestra play at Christian weddings and parties. For that agreement the Jewish musicians paid 10 Gulden annually to the Christian guild and two Gulden to the municipality's coffers. The municipality held the right to prohibit the admittance of new members without its approval. To that end, the Jewish orchestra submitted the list of its members [12] to the municipality.

[Pages 347-348]

Notes: – CHAPTER 4

All notes in square brackets [ ] were made by the translator.

1. Ł Charewiczowa: *Ograniczenia gospodarcze nacyj schizmatyckich i Zydow we Lwowie (kwartalnik historyczny)* t. XXXIX p. 226.

2. In that manner the renowned great scholar [gaon] Rabbi Majer ben Gdalia (MaHaRaM of Lublin) who had arrived at Lwów in 1599 as head of the religious law–court [Beth–Din], was made to leave it. A dispute arose between the MaHaRaM and the pupil of Falk, Rabbi Abraham Schrenzel [Szrencel] Kohn Rappoport, author of *Ethan Haezrachi* who kept at his own expense a Yeshivah and was collector of dues as well as fund raiser who transferred the funds to the Holy Land. In 1613, the MaHaRaM attended his son's wedding. When he left his house, Rabbi Schrenzel accompanied him as far as his home. The MaHaRaM was oblivious to the fact that he accompanied him, and when he got home his wife made him aware of that. The MaHaRaM retorted: Am I not worthy to be accompanied not only by him, but also by his Rabbi (Falk)? That remark angered Rabbi Schrenzel, and he brought the matter to the public meeting. With his influence and the help of his relative Rabbi Mardochaj [Marek] Nachmanowicz, it was decided to dismiss the MaHaRaM from the law–court, and he was forced to depart from the town straight away. From Lwów he went to Lublin where he served as Rabbi till his death in 1616. (S. Buber, *Anshei Shem* [*Men of Renown*] pp 12–13, 133.)

3. In *Anshei Shem*, pp. 222–224 of the *Lwów Notebook*, Salomon Buber published a copy from the Notebook of the Council of the Four Lands of Poland, the laws of fugitives (38 articles).. See also:
L. Lewin, *Neue Materialien zur Geschichte der Vierlaendersynode*. Frankfurt a/M 1905, Nr. 4, 5, 11, 13, 15, 17, 20, 28.

[Pages 349-350]

H. Nussbaum: *Historja Zydow*, t. V; pp. 204–209.
M. Schorr: *Organizacja Zydow w Polsce*. Lwów, 1899. pp. 71–72.

4. Dr. M. Bałaban: *Zydzi Lwowscy*, p. 430.

5. Dr. M. Bałaban: *Zydzi Lwowscy*, p. 434.

6. J. Ptasnik: *Miasta i mieszczanstwo w dawnej Polsce*. Kraków, 1931, pp. 355–356.

7. Władysław Łoziński: *Patrycyat i mieszczanstwo Lwowskie w XVI i XVII wieku*. Lwów, 1892. pp. 192–193.

8. Rybarski: *Handel Polski w XVI i XVII W*. Lwów 1892. pp. 254–257.

9. Mosze de Mozzo HaKohen [the priest: Mardochaj Kohen, Jakob Sydis, Dawid Passi, Josef Kohen from Crete, Chaim Kohen, Ezechiel ben Juda, Abraham Gambai, Izak Zabok, Mano Batormani, Dasaro Mosci, Mojzesz Tubiej

10. Dr. M. Bałaban: *Zydzi Lwowscy*. p. 468.
Dr. Łucja Charewiczowa: 1.c. Kw. hist. 1925, pp. 192, 193.

11. In the years 1552–1661, we know of 10 Jewish goldsmiths. They all excelled in the quality of their work and their artistic precision. see:
Ferdynand Bostel: *Przyczynki do dziejow zlotnictwa Lwowskiego w XVI i XVII wieku*. Sprawozdania komisji dla historji sztuki Akademiji Um., Kraków 1891, t. V, Nr. 4, 8, 44, 50, 90.

12. Dr. M. Bałaban: *Zydzi Lwowscy*. pp. 533–534.

[Pages 85-86]

Chapter 5: The Community Outside the Town

Translated by Myra Yael Ecker

Edited by Ingrid Rockberger

The Karaites' community. Employment of the Jews. The division between the Jews within the town and those outside the town. The Rabbis in the years 1599–1680. The fire of 1623. The agreement of 1624 to restore the Jewish Quarter. The controversy with the Ruthenian monastery about plots of land.

As previously mentioned, the Jewish community of Lwów was first settled in the Krakówite Quarter, and only after the fire did the old town turn into a suburb.

Adjacent to the Jewish community there was also a Karaite community. The Karaites resided in the Krakówite suburb at the foot of the castle (wysoki zamek). The area was subsequently referred to as "Karaites' Street" (Ulica Karaicka). The Karaite congregation was subject to similar rights and obligations as the Jewish community lower in the town (podmiejska). Together they paid joint taxes and property taxes to the castle. On the 27th October 1475, the two communities entered into an agreement, and regularized their mutual interaction with the authorities. The Karaites undertook city patrols, special tasks for the castle, such as: obligation to escort the thieves to the castle; patrol of the castle; provide the castle and the governing officials with a supply of horses, as well as food provisions during the King's visit to Lwów. In exchange, the Jews undertook to pay in cash all the taxes owed to the King and the Starosta. Both communities paid together the payments for the fortifications; both had a single cemetery shared also by the Jewish community within the town. The Karaites enjoyed also the privileges granted to the Jews by the kings of Poland: the privilege of Casimir the Great in 1364, and of Casimir Jagiellon in 1453. However, at the end of the 15th century, in 1475, the Karaites left Lwów for Halicz where a small Karaite community already existed.[1]

The Jewish community which most years grew and expanded,[2] developed also in the area of trade and craftsmanship. From the organizational–social aspect, the community formed the centre of ethnic life.

The life of the community customarily revolved around the synagogue (Vorstädtische Schul), where the community leaders and the law–court [Beth–Din] convened. In the suburb the Jews purchased plots of land and houses without special difficulties, since according to the royal privilege approved also by King Sigismund Augustus on the 1st October 1568, they were granted the right to purchase and sell houses. The privilege was rigorously maintained by the starostas, and one of them, Boniface Mniszek, declared in a special ruling of the 18th July 1618, that the Jews of the suburb were house owners who within the Krakówite suburb were entitled to purchase houses from Christians, and Christians were equally entitled to sell property to the Jews. That ruling obliged the Jews to pay the castle only the predetermined payments.

In time a division rose between the Jews outside the town and those within it, which divided them so that they regarded one another with derision and even contempt. The Jews outside the town (Vorstädtische) called the Jews within the town (Städtische) "dumb", and they termed the others "good–for–nothing". The schism was further increased since the Jews outside the town had synagogues, baths and fairs of their own and did not need the Jews within the town.

Jewish children at the beginning of the 18th century

The last Rabbi to serve both communities till 1599, was Rabbi Izak Eizyk ben Jechiel. After his demise, the joint rabbinate of the two communities ceased. Till 1680, each community was served by a Rabbi who acted as head of the rabbinic court, and each community had its own permanent ritual law–court. During that period, the community outside the town was served by Rabbi Mojzesz ben Mardochaj Askenazy (died in 1620), followed by Rabbi Jakob Koppelben Aszer HaKohen.

[Pages 87-88]

Soon after Rabbi Jakob Koppel took office he had a dispute with the scholars within the town, Rabbi Abraham Rappoport-Schrenzel] (author of *Ethan Haezrachi,* and Aron Aba ben Jochanan. The issue was trees whose branches spread over the cemetery practically like a Sukkah [ritual Tabernacles hut], and the restriction on Kohanim [ritual priests] to walk under the shade of trees. He died in 1630 and the rabbinical seat was occupied by Rabbi Mardochaj ben Cwi–Hirsz [Tzvi-Hirsch] Aszkenassy who was rabbi for just six years (1636). He was followed by Rabbi Josua ben Jozef, author of *Megine Schlomoh* and of the Responsa *Pneh Josua*, who was invited to serve as rabbi at Kraków; Rabbi Meszulam Salzburg ben Abraham Askenazy, who filled important roles in the Council of the Four Lands. After his death in 1645, the elected rabbi was the son–in–law of the great scholar [HaGaon] MaHaRam of Lublin, Rabbi Jozef ben Eliakim Goetz who was a leading authority in his day. He died in 1652 and his successor was the renowned rabbi outside the town, Rabbi David ben Samuel Halevy auther of *Turei Zahav* son–in–law of the great scholar [HaGaon] Rabbi Joel Sirkes (author of *Bayit Chadash*), known by the people as the "T–Z" after his book *Turei Zahav*. When Sabbataj Cwi [Shabbatai Zevi] came on the scene, he sent his son Rabbi Isajah and his stepson Rabbi Aryje Lew to test him. His sons returned enthused, but the T–Z was not impressed. The education of Sabbataj Cwi justified his position. At the rabbinate outside the town, the successor of the T–Z was Rabbi Jehuda Judel, son of Rabbi Mojzesz of Lublin, who was the last rabbi outside the town.[3]

The Synagogue's Beadle

Starting in 1680 a joint rabbi again served the two communities.

Until 1623, the life of the community outside the town had quietly developed with no particular interference. In the same year however, a great fire broke out near the synagogue which quickly spread throughout the Quarter and also destroyed the Christians' neighbourhoods.

Ritual Purim food dispatch

According to the chronicler Zimorowic almost 1,200 houses burnt down, including all the houses that belonged to the Jews, the synagogue in which a large library was consumed, and up to the Krakówite gate and the women's Benedictine church.

The municipality wanted to take advantage of the situation and to forbid the Jews from rebuilding their houses in that Quarter, and especially the synagogue. But the Jews did not rest and their lobbying led to an agreement on the 30th April 1624, according to which the Jews were allowed to construct a new road from the Poltva [Peltew river] eastwards, in the direction of the Benedictine monastery; to rebuild the ruined synagogue, but in a new location, at the foot of the Poznan castle[a]; to vacate the plots of land near the town–walls and to acquire instead new plots according to their wishes on which to build new houses. On the 10th July 1624, the King approved the agreement.

The Jews succeeded in obtaining a permit to build a synagogue also from archbishop Jan Andrzej Próchnicki, provided that the synagogue did not have a sumptuous exterior, and that it did not differ from the other residential houses.

Soon the residential houses were built around the Krakówite square. The construction of the synagogue was delayed due to lack of funds. In order to cover the expenses, the community used penalty fees from the religious law–court of Lwów and of its adjacent communities (przykahalki). Yet in 1632 the synagogue was erected, incorporating a women's section and a hall for the law–court [Beth Din]. In the "hallway" next to the stove was a prison cell (pillory). The building existed in its entirety until the Holocaust in 1941.

The community did not remain peaceful for long, however. In 1640, after the feast of Shavuot [Pentecost], again a fire broke out at the house

[Pages 89-90]

of the cantor Mardochaj with the flames quickly spreading to the neighbouring houses. A large section of the new synagogue was destroyed.

In addition to the conflagration disaster, plots of land adjacent to the Ruthenian monastery, which had belonged to Jews for over a hundred years, were stolen from them even before the fire broke out.

All attempts were to no avail, including the ruling by King Wladislaw IV of the 17th April 1640, that the monastery return the plots to the Jews.[4] Instead, the monks from the monastery together with hundreds of students attacked the houses of the Jews. On the 24th July 1640, while everyone was attending a wedding at the house of the Jew Eliyahu, they burgled their houses and caused great damage to the synagogue which had been restored after the fire.

When they saw it, the Jews chased the rioters, and when they learnt that most of the loot was in the house of Jan Podwysocki, they entered his house and gave it a thorough search. During the search, the [Jewish] lobbyist Zelig threw a few paintings of Christian saints and also broke a crucifix. When the Armenian archbishop Torosiewicz heard of that, he went immediately to the house of Podwysocki, assembled the fragments of the crucifix, put it together on the table and lit two candles as a symbol of mourning. A mass of Christians began to assemble around the house and to threaten the Jews. A delegation of Jews went to the castle to ask for help. In order to prevent a mob outbreak, Burgrave Gawłowski entered the house of Podwysocki, put out the candles and took with him the broken crucifix. The consistory demanded that he return the crucifix, and filed a legal case against the Jews for blasphemy.

The Voivode of Reissen, Jakob Sobieski, demanded that both parties appear at his law–court on the 8th August 1640. The friars did not appear however, claiming that they did not wish to litigate with wealthy Jews, and so the matter was dropped.

The Jews on their part submitted another court case against the friars demanding the return of their plots of land which after negotiations they got back in exchange for financial compensation. The overcrowding within the Quarter increased as did the dirt.

Due to the continual increase of population, there was unparalleled overcrowding within the houses. As the houses were built of timber, fires frequently broke out and destroyed the entire Quarter. In the Quarter within the town there was similar overcrowding, only unlike those in the Krakówite Quarter, there the houses were built of stone. The flats of the Jews were small and narrow. Due to the overcrowding and the absence of plots of land it was necessary to add further floor levels to existing houses, so that four and five stories were not uncommon sights. Flats were also formed in basements and attics, and partitions were placed inside rooms to let more families dwell there. Inevitably, even within the town under such circumstances, neither the cleanliness nor the required facilities for the health of the residents was available.

A room in a Jewish house

In the Krakówite Quarter, unlike the community within the town, lived mainly impecunious Jews, pedlars and craftsmen. A mob also assembled there, and not once were Jewish thieves caught there and even robbers such as Abraham Dankowicz, Heszel Juśko and the infamous murderer Dawid Moszkowicz Konfederat. He started off as a horse trader, later he stole horses and when he grew older he organized and led a gang of robbers who attacked merchants passing along the road to Glinyany. Izak of Lublinand Moszko "thief" who led a Jewish–Christian gang, struck fear in the Jewish Quarter and in those on the roads, and the attacks, clashes and thefts in the Quarter continued unabated.

Members of the underworld also helped the nobles to recruit new settlers for the settlements that were founded in the eastern regions of Poland.

[Pages 349-350]

Notes: – **CHAPTER 5**
All notes in square brackets [ ] were made by the translator.
[The spelling of most personal names were sourced from reference books listed by the author.]

1.   Dr. Majer Bałaban: *Studja historyczne*. Warszawa. 1927. pp. 15–17.

2.   In 1670, Ulryk Werdum wrote on his visit to Lwów: "Here (at Lwów) a great many Jews. They occupy the entire suburb West of the town, and maintain there a synagogue. In addition, Jews reside along a large street in the centre of town where they maintain another two synagogues." Xavery Liske: *Cudzoziemcy w Polsce*. Lwów 1886.

3.   Salomon Buber: *Anshei Shem*
Dr. Jecheskiel Caro: *Geschichte der Juden in Lemberg*. pp. 116. 122.

4.   Dr. M. Bałaban: *Zydzi Lwowscy*, pp. 224–227.

5.   Translation of [Wladislaw] Syrokomla: *Wilno* 1851, pp. 77–78.

6.   Dr. M. Bałaban: *Zydzi Lwowscy*, pp. 499–507.

Translator's footnote:

a.   It is possible that the author meant here: Lwów's High Castle, or castle hill

[Pages 91-92]

Chapter 6: Distinguished Families

Translated by Myra Yael Ecker

Edited by Ingrid Rockberger

Nachmanowicz family: Rabbi Isak ben Nachman, Rabbi Mardochaj and Nachman. "The Golden Rose". The businesses of the Nachmanowicz family. Rabbi Izrael Eideles (Złoczowski). Attitude of the Christians. Rabbi Jakob ben Wolf Gombrycht. Rabbi Jakob Doktorowicz. Rabbi Izak ben Samuel Halevy. The attacks by students. The issue of converts.

From the history of a number of Jewish families who, until 1647 held prominent roles in all aspects of the life of Lwów, one can also glean the development of the community and of the Jewish way of life.

From among those families the family of Rabbi Isak ben Nachmann (Nachmanowicz) stood out. He and his sons ruled the community and its institutions for some eighty years, and through their ambition and wealth they amassed a large variety of economic sectors in their hands.

It is not known whether the founder of that family, Rabbi Izak ben Nachman, was born at Lwów or whether he came from another town. He was first mentioned in a document from 1565,[1] where, as member of the religious law-court [Beth-Din] he was entered as "Doctor". Since he was not a rabbi, he was presumably given the title as a community leader on the Reissen regional committee. He also attended the meetings of the Council of the Four Lands, at Lublin and Jaroslaw.

Izak was talented and deft in his dealings. He had financial contacts with Konstanty Korniakt, one of the wealthiest men of his generation. Rabbi Izak loaned money with interest, against bills and mortgages, his own money as well as sums which he had received from wealthy townspeople, nobles and the clergy. Besides his financial business he also leased the revenue from customs, state and local road-taxes, a flour mill and trade in merchandise from the East. His businesses included many economic sectors during his lifetime. He rose to riches, was respected by the Jews and kept in close contact with the country's notables. Due to his status, in legal trials he was not obligated to take the Jewish version of the oath, instead he was sworn in as one of the town's residents. His wife, Chawale [Chwala], known to the public as *Bogata* [wealthy] or *Pani* [Mrs.], helped him in his business affairs. He was influential at the royal court of King Sigismund Augustus who, in 1571, helped him also obtain the house on the border of Ruska Street and the Jewish Quarter.

Rabbi Izak, who was involved in his community, also personally financed the building of a new synagogue after the old synagogue had burnt down in 1571. It was built anew, but it was too small to contain the large number of worshippers.

In 1578, he purchased Oleska Square (in the Jewish Quarter) from the municipality, and after he obtained the royal license he engaged the renowned architect, the Italian Paulus Italus [Paolo Romano]. to build the synagogue. In 1582 the building was constructed in the Gothic style. Adjacent to the synagogue, Paulus built for him a private residence which was connected to the synagogue by a single entrance-corridor. From 1604, the synagogue also served as the seat of the religious law-court and the archival storage of the community's records.

Rabbi Izak wanted to enlarge the synagogue and to add a raised gallery for a women's section, but during the preparations, in 1595, he died.

After his demise his affairs were managed by his wife, till her death in 1611, and by his two sons Rabbis Mardochaj and Nachman. His only daughter was married to the wholesaler Salomon, who conducted trade in crops with Armenians. His sons were scholars who, when not engaged in business affairs, dedicated themselves to the Torah. His assets in houses and plots of land were divided up between his sons Mardochaj and Nachman. Mardochaj received the house adjoining the synagogue, which he had enlarged by the architect Paulus.

Mardochaj who was a careful dealer with most of his business in leasing, especially the leasing of taxation, was also active in his community, and led its negotiations with the municipality about the rights of Jewish merchants. For that reason he was hated by the townspeople, and once, on his return from a fair at Sniatyn they even attacked him in the town square, during which attack he lost 500 Gulden. He did not deal in loans of any kind.

During many years he was head of the community as well as head and leader of the Land of Reissen [Ruthenia]. He represented both of those in front of the authorities and the King. He personally funded a hospital and a temple, built by Paulus. He also established a fund of "Hachnasat Kala" [ritual collection of funds for poor brides and grooms], a collection for "Gmilut Chassadim" [a ritual requirement to extend interest-free loans] (*pius mons*), clothing fund for poor boys, an alms fund for those out of work, as well as a fund for the ransom of captives. His home was open to visitors, and he always gave lodgings to Yeshiva boys, rabbis and scholars.

[Pages 93-94]

Unlike him, his brother Nachman was a more adventurous trader, quick-witted and undeterred even by risky business. He had strong links with the Christians who addressed him as "Mr. Nachman" Lwów resident (civis leopoliensis), and in documents he was even termed "Noble Jew" (*generosus judaeus*). His wife Roza was known by the people as "The Golden Rose".

The municipality treated him with admiration since the "Lwów Jew Nachman Izakowicz behaved well towards the town, and acquired major rights for the needs of the town." More than once when the municipality was in financial difficulties, he assisted with loans, and unlike the Christian patricians, such as Kampian, who received high interest, Nachman did not press the municipality when on occasion it had failed to pay the rates, affording it an extension of time so that the municipality felt obliged to treat him fairly.

Nachman was largely engaged in the business of loans with Christians, leases and management of public revenues such as: taxes, salt mines, fish ponds, mills, forests etc. A faithful assistant in his business was his wife Roza bat Jakob, a feisty woman who, after the death of Nachman in 1616, was able to manage the business and increase the family assets. Due to her wealth and beauty she was influential among circles of the nobility and the authorities, who referred to her as "noble lady" (*szlachetna pani*), although her official title was: 'infidelis Rosa Nachmanowa', and the municipality wrote about her in the unusual form: "the citizen of our town Lwów."

"The Golden Rose" was goodhearted and many legends about her were kept alive. She participated in the affairs of the community, contributing especially through her influence with Starosta Mniszek.

Roza played an important role in the trial between the Jesuits and the Jews, and from the legends spun about her by the people three versions remain:

> 1.   During the trial against the Jesuits Roza hosted a big banquet for the King and the nobles in order to win their hearts. She succeeded in receiving a written licence from the King, and when she went and handed the King's letter to the archbishop, she was killed and her body was dismembered. She had sanctified God and God will avenge her blood. (Suchystaw's version).

> 2.   When the Catholic clergy wanted to take the synagogue away from the Jews, the Jewish community despaired and begged God for mercy, and He helped them with the peasants' revolt against the King and the Church's influence (allusion to the Zebrzydowski rebellion), so that the Jews were able to call upon the help of the nobles. At the time a beautiful and wealthy woman named Roza lived at Lwów. She was the wife of a doctor. With her own money she engaged good lawyers, and taking advantage of the revolt she secured the return of the synagogue to the Jews by the law-court. When the priests turned the synagogue into a church, Roza found her way to the King who ordered the archbishop to give back to the Jews their prayer house. There was happiness and joy in the community, and the poet Izak, the brother of Dawid, composed a song of praise in honour of that woman.
> The Jesuits did not rest however, and blamed Roza of a crime. They tried her and sentenced her to death, and she was killed on the 26th September 1635. (the version of Natan Nata Samuely).

> 3.   When Roza came to see the archbishop, he demanded that she stay with him, and she replied: "I will do so as long as you first give me in writing that you are returning the synagogue to my brother, for I have no faith in you." He fulfilled her request. She dispatched the missive to the community leaders. There was happiness and joy in the Jewish street. Indeed, she had fulfilled her role without desecrating her honour. The archbishop found her lifeless. (version of Dr. Majer Bałaban).

There are other versions which ascribe the Roza affair to the period of the siege by the army of Khmelnytsky [Chmielnicki].

From these legends that have no historical basis, one can conclude that Roza was an energetic and influential woman who did many good deeds for her people.

After the demise of her husband she liquidated their financial affairs and demanded that the debtors pay off their loans. That was the background for the many legal actions brought against her, but she managed to collect the debts.

In 1625, the municipality brought a legal action against her regarding the lease of road-taxes, and accused her of exploiting the travellers and forcing them, with the aid of her servants, to pay higher rates than were set by law, and that consequently she caused price increases as well as raising the expense of the town.

After passing through all the different law-courts the case appeared in front of the King who decided that as a private person she was unable to appear before the King. The municipality realized then that it had lost the case and so withdrew its demands.

In 1635, Roza received from Starosta Mniszek plots of land in the Krakówite suburb, and wanted to build houses on them, but the municipality objected. Roza turned to King Wladyslaw IV who ordered the municipality not to interfere in the construction of her houses. Roza died on the 3rd October 1637, and left all her assets and capital to her only son Izak.

Her son Izak Nachmanowicz was also one of the prominent members of

[Pages 95-96]

the Jewish community. A trader with initiative and deftness who was brought up in the luxury of a wealthy home, he was used to being flattered. When the nobles and the townspeople were in need of loans, they came begging to the wealthy Jew, although he slighted them. He was a typical, resolute community member. Even commissaries in the country's Treasury sought his favour, once they realized that he was a wealthy man. In the financial life of Poland he played important roles: in 1626, when the war broke out between Poland and King Gustaw-Adolf of Sweden, Rabbi Izak provided the Treasury with funds, and helped the Polish army in Prussia. Consequently, when King Wladyslaw visited Lwów in 1634, Izak and his partner Abrahamowicz received on the 20th October 1634 a privilege from him, for their services to the Polish army in Prussia and for "continually" providing for the country. The privilege recognized them as "servants of the royal-court" subject only to the King's ruling. They had the right to trade and to erect goods' sheds at Lwów without any restriction, and to trade freely in all the towns of the rest of Poland and Lithuania, and they were released from all royal and private taxes and customs. They had the right to wear expensive clothes and to adorn themselves with a sword and a gold chain, contrary to all Synods' resolutions. Rabbi Izak traded wholesale in fabrics and bulls with Germany, and for the army. Together with his mother he also leased the revenue of Lwów's administration. Imitating the habits of a Polish nobleman, he oppressed the farmers and in 1635 the farmers in the village of Kowczycach near Komarno revolted against him, and Jan, their leader was killed by Izak's servants. But already in 1635 his standing started to decline due to leasing affairs which obliged him to borrow large sums (to the nobleman Jan Gardliński alone, he owed 17,000 Zloty). In 1643, Starosta Mniszek confiscated two of his houses in the Jewish Quarter, because he had failed to pay the Treasury the rates in accordance with to the leasing contracts. Along with the confiscation, a warrant was issued to apprehend him, and by and by the rest of the creditors put in their claims. Rabbi Izak, who still held the position of community leader however, was able to evade them. In 1645, one of his creditors stopped him in Podhajcach [Podhajce] while he had his goods with him, and he was incarcerated in the Jewish jail of Lwów. On the 9th February 1645, the Lwów community leaders released him and helped him escape, and he disappeared without trace. Thus ended the history of one of the wealthiest and most influential families of Lwów and of the whole of Poland.

The son of Rabbi Mardochaj Nachmanowicz, Izak ben Mardochaj, also dealt in leases. In 1634, he was granted by King Wladyslaw the privilege of dealer to the royal court. He too was a community leader, but he held no significant role and nothing is known of his life.

Among the distinguished families was included Rabbi Izrael Eideles who came from Zloczów and was therefore also known as Złoczowski. His business consisted of giving loans, and leases. In 1596 he leased from the nobles of Zloczów all the estates in the vicinity of Zloczów including mills, ponds, and distilleries of brandy, liquor, and dates. Although his affairs were centred around Zloczów, Rabbi Izrael lived at Lwów, where he was a community leader. He built himself a walled house, and had his daughter Bella married to the renowned great scholar [Gaon] Rabbi Jozue Falk Kohen, author of the book *Me'irath Eijnaim*. The latter managed his renowned yeshivah at Lwów, from where emerged: Rabbi Pinkas, the Rabbi of Fulda, author of *Magine Shelomo* [Defenders of Solomon]; Rabbi Isachar Ber ben Izrael Eilenburg [Öhlenberg] (1550-1623); and Rabbi Abraham ben Izrael Jechiel Rappoport-Schrenzel author of *Ethan HaEzrachi* [Ethan the Civilian].

His father-in-law, Rabbi Izrael donated generously to synagogues and communities; founded libraries and synagogues in small towns; married poor brides and also established a fund for Eretz-Israel; and enabled his son-in-law Rabbi Jezue to devote himself, in peace and comfort, to the study of the Torah and to teaching at the yeshivah.

Rabbi Izrael died in 1616, two years after the demise of his son-in-law (Nissan 5374, March 1614)

Also his brother-in-law, Jakob ben Wolf Gombrycht, the husband of his sister Hendla, numbered among the distinguished families. Jakob Gombrycht first appeared on the public scene in 1624. He too was one of the notable lessees of the period, but he got into financial difficulties and in 1634 he was on the brink of bankruptcy. He managed to avoid his creditors only after he had received a one year "deferment letter", from King Wladyslaw, issued during his visit to Lwów.[2] Based on that letter he was entitled to freely conduct trade throughout Poland, and during that year his creditors were prohibited from demanding any payment from him. That extension of time benefitted his financial situation, and in 1635 he tried to lease from the municipality of Lwów the roads and border fees. However, "the masses" refused to lease to Jews even a single franchise of the town.

Gombrycht also filled an important role in the life of the community, and in the years 1620-1634 he was the community leader. In 1634, he negotiated with the town Council and insisted that the Jews be released from paying taxes since the poll tax exempted them from any other tax. His son Efraim and grandson Samuel were oxen traders.

At the end of the 16th century, Jakob Doktorowicz was also a known figure. He was a tax lessee, and partner of Mardochaj ben Izak

[Pages 97-98]

Nachmanowicz. He was in charge of the customs stations at Chelm, Krasnystaw and Potylicz where, as sub-lessee, he leased the customs from the Polish nobles Waclaw Uhrowiecki and Pawel Orzechowski. In 1595, he was accused of blackmailing the trader Sebastyan Fogt of Danzig [Gdansk], and was dismissed from his position. A short time later however, he found a new partner and he leased three mills, fish ponds, market tax and drinks tax at Lwów and Przemyśl. It seems that he had amassed a wide range of businesses. He met with a tragic end: in 1607 he was attacked by his coachman Jan, and his servant Abraham, and after they killed and robbed him of everything, they fled. In 1618, his son Lewko (Levie), bought the house of the convert Jan Baptist Poletowicz, after the latter was forced to leave the Jewish Quarter outside the town.[3]

Of his generation were Rabbi Izak ben Samuel, poet and exalted scholar, and his brother Rabbi Dawid ben Samuel, author of *Turei Zahav* the interpretation of the Shulchan Aruch [an abbreviated form of the Jewish ritual law]. Dawid who had been the pupil of his brother Izak, was Rabbi at Potylicz near Niemirów, and in 1653 of the community outside the town of Lwów. To the people he was known as "The Turei Zahav". The Nachmanowicz synagogue was named after him "Turei Zahav", and on the entrance gate was engraved: "This is the place of worship of Turei Zahav". Rabbi David died in 1667.

Rabbi Izak, his elder brother, was the pupil of Rabbi Jozue Falk, and in 1609 he wrote *Shir HaGeulah* [The Song of Redemption], with an interpretation. That song was introduced into the prayers of the Saturday following Purim. Later, he was Rabbi at Chelmno and in 1627, head of the Yeshiva at Poznan. He also wrote an essay "Siach Jicchak" [Isaac's Discourse], an examination of the Hebrew grammar which was published at Basel in 1627 and at Prague in 1628. On that essay he had received the approbation of Rabbi Jom-Tob Lipman Heller, the author of *Tosafot Jomtob* ["Commentary on Yomtov"; commentaries on the Mishnah]. In 1736 the Responsa was also published.

During the years 1565-1642, these families served the community within the town as community-leaders and "good men", together with members of the families[4]: Jakob Treych, Jakob Zyskint [Susskind], Nachim ben Baruch, Moszko, Abraham Czech. One of the lessees of Reissen's customs, Abraham Czech was one of Izak Nachmanowicz's assistants. Jointly, he paid the Starosta and the Voivode the Jewish-tax due (manus judaicum charitativum). Aron Rubinowicz, the partner of Mardochaij ben Izak Nachmanowicz, together with Rabbi Nachman ben Izak, filled an important role during the trial with the Jesuits. In February 1606, he travelled with Rabbi Nachman and the lobbyist Mendel to Warsaw, and in April 1606, to Kraków and brought the affair to an end when, on the 15th November 1613, he paid the last instalment for the release of the synagogue from the hands of the Jesuits. Izak ben Abraham, the partner of Izak Nachmanowicz, helped the Polish army in 1626, and in 1634, together with Wolf Nachimowicz, Marek Bogaty, Aron and Jakob Giec all received a special privilege from King Wladyslaw.

The attitude of the Christians towards these families was courteous and better than towards the rest of the Jewish population. However, the masses regarded them as Jewish competitors to their own trade and products. They treated differently the wealthy Jews who were also connected to the above mentioned families, through partnership and trade.

The wealthy Jews and the wholesalers suffered with the rest of the Jews from attacks by the Christian mob and students. The religious affiliation was naturally stronger at the time than the economic factor. The masses who were incited by the clergy, were more responsive to the issue of religion, and even the slightest spark sufficed to motivate them to descend on the Jewish Quarter and attack the Jews under the pretext that they had stolen *Hostia*, or charging them with blood libel. In particular, claims intensified that the Jews stole sacred vessels from churches, when they took religious objects as security against loans, making a mockery of the Church's decisions. It was also claimed that wealthy Jews kept Christian servants in contravention of the Synods' decisions. For such attacks they always found support among pupils of the Jesuits and of the Cathedral school, who hated the Jews purposefully, and who were always ready to "invade" the Jewish Quarter, to rob, plunder, beat and even kill Jews, and to punish those Christians who were in the service of the Jews. These attacks were known as "*Schiler Galoif*" [students' run]. The bribes and donations the Jews paid annually to the schools at Lwów in order to prevent attacks, were of no avail. But the Jews did not remain indifferent and they knew how to protect themselves, and they did not recoil from catching students, beating them up and bringing them to jail, or to organize counterattacks in the students' residences, as happened in 1592, 1613, 1642.

A particular issue were the students' attacks on Jewish funerals during the years 1572, 1592, 1613, 1640, 1641, 1642 and 1643.

The Jews suffered gravely from military men who stopped at Lwów or passed through the town and demanded accommodation and money from the community. When the soldiers did not received their salaries, they always found an opportunities to enter the Jewish Quarter and rob what they wished from shops and houses. One Saturday in 1600, the officer Albert Osiecki burst in and killed the Jew Aron Kamchan] [Mączarz]. The Jews responded to the event by attacking every soldier of his company

[Pages 99-100]

who dared come into town. In retaliation for the Osiecki affair they injured several of his soldiers.

The Jews also reacted bravely in response to attacks by adventurous nobles on the Jewish Quarter.

Special types of attacks were organized by Jewish young men on converts who dared remain in the Jewish Quarter even after their conversion. In 1613, one knows of the case of the convert Jan Baptist Poletowicz who was attacked after he continued living in the Krakówite Quarter, and despite the order by King Sigismund III, that the municipality protect the convert from "pestering by the Jews", he was forced to sell his house to a Jew and to leave the Jewish Quarter.[5] On the 2nd September 1605, another convert Michal Michalowicz, sold the "place" he had in the synagogue outside the town, to the manager of the synagogue.

[Pages 349-350]

Notes: – CHAPTER 5
All notes in square brackets [ ] were made by the translator.
[The spelling of most personal names was taken from Bałaban's *Zydzi Lwowscy*.]

1. *Akta grodzkie i zeimskie* t. X Nr. 87.

2. Bałaban: *Zydzi Lwowscy* p. 168.

3. Bałaban: *Zydzi Lwowscy* pp. 385-386; 528.

4. Bałaban: *Zydzi Lwowscy* pp. 566-568.

5. Bałaban: *Zydzi Lwowscy* p. 528.

[Pages 101-102]

Chapter 7: The Massacres of 1648 and 1649

Translated by Myra Yael Ecker

Edited by Yocheved Klausner

Khmelnytsky at the gates of Lwów. His demand for the extradition of the Jews, and the municipality's refusal. Jewish participation in the defence of the town. The resumption of war in 1651. Extension of the contract between the Jews and the municipality. The siege of 1655. The trial to settle the debt owed by the Jews. The riots of 1664. The internal and the financial life. The influence of the Sabbateans.

1648 was a time of tragedy and trouble for the Jews of Poland, severely damaging also the Jews of Lwów. In April 1648, at the head of his army, Khmelnytsky [Chmielnicki] drove westward from the Zaporizhzhya region [Zaporozhian Sich], and during the 6th–15th May he defeated the Polish armed forces under the command of Potocki and Kalinowski. That brilliant victory signaled the outbreak of the general uprising by the Ukrainian citizens. They attacked Poles and Jews in the villages, towns and small towns, mercilessly destroying, robbing and killing everywhere.

The Jewish survivors fled westwards, with many successfully reaching Lwów before the siege. There they found refuge among the overcrowded community. The Jewish Quarter consisted of just two streets that contained forty nine houses; the facade of most of those had only two windows, 7 cubits wide. As the refugees numbered tens of thousands, they were housed with the community outside the town, around the great synagogue which was rebuilt in 1632.

In May 1648, the King of Poland died. The Cossacks took advantage of the interregnum and proceeded westward to Podolia and Volhynia, forging their way towards Reissen. The Polish armed forces under the leadership of Prince Jeremi Wiśniowiecki, retreated to Lwów where they hoped to withstand Khmelnytsky. On the 27th September 1648, Prince Wiśniowiecki assembled the civil and the religious leaders, and demanded that the citizens back the defenders and donate, each according to their means. The warlord's words stirred enthusiasm in the population. A great deal of gold and silver was brought out from the monasteries, the churches and the Jewish synagogues, besides money which the citizens gave to the municipality. The money collected by the Ruthenians amounted to 27,398 Gulden, by the Armenians – 24,502 Gulden, and by the Jews – more than 10,000 Gulden.[1] The value of gold and silver amounted to 300,000 Gulden.

Once the money had been collected and handed to the warlord, the armed forces left the town and news arrived that the Tatars were near Lwów. The town's residents had no option but to fend for themselves. The craftsmen allotted amongst themselves the defence shifts at the posts, the fortresses, and the town's towers. The Jews armed themselves too. They kept watch at those parts of the town–wall that bordered with the Jewish Quarter, and participated in the protection of the town's suburbs.

In September 1648, Khmelnytsky's army, now reinforced by Tatar battalions under the command of Tugay Bey [Tuhaj–Bej], stood at Lwów's town–gates. The chronicler Rabbi Natan Neta, the son of the holy Rabbi Moses Hanover, described the massacres of 1648 and 1649 in his book *JewenMezula* [or *Yeven Mezulah*; *Abyss of Dispair*] (first published at Venice in 1653). He wrote of the siege of Lwów: "After those events Khmelnytsky continued with all his army to lay siege to the holy community of Lwów, the capital which was one of the four great communities[2] of Poland. A large holy town of sages and scribes. And when the enemy arrived, they sat there at nightfall in front of the high fortress,[3] which stands outside the town of Lwów, and from the high fortress shot down at them and killed thousands of Greeks[4] and Ishmaelites.[5] But eventually, as they had no water there, they were obliged to leave the high fortress together with the Poles. And together they descended from the high fortress to the town of Lwów, and the residents set alight all the houses around the town walls, so that no enemy could hide around the town. Nonetheless, the enemy captured the high fortress, surrounded the town and laid siege to it. In the town terror spread, of leaving the house, for fear of the shafts of fire shot down from the high fortress into the town. Plague and great hunger was suffered within the town – outside the sword bereaves and indoors terror. Some ten thousand souls died in the town of hunger and the plague.[6] As time passed and they were unable to conquer the town, they blocked the springs[7] outside the town, which supplied all the water the town's citizens drank, so that there was no water for the community to drink. So the entire community said: Why die of hunger and thirst? Let us send a message to the enemy, perhaps he will accept our assets as redemption of our souls. So the townspeople dispatched messengers to the enemy to compromise

[Pages 103-104]

– they gave him silver and gold as redemption of their souls. As he approved of it, he told his servants: What do we gain from killing them? Let us take their assets as redemption of their souls. So he sent his captain of thousand, by the name of Głowacki, a minister in the Kingdom of Poland who, together with several Cossack ministers of the town, had pledged to him to rebel against the monarchy, to discuss with them a compromise." Till here the words of Rabbi Natan Neta Hanover.

According to Czechowicz,[8] all the town's suburbs and the synagogue outside the town were destroyed by the Cossacks. The townspeople defended themselves courageously and it was their resistance which prompted Khmelnytsky's decision to attack the town. Before his attack on the 10th October 1648, he sent a letter to Lwów's municipality in which he demanded that the Ruthenians hide themselves in their church, and that the municipality hand over to him Prince Wiśniowiecki and the citizens' assets. The townspeople replied that was not in town, and that the citizens who had sworn allegiance to the homeland would continue to protect the town, but they requested that he should not spill Christian blood in vain. To which Khmelnytsky responded that he believed the magnates were not in their hands, but he demanded the extradition of all the Jews with their wives and offspring, since they were the cause of the war, and the financial backers of the battles at Zaporizhia [Zaporoze]. "To that – wrote the mayor Martin Grosswajer in his report – we replied: We are unable to extradite the Jews for two reasons. First – they do not belong to us, but to the King, and they are subjects of the realm. Second – they bear all the burdens and hardships of the time, and they are ready to die with us and even for us". Khmelnytsky sent a further letter with the priest Teodor Rudkiewicz, in which he demanded 200,000 Red Gulden. In case of refusal, he would attack the town and completely destroy it. On that occasion he waived the extradition of the Jews. He wrote: "Those ugly and dirty Jews I leave you, I do not want them at all, they must however participate appropriately in the redemption payment, since they had raked many treasures in Ukraine."

During the letter exchange there was no lull in the fighting, but Khmelnytsky continued in his attempts to prevent the attack on the town. In response to his demand the municipality sent a delegation[9] made up of: the mayor – Czechowicz, alderman – Wąchlowiez, the Armenian – Zechnowicz, the Ruthnian – Lawrysiewycz, and the intermediary of the Jews – Szymon.[10]. After a protracted negotiation, during which the intermediary Szymon was insulted in the Cossack camp, they reached a compromise according to which Khmelnytsky would receive gold, silver and merchandise in the value of 546,276 Gulden. The Jews participated not only in cash, but also in expensive goods, in funds and properties of charitable enterprises as well as in mortgages they had received in exchange for loans, thus losing the capital as well as the interest. An entire year of deliberation with the municipality followed, as to the share of the Jews in the redemption sum. An agreement was only reached in 1649, in which the Jews pledged to participate in the sum of 84,000 Gulden.

Khmelnytsky received the promised sum and retreated toward Żółkiew [Zhovkva], but still there was no rest for the citizens of Lwów. For a long time they continued to suffer hunger, thirst and disease. In the Jewish Quarter a terrible overcrowding prevailed. Due to lack of space, the refugees were scattered in the streets, yards and at the gates of houses, exposed to the cold and rain, disease and epidemics. Abraham ben Samuel Ashkenazy, in his book "Sorrow of Many or Eulogy to Poland,"[11] complains, saying: "Over these I weep (Poland) day and night, over the blow to the holy community of Lemberg [Lwów], a great town, for there was no other like it in the diaspora. How those haters came and surrounded every path, to uproot the Nation like scattered lamb, and inside the blow is duplicated, epidemic and every mishap, even water there was none. For in ancient times a special device fitted with pipes let water from a single spring outside the town, into the town, and from there door by door. And now that the haters came and severed the spring, no cure or channel was found. So they made an excellent repentance, accepted by His throne. Six thousand[12] of the Chosen People died. And had they not given a great fortune to the wrongdoers, they would in their entirety have been like burnt offering, and you God stood still. Avenge the blood of the righteous who gave praise and adoration, and to you God the power and the glory."

The active participation of the Jews in the defence of the town was noted in the praises for their strength and bravery by the nobles at the *Sejmik* of Sudova Vyshnia [SÄ…dowa Wisznia].

On the 17th October 1648, Jan Kazimierz [John II Casimir the brother of Wladyslaw IV, was elected King of Poland.

But the peace and quiet had not yet arrived for the Jews of Lwów who had to accommodate and absorb the thousands of refugees as well as their livelihoods. In 1651, war broke out again between Poland and the Cossacks. Once again Khmelnytsky came out with slogans against the Jews, and his troops were given carte blanche to destroy whole communities and mercilessly to annihilate the Jews.

In 1652, the contract between the Jews and the municipality of Lwów had come to an end. The Jews wished to renew it, unaltered, but the town–Council saw here a convenient opportunity and tried to curtail their rights. When the King heard of it he ordered to extend the contract. The municipality refused to comply with his order, and when he visited Lwów on the 20th June 1653, the German merchant, Atelmaier, loaned the municipality money

[Pages 105-106]

to make presents to the King and his retinue in order to attain a ruling against the extension of the contract. The Jews did not rest and did not remain silent either, and eventually, on the 3rd July 1653, the chancellor, prelate Rożycki confirmed the contract despite the townspeople's lobbying. On the 29th September 1653, the community leaders were invited to the municipality and received a message that the Jews were forbidden all trade in merchandise made of Marocco [Saffian] leather. The community leaders strongly objected to the prohibition. On that occasion the delegates of the Jews were: Rabbi Izak ben Abraham Katz, Aron ben Cwi [Tzvi Segal Meszkisz, Jekusiel Zelman ben Eleazar, Cwi Hirsz ben Efraim the intermediary Fiszel Selman [Zelman], and Mardochaj ben Mojzesz.

In February 1654, the Jews and the municipality agreed on, and signed a new contract for an annual cost of 4,000 Gulden, valid for eight years. That contract included no negative changes in the condition of the Jews, and they were even granted some easements. They were permitted to trade in merchandise up to the value of 1,580 Gulden, at fairs outside Lwów. In case they required additional capital, they were to enter into partnership solely with Christian merchants. At the fairs they had to keep to the opening hours set by the municipality.

According to the contract the payment was destined solely for the defence of the town. Annually, the town Council elected two legal representatives who, together with the town's translator, were responsible for overseeing the precise implementation of the terms of the contract. The Jews were obliged to undertake not to buy the nobles' sympathy with bribes. According to the old custom they had to submit to the municipality's Council a detailed list of the merchants and the wealthy Jews.

The contract itself improved the relationship between the Jews and the townspeople, who had to withstand for the second time an invasion of Reissen by Khmelnytsky's army.

After he had surrendered to the Russian Czar Alexei Mikhailovich in 1655, Khmelnytsky went to war with Poland for a second time, and attacked it from the East. The Swedes took advantage of the situation and invaded Poland from the West, conquering several regions.

One of the Russian army corps which joined Khmelnytsky set out towards Lwów. The town commander, General Krzysztof Grodzicki, ordered to burn down the suburbs. On the 25th September 1655, the first companies of the enemy army were seen near the town, and the negotiation over a cease–fire began a short while afterwards. Among his conditions, the Russian General Buturlin demanded that all the Jews with their women, children and their possessions be handed over, as they were "haters of Jesus and the Christians."

Once again the municipality declared that such a demand would not be satisfied, but that it was ready to pay redemption money according to the townspeople's ability. After lengthy deliberations Khmelnytsky agreed to accept a ransom of 60,000 Gulden. Of that, the Jews paid 8,000 Gulden in cash, apart from merchandise and valuable mortgages.

In 1656, after that blockade was lifted, Lwów was attacked by Prince Rákóczi of Transilvania. He too received redemption money, a large part of which was contributed by the Jews, then he left the town.

The municipality demanded that the community pay off 26,520 Gulden, the remaining debt of the redemption sum which had been paid in 1649; contribution towards the defence expenses (ammunition, fortifications, guarding) 11,500 Gulden; redemption payment of 1655, 9,200 Gulden; fortification of the town in 1657, 7,800 Gulden; debt payment to the municipality, 23,043 Gulden; liquor payments from the Jews of the suburbs, 18,000 Gulden; a total of 96,162 Gulden.[13] The Jews replied that their financial situation had shrunk as a result of liabilities imposed on them during the siege as well as the damage caused by the fires, and consequently they were unable to bear the debt payments, at the time. The municipality paid no heed to their excuses, and sued them. The verdict handed down by the royal tribunal in the years 1663, 1666, was in favour of the town. After an appeal by the Jews however, the Chancellor delayed the execution of the verdict and appointed a new investigation committee in 1667. The relationship between the Jews and the municipality deteriorated due to the trial. Already in 1656, at the start of the disagreement, the municipality demanded that the King forbid the nobles from leasing out flats and shops in their properties, to the Jews. The King confirmed the demand and ordered that the Jews keep their shops and storerooms solely within houses of Jews.[14] In 1658, the municipality succeeded also in obtaining a royal decree forbidding the Jews from practicing medicine, except for doctors who had been accredited by Catholic universities. In the same year, King Jan Kazimierz issued a special instruction according to which the Jews of Lwów who had any legal claim, were forbidden from expropriating houses and real–estate from local Christians without an official court ruling.[15] Financially, the Jews found themselves in much reduced circumstances. Especially grave was the situation of the community outside the town which depended on the benevolence of the castellan ("burgrave") and his officials. In 1653, they were forbidden the trade in salted fish and liquor.

In the years 1658–1660, the authorities escalated their hostile policy toward non–Catholics, which led to inter–congregational tension. The 1658 decision by the *Sejm* to expel all the Aryans by the 10th July 1660, also increased

[Pages 107-108]

the hatred of the Jews. In the *Sejm*, demands were also voiced to expel the Jews, but due to representatives of the Church stating that the Jews owed them vast sums, no actual proposals were submitted.

That was followed by the period of blood–libel charges and attacks on the Jewish Quarters. In 1663, students from the Lwów Jesuit seminary attacked the Jews outside the town, insulted people, broke the windows of their flats, and led to fist–fights. The situation was greatly aggravated when at Lwów and the adjacent small towns suspected persons distributed letters, supposedly from the pope, the emperor and the King, that permitted the beating up of Jews.

Since the clashes recurred time and again, the Jews decided to resist the rioters. From the Starosta Jan of Groß Kuntschitz [Kończyce Wielkie; Great Kunchich as well as from the castellan, who were keen for the Jews to reside in the suburbs, they received an approval to defend themselves with firearms. The Jews bought the arms, learnt the proper way to use them, and kept guard day and night near the synagogue. The precautions by the Jews increased the anger of the thugs who burst in violently, on the 23rd May 1664. It was a Catholic holiday, the Jesuits conducted a festive procession and the Ruthenians arranged a reception for the new archbishop Zeliborski. The Jews, who feared a calamity, approached the Starosta in advance to ask for his protection. Before the holiday, a company of soldiers was sent from the castle to the Jewish Quarter. The holiday took place on a Saturday, but despite the sanctity of the day some 400 armed Jews, mostly young men, assembled in front of the Synagogue then split into three companies: one company, under the command of Leiser was stationed near the royal mills; the second company, under the command of Kuczka – near the butchers' shops, and the third company, under the command of Turczyn – at the Synagogue square. In the early afternoon, farmers from the surrounding villages together with apprentices and servants of the town's nobles began to throng. When they saw the Jews standing ready and armed, they mocked aloud and started to throw stones at them. The defenders hit right and left and succeeded in repelling the attack. The mob began to disperse, but the Jesuits' students who were armed, encouraged and urged them not to retreat. They attacked again, but again they were fought off by the Jews who fought heroically, according to the chronicler Józefowicz of Lwów,[16] who was not known for his sympathy for the Jews.

The victory of the Jews might have been complete were it not for the sudden betrayal of men, from the unit–corps sent by the Starosta, who joined the attackers. The defenders could not withstand the multitude that now outnumbered them tenfold, and they started to retreat. The rioters broke into the houses, robbed and ruthlessly murdered the old, women and children. Then they broke into the synagogue, destroyed all the contents, took out the Torah scrolls, tore and desecrated them. The cantor, Rabbi Szmul [Samuel] ben Jozef Chajote who was immersed in prayer at the time, was ruthlessly murdered. On the same day 102 Jews were murdered and over 200 were wounded.

On the 8th June, after the massacre, Stanislaw Potocki the Starosta of Lwów, sent a message to all the local authorities regarding the riots "which have erupted by the students and the craftsmen, during which they murdered Jews, took over their houses in the onslaught, carried out major robbery and even took children captive, and as I hear – the riots have not yet ceased." Since he learned that the ruffians fled from Lwów with their plunder, he turned to all the authorities with the demand to arrest any man found with booty, valuables or a Jewish child, and send him to his seat (at Podhajce [Pidhaitsi]).[17]

When the events at the Jewish suburb became known in the town, the Council sent beadles to calm down the rioters, but they too were beaten up. The survivors of the suburb managed with great difficulty to escape into the town and find shelter there. Among the survivors was Rabbi David Halevy, the author of *Turei Zahav*, who on that very day had lost two sons, Rabbi Mardochaj and Rabbi Salomon.

The rioters continued with their assaults and tried to break into the town, but by order of the municipality the gates of the town–walls were shut in their faces. At the Jews' request, the head of the Jesuit monastery stood in front of the gate to the Jewish Quarter within the town, in order to stop the students from passing the Quarter's gate before they had managed to shut it. These measures were of little avail. The students continued to threaten from the rooftops that bordered the Jewish Quarter, and even began to invade from there. As the danger increased, the town Council demanded funds from the Jews which, supplemented by funds from the town, paid for the mobilisation of one hundred armed soldiers. The Jews were not satisfied and turned to the chief military commander, Stanislaw Potocki. On the 8th June 1664, when the riots first started at the suburb, Potocki sent a notice to the town Council stating that the command of Lwów and its suburbs was handed over to the artillery officer Ferdynand Wolf, and that one had to stand by him. Following the Jews' petition, Potocki sent two cavalry companies under the command of Tarnawski. He gave them an explicit instruction not to stay with Jews, but only in the houses of Christians, within and outside the town – lodging under duress and coercion. This fact formed

[Pages 109-110]

an additional ground for the students to incite the masses against the Jews, accused of that burden.

The 12th June 1664 was another Christian holiday and there was fear of renewed riots. In order to preempt any trouble the Council convened a meeting of the craftsmen's guilds, to convince them not to join the rioters, but their response was total indifference. The mayor, the renowned historians Bartlomiej Zimorowic, visited the Jesuits and asked them to prevent the students from acts of violence. Although they promised to do their best, it was clear that they would not keep their promise.

The students assembled for prayer in the Dominican Church. The Council sent the town's beadles and assistants to participate in the protection of the Jewish Quarter, but many of them refused to obey the instruction. After the prayer the students left for the Jewish Quarter at the head of a mob of craftsmen's apprentices and the poor. They succeeded in breaking in, and with rage and fury they attacked the houses of the Jews. To prevent any mob outside the town from joining the rioters, the mayor ordered to shut the town gates. The town's citizens were recruited and a delegation was sent to the Catholic archbishop, Jan Tarnowski, as well as to the Jesuits, to employ their full influence on the youths to stop the riots. Meanwhile, Tarnawski and his cavalry had reached the closed town gates and forced them open, which allowed the mob outside to enter the town and increase the rows of rioters. Forcing the gates open led to a conflict between commander Tarnawski and the Council members, and consequently the armed citizens left their posts. The rioters prepared for a new attack. Tarnawski ordered his soldiers to beat the mob, and he even fired a cannon in order to disperse them, but all his efforts to control the situation were to no avail. The riots continued till dusk and their results – total destruction of the Jewish Quarter, pillage of money, collaterals and jewelry. "With spite and fury they killed and slaughtered over one hundred souls, scholars, renowned men, wealthy men, leaders, who were our protection on the day of wrath. And in the pandemonium they stole a few hundreds of thousands of their money and gold, and great rabbinical judges were also killed."[18] On that day 129 Jews were killed, among them rabbis, community leaders and scholars, such as the great scholar [gaon] Samson ben Bezalel [Bacalel];[19] heads of the Yeshivot: Menachem ben Izak,[20] Elieser ben Aszer,[21] Izak ben Samuel,[22] Moyses ben Haim,[23] Aron Jechiel ben Jozef,[24] Mardochaj ben Salomon;[25] the judge and head of the ritual law–court [Beth–Din] Rabbi Juda Leib ben Mojzesz

Margulies;[26] the community leaders and elders: Samuel ben Juda,[27] Salomon[28] and his son Abraham, Mardochaj ben Jechiel Kohn,[29] and Dawid [David] ben Daniel.[30] More than two hundred were injured, some of whom died later of their injuries.

A few days later the students tried to attack homeless Jews who roamed the streets. This time, men of the civil guard got involved, and using firearms they caught the attackers and handed them over to the municipal law–court. A civilian named Stontel, who sided with the Jews, the Armenian priest Szymanowiez and a few other Christians were injured and killed in the shootings.

A large number of the Christian citizens of the town showed some sympathy for the Jews, and many concealed refugees and saved them. Stanislaw Potocki, the Starosta of Lwów who was also the Voivode of Kraków, wrote to the Kraków municipality and demanded the extradition of the rioting students who had fled there.[31]

The authorities investigated forthwith. The municipality was accused of negligence and insufficient care to maintain order and prevent the outbreak of riots. The municipal law–court was instructed to collect evidence from the Jews about the extent of the damages. The community leaders within the town – Zelman Lewkowicz and Samuel Judkiewicz, and the community leaders outside the town – Aron Dawidowicz and Michał Judkowicz, appeared before the law–court and delivered the report about the damages in the presence of the Starosta and the clerks. In the suburbs outside the town some 1,000 persons from all strata of the Jewish community were injured – including: rabbis, merchants, craftsmen, and the extent of their damages came to 300,000 Gulden. The number of injured within the town was also large, and the damage had reached 700,000 Gulden. In the two synagogues, ornamental curtains to cover the front of the Holy Ark [Parochot], candelabra and some Keter–Torah, and holy vessels were stolen and destroyed. In the synagogue outside the town, which contained walls of the fortress, one of the pillars was destroyed and the damage amounted to 70,000 Gulden.[32]

The pogroms at Lwów shocked not only the Jews throughout Poland, but also the heads of the Polish clergy and nobility. The archbishop of Łuck [Lutsk] – Mikołaj Prażmowski, the Voivode of Sandomierz – Jan Zamojski, the priest Szczuka – on behalf of Queen Ludwika Maria as well as many magnates submitted written complaints about the injury to citizens loyal to the King whose rights, guaranteed in writing, were no less than those of the rest of the town's population. All of them stressed that these events defiled the name of Lwów, and that the municipality had to compensate the Jews, and were it not to do so shortly, steps would need to be taken against the town.

[Pages 111-112]

The *Sejmik* which convened at Wisznia [Vyshnia] at the time, demanded a thorough investigation. King Jan Kazimierz [John II Casimir Waza] was also astounded by the events at Lwów, and on the 22nd June 1664, 10 days after the riots, he sent from Wilno [Vilnius] an order to all the authorities and Councils announcing that irresponsible persons were passing through targeted areas with fake documents in their hands. They were inciting the population against the Jews, murdering and stealing from them. Such actions were against the law, and the local authorities had to take action against those people, as well as to suppress in advance any riots and disturbances.[33]

One of those magnates, Leszczynski, the Starosta of Lutsk, appeared at the gates of Lwów accompanied by his men, and attacked the townspeople. The civil guards succeeded in fighting off the invaders and in capturing some of them. Stanislaw Bieniewski, the marshal of the Lublin Tribunal, considered it a grave insult to the nobility, and on the 4th August he sent a harsh letter to the municipality of Lwów in which he demanded the immediate release of the captives. As the municipality did not fulfill his demand, Bieniewski filed a court case against it, in which the town's advisors were accused. The verdict was later annulled by the King since the matter was strictly under his own authority or that of the *Sejm*.

On the 30th June 1664, following the repeated demands of the Jews, the King appointed an investigation committee. The committee was made up of: two noblemen, two senators, two priests and the King's Secretary. The committee concluded that the municipality was guilty, of neglect in protecting the Jews, and of the rampaging of the rioters. The municipality argued that the students of the Jesuit seminary were solely responsible for the riots, since Tarnawski's squadrons had been sent to protect the Jews. Although those squadrons were ineffective, the municipality could not be held responsible for that, and besides the Jews, Christians were also killed during the riots. The committee was not swayed by the argumentation of the municipality, and continued to collect evidence, and once the enquiry was concluded all the information was transferred to the royal law–court. Behind the scenes rumours spread that the Jews bribed members of the committee, although there was no justification or proof.

On the 24th July 1668, a verdict was issued in which the town's Council was ordered to pay compensation *główcyzna*[34] to the families of the murdered, and to the injured, for grief and healing.[35] In addition it had to pay the King's Treasury a monetary fine for every Jew killed or maimed.[36] Four of the town mayors, four advisors and four members of the Council of forty, whose names were to be decided by the Jews – were to be punished by imprisonment for one year and six weeks.

According to the verdict the municipality was made to pay for all the damages to the synagogues, to dwellings, property, mortgages and cash, as well as for the cost of the court–case. The Jews were promised, that in future they would own their houses and the existing synagogues that required restoration, as well as the right to rent flats in the houses of Christians.

It is not known how far the verdict was carried out. One can only surmise that a compromise was reached since the Jews had no wish to see the reciprocal relationship strained once more, especially during a period marked by religious intolerance. At Lwów the municipality forbade all Protestant worship –consequently the Scottish merchants who had resided in the town for hundreds of years, were expelled. The way the Jews were treated was affected in no small measure by religious persecution, although the source of tension was not purely religious, but also economic.

It should be noted that in 1670 the *Sejmik* at Wisznia again debated the riots, and pleaded against the government which had not settled the matter of the "destruction of the Jews" – evidence that the verdict had not yet been executed. After the riots the *Sejmik* at Halicz [Halych] demanded the punishment of the "guilty of the blood–bath".

In 1669, Jan Kazimierz relinquished the throne. Mikhal Wiśniowiecki [Michael I] was elected his heir, a man with liberal views but helpless at holding on to the reins of power. Immediately after his coronation all the privileges of the Jews of Poland were confirmed, including the rights of the Jews of Lwów.

* *

What was the way of life of the Jews of Lwów during the pogroms, murder and robbery which lasted over thirty years?

The Jewish Quarter within the town remained in a state of overcrowding. The Jewish area only circumscribed 49 narrow plots of land which obliged Jews to reside also outside the Quarter. The process of leaving the Quarter started already in 1633. The population overflow moved to the community outside the town, at the Krakówite Quarter, which in time became larger than the community within the town. In the years 1648 and 1655, the community suffered greatly. Almost all the houses were burnt down in the fires that broke out, and the residents had to flee and find shelter outside the community. A great many refugees from towns, small towns and villages who had escaped from the sword of the enemies also streamed into Lwów, so that the overcrowding in the Quarter inside the town increased even further. The Jews of the suburb who were attacked by the enemies were also obliged to flee into the Jewish areas within the town, and there was no option other than to spread into the streets of the Christians, against their wishes. The townspeople considered it a breach of contracts and reacted harshly. On the 26th May 1656, under pressure from the town, King Jan Kazimierz issued a regulation according to which the Jews were not permitted to lease or rent accommodation or warehouses in the houses of Christians.

[Pages 113-114]

In case of contravention of the regulation the authorities were entitled to remove the Jews from the flats and to punish the Christian owners. These regulations were to no avail, since they were never kept.

The Lwów community–life was similar to that of other communities in large towns. The control was in the hands of a circle of distinguished men who by the system of voting were assured the final say over the management of the community, and the choice of the dues collector at institutions and companies. The annual elections mostly took place during "Chol HaMoed" of Passover. There were three separate ballot boxes: in one – names of the leaders, the respected, and community members called up to the Torah. In the second – names of the dues collector on

A Polish Jew

the community boards, and in the third – names of the rest of the tax payers. The beadle used to remove two slips of paper from the first ballot box, emptying the rest into the second ballot box. From it, he again removed two slips of paper, emptying the rest into the third ballot box. Lastly, two slips of paper were removed from it too. The six men whose names were extracted from the three ballot boxes were the voters, and they elected the new community leaders. Occasionally the authorities intervened in the selection of the men. There were incidences when the Jews lobbied men within the authorities to obtain jobs in the community, although according to the 1583 decision of the "Council of Four Lands", the candidates for Rabbi and community–leader were forbidden from lobbying the king or the authorities.

The ruling circle usually exploited its position for its own pleasure and benefit, such as: loading the yoke of taxes on the multitude, attaining monopoly and economic advantages, legislating regulations against the admittance of foreign Jewish merchants without the permission of the monthly community–leader. Thus for instance, the community of Lwów decided that Jews who came to Lwów to trade, were not permitted to sell leather or other merchandise directly to craftsmen, or to other Christian buyers. Instead, they had to sell such items to local Jewish traders. The community issued particularly severe regulations against foreign merchants who clandestinely sold their goods to hostelries in the suburbs. The community leaders were punctilious about the economic activity of the communities in the surrounding small towns (province). They were obliged to purchase their Etrogs [Citrus fruit required for the ritual celebration of Tabernacles] at Lwów; they were forbidden from selling liquor to Christians at Lwów, and so forth. From time to time such action led to conflicts, between the representatives of the small towns and the Lwów community–leaders, at the regional committee.

Within the autonomous organization of Polish Jewry, the Lwów community was the centre of the Reissen–Podolia–Braclaw province [Land]. Its community–leaders and elders were the Land leaders, mostly without any representation from the other communities in the Land. The 1692 ruling by Voivode Marek Matczynski (Clause 2), had already stated clearly that the leaders of the two communities of Lwów were the leaders of the Land, who fulfilled their roles in accordance with the set statutes and privileges.[37]

After the massacres of 1648, the situation had completely changed. The communities of Lwów which had been gravely hit by the riots, were economically greatly depleted and consequently their controlling influence and status decreased. In contrast, the communities of Brody, Tarnopol, Buczasz [Buchach], and especially Żółkiew [Zhovkva] rose greatly after 1648.

The names are known of those community–leaders who had signed the commitment to participate in the ransom payment in 1640, of those who had signed the contract with the municipality in 1654, and of those who were murdered in the riots of 1664. The names of some of the leaders who took part in the sessions of the Council of Four Lands are also known: Rabbi Jekutiel Salman, Rabbi Aronsz of Lwów (in 1661),[38] Rabbi Samuel ben Jakob of Lwów (in 1666),[39] Rabbi Izak Eizyk ben Rabbi Eliezer, Rabbi Aronsz of Lwów (in 1667 and 1671),[40] the son of Gaon [great scholar] Rabbi Salomon ben Reb Izak Abraham Charif (in 1672).[41]

Almost throughout the years of the [Jewish] autonomy in Poland, Lwów was the seat of the principal dues collector for the Eretz [Erec] Israel fund. His title was "President of Eretz Israel". The funds collected for Eretz Israel from the communities of Poland and Lithuania by the dues collector for Eretz Israel, were sent annually to Lublin, to the Council of Four Lands, and from there to Lwów for the "President of Eretz Israel".

[Pages 115-116]

The Presidents known to us, apart from Rabbi Nachman ben Rabbi Izak, the founder of the old synagogue within the town, were: the renowned gaon [great scholar] Rabbi Abraham ben Rabbi Izrael Katz Rappoport-Schrenzel [Szrencel], Rabbi Abraham Fiszel ben Rabbi Cwi [Tzvi] who had been head of the rabbinic court and leader of the Council of Four Lands (he died at Lwów in 1653), and Doctor Simcha Menachem de–Jonah.

Among the intermediaries active at the time are known: Rabbi Szymon who together with representatives of the town, participated in the negotiations with Khmelnytsky and the intermediary Mardochaj ben Mojzesz, who conducted the 1659 negotiations of the trade contract.

The Rabbis who served within the town were: Rabbi Majer ben Abraham (of sacred lineage), in the years 1638–1654, the Rabbi, Reb Naftali Herz ben Judah Zelki [Selki] of Kraków, died in 1669; Rabbi Cwi Hirsz ben Zacharyasz [Zecharja], Mendel Klausner, in the years 1669–1684. Born at Kraków, he played an active role in the sessions of the Council of Four Lands. In 1684, he was elected Rabbi at Lublin and left Lwów. The community outside the town was served by the following rabbis: Rabbi Meschulam ben Abraham Askenazy was elected after the gaon Rabbi Jozue ben Rabbi Jozef, author of *Megine Schlomoh*, had left Lwów; Rabbi Jozef ben Eliakim Giec [Goetz], son–in–law of MaHaRaM of Lublin, died in 1652; The gaon Rabbi Dawid ben Samuel Halevy, author of *Turei Zahav*, died in 1667. The last rabbi of that community was Rabbi Jehuda–Judel ben Mojzesz of Lublin, who died in 1697.

From 1680 onwards a single rabbi, Rabbi Mojzesz Pinkas ben Izrael served both communities. He was a native of Lwów. On his maternal side he was the great–grandson of Rabbi Jezaja [Jesaja] Horowitz [Hurwitz]. His wife was the granddaughter of Rabbi Abraham Rappoport-Schrenzel (*Ethan Haezrachi*). He participated in the Council of Four Lands, in 1673,[42] 1684,[43] 1687,[44] 1688,[45] 1697,[46] 1718.[47]

During that period the Rabbi received a weekly salary of 8–10 Gulden, a cost–free flat, and a special pay for two homiletic sermons on Great Saturday [Shabbat Hagadol = the Sabbath before Passover] and Repentance Saturday [Shabbat T'shuva = the Sabbath between Rosh Hashana and Yom Kippur]. The regional Rabbi received 5 Thalers for each homiletic sermon, while the town Rabbi received 2.5 Thalers.[48]

That period, fraught with tribulations and calamity, formed a suitable setting for the spread of Sabbataj Cwi's [Shabbatai Zevi's] movement among Poland's Jews. After the years 1648–1649, an anxiety spread among the Jews over the continuity of the Jewish people, and that movement which raised the hope of a return to Zion and the recovery of Jewish independence in Eretz Israel, found a response there, although its aims were not political but religious–mystical. A significant role in the successful spread of the movement lay in psychological factors. The general mood among the Jewish population was particularly suited for absorbing beliefs and mysticism. "For there is no country like Poland – wrote at the time the physician Tobiasz Kohn [Tuviyah Cohn *or* Katz][49] – where the belief in demons, jesters, sorcery and so on, is so embedded both among the Jews and the Christians." Interestingly, when the movement first spread in Poland, those who had been most affected by it, were the respected, and heads, of the Jewish population. One of the first to set off for Constantinople was Rabbi Berechyah-Berach Schapira, author of *Zerah Berach* [Birach's Seed], a relative and heir of *Magid Mesharim* [Preacher of Righteousness] at Kraków, Rabbi Natan Schapira, author of *Megale Amukot* [Revealer of the Depths]. From there he sent detailed information about the revelations of Shabbatai Zevi. After his demise (1666) at Constantinople, the Rabbi of Kraków, Rabbi Aryeh–Leib ben Zacharaya Mendel (author of *Tikunei Teshuva* [Prayers of Repentance] in Yiddish) got in touch with the people of the "messiah" and disseminated the writings of Natan HaAzzati. After a while letters and leaflets reached Poland relating the miracles and wonders which Shabbatai Zevi had performed in sight of the entire Jewish community. The rumours about the "messiah" also spread to Lwów, and their influence was so great that the rabbi, Rabbi David Halevy author of *Turei Zahav*, sent to Constantinople (Purim 1666) his son Rabbi Izajasz [Isaiah] and his step–son, Rabbi Arieh–Leb ben Cwi [Tzvi Hirsch] the rabbi at Komarno, to give praise and thanks to Shabbatai Zevi.

The two set out, and in June 1665 they reached the Gallipoli Fortress where they made contact with his disciple, Abraham Hichini [Yachini], and together with his "prophet," Rabbi Moses Servil of Prousa [later, Bursa], they set out a second time for Gallipoli. On the 26th of July, Shabbatai Zevi granted them an audience. When they told him of the massacres and the slaughter in Poland in the years 1648 and 1649, he responded: "You need not tell me anything, after all in front of me lies the book *Tsuk Haltim* [Distress of the Times][50] which contains all the massacres in all the communities." Then he added, "And why am I sitting in my red robes and my Torah Book is dressed in red? – For the day of vengeance is in my heart, and a year of redemption is coming." After that he divulged to them many secrets according to mysticism, and began to sing songs and praises and refrains in an alphabetical sequence. When he reached the 7th letter he cried out loudly: ["Zechor aniyaii umerudai"] "remember my poor and my wretched" and he wept profusely. He drew his visitors closer to him, held the hands of Rabbi Izajasz Halevy and said to him: "Are you the son of the author of *Turei Zahav?* and he replied: "Yes, our lord." Then he asked Rabbi [Aryeh–] Leib: "Are you the son of the wife of the author of *Turei Zahav*? And he replied: "Yes, our lord." He inquired after the elderly father, Rabbi David Halevy, and they told him: "Our lord!, our father is eighty years old with weakness in his hands and feet, and while we were at Constantinople an old man told us that he had fallen off the building, and was dying. And our lord the messiah sent him some food as medicine, and ordered to tell him that tomorrow he will walk with his stick, and that is what happened; may our lord give us something as medicine." Shabbatai Zevi gave them a piece of sugar and said: "Let him eat this and he will recover

[Pages 117-118]

immediately." After that, he gave Rabbi Aryeh Leib a silk shirt, and told him that his father should wear it on his body and say the verse "so that your youth is renewed like the eagle's." Rabbi Izajasz Halevy turned to him and said: "Our lord, I am his son, and his son comes first." To which Shabbatai Zevi responded in Yiddish "Be quiet"! Then he produced from his bag a kerchief coated in gold, and told him: "Take this and tie it around your father's neck, for his greatness, dignity and splendour." And he added: "The shirt in which Rabbi Leib will dress his father, is no great thing as it is solely for the body, but you will do something deserving of you, which is greatness and respect for your father." Afterwards, he ordered them to sit next to him, and a bowl full of fruit was set in front of them. He gave them two reddish gold, and after wrapping them in a gold embroidered kerchief he said: "I crown you my emissaries and ministers, in this world." After some song and dance he ordered his men to go and leave him with the messengers from Poland. When they were alone, Shabbatai Zevi revealed to them great secrets according to the Kabbalah, and the two declared that "we will be servants waiting upon his doors," and he replied that that was unnecessary, but that they had to deliver to their brethren "good tidings, salvation and comfort."[51] He sent a letter for their father, in which he promised to avenge the Jews' retribution, and he requested that the kabbalist, Rabbi Nehemiah HaKohen, should come to him. The two sons of Rabbi David Halevy left him with admiration, and when they returned to Poland they spoke much about his wealth and dignity.

After their return, Nehemiah HaKohen [52] who had "prophesied" that the days of the Messiah were nigh, set out to see Shabbatai Zevi. He was sent by several communities who bore his travel expenses, in order to ascertain if there was truth in the words of salvation and consolation apprised by Shabbatai Zevi. Nehemiah stayed three whole days with the "messiah". The splendour and the external glory did not change his views, and he created a deep rift among the followers of Shabbatai Zevi. After a stormy argument between them, he despaired of the "messiah," and when he realized that Shabbatai Zevi's men plotted to kill him, he escaped and informed the authorities of the fortress, that he wished to convert to Islam. His intension was to thwart Shabbatai Zevi, and save the Jews from the danger of the spread of his movement. At Adrianople [Edirne] he submitted his denunciation of Shabbatai Zevi as a rebel of the kingdom, which led to the final crisis before the conversion of Shabbatai Zevi to Islam.

Nehemiah HaKohen returned to Lwów, repented and returned to the bosom of Judaism. He did not talk of his plight, but only said that they should hope for the true Messiah and not for that one. The followers of Sabbateanism blamed him for bringing the great messianic awakening to a fatal end, and for causing the conversion of Shabbatai Zevi to Islam. They pursued him so far that he had to leave Lwów (1675).

Despite the deep disappointment caused by Shabbatai Zevi conversion to Islam, many in Poland remained faithful to him. It is not known how many of those were at Lwów, or what their influence was on the community.

The Sabbatean movement attracted a wide circle of people, and its extensive spread did not escape the notice of the Christians and even worried them. On the 22ⁿᵈ June 1666, Stanislaw Sarnowski, the bishop of Pshemish [Przemyśl] wrote a pastoral letter to his faithfuls, in which he ordered to ban the Jews from parading and distributing images of Shabbatai Zevi. In a special order of 4ᵗʰ May 1666, King Jan Kazimierz stressed the issue of rumours which circulated among the Jews about the appearance of their messiah (Sabbataj Cwi [Shabbatai Zevi]).

* *

Economically, as said, there was a substantial decline after the riots. Habitually, the Jews were mainly engaged in trade, but the foreign trade which had passed through Lwów, westwards, was no longer in their hands.

In the 17ᵗʰ century, crafts began to occupy a major part of the economic life. In 1627, a [Jewish] tailors' association had already existed. According to its regulations, apprentices were not permitted to accept work from Christian tailors. The tailors themselves, however, employed Christian apprentices. One after the other, more craftsmen's associations were established, such as: glaziers, goldsmiths, tanners, tinsmiths and furriers who had to withstand a tough struggle from the Christian furriers. The associations were organized in the fashion of the Christian craftsmen's guilds. They had the right to judge members on professional as well as the association's issues. The legal court of the association was made up of a patron, who was usually the association's rabbi, and principal members. The association's rabbi was elected by its members and approved by the deputy–voivode. Appeals against verdicts were heard at the law–court of the deputy–voivode. His office oversaw the jurisdiction of the associations as well as of their administrative practice. There was even an association of pedlars.[53]

The craftsmen had two Torah–study schools [Batei Midrash] of their own, and one knows of synagogues and Torah–study schools for bakers, tinsmiths, furriers,[54] tanners and singers. They founded also their own societies, such as the Psalm Society and the "Morning Guards" Society.

[Pages 349-350]

Notes: – CHAPTER 7
All notes in square brackets [ ] were made by the translator.
[The spelling of most names were sourced from books cited by the author.]

1.   Report according to the diary of the city governor Andrzej Czechowicz, and of the mayor Martin Grosswajer mentioned in Dr. J. Caro's book: *Geschichte der Juden in Lemberg.* p. 53.

2.   That is to say: Kraków, Poznan, Lublin and Lwów were the centres of Jewish autonomy in Poland.

3.   *Wisoki Zamek.*

4.   Cossacks.

5.   Tatars.

6.   According to Czechowicz's report, most of the Jews in the Krakówite suburb were burned to death in their houses which had been set alight by the Cossacks.

7.   According to Czechowicz's report, it was perpetrated by Ruthenians, residents of Lwów who switched allegiance to support Khmelnytsky [Chmielnicki]

8.   Czechowicz's report : Caro l.c. p. 57, n 2.

9.   Rabbi Natan Neta Hanover writes: "And afterwards many ministers and dignitaries and with them Rabbi Szymon, an intermediary from Lwów, arrived from town to discuss matters with Khmelnytsky and they reached a compromise that he would be given by the Jews and the ministers in town, two hundred thousand Gulden as redemption of their lives. Since they did not have such sums of money, they gave him silver, gold and other merchandise valued at much reduced rates comparable to wholesale prices at the time. And they weighed the silver and gold in bulk, like lead, at half price. And the holy community of Lwów survived like deep water devoid of fish."

10.   The lobbyist of the community within the town participated in the negotiation with the municipality over the (third) trade agreement, in the years 1636–1639. He was part of the delegation which travelled to Warsaw in 1636. In 1642, he represented the Jewish fur traders in their trial against the Christian furriers' guild.

11.   Jona Gurland, the publisher of the Contract, surmised that he was a pharmacist at Vladimir – Volhynia [Włodzimierz – Wołyński], who wrote "Elixir of Life," a book of morals composed in verse, with a Yiddish translation, published in 1590. That assumption seemed to him not sufficiently founded, and according to him the author was one of Poland's greatest, who fled to Venice with his writing in his hand. There he sought the approval of Rabbi Mojzesz Zacuto who wrote a short poem at the head of the essay. But the book was not published, and can be found at the British Museum, London, among the estate of Jozef [Giuseppe] Almanzi, until its publication by Gurland in 1888 (Kraków).

The Lwów community included also Jews who resided in the small towns in the Lwów region (Terra Leopoliensis), who were few in number. These included: Olesko, Pomorzany, Mikołajów, Sassów, Zółkiew, Gródek, Dunajów, Komarno, Bóbrka, Kulików, Gołogóry, Nawarya, Bruchnal, Kukizów, Podkamien, Młynówce, Brzezany, Busk, Tadanie, Knihinicze, Sieniawa, Narajów, Rohatyn, Potiorilcze, Jaworów, Kamionka, Swirz, Gliniany.

The affairs of the small towns which were known as "*przykahałków*" were managed by a committee made up of representatives from the two communities of Lwów and from the small towns in which later on, communities were established. The committee was termed "The Champions. Heads and leaders of state, and leaders of the holy community of Lwów," and in Polish *starsi ziemscy*, or *kahał ziemski*.

In the years 1623 and 1626, during the Tatars' invasion, the defence of Lwów was organized by its townspeople, in which the Jews also took an active part. They followed the orders of the town's leaders, and together with the rest of the citizens they put in special shifts day and night, at the ramparts and at the gates, transporting guns and weapons.

[Pages 351-352]

The participation of Jews during the siege when the Tatars attacked in 1590, is also known.

During the siege of 1648, the Jews were actively involved in the defence of the town. The lobbyist Szymon supplied weapons and the Jews together with the Armenians guarded the area from the Carmelites' Gate to the fortress near the Bernardine Church, as well as the Ruthenian Church. Together with the artillery corps, they participated also in the attacks against the Cossacks who robbed the Bernardine Church.

Fontes historiae Ukraino–Russiae. t. VI.

Akta grodzkie i ziemskie. Lwów t. XX, p. 91.

During the second siege (October 1655) and the invasion by Rákóczi's rebells in 1657, the Jews of Lwów also participated in the defence of the town. The coronation *Sejm* of 1675 stated clearly its determination that the Jews within Lwów and those outside the town were obliged to serve in the artillery corps, on the batteries.

12.   Rabbi Samuel Faibish the son of Rabbi Natan Faibish at Vienna, states however in his book *Tit Yeven* which was published in the *Book of Tears* by Dr. Simon Bernfeld, Berlin 1920; vol, 3; p.149: "and in the holy community of Lwów there were about one thousand five hundred house owners, and almost five hundred starved to death."

Rabbi Gabriel, the son of Rabbi Joshua Heschel of Rzeszów [Resche], sang in his lament "How can I bear my face and raise my head":

[The lament entered here was not translated]

And the community rabbi of Gnesen [Gniezno], Rabbi Henoch ben Abraham, mourns the Jews of Lwów in his lament "Gil Nekamot" [Age of Revenge] as follows:

"My heart's distress grew as siege was laid to the glorious town of Lwów against the wrath of the oppressor aiming to destroy a dispersed lamb and our souls turned into booty and our property into ransom, woe for war refugees dying within the town looking for bread. Withdraw your wrath and comfort them over the evil."

The lament was published by J. Gourland, in "The Treasure of Literature" of Shaltiel Gerber, Jarosław 1887; vol. 1; p. 57.

13.   Dr. M. Bałaban: *Ustrój gminy Zyd. w Polsce w XVI–XX wieku.* Glos Gminy Zydowskiej. Warszawa 1939 Rok. III, zesz. 1, p. 7.

14.   M. Bersohn: *Dyplomatarjusz*, Nr. 290, p. 163.

15.   M. Bersohn: *Dyplomatarjusz*, Nr. 261, p. 149.

16.   Ks. Józefowicz: *Kronika miasta Lwowa 1634–1690* (tlómaczenie Piockiego) Lwów 1854, p. 272.

17.   Dr. M. Schorr: *Zydzi w Przemyślu* Lwów 1908. Materyaly Nr. 99; p.180.

18.   From the "Yizkor" [memorial prayer] entered in the notebook of the great synagogue. Published in the book by Dr. Jecheskiel Caro. p. 162.

19.   *See* Salomon Buber: *Anshei Shem* [*Men of Renown*] p. 220.

20.   *ibid.* p. 140.

21.   *ibid.* p. 33.

22.   *ibid.* p. 116.

23.   *ibid.* p. 157.

24.   *ibid.* p. 23.

25.   *ibid.* p. 146.

26.   *ibid.* p. 77.

27.   *ibid.* p. 211.

28.   *ibid.* p. 201.

29. *ibid.* pp. 146–7.

30. *ibid.* p. 54.

31. M. Bałaban: *Historja Zydow w Krakówie.* t. II, pp.32–3.

32. The synagogue outside the town was robbed of 72 Torah scrolls; 18 silver Keter–Torah ornaments – 85 Liters each; 6 gold plated Keter–Torah ornaments; 15 velvet Parochets [ornamental curtains covering the front of the holy ark in the synagogue]; 160 curtains, tablecloths and covers; 4 candelabra each with 50 candles; one candelabrum with 100 candles; a large number of prayer shawls; 500 books. The synagogue within the town was robbed of 65 Torah scrolls; 25 silver Keter–Torah ornaments (125 Liters); 9 gold plated Keter–Torah ornaments; 36 Parochets; 135 tablecloths; silver candelabrum (70 Liters); 3 candelabra; 38 prayer shawls; 520 books.

33. Schorr: *Zydzi w Przemyślu* Nr. 100, pp 181–182.

34. Following to an ancient Polish law, the compensation was paid to the family of the person killed, according to her/his origin.

35. Wira.

36. According to the Statute of Kalisz by Boleslaw [the Pious], Article 9.

37. Pazdro: *Sady podwojewodzinskie Zydowskie* p. 117, Nr. 11.

38. Yisrael Hailpern: *Pinkas Arba Arazot* [*Notebook of Council of Four Lands*]. p. 99.

39. *ibid.* p. 103.

40. *ibid.* p. 109.

41. *ibid.* p. 136.

42. *ibid.* p. 141

43. *ibid.* p. 143.

44. *ibid.* p. 202

45. *ibid.* pp. 204–205.

46. *ibid.* p. 210.

47. *ibid.* p. 237 / XLII.

48. Bałaban: Ustroj kahalu w Polsce w XVI–XVIII w. Kwartalnik posw. Hist. Zydow w Polsce. Warszawa 1912 zes 2, p. 33.

49. *Ma'ase Tuvia* [Tuvia's Tale], Kraków, 1908, p. 18A.

50. For Rabbi Mejer ben Samuel of Zbaszyn (Kraków 1650).

51. David Kahana: *Toldot HaMekubalim, HaShabta'im vehaChasidim* [*History of the Accepted* [the Kabbalists], *the Sabbateans and the Hassidim*]. Tel–Aviv 1925, vol.6, pp.93–95.
Dr. Majer Bałaban: *Sabataizm w Polsce.*

52. Gershom Scholem: The Sabbatean Movement in Poland *The House of Israel in Poland.* vol. 2, pp.44–45. Dr. M. Bałaban: *Sabataizm w Polsce.* Kriega jubileuszowa ku czci prof. Dr. Mojzesza Schorra. Warszawa 1933, pp. 44–45.

53. "*Torbiarze*," after the satchels in which pedlars kept their merchandise.

[Pages 353-354]

54. In the approval of the Christian Furrier Union of the 30th March 1662 (by King Jan Kazimierz) were included also clauses regarding Jewish furriers, which included the 1629 agreement between the Jewish and the Christian furriers. (M. Bersohn: *Dyplomatarjusz*, Nr. 356, pp. 203–204).

[Pages 119-120]

Chapter 8: The Transition Period

Translated by Myra Yael Ecker

Edited by Ingrid Rockberger

The reign of King Mikhal Wiśniowiecki [. The dispute with the Christian shoemakers' guilds. The Jewish Trade. Dr. Emmanuel de-Jonah. The struggle with the townspeople. The community's financial situation and debts. The Rabbinate under "Sage Tzvi" and his opponents. The rabbis and Shabbatai Zevi's followers. The trial of the Reizes brothers. The students' onslaught. Polemics of Rabbi Jonathan Eybeschütz and Rabbi Jakób Emden.

Michał Wiśniowiecki [Michael I], who had succeeded in beating Khmelnytsky's forces, pursued a policy of tolerance towards the Jews of Lwów. Soon after he was crowned he granted the community leaders' wishes by allowing the Jews to keep stockrooms in their homes.[1]

Due to that, a dispute with the Polish and Ruthenian Shoemakers' Guild broke out under him.

In 1670, contrary to the royal provision, the Starosta (governor) Stanislaw Mniszek placed the Jews under his own jurisdiction and allowed unqualified craftsmen to undertake their work. He also granted them the right to reside within the nobles' jurisdictions, while forbidding the municipality from harming them. There were also Jews among these unqualified craftsmen. The governor permitted the Jews to settle below the urban castle, to sell liquor and ale and even to establish breweries and beeswax workshops. In 1673, under pressure from the Shoemakers' Guild, a royal verdict was passed to which the Starosta yielded.[2]

The Cossacks who were discontent that Wiśniowiecki had been crowned, succeeded in inciting the Turks to invade Poland. Their demand was that Poland give up the Ukraine region. On the 29th August 1672, they conquered Kamieniec–Podolski [Kamianets–Podilskyi] and from there they set out for Lwów. The municipality requested military assistance from the King. Jan Sobieski, the minister of the armed forces who came to Lwów, was able to defend the town with a limited number of infantry and cavalry men.

Following the King's order, women, the elderly and children left the town while jewellery and valuables were concealed. Those who fled included the rabbis, Rabbi Cwi [Tzvi] Hirsz (within the town) and Rabbi Juda Judel (outside the town). The one thousand men left in the town were mobilised, including Jews. The Jewish population of Lwów, like that of Rzeszow [Reisha], Przemyśl, Trembowla, Buczacz [Buchach], Tarnopol and Czortkow, was obliged to defend the town together with the Christians. For that purpose they were equipped with riffles and gunpowder, and at times even cannons. To protect the town, the suburbs were burnt down, destroying Jewish property. When the Turks approached the town they demanded its surrender. The municipality refused their demand and sent presents to the Turkish commander, Kapudan–Pasha. He refused the gifts and attacked the town with firearms from the 23rd to the 28th September 1672. As the siege debilitated the town, the King's emissary arrived carrying the order to negotiate with the Turks and to pay them ransom. The Turks demanded 100,000 red Gulden, a sum the townspeople were unable to raise, all they managed to collected with much difficulty was 5,000 Gulden. Once the Turks realized that they could not collect the entire ransom fee, they agreed to accept the 5,000 Gulden collected, in addition to 12 men of mixed–race, which included two Jews. Men who returned home only seven years later.

After the Turks retreated the Jews were in straightened circumstances. Poverty prevailed throughout the Jewish Quarter, and the refugees from the suburbs who feared to return home, preferred instead to wander through the overcrowded Jewish street in town. The community already laden with debts from the ransom payments imposed on it, was in addition obliged to pay a hefty interest and assist the refugees.

The nobles who had fled the town before the siege, and whose houses and castles in the suburbs were burnt down as a result of the war, were compensated after their return, following a law–court's decision. The Jews of the suburbs who had suffered destruction, were however given no compensation. The nobles understood the Jews' predicament and demanded that the *Sejmik* at Wisznia [Vyshnia], release the Jews of the suburbs, whose houses had been burnt down or destroyed for the protection of the town, from the payment of taxes. They also demanded the return of the mixed–race prisoners taken by the Turks. The townspeople, however, took no heed of the Jews' circumstance.

Despite their common war predicament, the townsperson hated the Jew, viewing him as an economic rival. All the townspeople wished for was to remove the Jews from the town, even by expulsion, especially when they saw the swift recovery of the Jewish trade after the war. But as the townspeople had no authority to expel the Jews, the traders and craftsmen settled for limiting the trade and crafts available to them.

[Pages 121-122]

New negotiations for a mutual agreement started, based on the earlier agreements. In 1676, the municipality decided that only a Jew who owned property or real estate be permitted to trade. Traders dealing in imported goods from abroad, or in fabrics, were obliged to prove that they owned at least 5,000 Gulden of assets. Petty trading required 3,000 Gulden; liquor trade required 6,000 Gulden and for ordinary wine and mead 3,000 Gulden were required. For beer brewers and liquor distillers 1,500 Gulden of assets were sufficient.

Consequently, Jews started to purchase plots of land – which benefited the townspeople who were in economic straits. Nevertheless, the townspeople continued to persecute the Jews. Influenced by them, the Sejm of 1676 decided that the Jews of Lwów be only permitted to trade in goods included in the agreement with the town council. As to the debts of the Jewish citizens, the *Sejm* ruled that in accordance with an ancient custom the Jews were obliged "To assist with the cannons situated on Lwów's town–walls."

King Jan Sobieski [John III], the heir of King Wiśniowiecki who died at Lwów on the 10th November 1673, appreciated the economic role played by the Jews. In his youth he knew the Jews of Żółkiew [Żółkiew], where he grew up, and recognized their importance to the state's economy. That led to his leniency with the Jewish population and his help in improving their circumstances. His court at Żółkiew included a large number of Jews, and he particularly trusted in his administrator and customs officer Jakób Bezalel [Becal] ben Natan, who settled at Żółkiew in 1685, and managed the customs office at Lwów.[3] His treatment of them was a cause for incitement against the Jews.

The municipality and the townspeople complained of the King's contempt for the Christians, and the magistrate at Warsaw commiserated with the Lwów municipality, lamenting that things had gone so far in Poland that "the Royal Customs was given to a Jew who oppresses and suppresses Lwów traders, an unthinkable situation in Warsaw."[4]

Jan Sobieski's court physician, Doctor Simche Menachem Emanuel, the son of doctor Jochanan Baruch de-Jonah,[5] was an exceptional man. His father had settled as a doctor at Lwów. His mother Eksa, who died in 1666, was the daughter of Doctor Menachem Zunsfurt of Lwów. His brother, Eliasza [Elieser], who died in 1672, was also a specialist doctor at Lwów. In 1678, his brother Jakob qualified at Padua as a medical doctor, together with his friend Levy Liberman–Fortis, of Lwów, and his brother Doctor Izak Fortis; his brother Józef was a merchant at Lwów and died in 1712. Their father, one of Lwów's community dignitaries, a great sage who closely followed the Torah and its commandments, died in June 1669.

The physician Simche Menachem de–Jonah married Nessia, the daughter of Reb. Pesach, and a short while after practicing at Lwów his renown as a doctor spread throughout the region. Besides his medical practice he also dedicated time to community affairs during the years of suffering following 1648.

The house of Dr. Simche Menachem
(Blacharska 19)

In 1670–1671 when King Sobieski fell seriously ill, he invited him [de-Jonah] to treat him and demanded he reside near him at Żółkiew. He remained there till the King died in 1696, after which he returned to Lwów. Here he built himself a magnificent house on the Jewish Street (number 19), and was respected by the community. Still during King Sobieski's lifetime he was "President of Eretz Israel," and in 1698, he was elected community leader by the Council of Four Lands. In this function he settled important issues, such as the dispute between the printer Uri ben Aron Feibisz Halevy who had moved a publishing house from Amsterdam to Żółkiew in 1690,

[Pages 123-124]

and the printers of Lublin and Kraków.[6] He also settled the dispute within the community of Żółkiew (1701). "Reb. Simche Doctor" – as he was known by the people – was accepted by all classes of society, both Jews and Christians. He was very learned in the Torah, educated and an art lover, as seen from the Renaissance building he built as his home. He was much appreciated for the generosity with which he assisted the poor and the wretched.

His first wife, Nessia, died in 1693. In 1696, after returning to Lwów from Żółkiew, he remarried but only lived a few more years. He died in March 1702.

King Sobieski was accepted by the Jews who considered him their patron, and legends circulated of his deeds and benevolence. One such tale recounted how during his reign Christians accused the Jews of Lwów, of blood–libel. At the time, Sobieski resided at Lwów and one night he stepped onto the balcony of his house and saw several Christians running away, one with a sack over his shoulder. The King ordered to stop the men, and the body of a Christian child was found in the sack. He instantly gave an order to punish the villains and to publish the facts in order to remove all suspicion from the Jews.

In February 1695, the Tatars invaded Reissen and arrived at Lwów. The Polish commander, Jabłonowski, was forced to retreat and to evacuate the Krakówite suburb. The Tatars then attacked the Jewish Quarter, killed most of its inhabitants, demolished and looted the houses. They retreated only after the onslaught by the Polish army.[7]

After the death of King Sobieski (1696), a new wave of wars erupted. The Swedes supported the candidacy of Stanislaw Leszczyński as king of Poland, and the Russians sided with Augustus [Frederick Augustus II] of Saxony. Mercenaries attacked Lwów and the town was obliged to pay ransom.

On the 23rd November 1703 a gun–powder store exploded in the Jewish Quarter (Boimów). Many buildings were destroyed and 36 Jews were killed. Among them was the messenger [HaMagid] Reb. Szmerl Katz,[8] the leader, Reb. Naftali Hersz son of Reb. Jechiel Rubel, the rabbinical judge [dayan], Reb. Aszer ben Reb. Ruben.[9] Hardly had the Jews recovered before they faced a new calamity. In 1704, the Swedes attacked and on the 6th September they occupied the town. The suburbs and their Jewish citizens were again the first to suffer, and the community outside the town was totally destroyed. Refugees from the suburbs fled to the Jewish Quarter within the town, crowding the streets. According to the chronicler Chodynicki,[10] the Jews participated very actively in the defence of the town. One Jew was killed while firing a cannon at the enemy. The Swedes, angered by the Jews who participated in the defence, decided to take revenge on them. When they entered the town, they rampaged through it, killed, and robbed private houses, churches and synagogues.

When the Swedish army left town only one garrison remained, led by General Stenbock. The Jews paid their share[11] of the ransom in addition to *munus judaicum* (present from the Jews) in the sum of 20,000 Thaler.

Suddenly a fire broke out, destroying the town's warehouses and the street of the Jews. Despite the calamity, General Stenbock demanded the "present from the Jews" payment. When they declared that they were unable to raise such a sum, he placed a hanging–tree in front of the synagogue and threatened the community leaders with hanging, were the tax not paid. Under those threats, the money was collected.

With Stanislaw Leszczyński's intervention, King Karl XII of Sweden agreed that the town of Lwów would pay just 132,000 Thaler, of which the Jews paid 40,000 Thaler.

The Jews of Lwów suffered greatly, their financial standing declined drastically even after the withdrawal of the Swedes, while expropriations and war–tax payments were still ongoing. In the years 1705–1711 the Jews were obliged to give their fair share of the 308,894 Gulden levied by the Swedes, since the nobles and the clergy counted on privileges and refused to partake in that payment. In addition, in 1709 the town paid 150,000 Prussian Thaler to Leszczyński, the Swedes' ally.

To make those payments which amounted to hundreds of thousands of Gulden, the community was obliged to borrow vast sums from Jew,[12] noblemen and monasteries.

The municipality brought legal actions against those Jews who failed to meet the obligation imposed on them in accordance with the 1683 contract which was extended to 1691. The trials continued for 40 years and there was no change in their circumstances till 1773. In 1709, all the "Classes and Nations" in town agreed a rule forbidding Christians from letting any accommodation or shops to Jews. The rule was confirmed by Augustus II in an addendum of the 11th April 1710, noting that anyone transgressing the rule would be fined 200–500 Gulden. The Jews were not surprised and managed to obtain a suspension to vacating the houses from the town's commander, Jaspres. The municipality, however, obtained an instruction from the King that Jaspres had no say in the town's affairs.

The dispute escalated further: the municipality had reached a verdict obliging the Jews to sign a new contract within a fortnight, otherwise they would lose their rights and their trade would diminish; they would be forbidden from owning taverns

[Pages 125-126]

and bars, and they would have to vacate the flats, stores and shops in Christians' houses.

The Jews of the suburbs were forbidden all trade and employment. After they appealed, the royal law–court at Warsaw decided, on the 14th February 1713, that the Jews had no right to sign any contract with the town; that their trade be restricted to four types, and that all their other merchandise be confiscated. Special commissaries were sent out to execute that verdict.

In 1732 (8th March), the municipality received a judgement permitting it to expel the Jews from all the streets and suburbs, other than the Street of the Jews. But the Jews managed to evade and prevent the execution of those judgments, with bribes and through connections. The Nobles backed the Jews and leased them their houses and plots of land, especially in the suburbs, and that due to the high rents they received from them.

The townspeople were embittered as the number of Jewish shops increased, and in 1738, 71 shops outside the Jewish Quarter were declared illegal. They obtained an order from the King handing the settlement of the dispute to a special committee, and after negotiations on the 21st July 1740, an agreement was signed between the Jews and the municipality in which the Jews pledged to follow their trades according to the 1592 contract. However, as the contract did not mention specifically that the Jews had to vacate their shops in town, they did not do so.

The Jews were also on trial against the Jesuits about a brewery they had leased from them. The 1611 contract between the Jews and the Jesuits was altered in 1722. Instead of pepper and saffron with which the Jews had previously paid the Jesuits, they now committed themselves to supply at each holiday: four turbots or carps, three pounds of oil from Danzig [Gdansk], three pounds of ginger, three pounds of pepper, one quarter of a fat calf and one Thaler, besides presents for the students: a container of liquor and a sum of money, quarterly. They supplied the Voivode's priest with four roasts for each and every holiday, and four jars for every new rector. All other taxes were eliminated.

Vast sums of money were required to cover the costs of, and the bribes associated with the trials, resulting in a heavy financial burden on the Jewish citizens.

The standing of the town declined, many of its houses stood vacant and even the Christians themselves let taverns to Jews. The Christians had 67 beer taverns in the town, some of which they let to Jews; the Christians had 71 plum brandy taverns, and the Jews had 31. Of the liquor taverns, 80 were managed by Christians and 16 by Jews. In the suburb there were 57 taverns, all in the hands of Jews. The number of taverns in the hands of Christians decreased further after the war with Sweden.

From every aspect, the condition of the Jews was difficult. There were 49 plots of land in the Jewish Quarter within the town, and after the war at the beginning of the eighteenth century, with the increased number of refugees who fled from the villages, it was impossible to house all the Jews within the Quarter. Consequently, they were forced to rent accommodation outside the Quarter in the adjacent streets (Ruska, Szkockiej [Scottish], Serbska, Boimów. Their shops were scattered all over town, including in Rynek 10, where, in the King's house, a Jew was selling honey.

The 1708 census shows that the situation continued into the beginning of the eighteenth century, when many shops in the town centre market (rynek) belonged to Jews.

The census showed there were 50 Jewish scrap metal vendors, 80 salt traders and 80 pedlars, 30 moneychangers, 30 money lenders with interest, 20 paramedics (compared with 19 Christians) and four physicians.[13]

The townspeople looked askance at the Jews and demanded to have the town cleansed of their competitors, but in vain. The nobles and the magnates as well as the Church who received high rents, had interest in keeping their Jewish tenants in town.

Although it was forbidden to sell any houses situated outside the Jewish Quarter to Jews, and despite the court hearings and verdicts regularly passed against the Jews, a few Jews still managed to break through the barrier and purchase houses from Christian nobles and townspeople outside the Jewish Quarter. Besides the tradesmen, also the Craftsmen's Guilds escalated their fight against the Jews. As their wished to secure cheap raw material for their men, they lobbied to forbid the Jews from exporting.

According to the 1708 census there were at Lwów 18 Jewish tinsmiths (there were no Christian tinsmiths); 44 Jewish goldsmiths (10 Christian); 50 Jewish butchers (eight Christian); 10 Jewish weavers (one Christian); there were no Jewish bakers within the town (20 Christian), 20 outside the town; 50 Jewish tailors (47 Christian).

The condition and management of the Lwów community was miserable. In 1703, as the authority of the community leaders had eroded so that they were unable to collect any dues despite imposing ostracism on the community, the Voivode Stanislaw Jabłonowski undertook to regulate the conditions.

On the 5th October 1703, in a special regulation given at Mariampol [Marijampole], the Voivode ordered that the community leaders be elected, and that they be vested with the power of jurisdiction. Concurrently,

[Pages 127-128]

he forbade any officer from interfering in the community affairs, other than in appeals at the district law–court.

The dismal situation the Jewish population had found itself in due to the events of war, lowered the public discipline. Consequently, it was appropriate to increase the community's authority,[14] especially in face of the heavy financial debt with which the community was burdened. In 1727, the community owed 438,410 Gulden to the municipality alone, as its share of contributions during the wars; all the synagogues were emptied out of all gold and silver they had contained. In order to fulfill its obligations, the community was therefore obliged to take out loans which entailed very high interest.

In 1707, the community took out a 4,000 Gulden loan from the "Discalced [barefoot] Carmelites", at 7% interest; and in 1714, a 15,000 Gulden loan from Benedykt Karkowski. The community owed also 42,000 Gulden to the Stauropegion Order; 4,000 Gulden to Magdalena Pruszkowska; 2,680 Gulden to the nobleman Aleksander Siedlecki; 12,600 Gulden to the nobleman Adam Karsz; 190 Gulden to the Christian Medics Guild.

In that drained financial situation new taxes were levied on the community. The meat taxes as well as "tenure" were increased in order to repay the debt of 52,000 Gulden to the Dominicans. But even that was of little avail and the community fell into debt with no way out.

While the Lwów community declined, a major mogul rose from among its ranks to succeed in encouraging, raising and returning it to its greatness.

In 1714, the great scholar [*gaon*] Rabbi Cwi [Tzvi] Hirsz ben Jakob Askenazy (the "Sage Tzvi") was elected Rabbi of the two communities, and was received with honour and great joy. He was also respected by the Christians, "and the Jewish community was not alone in receiving him with the greatest honour, for soon also the Gentiles were at his door and greeted him with gifts. And during the short time he was there, he established substantial regulations for the holy community, and raised its fame and glory. He adjudicated on men of violence, and the men of malice surrendered to him. He also removed the powerful community leader, Reb. Zelik from his appointment, after it was revealed that he had stolen community money and robbed the poor. And the latter went and delivered my sire, my teacher [of Jewish studies], the Rabbi of blessed memory, to the governor and the bishop. My sire, my teacher [of Jewish studies], the Rabbi of blessed memory was tried by them, and fear spread throughout the community since the Jews there greatly feared the governors. Yet, my sire, my teacher [of Jewish studies], the Rabbi of blessed memory went to see them, spoke with them in Italian, and the governors showed him such honour as he had never been shown before. The bishop then insisted he sat in the chair next to his own, and kept his hat on. God caused them to like him, and they granted him the right and power to judge almost capital law cases in his community whenever he saw fit, and he left them with great honour and in peace. All the principled as well as the malicious people present were filled with terror. They followed his orders and surrendered to him, of blessed memory, since they feared him, and to the entire congregation he was honour and glory and greatness.

The "Sage Cwi knew how to impose his authority on everyone. Reb Mojzesz Jechielis who imposed strict authority on his community members, accepted his precepts and surrendered to his authority. Even wealthy men who appeared in front of him in the law–court did not deter him, and he knew how to enforce his verdict upon them. The community members regarded him as a patron who safeguarded their interests since he knew "to ensure that everyone be content and be taken care of, be guided honestly in accordance with Jewish law, both in community affairs and the value of the heavy taxes; in the affairs of the many and the individuals; in general and in particular. That was his source [of wisdom], also in matters between man and man, to conduct an honest, unbiased trial.[15]

He was particularly involved in education and in the study of the Torah. He regretted that "some men, who had not even read the Bible and did not know the Mishnah [religious doctrine], men who were no experts in the fundamental issue, and who had not examined the first adjudicators, had become rabbis". As a consequence, he decided on fundamental amendments to the education and the methods of study. He assembled the teachers "and set them the method of Bible teaching, starting with grammar". But before he was able to establish the amendments, he died at Lwów on the 29th May 1718.

After his demise, the Rabbi of Lublin, Rabbi Simche ben Rabbi Nachman HaKohen Rappoport was elected, but he fell ill on his way to Lwów and died on the 4th August 1718.

He was followed by the great–grandson of Rabbi Jozue [Joshua] Falk, Rabbi Jakob ben Rabbi Cwi [Tzvi] Hirsz [Hirsch] (1681–1756), author of *Pneh Josua*, and son–in–law of Lwów's community leader Rabbi Salomon Segal Landau. He took an active part in teaching, and the community appointed him to oversee the teachers. [Some years earlier] on the 27th November 1703, his wife Lea, his mother–in–law Rösel, her father Schmerl Katz and his daughter, had all died from an explosion in the gunpowder store–room. The loss depressed him so much that he left Lwów. He took, Taube, the daughter of the wealthy Lwów Reb. Isachar Baer for his second wife, and served at the Rabbinates of Tarlow, Kurow and Lisko.

In 1718, according to Rabbi Jakob Emden's account, his wife's family attempted to obtain the Lwów Rabbinate for him. In September 1718, after his mother–in–law had spent 30,000 Zloty to attain that goal, he was elected Rabbi of the Lwów community and the region. No sooner had he returned to Lwów as head of the Rabbinate than one of the wealthy men lobbied on behalf of his son–in–law, Rabbi Chaim ben Lazer, who was Rabbi at Złoczów [Zelechów] but lived at Lwów, to be made the town's Rabbi.

Rabbi Chaim was the grandson of Rabbi Pinkas Mojzesz Charif who had been

[Pages 129-130]

rabbi at Lwów. His father–in–law who acted as mediator to Voivode Jabłonowski, was able to gain the latter's support as well as that of some community leaders. And so, in 1720 – once the tenure of Rabbi Jozue [Joshua] ben Cwi–Hirsz had come to an end – the community did not renew his tenure, replacing him instead with Rabbi Chaim ben Reb. Lazer, who was also approved by Voivode Jabłonowski. He was however unsuccessful in obtaining the Rabbinate for the region.

The two factions parted company and the disputes in Lwów led to the defamation of Rabbi Jozue and "they forfeited his money and assets losing him 30,000 Zloty which he had handed to the community to clear its debt". Rabbi Jozue was forced to leave Lwów in 1720 and he settled temporarily at Buczacz. He turned to the communities of the Lwów region, who determined in his favour and did not acknowledge Rabbi Chaim as the regional Rabbi, declaring that they would not comply with the Lwów community. On the 17th July 1720, at the regional committee session held at Kulików, a boycott was declared against Rabbi Chaim and his followers.[16] The verdict stated clearly that "we, members of the region, no longer have anything to do with the holy community of Lwów nor with any rabbi whom they elect. All of us as one, however, all the regional communities from one end to the other, owe respect to the above mentioned Rabbi, the Great Light, our great teacher and rabbi, Rabbi Jozue. He alone was our President, and which ever regional community he chooses to reside in, there he will remain, and we will follow him in all Rabbinical matters".

The Lwów community members were declared "transgressors" and Rabbi Jozue was granted the "authority" to boycott and banish the "sabotaging" Rabbi from all the communities of the region.[17] The Lwów community was sentenced to pay a 30,000 Zloty fine to Rabbi Jozue, a verdict which established him officially as the Rabbi of Lwów and the region. Despite this he did not return to Lwów but settled at Buczacz [Buchach] since Kinowski, the Starosta of Buczacz was in dispute with Voivode Jabłonowski, and so Rabbi Jozue was certain that there no harm would befall him.

Meanwhile his dispute was being deliberated by the Council of Four Lands. In 1724, the Council headed by Dr. Izak Chazak (Fortis), noted Rabbi Mojzesz ben Elejzer as "captain", and justified Rabbi Jozue's claim for 30,000 Zloty.

In 1727, when Rabbi Jozue left for Jaroslaw to represent the Lwów Rabbinate at the session of the Council of Four Lands, his opponents advised Voivode Jabłonowski who asked the Starosta at Jaroslaw to hand Rabbi Jozue to him. Only due to his friend Dr. Izak Chazak (Fortis), who at the time acted as comprehensive community leader of the Council of Four Lands, was Rabbi Jozue made aware of the matter. He then hid inside a wardrobe in his room till the detectives left. He was saved, left Jaroslaw and returned to Buczacz.

Rabbi Jozue continued to live at Buczacz under those circumstances till 1730, when he was invited to succeed Rabbi Michael Chassid as head of the Rabbinate at Berlin.

While at Berlin, he tried to have the verdict of the Regional Committee and of the Council of Four Lands, fulfilled, but to no avail. He also left power–of–attorney to his sons and daughter, but it is not clear whether they successfully obtained the compensation from the Lwów community.

At the time, Rabbi Chaim ben Izak Reizes served (1728–1737) as Head of the ritual law–court [Beth Din] of both communities, as well as the Lwów representative in the Reissen Regional Committee.

The number of Shabbatai Zevi's followers in Podolia and Reissen rose, and their influence increased particularly throughout the Reissen towns: Zloczow [Zolochiv], Rohatyn, Podhajce [Podhajze], Horodenka as well as Lwów. Many of his followers came from Podolia, which lay close to Turkey. They settled in towns and attracted the interest also of those from scholarly circles.

When the rabbis, who greatly objected to their actions, noted the undermining of the Torah and of the commandments, they gathered, by order of the Council of Four Lands, in the great synagogue outside Lwów on the 2nd July 1722. The regional and town rabbi, Rabbi Jakob Jozue [Joshua author of *Pneh Josua*, together with seven of his religious court–judges, declared the excommunication of the sinners by blowing the Shofar [Jewish ritual ram's horn] and extinguishing candles. The entire community stood trembling as they listened to the wording of the curse "and babes learning the Torah repeated after them, Amen… And several transgressing sinners of that accursed cult stood with us on the stage [Bimah] and while sobbing and wailing to heaven even they admitted their misdemeanours and recounted their actions, in accordance with the prayer book which they had put together. After leaving the synagogue on the 2nd July, they had to undertake a self inflicted mourning and ostracism for seven and thirty days, as laid down by the law; every precept pertaining to the outcast and the mourner, besides other penalties and reprimands set by us seven Rabbis, and that was just the beginning."[18] And afterwards they confessed their sins and publicly received their due.

Similar ostracism was declared in all other communities. Despite the ostracism however, the followers of Sabbataj Cwi [Shabbatai Zevi] could not be completely wiped out. On the contrary, the number of the cult followers increased, and some years later they joined Jakub Frank's faction.

Lwów's community life was not tranquil either. Since the controversy with Rabbi Jozue ben Cwi (author of *Pneh Josua*), the community–leaders tried to define the Rabbi's authority.

In 1726, they submitted a complaint to Voivode Jabłonowski that the Rabbi was introducing changes which were in contravention

[Pages 131-132]

of the regulations. They also requested that the Rabbi's authority and limits of operation be explicitly specified.

On the 20th July 1726, the Voivode issued the following regulations:

1. "The Chief Rabbi and the community–leader outside the town would reside alternately, three years within the town and three years outside it. The community–leaders cannot be appointed or elected from among relatives of rabbis. Rabbis are exempt from all taxation and payments. However, were they to undertake covert trade, or send merchandise to Breslau [Wroclaw] or elsewhere, they would have to pay the "burden" tax (community tax on goods and business).

2. The community is obliged to provide accommodation for the rabbis, but they are only permitted to provide sustenance in their homes for a single son, or a daughter with her husband, who will bs exempt from the payment of taxes and have only to pay the "burden" tax.

3. The weekly salary of the Chief Rabbi is 10 Zloty, and of the deputy Rabbi, three Zloty. For the two annual sermons they will be paid 10 Thaler; for weddings they will be paid 18 Grozky for every 100 Zloty received in dowery; for a Jewish legal divorce [Get], four Zloty, and they are not permitted to demand or receive over and above the set tariffs.

4. The rabbis are not permitted to assemble the community leadership in their homes. All community meetings will exclusively be held in the community house.

5. The title "Member [Chaver]", and "our Teacher [Morenu]" can respectively be granted three and six years after the marriage.

6. The rabbis have to ensure that the community–leaders and other appointees be elected according to the existing regulations.

7. The religious law–court [Beth Din] will convene at the residence of the law–court's president. And if the Rabbi is required to head the law–court, the judges will convene at the Rabbi's house.

8. Appeals against regulations set by the community–leaders or the rabbis, need to be submitted to the Regional Committee, and every Jew is entitled to appeal any decision at the law–court of the deputy–Voivode [*podwojewoda*].

9. By casting lots the Rabbi elects the appraisers to assess the taxes, and he swears them in to fulfill their tasks honestly, without malice or bias.

10. The Lwów community can have 12 [religious] judges within the town, and 12 outside the town. Only wise and mature men who have been married for more than ten years should be elected.

11. No public scripts can be kept at the Rabbi's house, nor is he allowed to purchase public copies from the community. He is not allowed to accept presents; they should be regarded as bribes."[19]

The community was in grave difficulty with the arrival of Jews from Lwów's vicinity, and sponsored by the nobles they resided in the suburbs that were under their protection.

Relying on the nobles' sponsorship they refused to recognize the community's authority or to pay the taxes it levied on them. Things led to conflicts and from time to time the community–leader, Izrael ben Reb. Lewi [Levi], was obliged to enter in his register appeals against "The Jews who reside within the suburbs under the auspices of Princesse Jablonowska and perform circumcisions in private houses, those who avoid paying community taxes, as well as births, marriages and tenure fees."[20]

Those Jews were mostly owners of shops within the town and therefore it was hard for the municipality to remove them, since their sponsors found endless stratagems to keep them there. The community found it difficult to withstand the hostile attitude that grew under the influence of the Catholic Church, which specifically at Lwów ended in blood–libel trials against Adela of Drohobych [Drohobycz], and against the Reizes brothers.

Miss Adela, the daughter of the head and leader Rabbi Mojzesz Kikenes, was a beautiful and very wealthy woman from the Jewish Quarter, and the subject of envy of the Christian neighbours. On the eve of Passover 1710 , soldiers and officers of the law–court broke into her house and found the body of a dead Christian boy that had been thrown there. The incited Christian mob wanted to attack the Jews, but Adela who wished to save her brother, took the blame on herself without the knowledge of the community, stating that she had killed the child. The law–court sentenced her to death. Once the sentence was published, her Christian cleaner confessed that she had put the murdered Christian child's dead body in her employer's house. The judges agreed to set–aside their verdict, on the condition that Adela become a Christian. She refused, and on the 21st September 1710, she gave her life for God's sanctity.

The trial of the brothers Chaim and Jozue Reizes [Reices] which was staged against a different background, echoed well beyond Poland, with detailed reports of it published in the "*Berlinische Priviligierte Zeitung,*"[21] the "*Gazette de France,*"[22] and the matter was also reported throughout the diaspora.[23]

The setting for the libel was the small town of Strusów, where the cobbler Jacko from Jaryczów announced that a person who had converted to Christianity and later returned to the bosom of Judaism, was hiding among the Jews. After a thorough investigation by the Church authorities it was discovered that Jan Filipowicz first converted at Lwów where he resided in the house of the painter Łukasz Wiśniowski, and later returned to Judaism. From Lwów he went to Dobromil and Drohobych before arriving at Strusów. There he was arrested, he was incarcerated in the church of Uniejów and later was transferred to Lwów.

Initially he did not wish to return to Christianity, but when he was made aware of the punishment, he agreed to remain a Christian. And then the investigation started into how and by whom he was tempted to return to Judaism. Severe torture induced him to reveal that a certain Jew named Moszko put him in the cellar of the rabbi's house where, in the presence of rabbis, the cross which he had carried with him was broken and the Christian faith defamed. Based on his revelation, the Starosta of Lwów ordered that the Rabbis of Lwów, Drohobych and Stryy [Stryj] be imprisoned. The Rabbi of the Lwów region, Rabbi Chaim, who was at Żółkiew when they came for him, was able to escape. In his stead, his mother, and the community leader of Żółkiew,

[Pages 133-134]

Isser ben Mardochaj were arrested as well as the head of the religious law–court of Lwów, Rabbi Chaim ben Izak Reizes [Reices] and his brother Jozue; also Dawid Reizes from whom they confiscated 8,000 Zloty, and Mojzesz who, according to Filipowicz's revelation, had tempted him to leave Christianity. The Rabbi of Szczerzec [now Shcherets] succeeded in evading the authorities.

According to an anecdote the Jews were tortured for 40 days but none of them confessed. Then, the archbishop made the prisoners stand in a line and together with Filipowicz he passed in front of them, and again Filipowicz was unable to recognize the culprit. But when Rabbi Chaim Reizes remarked to the archbishop, in Latin: You have kept them here in vain for forty days, Filipowicz retorted[24] "This is the one, I recognize his voice."

Thus ends the anecdote, the truth of which is hard to ascertain.

According to archival material, a law–court made up of Stanislaw Jabłonowski the Voivode of Reissen, Janusz Wiśniowiecki the Kraków castellan, Stefan Humieckie the governor of Podolia, and Stanislaw Potocki the Starosta of Lwów, sentenced Filipowicz to death by hanging. And to appease the Christian mob incited by the clergy, Rabbi Chaim ben Izak and his brother Jozue, were also sentenced to death, by burning. The elder brother was also sentenced to be dragged by a horse throughout the town before his death. The sentence was executed on the eve of Shavuoth [the Jewish Feast of Weeks].

According to Christian sources, Jozue committed suicide by cutting his own throat during his incarceration. The Jesuit priest Żółtowski still tried to entice Rabbi Chaim to convert to Christianity, promising him freedom, but in vain. Subsequently he was handed to the hangman. On the eve of Shavuoth (13th May 1728), he and Jozue were burnt to death.[25] Their property was confiscated and transferred to the municipality for repair to the fortifications.

The community redeemed their ashes for interment at the cemetery. Chaja,[26] the daughter of Rabbi Chaim Reizes, was also implicated in the trial, and was also killed.[27]

The murder was carried out without any protest from the Starosta, although it was his responsibility so to do since the Reizes brothers were citizens of the community outside the town which was under his authority. He probably did not dare oppose the omnipotent Church, even though the Starosta was predisposed towards the Jews. In 1729, a year after the Reizes trial, the Starosta leased all the taxes to Jewish merchants, and in disputes between the Jews and the municipality he always sided with them, probably against payment.

During 1732–1733 a wave of students' attacks (Schüler Gelauf [students' run]) hit the Jews of the suburbs, but in 1733, the students felt the response of the Jews who hit and struck them. After that, the students did not dare continue with their attacks.

At the time, Poland saw the spread of Hassidim and of active men who practised self–denial in the manner of the Safed Hassidim. 1690 saw the publication of HaAri's [Rabbi Izak Lurie ben Schelomo] version of the *Shulchan Aruch* [an abbreviated form of the Jewish ritual law] at Kraków and Frankfurt–an–der–Oder. At Dyhernfurth [Brzeg Dolny], with the endeavour of the rabbis of the Council of Four Lands, the *Shulchan Aruch Way of Life* was also published,

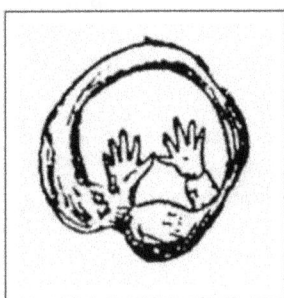

Seal of Izak ben Abraham HaKohen of Lwów. Dated 1654. Showing the mark of a Priest [Kohen] – priests's palms held in benediction.

A woman's signet ring from Poland. Single–stone. Inscription: "To light the Sabbath Candle", and candelabrum with three–arms carved and filled with gold. 17th century.

Seal of Aron ben Meszkisz HaLevy, Lwów. Dated 1654. Showing the mark of the Levi'im [Levis] – a jug for washing the hands of priests.

Seal of Józef–Salomon ben Jeruchim of Lwów. Dated 1629. Showing the sign of the owner who was born in the month of Sivan [the 9th month in the Jewish calendar, as it is presently arranged].

Seal of Jekusiel–Zalman ben MaHaRaR Eleazar of blessed memory, of Lwów. Dated 1654.

Seal of Józef–Salomon ben Jeruchim HaLevy of Lwów. Dated 1629. Engraved with Józef's birth sign; he was born in the month of Sivan. Twice enlarged.

Seals and signets belonging to Jews from Lwów

together with interpretation of *Turei Zahaw* by Rabbi Dawid Halevy of Lwów, and interpretation of *Magen Abraham* [Protector of Abraham] by Rabbi Abraham Abele of Kalisz, thus uniting all of HaAri's customs of the Halacha [Jewish ritual]. The state of ignorance in Poland encouraged the belief in secret faiths, demons, spirits, talismans, incantations, names and dreams. "Renowned figures", who also claimed to expel spirits and demons through the power of names, attracted the following of individuals willing to accept potions, folk remedies, amulets and incantation from them. Rabbis who perceived the influence of the Sabbateans in such actions, set out to wipe out the rest of that cult. Rabbi Jozue Falk the author of *Pneh Josua*, played a major role

[Pages 135-136]

in that struggle, especially after he had left for Berlin, by resolutely attacking Rabbi Jonathan Eybeschütz [Eibenschütz or Eibeschitz].

The controversy between Rabbi Jakob Emden and Rabbi Jozue Falk on the one hand, and Rabbi Jonathan Eybeschütz on the other, had attracted his disciples within Poland to a counterattack, which began with a declaration at the Lublin Synagogue, of a boycott against Rabbi Jakob Emden. The controversy provoked tempers in Poland, it was much discussed during the sessions of the "Council of Four Lands", and its echos reached Lwów and the region.

Among Rabbi Jonathan Eybeschütz's supporters at Lwów, one knows of the biblicist Reb. David Fest also known as Lemberger, who exchanged letters with Rabbi Jonathan Eybeschütz, whom he rated "pure and clean of purpose and perfect of mind."[28]

Unlike the rabbi, Reb. Chaim HaKohen Rappaport of Lwów who did not partake in the controversy, the regional rabbi, Rabbi Izak Landau was among Rabbi Jonathan Eybeschütz's sympathizers. He and his father–in–law, Rabbi Abraham ben Chaim, head of the Land of Lublin, and his son Rabbi Jakob, rabbi at Lublin who had been one of Eybeschütz's pupils, influenced the session of the "Council of Four Lands" which dealt with the controversy in 1753. The Lithuanian community–leader Abraham, and Baruch Jewen, King Augustus III's agent, sided with Rabbi Jakob Emden.

Swayed by Rabbi Izak Landau, a boycott was issued at Lublin against Rabbi Jakob Emden (28th July 1751). At Lwów, Rabbi Chaim Rappaport did not intervene in the controversy and did not sign the writ in favour of Rabbi Jonathan Eybeschütz which was published at Jaroslaw by the leaders and the rabbis of the "Council of Four Lands," on the 30th October 1753.[29] The position of rabbis and leaders of the Land and region of Lwów did not concur with that. At the session of the Council at Żółkiew – even before the conference of the "Council of Four Lands" at Jaroslaw – they signed a document in favour of Rabbi Jonathan Eybeschütz,[30] rather than the writ published by supporters of Rabbi Jakob Emden on the 30th October 1753. Rabbi Jakob Emden's supporters who were in the minority and defamed Rabbi Jonathan Eybeschütz, even ordained a boycott and burning of books which espoused his views.

As known, Kommissar Kazimierz Granowski, of Radom did not permit the "Council of Four Lands" to discuss the controversy between Rabbi Jonathan Eybeschütz and Rabbi Jakob Emden, as the matter was not under his authority.[31] Only after the Kommissar had left the meeting, that is to say after its official conclusion, did the supporters of Rabbi Jonathan Eybeschütz gather to decide in his favour. On the same day, the books of his opponents were burnt publicly in the Jaroslaw market place.

The following day, the supporters of Rabbi Jakób Emden also published a similar declaration which included a significant note describing the session and the debate: "All acts and affairs of that Council were controlled by strangers and the hand of a gentile meddled in it," and "due to that fact" we were unable to mend the generation's breaches, to enclose the matter in a rose strewn fence.

[Pages 353-354]

Notes: – CHAPTER 8
All notes in square brackets [ ] were made by the translator.
[The spelling of personal names was largely sourced from books cited by the author.]

1. M. Bersohn *Dyplomatarjusz* Nr. 290, p. 163. e.a. 1669.

2. Ptasnik: *Miasta i Mieszczanstwo w Polsce*, p.384.

3. Dr. Majer Bałaban: *Z historjii zydów w Polsce*, Warszawa 1920, p. 61.

4. One of the lampoons circulated about him was published in: Schuldt: *Jüdische Merkwürdigkeiten*. Frankfurt am Main 1714, t. I; p. 214.

5. Girona in southern France, after his father's birthplace.

6. Yisrael Hailpern: *Pinkas Arba Arazot* [*Notebook of the Council of Four Lands*], p. 238.
Dr. Bałaban: *Z historjii zydów w Polsce*, p. 50.

7. Yisrael Hailpern: *Pinkas Arba Arazot* [*Notebook of Council of Four Lands*], p. 238.
Czołowski: *Najazd Tatarow na Lwów w 1695 r.* Lwów 1902.

8. Buber, *Anshei Shem* [*Men of Renown*], p. 217; Article 1790.

9. *ibid.* p. 45; Article 1790.

10. Ks. Chodynicki: *Historja m[iasta] Lwowa*, pp 243–244.

11. One third of the 300,000 Thaler (1 Thaler = 7 Gulden, 15 Groszy).

12. In that manner the community leader Reb. Jakob Koppel ben Dawid funded out of his own pocket payments as well as interest to Polish noblemen, Dominicans and other priests. After his tenure as community leader was over, he sued the community and received judgement that the community had to reimburse him the entire sum and interest he had laid out. The community leaders did not implement the judgement, however. Instead, they demanded that he pay the community tax, and only deducted 50 Gulden from his debt. When he refused to pay, they took collaterals from him. Reb. Jakob Koppel appealed to the Regional Council which convened at Strelisk [Strzeliska Nowe] in 1708, and it confirmed the verdict of the Lwów rabbi: "Charge the champions and the leaders of the holy community of Lwów with the payment of the debt and the interest."
In 1715, Reb. Jakob Koppel was elected community leader, and spent even larger sums of money for the needs of the community. Several years later he sued the community leaders, at the Council of Four Lands which ruled in 1718, that he should be paid "the principal and interest with good money with no earthly delay or excuse." It also gave the lender permission "to extract the money from individuals or groups of Lwów citizens wherever he might find it within our region and beyond it and even through Christian law–courts." The debt amounted to 2636 Gulden and 40 Thaler, but due to its precarious financial standing the community failed again to pay.
In 1730, his son and heir Reb. Judah, a Torah and religious studies teacher at Kraków, claimed in front of the Council of Four Lands, and again he received the verdict signed by the Council's leader, Reb. Abraham Izak Chazak–Fortis. The documents were published in the article by Dr. Dov Weinreb: From the Community Leaders of Kraków. "Tav Betz," Jerusalem 1935, Vol. 8; p. 192, and in
Y. Hailpern: *Pinkas Arba Arazot* [Notebook of Council of Four Lands] 1806, pp. 276–277; 1861, pp 314–315.

13. Dr. M. Bałaban: *Dzielnica Zydowska – jej dzieje i zabytki*. Lwów 1909.

14. Pazdro: *Organizacja i praktyka*. Nr. 12a, pp 180–181.

15. Rabbi J. Emden: *Megilat Sefer*. Warsaw 1897, pp. 45–47.

16. Dr. M. Bałaban: *Dzielnica Zydowska*. pp. 49–50.

17. Rabbi J. Emden: Megilat Sefer. p. 67.

18. Dr. Simchoni [Simchowitz]: "Zur Biographie R. Jakob Josuas des Verfassers des Sefer Pnei Jehoschua". M. G. W d J 1910, pp 608–620.

19. Chaim ben Lazer. In 1728, he escaped to Chocim and died there.

20. The letter of Reb. Jakob Josua (author of *Pneh Josua*) to Rabbi Jakób Emden, appeared in his book Torat HaKanaut [The Doctrine of Zealousness] published at Lwów in 1890.
See Also the addendum "Le'Enei Kol Israel" [In full view of the entire community] p. 71;
David Kahana: *Toldot HaMekubalim, HaShaba'im veHafChasidim* [History of the Accepted [the Kabbalists], the Sabbateans and the Hassidim]. Tel–Aviv 1925, vol. 1, pp. 136–137.
Dr. M. Schorr: *Organizacja* P. 90; Nr. VI.
Pazdro: pp. 181–188; Nr. 11

21. 1728, Sheet 62, 68, 71.

22. 1728, pp. 302, 316.

23. According to the rabbi, Reb. Mojzesz Chagis, emissary from the Land of Israel during the years 1694–1704, preacher at Amsterdam in 1706–1718 and later at Altona, in his book: Misznath Chachamim (1733), p. 85.

24. See the section "Chevra Kadisha Notebook" in Caro *op. cit.* pp. 175–176.

25. The wording on the tombstone reads: "And the entire Jewish community will mourn the fire burnt by God, and the fire turned into a blade to part limbs and cut to pieces the head and the omentum to fragrant smell and the stringent law fell on us on that massacre day, the eve of Shavuoth, as an evening shadow fell to darken our faces in 1728. Alas we feared as fire broke out and consumed the foundation of the holy brothers. The Rabbi, the great light and great scholar our teacher, head of Yeshiva of the two communities, the crown and jewel of Israel was killed in a wicked fashion and his young brother, Pneh Josua, surveyed the moon for several years, sat fasting, and died of thirst and bitterness. The Rabbi and great scholar our teacher Josua, his son, our teacher Izak Halevy who courageously have both sacrificed their souls for the name of God and departed under the same decree. Burnt to death, unwilling to convert, great and awesome God, their soul departed holy and pure, and because of that their ashes rescued from the fire were collected and lie interred here like the ashes of Izak for eternal memory of martyrs. May their souls be cherished for eternity."

26. Her death is only known from the Parochet [ornamental curtains covering the front of the Holy Ark in the synagogue] which her mother Lipke donated to the synagogue outside the town, see:
Dr. M. Bałaban: *Studja historyczne*. Warszawa. 1927. pp. 134–140.

27.   Moshe–Arie Perlmutter in the book *Ve'avo HaYom El HaAyin* [and Today I come to the Spring] its relevance to Rabbi Jonathan Eybeschütz, and its significance to understanding the controversy between Rabbi Jonathan Eybeschütz and Rabbi Jakob Emden. Jerusalem 1943, p. 220; note 65.

[Pages 353-354]

28.   Hailpern: *Pinkas Va'ad Arba Arazot* [*Notebook of the Council of Four Lands*] pp. 391–395, para. 722.

29.   *ibid*. p. 390, para. 719.

30.   Articles by The Council of Four Lands, for the years 1733–1736, and 1753, in "Zion" Jerusalem 1936, pp. 158–159.

31.   [Hailpern]: *Pinkas*, p. 396, para. 723.

[Pages 137-138]

Chapter 9: The Situation in the 18th century
Translated by Myra Yael Ecker

The conflict with the municipality. The outset of the Frankist Movement. The debate at Lwów (1759). The conflict of the townspeople against the Jewish trade. The intervention of chancellor Andrzej Młodziejowski. The Jewish craftsmen and their organizations. The relationships within the community. The conflicts between the community elders. The election war. The accusations and lawsuits. The community–leader Moszka ben Icek–Mękis [Menkis]   and his seizure of power. Disagreements and confusion within the communities.

1.

In the 18th century a sharp decline occurred in the life of the town and the Jewish community. The municipality which had sunk into heavy debts did not take care of such essential needs as: the repair of roads and the town–walls, cleanliness and so on. The sanitation was in a deplorable state and endangered the health of the inhabitants. All building control was also suspended. The economic and cultural status was low and even renowned merchants and townspeople were illiterate.[1]

Due to the wars, many from the privileged sections of society left the town for towns in the East which had developed economically, such as Brody, Żółkiew and Buczacz. The town's poor state worried even King Augustus III who, on the 7th December 1735, ordered the Starosta and the municipality to investigate the reasons for the decline, and to start repairing the dilapidated buildings and roads. 300 houses had been abandoned by their owners due to the burden of taxes. As encouragement, the King reintroduced the freedoms and privileges of the townspeople, but to no avail. The municipality leaders continued to be occupied with court–cases against the Jews at vast expense.

On the 11th February 1735, during Augustus III's visit to Lwów, they obtained from him an order which severely charged the Jews to clear all roads outside the Jewish Quarter. Indeed, they were still granted to sell merchandise on Ruska Street for one whole year .

Concurrently a special committee was appointed to force the Jews to sign a suitable contract with the municipality. But the Jews refused to negotiate a new contract with the municipality on that occasion, as it did not offer them the freedom to trade, which they already had. They were aware that the municipality whose income declined daily, had no power to harm them.

Despite its weakness, the municipality continued its battles against the Jews, with the struggle reaching its peak in 1759. For the Jews of Lwów it proved to be a disastrous year during which negotiation with the municipality and the craftsmen's guilds about their right to live and trade in the town, had come to an end. As previously said, there were only 49 plots of land in the Jewish Quarter and the congestion increased daily.

Despite the prohibition forbidding Christians from selling to Jews real–estate outside the [Jewish] Quarter, in 1660 Jews purchased a large building at the corner of Serbska [Street] and *Szockim Targu* (Boimów No. 23–25) from Jakób Leszczyński, and managed to have their property registered with the land–registry. In 1692, once they had paid the relevant taxes, the property was registered in the names of his heirs, Symche Libermanowicz and Icko [Izak] Moszkowicz. Half the property passed down to Chaim, and later to Anczel Jakubowicz, who also purchased the other half, in 1751.

In 1742, the Drohobych [Drohobycz] Jew Abraham purchased (for 36,000 Gulden) the building on the corner Blacharska–Ruska, adjacent to the Jewish Quarter, from the nobleman Waclaw Karsza, It had been built by the Ruthenian Piotr Siemionowicz Affendyk ("kamieniczki Affendykowskie" [old Affendyk]). That caused an uproar within the municipality. In August 1745, a special committee ruled that the Jews had to vacate the building immediately, but Abraham of Drohobych who counted on his relationship with the nobles, did not move out. On the 6th February 1750, the community–leader Lewko Bałaban purchased the third house outside the Quarter, No. 7 Serbska Street.

The municipality pursued lawsuits over the title of those properties. The cases lasted for years. Investigative committees were launched, enquiries were conducted, the Jews submitted appeals and always succeeded in "settling their affairs," with the help of the Voivode, and Prince Augustus Czartoryski.

In 1757, decided to bring the matter to an end to its advantage, the municipality sent to Warsaw two representatives, Tomasz Frank and Franciszek Solski. According to them, money was required to placate the nobles, and so, on the 12th December 1757 the municipality decided to levy a special tax on the townspeople in order to pay for all the expenses related to those lawsuits.

The Jews engaged the lobbyists from the Council of Four Lands,

[Pages 139-140]

to influence members of the "asesoria królewska"[2] (the royal court of appeal at Warsaw). And it was decided to send to Lwów a delegate with the authority to reach a final decision, with no right of appeal by either side.

At the beginning of 1758, a royal commission headed by Feliks Czacki, royal cupbearer and Starosta of Nowogród,[3] arrived at Lwów. Azryel and Szlomą Malowany appeared for the Jews. After collecting evidence from the townspeople and the Jews, sentence was passed on the 12th February 1759,[4] compelling the Jews to vacate their accommodations and shops located outside the Jewish Quarter. Jewish house owners were ordered to sell their houses to Christians, within six months. A special committee was also appointed to supervise the execution of the sentence, by the 12th June 1759.

That sentence hit also hard the trading rights which the Jews had had, since they were now obliged to limit their trade and work. In accordance with contracts with the municipality, the Jews were permitted to trade solely in four types of merchandise, and craftsmen were almost forbidden from following their crafts.

Naturally, jubilation spread among the townspeople, and the municipality published its sentence to commemorate the complete downfall of the Jews.

The Jews did not surrender and took measures to delay meanwhile the execution of the sentence. Besides the house owners, the community also lobbied on the issue. On the 17th March 1759, Jan Krogulski representing the community, submitted a lawsuit against the municipality and its institution. Then, on the 17thApril 1759, an appeal was lodged with the court of appeal on the grounds that the verdict, to the detriment of the Jews, relied on false information.

Meanwhile, Lewko Bałaban and Aron Abrahamowicz attracted supporters and interceders among the nobility, and the Lwów lobbyist Reb. Chaim Kormis[5] travelled to Warsaw to represent the community.

Fearing that the Jews might be successful in having the implementation postponed, the municipality sent a special representative to Warsaw.

Immediately after the publication of the verdict however, and enraged over the Frankist libel claiming that Jews used Christian blood at Passover [Pessach], the Christian mob celebrated its victory and burst into Jewish shops, raided, robbed property and destroyed houses. On the 13th March 1759, the community–leaders submitted a memorandum describing the riots and damages which amounted to 247,901 Gulden.

The municipality was right to be concerned. The Jews did not move and did not consent to vacating the houses and shops. A whole host of new lawsuits ensued, which passed down to the Austrian rule.[6]

After that calamity, a serious crisis related to the dispute with the Frankists befell the Jews of Lwów, in 1759. It was spread over seven meetings in July, August and September of 1759.

The Frankist movement took no roots within the Lwów community although Frank's devotee, Lejb Krysa, had arrived there and started his propaganda in 1754. He did succeed however in attracting a number of believers who welcomed Frank on his arrival at Lwów in December 1755. Among those was a twenty years old man who had taken 50 Ducats from his parents in order to purchase honey, but then travelled to Salonika with Frank. At Lwów, Frank resided in a house near the Halicz [Halych] gate, known to the Jews as "house of darkness," and it was hard to tell what went on there. According to evidence he held there lewd gatherings.

Some of his sympathizers dared provoke the anger of the Jews with their actions. On a Saturday, one of them rode his horse in front of the house of Rabbi Chaim Rappoport, the town rabbi, and lit his pipe. Such misbehaviour angered the Rabbi and the Jews, and they complained to the archbishop, and asked for permission to punish the offender harshly. With his permission, the offender was placed in a pit according to the testimony of the Rabbi from Biala Podlaska. According to another version, he was sentenced to death and was not interred in the Jewish cemetery but under a tree on the highway.[7]

Due to the Jews' anger it appears that Frank was obliged to leave Lwów and go to Dawidow. His departure brought joy and satisfaction, and according to Birkenthal they were rid of a malignant disease, and the "house of darkness was burnt down to the ground and the woman who participated in the lewd acts died in her sin, while the house owner re–embraced Judaism and accepted penance for his sins."[8]

Faced with the mood of the Christian masses in 1759, and following the judgement by the royal commission, the community–leaders lobbied Lwów's priesthood, the nuncio and even behind the scenes, in order to delay the debate with the Frankists. And that, since the Frankists' representatives had declared their desire to prove openly and clearly from the Talmud, that Jews required Christian blood and used it.

Some 600 of Frank's sympathizers arrived from all over Poland, Podolia, Ukraine, Wallachia, Hungary and some even from Turkey. They were poor and barefoot, and Frank intended

[Pages 141-142]

to convert them to Christianity, but for the Jews they were like explosives.

Fear befell the Jews in the weeks between the debates, and especially prior to the debates of the 27th August and 10th September. In these the Frankists claimed that "the Talmud teaches of the need for Christian blood, and anyone believing in the Talmud is obliged to use it". Consequently, the town governor stationed military guards around the Jewish Quarter.

The peace was further disturbed when Frank arrived in town with all his possessions, on Sabbath the 25th August. On Sunday, the Church beadle invited Rabbi Chaim Rappoport and his associates to come to a debate, the following day. Directly after, the generals, the counts and the leaders of both communities of Lwów assembled and decided to declare a public fast on the Monday "Everyone, down to suckling babes will fast without redemption." They all agreed to the fast, but the debate was postponed to the 10th September. The Jews were glad that the storm they had feared did not materialise. The Frankists were convinced that the debate on the use of Christian blood would provoke the Christians to riots, so to confront the evil and its danger, Lwów's community–leaders assembled in the Rabbi's house on the 28th August 1759,[9] and decided to resort to bribes since they realized that they would not convince the priests of the truth, through argument.

The community members spent 1,026 Gulden on the debate with the opponents of the Talmud, a sum with which the Land's Council reimbursed the community when debts were settled in 1765.

The controversy with the Frankists aroused great interest in Lwów. Many Christians paid 15 Groszy entrance fee to attend those debates.[10]

1759 passed with only minor crises, but the struggle with the municipality over trade and dwelling rights, resumed. Not content with its 1759 victory, the municipality joined Poland's other towns in actions against the Jews. In March 1765, the municipality of Lwów together with the municipalities of Kraków, Poznan, Lublin etc., submitted a petition to the *Sejm* at Warsaw over the destruction of the town and its economics due to the trade, crafts and leasing by Jews.

Based on the petitions, the 1768 *Sejm* focused on the towns' problem.

The noblemen were unwilling to make concessions to the townspeople, and the *Sejm* increased further the starostas' authority over finance and jurisdiction. In order to compensate the townspeople for curtailing their authority, the *Sejm* agreed a statute forbidding the Jews to trade, distill or engage in any craft other than those within the framework of the agreements. Towns which had no agreements with the Jews were to follow earlier town agreements. That statute encouraged farther Lwów's townspeople to fight the trade and crafts by Jews, to confiscate their goods, to close down their shops and so on.

Despite the royal commission's ruling, the struggle continued between the townspeople and the Jews who did not easily surrender to it, and who found stratagems to continue their trade as before.

The Christian tradesmen and shop owners were naturally interested in eliminating the Jewish trade, and limiting it solely to the Jewish Quarter. But yet again they achieved no significant results. The wealthy merchants insisted on the rights they had been granted in the privileges, which permitted Jews to trade solely in merchandise not available in Christian shops. In particular, they were forbidden to trade in fabric, especially if sold by the cubit.

The Jews took no heed of that. In 1744, in its lawsuit against the Jewish wholesalers Dawid Hassles and Izak [Icek] (of Brody), however, the municipality was granted a decision by the podvoivode's law–court,[11] stating that they had to sell the entire fabric stock or remove it from Lwów by a set date. They were forbidden to bring any more fabric into town or into the suburbs to sell by the cubit. Their demand to prevent the Jews from any trade or sale was rejected by the law–court on the grounds that the Jews had debts and that they had to be given the opportunity to clear them. Also, preventing trade would damage the Orders and the creditors of the Jews. The Jews, just at that point, had bought silk fabrics, pearls, corals and goods from the East, and they were travelling back and forth to towns and small towns in Wolyn [Volhynia] and Ukraine.

The merchants' guild (confraternity) established at Lwów in 1767, had its regulations approved by King Stanislaw Poniatowski on the 26th September 1767. It was set up to secure advantages of import for its members, and it continued to oppose Jewish trade which it considered damaging. The merchants were particularly keen that any imports the Jews received from abroad – Frankfurt am Main, Danzig [Gdańsk], Leipzig, Breslau [Wroclaw] or Hungary – be sold retail to the town's Christian merchants, and not wholesale. According to their suggestion the goods should have been confiscated from the offenders, with half given to the treasury and half to the merchants' guild.

A special article (§24) discusses the Jewish merchants who had destroyed the Christian trade, and that consequently the Jews should be forbidden from trading within the town, unless, with the guild's agreement they would sign a contract (pact) with the municipality.

[Pages 143-144]

With no signed contract, all goods and objects should be confiscated from any Jew who dared trade within the town, except for on days of a fair.[12]

Article (§31) stated that the trade in grains, timber, dates and leather was permitted solely to the guild's members, apart from a quantity of skins which they would contractually allow Jews.[13]

The townspeople were unsuccessful in their attempts to eliminate the Jewish trade. And that, since the nobles and the clergy to whom Jewish individuals and communities owed vast sums – (in 1765, the Lwów community's debt to noblemen, clergy and Orders, amounted to 381,999 Gulden)[14] – were interested in collecting the capital as well as the interest. To this end, they tended to side with the Jews and enabled them to continue in their practices.

In the middle of the 18th century spiteful suits were brought against Jewish mediators (barysznicy) by Christian retailers, according to whom Christian trade was harmed and the price of goods increased. In 1742, a ruling reduced the number of mediators who required a joint license from the congregation and the deputy–voivode's authorities.[15]

The wholesale merchants who were interested in Jewish agents and mediators, for their own trade with foreign merchants, held a different view.

Since the Jews were also moneychangers, and they were blamed for distributing counterfeit coins,[16] the deputy–voivode [podvoivode] demanded from the community that only people known for their uprightness be permitted to be moneychangers.[17] The authorities announced that they would severely punish any Jewish moneychanger caught swindling.

Without a contract with the municipality in place, the economic life was in a strange state. Admittedly however, the authorities, especially the deputy–voivode's law–court, showed understanding for the resulting situation. When lawsuits were brought against Jewish merchants over illegal trading, the authorities took into consideration the debt burden of the Jews, and that they had no option but to deal[18] in any trade in order to make a living.

Shortly before the first partition of Poland, the relationship between the municipality and the Jews deteriorated again, on account of a special tax of 5,115 Gulden. The community–elder Zelman Pinkas submitted a letter in the name of Lwów's Jews, to Andrzej Młodziejowski, the chancellor of the Crown at Warsaw, complaining against the municipality, its treatment and the unbearable tax burden.

On the 7th January 1771, the chancellor [Kanclerz], instructed the Starosta to investigate the matter, since "the Jews are our colleagues and it is improper to demand unfair things from them." In his letter to the Lwów municipality he recommended they stop the special tax levy since the Jews were already burdened with heavier taxes than the rest of the town's population. Aware that the Jews did not lack patronage, the municipality had to pursue a sensible policy to prevent them from calling upon their protectors.[19]

In the 18th century, Lwów remained one of the principal Jewish trade centres. According to a census from 1764,[20] a fairly accurate list remains of the occupation of Lwów's Jews:

Of the 6,142 souls, 3,060 were men, of whom 1,460 were qualified to work. In fact, there were 834 breadwinners (57.3%), while 626 men (42.7%) were unemployed.

78 Jews (5.3%) were employed in trade and industry; 335 (22.9%) in crafts, 17 (1.1%) distillers and lessees; 295 (20.2%) employees, servants, coachmen, porters, assistants; 109 (7.8%) community clerks and various professions.

In 660 villages within the entire Lwów region, there were 6,783 Jews, of whom 3,400 were men, with 1,400 of them qualified to work. 1035 (69%) men were engaged in work: 764 (51%) of those were distillers and lessees; 14 (0.9%) in trade and industry; 29 (2.5%) in crafts; 190 (12.7%) in house and farm services; 38 (2.5%) Torah teachers and similar.

At the fairs, the Jews facilitated barter and leasing with estate owners. The trade in wine brought from Hungary through Lwów, was of great significance.[21]

The 18th century saw improvement in the organization of Jewish craftsmen's associations. Apart from the associations which had long existed, in 1727 were also established the Jewish tinsmiths', and glaziers' associations. The pedlars also gathered in an organization when their standing worsened.

On the 21st May 1754, the regional rabbi together with the leaders of the two communities, composed a special amendment to the satchel pedlars' association[22] (cechu torbiarze) to regulate their affairs and relationships.

In their satchels the pedlars carried panels, edging ribbons and haberdashery, on commission from traders. There were also women pedlars.

In 1761, the association's regulation was approved by the deputy–voivode's Office.

The congregation–elder Moszko Mękis [Menkis] was nominated association patron. In line with the practices of the craftsmen's associations, until the election the following were appointed association–leaders: Kisiel [Jekutiel] Kisielowicz, Abraham Józefowicz, Giecel Dawidowicz and Jakób Janklewicz.

All financial matters they litigated before the rabbi or the urban prefect, and all other issues, before the patron

[Pages 145-146]

and the association–leaders. Any appeals were brought to the deputy–voivode's Office.

Article 3 of the regulation warned the pedlars against unfair competition by reducing the price of goods. It was also prohibited to send women to sell goods.

Pedlars who had business and income, were removed from the association's list.

The organization of the craftsmen's associations was also established.

All internal disputes were settled by an internal law–court led by a patron. His judgement could be disputed at the law–court of the deputy–voivode who also oversaw the craftsmen's associations. Disputes between craftsmen and their apprentices exceeded the association's jurisdiction and were subject to his authority.

Whenever patrons exploited their position to the detriment of the association, the decision rested with the deputy–voivode's law–court. One knows for example of the 1770 case, when the furriers' association blamed its patron, Moszko Landys, for taking payments contrary to the association's custom: three Gulden for canopies used in Jewish weddings, and eight Gulden for letter writing. The matter was noted as gross extortion, besides the corruption he perpetrated for his own gratification. The law–court dismissed the patron and instructed the association, in accordance with the regulations, to elect another patron from among Lwów's citizens.[23]

The patrons and association–leaders paid strict attention to the maintenance of internal discipline and the association's authority, ensuring that no meeting took place without their knowledge, and no work was undertaken surreptitiously. In the tinsmiths' association, for example, it was customary for any work above 40 Gulden to be distributed among the craftsmen, by lot. The association–leaders safeguarded that craftsmen kept to producing products in their own craft and not subsidiary products.[24]

Indeed, the conflicts with the Christian guilds that were interested to undermine the existence of the Jewish craftsmen, increased.[25]

Trials against the Jews brought to the deputy–voivode's law–court by the guilds of leather workers, tanners, carpenters, glaziers and barbers are mentioned in documents.[26] The relationship with the tanners in particular was increasingly fraught. The Christian tanners accused the Jewish ones of illegally exporting leather abroad, and thus pushing up prices. In 1754, they sued the merchant Eliasza Moszkowicz, on the grounds that he bought and sold abroad all the leather.[27]

In general, the Christian craftsmen's guilds were keen to secure low–cost raw materials for their members, and were therefore interested to secure a ban over export.

On the other hand, they persecuted their colleagues who did not join guilds and produced shoddy work without permission. They adopted particularly stringent measures against the "non–experts" (*partacze*), persecuting especially the textile workers (*Flickschneider*) who helped the Jewish craftsmen.

With the decline and corruption in Poland generally during the Saxon dynasty, things did not run smoothly within the community either.

The Lwów community Council was made up of 4–8 leaders and 3–6 good–men; each great synagogue had 3–5 managers; 3–4 judges acted in the law–court; there were 3–6 appraisers; 5–6 arbitrators were elected to levy the Rabbi, cantor or judge. Apart from them there were 5 managers of the Eretz Israel [Erec Izrael] fund.[28] In the 1740s, the community–leaders were: Józef Cymeles, Józef Rabinowicz, Szmujł Dups and Icek [Izak] Minceles.

Rather than looking after the community's needs, they exploited their position to their own advantage. That was brought to a halt by the community treasurer Lewko Rawski, who filed a protest and complaint against them at the deputy–voivode's law–court since they had brought the community to bankruptcy.[29]

In 1742, the deputy–voivode's law–court was compelled to threaten the community–leaders Izrael Szmuklerz and Litman to relieve them of their office and fine them for the mismanagement they had introduced into the community administration, when they took for themselves 6,000 Gulden which they had received, on loan, to clear the community's debts.

In 1743 and 1745, Icek Minceles was accused of taking loans in the name of the community [30]without permission from the deputy-voivode, and was thus dismissed from his office of community–leader. Persistent disputes occurred between the community and the deputy–voivode's Office, which complained that the community did not observe its control and disparaged its orders. On occasion, it was even announced in the synagogue that anyone "who followed the deputy–voivode's instructions should be strangled, poisoned, and excommunicated so that they did not mingle with the community. His property and life should even be endangered, rather than surrender to the orders of Mr. deputy–voivode."[31]

When in 1743 the community–leader Józef Rabinowicz did not respond to the order to appear at the deputy–voivode's Office, he was dismissed from his post for three years.

[Pages 147-148]

One knows that the deputy–voivode's Office filled roles which affected most areas of Jewish life, and that the community contributed substantially towards his expenses.

According to the 1692 regulation, the community paid the Voivode 4,000 Gulden annually, 1,000 to the deputy–voivode, as well as to the Starosta. Besides supervising the community affairs, the election of the leaders and the supervisors, raising taxes and accounting, the deputy–voivode's Office had to supervise public order and security, as well as trade and crafts issues.[32]

The elections burdened the Office with quite a few problems. Nearly every election period gave rise to complaints against the ruling community–leaders, and against the rabbis who got involved and lobbied for their supporters. At times, the Office was obliged to intervene even in disputes between the community–leaders and the rabbis who overstepped their powers as defined in the 1726 ruling. The Office supervised all the community activities and its leaders, and did not shy away from taking severe legal steps against them.

In order to organize the community, when expenses were not correctly entered, and when people were relieved of their debts after a say so by the elders without the consent of the Office, the entire community was given 100 fines [grzywny], and the leaders were jailed for a week.[33]

With the rise of corruption cases, the community–leaders were forced to swear allegiance to the authorities that they would act in the public interest, that they would fulfill their duties honestly and that they would not relieve themselves,[34] their relatives or their friends of the payment of taxes. That seems to have been to no avail, since in 1745, Józef Rabinowicz and Herszko Cymeles (condemnation) were convicted by the law–court which removed them from the post of leaders,[35] and ordered that they never again be elected to any community office.

The number of accusations increased to such an extent that the officers could no longer cope with the complaints of the Jews. The prosecutor Ulanowski was also obliged to act against the mischief of the community–governors, to cancel elections and to remove the leaders from their posts.

In May 1743, the deputy–voivode accused the regional rabbi, Rabbi Chaim ben Symche (Rappoport), that on his initiative all those elected as leaders were his supporters, that he did not let Jews use the appeal courts, and that he boycotted those who did. He accused him generally of irregularities in the community, and of refusing to take part in meetings about the clearing of taxes.

Rabbi Chaim was also accused of inciting his supporters to submit applications to the Starosta, and that when the emissaries of the deputy–voivode's office came to the Jewish Quarter, he instructed to have them beaten up and to drive them out. He was further accused that "in one lawsuit (presided by the Rabbi), two contradictory verdicts were passed after he had received a bribe." [36]

Even Dov Ber Birkenthal [of Bolechów], his contemporary and assistant in the Frankists lawsuit at Lwów, wrote that he had heard complaints against him but did not believe them "when they say that they hate him, they freely discredit him out of jealousy. And when he was old, I held him as artless and honest, loved and accepted by most of the community. But now, with his disgrace revealed, we discover the truth that his misdemeanours during his rabbinate far exceeded those, so that he has no option but to flee Lwów" as he would be obliged to sue him.

The merchant Izrael Peyses's 1747 complaint against the verdict handed to him at Lwów, illustrates how severe the Rabbi's rule was over his flock. It was not impossible that the disagreements between him and the congregation, including individual members, drove Czartoryski, the Voivode of Reissen, to issue new regulations on the 3rd November 1751, and on the 1st January 1752. The preface specified that as a result of acts by the congregation, the Rabbi and the crowd were against the law and conscience, and in order to avoid incongruity and to maintain justice throughout, he reconfirmed the authority of Lwów's chief rabbi as set by Voivide Jabłonowski in the rule of the 20th July 1726. In fact, his ruling restated the 1726 ruling, leaving out Article 10 which considered the leave to appeal to the regional committee or to the deputy–voivode's Office, against the verdict of the rabbis, the community–leaders and their instructions. It stressed also that the Land rabbi and the house–owners had to act jointly, and obey the authorities.

Another Article (§16), forbade the rabbi from accepting gifts from the community members, or from organizing a reception at his own behest, paid for from the public purse.[37] On the 31st December 1771, a few months before the First Partition of Poland [1772], the Voivode Czartoryski introduced 7 additional Articles (§§ 17–23), which limited the authority of the rabbis: The rabbis are forbidden from granting the title "Our teacher [Morenu]" without a written approval from the congregation (§17); the rabbis and judges are forbidden from issuing a house–purchase certificate, without confirmation from the community treasury that house–tax was paid (§18); it is forbidden to marry anyone without a certificate from the community treasury, and the community–leader (§ 19); the regional rabbi is forbidden from providing any recommendation letter on innovations, to the towns or the villages, without first consulting and receiving written confirmations from both communities (§ 20).

In earlier years, the regional–leaders were elected from among Lwów's men, and they signed the summons.

[Pages 149-150]

As that privilege was repealed, the regulations stated that the regional–rabbi was forbidden from issuing summons to his law–court without signatures of the two community–leaders (§ 21). In a special register ("*dekretarz*"), the rabbi and the community–leader had to record all regulations passed by the rabbi, which will only be valid if entered in that register. In a second register the rabbis had to record every verdict, concession, payment, certificate and any legal negotiations (§ 22). Every three months these registers had to be submitted to the Voivode's law–court, otherwise a 100 fines [grzywny] would be levied (§ 23).[38]

Despite it all, the authorities were unable to improve the management or teach the community–leaders discipline.

Due to the reduced circumstances, the number of disputes and lawsuits rose, especially against the community treasurers for inaccurate accounting, collection of taxes and accounting on the settlement of debts. The Voivode's law–court was busy with cases of that controversy, which led it to dismiss treasurers and community–leaders for their actions.

In 1763, in between trials, the community treasurers were typically engaged in the following:

The deputy–voivode's office claimed that the community–leaders and elders appointed unqualified treasurers who did not manage the accounts, were not punctilious in settling the interest on time, and just caused confusion. The law–court decided to dismiss them and have them replaced by the previous treasurers: Szmelke Mojżesz, Mojżesz Manilowicz, Azryel Złoczowski, Marko Boruchowicz, Lewko Malowany–Mizes and Izrael Reis, who pledged to register the incomes and expenses, and meticulously to collect the taxes.[39]

In 1764, at the behest of prosecutor Ulanowski, the law–court's clerk criticised the community–leaders – Reb. Józef Cymeles outside the town, and Moszka Menkis within the town – for collecting tax on account of the Jesuit Order, and using it without the knowledge or consent of the Voivode's Office. The community–leaders and the supervisors received a financial penalty.[40]

Some extraordinary charges were laid against the appointed community appraisers who had reduced their own, their friends' and their relatives' taxes.[41] The instructions and orders which obligated the appraisers to be punctilious in the tax evaluation, had been in vain.

The podvoivode's jurisdiction can be gathered from a case of 1771. The prosecutor sued Icek Jakóbowicz, who had been fined by the congregation and by the town rabbi for having had a well dug on his property on Yom Kippur [the Day of Atonement]. Icek responded that at the houses of the community–elders, Christian tradesmen also worked on the Sabbath. The law–court determined that the accused had to admit, in the synagogue, that he had desecrated the Jewish custom, and that as ransom he had to donate 100 Gulden to the synagogue and the hospital. At the same time, the law–court warned the communities against acts of revenge or zealousness.[42]

The relations between the communities within, and outside the town, formed a special chapter.

The community members outside the town disregarded the authority of the community–leaders within the town. In particular, they objected to the portion of the taxes they were asked to pay, and evaded paying them. To justify their refusal they even laid serious allegations that the community–leaders used community funds for their own use and businesses.

For the community–leaders such actions manifested overt rebellion. They announced in the synagogues that the accusers should appear before the rabbis and prove, in the presence of those accused, the veracity of their accusations. In such a case, they would avoid any punishment. But were the result negative, the accusers would be punished and legal action would be taken against them at the deputy–voivode's office, for defamation of character and the spread of lies and deceit.[43]

The depleted status of the community's leadership is noted from the community elections of 1763, when Marko Wrocławski served as community–leader within the town, and Moszka ben Icek Mękis [Menkis], outside the town, as well as from the 1766–68 elections.

Moszko Menkis was a bartender, lessee and owner of a beer brewery. He was born at Brody, and through his connection with men of authority he rose to "prominence", became patron of the "backpack merchants," and knew how to surround himself with men who obeyed all his wishes and commands. Although he was an ignoramus, due to his connections with the authorities he was elected community–leader and ruled cruelly over his congregation. They endured his authority since not many sought the status of community–leader, considering the debt with which the community was burdened. In 1761, when the debt repayment was due, the coffers were empty. Mękis [Menkis] then took out a 20,000 Gulden mortgage on the synagogue, to general relief. Rumours spread within the community, however, that the community–leaders also benefitted from the loan, rumours which the community–leaders refuted while demanding that the "rebels" present proof to the rabbis. Menkis and his associates were convinced no one would dare openly rebel against them, but on that occasion they had miscalculated.

Leading the rebellion against Menkis was his competitor, the bartender and beer brewery owner, Dawid ben Eleazar Soboliszyn,[44] of Tyśmienica. As adventurous and uncivil as Menkis, his sole ambition was to be the congregation–leader. During Shavuoth [the Jewish Feast of Weeks], at the synagogue outside the town, Dawid Soboliszyn

[Pages 151-152]

did not permit to read out the congregation–leader's declaration. He and his gang ran riot and shouted against the congregation and brought to a halt the reading of the proclamation.

On the 28th May 1762, after the Holidays, Menkis and Mordechaj Wrocławski went to the deputy–voivode's office and submitted a complaint against those who provoked the riot.[45] Thus began the struggle for the congregation's governance, which lasted five years and unsettled the foundation of the communities' autonomy.

Moszka Menkis was a vengeful man who bore grudges, and he decided to mercilessly crush Dawid Soboliszyn who considered him a very dangerous opponent.

His revenge, assisted by the community–leader within the town, began by increasing the taxes. Dawid Soboliszyn and his faction remained silent while awaiting the 1763 election. Meanwhile, searching for those dissatisfied with Menkis – who was not much liked by the community – he recruited the distinguished families: Mizes, Lewkowicz, Byk, who had long wished to replace the community–leader.

Moszka Menkis, on the other hand, depended on his connections with the deputy–voivode who supported him. Despite it, however, Menkis did not achieve the total victory he had expected. Soboliszyn had failed, nevertheless, two of his men were elected. On the 20th April 1763, Soboliszyn's men submitted a protest to the deputy–voivode, regarding the arbitrators who had elected community–leaders who had failed to pay, or had paid reduced taxes. And that, despite the provision that the position of hospital leaders and collector–of–dues be open only to those candidates who had paid at least 75 Gulden in tax.[46]

The discussion over the election of the appraisers led to a dispute within the congregation. Menkis demanded that the previous appraisers, Szmul and Moszko Monyszowicz – who were his men – be reappointed. Neither of them was elected, but Menkis stubbornly obtained their endorsement from the deputy–voivode's law–court, dated the 25th August 1763. It included however an addendum he did not care for: that four inspectors from the opposing camp be appointed to assist them, Azryel Złoczowski and Marko Boruchowicz representing the town community, and Lewko Malowany Mizys and Srul [Izrael] Rais from outside the town.[47]

The relations within the congregation had worsened. Informing, complaints and charges were made which eventually reached the deputy–voivode's law–court. These were directed against Zelman Pinkas Rabinowicz, previously the community–leader who had been accused by Dawid Soboliszyn, Froimem [Ephraim] Daches, Lewko Byk, Mordechaj Fayglis, Aron of Drohobycz, Mordechaj Korzennik, Dawid Hassles and others, that during his leadership he indulged in: "financial intrigues of the elders, and did not account for his actions."

During the lawsuit the deputy–voivode ordered to inspect all the congregation's operations undertaken during the period of Zelman Pinkas Rabinowicz, and three years subsequently, since order in the community's economy was essential for the greater good.[48] The communities agreed, and even Menkis was satisfied since he believed the inspection would go solely in his favour.

The Pessach 1764 election was a total failure for Menkis. All those

elected to manage the congregation were his opponents: Dawid Soboliszyn, Szlomą Mizes, Lewko Mizes, Lewko Byk, Reis [Rais; Rays] and others.

Menkis did not dispair, He managed to obtain a decision from the deputy–voivode's law–court that due to irregularities in the election the new management was not approved, and that the previous community–leaders remained in their posts.

The elderly Józef Cymeles Mękis [Menkis] was appointed community–leader within the town. Outside the town, Libra Rabinowicz, Menkis's assistant, was appointed community–leader, as was the rest of the previous management members.[49] The issue was thus settled, but the people were angry and threatened the community–elders who feared assaults.

Total confusion reigned in both communities, and in the absence of anyone caring, not even the dead were buried.

The town rabbi tried to mediate between the sides, and succeeded in obtaining consent from the opposition to accept Cymeles as well as Rabinowicz as community–leaders. Shortly after, however, the controversy broke out again.

During Easter, the community–leaders bearing gifts, paid a courtesy visit to the Christian burgrave. Suddenly, the community–elders and the new (annulled) congregation representatives headed by Dawida Soboliszyn, appeared. Both delegations met, and when they left the castle Soboliszyn shouted at Rabinowicz: "Why are you following us, after all you are not the congregation–leader." It was only due to Menkis's intervention that no melee broke out.[50]

Rabinowicz was taken ill from irritation, and after lobbying by the burgrave, the prosecutor sued Soboliszyn. On the 17th May 1764, the verdict issued dismissed Szlomą Mizes from his post as elder for two years, and Dawida Soboliszyn, for one year; Jakób Byk was fined (three red Gulden). Izrael Reis and Lewko Mizes were released.[51]

The opposition surrendered and Menkis ruled again. The 1765 elections passed smoothly, and Menkis's entire roll was elected. Soboliszyn did not despair however, and after recovering from his setback he decided to get closer to Menkis, and turned into one of his frequenters. In 1766, he was elected as community–elder. His principal aspiration to become community–leader was yet distant, but he was slowly getting

[Pages 153–154]

there. 1765 was the third year of Menkis's community–leadership, and according to the rulings anyone who had served for three years had to vacate the post and could not even be elected community–elder.

At the time, Lewko Bałaban was community–leader within the town, and the elders who served with him were: Zelman Elowicz, Aron of Drohobycz, Mordechaj Boruchowicz, Anczlem Jakubowicz, Józef Cymeles, Boruch Mędlowicz [Mendelowicz], Izrael Józefowicz, Joelo [Joel] Moszkowicz, Efroim Abrahamowicz and Elą [Eliahu] Ablowicz.[52] Their relationship did not run smoothly either.

In 1766, a disagreement broke out between the community–leader Lewko Bałaban and the community–elder Eliahu Ablowicz.[53] It resulted from an altercation at the synagogue during Simchat–Torah [the last day of the Tabernacles Holiday], when Ablowicz insulted Bałaban. On the 7th October 1766, the law–court [Beth–Din] decided to remove Ablowicz temporarily from his office as community–elder until the final verdict. Bałaban accused Ablowicz that he divulged community secrets to the authorities, and based on his knowledge, the authorities imposed orders on the community, thus harming the community's existence.

Without contacting the congregation outside the town, Bałaban instructed that the law–court's directive be read out at the synagogues within the town, as well as outside Ablowicz's house. The following day, Eliahu Ablowicz submitted a lawsuit against him at the deputy–voivode's office.

The case against the Rabbi and the congregation whose verdict was illegal, took place on the 10th October 1766.

The deputy–voivode's decision confirmed the removal of Eliahu from his office as community–elder. In addition, he was fined 10 grzywny for offending Bałaban, and he had to apologise. Lewko Bałaban was imprisoned inside the synagogue's tower for two days and one night as punishment for accusing Eliahu that he had divulged secrets. The elders who took part in the judging were each sentenced to spend one day within the synagogue's tower.

Bałaban appealed the verdict in front of the deputy–voivode, as it debased the authority of the congregation–leader. The outcome of that appeal is unknown.

In 1767, the elections of the communities drew near. Soboliszyn took advantage of the opportunity and came to a compromise with Lewko Bałaban, contacted the Mizes family and the opponents of Menkis, and was successful. The arbiters led by Rachmil Mizys, elected the congregation made up of Soboliszyn's and Mizes's men alone.

Menkis did not rest, and on the 13th may 1767 two elders from his faction, Moszka Landys and Mędla [Mendla] Michlowicz, protested to the deputy–voivode against the elections.[54] They reasoned that a Jew from the congregation outside the town could not be elected arbitrator, unless he had lived within the town for ten years, while Rachmil Mizys had only lived in town one year. Soboliszyn, on the other hand, was not the right choice since he had leased taxes without the communities' knowledge. Their protest included also an appeal against the election of Lewko Bałaban since he had already served three years thus bringing his service to an end.

Soboliszyn's men submitted a counter protest in which they refuted all of the appellants' claims.

Soboliszyn was elected to lead the congregation. On the 1st July 1767, the deputy–voivode's law–court approved the elections despite the legal shortcomings. Instead of Soboliszyn however, the elder Józef [Joslem] ben Aron Nechles was declared the congregation–leader.[55] After five years of tense struggle, peace returned to the communities.[56] Nevertheless, the chapter of complaints over the validity of the elections did not end. Until 1772, after nearly every election period, the deputy–voivode's office received complaints and accusations over the elections and the unjust acts of the arbitrators.[57]

A dispute also broke out over the office of the rabbinate within the town. It had stood vacant since the demise of Rabbi Aryeh Loeb, the son of the great scholar [Gaon] Rabbi Symche Rappoport in 1759. Ulanowski, the deputy–voivode's prosecutor, found it even necessary to submit a complaint against the congregation–leaders Zelman Pinkas and Moszke Mękis [Menkis], as well as against the elders Azryel Złoczowski, Dawid Heslis, Józef Cymeles, Izrael Reis, Jakób Lewkowicz, Herszko Hulis, Marko Boruchowicz, Anczlem Korzennik and Major Rawski, for not following rules and postponing the election of the rabbi, a deferral which adversely affected the community's management. As a result of his complaint the elders of both communities were fined 50 Gulden for the treasury, and 100 fines [grzywny] for the law–court.[58]

On the 30th June 1765, Voivode Czartoryski appointed Berk Lewkowicz (Dov–Berof Rzeszów [Raisha]) Rabbi within the town for the following six years, provided that he were subject to the deputy–voivode's jurisdiction.

On the 3rd May 1771, in recognition of his good tenure and his honest judgement, his appointment was extended by six years.[59]

The two communities, their elders, leaders and rabbis sank among fights and disputes. The situation weighed heavily on the people who struggled for survival amid a hostile population aiming to suppress them financially. Internally – division and battles among family–factions that clung to the control of the community's governance; perpetual lawsuits against the community by creditors; expropriations and ostracism. Such was the Jewish Lwów of the second half of the eighteenth century, and the image was very grim.

[Pages 355-356]

Notes: – CHAPTER 9

All notes in square brackets [ ] were made by the translator.
[The spelling of most names were sourced from books cited by the author, especially those of Pazdro and Bałaban.]

1.   Ptasnik *op. cit.* p. 392.

2.   The High–Court of Justice which dealt with the municipal law–courts' appeals in the matter of privileges, boundary disputes and the royal estates, the nobles and the Church, was led by the chancellor [Kanclerz], while members of the law–court were referendar senators and managers of the King's Office.

3.   Dr. M. Bałaban: *Studja historyczne.* Warszawa 1927, pp 112–126.
Dr. M. Bałaban: *Dzielnica zydowska we Lwowie.* pp. 49–51.
Dr. M. Bałaban: *LeToldot HaT'nua HaFrankit.* [History of Frankism]. p. 214.

4.   Decretum Sacrae Regiae Majestatis Commisxoriale inter nob–ac spect. proconsulem civitatis Leopoliensis ab una atque infidels seniores totasque synagogs Judaeorum leopolienses anno 1759, prolatum.

5.   *See* his letter to Rabbi Dov–Ber [Birkenthal of] Bolechów, dated 23rd Elul [20.9.] 1802, published in my article "Three documents on the history of Frankism in Poland," in "Zion (Jerusalem) Year 2, Bk. 3–4, p. 328.

6.   Arch. Namiestnictwa Lwów. Castr. leopol. t. 604; p.2036–2127.

7.   Ber Birkenthal: *Divrei Binah* [Words of Wisdom] (Dr. Brauer) "HaShalach" 33, p. 384.

8.   Rabbi Jakób Emden relates the case in *Sefer Shimush*, sheet 2, sheet 3, column 1; sheet 19, column 2.

9.   Dov Ber of Bolechów's words of wisdom, by Dr. Brauer, "HaShalach" 1921, p.236.

10.   See my above mentioned article in "Zion (Jerusalem) year 2, Book 3–4; pp. 331, 332.

11.   Pazdro: *op. cit.* pp. 198–199, No. 26.

12.   i.e. on the 23rd January.

13.   Dr. Stanislaw Lewicki: *Konfraternia kupiecka we Lwowie za Stanislawa Augusta* Lwów 1910. pp. 34–36; 40.

14.   Archiwum główne Warszawa. Taryfy zyd. pogl. t. 64.

15.   Pazdro: *op. cit.* pp. 192–193 No. 19.

16.   On forgery and the trimming of coins and gold in those years, see: *Memoires of Dov Ber of Bolechów*, pp.32–33.

17.   Pazdro: p. 193, No. 20.

18.   Pazdro: p. 199, No. 26.

19.   Pazdro: pp. 276–277, Nos. 86–87.

20.   Archiwum główne. Taryfy zyd. pogl. t. 64.

21.   *Memoires of Dov Ber of Bolechów*, p. 29.

22.   Dr. M. Schorr: *Organizacja Zydów w Polsce.* Lwów 1899. pp. 94–95. No. VIII.

23.   Pazdro: pp. 257–260, No. 72.

24.   Pazdro: p. 201, No. 29; p. 201, No. 34.

25.   Pazdro: pp. 211–213, No. 37.

26.   Pazdro: pp. 229–230, No. 51.

27.   Pazdro: p. 207, No. 34.

28.   Dr. M. Bałaban: *Ustrój gimpy zed. Gmina zed.*, Warszawa 1937, No. 5, p,103,

29.   Pazdro: p. 190, No. 16.

30.   Pazdro: p. 196, No. 23 (1743).

31.   Pazdro: p. 192, No. 19 (1742).

32.   According to Stefan Czarniecki's regulation of the 17th March 1660, Article 8.

33.   Despite the regulations (porządki) the Voivodes set for the congregation's election procedures, conflicts broke out as to who was entitled to be elected according to the census. The census, as known, was set in accordance with the person's property and scholarship. According to a 1763 regulation, the community tax and the census cost to a community–leader candidate was 75 Gulden, and 50 Gulden to a collector–of–dues candidate.

34.   Pazdro: p. 195, No. 22. (1743)

35.   Pazdro: p. 200, No. 27.

36.   Dov–Ber of Bolechów, *Memoires*, pp. 33–37. It discusses the verdict passed by Rabbi Chaim Kohen Rappoport about the estate of a wealthy Jew at Komarno.

37.   Pazdro: pp. 181–88, No. 14.

38.   Pazdro: pp. 188–189, No. 15.

39.   Pazdro: p. 220, No. 44.

40.   Pazdro: pp. 230–231, No. 52.

41.   Complaints against the collector of dues, in 1771:
Pazdro: pp. 261–263, No. 73, 7; p. 269, No. 81, pp. 270–271, No. 82.

42.   Pazdro: pp. 271–273, Nos. 83–84.

43.   In 1762, for example: [Buber] *Anshei Shem* [*Men of Renown*] p. 60, Article 140.

44.   Pazdro: pp. 216–218, No. 41.

45.   Pazdro: pp. 216–218, No. 41.

46.   Pazdro: p. 219, No. 43.

47.   Pazdro: p. 220, No. 44.

48.   Pazdro: pp. 222–224, No. 47

[Pages 355-356]

49.   Pazdro: pp. 226–229, No. 50.

50.   Pazdro: p. 227, No. 50.

51.   Pazdro: p. 228, No. 50.

52.   Dr. M. Bałaban: *Z historji Zydów w Polsce*, Warszawa 1920. p. 162.

53.   Pazdro: pp. 240–243, No. 62.

54.   Pazdro: pp. 243–244, No. 63.

55.   Buber: *Anshei Shem* [*Men of Renown*], p. 95, Section 234.

56.   Pazdro: *op. cit.* pp. 245–247, No. 65.
see also: Dr. Izak Lewin: *Przycznyki do dziejów i literatury Zydów w Polsce.* Lwów 1935, pp. 27–35.

57.   Pazdro: pp. 283–285. No. 92.

58.   Pazdro: pp. 232–234. No.56.

59.   Pazdro: pp. 237–238. Nos. 59, 60.

[Pages 155-156]

Chapter 10: The Autonomous Jewish Institutions of Lwów

Translated by Myra Yael Ecker

The Lwów regional committee after the 1648 and 1649 massacres. The Żółkiew – Lwów controversy. Intervention by the Council of Four Lands. The 1740 decision by the Berezhany Council. The regional community–elders. The controversy over the regional rabbinate. Lwów's representation at the Council of Four Lands during the period 1589–1764.

I.

During the 16th and 17th centuries, as previously mentioned, Lwów was the sole large Jewish community in central Reissen. There was also a small number of Jews who lived in small towns and on estates where they were under the patronage of noblemen.

Since the [smaller] Jewish settlements were unable to establish their own communities, they were subject to the Lwów community's jurisdiction. Even small towns in which there was a community, such as Olesko in 1628,[1] or Sassów in which there were five houses,[2] were affiliated to the Lwów community (*przykahałki*). The Council which managed the affairs was made up of four principals, four good–men and a number of collector–of–dues. It represented the two communities of Lwów as well as the province, but its representatives were all men from Lwów. The official title of the Council was "The chiefs, principals and leaders of the Land and leaders of the holy community of Lwów"[3] (*starsi ziemscy*). The dependence of the province's communities meant that if a Jew wished to settle within a community outside of Lwów, the leaders of that community had to advise the Lwów congregation about it. The small communities were not permitted to set new taxes without submitting a financial report to the Lwów congregation. It was also via the Lwów congregation that they submitted all their taxes and payments to the kingdom in general, which from 1549, included also the poll–tax. That drive to concentrate power in the hands of the Lwów community was sustained by the congregation as well as by the authorities keen on that arrangement.

The rabbi of the community outside the town served also as the regional rabbi. He was appointed by "the Jews of Lwów and of the entire Land of Reissen" ("pospólstwo żydów lwowskich i wszystkiej ziemi ruskiej"), in accordance with Sigismund Augustus's regulations of 1571.

In time disputes broke out, between the rabbi within the town and the regional rabbi, over authority and over their standing with the leaders of the communities and the region. But so long as the Lwów community held sway in the Land of Reissen, it also picked the rabbi.

With the expansion of the outlying communities, however, the conflict between them and the Lwów community increased over the hegemony of the entire Land of Reissen. By and by, therefore, the Lwów community had to take into account the demands of the representatives from the smaller communities.

In the 16th and 17th centuries, all the communities within the territories of Reissen, Podolia and Wroclaw [Breslau] which formed a single Land,[4] (*ziemstowa*) were under the control of Lwów.

After the massacres of 1648 and the wars in Poland at the end of the 17th century, the Land too underwent a significant reorganization. Lwów declined economically, as did its influence over the communities.

Many citizens left the town for the neighbouring small towns. The surrounding communities of Zloczow [Złoczów], Lisko, Brody, Tarnopol, Buczacz and others developed largely due to help and support from noblemen who owned the towns. Nevertheless, the burden of taxes remained largely the responsibility of the Lwów community, which was unable to pay them on its own. In 1685, the matter was eventually brought to discussion at the *Sejmik* of Vyshnia [Wisznia]. The Reissen noblemen instructed their delegates to the *Sejm* to declare that: "The Jews of Lwów and Przemyśl are pestered with impositions of many taxes, and they are unable to bear the burden on their own. The *Sejm* must conclude that the Jews residing in the Royal towns and the villages of the Lwów and Przemyśl district should share in the tax burden together with the communities of Lwów and Przemyśl. For that purpose the Jews of Lwów and Przemyśl must be permitted to convene the Jewish representatives for a 'convention of Jews' (*Sejmik*) to calculate and organize the dispersal."[5]

Żółkiew, which in 1620 was still a small community affiliated to Lwów, underwent a rapid development driven by the town's proprietors, especially during the period of Jan Sobieski [John III] who was interested in its improvement and growth. In 1626, Żółkiew elected its own Rabbi, thus triggering its path to independence.

In 1672, Wreclaw and Podolia were severed from the Land of Reissen, and under the Peace Treaty signed at Buczacz between Poland and Turkey, they became part of Turkey. In 1699, when Podolia was returned to Poland under the terms of the Karlowitz Peace Treaty, the communities refused to be affiliated to the Land of Reissen, nor to accept Lwów's hegemony or her Rabbi. The communities of Podolia declared themselves a Land, with the Land's Rabbi at Satanów [Satanov].

[Pages 157-158]

A struggle also raged within the Land of Reissen itself, between Lwów and its subsidiaries that refused to recognize its primacy. Żółkiew, Brody and Buczacz led the resistance against Lwów's hegemony, and in 1664, during the Land Council's session at Swirz, they strongly attacked Lwów's community and its ambition to control the affairs of the communities. They particularly objected to Voivode Marek Matczynski's ruling of 1692, which declared that the leaders of Lwów's communities represented the Jews throughout Reissen.

In 1700, the small communities managed to insert their representatives into the Regional Council, so that the Council was made up of the following: Lazar [Eliezer] of Lwów, the Land's principal representative, Jakóbowicz of Lwów the Council's scribe, Izak of Żółkiew, Menachem of Brody, Samuel of Stryj, Mardochaj of Tyśmienica, Izak [Icek] of Czernelica [Czernelitse], Matisyahu of Kossów and Litman of Zalozce.

The composition of the 1720 Council of the Land, at Żółkiew, is also known. It included five representatives from Żółkiew, amongst them the Council's elder, the tax collector Gerson ben Bezalel, three representatives from Brody, one from Buczacz, one from another town and including the regional rabbi from Lwów, 15 members altogether.

The contrasting views between Lwów and the provincial communities over the composition of the Council, continued however. And that, since the provincial elders objected to the inclusion of representatives from Lwów in the Land's Council. Disagreements increased also with regard to organizational and financial issues. The authorities got involved in the matter once the poll–tax was not cleared. On 13th September 1725, the deputy–treasurer, I. Przebendowski, approached the regional–elder Chaim Reizes, cautioning him over the lack of coordination between the elders of Lwów and those of the province; that elders were unable to access the register of poll–tax distribution, and that consequently it was necessary to immediately convene a session at Białykamień [Bialy Kamien] in order to settle the portions of the tax which had to be paid to the treasury by 8th October 1725. The dispute over the Land's Rabbi as well as the organizational and financial issues continued until 1740. With the intervention of the Council of Four Lands at Jaroslaw, a final settlement was reached during its session at Berezhany [Brzeżany],[6] probably under pressure from the authorities who were interested in an ordered apportioning and collection of the poll–tax. That issue depended on fair relations within the Land's Council and its influence on the communities.

18 delegates participated in the session, including representatives from Brody, Lisko, Żółkiew, Stryj, Tysmenytsya [Tyśmienica], Chodorow, Janow and so on. The issues relating to the Land of Reissen were summarised in 15 clauses. The 1st clause determined that two appraisers from Lwów and five from the entire Land had to be present when the taxes were assessed and apportioned to the communities; that in accordance with the decision of the Jarizow session (§3), two leaders from Lwów and several Land representatives had to be dispatched to the election of the Land's elders; that in order to set the date for the Land's conference, a majority was required of six from Lwów and twelve from the region (§3). The Council of Four Lands at Jaroslaw had to include two leaders from Lwów and two from the region (§4). At the session to assess the poll–tax to the kingdom's treasury, the Council of Four Lands had to include three appraisers from the Land of Reissen: two from Lwów and one from the region, and alternately, one from Lwów and two from the region (§5); that Lwów would bear a greater portion of the poll–tax than any other town (§6). On 20th July 1753, during the Bóbrka session, that last clause was altered to the advantage of Lwów, due to the financial crisis of Lwów's community. The amount of tax, it was decided, would be set each time, separately. In clause 7, the right of Lwów's representatives to elect the Council's members was annulled and transferred to the Land's elder and to the regional rabbi. Clause 8 set the sequence of signatures on documents; the Council's decisions; the order of seating, as well as indicating the Council's composition as follows: the Land's elder, four leaders from Lwów, four from Brody, four from Żółkiew. And their seating was arranged as follows: at the head of the table, the elder; on either side of him leaders from Lwów (town), along one side of the table four leaders from Żółkiew and one from Lwów (the community outside the town), along the opposite side, four leaders from Brody and one from Lwów (outside the town). That meant that the Council numbered thirteen members. Clauses 9–12 considered the election of the Land's rabbi in the presence of four representatives from Lwów and seven from the region. The rabbi was elected from among four candidates presented by the Council's elder, who was always from Żółkiew, and one leader from Brody. Clause 15 determined that Lwów's leaders on the Council of Four Lands, as well as the poll–tax assessor, should be remunerated with expenses double those of other regional leaders.

Ever since the session at Brzezany, Lwów lost its pre–eminence of the Reissen region.

In the first half of the 18th century, Żółkiew was preeminent. For 30 years, the tax collector Gerson ben Natan ben Bezalel served as elder (marszałek ziemski). Energetic and forceful, he knew how to take control of the Council, especially in the conflict which broke out among the communities of Lwów and of the region over the Land's rabbi. He was followed as elder, by Izrael Isser ben Mardochaj of Żółkiew. In 1749, after his demise, the leaders of Żółkiew failed to hold on to the elder's office.

The Brody leaders successfully appointed Rabbi Ber Babad, the distinguished, wealthy man and the tailors' guild Rabbi. He took firm control over the the Land's affairs, and when the representatives of Lwów, Żółkiew and Tysmenytsya

[Pages 159-160]

refused to attend the session he convened at Brody, he apportioned the poll–tax according to his own calculation, and increased Lwów's payment share. Lwów's leaders submitted a complaint to the treasury minister who invited both parties to Konstantynów for a discussion. Meanwhile, he forbade Rabbi Ber from increasing Lwów's portion. Despite the warning, Rabbi Ber ruled as he saw fit, and Lwów's leaders had to pay the poll–tax according to his assessment.[7]

Complaints by Lwów's representatives were to no avail. The community–leaders Józef Cymeles and Zelman Pinkas, who attended the Council's session at Olesko in 1763, had to wait several days for the arrival of the other representatives, and eventually were obliged to sign the poll–tax register as Rabbi Ber had demanded.

Besides Lwów, other regional communities such as Zydaczow, Strelisk, Brzezany [Berezhany], Kalusz, Przemyślany, Narajów, Dolina, Drohobycz and Rozniatow, also opposed Rabbi Ber. The Lwów communities continuously sent complaints to the authorities against the regional Council, over the increased tax apportioning. Thus began the disintegration process of the Jewish autonomous institutions which started in those days.

The disagreement between the communities of Lwów and the Land, had reached its peak over the Land's rabbinate. Until the end of the 17th century, the regional rabbi for the Land of Reissen was always the rabbi of Lwów's community outside the town. That state of affairs continued till the election of Rabbi Jakob–Joshua (author of *Pneh Josua*) which sparked a disagreement that continued till the Austrian occupation.

After the rabbi, Rabbi Chaim ben Lazer, was forced to flee Lwów in connection with the lawsuit of the convert Jan Filipowicz, Rabbi Arje Leib [Lewko] ben Saul[8] (husband of Leah, the daughter of the Rabbi "Chacham Cwi" ["Sage Tzvi"]) was elected community rabbi (1735). Without the regional Council's consent, Lwów's elders attempted to obtain permission for him to officiate as regional rabbi.

On 20th November 1735, in his letter to Voivode Adam Czartoryski, King Augustus III expressed his indignation that the elders of the regional communities were splitting away from the Lwów community. He forbade them from disassociating from Lwów, and ordered that they accept Lwów's Rabbi as the regional rabbi.[9] But even the King's letter was to no avail. In the same year, the regional Council's elders elected the rabbi of Żółkiew, Rabbi Izak ben Cwi [Tzvi] Landau, son–in–law of Dr. Emmanuel de–Jonah, as regional rabbi. During 1714–1729 he was rabbi at Opatów, where his father, Rabbi Cwi lived. From 1729, he served in Żółkiew's rabbinate. Even after he was elected regional Rabbi, he continued to reside at Żółkiew. Inevitably, Lwów and in particular Lwów's rabbi, Rabbi Arje Leib ben Saul, objected to his selection. The disputes between the two rabbis terminated when Rabbi Arje Leib returned to Glogow [Glogau][10] in 1740. His departure from Lwów spurred the Żółkiew representatives to secure the rabbinical seat for Rabbi Izak Landau, but Lwów's community opposed it.

As a result, the session of the regional Council at Brzezany (1740) demanded that the regional rabbinate be split, half under the Rabbi Izak Landau, and half under the rabbi of Lwów who had yet to be elected. In the event that Rabbi Izak Landau, were to leave for Jerusalem, or were to be elected rabbi by another town, the rabbi of Lwów would take his place and act as rabbi for the entire Reissen region. The rabbi elected at Lwów was Rabbi Chaim, the son of the great scholar [gaon] Rabbi Symche HaKohen Rappoport, who was rabbi at Slutsk [Słuck].

His father, Rabbi Symche HaKohen, was elected rabbi of Lwów after the demise of "Chacham Cwi". On his way to the town of his posting, however, he died at Szczebrzeszyn. In the spirit of the agreement arrived at during the Council session at Brzezany, Rabbi Chaim became also rabbi of half the region. It is not known, however, which of the communities were subject to his authority, and which subject to Rabbi Izak's authority. At his election, Rabbi Chaim Rappoport pledged to the community–leaders: "When I become the overall regional Rabbi (that is to say in its entirety), and have the approval of the regional elders, and become the sole Rabbi of the entire Reissen region, and will receive the second half of the Lwów region salary, then I will receive not even one Szelag[11] from the Lwów congregation."[12]

Rabbi Chaim received his salary from the Lwów community as well as from the communities he oversaw as regional rabbi. Ever since he took office he and the community–elders were in dispute over the complaints brought against him.

In 1743, the deputy–voivode's official prosecutor accused him, that during the community–elders' election he lobbied for his own supporters who tended to evade paying any taxes; that he passed judgement against which he forbade any appeal proceedings, forcing both parties to agree in writing to maintain his prohibition. In general, the Rabbi disparaged all the old rulings and did not even recoil from ordering the expulsion and beating of Jews who did not obey him. In short, he was accused of being the cause for the irregularities in the community. He was in dispute with prominent families such as the Mizes–Kozimski family,[13] over the appointment of the head of the Yeshivah,[14] and who accused him of making deals with noblemen.[15]

When in 1754 his regional Rabbinate colleague, Rabbi Izak Landau, was elected the Rabbi of Kraków, the situation had reached a turning point.

The rabbi, Rabbi Chaim Rappoport, put himself forward for election as rabbi for the region's second half. On 6th October 1752, during the Council's session at Przemyślany, he was elected rabbi for the entire region, and with Voivode Czartoryski's recommendation

[Pages 161-162]

he was appointed by the regional–elders.

Peace lasted for but a short spell, however. In 1755, the regional–elders headed by Rabbi Dov (Ber) Babad elected, as a second regional rabbi, Rabbi Majer ben Cwi [Hersz] Margulies[16] who first resided at Tarnopol and later at Komarno.

Neither the Lwów communities nor Rabbi Chaim Rappoport could accept that decision in silence, and appealed to the deputy-voivode's judge. On 17th July 1755, the latter issued a declaration against "Berko Marszalek (Dov Babad) and Rabbi Majer Herszkowicz (Margulies))," that Rabbi Babad and the other regional–elders contravened King Augustus III's regulations, given to Voivode Jabłonowski of Reissen in 1730, stating the indivisibility of Reissen's Rabbinate. And yet, without a license from Voivode Czartoryski, they dared introduce Majer Hershkowicz into the Rabbinate granting him the title "subalternus Rabbinus [substitute Rabbi]", despite the fact that Chaim ben Symche (Rappoport) was the actual regional Rabbi.

Voivode Czartoryski who did not accept Rabbi Majer Margulies's election, considered Rabbi Chaim Rappoport the sole authoritative regional rabbi. On 30th May 1769, Czartoryski reappointed Rabbi Chaim Rappoport as the sole regional rabbi of Reissen.[17] In his pronouncement the Voivode announced that the Jews of Lwów and of the entire region had to bring all their lawsuits to Rabbi Chaim and provide him with a salary appropriate to a regional rabbi.

The regional Council ignored the Voivode's instructions as well as the Council's decision of 1752, and acknowledged only Rabbi Majer Margulies. Lwów's Rabbi and elders again registered their protest with the Voivode and also with the financial council of the crown ("*Rada ekonomiczny skarbu koronnego*") against Pinkas Swirski [Świrski], Berko Rabinowicz and the rest of the regional Council's elders, for choosing a second regional rabbi in contravention of the orders and regulations. That protest spurred the regional Council to write, on 3rd September 1765, inviting the leaders of the regional Council to appear before it at Warsaw.

Although the authorities acknowledged Rabbi Chaim Rappoport alone, the situation persisted until his death in 1771.

After his demise, in accordance with the Voivode's instructions and in the spirit of the mutual, Uniejow agreement of the 3rd October 1771, it was necessary to assemble the regional Council at Przemyślany to elect his successor on 1st November 1771. Although Lwów's representatives attended the meeting, the delegates from Brody and Tysmenytsya [Tyśmienica] did not arrive, on the grounds that the roads were defective due to a fair held in the town. Instead, they suggested to convene the session at Wyzlany [Wyżłany near Gliniany] at a later date, around the time of the contracts at Lwów. But that session did not take place either. On 12th November 1771, Lwów's elders submitted their protest against the communities of Brody, Tysmenytsya and Żółkiew,[18] and unilaterally elected Rabbi Solomon [Szloma] ben Mojzesz, who had been a rabbi at Chelm, as the regional rabbi[19]. On 31st December 1771, the Voivode sanctioned his appointment in accordance with the regulations of 1751 and 1752.[20]

The 1772 partition of Poland put an end to that rabbinate. Reissen in its entirety, including Lwów, came under Austrian rule.

II.

During the sessions of the Council of Four Lands, Lwów's elders represented the Land of Reissen. The representatives at the Council's initial session (1589), were the leaders Rabbi Izak [Icek] ben Nachman and Reb. Mardochaj ben Izak. Mardochaj ben Izak represented Reissen at the beginning of the 17th century, too. In 1589, Reb. Jakob Koppel ben Asher [Aszer] HaKohen, head of the religious law–court outside the town, also attended the session.

The list of the rabbis, rabbinical judges and community leaders who attended the sessions of the Council of Four Lands[21] was as follows.

In 1594: 1. Rabbi Abraham ben Rabbi Shabtai [Scheftel] Horowitz, father of the SheLaH [Isaiah Horowitz], author of *Chessed LeAbraham* [Grace for Abraham], an exegesis of Maimonides's eight chapters (Lublin 1578), *Brit Abraham* Abraham's Covenant] (Lublin 1578), *Emek Brachah* [Valley of Blessing] (Kraków 1596), *Yesh Nochalin* [There are heirs,] (Kraków 1616). 2. Reb. Baruch Dayan. 3. Reb. Mojzesz ben Jakob Izrael, known as Mojzesz Zipores of Lemberg.

1596: Reb Mojzesz ben Jakob Izrael Zipores.

1602, 1606: 1. Rabbi Jozue ben Alexander HaKohen, Descendant of the Priesthood (1550–1614), author of *Me'irat Einayim,* and *Kuntres al Ribit* [Pamphlet on Interest], head of the Yeshivah and community leader at the Council of Four Lands. He participated in composing laws about prohibited foods, garments, prohibited cloth composition [shatnez], and interest laws which were passed by the Council of Four Lands, in 1607. 2. Rabbi Jakob Ber Elyakim Heilpern.

Prior to 1613: Rabbi Jozue ben Alexander Falk (author of *Me'irat Einayim*).

1613: 1. Rabbi Solomon [Szloma] ben Izak Charif, head of Yeshivah, and Judge at Lwów's Jewish lawcourt. 2. Rabbi Jakob Koppel ben Asher Kohen.

1616, 1617: 1. Reb. Alexander ben Reb.Mojzesz HaKohen Askenazy, known as Susskind. 2. Rabbi Samson ben Izak Bachner, Judge [Dayan] and head of the Yeshivah at Lwów. 3. Rabbi Jakob Koppel ben Asher Kohen.

1626, 1627: Rabbi Abraham ben Mojzesz Heilpern, head of Lwów's rabbinical law–court, author of *Ahavat Zion* [Love of Zion].

[Pages 163-164]

1638: Rabbi Majer ben Abraham ZeK [of sacred lineage], leader of the rabbinical law–court, head of Yeshivah, within the town of Lwów.

1639: Thirty rabbis signed a proclamation that no rabbi should lobby to attain the rabbinate for money, a loan or a gift, either by himself or by others. The signed Lwów rabbis: 1. Rabbi Jozue Falk author of *Me'irat Einayim*. 2. Reb. Koppel Katz, leader of the rabbinical law–court for the community outside the town. 3. Rabbi Izak Eizyk ben Jechiel, head of Yeshivah, and leader of the rabbinical law–court of Lwów. 4. Rabbi Chanoch Hendel ben Shemarja [Szmarja], author of *Mano'ach Levavot* on *Chovot HaLevavot* (Lublin 1596 (who, together with Jozue Falk (author of *Me'irat Einayim*), was one of the Vienna divorce arrangers.

1641, 1643: Rabbi Abraham ben Izrael Jechiel Katz Rappoport, also known as Schrenzel [Szrencel] (named after his father–in–law Schrenzel), author of the Responsa *Ethan Haezrachi* and *Gaba'eh Tzedaka Mara Dear'a DeIsrael*.

1645: Rabbi Jozef ben Eliakim Giec [Goetz], son–in–law of MaHaRaM of Lublin.

1654: Rabbi Dawid ben Samuel Halevi (author or *Turei Zahav*).

1660, 1661, 1663: 1. Rabbi Jekusiel Zelman Rabbi Arons. 2. Rabbi Dawid ben Samuel Halevi (author of *Turei Zahav*

1665: Rabbi Samuel ben Jakob of Lwów.

1666: Rabbi Izak Eizyk ben Eliezer Rabbi Arons

1670: Rabbi Cwi [Tzvi] Hirsch [Hirsz] ben Zecharja Mendel, known as Rabbi Hirsch Rabbi Mendels. Leader of the religious law–court [Beth Din] and Head of the Yeshivah within the town.

1671: 1. Rabbi Izak Eizyk ben Eliezer (Reb. Arons). 2. Rabbi Asher [Aszer] ben David [Dawid], from the house of Levy.

1672: 1. Rabbi Izak Eizyk ben Eliezer, known as Rabbi Eizyk ben Arons of Lwów. A signatory to the boycott declaration against "those belonging to the sect of Sabbataj Cwi [Shabbatai Zevi]." 2. The youngest in the House of Levy (Izak), son of the great scholar [gaon] Solomon Charif, leader of the religious law–court at Lwów.

1673: 1. Rab Mojzesz ben Izrael Charif (the second). Leader of the religious law–court and head of the Yeshivah of the holy community of Lwów and the region. 2. Rabbi Cwi Hirsch [Hirsz] Mendel, known as Rabbi Hirsch Rabbi Mendels. Leader of the religious law–court [Beth Din] and Head of the Yeshivah within the town.

1677: 1. Rabbi Izak Eizyk Rabbi Arons. 2. Rabbi Abraham Eberles ben Shemarja, a great [religious] judge at Lwów. 3. Rabbi Jehuda Leib ben Jakob, leader of the religious law–court and head of Yeshivah. 4. Rabbi Arje Leib ben Mojzesz of Ludmir [Włodzimierz Wołyński], a celebrated Kabbalist in his day, leader of the religious law–court and head of Yeshivah of the holy community of Przemyśl and of the holy community of Lwów (outside the town). He was known as "Rabbi Leib Chassid, grandson of our late rabbi, Rabbi Mojzesz Isserles" (*Shem Hagdolim* [Name of the Renowned]) Article 57). 5. Rabbi Cwi [Tzvi] Hirsch [Hirsz] ben Zecharja Mendel, known as Rabbi Hirsch Rabbi Mendels. Leader of the religious law–court [Beth Din] and head of the Yeshivah within the town.

1678: 1. Rabbi Cwi Hirsch [Hirsz] ben Zecharja Mendel, leader of the religious law–court [Beth Din] of the holy community of Lwów. 2. Rabbi Asher [Aszer] ben David Halevy [Dawid Halewi]. 3. Rabbi Menachem–Mendel ben Jechiel Mechel prayer leader from Lwów, leader of the Land of the Lwów region. 4. Rabbi Jozue Heshel ben Rabbi Cwi [Tzvi Hirsch, leader of the religious law–court and head of Yeshivah of Lwów and of the region, leader at Lwów.

1680: 1. Rabbi Cwi Hirsch ben Zecharja Mendel, leader of the religious law–court [Beth Din] of the holy community of Lwów. 2. Rabbi Solomon.

1681: 1. Rabbi Cwi Hirsch ben Zecharja Mendel, leader of the religious law–court of the holy community of Lwów. 2. Rabbi Arje Jehuda Leib ben Mojzesz of Ludmir. 3. Rabbi Juda Abraham ben Izak of the house of Levy, leader of the religious law–court and head of Yeshivah at Lwów.

1683: 1. Rabbi Mardochaj Gimpel ben Jakob, head and leader. 2. Rabbi Menachem–Mendel ben Jechiel Mechel, leader of the regional Land of Lwów.

1684: 1 Rabbi Menachem Mendel ben Jechiel Mechel, leader of the regional Land of Lwów.

1685: 1. Rabbi Hillel ben Naphtali stationed at Żółkiew, arbitrator for the holy community of Lwów (Author of *Beth Hillel* about *Shulchan Aruch*, "Yore De'ah" and "Even HaEzer," Dyhernfurth [Brzeg Dolny] 1681). 2. Rabbi Mojzesz ben Izrael Charif, leader of the religious law–court, and head of Yeshivah of the holy community of Lwów and of the Region.

1687: 1. The leader, Reb. Ze'ev [Sew Wolf] ben Meikisz. 2. Rabbi Mojzesz–Mechel, leader of the regional Land of Lwów. 3. Rabbi Mardochaj from Lublin, leader of the Lwów Region. 4. Reb. Menachem named Mendel, known as leader of the regional Land of Lwów, foremost of the leaders of the Four Lands. 5. Reb. Ze'ev [Sew Wolf] ben Meikisz, first leader of the regional Land of Lwów.

1688: 1. Reb. Menachem named Mendel, known as leader of the regional Land of Lwów, foremost of the leaders of the Four Lands. 2. Reb. Chaim ben David Mach, leader of the regional Land of Lwów.

1689: 1. Reb. Chaim ben David Mach, leader of the regional Land of Lwów. 2. Reb. Chaim of Jaworow, leader of the regional Land of Lwów.

1690: 1. Reb. Menachem Mendel, leader of the regional Land of Lwów. 2. Reb. Ze'ev [Sew Wolf] ben Meikisz, Land's leader. 3. Reb. Samuel [Szmul] ben Izak (Icko) of Lwów.

1691: Reb. Pinkas Mojzesz ben Izrael Charif (the second), leader of the religious law–court and head of Yeshivah in both communities.

1692: Reb. Pinkas Mojzesz Charif (the second).

1693: 1. Reb. Pinkas Mojzesz Charif (the second). 2. Reb. Chaim ben Reb. David Mach, leader and head of the Council of Four Lands. 3. Reb Ze'ev [Sew] Wolf ben Pinkas.

1698: Reb. Pinkas Mojzesz Charif (the second).

1699: 1. Reb. Jakob ben Mojzesz of Lwów. 2. Reb. Mardochaj of Lublin, of the Lwów Region (took part in the 1696 session).

1700: Reb. Menachem Mendel, known as leader of the regional Land of Lwów.

1702: Reb. Mojzesz ben Mardochaj, leader and legal representative of the community and the Region of Lwów.

[Pages 165-166]

1713: 1. Rabbi Joel ben Izak Eizik Heilpern, leader of the religious law–court [Beth Din] and head of Lwów's town, and regional Yeshivah.[22] 2. Reb. Zelman ben Mojzesz Arje Jehuda of Lwów.[23]

1718: 1. Reb. Abraham ben Sholem–Szachna Kahane arbitrator for the entire community of Lwów and the Region.[24] 2. Reb. Eliahu ben Abraham of Lwów. 3. Reb. Chaim a noteworthy judge at Lwów, outside the town. 4. Reb. Jekutiel [Jekusiel] Lazel Margulies.

1724: 1. Rabbi Jakob ben Reb. Cwi [Tzvi] of Kraków, of the holy community of Lwów and of the Region (author of *Pneh Josua*). 2. Reb. Jakob Aron ben Mardochaj of Stryj, arbitrator for the Lwów Region. 3. Rabbi Zecharja] Mendel of Lwów.

1727: Rabbi Jakob Jozue author of *Pneh Josua*.

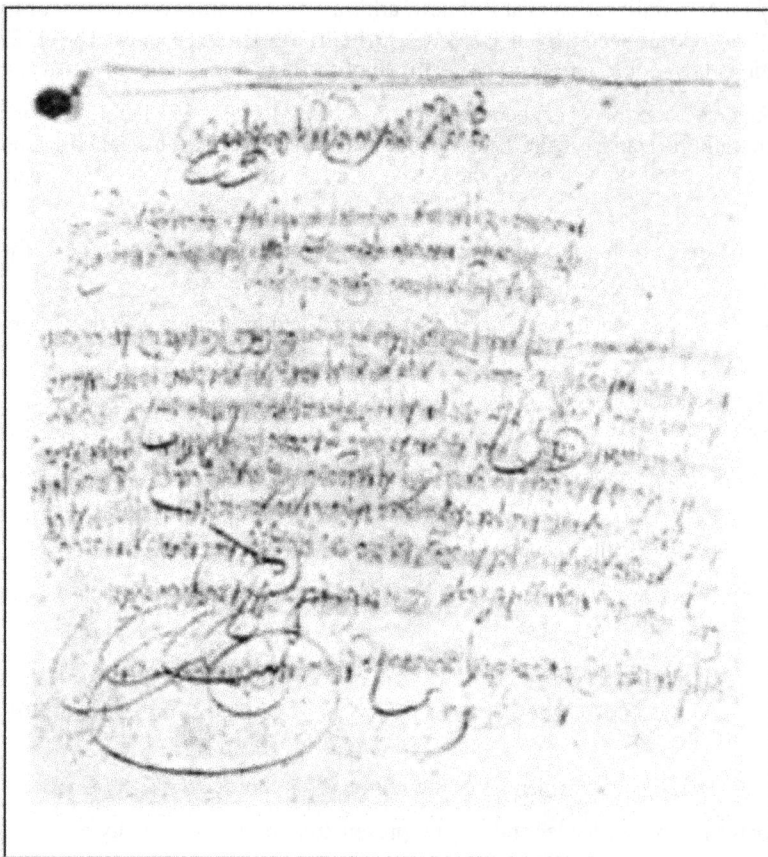

Missive of Reb. Mardochaj Ze'ev [Sew] Ornstein to Reb. Ezechiel Landau (*Nodah BeYehudah* [known within Judea]) dated 1781

1730: 1. The judge Reb. Jekutiel Zelman ben Benjamin Ze'ev Epstein. 2. Reb. Arje Leib Segal Landau.[25]

1731: Reb. Izak Segal Landau, stationed among the holy community Żółkiew, arbitrator of Lwów, Rabbi of the Reissen Region.

1738: Reb. Lazar Litman, arbitrator from Lwów.[26]

1742: Reb Arje Leib Landau *S'gan Levi* [Levi's deputy].

1750: The Rabbi, Reb. Izak Landau, leader of the religious law–court and teacher of Jewish law [*moré zedek*] for the Lwów region. He, together with Rabbi Ezechiel Landau —leader of the religious law–court and teacher of Jewish law at the holy community of Jampol [Yampol] (Wolyn [Volhynia])— were elected "collectors–of–dues, for the Judaic studies programmes of married men [Kollel] within the Four Lands of Poland, and for the learned Presidents of Eretz Israel."

1755: Rabbi Chaim Kohen Rappoport.

1762:[27] Rabbi Chaim Kohen Rappoport.

1763: Rabbi Chaim Kohen Rappoport was the deputy of the presidency committee's elder.

1764–1765: In 1764, the three Land leaders of the Reissen region participated in the session of the Council of Four Lands. Their names are not known.

On 1st June 1764, during the *Sejm*'s session at Warsaw, a proposal was put forward to liquidate the Jewish communities' autonomous institution (Council of Four Lands, and Regional Committees), and to collect the Jewish poll tax (four Gulden from every adult and one Gulden from a child) directly, and not via the Jewish institutions.

On 6th June 1764 it was decided by the Senate, by 16 votes to 13, and by the *Sejm*, by 66 votes to 36, to abolish all the committees; to organize a census of all the Jews in the country; to eliminate the collective poll tax which had been determined in the 1717 constitution, but to charge them instead a personal poll tax, of 2 Gulden annually.

In order to manage and settle the debts of the Jews, the Land's leaders charged the Council of Four Lands, the Regional Committees and the communities, "to appear without delay before the Treasury Council which convenes quarterly, and which is due to meet in February 1765, bringing with them documents, notes and registers which indicate the debts accrued, so as to inform and clarify, under oath if necessary, and to determine and find ways for the Jews to clear them in future."

According to the record of debts prepared by the liquidating committee of the royal Treasury, the debts of the Reissen Region (the Jewish population numbered 95,413 souls) amounted to 249,316 Gulden, and the debt of the Council of Four Lands was 42,405 Gulden. Lwów's community owed the municipality 820,409 Gulden, and together with interest the sum amounted to over a million Gulden at the end of the 18th century.[28]

Those debts still occupied the Austrian authorities long after 1772.

[Pages 357-358]

Notes: – CHAPTER 10

All notes in square brackets [ ] were made by the translator.
[The spelling of a large number of names was sourced from books cited by the author, especially those of Pazdro and Bałaban.]

1.   2 houses. Libek was the leader of the congregation.

2.   Tobiasz [Tuvia] ben Jakob, leader of the congreagation.

3.   S. Buber: *Kiryah Nisgavah* (Żółkiew) pp. 84, 85.

4.   Dr. M Bałaban: *Z zagadnien ustrojowych zydostwa polskiego*. Lwów, 1932, p. 6.

5.   *Akta grodzkie i ziemskie*. Lwów, 1911, t. XXI, No. 144, Cl.s 91, 93.

6.   Dr. J. Schipper: *Beiträge zur Geschichte der partiellen Judentage in Polen um die Wende des XVII. und XVIII Jahrhunderte*. M. G. W. d. J. 1912; pp. 458, 606–607.
Dr. M. Bałaban: *Z. zagadnien* pp. 8–10.

7.   The poll–tax for Lwów was set at 4,100 Gulden on 24th July 1753.

8.   He was Rabbi at Rzeszów [Resche] in 1724, and of Głogów [Glogau] in 1734.

9.   Dr. M. Bałaban: *Z. zagadnien* pp. 15, 17.

10.   While at Głogów [Glogau] he was invited by the Ashkenazi Congregation of Amsterdam, and was subsequently known as Reb. Arje Leib Amsterdamer. His daughter Nehama was married to the grandson of the tax collector Bezalel [Bazyleja], Reb. Mojzesz ben Jozef of Żółkiew, himself the father of Mardochaj Cwi [Tzvi] Ornstein, Lwów's Rabbi.

11.   A polish coin. In the 14th century it was worth 12 Grosz, and the 17th century half a Grosz.

12.   Pazdro *op. cit.* No. 35, p. 209 (Cl. 2).

13.   The Mizes [Mizys] family had a rich past in Lwów's history. The name Mizes was derived from Mize [Mizy] the wife of the community–leader and elder, Rabbi Cwi Hirsch [Hirsz] ben Mojzesz. Prior to that the family name was Buzimski, and in the community records the family name was Koziner or Mizes–Koziner [Mizys–Koziner] until the end of the 18th century. Among the early community–elders of that family one knows of, was Reb. Mojzesz ben Eliahu or Reb. Mojzesz Koziner who was, at the end of the 17th century and later, community–elder and leader of the community outside the town. He took part in the regional Council at Lwów on 19th November 1700, and was signatory to the resolution against those who negligently opposed the congregation's regulations and the tenure of the 9th February 1718. His son was also an elder and leader of the community outside the town for many years. His wife Mize was the daughter of the community–elder Rabbi Arje Leib Segal (the son of Reb. Naftali Hirsz [Hirsh], author of the book *Seva Ratzon* [*Satisfied*]). In 1737, Rabbi Cwi Hirsz visited one of the community's villains, who beat him to death. His tombstone bears the following saying: "Congregation elder and leader, faithfully engaged in public service, who gave his soul to the hall of ministers for God's people, even so far as a beating, and the Israelite overseers were beaten. Sunday, 26.10.1737." His wife Mize passed away some six months later and was buried next to her husband. They were given a joint tombstone. Their three sons played significant roles in the community. Rabbi Arje Jehuda Leib (Lewko Malowany in Polish documents) acted as ritual judge at the law–court of Rabbi Chaim Kohen Rappoport, as well as community–elder for over twenty years. In 1763, judge Orlewski appointed him additional appraiser for the community outside the town, together with Reb Izrael Rais [Reis], outside the town, Reb. Aryel of Zloczow and Mardochaj Boruchowicz of the community within the town, in order to assess the income of all the congregation members, so as to clear the interest of the community's debts. His brother Jerachmiel

[Rachmil] was forceful in his community, and after his marriage he settled within the town and bought himself a large house, number 46 Boimów Street. He was in a protracted dispute with the community, over his nomination as the community arbitrator within the town, for the congregational elections. The congregation leaders within the town objected and refused to recognize him. They filed an appeal against his appointment under the claim that only a resident within the town who had lived there for over ten years was eligible to undertake such a role. The arbitrators responded to the appeal with a protest letter against it, but the judge of the deputy–voivode revoked his appointment on 1ˢᵗ July 1767. In 1771, he was appointed community–leader within the town, and was its representative at the regional Council. He was the last community–leader during the Polish period.

14.   Rabbi Chaim Rappoport wanted his son, Rabbi Arje Leib, to be appointed head of the Yeshivah. Mojzesz, the brother of Rachmil Mizys, the community–leader outside the town, was however appointed. He died suddenly after his first address (1752), and was followed by the son of the rabbi, Rabbi Chaim Rappoport (died 1759).

15.   On 4ᵗʰApril 1761, he was arrested for a debt of 147,300 Gulden he owed Prince Michał Radziwill [Radziwiłł, lord of Slutzk. Bałaban: *Zagadnienie* p. 17.

16.   Reb. Majer Margulies was the son of Reb. Cwi [Tzvi] who had been Rabbi of Horodenka and later of Jazlowiec [Yazlovets] and Zaleszczyki [Zalishchyky], the estates of the Poniatowski family. His father was in touch with the town's lords which helped in getting his son elected to regional rabbi. His brother Izak–Ber, who after their father's demise was elected rabbi at Jazlowiec and Zaleszczyki, was also appointed regional rabbi of Podolia, with King Poniatowski's support. In 1757, he assisted in a debate with the Frankists at Kamieniec Podolski.

17.   Pazdro *op. cit.* pp. 247–248; No. 66.

18.   Pazdro *op. cit.* pp. 272–276; No. 85.

19.   Author of *Merkevet HaMishnah,* on the glory of Maimonides, which was published at Frankfurt–an–der–Oder in 1750; *Shulchan Azeh Shitim,* about Sabbath ritual laws (Berlin 1763); and the book *Sha'areh Ne'ima al Dikdukeh Neginot veTeamim* (1767). He was born at Zamosc [Zamość]. His father was a well–to–do rabbi, son–in–law of Mojzesz, the influential community-elder, chief and leader in Lithuania. Dependent on his father–in–law, it was from Lithuania that he was appointed head of the rabbinical law–court at Chelm [Chelmas] and later became rabbi of the Judaic studies programme at Zamosc and of the region. Influenced by Rabbi Izrael of Zamosc author of *Netzach Israel,* he advocated secular studies. At Lwów he only served six years, leaving the rabbinate to go to Eretz Israel in 1777. In February 1770, he passed through Constantinople on the way to Salonica where he took to the printers his essay on innovations to the rules of the Mishnah. The second edition of his two–parts book *Merkevet HaMishnah* [Chariot of the Mishnah] about Maimonides's entire book *HaYad HaChazakah,* was also published at Salonica. He died at Salonica in 1785. (*see*: Dembitzer , *Klilat Yofi* Part 1, pp. 140–144 b).

[Pages 359-360]

20.   Pazdro No. 67; p. 248.

21.   Arranged according to: *Pinkas Arba Arazot* [*Notebook of Council of Four Lands*], compilations of religious rulings as well as arranged and annotated lists by Yisrael Hailpern, Jerusalem 1945. pp. 10, 11, 13, 16, 23, 32, 35, 53, 58, 61, 62, 67, 74, 75, 98, 99, 109, 116, 126, 136, 137, 138, 141, 153, 156, 159, 160, 164, 165, 168, 169, 171, 177, 179, 183, 184, 194, 201, 202, 204, 206, 207, 208, 212, 215, 230, 231, 243, 256, 268, 275, 279, 281, 284, 285, 305, 313, 317, 329, 334, 405, 437, 442, 456, 490, 496, 499.

22.   Was rabbi at Lutsk [Łuck], Ostroh [Ostrog], and Pinsk. In 1760, he was appointed head of the rabbinical law–court, and head of the Yeshivah of Lwów and the region. He numbered among the great scholars of the Council of Four Lands. He had already taken part in the sessions of 1691, 1693 and 1698

23.   Probably Reb. Mojzesz son of MaHaRaM Kikenes who at the time was ritual judge at Lwów. (Buber: *Anshei Shem* [Men of Renown] pp. 164–165, February 1655, 1657

24.   Was head of the rabbinical law–court at Brody (1706–1718), as well as at Ostroh [Ostrog], and at the end of his life at Dubno, where he died in 1740.

25.   Probably, Lewko Landys who was the agent of the archbishop of Lwów.
Pazdro *op. cit.* No. 17; p. 191.

26.   In 1742, he was removed from the post of community–elder due to irregularities in the community's accounting. Pazdro *op. cit.* No. 17; p. 191.

27.   The Council of Four Lands convened at Pilica.

28.   Akademja Umiejetnosci Kraków.
Manuscript: *Hauptpassivstand der galizischen Judenschaft.*

[Pages 167-168]

Chapter 11: The Austrian Occupation

Translated by Myra Yael Ecker

Edited by Yocheved Klausner

The Austrian army marches into Galicia. The ceremonial swearing in, at Lwów. The restrictions and the commander. The 1776 regulations. The taxes and the officials' attitude. The Jews' problem with Pergen's memorandum of 1775. Expulsion of the Jewish bartenders and the community's lobbying. Community disputes and the Jewish council. Establishment of agricultural settlements. Army recruitment. Galicia's Jewish delegation to Emperor Leopold. The community's appeal over reinstating the Jews in the Jewish Quarter. Growth of the Jewish population 1772–1800. Meat and candle tax lessees. Berl Joselowicz at Lwów and the Jewish Brigade affair.

In 1772, Poland and Jewish life in particular underwent dramatic changes.

Maria–Theresa, who first objected to the partitioning of Catholic Poland which she considered a buffer between Orthodox Russia and Protestant Prussia, was persuaded by the Chancellor, Prince [von] Kaunitz [–Rietberg] who had succeeded in gaining the support of her son, Joseph II. She agreed to the partitioning once Russia and Prussia had contractually agreed on its implementation.

On 14th May 1772, the first platoons of the Austrian army marched into Poland from beyond the Carpathian Mountains and progressed towards Stryy [Stryj]. On 21st June 1772, Austrian brigades advanced from the Silesian border, and in September Lwów was "conquered" without any resistance from the town. The Russian army which since 1764 had battalions stationed there under the command of General Kaminski, handed over the town to the Austrian Commander Schröder. On 19th September 1772, the Austrians entered under the command of General Hadik [von Futak]. Right away Count Anton [von] Pergen, who had been an envoy to Mainz and London for several years, was appointed to manage the administration of the new territory named Galicia and Lodomeria. On 4th October 1772, at Lwów, he was made governor of Galicia. After the Austrian authorities had concluded the initial administrative arrangements[1] they decided to organize celebrations throughout the country, during which the citizens would swear allegiance to the Austrian Empress and Kingdom, in the following sequence: 1. the clergy; 2. the property–owning nobility; 3. towns; 4. small towns and villages; 5. Jewish communities. During those celebrations termed "Homagium" (*Eid der Untertan und Vasallentreue*), everyone of the above listed had individually to swear allegiance.

At Lwów the swearing allegiance celebration took place on the 4th October 1773. The Jews did not swear allegiance in the synagogue, as at Brody, but in the square facing the Catholic Cathedral.

Fear descended on the Jews with the arrival of the Austrian rule.

In August 1772, Joseph II ordered to dispossess the Jews of any leasing of brewing, taxes and taverns. In December 1772, a census of the Jews undertaken by the army showed there were 6,339 souls within the confines of Lwów's Catholic Church. In 1774, the community–elders declared that there were 6,664 souls at Lwów.[2] In 1773, a ban was imposed on their marriage ceremony, obliging them to first obtain a license from the governor, at the cost of 20 Ducats. The Jews were gravely affected by these restrictions. On his visit to Lwów from 31st July till 6th August 1773, Emperor Joseph II tried to familiarize himself with the situation in the country and its administration. In a special memorandum on the required improvements for the advancement of the country, he also dedicated an exclusive clause to the problem of the Jews, which was a new topic for the Austrian administration since in no part of the monarchy was there such a large number of Jews as in Galicia. The Emperor believed that the Jews were engaged in fraudulent businesses, and that they should not be given preference over the good, hard working Protestants.[3] Joseph II who sought to centralize all government at Vienna, proposed a programme for the form of administration in Galicia, and the implementation of economic and social advancement in order to improve the status and condition of the farmers; to shrink the Jewish, urban middle–class, and to establish a Christian middle–class. His salient improvement was however to advance the economic element, the issue of taxation and to gather the support of the authorities against the Polish nobles who were not loyal to Austria.

The authorities' order to undertake a census, worried the Jews of Galicia and especially at Lwów, since they feared that new taxes would be levied on them. The Austrian authorities were interested to displace the poor from among them by imposing marriage taxes, orders ([letters]patent) and by decreasing the number urban and rural residence licenses.

[Pages 169-170]

Although the aim of the enlightened government was the productivity of the Jewish masses, it found no means to implement it since the financial and budgetary factors obliged the authorities to conduct a policy totally opposed to productivity.

With the onset of the Austrian occupation, the 16th July 1776 "Jewish Code" (*Judenordnung*)[4] of Empress Maria–Theresa regulated the legal status of Galicia's Jews. At the head of each district, of which there were six in Galicia, was placed the district–elder elected by the district minister and approved by the governor, selected from the two candidates put forward by delegates of the communities. The Jewish denomination was assigned "the Jews' management" (*Judendirekzion*) made up of: six district–elders, six state–elders and the state's rabbi, elected out of the three candidates put forward for the Empress's approval.

Rabbi Arieh Leib Bernstein from Brody was elected state's rabbi, with his deputy, Rabbi Mordchai Ze'ev Ornstein, from Lwów. Like the Council of Four Lands, and the regional committees, the Jews' management had the authority to apportion the tax quota for the communities which they imposed on their members. For that purpose a system of officials was required.

The Austrian occupation imposed new taxes on the Jews of Galicia. In 1774, the poll–tax (*pogłówne*) which in Poland had been 30 Kreuzer per Jewish soul, rose to one Gulden. On 6th July 1776, the tolerance tax (*Schutz–und Toleranzsteuer*) as it was termed, was set at four Gulden per family. Apart from that, the Jews had to pay according to "the Jewish order" (*Judenordnung*), employment and property tax (*Gewerbe– und Vermögenssteuer*) four Gulden per family, and marriage tax according to the value of property, aimed to reduce the number of Jews. In order to obtain a special marriage license from the governor, proof had to be presented of the couple's source of income and of the value of their assets. Maria–Theresa's code also included a prohibition for the Jews to have a monopoly on trade. The grain merchants were worst hit when a directive of 23.12.1772 forbade them any trade in grain.[5] Lwów, as one knows, was the grain trade–centre of all Reissen, where, during the period of trade contracts the acquisitions by landowners and Jewish merchants concentrated on exporting the grain abroad. The grain trade suffered heavily when the price of grain slumped in the markets of northern Europe. During the Polish rule, Lwów supplied the whole of Poland, but after the occupation acquisitions moved away from Galicia to fairs at Dubno, while Lwów retained only the trade with the landowners of Galicia. The Jews of Lwów also held the trade in timber and meat,[6] as well as the majority share in beef import, especially to Germany, from where they brought goods to sell in Russia and Turkey. Many of Lwów's merchants went to the Leipzig's fairs.

By and by economic life returned to normal and the Jews re–established their trading status, especially in the export trade. The retailers and pedlars encountered greater difficulties than wholesalers who had a wider scope of action and were also better supported by the authorities.

Among the Jewish wholesalers at Lwów one knows of: Rachmil Mizys, Gabriel Reizes, Mojsesz Barach, Jakob Kitaj, Aron Rechen, Berl Weber, Ben–Zion Parnas, Izrael Jalis, Izyk Jalis, Jakob Wallach, Samuel Schnit, Menasche Reizes, Hirsch Weber, Izak Silberstein, Mojsesz Reizes, Jakob Zipper, Nissan Joles, Izak Reifenscheid and Izak Koliszer who, in 1794, tried to undertake the leasing of Kosher meat taxation. To that end, he even proposed a leasing fee of 10,000 Gulden greater than the offer submitted by the partnership of Heinzman, Krater and Solomon [Szloma] Kopler. Nevertheless, the leasing was granted to that partnership.[7]

For a foreign Jew to obtain a license to settle in Galicia required proving they possessed 5,000 Gulden, 10% of which was the cost of the residency–license.

In places where Christian craftsmen were available, Jewish craftsmen were forbidden from undertaking work for Christian customers. Lwów's Jewish bakers were badly affected when, at the beginning of November 1772, the urban authority ordered to discriminate against them in favour of Christian bakers and to prevent free competition between Christian and Jewish "non–expert" ("botcher") bakers. Other prohibitions against Jewish craftsmen who had lived there since the Polish rule were thus all kept, other than in cases where the state benefitted financially from Jews engaged in forbidden occupations.

Zipora Perszlin, for example, applied in September 1775 for a Post Office franchise within the Jewish Quarter, noting that at Prague too the Jewess Perle Taussigen maintained the Jewish Post Office. On 21st December 1775 after the governor had supplied a reference, the Vienna postal ministry (*Oberpostamt*) agreed to establish a Jewish Post Office at Lwów,[8] due to the heavy postal exchanges between the Jews.

A special order was issued to limit the activity of surgeons (doctors) to only treating Jews. There were 19 doctors (non specialists) at Lwów alone, and in 1773 special courses were prescribed for them. Of those who had completed them, only four were permitted to remain at Lwów while the rest were transferred to provinces where there was a dearth of doctors.

[Pages 171-172]

Concurrently, in a report of 17th December 1778, the medical collegium suggested permitting the Jews to work in the professions of hairdressing, bloodletting and cupping, since both the Jewish and Christian poor could not afford the heavy fees levied by the (non specialist) Christian doctors. The governor approved the suggestion so long as the number of non–specialist Jewish doctors did not exceed four.

Regional doctors were appointed to maintain the state of health. For the entire Jewish population of Galicia the authorities appointed twelve Jewish doctors. At Lwów, the Jewish *physicus* Solomon [Szloma] Benjamin Freschel was appointed.

The situation persisted till 1784, when Kaiser Joseph II decided to repeal the discrimination against the Jews and to include them in the general population. The role of health inspectors (Jewish physicus) was abolished and they were inspected by general doctors that included Jewish doctors.

Shortly after the occupation, the Austrians issued a decree ordering the Jews to clear the flats and shops they had in the town centre. The community's vigorous requests to delay the decree's execution were rejected. The Austrian administration was from the start openly hostile to the Jews, referring to them in documents as "state infestation" (*Verderben des Landes*); as "leeches sucking the blood of the population"; as well as considering them cheats and crooks. Milbacher the governor of Lwów, was fully aware that the Jews were hated because of their control over trade, nevertheless he emphasized the fact that the Jewish merchants were hardworking and frugal. "A Galician Jew spends on his sustenance just 30 Gulden annually" and consequently he was able to lower the price of goods, unlike Christians who spent four times their income.

The Austrian officials did not understand the Galician Jews who were used to the Polish regime and were unable readily to adapt to the new administrative system.

The Lwów community managed its affairs according to the old system since in fact the authorities had not touched its administration; they were solely interested in the tax income.

The first governor of Galicia, Count Johann Anton [Graf von] Pergen, from the school of thought of Prince Kaunitz who was expert in organizational skills, began his mission with investigating the state of the country. On 6th November 1772, prior to leaving Galicia, he was given instructions for his mission that included clauses on decreasing the number of Jewish marriages and dispossessing them of taverns as well as of the customs and postal services. He ordered a census of the Jews in order to familiarize himself with their living conditions, and on the basis of his findings he sent Kaunitz a detailed report on Galicia, on 8.8.1773.[9]

In 1765 according to the report, there were 140,000 Jews in Galicia, and their number rose despite the wars. Apart from that, at Kokiche and Halicz [Halych] there were some 150 Karaites.

The Jews of Poland constituted a special political unit with organizational and representational rights. Due to their economic status they became a vital element in the state's economy, especially with regard to credit. The communities acted also as a bank where the nobles and the clergy deposited their monies at an interest of 7%. On the other hand, the communities owed them, substantial sums. Lwów's community alone owed 57,581 Gulden, and declared it was unable to clear it.

The Jews of Lwów faced a difficult struggle with the townspeople who had obtained 18 verdicts against them, none of which was ever executed. According to Pergen's report, the Jews brought about corruption and damage by purchasing stolen goods; caused damage by importing inferior goods from Germany; reduced the currency value, and supported riots in order to avoid the payment of taxes; the rabbis and the community leaders ruled firmly, collected monies without accounting for it; and a system had to be established to systematically regulate an arrangement to best benefit the State Treasury.

In May 1773, Kuczian the imperial court advisor was sent from Vienna to organize the Galician administration according to specific instructions. Chapter 2 Article viii, stated that the district ministers should determine the number of Jews, taking into consideration "that with support of the nobility and the laxity of the Polish nation, that race had greatly increased in number," the issue required "to pay attention to restrict their proliferation and the greed among them."

On the whole, the overt Austrian policy was to reduce the number of Jews, and consequently by imposing a special license they tended to limit the number of marriages; to expel from Galicia the poor who were termed "Bettel–Juden." To that end rules were issued on the 8th March and 28th June 1773.

On the face of it, the aim was to improve the life of the Jews and to turn them into useful citizens of the monarchy. To that end, proposals and schemes were presented such as employing the Jews in road construction and establishing Jewish agricultural settlements, but every scheme failed right from the start.

[Pages 173-174]

Among those schemes was suggested the removal of the Jews from the estates, a plan which would adversely affect both the Jews and the interest of the landowners who objected, claiming that the vacuum in farming created by the dispossession of the Jews could not be filled by Christians. On 8th August 1783, a group of nobles submitted to the governor a memorandum, noting that the Jews were an ineffectual part of the population who did not full fill their obligations to the state; they did not contribute towards development in agriculture; they evaded army service and engaged in fraud; they had always damaged the state and damaged the townspeople's status. From a religious aspect too, they were a damaging element as was shown in the blood libel lawsuits. As bartenders in the villages, where they intoxicated the farmers and extorted their funds, they were an especially negative element. It was thus advisable to expel them but not immediately or legally, but rather by a sudden stop of tax payment. Only after a gradual process should a dispossession law be passed against them. According to the authors of the memorandum, Christian lessees could be found to replace the Jews.

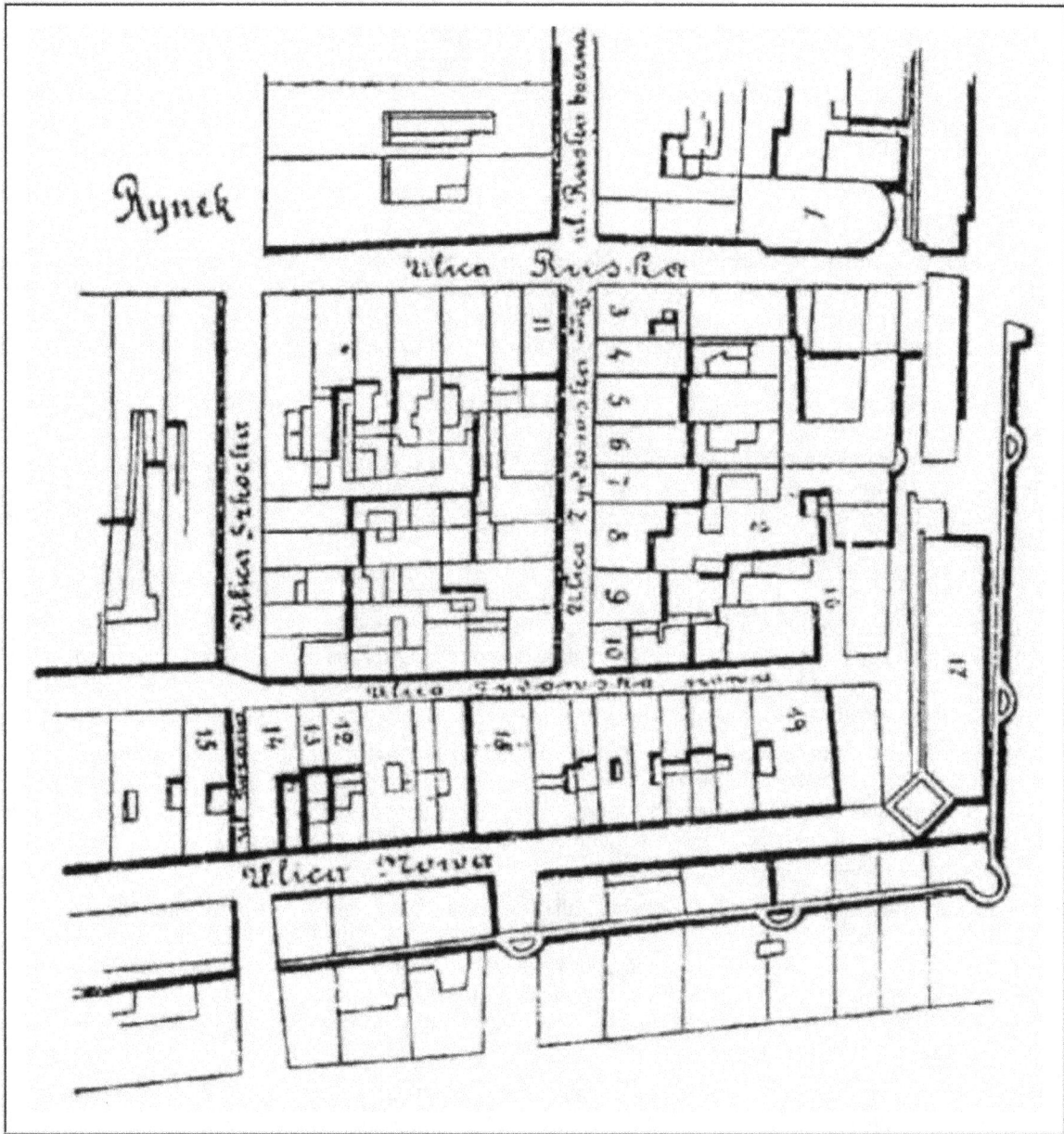

Plan of the Jewish Quarter in the 18th century

Early in the occupation the administrative leaders took the view that primarily the number of Jews had to be curbed. That view was also accepted by Vienna, spurred by governor Graf Brigido and by the commissioner's advisor, Kortum, without taking into consideration the possible adverse effect on the state's economy.

At Lwów the Jews were permitted to reside in the Jewish Quarter as well as on Ruska, Szkocka (Serbska) Boimów and Nowa streets, to which they were forced to move from all other streets. In 1793, after the authorities agreed to demolish 68 Jewish houses in the Żółkiew suburb due to fire hazard,[10] the living condition in town worsened and the congestion rose in the other suburbs in which Jews resided.

In the Jewish neighbourhoods the police had Jewish police inspectors (Polizei Revisoren). At the time there were two Jewish inspectors, Samuel [Szmul] Rays and Abraham Kormis as well as a special Jewish postman.[11] Jewish judges who acted in law–courts of commerce and exchange (*Merkantil und Wechsel-gerichte*) held at Lwów and Brody, counted as government officials

The governor also appointed a special beadle, to bring a Torah scroll for the swearing in of witnesses in the law–courts. His salary, paid for from the penalty fund, was 12 Florins per annum. At the time, Leibl Najer was the beadle.

The July 1784 request letter from the Lwów community indicates how far the prohibition to keep distilleries had affected the Jews of Lwów. In it, the community requested that the prohibition should not extend to houses where the Jews were permitted to pour and sell liquor. It stressed that the prohibition would deplete a number of Jewish families who had the privileges to serve drinks. The community's request was granted and serving drinks[12] was permitted in those houses.

LewBałaban, Rachmil Mizys, Herschel Rays, Abraham Berlach, Herschel Eliahu Lewit, Markus Faigels and Joel Bodek were at the time leaders of the Lwów community.

Due to the economic hardship the management faced grave difficulties. Apart from the debts with which the community was burdened –the debt to the Jesuits was 575,861 Gulden– the community was also charged with the responsibility to collect taxes. Matters had reached conflicts[13] with the authorities and the Jewish Council (*Judendirektion*). In 1784, the community-elders bribed the Council's member Jakob–Aron, and the Christian official (*actuarius*) Kulig with 130 Ducats, so they would lower the tax portion of the Jews. The governor who heard of it, started an investigation as a result of which Jakob–Aron was fined 260 Ducats, was removed from the Council and was denied the right to hold public office. Kulig, the Christian official, was fired, and the community management members, Josef Dawid, Lew Bałaban, Markus Faigels, Joel Bodek and Efraim Samuel were fined 130 Ducats each. Majer Herschel, the scribe of the Jewish community who had benefited from the bribery, was fined 360 Ducats and was dismissed from his post. During the investigation it was found that the community had used 1,500 Florins from the leasing of the meat–tax without accounting for it, and that there were irregularities in the collection of taxes and in the leasing fees.

[Pages 175-176]

The investigation commission found there were "fights, strife and controversy, mutual hatred, coordinated revenge and a tendency to oppress the weak", within the Council, and that instead of caring for the good of the community, those involved tried to release their relatives, friends and their supporters from the payment of taxes. The distribution of taxes was neglected, leading to arrears in collecting them and in the revenue.

The situation led to complaints not only from the Lwów community, but also from the rest of Galicia's communities. The governor took no notice of the complaints however, although in a report to the Emperor, dated 24th April 1781, he acknowledged that he did not agree with all of the Jewish Council's actions.[14] The report emphasized in particular that the Jewish Council, in its desire to lower the taxes of the rest of the communities, and with the aim to suppress Lwów's community, unfairly overburdened the Jews of Lwów.

The end of the report indicated specifically that "not all the Jews complained, only the wealthy, since the poor complained about the complainants from time to time. Although we far from agree with all of the Council's doings, and we have opposed it more than once, we are nevertheless convinced that Your Highness will concur that the Jews' complaints are unjustified.". According to the governor, the complaints included disingenuous and false facts. The complainants were wealthy Jews who, as one knows, prefer to pay fines rather than be considered wealthy by the authorities, and they prefer to be forced to pay so long as they do not have to pay of their own accord.

The reports and complaints from Galicia about the Council, were meticulously treated by the central authorities at Vienna. In time they led the government to liquidate the Jewish Council, since the regulations had not resolved the Jewish problem, of turning them into useful citizens.

In 1786, when in response to an order from Vienna, the governor was forced to close down the Jewish taverns, the issue of the Jewish bartenders resurfaced.

In October 1786, in the name of all the Jews of Galicia, the Lwów community–elders submitted a petition to permit those Jews who made their living from taverns, to retain them. For their own reasons, the meat–tax lessees also requested that the Jews not be dispossessed of the taverns.

Although clear instruction had already been issued, the governor passed on the petition to Vienna and recommended to fulfil the request, as executing the instruction would leave thousands of Jews without an income which would lead them to engage in even worse occupations. The governor suggested that the privileges of the taverns be extended by another three years, and that the bartenders born before 1772, be permitted to maintain them to the end of their lives. In his reasoning the governor stressed that the Jews were not responsible for the farmers' drunkenness, but rather, that the landowners wishing to increase their income, and realizing that the Jews knew how to run their business, they preferred to lease the taverns to them. The central authorities at Vienna (*Vereinigte Hauptsellen*), who failed to recognize the governor's reasoning, claimed that the Jews had sufficient time to find new employments since 1772. In their reply, the authorities stressed that they would suggest one concession to the Emperor – to postpone the date to the end of 1787 without issuing a proclamation, so as to avoid looking bad publicly. The authorities' proposal was not accepted however, and on 29th January 1787 Emperor Joseph II passed the resolution "to remove the taverns from the hands of Galician Jews, without delay; and the landowners who will keep Jewish lessees despite the prohibition, will be heavily fined with no favouritism."[15]

As part of the strategy to make the Jewish masses productive, Joseph II who realized that regulations would not easily do away with the beggars ("*Bettel Juden*"), he ordered in 1782 to employ them in road construction for which land on the royal estates was provided for them. That led to the idea of creating Jewish agricultural settlements. In 1781, Joseph II requested the governor's opinion on the matter, but meanwhile that programme was no longer pursued. Only after the ruling (patent) of 24th January 1785, which denuded thousands of Jewish families of leasing estates and land, leasing of taxes, salt export, maintaining liquor distilleries, or mead and liquor blending, did the government recall the Jewish settlement programme. On 16th July 1785, Joseph II ordered to start immediately the establishment of Jewish settlements,[16] where 1410 families were to be settled. The cost of settling a family was 250 Gulden, and the expenses were to amount to 35,259 Gulden, a sum which was split between all the communities. In conjunction with that programme, the congregation of Lwów was ordered to fund the cost of settling 136 families.

The 7th May 1789 ruling (*Toleranzpatent*) by Joseph II, which abolished the Jewish Council and rearranged the affairs of the Jews in seven chapters made up of 64 clauses, determined that it was the Lwów community's responsibility to maintain the regional rabbi who received an annual salary of 400 Florins. Seven community–elders, elected on 15th September in the presence of a government official for the period of three years, would head the community.

[Pages 177-178]

Actually, the community was to elect 14 candidates out of whom the local government would pick seven. The community-elders whose authority was now reduced to synagogue matters and welfare (*in synagoga-libus et beneficiis*) would receive a monthly salary from the community purse, they would be reliant on the district government and would follow its directives. Despite its reduced authority, the community was collectively responsible for the collecting of taxes. On 18th February 1788, even before the ruling was released, a directive obliged the Jews to enlist in the armed forces.

In order to encourage the Jews to enlist, the Lwów community promised 15 Zloty to every Jewish soldier, but to no avail. In 1790, despite Jewish opinion and due to the war against Turkey, the government was forced to introduce conscription.[17] Once Leopold was crowned Emperor of Austria, the community of Lwów decided to send a delegation to Vienna with a list of requests to improve the condition of the Jews. At first, the community–elders considered that the delegation would represent the Jews of Galicia in its entirety, and to that end they approached the communities of the regional towns, to send authorised representatives to Lwów, to take part in the consultation. The representatives were chosen in consultation with Rabbi Hirsz Rosanis, the representative from Lwów, Jakobka Landau from Brody, and Scheiner from Buczacz, who travelled to Vienna at the expense of the community. The government looked kindly on the delegation, since "a calming of the citizens had been achieved, which benefited the Kingdom."

In June 1790, the delegation reached Vienna and submitted its petition to the Emperor, requesting to introduce redemption–money instead of personal service in the armed forces, since the Jews were not fit to serve in the armed forces, and it was hard for them to keep their religious commandments in the military. They noted in particular the phenomenon which threatened to demolish the economy, as craftsmen, employees and labourers fled Galicia in order to evade military service.[18]

The Emperor took no account of the Jewish delegates' claims, and sent his decision to Lwów: "The Jew, as a person and as a citizens of the kingdom, will serve in any service just like the rest of the citizens. He is not affected religiously, since he can eat what he wishes, and on Saturday will hardly have to do any work, just like the Christian on Sunday. The Jews of Galicia are given all the civil rights, excepting the leasing of taverns, and they are even permitted to acquire noblemen's estates and to serve in any position, accordingly, they must participate in all the country's debts."

The communities' representatives did not rest, and in July 1790 they submitted two new petitions in which they repeated their request to annul the personal service in the armed forces, and replace it by redemption–money for each Jewish recruit. They also presented the Emperor with the request to permit them to maintain the Jewish law–courts, and reinstate their right to lease taverns.

The lobbying succeeded, and on 28th July 1790 Emperor Leopold II issued a directive which released the Jews from personal service in the armed forces. Instead, they had to produce an equivalent number of stand–in recruits from among local or foreign volunteers, or pay 30 Florin redemption–money per recruit, to ensure the military authorities could enrol replacement recruits.[19]

The delegation tried to attain also mitigation regarding distilleries, the reinstatement of rabbinical judgement as well as education. They were unsuccessful except for the permission to provide Kosher food for Jewish prisoners in jails.[20]

Prussia, fearing land occupation by Austria during the Austro–Turkish war (1789–1790), strove to incite the Polish nobility of Galicia against Austria, with a view to a new war. The Polish nobility distrusted the Prussian conniving, however. Nonetheless, they took advantage of the war in order to organize committees at Lwów and the provinces. On 23rd April 1790, their representatives submitted to Emperor [Kaiser] Leopold II a reminder made up of 53 clauses, which included grievances and political demands to improve the situation in Galicia. Among those they demanded to convene the *Sejm*, a national autonomy in the manner of Hungary, led by a Polish commissioner, and a Polish national army. As part of the constitution they demanded affirmation of the farmers' citizenship, the granting of civil rights to Jews, apart from the acquisition agricultural estates or the right to be elected to public office.[21]

The Galician nobles' negotiations at the Emperor's court in Vienna lasted three years without any positive outcome. After the death of Leopold, his son Franz I had no interest in granting Galicia special political status.

The war brought worsening economic conditions which affected the Jews in particular due to the difficulty of trading with Silesia and Prussia.

In 1791, the dispute between the Jews and the municipality started again.[22] In May 1791, the Christian traders submitted a petition to the Court Council at Vienna: 1. That the Jewish traders be removed from the town–centre to their own streets;

[Pages 179-180

2. To demand documents from Jewish traders to prove that they had studies and were practised in trade; 3. To demand that their books and accounts be in the German language; 4. To prove that they possessed sufficient capital for their affairs; 5. To forbid the Jews from peddling, whether among Jews or Christians.[23]

With the 3rd October 1791 constitutional statute passed by the Polish *Sejm* granting rights to the townspeople, the Emperor ordered the governor of Galicia, Graf Brigido, to report to him "what will best benefit the townspeople and farmers of Galicia, in view of the constitutional situation created in the Polish Kingdom." In November 1791 Brigido submitted his view, proposing a list of changes to improve the economic situation, as well as his view of the Jews who were the principal cause inhibiting the development of towns, especially Lwów. In his view, there was such danger at Lwów and other towns' Judaization (*Verjudung*), that the Christian population – the traders and craftsmen – would leave Galicia for Poland in order to take advantage of the new constitution. Consequently it was necessary to turn the Jews and especially the youth, to a productive element of society. One necessary measure was the expulsion of all unregistered Jews ("conscripts") those not in permanent employ; prohibiting them from residing in villages, unless they were employed in agriculture or craft; prohibiting entry to Jews from abroad who had no capital (minimum of 10,000 Florins); restricting their marriages and change to their way of life: to begin with – change of the Jewish garments for European dress. A useful means of alteration, according to him, was their conscription in the armed forces.[24]

Governor Brigido's report, also required in the negotiation with the nobles' representatives, failed to pass and remained in the government's files with no attempt to execute his suggestions.

Lwów's townspeople did not rest and did not let up their demands to remove the Jews from town to their own dwellings. When their demands were rejected by Vienna, the representatives of the Christian merchant's guild: Anton Fischer, Simon Werner, Herman Bürger, Jakob Danilwicz, Johann Poprop and Simeon Gehrzin, submitted on 15th November 1793 a new request to limit "the excessive trade rights of the Jews of Lwów," who bring destruction on the Christian traders and take away their livelihoods.[25] The Christian craftsmen's guilds also renewed their conflict with the Jews.

According to Maria–Theresa's 1776 rules,[26] the Jewish craftsmen were only permitted to work for Jewish customers. In 1784, Joseph II repealed that restriction in order to encourage the Jews to engage in vocational work, and he also permitted Jewish craftsmen to sell their wares at the fairs. They were granted permission to join the craftsmen's guild and to participate in electing their leaders, as well as to establish Jewish associations. Inevitably, the Christian craftsmen were dissatisfied with the situation.

In 1793, the Christian tailors' guild requested to stop the Jews from participating in elections and from filling posts in their guild, as well as stopping them from employing apprentices who did not have German school certificates. Under those circumstances the Vienna authorities ordered, on 7th October 1793, that the governor support that complaint.[27]

On 31st December 1793, among the restrictions on the Jewish population enacted by the government, they were forced to vacate the houses in town and reside solely in the two suburbs – Kraków and Żółkiew suburbs. The Jews in all other suburbs were ordered to join them there within three years. Where the Jews were house–owners, they were permitted to retain those so long as they did not let any flats or shops to Jews. Jews who kept taverns in the suburbs, were permitted to remain and continue in their vocation, but their privilege would not pass down to their heirs who would be obliged to sell the houses.[28]

The Jews did not rush to vacate any flats or shops within the town–markets. They found support from Christian house–owners who, in a memorandum of January 1795, demanded also in future to be permitted to let to Jews shops in the town markets and other streets, as they had been allowed previously. The Governor advised the Vienna authorities to defer the request.

Even industrialists in Lower Austria requested from the Vienna government not to curtail the trading freedom of Lwów's Jews, who were their clients. In their response of February 1794, the Vienna authorities stressed that the Jews of Lwów had cleverly acquired the best flats and shops and displaced the Christian tradesmen. The purpose of the ruling was to return the Jews to their place, no change would be made and the ruling would be executed in its entirety. The Jews did not relinquish their rights, and Jakob Kitaj and Simche Rappoport submitted to Emperor [Kaiser] Franz I a special petition in the name of the Jewish tradesmen and house–owners,[29] to permit them to remain in their abodes considering that they had legally acquired their houses, and moving them to the Kraków and Żółkiew suburbs would ruin them financially and deprive them of their livelihoods.

[Pages 181-182]

The Governor took no notice of their request and instructed to enforce the regulation, excluding wholesalers of national products who had invested some 30–40 thousand Gulden in their trade.[30] The Christian tradesmen's representatives also appealed that permit, and demanded to have also the wholesalers removed from the town.

Their demand was however rejected by the authorities, and in October 1795 they submitted a further petition to remove the Jews from their abodes without delay.

The community, on the other hand, appealed to the Vienna central authorities over the execution of the 1793 regulation, and requested that the Governor be instructed to defer the evacuation till the conclusion of the appeal.[31]

The Lwów union of Christian tradesmen sent to Vienna reports that the Jews of Lwów were amassing large sums in order to find means to have the regulation revoked. After investigation the Governor accounted that the reports were baseless. The Vienna authorities responded, noting that in their written requests the Christian tradesmen had to be truthful, otherwise they would be punished.[32]

With its lobbying, the community succeeded in having the evacuation deferred by three years with the proviso that Jews were forbidden from purchasing property other than within the Kraków and Żółkiew Quarters.[33] In the Halicz and Brody Quarters Jewish bartenders with a license were permitted to remain, but their heirs as well as the house owners who had no bar–tending license, had to move to the permitted Jewish Quarters, within six years.

In 1792, the Jews of Lwów numbered 11,765 souls (2,774 families); in 1795: 11,966 (2,875 families); in 1800: 13,302 (3,372 families); and in 1803: 13,297 (3,395 families). In 11 years the number of Jews grew by 1,532 souls (621 families), and the issue worried the authorities to such an extent that the Governor received a notice from Vienna stating that "such significant proliferation of Lwów's Jews is worrying and we hope that the Governor will rigorously execute the Emperor's regulation against an increase in the number of Jewish families."[34] The Jews of Lwów suffered further due to the Kosher meat tax–lessees, who brought about complaints and complications in the community's life as well as the involvement of the authorities.

The band of lessees took no account of the population's predicament nor of the public needs. In November 1792, the community–elders submitted a complaint that the lessees increased the meat price in contravention of the contractual obligations.[35] It became clear that two community–elders, Solomon Luber and Jakob Taubes, were involved in the conspiracy, and they were dismissed. In December 1792, they asked the Governor to reinstate them in their posts or to appoint an inquiry commission to look at the accusation charges which Joseph Zellermayer had brought against them.[36] On 29th January 1793 however, their request was rejected when a negative response to their request arrived from Vienna.[37] There were many such cases, and the authorities received denunciations and submissions on the irregularities by the tax lessees.

In 1794, complaints were submitted to the Governor and the authorities, against the community–elder Zelig Hulis and his partner as tax lessee, Mojzesz Schiefer, for not entering the required deposit. The authorities investigated the matter and decided that Zelig Hulis was not fit to be a community–elder. Due to that affair the community scribe, Pinkas Dietersdorf, was also dismissed. Hulis and Dietersdorf were dismissed from their posts and their dismissal was confirmed by the Governor.[38] During the investigation, the community–elders Leibel Schneier, Zusman Bałaban and Herschel Witeles were also accused of embezzling 195,000 Florin from the community purse. The accusation was brought by Joseph Zellermayer who was in the habit of informing. The accused appealed and requested a deferment till the matter was brought to court. The inquiry commission took its time and Zellermayer reported it to the Vienna authorities which demanded a report from the commission about its negligence, as well as the appointment, without bias, of a new inquiry commission.[39] The Governor notified that he would ensure the inquiry came quickly to an end. The archival records make no mention of the inquiry commission's outcomes. It seems that the community–elders managed to cover up the entire affair.

In the years 1796–1798, the Jewish community proposed to erect a Jewish hospital. The authorities let it be known that so long as the Jews had not cleared their tax debts and had not participated in the war loan, they would not be able to spend money on building a hospital, and in the absence of a hospital, the community leaders were responsible for the destitute patients,[40] The community wanted also to build an almshouse for the poor, and it approached the authorities with the request to be permitted to levy one Polish Groschen on every kilo meat, to be paid for by the meat tax lessees Heinzman, Krater and Kopler.

In 1797 Solomon Kopler, together with his meat tax–lessee partner, the Christian Ignaz Krater, suggested that the tolerance tax be replaced by a tax on Shabbat candles: two Kreuzer for each candle; six Kreuzer per memorial candle; ten Kreuzer per Yom Kippur candle; one Kreuzer for holidays; half a Kreuzer per Hannukah candle, and at weddings, one Florin per candle and one Florin per torch. The government hesitated since Emperor Franz I considered such a tax would be a form of religious suppression. Influenced, however, by Herz Homberg (Kopler promised him a net income of 2%), who claimed that it was not a suppression of lighting candles, but rather a proposed special tax on them, the Emperor agreed to his proposal.

[Pages 183-184]

In Eastern Galicia, the government leased the collecting of the tax to the partners Kopler and Tuvie Steinberg, at the annual cost of 194,409 Florin. That tax weighed heavily on the Jewish community and the sub–lessees (candle–lessor) were hated by the masses for their cruelty and spitefulness.

The voting rights within the community were linked to the payment of the candle tax. At Lwów the voting right was fixed to the tax payment on seven candles; the right to be elected was contingent on the payment of tax on eight candles; to be elected community leader or rabbi, depended on the tax payment on ten candles.

Munis Finkelstein and Menachem Schneier of Lwów, in particular, bothered the authorities with their proposals. Schneier suggested how to raise the war loan and the drink tax. With regard to enlisting, he proposed to release the Jews from the armed forces, if they were to recruit 300 volunteers from abroad and pay 50,000 Florins to the treasury. He also proposed changes to the candle tax, and requested to determine a commission to investigate the behaviour of the candle–tax lessees and find means to increase the income from the tax to 50,000 Florin without affecting the poor, and to use the proceeds to raise the education of the Jews.

The Governor sent his proposals to the Vienna authorities where they were discussed by the commission of the royal–court, but were rejected. Instead, on 24th September 1798, Emperor Franz I ordered to inform the Lwów Governor that "The Jew Menachem Schneier of Lwów should not in future bother the offices of state and the royal–court with his proposals."[41] For several years Menachem Schneier refrained from bothering the authorities, but in 1805 he again proposed suggestions.

On that occasion he proposed a programme to turn the Jews into useful and happy citizens of the empire. According to him, the Jewish education affected adversely the character, and consequently the state should check the religious studies, the "Talmud," which compelled to hate the gentiles. The education of the Jews of Galicia prevented progress and the youth needed to be taught in German. To implement the improvements it was advisable to appoint a cross–country leader (*Oberlandesältester*) at an annual salary of 20,000 Florin, and a Christian deputy to assist him. Their remit would be to undertake a detailed census of the Jews, and the communities would be abolished and be placed under the authority of municipalities. The communities of Lwów, Brody and Kraków would be led by two elders, while a single elder would serve each of the other communities.

The scheme intrigued the authorities, and its proposals seemed to them "perfectly purposeful and worthy of consideration in conjunction with the new Jewish regulation."[42]

The Governor received an order to inform Schneier that his proposal to be invited to Vienna and that his travel should be paid for on account, was rejected since he was able to deliver all the details to the Lwów Governor, in person.

The authorities also received information that a criminal investigation over theft had been undertaken against him. Although the investigation was quashed, the authorities deemed it necessary "to keep him under special political supervision," and according to information he tried "also to infiltrate the community management, which is quite impossible." Thus ended the Schneier affair, and there is no mention of him in the government files. He was in fact one of the corrupt characters who were the by–products of the Austrian regime of the time.

In 1796, Berl Joselowicz, the Jewish major–general who had established the Warsaw Jewish Volunteer Regiment during the Kościuszko uprising (1794), visited Lwów. In September 1796 while at Lwów, Berl Joselowicz approached the Governor Graf [von] Gaisruck in a memorandum, in which he suggested to the Austrian government –which at the time was in a state of war with France – to form a voluntary Jewish military division of 6,000–8,000 soldiers to serve in the war against the French. In his memorandum he detailed how to organize and equip the Jewish division.

The proposal was favourably received by Graf Gaisruck who forwarded the memorandum to the Vienna authorities, with warm recommendation, expressing his positive estimation of Berl Joselowicz due to his sense of honour and pride.[43] The

Vienna war commission viewed the matter differently however, believing it was beneath the honour of Austria to use a corps "composed of naughty Jewish young men, idlers who were a liability to their parents and relatives." The war commission informed the Governor at Lwów that "One cannot expect any good to come of such a suspect corps," and it was unable to make use of Berl Joselowicz's offer to establish a Jewish volunteer army.[44] Berl Joselowicz left Lwów and turned his back on Austria, and after a period he joined the Polish legions of Dombrowski [Jan Henryk Dąbrowski], in the French armed forces.

[Pages 359-360]

Notes: CHAPTER 11

All notes in square brackets [ ] were made by the translator.

1.   The Polish poet Karpiński describes the administrative tangle inflicted on the Galician residents with endless rules, instructions and decrees, in the following lines:
Po wesolej w Polsce chilli
Juzesmy prawie wkroczyli
W kraj gdzie smiac sie zapomniano
I gdzie glakac zakazcno
W kraj pelny uniwersalów
Wiecznych prawnych foljalów
I cursory instruktarzôw
Ostrzezen i cyrkularzów.

2.   Archives of the Ministry of the Interior in Vienna. ex. 1; T IV; Nr. 138. January 1776. According to the commander the entire Lwów district contained 42 Parishes (Pfarrsprenge), 25 towns, 26 small towns, 647 villages, and of the citizens 120,456 were Christian, 66,264 were Jewish.
Wiener Staatsarchiv. Staatsratsakten 1773 Z 2940.

3.   Arneth: *Maria Theresias letzte Regierungszeit.* Wien 1877; t. II, pp. 418–421

4.   At first they thought – as suggested by Count Auersperg – to implement in Galicia a Jewish statute of the 1754 Law. (Archiv d. Min. d. Innern, Wien Galizien Protokolle, 1774), but his suggestion was rejected and a specific statute was created for Galicia.

5.   Archive of the commission at Lwów: Protokolle e.a. 1772 Nr. 1082.

6.   Pergen's report, in Ossolineum Manuscript 525 Chapter IV.

7.   *Protokolle Galizien 105*; 1791, Mai Nr. 105. sed eius index indicium in eis (judaeis) exercebit.

8.   Archive of the Ministry of the Interior, Vienna: *Protokolle Galizien e.a.* 1775.

9.   A 122 sheets (224 pages) manuscript titled:
Beschreibung der Koenigreiche Galizien u Lodomerien nach dem Zustand in welchen sie sich zur Zeit der Revindicirung durch Ihre Kaiserl. Koenigl. Apostolische Majestaet. und besonders im Monat Julius 1773 Befunden haben. And these are the chapters: 1. On the condition of the population and the country's produce (pp. 1–29); 2. On the nobility (pp. 30–71); 3. On religion and the priesthood (pp. 72–121); 4. On the towns and the urban industry (pp. 122–165); 5. On the status of the farmers (pp. 166–207). 16 manuscript 525 (p. 208); 6. On the Jews (manuscript 525, pp. 208–240). The draft document is in the collection of the "Ossolineum" Library, Lwów, Manus. No. 525 and a copy at Vienna: Staatsarchiv Wien, Staatsratsakten 1773, Nr. 2388. On the report *see also*: Dr. Ludwik Finkel: Memorjal Antoniego hr. Pergena kw. hist. t. XIV.

10.   *Protokoll. Galizien* 1793 Mai Nr. 23.

11.   IV T 5 Juli 1795 Nr. 7

12.   Archive of the Ministry of the Interior: IV T 11, Carton Nr. 2657. Nr. 11 ex August 1784 Galizien.

13.   In 1775, the community became embroiled with the authorities over the assistance the community had extended to the Stryj community after the fire there caused destruction. When Empress Maria–Theresa agreed to support the Jews of Stryj who had suffered from the fire, just as the Christian citizens, the Governor appealed claiming that it was groundless since the Jews were assisted by the communities of Lwów, Brody, and Kazimir. As a result, an order was given from Vienna to investigate the communities' accounts regarding the joint assistance in such cases.
Protokolle Galizien e.a. 1775.

14.   IV T 11 Carton Nr. 185, ex. Majo 1784 Galizien.

15.   IV T 11 Carton 2658 (1786–1792).

16.   *see*: Dr. A. Breuer: "Joseph the Second and the Jews of Galicia." *HaShelach*, 1910; pp. 336–343.

17.   1,060 Galician Jews served in the Austrian armed forces during the Austro–Turkish war.

18.   Archive of the Ministry of the Interior: Carton 2579; IV T 11 Judensachen IV T 11 Judensachen; Carton 2659 I.

19.   Carton 2579; No. 106, ex. Julio 1790.

20.   IV T 11 Carton 2659

[Pages 360-361]

21.   "Ossolineum" Library, Manuscript No. 525; pp. 616–619.
see: Stanislław Starzyński: *Projekt galicyjskiej konstytucji 1790*, Lwów 1893.

22.   On 18th October 1786, the Lwów municipality also underwent a reform. A president was set at its head (at an annual salary of 1,800 Florin); his deputy (on 1,200 Florins); 12 advisors on civil and criminal issues; four advisors on political affairs (eight of them received 800 Florin annual salary, and eight, 700 Florin); four secretaries (two on 600 Florin, and two on 500 Florin) three protocol directors; a deputy (300 Florin); registrar (500 Florin); expediter (600 Florin); treasurer; supervisor; and another 18 clerks; 21 judges; and one hangman. The municipality was also responsible for criminal jurisdiction till November 1787, when special criminal law–courts were established in Galicia.

23.   Archive of the Ministry of the Interior: Protocoll Galizien 1791. Juni No. 791.

24.   Manuscript in Ossolineum 525; p. 674.

25.   IV T 1 Carton 2580, 72 ex. Dezember 1793.

26.   IV Abschnitt 4, Art. 1.

27.   Protokoll 1793 Oktober No. 16.

28.   Archive of the Ministry of the Interior: IV T 1. Dezember 1793. No. 72.

29.   A power of attorney was appended to the petition written in Yiddish: "Power of attorney which we the undersigned, the Lemberg house owners tradesmen entrust with power and permission the venerable master, the elder [Nagid] our teacher and rabbi, Rabbi Jankel Kitaj, as well as the venerable master Rabbi Simche Rappoport, so that in our name they will come to an accord with his majesty, that in accordance with the freedom granted by the late Emperor Joseph, our property of shops and built houses and the benefits from them may continue to be protected. Lemberg 23rd April 1795."

30.   IV T 1 Carton 2580. Januar 1795. No. 76; 1795. No. 39.

31.   Protokoll 1795. November No. 35.

32.   Protokoll 1796. März No. 105; Nov. No. 39.

33.   IV T 1. 1795.

34.   Dekret an das galiz. Gubernium v. 19/VI 1804. No. 10. 155. IV T 1. Carton 2580. 155 ex. Junio 1804.

35.   IV T 12 ex. a 1792.

36.   Protok. Galizien 1792, Dezember No. 24.
Janua. 1793, No. 41.

37.   Prot. 1793. Januar No. 82.

38.   IV T 10. Februar 1794. No. 69.

39.   Prot. 1795. September No. 112.

40.   IV T 14 1798. Sept. 125.

41.   IV T 11. Judensachen, Carton. 2659 II.

42.   24 October 1805, order to the Governor: IV T 11. Carton. 2581. 181.

43.   Archive of the Ministry of the Interior: Protokoll Galizien 1796. September No. 122. Freikorps aus Juden: Oktober No. 41.
Vienna War Archive: Hofkriegsakten e. a. 1796 No. 9. 1311.
In his letter of recommendation Graf [von] Gaisruck writes:
"Berl Joselowicz, a Jew who, as Colonel, has already led a corps of Jews against the Russian at Warsaw, and who has the loyalty of the Jews, has made himself available to assemble at short notice that existing corps made up solely of Jews, and produce it for the required exercise, conditional however on his title of Royal & Imperial [K.K.] Colonel, and he requests that were he to be injured he would receive a most gracious pension. The Jew in general has his own pride, and due to that pride Berl Joselowicz can assemble that corps more easily with the honour and emulation of the title of Colonel."

44.   Message to the Governor of East Galicia, dated 13 October 1796: Protokoll Galizien 1796. Oktober No. 41. acta 102 Frey–Korps.
see also my book: *Aus Zwei Jahrhunderten*. Wien 1924, pp. 11–13.

[Pages 185-186]

Chapter 12: Education and Culture

Translated by Myra Yael Ecker

Edited by Yocheved Klausner

The state of education in Lwów. The attitude towards the Jews and proposals for amendments. The organisational action of Herz Homberg. The state of the schools and the teachers. Sabotage against Homberg. Establishment of the Aron Friedenthal seminary. The Galician schools' fund. Liquidation of the Jewish education network. Early signs of the Enlightenment in Lwów.

Education was concentrated in the hands of the governor's educational commission, headed by Graf [von] Gallenberg, but its progress was very slow.

In 1783, a state elementary school and four preparatory schools (*Trivialschulen*) were established. Apart from those, there were also schools for Officers' children, taught by deputy–officers who had ended their military service. While the monasteries still existed, teaching continued at the Latin schools they had established. The first, secondary school of the state educational service, was opened at Lwów on 1st September 1784. On 3rd July of the same year the university was also established, with faculties in philosophy, law and medicine, taught to begin with in Latin, and later in German.

In 1785, with the arrival of the Bohemian education pioneer, Kindermann, who introduced structure to the education of Galicia, fundamental reforms in education were undertaken. Within the framework of that reform the question of the Jewish education was also considered.

With the authorities' failure to rid Galicia of its Jews, despite the repressions, the restricted employment, the restrictions on marriage, the expulsion from the villages and from the border regions, they decided on a method of turning the Jews into model citizens through education.

During the period of Maria–Theresa and Joseph II, education underwent fundamental changes as schools were placed under the supervision of the kingdom. The monastic educational establishments were replaced by state schools where secular teachers were appointed.

In accordance with that educational system, Joseph II demanded from the Galician authorities a report of the state of education, and proposals for its improvement.

The Jewish statutes of 16th July 1776 established three types of schools in the communities: the first school, with compulsory reading and writing lessons in the German language; the second school, for Talmud studies; and a higher educational school, for the training of rabbis and judges [Dayanim]. The state Rabbi was given the overall supervision of education.[1]

After years, Jewish children were permitted to enrol also in state schools (Normal– und Trivialschule).[2] Study at the state school lasted for four years, in four classes.

In 1785, the government ordered that each community appoint a teacher experienced in state–school education, at an annual salary of 100 to 200 Gulden. That statute set the foundation for the Jewish elementary schools whose supervision was removed from the state Rabbi and transferred to governmental authorities.[3]

To finalize the new method all the communities were obliged to provide school education for Jewish boys up to the age of thirteen [age of Bar–Mitzvah]. In the 1785–1789 debates on changes to the Jewish statute, stress was laid on the improvements it required in order to achieve the "Enlightenment of the Jewish People, education of the youth and change to their moral character", with the aid of improved education undertaken at regular schools. The "overfeeding of Jewish youths with Talmudic musings" (*Talmudistische Träumereien*) had to stop, and schools of that nature should be abolished. The authors of the statute proposed to impose on Jewish children an education first at state schools and later they could study at "Talmudic schools," which would ensure that Jewish youths would find no point in the Talmud and its teachers, and would aspire to adapt to the other state citizens. In their innocence the proposers were convinced that that would lead to increased numbers of Jewish converts to Christianity. Apart from education it was also important to pay special attention to spreading the Enlightenment among the Jews.[4]

The principles of the proposals were also integrated into the statute, thus highlighting the government's aim to change the character of the Jew of Galicia through education.

Clauses 11–14 of the statute dated 7th May 1789, stated clearly that each community had to erect a German speaking school similar to the elementary school and impose on the youth, both boys and girls, the compulsory school education.

The Jews considered that statute a harsh decree.

A special training course to qualify suitable teachers was established at Lwów under the authorities' supervision.

[Pages 187-188]

The Vienna government handed the organization of the educational network to Herz Homberg who arrived at Lwów from Prague. Herz Homberg was born at Liben (Bohemia), in 1749, he studied the Talmud at Prague and began to learn German at a more advanced age. Later, he studied at Pressburg [Bratislava], Breslau [Wrocław], Berlin and Hamburg, concentrating particularly on the study of pedagogy. In the years 1778–1782, he taught at the house of Moses Mendelssohn, and also participated in his translation *HaBiur* ["The Exegesis"] of the Torah.

After Joseph II's statute was published, Homberg returned to Austria and taught at Graz [Gratz] and Trieste. From there he returned to the University of Vienna, and with the Emperor's special permission he passed with distinction the examinations in Philosophy, and was appointed lecturer at Prague University. The Emperor did not approve that appointment and made him inspector of the Jewish schools in Galicia. When he got to Lwów however, he was greeted by overt hostility by the Jews who considered him the executor of a harsh decree imposed on them. With difficulty he got accommodation at Lwów, not in a Jewish house but in the Christian Quarter, and a military guard watched his flat against assault. On his arrival in Galicia, Homberg wrote a missive written in Hebrew, addressed "To the shepherds of the dispersed lambs of Israel, the rabbis as well as the religious and Torah teachers, and to you the influential people leading all the congregations within the Kingdom of Galicia and Lodomeria."

In his missive Homberg elaborated on the benevolence of the Emperor, who "derived satisfaction from teaching our sons in their youth, intellectual morals, knowledge of our German language, and the use of arithmetic; and besides necessary, courteous and political matters he ordered to build or prepare schools (to be distinguished from the religious and Torah schools) where, for a few hours daily he placed Jews like us to teach the Jewish children everything mentioned and written in a normal school." The purpose of the directive was "to benefit our sons and our sons' sons after us, to raise their standing in the eyes of the ruling nation and to rid them of any disgrace and contempt." He explained the shortcomings of the old form of education and stated that the rabbis and leaders should reorganize the children's education and teach the youths crafts. Were the rabbis and leaders to agree with him, so much the better, but if not he would set his words in writing and create a programme he would submit to "the glory of the ministers in the first rank of government who will decide and be our eyes."[5]

Since his arrival till 1788 he established 41 schools in Galicia, with two at Lwów. Isser Minden was appointed manager at Lwów, and was followed by Nathan Morgentau.

In 1790, four schools (Deutsch–Jüdische Schulen) existed at Lwów, and one school for girls. Two of the four schools were situated in the Krakówite Quarter and one in the Halicz Quarter. The fourth was an elementary school with three classes, a principal and two teachers. In 1793, two additional schools for girls were added. In the years 1790–1795, apart from the supervisor Herz Homberg who received an annual salary of 1,000 Florin, there were at Lwów seven teachers: Nathan Morgentau (300 Florin), Hirsch Seligman (300 Florin), both of them at the elementary school with three classes. Mejer Epstein (200 Florin) Levi Popper (200 Florin) both at the school in the Krakowite Quarter, Benjamin Grünbaum (200 Florin) at the school in the Halicz Quarter, Bertha Mendelssohn (200 Florin) at the school for girls.[6]

The Teachers' Council (Jüddisch–Deutsche Lehrer–Konferenz) was led by the seminary's manager. In administrative matters the Council was subject to the ministerial office (K. und K. Ostgalizischer Studien–Konsens) which was made up of: the university rector, chairman, four deans, the representative of secondary schools, inspector of the state schools, the university librarian and the inspector of Jewish education (Homberg), who had been entrusted with, and granted the decisions over all matters concerning the Jewish schools.

The teachers were also unwelcome by the Jewish congregation, and the community requested from the Governor to be rid of the obligation to provide them accommodation free of charge. On19[th] September 1791, the Governor received instruction from Vienna not to release the community from that obligation, since Christian teachers also benefitted from free accommodation and consequently the community had to bear that burden.[7]

Education at Lwów was not on the desired level; the disputes between Homberg and the teachers brought no honour to the schools. By appointing his brother Simon as teacher, Homberg's use of nepotism led to the unfair dismissal of another teacher. He also established a second girls' school in order to provide an income for his sister–in–law, as its headmistress.

After Morgentau resigned, Nathan Gunzenheusen was appointed headmaster of the elementary school. His job was however immediately transferred to Homberg's brother.

Homberg faced many difficulties in his efforts to attract Jewish children to the schools. The parents evaded the obligation to send their children to school for fear that they might leave the fold and be led astray while they were removed from the Torah and the tradition. They employed all manner of means: they sent requests to which they appended doctors' certificates about the ill health of the child, in order to exempt him from school obligation; others brought proof that their children studied with private teachers; there were those who submitted certificates of departure from town, or marriage certificates. Despite the small number of pupils,

[Pages 189-190]

when Emperor Joseph II visited the schools he saw classes full of boys and girls, since Homberg knew how to deceive him by moving pupils from one school to the next, during his visit.

The fact that the Jews used every ploy to prevent their children from attending school was also known to the authorities, who sent detailed reports to the Vienna authorities.

After the demise of Emperor Joseph II, a delegation of representatives from Lwów, Brody, and Buczacz travelled to Vienna to attain improvements for the Jews of Galicia. Those included the request to exempt the Jews from the heavy burden of schools. In their petition they complained about the teachers, who spurned the religious laws and whose teaching was faithless and reckless. Their effort was however in vain.

At the end of 1792, an order was issued that young men and women who had not completed their schooling or who had not passed their examinations, would not receive marriage licenses. On 31st July 1793 an order was also issued to the schools' board, to take measures against parents whose children did not attend school regularly, and to fine them financially, and were that to no avail, to punish them also physically.[8]

Twice yearly during examinations, members of the "*Studienkonsens*" visited the school, and each time they reported on neglect of the children who showed no progress in calligraphy etc. In 1793, based on those reports, Emperor Franz I expressed his disappointment of the state of Jewish schools which did not measure up to the task they had been set, and he ordered to paste his message in every synagogue. Under threat of punishment all the Torah teachers were ordered to urge their pupils to attend school. To rectify the situation an enquiry commission was set by the Governor, led by von Felsing, and it returned a severe report that for three years the community had failed to collect any fines from the parents. In its conclusion the commission proposed that in the absence of a child from lessons, parents should be punished, be it by a financial fine or four days' imprisonment. The children would have to copy 66 times the list of the evaders, and the community leaders had to paste the lists in the synagogues and Minyanim.

In September 1797, 67 parents and one Torah teacher faced jail punishment for preventing children from attending school.[9] The dismal situation spurred some individuals to submit strange suggestions for amendments to the authorities. One such suggestion submitted by the Lwów merchant Chaim Menschel, proposed to also include religious studies in the school curriculum, and to forbid Jews unable to read and write German, any trade or crafts.[10] Another Jew, Menachem Schneier, suggested that he himself be appointed inspector of Torah teachers. As recommendation for his appointment he submitted a list of recalcitrant parents and Torah teachers. The government rejected his request but ordered the Governor to punish the parents and Torah teachers on his list.[11]

The teachers themselves brought about the dismal situation. Instead of working diligently and maintaining good relations with the population, they isolated themselves so that even those inclined towards the Enlightenment approached the authorities with complaints that the teachers were the cause for the parents' objection to education. Most teachers lacked the appropriate education to be teachers. They took no account of the feelings of the Jewish population, they disparaged Jewish laws and customs, they smoked and wrote on the Sabbath, and in all their behaviour they opposed the spirit of tradition. Homberg himself did not refrain either from offending the feelings of the population as regarded religion and tradition.

In November 1795, the Vienna authorities demanded the opinion of Gunzenheusen, the Lwów school principal, regarding those complaints. He evaded them however with personal excuses that he was not responsible for the situation.[12] In fact, the teachers were deeply involved in intrigues, denouncements and quarrels with Homberg, on the one hand, and among themselves, on the other. There were also complaints that the supervisor and the teaching staff spent their time on financial business[13] and on demands for increased wages.[14]

Due to the poor study results the education authorities took every opportunity to turn the teachers' attention to the demands "to keep close watch over the school classes." They were particularly dissatisfied with the handwriting samples from the seminary pupils. According to clause 14 of Joseph II's statute, the necessity to improve the educational organization required the establishment of a teachers' seminary at Lwów. To begin with, teachers' training courses (*praeparandi*) were established, directed by Aron Friedenthal, who was paid an annual salary or 200 Florins plus inspection fees and travel expenses. Ten apprentices participated in each of the two–months' courses. In 1793, the courses were confirmed as a teachers' seminary, and the director was granted the title "Seminary Director."

Aron ben Zecharja [Zacharyasz] Friedenthal was born at Jaroslaw and studied at Berlin. He numbered among Moses Mendelssohn's circle, and took part in his *Biur* ["Exegesis"] of the Torah. The exegesis of the "Book of Numbers" was written by him, and he also published the *Milot HaHigajon* ["Words of Logic"] by Maimonides with interpretation by Mendelssohn.

The students and teachers at the seminary were largely from Bohemia, Moravia and Germany, and found it difficult to adapt to life in Galicia. The young men entered the seminary with the expectation to

[Pages 191-192]

find teachers' posts at the end of their studies; at the institute they also received accommodation, provisions and financial help. Each of the students committed themselves to serve three years as teachers, and to reimburse all the expenses of their study period.[15] The pupils were greatly influenced by their instructors and turned more "heretical," an issue which gave rise to complaints from the community over the [students'] desecration of the Sabbath.

Friedenthal "believed" himself an educator and director, and submitted numerous requests to increase his salary as well as his "supervision and travel fees." He stood in for Homberg, in the latter's absence, and on his return they fought and quarrelled to the extent that in 1798 the supervisory authorities appointed Kazimierz Wohlfeil, principal of the general school within the town, to investigate the background to the conflicts. The investigation uncovered that students at the seminary were obliged to seek employ as the 81 Kreuzer a day did not suffice for their livelihood. Instead of choosing candidates from among the best students, Homberg preferred to accept the children of teachers he knew, and of his family, and Friedenthal objected to it.

To set–up the seminary's budget which existed solely on taxes paid from the Jews' taxation, Friedenthal proposed to impose a 50 Florin annual fee on every "Minyan." In 1793, the pay was reduced to 25 Florin (Lwów had 41 Minyanim).

The authorities were dissatisfied with the seminary's teaching results and highlighted their derogatory opinion in a report to the Vienna authorities. They complained in particular over irregularities and over the escapes of pupils from the institute. The responsibility was naturally laid at the door of Aron Friedenthal. The authorities wondered about the sudden decline in the number of pupils, of whom only one remained in 1798. On 27th September 1798, the Vienna authorities demanded an explanation from the Governor "Why is there only one student in the Jewish teachers' seminary?"[16]

The number of pupils in the girls' school remained constant, on the other hand, and the headmistress, Dornbach, was even granted full recognition by the Governor.

The authorities had reached the conclusion that "the teachers themselves are guilty of the errors and weaknesses at the schools, and for the objections of the parents." To improve the situation they ordered to determine the identity of the culprits and to dismiss them.[17]

The authorities relied on information submitted by the teachers Joel Turnau, Samson Popper and Benjamin Grünbaum, who pointed out the obstacles which inhibited the progress within Lwów's schools, and which attracted the objections of the congregation.[18]

Once the Jews realised that Homberg influenced Kaiser Franz I to agree to impose the candle tax, they loathed him. The trial revealed that the national tax lessees ("*Lichtverpächter*"), Salomon Popper and Tobias [Tuvia] Steinberg, paid him 2% of the net income.[19]

In 1801, to evade the legal enquiries which were submitted against him, Homberg decided to leave Galicia and go to Vienna. Here he found a protector and advocate in Graf [von] Rottenhan, who valued his performance in the field of education, and suggested to transfer him to Kraków, the capital of West Galicia. But according to Turnau's informing, the Emperor ordered to return him to Lwów. Homberg submitted a medical certificate stating that he had to stay in Vienna due to ill health. The Court–

cabinet did not accept his pretext and ordered him to return to Lwów. Homberg approached the kingdom's Council (*Staatsrat*), where his request was granted and he remained in Vienna, thus ending his educational activity in Galicia. The authorities accepted that he "had been accused by his own people for immoral and dishonest actions in his post as chief inspector over the Jewish schools of eastern Galicia."[20]

His influence on Galicia's Jewry was marked by the textbook *Bnei Zion* ["Children of Zion"] (1812), on which the regional office tested each bride and groom, for their attainment of a marriage certificate. Homberg's departure brought no change in the attitude of the Lwów Jewish community to schools. On 26[th]June 1806, Kaiser Franz I affected the teachers' seminary which was closed down together with all the schools. In 1806, 389 Jewish children attended Lwów's Jewish schools, it is unknown however, how many pupils graduated from the seminary and chose to become teachers. The schools' fund of 259,088 Florins which had been collected from the Jews' taxation, was entered into the general schools' fund of Galicia (Galizischer Normalschulfond).

Once the schools had closed down and the Jews were released of the need to obtain their qualification as a condition to acquire a marriage certificate, they were hit with a new adverse edict. Instead of the school test, those who wanted a marriage certificate were now required to pass a religious examination, based on Herz Homberg's *Bnei Zion* (: Ein religiös–moralistisches Lehrbuch für die Jugend israelitischer Nation) which had been approved as textbook for the Jewish schools of Austria, by order of the Emperor. The examinations were conducted by a regional Committee made up of the regional clerk, the municipal governor and the rabbi or the religious teacher. To avoid the inconvenience of acquiring the licence demanded by the new edict,

[Pages 193-194]

marriages were arranged covertly. The couples were obligated to purchase the book at two Gulden.

In 1806, parents were granted total freedom regarding education, and the general schools were naturally open to them. Only rarely did Jewish children attend general schools. One such was Izak Reuben Pinkas, who was admitted to secondary school [Gymnasium] and was even granted permission to appear in his Jewish outfit. His impoverished parents were unable to purchase the school uniform for him. The wealthy Jews did not wish to support him due to their contempt for the secular schools. In October 1787, he turned to Kaiser Joseph II to request his assistance. His request was passed on to the studies' commission of the Court–cabinet which granted him a new pupil's uniform. A few Jews also studied at Lwów University. The students Salomon Wolf and Moses Piper even received an annual scholarship from the Jewish Fund (*Domestikalfond*) of 50 Florins, which rose to 100 Florins in 1797.

As it happens, the first candidate who graduated from the University of Lwów with a doctorate degree, was Jewish.[21]

* *

Unlike Brody or Tarnopol [Ternopil], Lwów was not in the vanguard of the Enlightenment movement, and only few of its circles were influenced by it. Lwów's early pioneers of the Enlightenment were Homberg, Friedenthal and the teachers, and to some extent also the officials who mostly came from Bohemia, the birth place of Homberg and his friends.

Even prior to the Enlightenment, however, there were at Lwów a few individuals who strove to acquire a general education. It is worth noting that in the middle of the 18th century even among rabbinical circles there were visible ambitions for knowledge of secular subjects. In his youth at Zamosc, Rabbi Salomon ben Mojzesz Chelma (1720–1781) acquired a wide knowledge of secular sciences: Philosophy, Mathematics, and Natural Sciences. In 1761, he published the book *Merkevet HaMishne*, an interpretation of Maimonides's *HaJad Hachazaka* ["The Strong Hand"], where in the introduction he specifically stressed the need – even from the religious aspect – to engage in secular sciences, which were the sole means by which ambiguous areas of the Talmud might be resolved. He was one of the first rabbis to be interested in secular sciences and to encourage their study.[22] In that vein he also influenced his pupils during his 1772–1777 years at Lwów's rabbinate.

By the middle of the eighteenth century an increased interest to examine the Hebrew grammar spread even among Lwów's [Jewish] scholarly circles. Rabbi Aron–Mojzesz [Ahron–Moses] ben Cwi [Tzvi] Lwów (also known as Graiding) composed a grammar book in verse, titled *Shirah Chadasha* (Żółkiew 1764), as well as a complete grammar *Ohel Mosche* [Moses's Tent] (Żółkiew 1765).

In the nineties, after the Austrian occupation, Rabbi Pinkas. Eliahu ben Mejer Wilno [Vilna][23] wrote "*Sefer HaBrit Hashalem* which includes all world wisdom and knowledge. Enclosed in it are Torah innovations, morals and the true wisdom, and the details of its content are entered in the second title–page… Written by our teacher and rabbi, the sage, sound, artless, honest and God–fearing Rabbi Pinkas Eliahu, son of that righteous *Tzadik* of blessed memory, our teacher and rabbi, Rabbi Mejer of the holy community of Wilno, may God protect it." The first part contained information on Geography, Natural sciences and Physics according to eighteenth–century discoveries. The second part discussed "Man who rises above all creatures." His views were rooted in the teachings of the Kabbalists, our master, Rabbi Izak Lurie Askenazy [Aszkenassy], and his disciple Chaim Vital, and he unveiled his aspiration to reveal how Man could attain the Holy Spirit, even in our lifetime.

Pinkas Eliahu Horowitz (known as Otor) was one of the first exponents of the Enlightenment in Galicia and Poland. Born at Lwów on 23rd February 1765, he wandered in Poland and Germany before settling at Lwów and later at Buczacz. There he began writing his book *Sefer HaBrit*, but due to ill health he moved to Lwów and lived in the house of his wealthy follower and supporter, Nachman Reiss. He left for Pressburg [Bratislava] where, at the house of his friend Ber Oppenheimer, he finished his book and published it at Bryn in 1797.

At first he wished to publish the book "in my mother tongue, which is the everyday tongue spoken by the Jews of Poland". Affected by the French Encyclopedists, the book was written in a clear style and in the spirit of tradition and the fundamentals of religion. His goal was to inculcate knowledge and natural sciences in the Jewish population. Having no knowledge of foreign languages himself, he stated that his friend Ber Oppenheimer[24] "read to me the contents of the Nations' books written in their languages, and everything he read to me I wrote down. First, from every foreign language I wrote down on paper in my mother tongue, and from there to the book in the Holy tongue."[25]

His book *Divrei Emet* included also remarks on actual Jewish life in Poland. He laid special stress on the masses' lamentable situation, and the superstitions they latched on to. He also condemned the education in Poland where children were not taught any crafts, and every father wanted his son to be a rabbi or a rabbinical judge. Those incapable of attaining such status turned into toddlers' teachers, and since "The number of Torah teachers is greater than that of pupils, they only earn half the salaries and there is no bread or dress in their homes"[26] and they too joined the unemployed. Therefore, there was need to alter the education and teach the youth crafts to refute the

[Pages 195-196]

Nations' misconception that the Jews were not engaged in work but only in trade, and spur hatred of the Gentiles. The means of employment and the vocations of the Jewish masses had to change.

His book included also comprehensive information on the philosophy of Immanuel Kant, who used his rationale to contradict the methods of Wolff and Leibniz. His writing *"Ahavat Re'im veChovat Chibat Chevrat Min HaEnoshi"* ["Love of Friends and Duty of Affection of Mankind"] was also affected by his epoch. Although he objected to heretical thoughts which spread throughout Galicia under the influence of Berlin scholars, and he took a clear stand on tradition, his book met with objections and derision from orthodox circles due to his aim to stimulate interest in secular sciences. And indeed, his book fulfilled an important role in advancing the education of Jewish youths who read it in secret and stealth and drew their secular education from it. Its influence spread beyond Galicia, to Poland and Hungary, the Balkan States and the East, and it was also translated into Ladino, the spoken language of Sephardic Jews.

In his latter years, Pinkas ben Eliahu resided at Kraków and died there on 21st April 1821.

As he mentioned in his book *Divrei Emet*, he had also authored the books: *Matmonei Mistarim* ["Hidden Treasures"] the secret combination of letters "Ta'am Etzo" ["Flavour of his Tree"] on the book *Etz Chaim* ["Tree of Life"] by Rabbi Chaim Vital; and "Mitzvot Tovim" on the reason for the Mitzvot [commandments]. Those written essays remained unpublished. Indeed, one need mention the fact that the book *Sefer HaBrit* boosted the youths' desire for education, despite the fact that it had not yet reached the Enlightenment founded by Mendelssohn. While Homberg and his teaching staff strove to disseminate the Enlightenment, their tactics largely undermined their efforts due to their "constant requests" from the authorities to help them in implementing changes to education and culture. In that fashion they aroused the hatred of the Jewish masses, even of the few Lwów supporters of the Enlightenment.

The fact that the tax lessees who oppressed the people were also considered *Maskilim* ["Hebrew Enlighteners"] – since they had to understand the national–language, and be literate in German – did not enhance any sympathy for the Enlightenment. That was perhaps also the reason for the secret meetings and closed circles of Lwów's early *Maskilim*, to avoid arousing public rage against them.

1816, when Rabbi Cwi Ornstein the rabbi of Lwów boycotted the *Maskilim*, and Salomon Jehuda Rappoport published the pamphlet against the Hasidism, saw the start of open conflict against the *Maskilim*. In the years 1772–1816 hardly any literary output by the *Maskilim* of Lwów can be reported – unlike the state of Enlightenment at Brody.

During the early period, Lwów's few *Maskilim* focused on reading and on the study of secular knowledge and foreign languages, especially German which also impacted on the Austrian officials in maintaining social contact with the *Maskilim* and drawing their support for the Habsburg kingdom, in which they succeeded.

The officials, the school teachers as well as the military officers, willingly taught the *Maskilim* and supplied them with German literary reading material. The schools and university graduates contributed much to the dissemination of the

Enlightenment, and influenced the youths from well to do homes to adapt to European customs, and in particular, to remove the traditional clothing and exchange those for clothes such as those worn by the Ashkenazi [German]. Consequently, the *Maskilim* of Galicia were labelled "German" (Ashkenazi). The change of clothing stirred up the orthodox Jews since one recalls how the Jews of Galicia fought against the 1789 ruling which dictated that from 1795 onwards, all, apart from rabbis, had to adopt the Gentiles' dress code, which was only annulled after their representatives petitioned Kaiser Leopold II.

The period of the Enlightenment began in fact only in the first decade of the nineteenth century.

[Page 362]

Notes: – CHAPTER 12
All notes in square brackets [ ] were made by the translator.

1.   The Lwów Census of 1782 showed that there were 60 teachers of Torah, 21 of whom in Cheder for young children, with 105 assistants (*Behelfer*) and 735 pupils, 22 Chumash teachers with 280 pupils, 11 Gemarah teachers with 132 pupils, six adjudicators' teachers with 36 pupils, 1,183 pupils altogether. Income from all the Cheders came to 20,150 Gulden, and only 43 pupils' education was paid for by "Talmud–Torah" which paid their tuition fee of 412 Gulden. The salary of a Torah teacher for young children was 175 Gulden "for a period" including the salary of the tutor, Chumash teacher got 220 Polish Gulden, Gmarah teacher 216 Gulden, and adjudicators' teacher 304 Polish Gulden.
(*see* article by Dr. Abraham Jacob Brauer "Inspector of Cheders at Lwów in 1782" *Reshumot*, Vol. 1. Tel–Aviv, 1925. pp. 419–428. The census certificate was published by Dr. Gershom Wolf in *Zeitschrift für Geschichte der Juden in Deutschland*, Vol. V., pp. 147–148.
According to Wolf, however, the Chumash teachers numbered 14, (According to Brauer 22), 280 pupils (according to Brauer 484); The 735 pupils in Cheders included also girls, according to Wolf.
In 1795, 85 Torah teachers were engaged in Lwów's Cheders, and 183 as tutors, and there were 1,574 pupils. The salary of the teachers and the helpers came to 13,420 Gulden.

2.   The term "Trivial" schools was derived from the teaching programme which included reading, writing and arithmetic (*Trivium*).

3.   Michael Stöger Loc. cit. 1 prg. 70, p. 113.

4.   Skizze einer allgemeinen Judenordnung für Galizien. Ein Gesetzentwurf aus prg. 69.
IV. T. 11 Carton 2579 Galizisches Judensystem 1785–1790.

[Page4 363-364]

5.   The pamphlet was published at Lwów and by order of the authorities was sent to all the communities. Published eariler in "Hame'asef," p. 227. Mentioned in S. Assaf *Sources of the History of Education in Israel*. Tel–Aviv, 1925, Vol. 1, pp. 250–253.

6.   Status Salariorum der jüdischen Normalschullehrer mit Ende 1790.

7.   Archives of the Ministry of the Interior
Galizien Prot. 1791, No. 46 September.

8.   Archives of the Ministry of the Interior:
IV T 7. Jüdische Schulen e.a. 1793; 68.

9.   IV T 7. Sept. 1797; 59.

10.   IV T 7. Jüdische Schulen 28/XI 1793, No. 79; 102.

11.   IV T 7. 24 Jan. 1794. 67.

12.   IV T 7. Jüdische Schulen October 1795. 9.

13.   The teacher Joel Turnau denounced Homberg, claiming that he pocketed the funds intended for buying equipment, and that he took bribes from teachers in order to raise their salaries. A separate affair was the dispute between Aron Friedenthal and Homberg, who accused him of receiving bribes, negligent work, etc.
Archive of the Lwów Commission, Judensachen Fasz 11.
The teachers' loathing of Homberg was reflected in the fact that when submitting their proposals, they asked the authorities not to pass these to him; as for example the January 1794 proposal by the Drohobych [Drohobycz] teacher Zeckendorf, for improvements in the lives of Galician Jews.
Archive of the Ministry of the Interior, Vienna, IV T 2 ad Carton 2580. 1792–1804.

14.   Prot. Galizien 1793, No. 631; 1793, No. 23.

15.   Archive of the Ministry of the Interior, IV T 7. 1794, 59.

16.   IV T 7. December 1789, 109.

17.   IV T 7. Juli 1795, 43.

18.   IV T 7, Dec. 1791, 67.

The matter is clear, since the teachers undertook also spying roles. Thus for example, Aron Ornstein, the school director at Bochnia, informed that in the synagogues there was a large number of silver objects which were not required. Instantly, the government demanded that they be handed over in exchange of "loan certificates" for the war against France. Prot. Galizien. Sept. 1796, 145.

19.   Dr. M. Bałaban: Herz Homberg; *Z historja Żydów w Polsce*, Warszawa 1920, p.205.

20.   A. F. Pribram: *Urkunden und Akten zur Geschichte der Juden in Wien*. Wien 1918, II, No. 325, pp. 161–172.

21.   F. Kratter: *Briefe über den jetzigen Zustand von Galizien*. Leipzig 1786, Part II, p. 57 remark.

22.   Dr. M. Weissberg: *Die Neuhebr[äische] Aufklärungs Literatur in Galizien*. Wien 1898, pp. 81–83.

23.   According to Mejer [Max] Halevi

Letteris, Rabbi Pinkas Eljahu Vilna [Wilno], author of *Sefer HaBrit*, was born at Lwów; see: History of my dear father, parent, teacher, light and salvation, the wise Rabbi Gerschom Halevi Letteris of blessed memory, in *Bikurim* by Naftali Keller, Vienna, 1864, p. 51. Gershom Bader (*Medinah veChachameha*, New–York, 1934, p.80) states that his father Mejer and his mother Jente were born at Vilnius [Wilno], and that in 1765, wishing to settle at Buczacz, they had reached Galicia via Lwów, where Pinkas–Eliahu was born. He heard that detail from his grandfather who had known Pinkas personally.

24.   Ber Bernhard Oppenheim (1753–21/9/1853) born at, and citizen of Pressburg [Bratislava], author of the Responsa *Mei Be'er*, contributed also to *Bikureh HaItim*, his translation of Herder's poem "Sonne und Mond" Vol. IV, 1823, pp. 138–141, as well as "Poem of Gratitude" to the minister Leopold Graf Pálffy (Vol. IV, pp.175–179)

25.   *Sefer HaBrit*, Bryn, 1797. Intro. p. 4.

26.   *Divrei Emet*, p. 41.

[Pages 197-198]

Chapter 13: The Reign of Kaiser Franz I

Translated by Myra Yael Ecker

Edited by Ingrid Rockberger

The changes to Lwów and the Jews. Napoleon I's Eretz Israel plan. Napoleon's victory celebrations. Jewish immigration from the conquered territories and its effect. The accommodation issues and difficulties. The authorities' regulations. The 1812 Census. The Joseph Schwamberg Affair. The tax–lessees' takeover of the community. The community elections of 1817. Failure of the opposition's appeal. The economic state according to the 1820 census. Demands to alleviate the tax burden. Issues with improvements to the way of life. Menachem Schneier's proposals. The issue of traditional Jewish clothing.

Early in the nineteenth century, Galicia experienced many political changes which also affected the life development process of Lwów's Jews. In 1796, the Austrians conquered Kraków, where they remained till 1815. During 1815–1816, Kraków and its environs functioned as an independent republic. In 1809, Lwów was temporarily conquered by the Russians, Napoleon's allies. During 1796–1809, the land between the Vistula [Wisla] and the Bug, which included Lublin, Zamosc [Zamość] and Sandomierz, was also attached to Galicia. During 1809–1815, the Russians also ruled over the Tarnopol region, and till 1848, Bukowina too was linked to Galicia.

During Galicia's transition years, the town of Lwów was ruled by multiple authorities. On the one hand were the Austrian authorities with an administrative organization of Czechs and Germans, and on the other, the Polish population sympathized with the national movement led by Kościuszko and the legionnaires. At the clubs established by the advocates Węgliński, Nowakowski and Walerian Dzieduszycki, help agencies for the legionnaires, organized and recruited volunteers to the battalions of Napoleon whom they considered Poland's saviour.

Among the Jews of Lwów some were also attracted by Napoleon who, in 1799, had published a proclamation to the Jews promising them that were they to assist him, he would re–establish a Jewish State in Eretz Israel. The Jews of Lwów were influenced by him, and one of the newspapers stated explicitly "A written proposal (Napoleon's Pronouncement) disseminated throughout the world and encourages the Jews to return to Jerusalem, has already much influenced the Jews of Lwów. They frequent restaurants a great deal to read newspapers, and one sees them huddle together, whisper and consult over their travel to Jerusalem".[i]

It is hard to imagine, however, that the political events stirred up the Jews of Lwów. They were still far removed from any public interaction especially with strangers. In 1809, just when the polish army victoriously entered Lwów under the command of Prince Jozef Poniatowski after conquering Zamosc, the Jews welcomed him, not so much with genuine enthusiasm as from resentment towards the Austrian authorities.[ii] The community of Lwów sent food and spirits to the Polish encampment and collected funds for the army.

The Polish army organized, amongst other things, a national rule which included a department for Jewish affairs managed by Jan Tarnowski. One of the Polish government's early acts was to collect half of the 1809 tax from the Christian as well as the Jewish population.[iii] They were unable to complete that act, however, when on 15th June 1809 an Austrian army brigade entered Lwów to the enthusiastic welcome of the German citizens. They were followed by the Russians who at the time were Napoleon's allies, and remained at Lwów till the Austrians captured it again on 14th December 1809.

Under the Austrian rule life returned to normal and the Jews, together with all the empire's nations, were pleased with Napoleon's defeat (1814), and according to Mayor Lorenz, they participated in the celebration of that victory on 29th June 1814. They lit up the windows of their homes in celebration, and under the community's initiative a song of praise in German was published, entitled "The sentiments of Lwów's Jewish congregation on 29th June 1814" ("Die Gefühle der Israelitischen Gemeinde in Lemberg am 29 Juni 1814"). In the evening, a celebratory prayer was said at the synagogue, and Rabbi Jakob Ornstein delivered a sermon which was published in the addendum to *Shir Hilulim* ["Song of Praise"] which the school choir also sang in German.

With the emergence of a new policy, the composition of Lwów's Jewish population underwent changes due to the increased number of Jews from the new territories whose economic situation there was quite difficult. By moving to Galicia's capital, they had hoped to improve their economic as well as their social–cultural situation. A large number of young people in particular, came to Lwów hoping for the opportunity to study.

[Pages 199-200]

That population movement affected the social and cultural integration of Lwów's Jewish circles. To begin with, the new elements adversely affected community life, especially in respect of accommodation, income and the way of life.

From 1794 to 1808, 998 Jewish families which numbered 2,512 souls, arrived at Lwów from elsewhere,[1] and Lwów's Jewish population evolved between 1796 and 1826, as follows:

Year	Jews
1796	12,486
1800	13,412
1810	14,979
1815	16,125
1820	17,931
1825	18,689
1826	19,277[2]

The authorities were surprised at the rise in the number foreign Jews, and took measures to curtail the increase. The municipality also took steps, by sending memorandums to the Governor demanding that he reduce their residential zone. In the past, as previously mentioned, the municipality had already tried to dispossess the Jews of their shops and flats within the town.

Nevertheless, in 1795 the Jewish community responded that the area in which they could dwell had been extended through the legal purchase of houses. Removing the Jews to the Żółkiew and Kraków Quarters would be economically detrimental to themselves as well as to the Christian house and shop owners who would lose large sums in rent.

The dispute with the municipality over the dwelling rights continued for many years.

Under pressure from the townspeople and the Governor, the Viennese authorities gave strict orders to delay the flow of Jews into Lwów, and to forbid the marriage of men with young single women and widows from outside the town, in order to prevent an increase in the Jewish population.

In accordance with the Kaiser's order of 4th April 1805, only in exceptional circumstances were the authorities permitted to grant entry licences to teachers at the Jewish schools as well as to specialised craftsmen in essential industries, where no comparably qualified person was found in town.[3] The order was published in a printed message that warned against the entry of foreign Jews, under threat of fines or beatings. Under those circumstances the Jews who resided in the Brody and Halicz [Halych] suburbs were obliged to move to the Żółkiew and Kraków suburbs.

In 1807, there were 14,371 Jews among the 43,614 citizens of Lwów. The prohibition of entry to Jews into the town is clear from the 1812 census: of the 3,709 Jewish families residing at Lwów, 7,237 were men and 7,736 were women, totalling 14,973 souls. During five years the Jewish population only increased by 602 souls. The number of Jews in the entire Lwów region was 4,420 families, of whom 8,764 were men and 9,288 were women, totalling 18,052 souls.[4]

In 1811, the issue of the rise in the Jewish population was again addressed by the authorities, this time for sanitary reasons. According to the Governor's report, Lwów had 4,436 Jewish families with 30,000 people who resided in 314 houses, in which there were 1,974 rooms and 629 cubicles, that is to say, 8–12 persons per room or cubicle.[5]

Apart from the accommodation question on which the municipality focused, the Governor, in accordance with the Order (patent) of 17th May 1789, also picked on Jewish issues in the neighbouring small towns which had previously been under the regional offices' jurisdiction.

The municipality appealed against the Order, claiming that the issue was not its concern, and that handling such matters would place the municipality under the jurisdiction of the regional office, in contravention of the town's constitution. On 22nd June 1826, the Vienna authorities approved the Governor's decision of 13th January 1826, to centralize all of Lwów's Jewish issues in the hands of the municipality, including

1.   To supervise the apportioning, as well as the collecting, of Jewish taxes.

2.   To deal with complaints by Jews against the supervisors.

3.   To register the Jews who were in Lwów.[6]

Due to congestion as well as difficulties from the townspeople and the authorities, the housing conditions in the Jewish Quarters worsened daily. During the Austrian rule, Lwów turned into a town of trade and industry to which new citizens flocked from all over Galicia. The townspeople did not tolerate the invasion of Lwów by the new crowds who would endanger the citizens' trade and crafts. The authorities too were against the rise in the Jewish population, and plotted to add further restrictions which were set in the Orders (patent) of 1793, 1797.

At the beginning of the 19th century, the situation was as follows: the Jews were permitted to reside at the Kraków and Żółkiew suburbs without restrictions; those residing at any of the other neighbourhoods, had to move there. The Jews were permitted to reside within the town but they could not purchase without permission, property on Szkocka, Ruska, Serbska and Nowa Streets, or in the adjoining alleys, except for special circumstances where the house–owners owed them sums equal to the value of the house.[7] They were permitted to keep shops on Ruska, Szkocka and Serbska Streets.

The authorities allowed for some exceptions: wholesalers who traded in foreign merchandise valued at 30,000 or 40,000 Gulden, were permitted to reside outside the Jewish Quarter,

[Pages 201-202]

and they had to be supervised by the municipality to ensure that a Jew whose assets were reduced, would move to the Jewish Quarter.[8]

Jews who owned houses outside the Jewish Quarter were granted an extension till 1803 to live in them, before moving with their families to the Jewish Quarters. They remained the house owners with the proviso that they did not let the accommodations or shops to Jews.

According to the 1825 census there were 25,117 inhabitants within the town, 954 of whom were Jews; the Halicz Quarter had 2,000 inhabitants, five of whom were Jews; the Kraków Quarter had 2,556 inhabitants, 1,247 of whom were Jews; the Brody Quarter had 1,256 inhabitants, five of whom were Jews; the Żółkiew Quarter had 3,033 inhabitants, 2,001 of whom were Jews.[9]

In order to check the growth of the population foreign Jews were not permitted to move to Lwów and register with the community, after 24th July 1804. In addition, Jews of Lwów were not permitted to marry foreign Jews, and any contravention would lead to a 100 Ducat fine.

On 22nd January 1805, the mayor of Lwów Franz Anton Lorenz, published an Order imposing a 12 Ducat fine on house owners who let flats to Jews expelled from Lwów, or not permitted to reside in the Christian Quarter. Any informer on such cases,[10] was promised a fee of 25 Florins. The Order also forbade any exchange of flats between a family at Lwów and one residing outside the town, except for exceptional cases of specialist craftsmen, printers etc.[11] The restriction also did not apply to teachers who came to Lwów and had been employed by the Jewish schools.[12]

Adopted children who had reached the age of majority, had to leave the town and return to the community whence they had come. (In the years 1814–1816, the Jews of Lwów had only adopted 14 children). The authorities considered the adoption of children a ploy to "smuggle" them into Lwów and increase the Jewish population. In August 1815, the Governor[13] proposed to the Vienna authorities to permit the adoption of a Jewish child in exchange for two large families who had left Lwów. The Court–office refused and gave instruction to follow the existing ruling. On 16th February 1816, the Governor sent the Kaiser a special request to delay any plea for the adoption of Jewish children until the approval of the new Jewish regulations being discussed by the government. The Emperor–office's reply stressed that in the previous two years only 14 children had been adopted, and that that could not be considered a threat of increasing Lwów's Jewish community, and that consequently there was no reason for the proposed change.[14]

When a Jew was permitted to move to Lwów, he had to provide an exit certificate from his community and a declaration from Lwów's community committee that there was no reason to refuse his acceptance. In addition, two families from Lwów would have to forego their right of residence and would have to leave the town. The transfer of the Jew was granted only after the two families who were leaving, had provided a certificate of acceptance from the other community.

The prohibitions and restrictions also led to corruption. The community officials, especially the managers of the population register, were bribed to enter foreign Jews in the population list. The registrar Ber Chaim Modlinger in particular, grew rich from such transactions, as was demonstrated in his trial of 1817.

A further issue arose when the *Maskilim* [Hebrew Enlighteners], dressed in European clothes, approached the authorities with requests to allow them to reside in a non–Jewish Quarter. In many cases the authorities agreed to their move, on condition that not only the head of the family but all its members, men and women, be dressed in the European fashion. In October 1815, when Joseph Schwamberg who wore European clothes requested a licence to reside in a non–Jewish Quarter, the police rejected his request so long as his wife and the rest of his family did not cease wearing the Jewish traditional clothes. In March 1816 Schwamberg renewed his request, now appended by a police certificate that his entire family wore European clothes, but again his request was refused. He then appealed and provided proof that his son Izak was studying medicine at Vienna, that his second son, Karl, was working for a Vienna trading house, that his two daughters were enrolled at a Benedictine convent school, that he and his entire family had rid themselves of Jewish habits, that he was despised by the Jews and was unable to reside among them. In his business too, he was associated with trading houses outside the Jewish Quarter. In his written request he also stressed that Jews from Lwów: Johann Seligmann, Paul Mendelssohn and Zadok Hirsch Goldberg, had already been granted transfer licences. With the Governor's recommendation, the Vienna Court–office agreed to grant Schwamberg a licence to transfer into town.

The municipality did not approve of Jews moving to Christian Quarters. In January 1818 the townspeople complained to the authorities that Jews stayed in town, married and constituted a general danger. The authorities however rejected those accusations and demands as exaggerations. On the contrary, in September 1818 a number of Jewish merchants who excelled in cleanliness and order, who had replaced their Jewish garments and who adopted a way of life similar to the rest of the population, were granted permission to reside in town, outside of the Jewish Quarter.[15]

[Pages 203-204]

The community leaders did not accept the restrictions and made every effort to get the authorities to ease the terms of entering and residing within the town. The community leaders appointed by those who paid the candle tax, were supporters of the candle tax lessee. He was in charge of granting certificates to the candle tax payers as well as appointing the leaders and elders. He was also in a position to issue fake certificates,[16] and had a deciding vote in the elections in which the candidates were usually the lessees themselves. Although after each election appeals were submitted to the authorities by those opposing the lessees, those appeals remained unresolved.[17]

Till 1817, the community leaders were Joel Rappoport, Lieber and Rosenthal. Their objectors, Leib Bałaban, Kalman Berger and a number of the community members, claimed that when they had left the community before the new elections, they had taken some of the community tax money, for their own use, leaving the community indebted to the kingdom's treasury by that sum.[18]

Those accusations enabled the tax lessees to elect their representatives with ease. In 1817, the elected community–elders were Józef Pineles, Gershon Kurzer, Chaim Blumengarten, Berl Schönfeld and Chaim Joschoua Glanz, four of whom were in partnership with the candle tax lessees. A group of known merchants, headed by Joseph Barach,[19] Schmelkes, Waldberg, Goldenblum, Ahlenberg, Joel Rappoport and Leib Mendrokhowicz opposed those elected, and presented a counter list which included Hersz Rektor, Abel Fischler, Nathan Sokal, Aron Chaim Rappoport, the father of Salomon Jehuda Rappoport who for several years had been an appraiser for the authorities, and Moses Waag.

Forgery tricks and the lessees' hoaxes led to the list's rejection. The group of merchants did not accept the situation however, and appealed to the Governor stressing that the official candidates were corrupt, informers and devoid of education. In their written appeal they pointed out that Józef Pineles, who headed the list, had collected 13,000 Gulden for the establishment of a Jewish agricultural settlement in 1806, funds which he did not hand over to the community, and that he faced a criminal investigation; that Gershon Kurzer was a man devoid of a conscience, rude, and a known informer who had been in jail since 1810, was nonetheless a partner of the tax lessees; that Chaim Blumengarten was a veteran bartender devoid of any education; that Berl Schönfeld was a known loan–shark.

The appeal prompted the Governor to order new elections to take place in March 1818. Nevertheless, the results remained unchanged. Again, the supporters of the tax lessees were voted in by an overwhelming majority, with the opponents failing completely.[20] Despite the population's loathing of the lessees who in 1808 requested permission to reside outside the Jewish Quarter for fear of revenge and retribution, their influence on the community's affairs increased with help from the authorities and they controlled the community until the revolution of 1848. The increased loathing of the lessees was such that in 1808 the authorities were obliged to grant them permission to reside outside the Jewish Quarter, since they were been in constant fear of their lives.

The community's powers and scope of transactions remained unchanged apart from a rise in the candle tax: in 1800, by 50%; in 1806, by another increase. The meat tax rose by 50%; in 1802 the price of 1/2 kg. Kosher meat was 19 Kreuzer; 12 Kreuzer in provincial towns; non–Kosher meat cost 7 1/2 Kreuzer in Lwów, and 5–7 in provincial towns. Apart from the meat price and tax, the Jewish consumer also paid expenses and interest to the tax lessees.

Besides the general taxes, the Jews paid marriage tax, tolerance tax, Kosher meat tax, candle tax, Minyanim tax as well as a tax on the building of synagogues and to establish cemeteries.

The system of taxation was based on personal tax (Klassensteuer [class taxation]) which included: 1. A special tax on house and land, 2. Head of family tax, 3. Poll tax, which was subject to change. In 1802, the Jews paid 112,000 Florins which was apportioned according to family and property. In 1804, a five–florin tax was levied on every head of family as an overall rather than a personal amount. In 1806, an increase of 30 Kreuzer per Gulden of tax was introduced. Under the 20th July 1824 Order (Decree), however, besides income tax an overall tax was levied on all of Galicia's Jews, totalling 836,000 Florins.

Besides tax collecting, the community was also responsible for the upkeep of the charitable institutions. With the authorities setting more stringent sanitary standards, 18 Jewish prisoners were employed to clean the Jewish Quarter, each at a monthly salary of six Gulden. Due to the spread of disease in the Jewish Quarter, the sanitary authorities fined the community heavily for neglect of cleanliness in the streets.

From 1801, the Jewish community kept a Jewish hospital with a doctor, two surgeons, a midwife and several medics. The hospital also kept two bathhouses which were let out. The hospital's management was appointed by the community and the expenses were paid for from the

[Pages 205-206]

bathhouses' leasing fees as well as from donations from the meat tax lessees and from individuals.

Ten police inspectors (*Polizeirevisoren*): five Christian and five Jewish were employed to maintain order within the Jewish Quarter. According to Lwów's management report, the Jewish inspectors fulfilled "useful and successful services, not only in Jewish affairs but also in other matters." As a result, in 1824 their annual salary was raised from 200 to 300 Florins.[21]

One of the community's special enterprises was the collection of funds for Eretz Israel. The dispatch of funds to Eretz Israel was closely monitored by the authorities who forced Lwów's elders and its rabbi, Rabbi Izak Ornstein, to submit a detailed report on each dispatch.

In May 1818, the community–elders submitted a complaint against the elder Ber Chaim Modlinger, known for his employ as registrar of the citizens' census, who collected funds for the Jews of Eretz Israel.[22] It is not known what the authorities did about that complaint, nevertheless, during the inquiry it was revealed that the funds were collected by one Kolikower. who had used receipts signed by Rabbi Jakob Meschulam Ornstein, and by Lwów's community secretary, Ber Chaim Modlinger. According to Abraham Kahane's report to the authorities, Modlinger had pressured him and three other Jews to emigrate to Eretz Israel, and to collect funds for that purpose. An anonymous report was also submitted claiming that Ber Chaim Modlinger and Rabbi Meschulam Ornstein engaged in collecting funds for Eretz Israel, but the inquiry was repealed due to lack of evidence.

The economic composition of Lwów's Jews had not undergone great change. In town, the shopkeepers and the peddlers, who were particularly active during the fairs ("Kontracts") which took place annually during May and October, were still there. The fairs kept going till the arrival of the railway and communication with the West.

The 1820 census contains interesting facts about the Jews of Lwów, their occupations and professions. The entire town population numbered 45,162, of which 17,932 (38.7%) were Jewish. Of the 2,140 who were engaged in trade and industry, 1,308 were Christian, 832 were Jewish. The percentage of Jews engaged in trade was 55.2%, and in crafts 24.5%. Among the 262 merchants, 200 were Jews, and among the 290 shopkeepers, 265 were Jews. Out of the 381 bartenders, restaurant and coffee house owners, 58 were Jewish.[23] Next to the restaurants were also hotels and simple hostelries where impoverished nobles, and Jewish merchants stayed during their stay at Lwów in the winter months, for the "Kontracts" season.

Among the occupations of Jews one notes salaried employees, servants, coachmen and porters who were known for their agility and honesty.[24] Lazar Zucker and Izak Heilpern were known coaching–contractors for the route Lwów–Olmütz [Olomouc]–Vienna.

Among the 745 Jewish craftsmen, 249 were tailors, 22 glaziers, 51 bakers, 133 furriers, 34 silversmiths, 28 twiners, 19 bookbinders, 9 carpenters, 9 belt makers, 8 candle makers, 1 watchmaker, 28 goldsmiths (jewellers), 7 mead distillers, 3 weavers, 13 whitewashers, 3 blacksmiths, 3 cotton–wool processors, 8 upholsterers, 5 wax pourers, 1 printer, 3 brick–makers, 1 sock–maker, 2 mirror polishers, 3 hatters, 2 engravers, 1 shoemaker, 99 were engaged in other occupations such as: butchers, liquor distillers, soap makers, coppersmiths, carvers, woodcutters, painters [decorators], tanners, beer brewers, hairdressers.[25]

The wholesale trade from Vienna to Russia was in the hands of Jews. A number of Jewish wholesale traders from Lwów frequented the fairs at Leipzig. By and by, however, they were displaced by Jews from Brody who in time represented Galicia at the fairs. In 1829 for example, of the 226 merchants representing Galicia at the Leipzig fair, all were Jews from Brody.

Among the wholesalers one knows of Moses Pinkas who was in charge of most of eastern Galicia's timber trade, which he transported to Danzig by rafts along the Vistula [Wisla]. Lwów's Jewish timber merchants kept large warehouses at Józefów and Krystynopol [Czerwonogród] and supplied goods to Moses Pinkas and Joseph Mendel of Kraków, and to Izak Hirsch of Brody.[26]

Josef Mizys managed wholesale trade in wax, and Gabriel Reizes, in fur.

A number of Jews engaged in brokerage and in the maintenance of warehouses. Zadok Bałaban and Gezl were known as large–scale shop owners who supplied fashion items to Polish nobles of Galicia and Poland. There were also Jews who supplied the armed forces, among whom one knows of Izak–Ze'ev Rappoport, a wholesaler in tobacco, grains and salt. The authorities valued his economic operations, and backed him when Chaim Hainisch of Lwów reported him, and they proved that the denouncements against him were untrue, and that the Jewish merchants of Lwów benefitted the country[27] as suppliers, wholesalers and industrialists. At the time, several of Lwów's Jews took part in the development of industry, establishing workshops and the first factories, including the liquor factories of Leib Mimels and Fischel Dobs, Baczeles and Margulies, and a beer brewery of Bruner from Lwów. Large flour mills were also established by Jews.

[Pages 207-208]

The economic standing of the [Jewish] population was so depleted that the community requested a reduction in taxes. Even high government officers submitted reports stressing that the tax burden levied on the Jews was too heavy, and was considerably greater than the taxes levied on the rest of the population.[28]

In October 1816, the Lwów community requested that the Governor consider the situation of the Jews, and ease their tax burden. The memorandum highlighted that as an outcome of the wars the value of money bills had fallen and the assets of the wealthy had shrunk due to the restrictions barring them from the purchase of properties and estates, which had kept their value. Jewish trade plummeted when the relationship with Russia, the major buyers' market, was cut off by the Russians. The war had ruined the fundamental existence of Lwów's Jewish population and consequently it was unable to meet the tax burden.

Governor Hauer took no account of the community's arguments however, and rejected its request. That refusal to ease the taxes prevented any improvement in the economic situation of Lwów's Jews. Their standing was reduced year by year to such an extent that, according to the community commission, by 1817–1822 the number of those able to pay tax had fallen from 1800 to 900.

In its request the community pointed out to Kaiser Franz I the grim reality that a large number of heads of families who had previously paid taxes, could hardly support themselves while they and their families suffered hunger.

In 1821, the community's Jewish tax debt amounted to 39,419 Florins, and the general taxes debt amounted to 60,000 Florins.[29] Even then, the authorities rejected the request to ease their tax burden.[30]

The general economic reality of Galicia weighed heavily on the Jews' circumstances, especially due to the devaluation of the currency. The 20th December 1811 decree, reduced the value of banknotes (Bankzettel) by 20%.

The reduced credit and investment of funds was especially felt in the grain and timber trades, and it became difficult to export them to Danzig.

On numerous occasions in its messages to the Vienna authorities, the Galician *Sejm* pointed out the difficult economic situation. Prince [von] Metternich who due to his sudden illness spent an extended period at Lwów, also wrote to his wife that Galicia was a fertile country rich in natural resources, but that the lack of funds and transportation hindered export and led to an excessive reduction in the price of goods. The commissioner Prince [von] Lobkowitz, who became Governor in 1826, tried nonetheless to amend the economic situation by improvements, and he also recognized the injustice done to the Jews.

After years even the authorities had to recognized the reality, and enlightened officers awakened the central offices' attention to the reduced situation of the Jews of Galicia and of Lwów. By and by even the Vienna authorities took note that the policy of taxing the Jews to destruction had to stop. In 1830, the Court–cabinet (Hofkanzlei) proposed to abolish all the taxation on Jews, and place them financially on a par with the rest of the population, but the proposal was not approved by the Emperor, saying that the time had not yet come for such changes.[31] Most of the administrative staff considered the reduced state of the Jews, not due to external conditions –economic circumstances, taxation etc.– but due to their internal way of life.

The central authorities also debated the restrictions of habitation within Lwów and asked the Governor the following questions: 1. Should one continue to restrict the habitation of Lwów's Jews? 2. Should one annul the prohibition on acquiring houses and plots? and 3. Should one allow Jews to purchase houses in the Jewish Quarter from Christians?

The Governor replied in the positive to questions 2. and 3. only, stating that as for question 1., each case had to be considered on its own merits.

The Vienna Court–cabinet concluded that the attractive sections of town should be devoid of Jews. With regard to questions 2. and 3., it agreed with the Governor. The Governor's proposals of 12th December 1828 and of 26th March 1830 –regarding the reduction of Lwów's Jewish population, and the organization of the Jewish Quarters– were decided in the negative, since "after detailed consideration we have reached the conclusion that one need abandon the old system to turn the Jews into useful citizens through restrictions, and that it is preferable to turn them into useful citizens through religious, moral and intellectual education, and by and by eliminate the restrictions which would become redundant."[32]

The issue of amending the way of life of Galician Jews also occupied the authorities, just as it had in earlier periods. They accepted every proposal submitted to them, hoping to arrive at the right means to implement the alterations they were after. From time to time the Vienna officials troubled the Lwów Governor with demands for

[Pages 209-210]

suggestions that would at least accomplish the alterations they had achieved in Bohemia and Moravia.

There were inevitably some bothersome Jews who submitted endless proposals on the issue to the Governor. One of them, Menachem Schneier, submitted a programme in 1805 to turn the Jews into "productive, happy citizens." His intention was to receive the fare to Vienna and a licence to stay there in order to submit the details of his proposal, but the Governor replied that he could submit his proposal, in person, and it would be forwarded to Vienna. Already in October 1805, his programme was in front of the Court–advisor Reichmann, who considered it very interesting since for the first time he found "a true and unflattering description of the Jews and their character."

Schneier reported details of the children's education and its failings; he stressed specifically that the Talmud taught Jews to hate Christians; that the prayers included curses of non–Jews; that the education led to savagery and to distancing from the rest of the population. Change would come about through secular education of mixed Jewish and Christian youths; dissolving of Jewish schools; teaching the Torah in the German language; abolishing the Jewish traditional dress and forbidding sidecurls [payot] and beard; appointing a national Jewish elder (Überlandesältester), a *Maskil* [Hebrew Enlightener] who, as a governmental officer at an annual salary of 2,000 Florins, would represent the Jews. Apart from him one had to appoint a Christian clerk. Both would appoint Jewish commissars who would organize a census with an index card for each individual.

For administrative reasons, it was preferable for the municipality to have the authority over the Jews. Every community would be led by a single elder, apart from the towns of Lwów, Brody, Kraków and Lublin, where two elders would be appointed.[33]

The author of the programme, Menachem Schneier, was a Lwów restaurant owner, who had an adventurous past. He had been accused in the past of theft and burglary, found not guilty and placed under police supervision. He tried to insinuate himself into the community's committee and become a member, but he was expelled. It is unknown whether he associated with any Enlightenment circles. From time to time he bothered the authorities with his proposals which remained filed in clerks' desks. He was one of many bothersome characters who flooded the offices with suggestions and programmes "for the good of the Jews."

In 1813, talk among the clerical circles of Lwów and Vienna considered the need to improve the condition of the Jews of Galicia. The Court advisor, Johann Fidelis von Erggelet, wrote a comprehensive memorandum the principal conclusion of which was that one had to bring them [the Jews] out of their isolation, ease the harsh restrictions on them, and place their rights and obligations on a par with the rest of the population.

The officers claimed that it was impossible to give up the Jews of Galicia and expel 40,000 families from the country. Under those circumstances and despite their shortcomings, one had to treat them as fairly as the rest of the population.

Their proposals laid stress on improving the education of the youths which, except for religious studies, should be taught

at state schools.[34] Von Erggelet's memorandum was given to the members of the Court–committee for their opinions, and most of them concurred with him that the Jews should be granted the same civil rights as the rest of the population if they were required to fulfill all the obligations of the state's citizens. So long as no such policy was in place, the Jews' evasion of fulfilling their duties, and their stratagem to circumvent any laws which were to their detriment, was justified. Some of them claimed that as long as rabbis who lacked any general education were leading the Jews, no improvement was possible. On the other hand, the authorities had to realize that regulations and administrative arrangements alone could not alter the character of a people, and therein lay the mistake of tackling the Jewish issue. Although radical changes could not be implemented at once, one had to strive to prepare the Jews to embrace equal rights, by and by.

First of all, by eliminating the restrictions one had to allow them an

economic living condition that would forgo their need for deception and immoral living. Despite those proposals submitted to the central authorities and to Kaiser Franz I however, they remained deaf to any request to lighten the living conditions of the Galician Jews.

Besides the principal issues, in the 1820s tradition dress surfaced again, with the aim to apply the 16th May 1781 prohibition against the traditional Jewish clothes, that the authorities had abolished in 1790 due to an inability to implement it. The authorities were greatly interested in the question of dress once certain wealthy circles and admirers of the Enlightenment had removed their traditional dress, out of their own volition.

The *Maskilim* of Brody were largely responsible for that. Several members of Brody's community submitted a memorandum to the authorities[35] in which they requested that in conjunction with the new Jewish regulations a new law should be enacted to oblige the Jews of Galicia to replace their traditional dress which was a principal hindrance to their relations with the Christian population. The *Maskilim* requested to hasten that process even though, "elderly Jews were attached to their traditional dress, whether from ancient law or from habit."

The Brody *Maskilim*'s request encouraged the Governor to draw the attention of the Vienna authorities to the question of clothing.

[Pages 211-212]

In July 1816, in a report after his voyage throughout Galicia, the commissioner Freiherr von Hauer stated with satisfaction that replacing the traditional clothing was raised among the Jews of Galicia, especially by the well to do. It was however advisable for the authorities not to get involved, "so as not to arouse the zealots' wrath."[36]

During the 1820–1821 debate over the new Jewish regulation, the advisor von Widmann proposed the following questions in his summary to the commissioners:

1.   Is it necessary to abolish the traditional Jewish clothing with a law or was it preferable to leave the matter to the Jews themselves?

2.   Should one separate the improvements regarding dress from the Jewish regulation?

3.   Need a date be set for abolishing the traditional clothes, while permitting only rabbis and religious officials to wear the traditional dress?

Blacharska Street

According to commissioner Hauer it was advisable to bridge the existing abyss between the Jews of Galicia and the rest of the population, specifically concerning their peculiar dress, and to bring them together as soon as possible. Considering the situation, however, justice and law should not be mixed with habits and tradition. Although it was advisable to introduce improvements to the Jews' lifestyle, it was difficult to force them to alter their habits –of which dress made part– just as it was impossible to force the nobles and farmers to give up their national dress. After all, till then the Jews of Galicia appeared in their traditional dress in front of the nobles, and travelled in it to the fairs of Germany where they received credit. Since Galicia had several national costumes there was no good reason to demand from the Jews in particular to wear European clothes. The argument that the change of dress would encourage the process of bringing them closer to the rest of the population and to secular Enlightenment, was fundamentally flawed and consequently he believed that it was better to start the improvement by granting them permission to engage in occupations from which they had been barred, to live outside the specified Quarters, to establish elementary schools for them and admit them to secondary schools without hindrance. Every aspect indicated that no law should be enacted to force the Jews to give up their traditional dress.

Despite his opinion, and since the Jews had not responded to the 1817 authorities' call to alter their clothes voluntarily, the Governor proposed to combine the Jewish regulation with renewal of the decree on Jewish dress, under the assumption that it would prepare the ground for general alterations to the lifestyle of Galician Jews, and that the Jews were unlikely to alter their clothes voluntarily.

The Governor was also guided by the Jews' wishes to prohibit the Jewish traditional dress which delayed the Europeanization of their people. Based on the Governor's proposals the Vienna authorities ordered that Jews replace their dress with European outfits. At Lwów, according to the Governor's instructions, the timetable for the changes was:

1.   For those on third–level income and for community leaders three months;

2.   For those on second–level income six months;

3.   For those on first–level income eight months.

Once Jewish merchants who paid heavy taxes were made aware of the government's proposal regarding dress, the most respected and affluent among Lwów's community: Fischel Mizys, Leib Mendelssohn Hirsch Rappoport, Ber Modlinger and others submitted a petition "against some proposers, regarding the change to Jewish traditional dress which is hazardous and will bring no benefit to the country while jeopardizing property, trade, morals and the Jewish religion in Galicia." They requested to maintain the Jewish dress also in future, so that Jewish youths should not be led astray, since European dress would more easily and covertly lead them to abandon the precepts of their religion. It pointed out that the simplicity and unity of women's traditional dress did not depend on luxury and allowed their husbands to maintain frugal lives and the payment of taxes, while change in the situation would lead to damage to the Kingdom's treasury. The authors

[Pages 213-214]

of the memorandum stressed the fact that traditional dress also saved on foreign currency.

The authorities made no changes, yet the number among the Jewish public wearing European dress rose under the influence of the *Maskilim* on the youth and on the affluent strata. That process also led to a bitter conflict within Lwów's Jewish public, the majority of whom saw in the Enlightenment a danger to Judaism.

In 1826, the central authorities also began to debate the right of citizenship of Lwów's Jews. Galicia's *Sejm* committee (*Wydział krajowy*) made up of six *Sejm* delegates: 1. The clergy; 2. estate owners; 3. the nobility, (two from each category) and the commissioner of the town of Lwów, decided in 1828 to grant Jews the right of citizenship in the following categories: 1. Wholesale traders or industrialists; 2, Merchants who were members of the merchants' organization; 3. Artists; 4. Anæsthetists and medical doctors; 5. Craftsmen who had attained craftsmen's accreditation who excelled in patriotic and humanitarian acts or who encouraged trade, culture, industry and science.

The Governor's view was that the question of acquiring estates and the right of citizenship were not connected, and that the right to acquire estates should be granted even without the right of citizenship. The *Sejm* committee wholly rejected that view.

The Emperor's decision was to grant Jews citizenship in Galicia only on rare occasions, irrespective of the ownership of estates.[37]

[Page 364]

Notes: CHAPTER 13
All notes in square brackets [ ] were made by the translator.

     i.   Magyar Konywhaz 1799 XII, pp.48–58.

     ii.   Aleks. Fredro: *Trzy po trzy*. Dziela t. XI, pp. 108–112.

     iii.   Ossolineum Lwów manuscript, 1875, p. 113.

     1.   Archive of the Ministry of the Interior, Vienna IV T 2 Carton 2581. 98 ex Majo 1808.

     2.   IV T 1 Carton 2582 No. 8038, 1828 12/XII.

     3.   IV T 2 Carton 2581. 49 ex Mayo 1805: No.8459/624. 175 ex Augusto 1805 1805 No. 15, 928/1250.

     4.   IV T 1 Carton 2582.

     5.   IV T 2 Carton 2580 150 ex Dez. 1811.

     6.   IV T 2 Carton 2580 123 ex Junio 1826.

     7.   Hofkanzlei Dekret vom 26 Dezember 1811.

     8.   Hofkanzlei Dekret vom 27 Februar 1806.

     9.   M. Stöger *Loc. cit.* [*Darstellung der gesetzlichen Verfassung der galizischen Judenschaft*] I, p. 35.

    10.   IV T 2 Cardon 2605 No. 780.

    11.   Lwów's printers were granted the right in an decree dated 26th June 1806.

    12.   In 1819, there was an incident involving the teacher Moses Rosenzweig who had accepted the government's offer to become the teacher at the Jewish school of Chodorów [Khodoriv]. After the school was closed down, he requested a tansfer license to Lwów. After much persuasion the Governor was authorized by the Vienna central authorities to grant him that license. Archive of the Ministry of the Interior: IV T 3, No. 18799/1043, 149. Juni 1819.

13.   During that period the commissioners heading the Galician Governor office were: 1. Graf Johann Gaisruck (1795–1801); 2. Józef [von] Úrméni Kermeny (1801–1806); 3. Graf Christian Wurmser (1807–1810); 4. Graf Peter Goëss (1810–1815); 5. Graf Franz Hauer (1815–1822).
In 1797, a special Vienna Court–Office for Galician affairs was established, under the management of Joseph Mailott; 6. Graf Ludwig Taaffe (1823–1826); 7. Fürst August [von] Lobkowicz (1826–1832).

14.   IV T 1 6277 ad 166, März 1816.

15.   Gubern–Dekret v. 31 Dez. 1819, Loc. cit. I. p. 38.

[Pages 365-366]

16.   IV T 1 No. 23112 Polizeisachen ad. Juli 1816.

17.   IV T 1 Carton 2582. 1787 3/916. 40. Sept. 1818.

18.   Governor's Archive, Lwów:
Gubernial–Akten Allg. Sachen. Fasz. 11 Judenordnung 20407, Mai 1817.

19.   In 1817, Joseph Barach converted to Christianity and moved to Vienna. He approached the government requesting that his wife be released from the candle tax from the time of his conversion. On 29th April 1830, the Court–Office replied that as his wife Feige had left Lwów's community, she was not subject to the taxes imposed on Jews and that with Barach having abandoned the Jewish community, his family was also exempt from any taxes on Jews.
IV T 1 Carton 2582. ad. 19257 ex. 1828.

20.   IV T 1. 1815–1828. Carton 2582 Galizien.

21.   Archive of the Ministry of the Interior: IV T 3. 2615. ex 1824.

22.   Stattaltereiarchiv Lemberg Fasz. 11 Juden allgemeine Sachen. No. 26467/2589, 26 Mai 1818.

23.   The Jews were gravely affected by the 15 February 1827 statute which ordered that in Jewish restaurants and taverns one was only allowed to sell to Jews, at the table, and that the number of restaurants should not exceed 50. The Jewish tavern and restaurateur owners submitted an appeal claiming that since many Jews wore European dress and spoke German, it was difficult to know who, among the restaurant users was Jewish. For once, Lwów's municipality supported the Jews and announced that it was impossible to execute such a statute. On the other hand, however, it supported the restriction on the number of restaurants and taverns, and that after the demise of a restaurant owner the license would not be transferred to another Jew. The appeal was refused and the statute remained in force.
Arch, Min. d. Innern [Archive of the Ministry of the Interior] Fasz. 282 Prot. No. 12881, e.a. 5/VI 1828.

24.   Joseph Rohrer: *Versuch über die jüdischen Bewohner der Österreichischen Monarchie.* Wien 1804.

25.   Arch, Min. d. Innern [Archive of the Ministry of the Interior] IV T 1 Carton 2585 e.t. 1815–1828.
M. Stöger Loc. cit. 1 prg. 127.

26.   Joseph Rohrer: *Bemerkungen auf einer Reise* von der Türkischen Grenze über die Bukowina durch Ost und Westgalizien, Schlesien und Mähren nach Wien. (Wien 1804).

27.   IV T 4. 26077/2817 17 November 1817.

28.   In an 18 May 1809 report submitted to Kaiser Franz I by the Governor regarding the new statute for the Jews, was stated that:
"The Jews of Galicia, as had been proven from the start, pay the State a truly large and somewhat prohibitive tax burden, and were each and every subject to pay but half the tax that the Jew has to bear, then the income of Galicia, excluding the yield from the regalia, would approximately amount to 25 Million Gulden."
(Archive of the Ministry of the Interior IV T 11 Carton 2659 II No. 466 ad 18 Mai 1809).

29.   (Wiener St. A. Kabinettsarchiv 1819 No. 332).
In a section from the Lwów police report concerning the economic decline among the Jews, submitted to Kaiser Franz I. on 1st February 1819, was stated that:
"On 13 January, an eight months' old dead female baby was found at the synagogue. Her mother was not yet uncovered. The police director noted that among the Jews it had become a frequent method of putting away children, but an unprecedented occurrence otherwise, and that it can be taken as proof of the misery under which the highly taxed Jews must be."
The Emperor's response to that section was:
"Deserves the police's excellent attention, and in this specific case should, if possible, be further investigated."

30.   Wiener Staatsarchiv 2320, 9 April 1822.

31.   Vienna State Archive 960, 22 Februar 1830.

32.   IV T 1 Carton 2582, ad. 1564 Nachlassantrage der Gefälle.

33.   IV T 1 Carton 2581. 181 ex Oktober 1805, No. 25398/1655.

34. IV T 1 Carton 2583. e.a. 1813–1827.
Spezialia Vota der K.K. Hofräthe über das Operat des Hofrats von Erggelet.

35. Nr. 9450 ad 126 Mai 1821.

36. IV T 1 Carton 2581. 11366/591 April 1821.

37. IV T 1 Carton 2582. ad 14688–1832 III, p. 1251.

[Pages 215-216]

Chapter 14: The *Haskalah* Movement

Translated by Myra Yael Ecker

Edited by Ingrid Rockberger

The emergence of the *Haskalah* at Lwów. The first group led by Salomon Jehudah Rappoport. The early *Maskilim* and their conflict with the Orthodox and with the *Chassidim*. The 1816 boycott. Jehudah Leib Mizes the zealot *Maskil*. The emergence of *Chassidism* [Chassidut] at Lwów. The *Maskilim* and the state's policies regarding the Jews. The memorandum on the improvement of the Jews' circumstances and the state's response.

Brody and Tarnopol were known centres of disciples of the *Haskalah* [Hebrew Enlightenment], with some *Maskilim* arriving from the new territories, from Zamosz [Zamość] etc. At the end of the 18th century there were *Maskilim* groups at Lwów, but their influence did not spread beyond their own circles, until the early 19th century.

Well–to–do Jews were in contact with German officers who included educated men, teachers and scholars. As they spoke no Polish, they were forced closer to the Yiddish speaking Jews whose language they understood to a large extent. The officers gave German lessons to the families of those Jews with whom they were in contact, and they considered the dissemination of the German language and culture, a noble mission.

Among the disseminators of the Enlightenment were also Jewish merchants, who visited fairs in Germany and who brought back News of the Berlin Enlightenment, and who at times even circulated pamphlets and Enlightenment books. Those *Maskilim* joined closed circles where secular books were studied and read. Among the disseminators of the Enlightenment were also university students.[1] (Among the 320 students of the Law Faculty, there were 4 Jews). The Jewish medical doctors, Dr. Aron Gussman, Dr. Jakob Rappoport (1772–1855) and his son–in–law Kasowicz also played a major part in disseminating the Enlightenment. Secular studies were already widespread among the families of affluent merchants who were in touch with the authorities.

Among the early *Maskilim* were teachers of young children, who taught the Bible according to Mendelssohn's *Biur* [*Exegesis*] and spurred their pupils to study erudition and languages. One of those, Reb. Benjamin Zvi Natkis, was among the first to fight the Orthodox over their ignorance and over their objection to secular studies. To the group of youths who gathered at a small house on the same street as the hospital, behind the cemetery, he read out Hebrew and German books, and taught them Hebrew grammar, the Bible as well as foreign languages, He thus educated a young generation of Enlightenment sympathizers. From among that circle also sprang the awakening of research into the science and history of Israel.

The circle of Natkis, who was a teacher in the house of Rabbi Jakob Ornstein, was joined by Izak Erter (1791–1851), a languages, mathematics and history teacher who lived at Lwów from 1816 to 1819; Jehudah Leib Pastor, Salomon Jehudah Rappoport [aka. *Shir* = song] and Jehudah–Leib Mizys [Mizes], an offspring of one of Lwów's distinguished families which produced community–leaders and leaders of Reissen's Jewry (Mizys established a company to support youths who wished to undertake secondary–school education, as well as for medical students)[2]; Reb. Mardochaj Cwi [Tzvi] Jalisz (father of Zacharyasz [Secharja] Izajasz Jalisz, 1814–1852, who later moved to Minsk and became one of Dr. Lilienthal's assistants) scholar and scientist; Chaim Lerner, native of Lwów, a friend of Izak Erter and Mejer [Max] Halevi Letteris, who was knowledgeable in foreign languages. Once his circle of friends was under boycott, he left Lwów for Jaroslaw where he was a teacher, wrote articles and translated Schiller's Poem "Der Taucher" ["The Diver"] into Hebrew.

The *Maskilim* circle also numbered 1. the son of David Barda,[3] Eliahu (1793–1864), the uncle of Salomon Jehudah Rappoport, author of *Shorashei HaLashon HaIvrit* [*Roots of the Hebrew Language*], *Ma'arich Ma'arachot* [*Systems Appraiso*] and translator of Metastasio's Italian libretto *Isacco*. 2. Solomon ben Chaim Boruch Berik, born at Lwów on 7th May 1790, lived in Germany and Vienna and died at London on 10th June 1846. He wrote his autobiography *Chakirat HaEmet* [*Investigation of the Truth*], where he also investigated the concept of Truth (it was published at Altuna in 1838, and at Vienna in 1841). His second book, *Chezionei La'il* [*Night–time Visions*], was published at Vienna (1873), by his son Izak Levy Berik. 3. Josef Tarler (Tarla, 1794–1854), born at Gologory [Holohory], was a renowned scholar. Married to the daughter of the Rabbi of Wielkie Oczy[4] near Pshemish [Przemyśl], he grew wealthy, turned heretical and loathed the rabbis and the *Chassidim*, and in particular the Rabbi of Belz, Zvi Elimelech from Dinov [Dynów]. His sharp sarcastic writings eventually forced him to leave his father–in–law's house and move to Lwów as a private teacher. He got into trouble with a Polish noble for counterfeiting bills, and was liable to a severe punishment, but the suit was dropped with the proviso that he converted. And so, Tarla together with his wife and offsprings, converted, and he was appointed the first censor of Hebrew books published in Galicia. As censor he took his revenge

[Pages 217-218]

on the *Chassidim* and banned the publication of books on *Chassidism*. Despite his conversion, he remained a faithful Jew associated with Lwów's *Maskilim* and joined the circle of Salomon Jehudah Rappoport. Later on he repented and returned to the bosom of Judaism. Tarla was a tutor to Izak Erter and encouraged him to study medicine. Tarla wrote articles for "Jeruschalajim" the compilation by Nachman Fischmann, as well as a sharp satire *Ja'alizu Chassidim Be'Chavod* [*Let the Chassidim rejoice in honour*], against the *Chassidim*.[5]

The *Maskilim* also gathered on Szpitalna Street at Salomon Jehudah Rappoport's house where he lived with his father, Rabbi Aron Chaim Rappoport who was a *Chacham* [Sage] and kept a Yeshivah for pupils from the towns of Galicia. After he married the daughter of the children's Torah teacher, Rabbi Arieh Leib[6] who was subsequently elected rabbi of Stryj and was known as the author of *Kezot HaChoshen*. His spiritual development was much inspired by his mother, Zirel Etel, who was a gentle woman known as "The Pearl of Women", as well as by her brother Eliahu Barda. At home, Salomon Jehudah Rappoport, lectured to the *Maskilim* circle on research into Jewish history.

Rabbi Salomon Jehudah Rappoport [*Shir*]

Inevitably, by and by rumours spread about the young *Maskilim* circle. The Orthodox began to cast aspersions on them as heretics who degraded the Torah, especially once the critical comments by Salomon Jehudah Rappoport on "the innovations" published by Rabbi Jakob Ornstein in his book *Yeshu'ot Ja'akob*(1809) became known. They also claimed that not a single original idea appeared in his books. Due to his comments, Salomon Jehudah Rappoport was detested by Rabbi Ornstein.

There was also the incident when by mistake Benjamin Natkis left a Hebrew translation of Mendelssohn's book, at the Rabbi's house, a matter which sparked an explosion.

One night, on 10th May 1816, an announcement on behalf of Rabbi Jakob Ornstein was pasted onto the entrance of the Great Synagogue, to banish and ostracize Salomon Jehudah Rappoport, Izak Erter, Natkis and Pastor. They did not dare ostrocize Mizys. The *Maskilim* complained to the authorities about Rabbi Jakob Ornstein who had banned them without a special licence from the authorities, and submitted a German translation of the banishment announcement. Their complaint asserted that all ostracism had been outlawed in Austria ever since Joseph II,

The authorities compelled the elderly Rabbi to publicly revoke the ban within the Great Synagogue, and to declare in a sermon given in German that, according to the Torah, learning the German language and secular studies was permitted. In their conflict the *Maskilim* were assisted by the commission–officer Sacher, who liked and admired Salomon Jehudah Rappoport, and consequently demanded an apology from their zealot persecutors[7].

In a letter to a friend, an anonymous *Maskil* described the lifting of the ban, as follows:

"This Sabbath, our venerable master, Rabbi and great scholar [*Gaon*] cloaked in a *Tizlik* [a costly, long silk coat that reached the ground] and tied with both straps in front of his throat, was led by state–officers, one on either side of him, who placed him in front of God's Ark. There, with trembling hands, he took the sermon written in a foreign script and language, known as Germanish, which strangers had prepared ever since Friday evening, and with his head covered, a terrified expression and moving lips he read the following: Concerning the boycott scrolls which soared this summer over those seeking knowledge and the Gentiles' tongues, especially over four people noted by their names so–and–so etc., and over the towns of Brody and Tarnopol, in which schools were established for their youth. Not only were His Excellency the Emperor's statutes broken, they breached the country's religious code which did not permit the boycott of men. Consequently, if even in days to come the scoundrels of that abomination will not clean up, in the spirit of ethics, and together leave behind the rebellious criminals, who do not follow the Emperor's laws, as they also transgressed the laws which were passed to teach us that it is necessary and befitting for each and every Jew to learn languages of the nations under whose rule and mercy they might complain."

Present at the synagogue were "the leaders, heads of the community," as ordered by the Governor's ministers with a 50 Reinisch fine on anyone who abstained from hearing the sermon of our Rabbi the great scholar, and they wisely requested, from those who had issued the orders, that he hold his sermon after reading the Torah, believing that afterwards each member of the community would go home. They were mistaken however, with their request turning into a stumbling block and to the accuser's successful action, when after the Torah was read, the entire congregation from the youngest to the old, wealthy and poor together, from all the synagogues, a large crowd as at a celebration. They were pressed together in the synagogue as well as the small hall of the house, too tight to contain all the crowd that rushed there, so they climbed on the roof and looked through the windows to see the splendour of our honoured Rabbi the great scholar's face, and to hear

[Pages 219-220]

gracious words from his blessed mouth. And when he sighed to deliver the sermon in a small voice (since the anger, grief and shame that raged in his soul also choked his untarnished throat) the regional commissar Därnfeld read out that sermon, a second time, in a loud voice. And whoever had not heard the words of the our honoured Rabbi the great scholar, the first time, clearly heard the words the second time, from Mr. Därnfeld.

"It took place at the synagogue outside the town, and at the two synagogues within the town the rabbis and the community–elders also read out that sermon, and to their right, translators who spoke German (for the honoured community–elders would not be drawn thus to speak) most of them, fearful of foolishness, were sickened and angry, but put a hand to their mouth and held their tongues, for fear of watchful eyes. But in the secrecy of their own homes they swore and cursed the criminals who took revenge on, and repaid in kind the honour of our righteous Rabbi who hates [secular] wisdom and its preachers, and who disgraced and persecuted it within the community, and some sinning in their knowing souls, and whose sins of leprosy of knowledge shone on their foreheads to understand from the Bible – rejoiced in his downfall and read the Biblical saying about him: The wise shall inherit glory, but shame shall be the promotion of fools. Till here the words of that writer."[8]

Such cases inevitably increased the objection to the *Maskilim* since the Orthodox led by Rabbi Ornstein upheld their offence against the *Maskilim*, especially against Salomon Jehudah Rappoport and Mizys; the gulf widened between the Orthodox and the *Chassidim* and between the *Maskilim*. Arguments within families and disputes between parents and children led to actual segregation, with some 50 women forced by their parents to divorce, since their husbands were suspected of heresy. Jehudah–

Leib Mizys was also obliged to divorce [give a *get* to] his wife who, according to his request, married his friend Natan Rosenstein whom the Orthodox did not consider a suspect.

The *Maskilim* were led by Jehudah–Leib Mizys (1792–1831), descendant of a renowned, wealthy family whose sons numbered among the scholars, leaders and elders of Lwów's community as well as regional committee. Jehudah–Leib did not abandon his fight with, and hatred for *Chassidism*, neither did he recoil from turning informant, especially following the ban on the *Maskilim* of Lwów, Brody and Tarnopol. In his loathing for *Chassidism* he was greatly influenced by Joseph Perl who had befriended him and was a guest at his house on his stays in Lwów. In his contact with the authorities he had a hand in the persecution of Kulikow and Modlinger regarding the collecting of funds for the poor in Eretz Israel. During 1823–1825, Mizys together with two other *Maskilim* –Markus Hiller and Mojżesz Rabe– submitted complaints to Lwów's authorities over the communities which, in contravention of the law, granted licenses for arranging *Minyanim* for the Chassid Rabbi Joseph ben Rabbi Jakob ben Izak of Lublin. Mizys, who was a stubborn and jealous man, was always ready to help his fellow *Maskilim*: Izak Erter, Mejer Letteris, Natkis, Samson Halevi Bloch and Nachman Fischmann as well as others. Apart from his knowledge of the Talmud and the Midrash, Mizys also excelled in general knowledge. In 1823, in Letteris's collection *HaTz'phira* ["The Siren"], he [Mizys] published the article "On the Reason for our People's lack of Human Knowledge," which harshly criticised Poland's Jews "who scorn human knowledge." That article spurred the rage of the Orthodox, and even angered some among the *Maskilim* circles that Letteris had published Mizys's harsh words. Among the sympathisers of the Enlightenment in the Mizys family, one should mention Fischel Mizys who loved the Hebrew language and literature. He published Rabbi Moses Chaim Luzzatto's book *LaJesharim Tehila* [*Glory to the Righteous*]. The author Mejer Levy Letteris lived at Lwów as a university student in the years 1826–1836, when he formed contact with the *Maskilim* circle and specially with Mizys.

On the death of Baron [von] Hauer in 1827, the community had to publish a lament for his death. Rabbi Jakob Ornstein turned to Letteris to write a lament in Hebrew as well as in German, in which the Rabbi who would bear the printing cost, would be mentioned by name. Due to his honour, Letteris agreed and wrote the lament *Palgei Mayim* ["Water Streams"] (Lwów 1927), for a fee.

Mizys's book *Kinath HaEmeth* [*Zeal for the Truth*] (Vienna 1828), is a kind of dialogue between Maimonides and his interpreter, the author of *Merkevet HaMishnah*, written in the spirit of the rationalism characteristic of the period of Enlightenment, filled with bold views which angered Salomon Jehudah Rappoport.

In his comments on the translation of the book *Techunath HaRabanim* [*The Rabbis' Trait*] by David Caro (1782–1829) from Zhupany [Żupanie], Mizys demanded to introduce amendments in education, in the spirit of [Naftali Herz] Wiesel's [Wessely] proposals; changes in the economic composition of the Jews through their employment in agriculture. He also demanded that they amend their way of life and get closer to the rest of the population. Mizys's major work was his fight against *Chassidism* which he whole heartedly despised – a fight which angered Jacob Shmuel Bik. who considered it a quixotic act.

Mizys died (26th June 1831) on Izak Erter's lap, of the cholera epidemic which had spread through Galicia. His funeral was attended by his enemies, the Orthodox and the *Chassidim*, whistling and shouting for joy.

Mizys had not established a special school. His extremism found no supporters even among the *Maskilim* circles that objected to the tactics of the *Chassidim*. They did not wish to escalate the conflict with the Orthodox

[Pages 221-222]

as well as with the *Chassidim*, at the same time, since the Orthodox also opposed the *Chassidim*.

We have no precise details on the development of Lwów's *Chassidism* at the end of the 18th century. Lwów's community, led by Rabbi Hirsch Rosanes, strongly objected to it. In 1792, on his initiative, a ban was issued against the *Chassidim* and against the ritual butchers [*Shochtim*] who were their sympathizers. The ban forbade the *Chassidim* from holding their own *Minyanim* (Schtieblach). Besides Rabbi Hirsch Rosanes, the signatories to that proclamation were the community–elders Hirsch ben Moses Witeles, Süsskind Zusman Bałaban, Abraham ben Eliaezer Menkes.[9] Despite their objection they were unable to prevent the progression of *Chassidism* which surrounded most Jews of Eastern Galicia. At Lwów however, those objecting to that sect did not rest and fought its rabbis. In 1794, when Rabbi Meszulam Igra stopped at Lwów on his way to Pressburg and saw the influence of *Chassidism*, he addressed the community leaders in a letter of 8th February, calling "to rehabilitate the rejected sheep and stop them spreading in all directions." Avoid forming factions, avoid forming sects, groups that will alter the traditions of our forefathers, the great world scholars in our country and in our Torah. Their virtue will save us and I went out "toward them to zealously protect the Lord and his Teaching so that the Torah will not be lost."

Jewish shops

Rabbi Cwi [Tzvi] Hirsch Rosanes and the community–elders of the two communities agreed and replied "To release us from this obstacle which has alienated us from the glory of our exalted Torah that lies neglected."[10]

The rabbis and the community leaders did all they could to halt the spread of *Chassidism* and to expel its followers from any influence on the community's affairs.[11]

Only in the 1840s did the *Chassidism* movement turn into an element which affected Lwów's community. Prior to that the *Chassidim* had no leader at Lwów. They maintained three prayer *Minyanim* (Schtiblach) which turned into propaganda cells whence *Chassidism* spread among the population. Jacob Glanzer rose as their leader.

With the emergence of *Chassidism* as a mass movement, Rabbi Jakob Ornstein came out against it. At the same time it was necessary to open a second front against the *Maskilim* who inculcated their knowledge from their centres at Brody, Tarnopol and Lwów to the communities spread all over Galicia, and attracted the youth by opening to them new spiritual avenues and opportunities for new lives rather than the ones in which they had been immersed.

Unlike Mizys and Perl, Lwów's *Maskilim* were rooted in traditional Judaism. They injected a national aspect into the Galician Enlightenment, remained faithful to the Hebrew language, the mainstay of their national outlook. Although some of them had already rejected the commandments –not publicly but secretly– their number was small. There was also an unusual kind of *Maskilim* who wore traditional Jewish clothes and put on a *Schtramel* [fur hat] on Sabbath, but who were heretic at heart. An opinion prevailed[12] that the Jews of Lwów excelled in "excessive naiveté, humility, love of mankind." They lacked the arrogance of the Jews from Galicia's small towns who enjoyed upsetting their friends with stinging jokes, They were also naive, not quick enough to deceive their friends. Those from small towns said of them that "their wisdom would expire" beyond the town's gates.

One need realize that the spread of *Chassidism* was actually assisted by "Josephinism," which for scores of years after the demise of Joseph II still formed the conceptual bedrock of Austria's Enlightenment policy for the Jews.

The grave demands for assimilation, without the actual implementation of Jewish civil parity, wholly contradicted the Jewish way of life. A wholesale revolution was required in the lives of Galicia's Jews–something that could only be achieved through an historical process. Lacking any understanding of the Jewish problem, and by considering it solely a religious issue, the authorities alienated the Jewish masses from a desire for Enlightenment, and pushed them into the arms of *Chassidism* and its rabbis, where they sought refuge for their souls' yearnings.

The authorities did everything –contrary to the aspirations of citizen–rights, to equality and to the dissemination of the Enlightenment among the masses– to restrict the legal economic basis of Jewish existence.

The Vienna government's method of repression was however guided by its political interest in Galicia's Jews, through whom it aimed to weaken the Polish national–political element which, since the 1831 revolt had begun to take root in the country, and in its capital Lwów in particular.

[Pages 223-224]

The Austrian government's policies regarding the Jews was also guided by the failed attempts to involve the Jews in agriculture as well as to increase their German assimilation. In short, "Josephinism," the government's policies regarding the Jews, had totally failed since the Jews of Lwów and Galicia were not swept by the current of assimilation, but remained faithful to traditional Judaism.

Lwów's *Maskilim* looked for ways to lighten their brethren's circumstances. In 1820, they started to make plans for improving the situation of the masses, and in a memorandum to the Governor they submitted proposals how to amend the Jewish education: 1. To establish Jewish educational institutions. 2. To enforce by law the abolition of Jewish traditional dress. 3. To make the appointment of the community–elders unrelated to the payments of candle–tax. 4. To collect from, and to allot the Jewish taxes to, the entire community. The Vienna central government responded that those issued had been debated in the proposals for the new Jewish–statute, and that consequently the issues did not require debate but rather to be used to that end.[13]

Clearly Joseph II's heirs continued with his Jewish policy, without taking note of the Jews' fundamental needs. The tax burden and the economic discrimination were greatly increased under Franz I, and remained in force till the revolution of 1848, and even then the special situation in which the Jews found themselves was not brought to an end.

[Page 366]

Notes: CHAPTER 14
All notes in square brackets [ ] were made by the translator.

    1.   Lwów University was established in 1784 and functioned till 1805, when the professors were transferred to Kraków University which was located within the Austrian territory. At Lwów, a Lyceum for the study of theology, law, philosophy and surgery was established. The Lyceum was not entitled to grant doctoral degrees. In August 1817, the University was reopened by Kaiser Franz I, and was named after him.

    2.   A. Sares: History of the rabbi the great Scholar, Rabbi Salomon Jehudah Leib Rappoport. *HaShachar* 1929, p. 26.

    3.   His sister, Zirel–Etel, was the wife of Rabbi Aron–Chaim Kohen Rappoport, the father of Salomon Jehudah Rappoport, who inspired him in the way of the Enlightenment.
Eliahu Barda married the daughter of Rabbi Izak–Arieh Margulies, bookseller and housekeeper to Rabbi Fischel Mizys.
In 1829, Eliahu Barda moved to Vienna as housekeeper to Mizys, and was appointed as commercial dealer, but since he had no right to remain at Vienna he lived at Eisenstadt till 1838. He contributed to *Avnei Nezer* and *Wiener Vierteljahrschrift* [*Vienna Quarterly*] of Dr. Mejer Letteris, and to *Kochbe Jizchak* ["*Isaac's Stars*"]. The book *Ma'arich Ma'arachot* includes all roots of the past tenses according to the Bible with interpretation and translation. He also participated in Vienna's public life and was the leader of the synagogue of Poland's Jews.His son Daniel wrote comedies and articles in German; and his

[Pages 367–368]

second son, Jakob, was a builder. His daughters, 1. Channah was married to David Weiss Benisch; 2. Jentel, to Mechil–Leib Benisch; 3. Zila, to Tibia Gottlieb.

    4.   In the book *Ohel Naftali* [*Naftali's Tent*] (Warsaw 1911), p. 99, it is said that Rabbi Zewi–Elimelech of Dynov [Dynów] (author of *Bnei Issachar*: [*Sons of Issachar*]) spent one Sabbath at Wielkie Oczy, "Where a great Chacham and prodigy named Josef Tarler, was continually laughing at the above mentioned holy man who at the time was reading the *Sidrah* [Bible weekly portion] – Therefore the Jews will not eat the thigh tendon– and the holy Rabbi of blessed memory read enthusiastically and sweetly from the Bible as was his wont. And the prodigy Josef Tarler joked, not in an entertaining way: What luck the Angel has not touched upon devouring the best, for alas if he had, you would not be permitted to eat brisket [based on a pun in Yiddish]. When later Josef Tarler's words were repeated to the holy Rabbi, he retorted with, Is that what he said?, so I have no doubt he must be an infidel, etc. When later this was related to Josef Tarler of Sathmar [Satu Mare], it sparked in him an envy of greater defiance, and he travelled to the holy Rabbi of Ropczyce [Ropshitz]. And he said to the holy Rabbi at Ropczyce: there is a rebel who thinks of himself a rabbi, who said of me that I must be an infidel. So the holy Rabbi of Ropczyce asked, Is that what he said?, what a *Mitzva* [commandment] to hear the words of sages. For the holy Rabbi of Ropczyce, in his holiness, knew that Josef Tarler was inside an infidel. Instantly, Tarler's face fell and he ran for his life, and soon after there was no villain. And in bad times he transgressed from the essence, and converted [to Christianity] God save us. He rose far among the nations and was appointed censor at the town of Lwów. When the book *Ben Issachar* was printed he refused to grant it a license, saying that according to it ["]I must be a transgressor.["] It was first published without introduction or title page. It later emerged that even in his youth Tarler was friends with a corrupting man, Letteris, his name be damned, and even in the past Minian books fell out of his lap, God save us."

5.   Dr. Simon Bernfeld: Memoires, *Reshumot* [*Records*]. Tel–Aviv, 1926, Vol. 4. pp. 186–187.
Dr. M. Weissberg: *Die neuhebr. Literatur* M. G.W. d. J. 1928. p. 185.

6.   In 1823, Izrael Piklanzer reported Salomon Jehudah Rappoport who had married the Jewess Friede against Austrian Law and Justice. The authorities investigated and found that the report was unfounded and untrue "that Rappoport lives in a wild marriage" (Dünaburg; Daugpilis) From the Archives of Salomon Jehudah Rappoport. "Kiriat Sefer" Vol. I, Jerusalem. 1925, pp. 151–152].

7.   Later, when he was appointed Tarnopol's regional minister, he protected Salomon Jehudah Rappoport, who served there at the Rabbinate.

8.   Appeared in Israel Weinlös's introduction to the book *Joseph Perl, Jewish writings*. Wilno. 1937, p. ixxx, note 1.

9.   The ban was published in the book *Cherev Chada* [Sharp Sward] by Ephraim Deinard, Kearny, 1904, p. 122; from a manuscript at Oxford *This is the Doctrine of Zealousness* by an unknown.

10.   Two letters were published in the book of S. Dubnow *History of Chassidism*, Tel–Aviv. 1840, Vol. III, pp. 452–453.

11.   In 1798, Israel ben Jehudah–Löb (Löbel), the tycoon [*magid*] elder from Slutzk, and one of the fiercest active opponents of *Chassidism*, came to Galicia. When he was at Kraków, his books were banned by the tax–office after lobbies by the *Chassidim*. When he came to Lwów in September 1798, the *Chassidim* met him on Janowska Street, and beat him up. When afterwards, at the beginning of 1799, he had an audience with Kaiser Franz I, Löbel submitted a written complaint against the *Chassidim*. The Kaiser promised to investigate the matter. As a result, the *Chassidim* were badly affected: the authorities issued a prohibition on public gatherings, and the Chassidic rabbis left Galicia for Poland. In addition, books of *Chassidism* were banned in Galicia.
Israel Löbel. Glaubwürdige Nachrichten von einer neuen Sekte unter den Juden in Polen und Litauen die sich Chssidim nennt und ihren. die Menschheit empörenden Grundsätzen und Lehren. Frankfurt an der Oder 1799.
Appeared in: *Sulamith*, Dessau 1807. Vol. II, pp. 308–333.

12.   Dr. Simon Bernfeld: Memoires, *Reshumot* [*Records*]. Tel–Aviv, 1926, Vol. 4. pp. 170–171.

13.   Archive of the Ministry of the Interior, Vienna: Carton 2580 ad 48. Febr, 1820.

[Pages 225-226]

Chapter 15: On the Eve of Revolution

Translated by Myra Yael Ecker

Edited by Dave Horowitz–Larochette

The 1829 earthquake. The 1830 Cholera epidemic. Demonstrations against food–tax. The association for the distribution of industry and crafts among the Jews of Galicia. The 1828–1834 debate and its rejection. Mordechai Bernstein invited to Lwów. Lwów Jews' housing problems. The social changes. The unrest among the *Maskilim* circles. The government's involvement in appointing the enlightened to the community's committee. The community committee's members led by Dr. Emil Blumenfeld. The construction of a synagogue (the Temple) for the Enlightened. Dr. Jakobka Rappaport. The debate on the creation of a Jewish school. Establishment of a children's nursery and a health organization. The school syllabus and its budget. Appointing the preacher Abraham Kohn. The school staff. The number of pupils in the years 1844–1847. Protest by the Orthodox. Delay in the new ruling regarding Jews. The government's stance on the Jewish issue. The Polish public and its attitude toward the Jews. The Jews and the Polish revolt of 1830–1831. The *Maskilim*'s stance. The Jews of Lwów and the **events** of 1846. The community's proposal to establish a Jewish brigade and the government's response. Stadion's appointment as Galicia's governor. The 1847 Lwów convention of the communities' representatives. Lwów community's petition. The issue of Jewish traditional dress and the community's opinion. Abraham Kohn and Meier Münz. Protests and informing by the Orthodox.

The years prior to the 1848 revolution known in Austrian history as "*Vormärz*" ("pre–March" [German Revolution] 1848), were extremely difficult.

On 26th November 1829, Lwów was hit by an earthquake. In 1830, its citizens suffered drought, typhus and cholera which raged between May and September 1830 and claimed a large number of casualties. Special hospitals were then erected for Christians and Jews.

Their congested living conditions at the outbreak of the epidemic resulted in a much larger number of casualties among the Jewish population, despite the efforts of the Jewish doctors, especially Dr. Jakobka Rappaport. On 7th June 1830, the authorities ordered to move 300 families to green fields outside the town. At the Jewish hospitals, excluding the patients who were treated privately, there were 803 patients, 415 of whom died and only 388 recovered. Not only the doctors distinguished themselves, but also two young Jewish assistant medics, Izidor and Henrik Papo.

Lwów's citizens, the Jews included, were economically hit when precisely in 1830 the government introduced a special tax on the import of food. The tax imposition led to citizens' demonstrations in which the Jews also took part, and which at the town periphery reached even clashes and attacks on the tax officers and the police, as well as on the tax administrator Franz Helm. As a result of the demonstrations Lwów's citizens managed to secure a release from, and reduction in the food tax depending to type.

On 4th September 1838, a great fire broke out in the Jewish Quarter. On Boimów Street 11 houses were burnt down in the fire which also killed 11 Jews. Hirsch Taitels distinguished himself among the rescuers, successfully saving his sick mother from the burning house.[1]

The rigid and decadent bureaucracy that gnawed at files with no regard for people's needs, further exacerbated the Jews' adversity. A few officers tried however to convince the Vienna central authorities to introduce crucial changes and improvements to the living conditions of Galicia's Jews. Their efforts were however in vain since the Vienna authorities did not care to hear of such suggestions.

As far back as1790 the Galician *Sejm*, the ostensible "Parliament", had already debated granting civil rights to the Jews, but its proposal was derived from self–interest. In the thirties the Poles realized that the Jews, whose loyal support they hoped for, in fact sympathised with the Austrian regime. Without explicitly voicing the view that the Jews were enemies of Poland, it was clear that they did not consider the Jews[2] an element supportive of the Polish national spirit and movement. The national movement gained strength especially during the (1826–1832) governorship of the Poles' sympathiser, Prince Lobkowitz [Lobkowicz], and at Russia's request he was removed from that post due to his stance. In his treatment of the Jews Lobkowitz also showed complete understanding, in an attempt to improve their situation and support the *Maskilim*'s request for a licence to establish an "organization for the distribution of industry and useful crafts among the Jews of Galicia."

In 1828, the renowned *Maskil* Josef Perl of Tarnopol, and his friend Reb. Mordechai–Berisch Margulies of Lwów, member of the mercantile law–court and agent of the savings fund, together with Dr. Kolischer, prepared a plan for the establishment of the above mentioned organization in honour of

[Pages 227-228]

Kaiser Franz I's 60's birthday. On 9th February 1828 Perl and Margulies were granted an audience by Prince Lobkowitz, and submitted the memorandum for establishing the company.[3] Prince Lobkowitz allowed them to hold a founding meeting which took place on 12th March 1828, and included Dr. Jacob Rappoport, D. Epstein, Nathan Kolischer, Dr. Kolischer and Herz Ettinger –all from Lwów. The membership fee was established and a committee of three members was elected to draught the regulations.

As the endeavour for an approval of the regulations took a long time, it was decided to accelerate the approval at Vienna. When on 1st June 1829 Perl was seen by the Kanzler Prince [von] Metternich, he asked for the approval to be speeded up, but the matter did not progress.

On 24th July 1832,[4] the Court–office prepared a report which determined that every association member should contribute 200 Florins, or a mortgage of 5% of the value of a house. Jews outside Austria would also be entitled to become members of the association.[5] The association would be responsible for placing industrious and talented poor children to learn a craft useful to craftsmen, under the auspices of craftsmen; to maintain their provisions and clothing, and to pay their tuition fees as well as the craftsmen's association fees.

According to the report some "affluent" Jews had already joined the association, pledging to pay the membership fees of specific individuals as well as donating funds to the association's management authority, headed by a member of Lwów's mercantile law–court, Markus Margulies, and others. The association determined to begin operating once it had collected a sum of 20,000 Florins.

On 11th April 1833 – ten months after the report was submitted to the Court–office – the Emperor ordered to hand it over to the Minster of Police [Josef von] Sedlnitzky [Sedlnicky] for his opinion, whether there were under the existing circumstances any doubts about establishing the association. On 4th May 1833, Sedlnitzky turned to Lwów's Police Commissioner, [Leopold] von Sacher-Masoch, requesting his opinion on the association's regulations as well as a report on its proponents.

On 8th September 1834, the report[6] was submitted to the Kaiser by the Minster of Police Sedlnitzky, with his observations. According to the Police Commissioner's report, Sedlnitzky noted: there is no objections to the establishment of the requested association for political or managerial reasons, and it constitutes a major step forward in the Jews' civil integration. There is also no objections by the police to the establishment of the association, considering that the Jews of Galicia supported the existing regime. Accepting associate members from abroad is to be opposed however, and a demand must be made that a government commissioner be present at every association meeting to safeguard the government's interests. It is in the government's interest that the Jewish citizens gradually achieve parity with the rest of the population and become part of it. That is only attainable by influencing their religious, moral and intellectual education, as well as by encouraging them to engage in useful and desirable trades. The association is one of the active means by which to attain this aim, and consequently its establishment is no cause for concern. Moreover, as the association members take upon themselves all expenditure, the government will not be burdened by any financial outlays.

Despite his earlier recommendation, the Kaiser delayed the approval of the licence to implement the association, till 11th April 1848.[7]

Prince Lobkowitz also supported the request put forward on 10th June 1828 by Mordechai Bernstein of Brody to establish a vocational school and a rabbinical seminary at Lwów. On 12th August 1828, Prince [von] Lobkowitz responded that he considered the proposal commendable and worthy of support, and he invited Bernstein to come to Lwów. Due to the difficulties he faced from the Orthodox as well as the bureaucracy, his project only came to fruition in 1864.[8]

The officials looked askance at Prince [von] Lobkowitz and his sympathy for the Jews, whom they only considered a means of extorting bribes, while detrimental to the state and society. There was also an apparent "Intolerance by the Christian population which delays and destroys every extension of human principle, not only the government, but also the citizens spread the seeds of hate."[9] In 1837, one officer depicted the Jews' circumstances in the following manner: "The learned Jew one mocks and saddens, the uneducated Jew one ridicules and expels; one belittles the dignity of the esteemed Jew, and humiliates the ignoble; one laughs at the rich and hates the poor. Every good thing done by a Jew is considered repulsive; every great thing – one demeans its worth; every favour is only regarded as malice," and no progress will do any good nor will it appease those who hate the Jewish People.[10]

In the period 1838–1840 the resentments intensified when Lwów's municipality reawakened the issue of foreign Jews' residency within the town, especially with regard to Lwów's Jews who had married women from other towns.

In 1823, as previously mentioned, the Governor had expressed his view that it was advisable to abolish all restrictions on the entry of foreign Jews into the town of Lwów, since their residence at Lwów was no more pernicious than at any other town. In 1826, with Prince Lobkowitz's approval, the restriction on the entry of Jews into the town was upheld as well as preventing an increase

[Pages 229-230]

in the number of Jewish families. Orders were issued to prepare a list of all the Jews present at Lwów, and to sort the Jews who were community members from the foreigners who illegally resided in the town. Any transgressors of the right of residency had to be expelled from Lwów. The proposals were sanctioned by the Court–office and executed by the municipality with consent of the police.[11]

During the *Vormärz* ("pre–March" [1848 German Revolution]) years, the social composition of Lwów's Jews had undergone considerable changes:

Compared with the Orthodox Jews, the enlightened section of the *Maskilim* grew in number. Among them were medical doctors, lawyers and others with academic education who excelled in the arts and sciences and reached significant positions in their fields.

In 1839-1840, there were at Lwów 15 Jewish medical doctors and a number of surgeons. Renowned among those were: Dr. Jakobka Rappaport, his sons–in–law: Dr. Kasowicz and Dr. Barda, Dr. Abraham Natkis and Dr. Gussman, the writer Dr. Moritz Rappaport, Dr. Dubs, Dr. Epstein, Dr. Goldberg. Among the known lawyers were: Dr. Blumenfeld, Dr. Menkes, Dr. Klahr, Dr. Mahl, Dr. Maximilian Landsberger, J. Pfeffer. One need also mention Leo Kolischer, a Dr. of philosophy and a highly cultured man. The *Maskilim* were also joined by wide circles of cultured merchants whose cultural standing was however not on a par with that of Brody's merchants, as well as by functionaries in Jewish institutions whose meagre salary prevented them from devoting themselves to the Enlightenment as they would have desired. Some Jewish families sent their children to state schools, and the number of pupils at secondary schools and university increased year by year. On the other hand, the influence of Chassidism increased among the common people. An indifference and lack of concern for the needs of the general public prevailed among those circles not touched by Chassidism.[12]

During 1827–1847 a turmoil stirred among all strata of the *Maskilim* circles, who expressed grave objections to the community management's prevailing reliance on the kindness of the candle–tax lessees who were interested in the sole appointment of their supporters. Their demand was not willingly heeded, but in time the authorities also realised the need to introduce changes in the organization.

For the first time, at Brody, some medical doctors and lawyers from among the *Maskilim* were appointed extraordinary community–elders.

In 1839, Lwów's community faced a crisis. The rabbi, Rabbi Jakob Meschulam Ornstein died. The community's *Maskilim* considered it best to appoint a temporary rabbi till 1846, when a well educated rabbi would be appointed.[13] Opposers [*Misnagdim*; of Chassidism, from among the Orthodox Jews], led by Hirsch Bernstein, appointed Rabbi Hirsch ben Mordechai Ze'ev, as the Rabbi's successor. Rabbi Hirsch's candidacy rested on the support of his maternal, Mieses [Mizys] family. But the Chassidim, led by Rabbi Jakob Glanzer who built the Chassidic Beth–Midrash [religious study house], opposed that appointment.

In 1838, the community was led by Meier Münz, a *Maskil* who spoke a stylish German. He was on friendly terms with the Orthodox as well as with with their leader Hirsch Bernstein, and wrote all the announcements and written requests on their behalf (he also maintained good relations with the Polish Democratic Society and even held a political position in 1848).

The appointed committee members included: Osias Meier Goldbaum (an opposition veteran during 1817–1820), Fischel Dubs as well as David and Herz Sokal, Meier Rachmiel Mieses, Leib Sternklahr, all moderate *Maskilim* who were also accepted by the Orthodox. They were supported by the Police Commissioner, Ritter von Sacher-Masoch, who was keen for the intelligentsia to attain the leadership of the community. The committee pursued a moderate policy, avoiding any changes that might shock the Orthodox or the Chassidim. Its mission was: to reorganize the hospital which was in very poor condition; settle the taxes and organize the charitable institutions.

Leib Sternklahr, head of the hospital founded by Izak Ohringer (1741–1818), succeeded in improving the institution's situation and in increasing its income from 8,000 to 13,200 Florins.

Meier Rachmiel Mieses who supervised the tax affairs, held a moderate stance in–between the conservatives and the progressives. He was joined by merchants keen to have their children educated in the spirit of the time.

Fischel Dubs, a founder member of industry, was a wise practical man who did much to organize the neglected and abandoned charitable affairs.

David Herz Sokal, the son of Nathan–Neta Sokal, a prominent merchant known for being active against the tax–lessees, managed the hospital's affairs together with Sternklahr. Their work was also approved of by radical *Maskilim* who appreciated their bravery of not yielding to the Orthodox nor to the Chassidim.

The *Maskilim*s' standing enjoyed a significant rise when Meier Rachmiel Mieses, Fischel Dubs, Meier Münz, D. H. Sokal, Leib Sternklahr and Goldbaum accepted Dr. Jakobka Rappaport's invitation to participate in the meeting of 4th October 1840, at Dr. Blumenfeld's apartment, where it was agreed to erect a "Temple" (Temple, a synagogue for the Enlightened).

One of the committee's earliest actions was to entrust Dr. Blumenfeld and Dr. Kolischer with the task,

[Pages 231-232]

during his October 1840 visit, to present Franz Karl, Kaiser Ferdinand's brother, with a memorandum on the condition of the Jews and to request an annulment of the candle–tax, as well as an easement on the employment of Jews.

The community's conditions had in fact shown signs of improvement. In culture and education Lwów lagged behind Brody and Tarnopol where schools already had trained and experienced teaching staff. At Lwów, not even one Jewish school existed despite the relatively good financial situation.

Antrittsrede,

gehalten in der großen

Vorstadt-Synagoge

zu

LEMBERG,

am 11. Mai 1844.

von

Abraham Kohn,

Religionsweiser und Prediger der hiesigen Israeliten-Gemeinde.

——————

Der Ertrag ist dem Ausbaue des Israelitisch-Deutschen Bethhauses allhier gewidmet.

LEMBERG,

gedruckt bei Peter Piller.

1844.

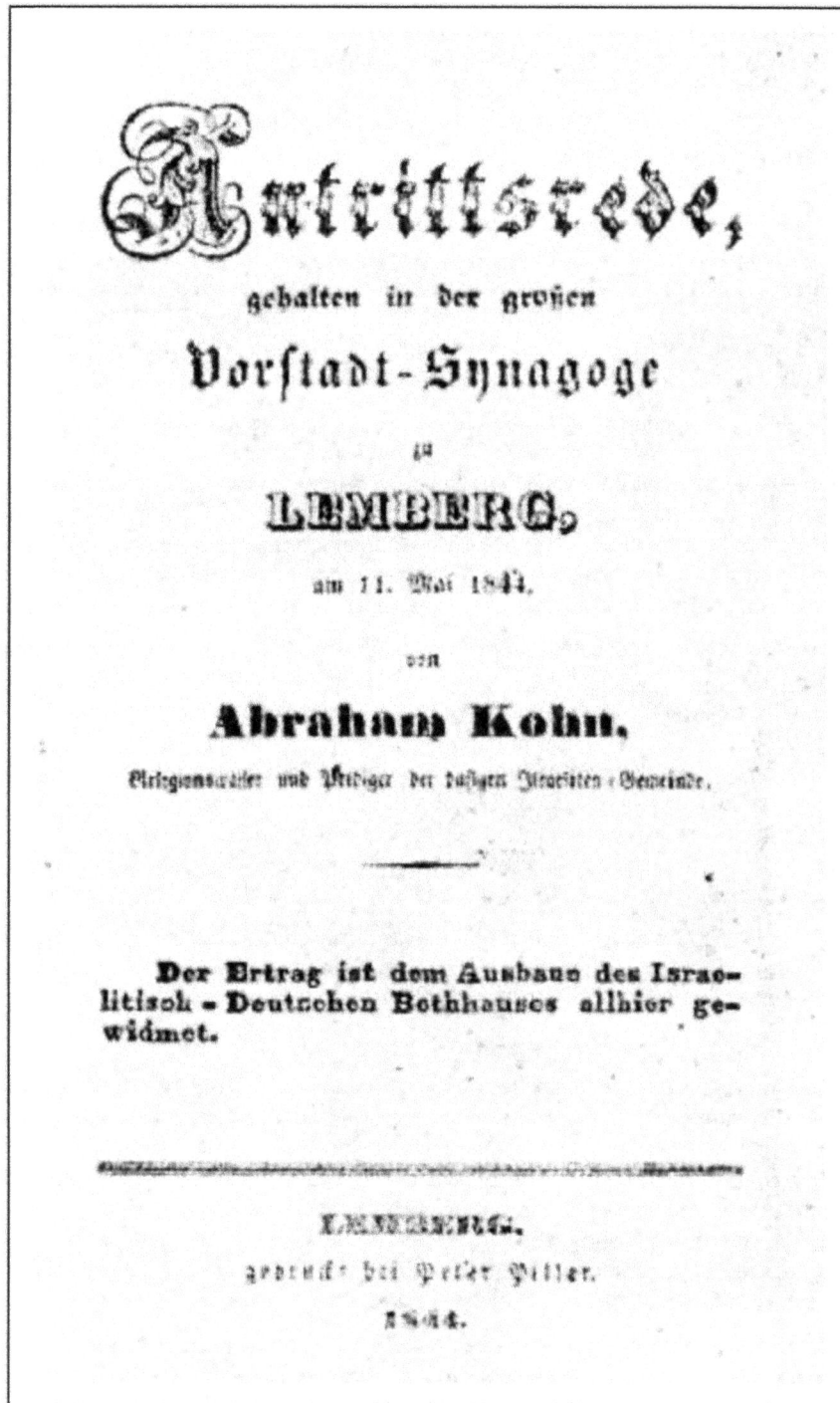

Pamphlet. Rabbi A. Kohn's Synagogue address

1840 was set for new elections, but concern that the candle–tax lessees' influence might impede the candidates, led to the postponement of the election. It appears that even the authorities who did not get involved in any conflicts between the *Maskilim* and the Orthodox, the opposers [*Misnagdim*] or the Chassidim, did not want to see the tax–lessees' people on the Community Committee. Instead, they preferred to consider the Jewish intelligentsia. Consequently, in 1842 without any elections, the authorities appointed a new Community Committee which included: Emanuel Blumenfeld, Dr. Oswlad Menkes, Dr. Abraham Barach–Rappaport, Markus Dubs, Isak Aron Rosenstein, S. Rappoport. To the Board were appointed: Michael Kehlmann, D. L. Kronstein, Meier Rachmiel Mieses and Leib Meller.

A year prior to the appointment, Lwów's *Maskilim* were spurred into action by the scholar Josef Perl who lived there. His medical doctor, Dr. Jakob Rappoport, was in fact the spiritual leader of Lwów's Jewish intelligentsia. Dr. Rappoport (1772–1855), born at Uman [Humań], Ukraine, was from a rabbinical family. His father, Rabbi Mordechai ben Shabbatai Rappoport, was rabbi at Oleksince [Oleksyntsi] and Uman, great–grandson and grandson of Benjamin, author of *G'vulot Benjamin* ["Benjamin's Bounds"] (Lwów 1789), religious judge [*Moreh Tzedek*] at Brzeżany, the brother of Lwów's rabbi, Rabbi Chaim HaKohen Rappoport, known for participating in the 1759 dispute with the Frankists.

Rabbi Mordechai, Dr. Jakob Rappaport's father, the regional Rabbi for Podolia, also practiced medicine. At the end of his book *Imrei Noam* [*Words of Pleasantness*] (Oleksince, 1767), he published an addendum "Children's Medicines" with "recipes" in Latin. His mother, Sara, the daughter of Rabbi Jakob of Dubno, had published in Yiddish the book *Tehinah far Imahot* ["Plea to Mothers"] (Lwów 1804). Rabbi Mordechai who lived at Horodenka, moved to Kraków and practiced medicine there too. On 18ᵗʰ April 1781, Galicia's director of medical services, Dr. Andrzej Krupiński, issued him with a certificate which entitled him to treat patients throughout Galicia. In 1782, the certificate was approved by the faculty of medicine of Kraków University, and for a while he was a doctor at Kazimierz, the Jewish Quarter near Kraków.[14]

His son Jakob, who was traditionally educated, studied philosophy too. He married Juliana, the daughter of Ber Birkenthal from Bolechów [Bolekhiv], known for participating in the dispute with Jakob Frank. Jakob passed the entrance examination of the philosophy faculty and later that of the medicine faculty. In 1804 he ended his studies as a doctor of Medicine,[15] settled at Lwów and was very successful as a doctor. He was liked and accepted by people from every walk of life. As a doctor he forewent any payment from paupers and even gave poor patients of his own money as well as providing them with medication. Dr. Jakob Rappoport was a proud Jew who was interested in the life of his community. In his view, "We have no need to be ashamed of our People (nationality) when we are among other people and nations." He objected to deprivation of the Hebrew language; to changes in the Jewish prayers; and to praying in German in the synagogues, as demanded by radical reformers in Germany. He was also one of the instigators and founder members of the Enlighteners' synagogue (Temple).[16]

The new community leader, Dr. Emanuel Blumenfeld,[17] was a descendant of the Reizes family who were martyred. He and his colleagues on the community management went briskly into action. In March 1842 they approached the governorship with a request to authorise the community

[Pages 233-234]

to set aside funds for 10 bursaries for craftsmen, and to use the "Talmud–Torah Fund" for the construction of an orphanage for 12 of the institute's orphaned pupils. According to the plan, the orphans would study secular studies at the orphanage, and would sit the annual examinations at a state school. The request included the proposal to allocate a post to a Jewish–religion teacher at the secondary school, who could also act as preacher. The request was supported by the municipality as well. In his reply the Governor reminded the community that the matter had already been debated in 1835, and based on the assessment of Josef Perl and Herz Homberg, the Vienna Court–office ordered on 2ⁿᵈ September 1837 that Lwów's community should establish an elementary school similar to that at Tarnopol, and should use the budget to pay the teacher's salary. The Governor had thus returned to the issue of establishing a school.[18]

At the beginning of 1843 the community committee submitted a petition to abolish the candle–tax,[19] together with a detailed description of the hardship caused by the taxes which constituted an affront to conscience and religious feelings. The additional taxes and the injustice, it stressed, were the principal reasons for the poverty of Galicia's Jews. A counter–memorandum was concurrently submitted by a group of Jews, initiated by the tax–lessees.[20]

The Governor ruled that the Jews of Galicia had to pay all the direct and indirect taxes like the rest of the population. The candle–tax, however, was loathed for its malevolent collection and in particular its pernicious effect on the poorest.

Indeed, the Finance department decided that the candle–tax would be debated as part of the general discussion of the Jewish taxes, but that it should remain in force for the time being. The "temporary arrangement" continued for many years; only on 15ᵗʰ March 1843 did the Court–office propose to abolish the candle–tax. Despite that, the Court–office insisted that due to the monarchy's economic situation and requirements such an income could not be waved, and that the Emperor should not abolish the candle–tax unless a substitute income was found. On 19ᵗʰ May 1843 Kaiser Ferdinand sanctioned the Finance department's demand,[21] thus deferring the community's request.[22]

Once Dr. Blumenfeld and members of the community management had tried to introduce order into the administration, they turned to reorganizing the Orthodox junior–school where they also introduced general studies. The syllabus also included Bible classes in German translation, arithmetics, writing, Hebrew grammar and the German language. There were 130 pupils. The 800 Florins income from one of the community houses sufficed to cover the costs. The orphanage [female] director also supplied food and clothing for those in need.

On 30ᵗʰ May 1842 the orphanage was opened with the active support of Hersch Zipper (1796–1858), the Police inspector for the Jewish Quarter who donated his entire wealth to the cause.[23] The wealthy Orthodox citizens refused to contribute financially towards its maintenance as they objected to the institute's aim. The government contributed 10 pupils' stipends for the study of crafts and professions.

Concurrently, the upper war commissioner (K. K. Feldkriegs–Oberkommissar), Willibald Schiessler, donated a building which was made into Lwów's first Jewish children's day–care centre. 170 children were accepted by the institute.

The annual income of the hospital increased from 13,200 Florins to 20,000 Florins. During 1843, 1304 patients received medical care there, of whom 1117 recovered and 187 died. In 1843, with the help of B. Goldstern's heirs, a sanitarium for 79 individuals was established next door to the hospital.[24] On the community's initiative a women's association was established to provide food and clothing for the orphanage.

Indeed, the community committee devoted much of its efforts to establishing an elementary school–. The authorities' response regarding the appointment of a teacher, of [the Jewish] religion, reiterated the Court–office's ruling of 1837 instructing the community to establish an elementary school, a project which Dr Blumenfeld consequently set out to implement.

At the beginning of 1844 the community submitted a detailed memorandum on creating a German–Jewish school (Deutsch–Israelitische Hauptschule), after proving that the overcrowding in the Christian schools necessitated the establishment of a special school for Jews, whose number had reached 17,043 souls of which 1,704 were children of compulsory education age. ["]The *Cheders*, the Torah teachers and the teachers' assistants (*Belfer*) are the source of the ignorance, and they are unsuited to provide the children with regular education. The Torah teachers are ignorant and lack knowledge. Most of them are men who found no livelihood and became Torah teachers out of necessity.["] The community expressed its desire to establish a regular school similar to Perl's school at Tarnopol. They tried for long to establish the school, but their efforts failed due to the anti–Enlighteners (Obskuranten) who lobbied the authorities' offices against such projects.

The community's request was sent to the Court–committee for education (Studien–Hofkommission) which decided on 16ᵗʰ April 1844 to approve the community's plan, as follows:

The community undertook to collect funds to purchase a plot for the school. To reach the required sum they set out to collect it from: A. One extra Gulden on Kosher ritual slaughter – 4,400 Florins. B. Tuition

[Pages 235-236]

fees depending on the pupil's parental status – 20 Kreuzer [Kreutzer], 45 Kreuzer, or one Florin; and pupils from outside the community – 3 Florins; children of the poor were exempt from tuition fees. Any budget deficit would be filled by a special tax.

At the suggestion of the regional office, one director and two inspectors appointed by the Governor would head the institute. The teachers would be appointed by the director and the inspectors, and approved by the Governor. The entire staff would be Jewish.

The German and Polish languages would be taught according to the state schools' syllabus. The Hebrew studies – according to Perl's school syllabus. The school would be under the authority of the regional office, and subject to the general schools' legislation. No classes would take place on the Sabbath and Jewish holidays, but would be held on Sundays and Christian holidays. The duty of study would also extend to girls. The community's proposal to name the school "Model Elementary School" ("*Muster Hauptschule*") was rejected. Instead, it was given the name "Ashkenazi–Jewish School at Lwów" [Ashkenazi = German, in archaic Hebrew] ("Deutsch–Israelitische Hauptschule in Lemberg").

On 16ᵗʰ April 1844, Kaiser Ferdinand I approved the Court–committee for education's proposal, with the proviso that the additional tax on the Kosher ritual slaughter be charged until such time as it was necessary to abolish it.[25]

The community leaders wished to invite a progressive preacher to undertake the school's management. They decided to implement the decision, of 4ᵗʰ October 1840 made at Dr. Blumenfeld's home, to establish a synagogue for the Enlightened which despite the efforts of "the Temple Committee" headed by Jakobka Rappoport, had not materialized. They considered it the right time to realise that decision.

The licence application to build "a Modern Temple," in the manner of Vienna and Prague, had long been submitted to the Governor – on 20th June 1842. Once they explained to the Governor the means by which they would pay for the building, the regional minister [von] Millbacher who supported the *Maskilim* to the dismay of the Orthodox, granted the licence on 18th December 1842.

In July 1843, land was purchased and entered in the land–register as: "Ashkenazi–Jewish Synagogue" ("Deutsch–Israelitisches Bethaus"). Once all the funds were collected the donation of 900 Florins by Jakub Glanzer, the leader of the Chassidim, was revealed among other; a sum he was obliged to contribute toward the "Temple," in order to obtain approval from the community and the regional office for constructing the "Innovation [Chidushim] Shul." To build the "Temple" required greater investments than the 4,000 Florins capital from Isak Rosenberg's 1798 estate. Consequently, the 5,503 Florins & 42 Grozky capital of the orphanage was also used, and was entered as a loan. Rabbi Abraham Kohn of Hohenems was invited as preacher. On Saturday 8th August 1844, at the synagogue outside the town, he delivered his first homily which was enthusiastically received by members of the community committee as well as by the committee of the "Temple," and the contract of his appointment as preacher, teacher of religion and school director was signed on 20th August 1844.[26]

The school, made up of three classes and one elementary class, similar to the state schools, was opened in November 1844. The school council was made up of: two inspectors, the community–elders Dr. Blumenfeld and Dr. Kolischer, as well as the preacher Abraham Kohn as the school master. The elected teachers were Pessach [Psachje] Grünes –Hebrew language;[27] Hersch Glasgall –calligraphy, both of whom had taught at Perl's school; Michael Wolf ([28] –Hebrew; Leo Volländer–Riesberg –German Languae; Akiba (Karl) Lodner[29] –Arithmetic; S. Schlesinger, Igolnitzer –Hebrew; Bernhard Frenkel –Polish. In addition, Dr. Bernhard Sternberg was appointed teacher and deputy director.

Once the school had opened, a large number of boys and girls enrolled. During the first academic year (1844–1845) it catered for 427 pupils. During 1845–1846 there were 583 pupils (in seven classes), and during 1846–1847, 738 pupils.

Rabbi Abraham Kohn himself wrote some handbooks on the study of Judaism: *Sefer Limud Toldot HaYehudim* ["History of the Jews Textbook"] up to the destruction of the second Temple, and a book for the study of religion *Chanoch LaNa'ar* ["Train up a child…"].

The establishment of the school, the erection of the "Temple" and the appointment of Abraham Kohn had so enraged the Orthodox that they submitted an appeal to the Governor, signed by their leaders Josef Hersch Rappoport, Mordechai Zeeb Ettinger, Jacob Herz Bernstein, Hersch Ornstein, Samuel Goldstern and Meier Münz. Their anger was particularly inflamed when they realized that the preacher, Abraham Kohn, was elected the community Rabbi to occupy the seat of head of the Rabbinate, a post previously held by such great scholars as Kalman of Worms, Meschulam of Salzburg, David Halevy author of *Turei Zahav* "Chacham Cwi ["Sage Tzvi"] Zvi Hirsch Rosanisch [Rosanes], and last, Rabbi Jakob–Meschulem Ornstein. The Orthodox, who could no longer hold their peace, decided to come out vociferously and prevent such a move. The appeal, probably penned by Meier Münz, described Abraham Kohn as a man ignorant of the Talmud, who did not keep the religious precepts [Mitzvot] and who disparaged the Law of the Torah. The petition with hundreds of signatures protested against the establishment of the school. The petition, together with the positive opinion of the regional minister Millbacher, were sent by the Governor to the Vienna authorities who passed the appeals to the accredited office at Dornbirn, Tirol, with a request

[Pages 237-238]

for a report on Abraham Kohn's character. The office invited Hohenems's community leader, Philip Rosenthal, who provided a favourable opinion about him. Based on his opinion, the Vienna central authorities rejected the petition submitted by the Orthodox.[30] Shortly afterwards the authorities appointed Abraham Kohn, Rabbi for the Lwów district (Kreis–rabbiner), as well as the registrar of the Jewish population, replacing Abraham Korkis.

Once Abraham Kohn uncovered forgeries in the registration books, the resentment of the Orthodox rose even further. In his sermons he criticised the zealousness and ignorance of the rabbis and of the righteous men. In his letters which he published at Vienna in *Lu'ach Bosh* ["List of Shame"], he mocked certain customs. Their opposition peaked when, in December 1846, he conducted a Bar–Mitzvah and a "Bat–Mitzvah" celebration at the "Temple" synagogue.

For the Orthodox that signified a slide towards annihilation; unrest ensued, which had to lead to an outburst.

The community committee continued in its operational activities and in its endeavour to replace the outdated practices and breathe new life into the community and make it relevant for the time. The community–elders attempted to convince the authorities of the need to introduce legal amendments to improve the economic and cultural status of Galicia's Jews.

Once they had succeeded in establishing a synagogue and a school in the spirit of the age, and to organize the institutions' welfare, the community–elders turned to finding solutions to the pressing problems in the relations of the government with the Jews.

Ever since Kaiser Franz I had ordered a new Jewish code in 1803, "which did not focus on taxes alone" (*Deren Zweck nicht allein das Steuerwesen ist*), the authorities considered the time and circumstances appropriate. Although the Kaiser ordered to speed up the issue, they spent years preparing the new code since, according to Kanzler [Chancellor] Graf Ugarte (1812), the Jewish issue required a prolonged investigation. In 1820, the Emperor firmly ordered to work towards removing any segregation between the Jews and the rest of the population. He also ordered to impose on the youth the study at general schools, and to make the appointment of rabbis contingent on their general education.

In 1833, the Court–office announced that it was still investigating the regulations regarding the Jews, and that the responsible Court advisor, von Widmann, had not yet terminated his investigations, constantly requesting additional information from the Governorship: regarding the regulations of the drink pourers; concerning the establishment of an institute to instruct rabbis, in philosophy; what was the difference between a rabbi and a teacher of religion, etc. The Governor for his part passed on the questions to the regional ministers for their opinions, and none of them was in a hurry to reply, thus endlessly extending the debates and the files.[31] The authorities who were assigned the Jewish issues, collected memoranda and opinions from enlightened Jews and specialists in the fields – and matters remained unchanged.

The Galician authorities started to note the value of the Jews and deemed them Galicia's "Third Estate" (*tier état*), that might strengthen the German constituency which supported Vienna's centralization of power. Galicia's Polish leadership, on the other hand, also began to fathom that the Jewish issue should not be underrated. Among Galicia's Polish population the realization arose that with the growing "emigration", especially after the 1830–31 Polish revolt, the Jews of Galicia had

to be mobilized for the "Polish cause." Experience had taught them that unlike their brethren in Congress Poland, the Jews of Galicia had manifested no enthusiasm for the national revolt, and the number of young volunteers from Galicia was very small.[32]

Although only few among the [Jewish] young sympathized with the Poles, the government suspected the Jews of Galicia and especially those of Lwów, of assisting the Polish nationalists. During 1835–1837 the suspicion increased after the emigration envoy Józef Zaliwski, on his own initiative, had organized in March 1833 a partisan invasion into Congress Poland which ended in total defeat. The Polish insurgents were driven back by the police with assistance from the armed forces, as well as through searches on the roads and in forests, and mass arrests. In its persecution campaign the police had also employed Jewish spies, but only a very small number of Jews was willing to spy on the Poles for the authorities. On the contrary, to the Poles' surprise the Jews of Brody and Lwów showed great sympathy for the Polish cause and helped the Polish insurgents hide from their persecutors. As is known, many Poles faced prosecution. Among them were Jan Lewandowski and Karol Borkowski who were accused of treason against Austria, and during their lawsuit the authorities uncovered details of the help Jews had extended to the Polish movement. Based on the police report, searches of Jewish *Maskilim* were carried out.[33] At the bookshops of Mendel Bodek and Samuel Igel they found the pamphlets by Polish emigrants in Paris. The authorities considered the events so suspicious and important that on 25th January 1835, the president of the Vienna Ministry of Justice, Graf [von] Taaffe, handed the Kaiser a special report about the searches.

[Pages 239-240]

Berman Birkenthal of Bolichów, probably part of Ber Bolichow's family, passed detailed information on the existence of Polish revolutionary associations. For his services he received 600 Florins, in 1835 alone.[34]

While Polish leaders began to regard the Jews as a political element, no signs of closer Jewish–Polish relations were yet visible in Galicia. Although the *Maskilim* circles stressed that Jews owed gratitude to the Polish people for letting them into Poland when they were expelled from Germany, "In modern life, memories of the past fade in the reality of the present, and in the interest of future existence. Consequently, the Jews must reserve any fondness for Poland", since "our future is in the hands of Austria, and our politico–spiritual existence can only be German despite the systematically cold manner in which the German people reject us."[35] Nevertheless, the *Maskilim* insisted that Polish [language] also be taught at the Jewish schools.

No defined political orientation had as yet evolved among the Jewish intelligentsia whose prime aspiration focused on attaining emancipation which the community leaders desired, without giving much consideration to any other problems. Believing that the future of Galicia's Jews was firmly linked to Austria, Lwów's community committee considered itself under obligation, with regard to the Tarnów [Tarnau] peasants' corruption and their riots in other regions during the 1846 revolts,[36] to ask the government to establish a Jewish Brigade in the service of Austria.

On 3rd March 1846, the Governor replied that since there was no risk to the country nor its capital, the government had declined the offer to establish a Jewish Brigade. In case of danger, however, the government would take into account the community's "patriotic offer." The regional minister expressed his hope that all preparation be made to establish the Brigade, were a danger to arise.[37] Besides its suggestion of the Jewish Brigade, the community committee donated 4,000 quarts of liquor to the soldiers "who undertake difficult service." For "that patriotic donation", General Festenburg sent the community committee a letter of appreciation from the army headquarters.

On 3rd April 1846, based on the "loyal stance" of Galicia's Jews during the bloody uprising, the community submitted a petition to Kaiser Ferdinand I (signed by Dr. Blumenthal, Rosenstein, M. Dubs, I. L. Kolischer and Dr. Kolischer) to abolish the restrictions on the occupations available to Jews, especially the prohibition to settle in villages. In their petition, the alliance and loyalty the Jews had demonstrated during the 1846 bloody uprising was emphasized to justify such a demand, also, that due to the urban congestion some of the Jewish population should to be moved to the villages, thus increasing the German element on which the authorities laid great stress. To the petition the delegation (Pillersdorf and Zaleski) appended a letter which confirmed the "patriotic conduct" of the Jewish population and their full assistance during the uprising, and it recommended to grant the Jews the easement they were seeking. On 26th May 1848, the Vienna Court–office submitted a recommendation to the Emperor that that petition be taken into account when the new rules concerning the Jews of Galicia, were considered.

The Jews greeted with satisfaction the appointment of Count [Franz] Stadion [Graf von Warthausen] as Governor of Galicia, since his sympathy towards the Jews was revealed during his period of tenure as officer at the Sambor regional office in 1829, when the Jewish teacher Löbl Grabscheid taught him Polish and Hebrew.[38]

In 1847, with the change of governorship, Dr. Blumenfeld initiated a political move that proposed to grant Jews the rights of citizenship within the town, but his proposal was met with stormy resistance from the Christian townspeople. Dr. Blumenfeld and his colleagues concerned themselves not only with the local Jewish community, and decided to take care of Jewish affairs in the whole of Galicia. With that in mind, in the summer of 1847 Dr. Blumenfeld assembled the representatives of the large communities of Lwów, Brody, Tarnopol, Stanislawow [Stanisławów], Stryy [Stryj] and Sambor, to discuss the situation, and they decided to submit a memorandum to the government, detailing the lamentable situation of the Jews and to request an annulment of the restrictions on habitation, and of the special taxes, especially the candle tax and the tax on Kosher meat. Since it was against the law to submit a joint petition from the different communities, it was decided that each community should submit its own petition, directly.

On 22nd August 1847, Lwów's community submitted the first petition, signed by Dr. Blumenfeld, Dr. Adam Barach–Rappaport, Marek Dubs, Dr. Leo Kolischer, I. L. Kolischer, I. A. Rosenstein, as well as the committee members: Jakob Gottlieb, Feiwel Weitz, Leib Russmann and H. Gruder.[39]

The petition highlighted the issues arising from the Jewish taxes: the candle tax and the tax on Kosher meat. The insult to the Jews prompted by those taxes was heart–wrenchingly described. Apart from the distress they inflict –it reported– it is hard to recount the howls and cries when the tax collectors confiscate the mattresses from the homes of the poor, remove the most essential housewares, and even the prayer books. The taxes cast fear and horror and shatter the tranquillity of the population. The horrific scenes, of the tax lessees and their factotums accompanied by

[Pages 241-242]

soldiers inside the dwellings of the poor, investigating whether more candles had been lit than tax had been paid on, were indescribable. The situation concerning the taxes on Kosher meat was identical. The memorandum also considered the political and civil conditions, the prohibitions and restrictions on trade, crafts and the free professions.

The delegation that included Rabbi Abraham Kohn, set out for Vienna to deliver the petition but its effort was in vain. The central authorities refused to annul the taxes, or to agree to any concessions which would benefit the Jews. All the petitions from Lwów, Brody (19 Sept. 1847), Tarnopol (1 Oct. 1847), Stanislawow (25 Oct. 1847), Stryj and Sambor (2 Nov, 1847) were returned to the Governor and filed with no further action.

The only issue which attracted the governorship's attention on several occasions, regarded the abolishing of Galician Jews' traditional clothes and the means how to force them to wear European dress.

In 1791, Kaiser Joseph II demanded to put an end to the Jewish traditional dress. The demand was not carried out however, after the Jews of Galicia lobbied Christian cloth and velvet manufacturers, at Vienna and Bohemia, who in turn petitioned the government with claims that they had amassed stockpiles and in order to prevent the destruction of an industry in which 11,000 men were employed it was best to delay the execution of the ruling. The Governor of Lower–Austria supported the petition with the argument that following the ruling would destroy an entire industry employing 250 precious machines. Under such pressure, Kaiser Joseph II withdrew the regulation.

Nonetheless, in 1804 the issue resurfaced in conjunction with the ruling to stop Jewish women from wearing coifs. The debate continued for some while when, on 5th April 1941, the Emperor ordered to maintain the Jewish traditional dress.

Still, the issue of dress arose again.

On 2nd July 1847, the community committee was ordered by Lwów's police to provide its opinion on the issue of Jewish traditional dress. The community committee agreed to replacing the traditional dress, as it believed it would remove any barrier between the Jews and the Christians and would also greatly contribute towards order and a sense of cleanliness, quelling women's desire for luxury, thus bringing an end to the Christians' envy. The outfit should therefore be abolished in accordance with the rulings of 29th March 1789, and 3rd March 1820, especially since many Jews had already changed their dress style of their own accord, while many avoided so doing for fear of their parents and in–laws.[40] To the memorandum, the community committee appended declarations of hundreds of Lwów's Jews requesting to abolish the traditional dress.[41]

One Sabbath, many among the youth wore European clothes and paraded in the streets, in protest.

The Orthodox, noting the growth of the movement and fearing that the authorities would fulfil the wishes of the Enlightened [Maskilim], organized a counter action. Through the communities they mobilized mass requests to maintain the traditional Jewish dress, claiming that merchants and tailors had large stocks of silk suitable solely for the Jewish outfit. They also requested that the women's coifs should not be abolished, as at times those were the sole valuables of a Jewish family.

The governorship decided to seek the opinion of Rabbi Abraham Kohn, who disclosed that all Jews, apart from Rabbis, ritual judges and holy–vessels, should be obliged to wear European clothes. Rabbi Kohn insisted in particular on forbidding the wearing of "*spodeks*" [men's traditional tall] Sable fur hats, or women's coifs set with pearls and gemstones, which led to the financial ruination of many a family pretending to be wealthy by wearing luxury goods. He suggested that the granting of trade, crafts, industry, and especially marriage licences should be conditional on changing the [traditional] clothes. Rabbi Kohn's proposal to abolish the traditional Jewish dress in Poland demonstrated the need for such amendments in order to eliminate the Chassidism which had spread through Galicia since the arrival from Russia to Austria of its "patron," Rabbi Israel Friedman [Ruzhiner Rebbe].[41]

Not content with that response, the governorship sought the opinion of the Jewish intelligentsia that was close to the Orthodox. Consequently, on 17th November 1847, Meier Münz was asked to provide the regional office with his opinion on the reasons for the poverty, the moral decline and the unlawful marriages among the Jews.

In 1848, Münz's memorandum was published as:

Ein Wort zu Zeit. Gutachten über die Verhältnisse und Übelstände der Galizischen Juden in Folge einer löblichen K.K. Kreisamtlichen Aufforderung von V...v. M...tz.[42]

His memorandum presented a clear depiction of the condition of the Jews and ascribed the blame for the poverty and economic decline solely to the government which restricted their rights, and limited their rights of residency to specific quarters, thus blocking the path of culture and advancement. Unlike the *Maskilim* who laid stress on the Enlightenment, the establishment of schools etc., Münz in his memorandum claimed that under the existing political circumstances Enlightenment brought great disappointment to the Jews once they realized their wretched circumstances. It was not Enlightenment the Jews required, but equal civil and economic rights

[Pages 243-244]

which in turn would lead to changes in education. Münz, who was an opponent of Rabbi Kohn, encouraged the protests and reactions of the Orthodox. He composed and wrote their memorandums and complaints which accumulated at the offices of state.

The authorities' sympathy, especially that of the regional office headed by the enlightened officer Millbacher, lay with the Enlighteners' aspirations. The Orthodox endlessly petitioned to remove the population's registration from the hands of Rabbi Kohn. They libelled the head of the congregation as well as the institutions' social workers, and claimed that the Jewish Police–inspector, Hersch Zipper, took bribes from foreign Jews to benefit the orphanage and the "Temple." The authorities also received anonymous libel letters which exacerbated the relationship between the Orthodox and the Enlightened, even ending in conflicts and assaults.

The cultural life of Jewish youths underwent a marked change and a large number of *Maskilim* studied Enlightenment books and German literature, which they considered the epitome of spirituality.

The youth found no contentment however in the scientific strand of Enlightenment literature, nor in the Jewish studies guided by Rabbi Salomon Jehudah Rappoport [Shir], Reb. Nachman HaKohen Krochmal, Reggio, Samuel David Luzzatto, SaDaL, etc.

The youths rebelled against the scientific strand, longing instead for an artistic direction. There were at Lwów a number of talented young *Maskilim* and poets who wrote in Hebrew and German. One of them, Moses Reizes [Reices], wrote poetry in seven languages: Hebrew, Aramaic, German, French, Italian, English and also Polish. At the age of 17, the young, Lwów born author Nahman Isaac Fischmann published a volume of poems *Eshkol Anavim* ["Bunch of Grapes"] (Lwów 1827), with the help of Jakob Samuel Byk who recognized his talent and encouraged him; the publication made a great impression. The medical doctor Dr. Abraham Natkis, a son of the *Maskil* Benjamin Natkis whom Rabbi Jacob Ornstein had boycotted in 1816, published lyrical poems in *Bikureh Haltim* (Pamphlet 6–7) and in *Jeruschalajim*. While still a secondary school pupil, he published poems in Lwów's German monthly, "*Mnemosyne*". After 1848, the talented author Abraham Mendel Mohr (1813–1868), together with his brother–in–law Bodek, attacked the *Charedim* in the pamphlet *Etzah Tova* ["Good Advice"] in which they warned the Orthodox leaders and the tax lessees who took advantage of, and deprived, the Jewish population. They also published Lwów's first Yiddish weekly, *Lemberger Jüdische Zeitung*, as well as geography and history books written in a popular style.

There was a significant discontent among the youth against the scientific strand of the Enlightenment literature. A group of youths led by Jakob Bodek (1819–1855), aspired to topple from their pedestal the authors of wisdom and science: Salomon Jehudah Rappoport, [Leopold Zunz [Tzuntz], Samuel David Luzzatto. I. S. Reggio, whom they had previously regarded prominent figures in science and literature, and whom they had greatly honoured.

Jakob Bodek joined his brother–in–law Abraham–Mendel Mohr, Nahman Isaac Fischmann, known by his Hebrew poems, as well as Jakob Mentsch, and in 1837 they published the first annual critics' pamphlet titled *HaRoé uMevaker Sefer Mechabrei Zemanenu* ["Which Notes and Criticises Books by Contemporary Authors"]. The annual was no biographical–theoretical review of published books, but rather a platform dedicated to polemics – probably guided by the personal envy of the authors whose scientific works had gained recognition and honour.

The articles published by the four youths in their annual, were derogatory reviews of all the innovations by the Enlightenment [*Haskala*] scholars in the history of the Jewish People –especially Salomon Jehudah Rappoport, Reggio, Zunz and Samuel David Luzzatto. Those articles were not written in an objective, scientific vein, but rather to demean them and besmirch their names, with the aim to offend and demean them in the reader's mind.

When they submitted the pamphlet to the censor and J. H. Schorr of Brody found out its content, he spared no effort to convince the former to assign *HaRo'é* to oblivion. Due to his efforts the second pamphlet in which they treated Salomon Jehudah Rappoport with contempt and abuse, they were unable to publish at Lwów. In 1839 the pamphlet was therefore published under the title *Emek Shoshanim* ["Valley of Roses"] in in the Hungarian style, which was not subject to Austrian laws, and where Emanuel Rosenthal[43] joined the group. When the Lwów censor became aware of the matter, he ordered to destroy all the published issues that were brought to Galicia, and to fine the authors 25 Ducats.

In their fight against Salomon Jehudah Rappoport, his young opposers did not even stop from harming his livelihood as rabbi. When he was offered to head the Prague Rabbinate, they wrote to the community dignitaries to spur them to cancel his candidacy. Salomon Jehudah Rappoport responded to their attacks with two letters in *Kerem Chemed* ["Charmed Vineyard"] 11–12, 1841. Due to its negative, personal polemics, *HaRo'é* made no positive contribution to the development of literature. Its hostile attitude made Jakob Mentsch leave the group. At Żółkiew (1844), Lwów and Prague (1845), Bodek, Fischmann and Mohr published three pamphlets in the collection *Jeruschalajim* constructed as a town united by words of wisdom and knowledge, poems and riddles, explanations of Scriptures and everything sacred in the Holy Language.[44]

After returning to the bosom of Judaism, Josef Tarler also contributed to this collection with the sharp rebuff against Chassidism in his

[Pages 245-246]

Ia'alizu HaChassidim "Let the Chassidim [*also* righteous] rejoice." Fischmann contributed to the collection poems with a religio–patriotic content, and articles on the history of the Jews. Articles by Bodek and Mohr focused on Hebrew literature during the middle–ages; Bodek published also humorous travel reports, and Naphtali Mendel Schorr, published his poems in that collection.

Jeruschalajim was free of the aggressive–personal tenor which characterized *HaRo'é*. On his own initiative Fischmann abandoned any negative criticism and adopted a positive literary style. He published plays on biblical subjects such as *Mapeleth Sisra* ["Sisra's Fall"] (1841), commentary on the Book of Job *Safah LaNe'emanim* ["The Speech of the Trusty"] (1854), the poem "*HaEt veHaMeshorer*" ["The Epoch and the Poet"] (1870) and from time to time he also contributed to Joseph Kohn-Zedek's *Meged Jerachim* ["Pleasant Months"].

By the middle of the nineteenth century the *Haskalah* was deeply engrained among the Orthodox youths who wished to abandon the grey alleys of their lives, for new lives.

The poet Moses–Hersch Enser, who was born at Lwów in 1804 and died there in 1871, also numbered among the *Maskilim*. He excelled at languages, German, French and Greek. His spiritual development was influenced by Dr. Isaac Erter, Salomon Jehudah Rappoport and S. Bloch, with whom he was on friendly terms. Ever since 1845 he published poems in *Kochbe*

Jizchak ["Isaac's Stars"] and in 1854 he published a grammar book on the past–tense, titled *Misat Moshe* or *HaMetzaref* ["Moses's Gift" or "The Purified"]. In his estate were left the manuscripts of *"Igrot el Assaf"* ["Letters unto Assaf"] (about the Hebrew Language), and *"HaNoten Zemirot"* ["The Giver of Tunes"] (on Discernment) as well as an interpretation of *Sefer HaNefesh* ["The Book of the Soul"] by Shem–Tov ben Joseph ibn Falaquera (1224–1270) and a collection of poems *Zera Kodesh* ["Holy Scion"].

Menachem Manisch König (1825–1848) published poems in *Kochbe Jizchak* ["Isaac's Stars"] and left a collection of poems in manuscript form, which was posthumously (1848) published at Lwów by the *Maskil* Salomon Rubin. Another *Maskil*, Moses–Leib Lejbowicz, published poems in *Kochbe Jizchak*, as well as in *HaNescher* ["The Eagle"] edited by Kohn-Zedek.

The *Maskilim* also included among their number Jente Kehlmann, the daughter of the renowned *Maslkil* and merchant, Michael Kehlmann, member of the community committee headed by Dr. Blumenfeld. She was born in 1810 and learnt the Bible and Hebrew grammar by listening in on her brother's lessons in childhood. Over time she acquired an extensive knowledge of the Hebrew language, read poems by Wessely and Enlightenment books. Aged fourteen she was betrothed to the *Maskil* L. Rosanisch of Brody with whom she corresponded in Hebrew. Rosanisch died shortly after the marriage, and she married the merchant Samson Wohllerner, who also died young, and three weeks later her only son, Kalonymus also died.

She kept her letter–exchange with Rosanisch, but her Orthodox mother took the letters away from her and burnt them. Her letters excelled in their Biblical style; she expressed all her thoughts in the Hebrew language and its literature.[45]

The *Maskilim* had no political agenda, but the events which loomed over the political horizon of the Austrian Monarchy, brought fundamental changes to its Nations, including to the Jews.

[Page 368]

Notes: – CHAPTER 15
All notes in square brackets [ ] were made by the translator.

1.   In 1494, 1504, 1571, 1616, 1626, great fires broke out in the Jewish Quarter.

2.   Memoires of Baron Ludwik–Joseph Jabłonowski. Manuscript at the Ossolineum (Lwów), III, 4793.

3.   Lwów Governor's Archive:
Fasc. 11; Allgem. Sachen No. 14690, 1830.

4.   Wiener Staatsarchiv: S. A. 4200, 24.7.1832.

5.   The Vienna government objected to this Clause for fear of infiltration by foreign Jews (*Die Einschleichen fremder Individuen erleichtert werden*), and changed the Clause so that only wealthy members could join the association.

6.   Archiv des Min. d. Innern. [Archive of the Ministry of the Interior], Police files, No. 3348.

7.   Dr. Gerson Wolf: *Joseph Wertheimer*. Vienna 1868. p. 105.

8.   Report by the institute named after Bernstein. Lwów 1864.

9.   *Galizisch–jüdische Zustände* [Jewish–Galician circumstances] (Anon.) Leipzig. 1845, p. 44.

10.   Allgemeine Zeitung des Judenthums 1837, No. 105, pp. 419–420.

11.   Archive of the Ministry of the Interior: IV T 1, 1828–1848; Fasz. 278, 279.

12.   *Allgemeine Zeitung des Judenthums* 1840, No. 1.

13.   Article signed: A. Barach, *Allgemeine Zeitung des Judenthums* 1839, No. 41.

14.   Dr. Mejer Bałaban: *Historia Zydów w Krakówie i na Kazimierzu*. Vol. II. pp. 537–538.

15.   Wurzbach: *Biographisches Lexikon für das Kaiserreich Österreich* Vol. 24, pp. 355–356.

16.   Dr. Rappaport's only son, Chaim, who had studied medicine at Vienna, drowned in that bathhouse. His daughters: 1. Jura (1808–1841) married Dr. Isak Goldschmidt, a doctor who practiced at Brody; 2. Zophia married a medical doctor, Dr. Kaschowicz, and after his demise, the banker Morizi

[Pages 369-370]

Klar; 3. Sara was married to the lawyer Oswald Menkes. His fourth daughter married the renowned doctor, Dr. Adam Barach, who was also known as Dr. Rappoport, after his father–in–law.

17.   In 1824, Dr. Blumenthal married Leah Pranger of Tarnopol, for whom he was granted a licence to live at Lwów, only after two Jewish families had moved away to a different town. In 1844, after her demise, he requested an entry licence for Rivka Landesberg, with a view to marriage. The Galician authorities supported his request and suggested the prohibition be scrapped in

its entirety. On 6th December 1846, the Court–office recommended his request, but the Kaiser's approval was only granted in 1848, stating: "*Allerhöchste Entschliessung vom 5. Dezember 1848*; Prot. No. 41.198.
"Von den in dem Hofkanzleidekrete vom 4. April 1805 enthaltenen Beschränkungen der Lemberger Israeliten in Ansehung der Wahl ihrer Gattinen aus anderen Inlädischen israelitischen Familien hat es für die Zukunft abzukomen. Ferdinand"

18.   Lwów Governor's Archive: Folder 11/2.
Archive of the Ministry of the Interior: IV T 1, 1828–1848; Fasz. 278.

19.   Wiener Staatsarchiv S. A/1866.

20.   Allgemeine Zeitung des Judenthums 1843, No. 17, p.256.

21.   Wiener Staatsarchiv S. A/2075 19 Mai 1843.

22.   And his decision was worded:
"Dem Gesuche der israelitischen Gemeinde zu Lemberg um Aufhebung des Lichterzündungsaufschlages finde Ich unter den dermaligen Verhältnissen keine Folge zu geben   .
Schönbrunn, den 22. Juli 1843. Ferdinand.["] Staatsarchiv S.A. 2871.

23.   Orient 1842, p. 237.

24.   Allgemeine Zeitung des Judenthums, 1843, No. 17, p. 256; No. 24, Orient 1844, p. 254.

25.   And his decision was worded:
"Die Anträge der Studien Hofkommision zur Errichtung einer eigenen deutsch–israelischen Haupschule in Lemberg erhalten Meine Genehmigung mit dem Beisatze, dass Ich für die Erfordernisse dieser Schule die Einhebung der angetragenen Abgabe vom Koscher geschlachteten erwachsenen Hornvieh insolange gestatte, als nicht öffentliche Rücksichten der Aufhebung oder Cnderung dieser Abgabe nothwendig machen. Wien. 16. April 1844. Ferdinand.["]
(Archiv Kultus. Min. 23a Lemberg ed. 2721
Z. S. 274–4540).

26.   On the establishment of the "Temple" and the deeds of the preacher A. Kohn, *see* Tzvi [Cwi] Karl's article in this volume.

27.   His son, Isaak Jonah Grünes, was a censor of the Hebrew language, for the police, and a Hebrew language expert, at Lwów's law–court.

28.   Michal Wolf who was a Hebrew–language teacher, was born at Gewitsch [Jevíčko] (Moravia) on 2nd January 1807. After the demise of Abraham Kohn several community–leaders wished to appoint him rabbi and preacher, but they failed, and for the next forty years or more he remained a teacher at the Jewish–school and taught religion at the general schools. He also published books: a German translation of Maimonides's "Eight Chapters" (1871); Supplement to *Ozar HaSchoroschim* ["The Treasure of Wisdom"] by Ben-Zew (Lwów, 1880); as well as articles and notes on the translation of the *Pshittah* [standard version of early translation into Syriac of the Bible and the New Testament]. He also published poems in the Syrian language, in *Ozar HaChochmah, HaBoker Or* and *Beth Ozar HaSafrut*. His only son became a hight–court judge and converted [his religion].

29.   After Josef Tarler's demise (1854) he became censor of Hebrew books.

30.   Staatsarchiv SA/836, 1846.

31.   Such as the Vienna Archive records of the Ministry of the Interior, IV T 1 Galizien Fasz. 277, 278 (1828–1848).

32.   Among Galicia's Jews who left for Poland to join the uprising were: 1. Markus Frenkel, a philosophy faculty student at Lwów University; 2. Josef Krochmalnik a surgeon from Brody (it is possible that he was the son of Reb Nachman Krochmal; it is known that the latter had a son, Josef, who studied medicine and later left for Russia.).; 3. Dawid Rottenberg, surgeon; 4. Abraham Steiner, surgeon; 5. Baruch Maurycy. Law student at Lwów University; 6. Adolf (?) Kornberger, Law student at Lwów University; 7. Ludwig (?) Grünfeld, Law student at Lwów University; 8. Jakob Hiller, a surgeon from Brody; 9. Viktor Brodzky, from the Stanislawow [Stanisławów] district; 10. Ignaz Brodzky, from the Tarnow district; 11. Samson Ball, from the Sanok district; 12. Joseph Eisner, from the Zloczow district; 13. Eduard Kurzweil, of Lwów; 14 Dawid Rottenberg, a student of medicine from Brody; 15. Ignacy Karger, of Lwów; 16. Abraham Schwabe, secondary school pupil from Lwów.
Józef Białynia Chołodecki: *Lwów w czasie powstania listopadowego*, Lwów 1930, pp. 36, 37, 42.
Mgr. Karol Lewicki: *Uniwerzytet lwowski a powstanie listopadowe*. Lwów 1937, pp. 143, 146, 149.

33.   Wr. Staatsarchiv; Zentrales Informationsbüro, 20/59 Vortrag Gf. Taafe.

34.   Informbüro Prot. CLXX 688 e.a. 1834.

35.   A. Z. d. J. 1846. p. 659, 667–670. "Ein Schreiben des Verfassers der Wanderungen über Galizien etc."

36.   In 1844 Teofil Wiśniowski appeared in Galicia as an emissary on behalf of the Polish Democratic Society at Versailles, to collect funds for Polish military schools in emigration. In 1845, the Polish emigration emissaries operated an underground resistance to spark a revolt with the aid of the peasants. One of the emissaries at Lwów, Edward Dembowski, proposed to the Polish statesman Franciszek Smolka, that he himself would undertake the central administration of the revolt, and he promised to raise 60,000 peasants from Galicia to join the revolt. Smolka immediately realized the danger such an operation entailed and declined

the offer to join, claiming that the peasants who would take it for a revolt by the nobles, would consequently join the government to suppress the rebellion. Nearly all the Polish leaders of Eastern Galicia objected to such a venture and expressed their view that what was required first was to win the peasants' hearts by releasing them from the permanent enslavement to their estate owners. In September 1845, rumours spread through Lwów that the revolt would soon break out. The governing president, Franz Krieg von Hochfelden, declared to some *Sejm* delegates that the revolt would only last three days, followed by one hundred years of peace. In January 1846,

[Pages 371-372]

a secret meeting of emissaries from the whole of Poland was held at Kraków, during which a national government was elected. The elected revolt leader, Ludwik Mierosławski, also submitted a "combat plan." A revolutionary committee established at Lwów, published the magazine *Kosa* ("Scythe"), and it was agreed to announce the revolt on 20–21 February 1846, to arrest the government leaders during a ball held at Archduke Ferdinand's palace. But Mierosławski was arrested together with some 1,000 Polish rebels, at Poznan [Posen]. The revolt broke out only at Kraków and in the Tarnow district, but the peasants led by Jakub Szela from the village of Smarżowa, attacked the rebels, the priests, the churches and the estate–owners; they killed, robbed and destroyed without mercy. The peasants delivered the bodies of the murdered on wagons, in order to collect the payment which Starosta Breinl had promised them. The peasants of the Rzeszów district were also prepared for similar action, but General Lagdiez (a Hungarian) disbanded the gangs. On the other hand, Lieutenant General [von] Benedek, Krieg's son–in–law, organized such a massacre at Bochnia. In Eastern Galicia there were riots near Narayev [Narajów] and at Horodzow.

The rebellion was confined to the Kraków republic headed by the dictator Tyssowski. A few days later the riots were quelled and on 11th November 1846 Kraków was annexed to Austria.

The Galicia uprising as seen in archival records, was masterminded by Austrian officials in Galicia, led by Krieg, Kraus, and Sacher–Masoch, and forced the Vienna authorities to concede the administration's culpability. Krieg was removed from his post as Galicia's representative and was replaced by Graf [Count] Franz Serafin Stadion who attempted, in the area under his control, to embark on a new Austrian policy. On 31th July 1847, the day he arrived at Lwów, the Polish revolutionaries Teofil Wiśniowski and Józef Kapuściński were executed by hanging.

38.   The government's reply was as follows:

No. 153/pr. Lemberger Israelitischer Gemeindevorstand.

Auch das fernere Anerbieten der Errichtung eines bewaffneten Korps von Juden wurde gnädigst mit dem Beisatz aufgenommen, dass es gegenwärtig wo die Ruhe der Provinz und der Hauptstadt in keinem gefährlichen Grade bedroht ist nicht angenommen werde, dass jedoch die Regierung in dem Gottlob unwahrscheinlichen Falle einer Gefahr von dem Patriotischen Antrage der hiesigen Judengemeinde Gebrauch machen würde.

Es gereicht mir zum Vergnügen dieses dem Vorstand der israelitischen Gemeinde zu eröffnen, und ich erwarte dass Alles werde vorbereitet werden um bei eintretender Gefahr des betreffende Korps aufstellen zu können. Milbacher mp. vom k.k. Kreisamt. Lemberg am 3. März 1846

An den isr, Gemeindevorstand Hier

A. Ztg. d. J. 1847 No. 36.

Archiv d. Min. d Innern. IV T 1 Consignation No. 979 e. a. 1846.

39.   [forms part of the entry for [37]]

40.   Fascicle 11 Allgem. Judensachen No. 48, 122 e. a. 1847.

41.   Fascicle 11 Allgem. Judensachen No. 345 Z 57140 e. a. 1847.

42.   Fascicle 11 No. 1403, 11252.

43.   Manuscript of the memorandum held at Lwów's Archive of the Representative, 1819–1847. Fasc. 11/2.

44.   Menachem Mendel ben Dov–Ber (Emanuel) Rosenthal, born in 1799, was a merchant and later a teacher at Güssing, and towards the end of his life, at Varaždin, where he died in 1871. He contributed to *Kochbe Jizchak* Pamphlets 19, 22, 23; published the notebook *Emek Shoshanin* ["Valley of Roses"] (Ofen [Buda], 1839), against Salomon Jehudah Rappoport's contempt for Talmud scholars. He travelled to Prague and forcefully confronted Salomon Jehudah Rappoport till the community–elders asked the authorities to expel him from Prague.

45.   *Jeruschalajim* set its agenda in its first published issue, in the following rhymes:

> History of ancient days
> for Hebrews and for all the Nations
> Words of reason and knowledge
> pleasant to a listening ear.
> Trope, riddles and allegories
> to awaken the hearts of the cunning.
> Pleasant and lofty songs
> in morals entwined.
> Concealed Creation and its mystery
> shows favour to those seeking its guidance.

> The work of cunning artificers
> and new science books.
> Olden Holy books
> that were shrouded in darkness.
> Exegesis of concealed phrases
> by the wise and learned.

46.   Some of the letters were published in *Kochbe Jizchak*, pamphlet: 18, (pp. 39–40); 28, (pp.73–74); 35, (p. 49), *Beth Ozar HaSifrut* (Jaroslaw pp. 60–62.) In *HaBoker Or* ["The Morning Light"] and in *Jbri Anokhi*. Jente Wohllerner died at Lwów in 1891.

[Pages 247-248]

Chapter 16: 1848

Translated by Myra Yael Ecker

Edited by Yocheved Klausner

Events at Vienna on 13th March 1848. The Equal–rights petition. Establishment of the National Committee. The Jews in the delegation and on the Vienna National Council. Jewish delegates to the Galician *Sejm*. Declarations of brotherhood by the Poles and the Jews. Stadion's proposal to annul the taxation on [Kosher] meat and on candles. The conflict between the Orthodox and the Enlightened. The Anti–Jewish mood. The proclamation to the village residents. Elections to the "Reichstag." The political factions of Lwów's Jews. The communities' memorandum to the "Reichstag". The controversy over Rabbi Abraham Kohn and its bleak outcome. The Jewish debate at the "Reichstag." The riots at Lwów. The onset of the reactionary regime. The legislation of 4th March 1849. Thanksgiving prayer at the Temple of the Enlightened .

A.

The 1848 Spring of European Nations had a significant effect on the lives of Austrian Jews too, and even on the way of life of the Jews of Lwów. The 13th March 1848 shooting at Vienna (*) and the barricades in the streets alarmed the population throughout the lands of the Austrian Empire, and for its own preservation, the Kaiser's House was forced to make concessions to the people. Those included the dismissal of Prince [von] Metternich who embodied tyranny at the time.

On Sunday 19th March 1848, Lwów's Jewish congregation first heard of the events at Vienna. Crowds in high spirits gathered in the streets, especially near the governorship.[1] The Jews too welcomed the events at Vienna, which they considered the harbinger of a new era. They came in droves and were welcomed, with Poles walking arm in arm with "their brethren of the Jewish faith." Governor Stadion's announcement that the Constitution was approved at Vienna on 15th March 1848, was met with jubilation.[2]

Prior to establishing the National Committee during the night of 19th March 1848, the Polish politicians Franciszek [Franz] Smolka, Robert Hefern and Floryan Ziemiałkowski, had prepared a written petition to the Emperor, which the citizens were asked to sign in order to dispatch it to Vienna.

On 19th March the signing began in front of the publishing house of *Dziennik Mód Paryskich* ["Journal of Paris Fashions"], on 301 Halytska Square [Plac Halicki] (opposite the "George Hotel"). "Thousands of citizens crowded around the publishing house and waited patiently for their turn to sign, after Smolka had read out from the balcony the wording of the petition. The first to sign was Archbishop Wacławiczek, followed by the mass of the citizens. The Jewish leadership soon appreciated the significance of the petition which included some demands of interest to the Jews, too. Marek Dubs, Rachmiel Mieses and Rabbi Abraham Kohn ordered the Jews to sign the petition, while stressing that "The Poles are liberal and back the Jews." The Jews followed their advice and the first to sign were Dr. Oswald Menkes, M. Dubs, Joschua Leib Horowitz, Rabbi Abraham Kohn and Meier Rachmiel Mieses."

Till five in the afternoon the ceremony continued peacefully, when suddenly the municipality's clock sounded and rumours spread that a fire broke out in the Zólkiew suburb. With Governor Stadion fearing a possible mayhem among the crowded masses, military companies were immediately on the scene. The presence of the military caused unrest, but the Hungarian cavalry companies were greeted by cries of "*Éljen!*" (Hurrah), and the crowd calmed down. Some twenty thousand persons from all walks of life, with many Jews among them, turned toward the Governor's Palace, and the representatives from all strata of the population headed by Prince Leon Sapieha, Smolka and Mieses reached the palace to hand to Governor Stadion the signed petition forms. The delegation's Jewish representatives were Rachmiel Meier Mieses and Rabbi Abraham Kohn.

The Petition required the Kaiser to grant autonomy to Galicia as an independent entity; general amnesty to all political prisoners; establishing a national education system; annulment of the peasants' serfdom (*Leibeigenschaft*). Clause 9 of the petition demanded that the Kaiser grant equal rights to all strata of society, irrespective of religion, civil, judicial or political stance; revocation of all taxes associated with religion, such as candle tax,

(*). The 15 killed included two Jews: Heinrich Spitzer and Bernhard Hirschmann.

[Pages 249-250]

Kosher meat taxes and any restriction stemming from the affiliation to a religion, and granting equal rights and status to the Catholic, Roman and Greek clergy as well as to the leaders of all other religions.

Rabbi Cwi Hirsch Ornstein

Governor Stadion promised to send the petition to Vienna, but feared that the incidents at Lwów might adversely affect the country's situation and the Poles' attitude towards the central authorities. So the following day –20th March 1848– he sent a secret circular to the regional ministers, pointing out the possible dangers the authorities might expect from the Lwów protests which, according to him, had been promoted by the political party that aspired to social changes and to incite the population to revolt.

Nevertheless, he hesitated to establish an armed "National Guard" as proposed by the population's representatives. His opinion on the matter was guided by the Police–director Leopold [von] Sacher-Masoch who despised the Poles and was keen on their outbursts.

On 20th March 1848, "Kol Kore Davar Be'Ito", a small pamphlet addressed to the Jewish citizens of Galicia, (^) was published at Lwów by Izak Jehuda ben Abraham who considered himself someone who loved the Jewish People and was fond of all Nations. The pamphlet which was also published in Polish, German and Yiddish set out to explain the events at Vienna. In simple terms it reported that the Kaiser's "good hearted" advisors did not wish to inform him of his Nation's request, and so conceal from him the population's condition. But under pressure from the students, a memorandum was submitted to the "Landtag," and before it had reached the Kaiser, the Vienna events broke out. Having described the events up until the Kaiser fled, the author focused on the events at Lwów, after the Vienna events had become known –on Purim– 19th March 1848. In his description of the petition with 13 Clauses, of which the 9th Clause focused on granting equal rights to the Jews, the author praised Governor Stadion as "Father of the citizens" who dismissed an officer who hated the Jews. The pamphlet aimed to ascertain that the time was right for the Jews to abide by the saying "Love thy neighbour," because the Christians refrained from hating the Jews.[3]

On 21st March 1848, some forty men – representatives of the Poles, the Ruthenians and the Jews, craftsmen and the clergy –assembled at the Municipality and established a committee to arrange the management. When Governor Stadion became aware of the meeting, he came in person and ordered to clear the hall. Organizing the management was handed to a Polish estate–owning nobleman, Count Agenor Gołuchowski who was a governorship–official and was appointed deputy mayor, replacing mayor Festenburg who was hated by the entire population and who resigned from the mayoralty. Part of the disbanded committee continued consulting in a private flat and decided, in face of Governor Stadion's hostile stance, to hand the petition compiled by Franciszek Smolka, to the delegation sent to Vienna rather than rely on the Commissioner to deliver it. They immediately elected a delegation of forty members some of whom were Jews.

Rabbi Abraham Kohn,
the first rabbi of "The Temple" synagogue

There is conflicting information as to who the Jewish members were. According to Stadion's report to Pillersdorf, Abraham Mieses, Dawid Horowitz,[4] Rabbi Abraham Kohn, Herz Bernstein and Meier Münz represented the Jews of Lwów. Prince Sapieha, in his memoir, recalls that the banker

(^). "What are those interminable events at Vienna and Lemberg."

[Pages 251-252]

Nirenstein was also part of the delegation; the Polish historian Schnür-Pepłowski mentioned also Klemens Kolischer.[5]

The delegation which reached Vienna on 31st March, included delegates also from Kraków, with Rabbi Dov–Berisz Meisels representing the Jews. The preparation and translation of the petition into German was undertaken by the lawyers Dr. Ziemiałkowski, Dr. Aleksander Sękowski [Senkowski] and by Rabbi Abraham Kohn who knew German well; he also drafted clause 9 which dealt with equal rights of Jews and the annulment of their taxes.

The audience with the Kaiser was set for 6th April. As it was not possible to present the entire delegation to him, a 13 members committee was elected, with Meisels representing the Jews.

Lwów's Jewish representatives at Vienna were ignorant of the Poles' aspirations. Unlike Rabbi Meisels of Kraków who fully supported the Poles, Lwów's Rabbi Kohn overlooked the two clauses and did not concur with all of the Poles' demands for full autonomy. His great attachment to Austria caused the Polish leaders, especially Floryan Ziemiałkowski, to distrust him, whereas they considered Rabbi Meisels "a loyal and true Pole."[6]

Floryan Ziemiałkowski wrote of Rabbi Kohn that he was "a dishonest man, who joined us for fear that we might slaughter the Jews, or with the hope of some benefit. He belittles us and our aspirations to such an extent that despite his cunning he is unable to cover it up."

Under his influence, Mieses and Horowitz did not side with the Poles either, unlike Rabbi Meisels. The Poles suspected Rabbi Kohn who did not wish to sever relations with the government, unlike Rabbi Meisels who actively opposed the government, which was welcomed by the Poles.

On 6th April 1848 the delegation was received by the Kaiser, and delivered the petition. The Kaiser promised to study it. The delegation remained at Vienna and awaited a reply from the government, which in turn approached the Governor Stadion and demanded his opinion.

To minimize the delegation's activities at Vienna, on 26th April 1848 Governor Stadion called a regular session of the Galician State *Sejm* ([*Galicyjski*] *Sejm Stanowy*) in which he implemented a change by increasing the number of urban representatives. Among Lwów's twelve delegates, two were Jews – Rachmiel Mieses [Mizys] and Nathan Sokal – and another two, Majer Kallier of Brody and the physician Dr. Roseneck of Kolomyea [Kolomyja]. In addition, apart from the Catholic and Evangelical legates, the Jewish Rabbinate's envoy, Rabbi Abraham Kohn, was also elected. The Jews were thus represented by five delegates. By means of the *Sejm*, Governor Stadion hoped also to solve several urgent issues regarding the Jews.

On 25th April 1848, the Pillersdorf Constitution (*Pillersdorfsche Verfassung*) was published at Vienna, and formed the basis for the Austrian National Diet [Reichstag].

The Constitution's publication brought joy to the Jews of Lwów, in particular clause 17 which promised "to all the kingdom's citizens, full freedom of religion and conscience as well as personal freedom," and Clause 27 which determined that a bill would be brought during the first National Diet, regarding the lifting of all civil and political restrictions from the religious denominations.

On 28th April 1848, the Polish established a National Council (*Rada Narodowa*) made up of 25 members.[7] Since it was prohibited to sustain political organizations, the newspaper *Rada Narodowa* was launched and the National Committee was declared its editorial committee. Dr. Oswald Menkes, Abraham Mieses, Meier Münz and Rabbi Kohn were invited to represent the Jews. The Council oversaw the national management which also included a Jewish company of 300 men under the command of Emanuel Gall. Every Polish management member had to sign the declaration "acknowledging the German and Jewish students, as citizens of equal rights."

On 20th April 1848, the National Council appealed to the townspeople to consider the Jews as equal citizens, "whose sole ambition is the resurrection of our homeland, where we will live as brothers of one family," and to expunge any hate and resentment from their hearts. And the Jews were asked to disregard the words of villains whose aim was to drive a wedge between Jews and Poles.

When an Italian named Ricci displayed in his Lwów shop caricatures of Jews from among the administration, Poles smashed his shop–windows and forced him to apologize. Once Governor Stadion was forced to abolish the censorship – brought to an end by the Constitution – Abraham Mohr published the newspaper "*Die Zeitung,*"[8] written in Hebrew script.

Concerned that not many Jews joined the Poles, the National Council addressed the Jews in a proclamation on 13th May 1848, pointing out that during the recent events the Poles reached out to the Jews and that Poland received them with open arms after they had been expelled from Germany and other countries. In the petition submitted to the Kaiser, they demanded to grant the Jews rights equal to the rest of

[Pages 253-254]

the population, therefore the Jews should willingly accept the hand of friendship extended to them.

The union with the Poles also required the establishment of a linguistic union, just as the Jews of France, Italy and Germany speak the national language, so the Jews of Poland should speak Polish. That demand probably appeared in conjunction with Abraham Mohr's new publication of the newspaper *Die Zeitung*, and the fact that most of the Jewish intelligentsia was predisposed to the German language and culture.

Unlike the Jews of Western Galicia who supported the movement of the Polish Federation, Lwów's Jewish intelligentsia preferred Vienna's centralization of power. The intelligentsia formed included also a group predisposed towards Polonization; the group formed an association which strove to impart to the younger generation the Polish spirit and encourage it to adopt the Polish language as the national language. Committees and societies were formed to spread the Polish language and literature. A few were even fully inclined towards the Poles, such as the physician Dr. Johann Beiser, a [Jewish] administration member who published a poem –in German– in praise of Poland,[9] which was translated into Polish by Count Leszek [Aleksander] Dunin–Borkowski. The physician Moritz Rappaport, whose renown as a poet rested on his opus *Mose*: [*Episches Gedicht*] (1842), and who was brought up on German culture, found himself attracted to the Polish and to the Jewish People, and expressed the emotional rift in the poem *Bajazzo* (1863),[10] in which he effusively stressed patriotism to Poland. In an enthusiastic poem he lauded the release of Polish political prisoners from the jails at Spielberg [Špilberk] and Kufstein.

This pervading mood drove the youth of Lwów's Jewish intelligentsia to join the Polish faction, and laid the ground for the future movement of assimilation. The trend towards Polonization affected only limited circles, however, and did not reach the circles of veteran *Maskilim*, let alone the masses. Supporters of the Hebrew Enlightenment (*Haskalah*) did not see eye to eye with the circles of the assimilated, and by circulation of leaflets they made every effort to guide the masses in the spirit of Judaism.

Governor Stadion acted against the National Council which in his opinion undermined the authorities' power. When he realised that members invited to the *Sejm* session on 26th April 1848 planned to boycott him, he decided to abolish the National Council with the excuse that it was an illegal institution. He failed, however, when news from Vienna announced the granting of the Constitution (25.4.1848) which, in Clause 22, granted to all citizens of the Empire the right to petition and to establish companies and associations. His decisions were thus thwarted and the Council turned into a legal institution.

On 27th April 1848, Governor Stadion announced he was willing to recognize the National Council with the proviso that he would head it. When his proposal was rejected, the National Council appointed from among its members an advisory committee (*Beirat*), made up of three Ruthenian priests, a (Polish) Catholic priest, a German townsperson, six estate owners, five Polish government officers (led by Gołuchowski),[11] and two Jews (Rabbi Kohn and Mejer Rachmiel Mieses).

At every opportunity subject to the amendments, Governor Stadion showed his willingness to fundamentally and comprehensively improve the legal and political status of the Jews. He consulted with Rabbi Kohn on all matters, which the Poles viewed with suspicion.[12] They feared that he supported the Ruthenians and encouraged them to submit a petition to the Kaiser, on 19.4.1848, with the request that the Ruthenian language be accepted by the State offices and by schools, and that the Uniate clergy be granted equal rights; that he wished to cultivate the Ruthenians and the Jews as counterbalance to the Poles and their aspirations.

The Council also discussed the taxes with which the Jews were burdened. In one of the early sessions Rabbi Kohn proposed the annulment of the restrictions on marriage, and the taxes levied on the Jews. Governor Stadion's plot to use the Council as counter balance to the National Council, failed however, once he was appointed minister of Internal Affairs of the Vienna central government.

On 4th June 1848, he surreptitiously left the town of Lwów.

Even Lwów's municipality which only a year earlier had refused to grant Jews the rights of urban citizenship, elected eight Jews among its 40 members: Dr. Blumenfeld, Mardochaj Dubs, Meier Mieses, Dr. Barach–Rappaport, Osias Meier Goldbaum Dr. Kolischer, Meier Münz, Elischa Mendrochowicz. Their active involvement on the committees' works included, Dr. Blumenfeld, M. Dubs and Meier Mieses on the Finance committee; Dr. on the Health committee; I. M. Goldbaum, Dr. Kolischer, Meier Münz and E. Mendrochowicz on the committee of Police Affairs. The municipality conferred on new regulations for election. The Jews were represented on the Regulation committee by Herz Bernstein, Dr. Emanuel Blumenfeld and Rachmiel Mieses, who had to sanction 15 Jews among the 100 municipality members, as well as five Jews among its 30 deputies. After the regulations had been confirmed in July 1848, the election took place in October 1848, and only progressive candidates were elected. Candidates from among the Chassidism and the Orthodox, failed.

The Constitution gave rise to the question whether

[Pages 255-256]

it was necessary to continue applying the Jewish taxes. The community sent a delegation to Governor Stadion, to relate the affair to him, but he retorted in jest: "He who consumes non–Kosher food pays little, and he who eats Kosher food has to pay more."[13]

The response astounded the community's representatives.

Despite the excitement generated by [political] events, the masses remained indifferent. It was left to the *Maskilim* to explain to the population the meaning and importance of the revolution and its benefit for the Jews.

Nevertheless, Governor Stadion was obliged to send to the Vienna Treasury, with his endorsement, the Jews' demands to annul the taxes and he proposed to annul the Jewish taxes forthwith since the Jews refused to pay them, citing Clause 25 of the Constitution, and "due to the desire to attract the sympathy of the Jewish section of the population."[14]

The government accepted his recommendation and debated it during its 24th May 1848 session. The minister of Finance, the Lwów born Baron Philipp [von] Krauss who was familiar with the situation of Galicia's Jews, maintained that it had to be expected that soon the National Diet would revoke the Jewish taxes. Due to the government's fiscal situation, however, it was difficult to forego the annual 80,000 Florins income. Following his direction, in order for the Treasury to avoid becoming embroiled in legal compensation with the tax lessees, the Cabinet decided to maintain the tax collection till the end of 1848. That did not contravene the 25th April 1848 Regulation,[15] which determined that the final decision would rest with the Reichstag which had yet to be convened at Vienna.

Leaflets written in Yiddish explained the significance of the change brought about by the Constitution which had been granted to Austria's Nations. Abraham Mohr and his brother–in–law Iakob Bodek published a pamphlet titled "Good Advice, [followed in Yiddish] Good counsel and advice, what one should do at this time, here at Lemberg [Lwów] as well as at all the smaller communities and towns," which called the Jews to participate in the freedom proclaimed in the world. They should converge on the parliament rather than deal with minor issues. They strongly attacked the wealthy Orthodox and the tax lessees whose wealth had derived from exploitation of the population. The text of the Constitution was published in Yiddish, in a pamphlet titled [in Yiddish] "The Constitution. The Empirical Licence with all the 50 Clauses of the Constitution. This Constitution brings to an end many offices and taxes which had oppressed the public, including the two damaging taxes, the candle and [Kosher] meat leasing, and the 1000 Gulden coin–tax… and one will have additional freedoms too." (Lwów 1848)

One of the pamphlets was the biography of Prince Metternich titled [in Yiddish] "Biography of the swindling Minister Metternich" (1848).

Influenced by events, Jewish cultural clubs were established at Lwów and other towns of Galicia for the advancement and the spread of Enlightenment. Lwów's club was headed by Iakob Bodek, Abraham Mohr and Izaak Aron Rosenstein. It was the venue where all political activities were held, and it also initiated evening classes for craftsmen, apprentices, merchants' assistants and labourers. The Orthodox congregation objected to those activities of the Enlightened. In response they published a pamphlet against Mohr and Bodek titled: "Cancelling the advice of the evil… A call to uncover evidence of ignorant advice." [then in Yiddish] One should not follow nor listen to the false advice which the wicked wrote in "Good Advice" (in the year of the beard shavers and traitors, consumers of kosher and non–kosher food – together they will perish)" In that pamphlet the Orthodox resumed their attacks on Rabbi Kohn that he was a sinner, a heretic etc, and on the community management, the "Temple" and the Enlightened.[16] The *Maskilim*'s counter–articles in the Vienna newspapers *Allgemeine Zeitung des Judenthums* and [*Oesterreichisches*] *Central–Organ* [*für Glaubensfreiheit, Geschichte und Literatur der Juden*],[17] denigrated the Orthodox Herz Bernstein and Hirsch Ornstein, and blamed them that together with the tax lessees they had submitted a petition against the revocation of the candle–tax and the tax on Kosher meat. The Orthodox published a denial, stating that they had no hand in the petition, the shameful doing of the candle–tax lessees and their supporters.

The anonymous writer,[18] however, insisted on his accusations and reproached the lawyers Dr. Landsberg and Mahl who, for money, "had lent their pens" to the Enlightened rebels. The Orthodox who worried that the Enlightened might gain control over the Jewish population, decided to submit a petition to the Kaiser and to the National Diet against Rabbi Kohn as the source of all evil whom they wished to have fired, and for the dispersal of the community management which was controlled by the Enlightened "under whose yoke of arbitrariness, the Jewish citizens sigh."

Seven members on the community administration had been appointed by the district minister Milbacher around the year 1848. In their struggle against the community–committee, the Orthodox were also supported by the lawyers Dr. Landsberger and Dr. Mahl and Meier Münz who were offended for not being appointed community members.

While one of the Orthodox, Grünfeld, was collecting signatures, the petition of the Orthodox had reached the community officer Bernhardt Pipes.

Pipes ordered to jail him and to ban the

[Pages 257-258]

petition. On 23rd April 1848, after his return from Vienna, an angry Orthodox crowd burst into Rabbi Kohn's flat at the Bernadine Courtyard, and shattered his windows with stones. As the Jewish Company of the national elite started to disperse the Orthodox, the latter attacked them, and only with the aid of an army company did they succeed in restoring order, detain the rioting protestors and put them behind bars. The incident spurred the moderate Orthodox to meet the community leaders at Natan Sokal's house in order to reach a compromise. The Orthodox were unwilling to relinquish their demand that Rabbi Kohn leave Lwów, and agreed only to pay him compensation. The Enlightened rejected their proposal, however, leaving the matter unconcluded. Relations worsened further, the Orthodox even disrupted funerals in which the "Temple" cantor ([Osias] Abras) officiated, and intensified their fight against Rabbi Kohn. The petition they wished to present to the Kaiser was handed to the commission and was published as a pamphlet.

The attacking Orthodox were supported by the tax lessees who opposed Rabbi Kohn for his refusal to confront the candle–tax and Kosher meat–tax transgressors. A few of the leading Orthodox were themselves tax lessees and they found it easy to incite their followers against the community management and Rabbi Kohn. All their efforts to be rid of Rabbi Kohn were however in vain, and the government refused their petition. The Orthodox representatives then tried to attract the support of the Poles to their demands, and raised the question of Rabbi Kohn with the National Council, contesting that he was not a native Galician, and pleading: "we wish to have a Polish rabbi". They even asked the Reichstag representative, Count Aleks[ander] Borkowski, to lobby for the rabbi to be elected without government intervention, and that the government should grant rabbis the right to punish any Jew who transgressed Jewish Law.

The *Maskilim* were angered by what they considered a gross act of denunciation, and the mutual relationship greatly eroded.

Lwów Jewry suffered from lack of political unity and from an internal division. The Orthodox with their spiritual leader Rabbi Hirsch Ornstein –grandson of Lwów's Rabbi, Seb Jakob Ornstein– strongly objected to the demands of the Enlightened.

The leader of the Orthodox was in effect Naftali–Herz Bernstein, great–grandson of Rabbi Arieh Leb Bernstein from Brody, the first Rabbi of the Land of Galicia. He was wealthy and independent and his talents superseded those of Ornstein. He considered that his role was to maintain the interests of the Orthodox; he despised the *Maskilim*, especially after 1848 when the *Maskilim* began to wear European outfits – nevertheless, his children's education also included a general education. He considered every "Deutsch" (*Maskil*) a criminal nonentity. He was known for his saying "A Chassid might be contemptible, but the "Deutsch" is inevitably contemptible."[19] He despised Rabbi Kohn personally and considered him the root of all the community's evil, and would have supported any plot against him.

Some of the *Maskilim*, Meier Münz etc., who were truly attached to the Jewish tradition, supported the Orthodox, especially in matters of the local community. The contrasts were accentuated not only due to Rabbi Kohn, but also due to the political struggle for Jewish rights. The two–way split of Lwów's Jews harmed the entire Jewish cause and prevented them from presenting a united front at the elections to Vienna's first National Diet [Reichstag].

But just when Jews and Poles celebrated fraternity, clear signs of an Anti–Jewish movement loomed over Galicia's political horizon.

On 19th June 1848, a leaflet by an anonymous Ruthenian was disseminated throughout Lwów, demanding that the Jews be granted emancipation only when they were worthy of it. First, however, the government had to treat the morals of the unkempt and neglected Jewish People.[20] Dr. Leo Grünberg, a founder member of the "Hechal [Temple]," secretary of the first committee and a prominent Jewish Enlightened, responded to that leaflet with a pamphlet, in German:

"Are the Jews ready and mature for emancipation? Retort to some wishes of a Ruthenian, made public in a leaflet of 19th June 1848, about some Galician Jews' advancement from an association – July 1848."

The depth of Anti–Jewish sentiment despite the brotherly demonstrations and enthusiastic affirmations towards the Jews, is evidenced in the following: Galicia's delegates to the Reichstag received petitions from their voters, that when debating urban–law, they should propose transferring a large portion of Galicia's Jews – to Hungary, Dalmatia and Austria, where the population was sparse, and that they be settled in agricultural settlements[21] specific for them.

On 26th May 1848, the reactionists who wanted to block the achievements of the revolution, incited on the streets of Lwów the rebells against the Jews, as traders, restaurant owners and tradesmen refused to accept payment in banknotes according to the official rate; the Jews were only saved from riots by the National Guard. News reached Lwów of the peasants' confrontations even with estate owners' officials

[Pages 259-260]

due to incitement by government officials. The Jews in the villages were also affected by the conflicts. During the June 1848 Reichstag elections, government officials incited the peasants against the *Szlachta* [Polish nobility]. For fear of riots similar to those of 1846, the Jews of Lwów were asked, as in 1848, to instruct the lessees and the owners of taverns in the villages, to explain the true situation to the peasants.[22] The proclamation "To our Jewish brothers who reside in the villages,"[23] stressed in elementary Yiddish that thus far only the government officials' opinions had been heard by His Majesty the Kaiser and it was they who discriminated against the peasants and maintained the peasants' subjugation. The forthcoming legislative elections called for unity and peace among all strata of the citizens. "The masters" (*Szlachta*) abolished the peasants' serfdom and made also peace with the Jewish people, promising to support their demands "to relieve us of the yoke of exile and also permit us alternative livelihoods." Therefore, "our entire redemption relies on peace." Let no Jew from the villages believe "the deceit of rioters, but rather, that it is appropriate and necessary to make peace among men. And especially you, villagers, whose words are listened to by the farmers, you must secure peace between the Gentiles and the masters, and explain to the Gentiles that there is no intention against His Majesty the Kaiser but only the desire to make peace. After all, one knows that the Polish landowners have actually proclaimed to the entire world that they would abolish serfdom (*Pańszczyzna*)." The proclamation ended by emphasizing that "It is incumbent upon us, fellow Jewish People, to make peace. After all, our livelihoods and subsistence have always depended on the noblemen, and on their peace rests also ours." The Jews expect favours from the Kaiser, and those would materialize when "the nobles will testify in our favour as they have done thus far, and as they have published in all newspapers that they would support us in the *Sejm*, but everything rests on peace, and peace will bring us the Redeemer."

Dr. Kolischer again proposed to the community committee the plan that the Jews should take up agriculture, but due to opposition from the *Charedim* [the ultra-orthodox] the plan was abolished from the start.

It seems that events of the period drove the Jews to the conclusion that gradually their situation was disintegrating. Between July and September 1848 another calamity hit Eastern Galicia with the outbreak of cholera, to which 843 persons succumbed at Lwów alone, of whom 371 died. The financial condition deteriorated and trade plummeted. The desire increased to leave Galicia, for America. On 3rd June 1848, the Vienna publication *Central–Organ* carried the Lwów proclamation to support the emigration enterprise. The desire to emigrate was probably also influenced by the Vienna events of May 1848, and the anti–Semitic movement. Notices were put up on the streets of Vienna, inciting to attack Jews.

Debates within circles of the Jewish intelligentsia questioned whether in face of the anti–Semitic manifestations, at Vienna and the provinces, it was not advisable to abandon that ungrateful homeland and immigrate to America.

On 6th May 1848, the author Leopold Kompert published a proclamation in *Central–Organ* (Issues 6; 7) to assist in the immigration of Jews to America, for although "The sun of freedom shone over the homeland, over us Jews, however, it only appeared as the blood–stained northern Venus." According to the statement by the Jewish author [Simon] Szántó, an emigration committee was also established at Pest.

At Vienna, the 14th May 1848 saw the publication of the programme of "The Association of Jewish Emigration to the United States" by Dr. Max Engel and Dr. Ludwig August Frankl.

In the strongly worded article: "Remain in the Country",[24] David Mendel and Rabbi Dr. Schmiedl from Moravia objected strongly to the emigration movement. At Lwów too, the Enlightened circles discussed the schemes and an emigration committee was established which requested detailed information from the Vienna editorial board of the *Central–Organ*. At the beginning of 1848, Dr. I Pollak of Vienna was interested to establish a Jewish settlement in America, and even submitted suggestions to the Galicia authorities for the training of Jewish candidates The project failed, however. The question of emigration to America, which was initiated by the Vienna committee, was debated at Lwów in a meeting where doubts arose and counter proposals were put forward of settling in villages rather than emigrating to America. The Lwów committee expressed the view that it was preferable to consider Jewish agricultural settlements within Galicia itself, where Jews were permitted to purchase land. The emigration cost per family would suffice to settle it on the land in Galicia.[25]

As said, the agricultural settlement was also debated by the community committee, but it was rejected due to opposition from the *Charedim*.

The Jewish leaders were so embroiled in dispute that they had taken no measures to secure a Reichstag delegate for Lwów's Jews. Subject to the electoral areas, Lwów's Jews were assured one mandate. The Jewish arbitrators wished to hand the mandate to Meier Münz, but the Enlightened who opposed him since he supported the Orthodox,[26] passed a municipal ruling that the town be split into three electoral areas, thus annulling the possibility of electing a Jewish delegate.

On 2nd July 1848 elections were held at Lwów: the progressives preferred to support the candidacy of the Polish

[Pages 261-262]

"supporters of the Jewish People," Dr. Marian Dylewski, Dr. Floryan Ziemiałkowski and the Baron Leszek Borkowski.[27]

Although the leaders of the Enlightened and the *Maskilim*, such as Mohr and his newspaper sided with the concentration of power, they supported the Poles and took part in all their national demonstrations. On 4th May 1848, crowds of Jews joined the funeral of the Polish émigré Edward Morgenbesser, who came from France to Kraków where he fought at the barricades and was wounded on 26th April 1848. From Kraków he was taken to Lwów where he died. On 31st July 1848, the anniversary of the execution of Teofil Wiśniowski and Józef Kapuściński, the Enlightened held a memorial in the "Temple" at which Rabbi Kohn gave an address.[28]

The Jewish leaders were certain that the Polish Reichstag delegates would protect Jewish affairs and would support their demands for full equal rights and the abolition of Jewish taxes which had not been annulled despite the Constitution.

The issue of taxes exacerbated the relationship between the community leadership and the Orthodox, since wealthy Orthodox Jews were among the tax–lessees who influenced their friends and submitted to the Vienna authorities a memorandum against the annulment of the taxes: according to the Constitution the Reichstag set for 3rd July 1848 was scheduled to discuss the matter, but meanwhile the Jews had to pay the taxes.

The community sent to the Governor representatives, who explained to him that according to Clause 25 of the Constitution there was no ground for the collection of taxes. The masses had stopped paying the candle–tax and buying meat.[29] That angered the lessees who stood to lose much and hoped to convince the government in their favour. Brazenly, the lessees stated in their memorandum that the Jews themselves were asking for the tax to be maintained. To substantiate their claim they supplemented signed pages which they had appended at the time to the petition in the Rabbi Kohn's affair. The lessees asserted to the masses that by paying the special taxes one could count on the authorities' patronage. They further justified their position with the claim that by annulling the taxes thousands of Jews would lose their income as clerks, sub–lessees, supervisors and assistants.

The Polish representatives, Archbishop Wierzchleyski, Dr. Smolka and Dr. Ziemiałkowski opposed the petition.

Not satisfied, however, the Lwów community summoned the representatives of all Galicia's communities to a meeting at Lwów, where it was decided to send a memorandum[30] to the Vienna Reichstag set for 26th July – 7th September 1848.

The memorandum opened with: Galicia's Jews hope that the National Diet will not only decide on the future and the direction of the Kingdom, but also on the civil existence of the Jews and their future. Under the Polish rule, prior to the Austrian occupation, Galicia's Jews enjoyed privileges that granted them full freedom in their economic lives, and they were entitled to purchase houses and even estates. They enjoyed the right to purchase land even under Joseph II. Here the memorandum entered in detail the restrictions and levies imposed on them, with which the Emperors had been confronted on several occasions during the Austrian Rule. Although the Constitution of 25th April 1848 proclaimed the granting of civil and political equal rights, the Jews were subject to certain restrictions and they had to pay special taxes which were collected with full legal backing, and which led to the impoverishment of the masses. Galician Jews' hope rested wholly in the Reichstag's effort to bring to an end the injustice done to the Jews. Is it not time to grant them equal rights and complete freedom? For tens of years the press and the national diets have spoken of the Jews' emancipation, which was also their demand. In the petition of 18th March and 6th April 1848, Galicia's residents demanded equal rights for all Nations and faiths and the National Diet need comply with the demand.

The Orthodox were quite unable to face the reality that Abraham Kohn was acceptable to the Jewish and to the non–Jewish population.

Bernstein, the leader of the Orthodox, was unable to forgive him for heading the delegation to Vienna, in autumn 1847, which submitted the community's memorandum on the annulment of taxation on candles and on [kosher] meat. Bernstein even offered him compensation if he were to leave his position in Lwów, but Rabbi Kohn rejected that offer.[31]

Having run out of options they started to adopt immoral means to harass him. In January 1848, on his return home with a group of teachers, the Orthodox waited for him at the school gate, attacked him and wounded his hand.[32] They also bribed the Jewish pauper, Joel Schorr, to testify that Rabbi Kohn falsified the residents' register, ate non–kosher food and desecrated the faith. The investigation disproved Joel Schorr's testimony, for which the authorities jailed him, and he was only released on Rabbi Kohn's personal request. His situation worsened daily. His wife urged him to leave Lwów and he almost agreed, but the *Maskilim* asked him to stay, for they realised that his departure would result in the destruction of the "Temple" and of all the community's undertakings attained with great effort, with his assistance.

His foes continued searching for stratagems to be rid of him. And then they happened upon the thug Berl Pilpel, who was

[Pages 263-264]

willing to execute their scheme. On 6th September 1848, the Orthodox spread the rumours along the Wide Street (Breite Gass) that Rabbi Kohn and his family had contracted Cholera. The Rabbi and his children went for a walk to the Wysoki Zamek [High Castle] hill, and his wife went to the market. On her return, the doctor arrived to see Theresa, their young daughter. There was no one in the kitchen when Pilpel entered and put poison in their soup pot.

Oblivious of that, the entire family had their midday–meal and soon fell ill. The doctors were alerted but all their efforts were in vain. The Rabbi and his daughter Theresa died.

The news that the Rabbi was poisoned stunned the entire town,[33] Jews and non–Jews. Governor Zaleski sent a report to the Vienna authorities and ordered the police immediately to investigate the matter thoroughly. A number of Orthodox men were arrested, with Hirsch Ornstein and Herz Bernstein among them. Pilpel concealed himself, but on the day of the funeral he went to a barber and requested to have his beard and hair shaven off. His request raised suspicion, and the barber called the leaders who arrested him. The Rabbi's daughter and the maids recognized him as the man who had entered the Rabbi's house and kitchen.

The tombstone of Rabbi Abraham Kohn

Large crowds, including leaders of the authorities and the military, attended Rabbi Kohn's funeral. On behalf of the community, Dr. Emanuel Blumenfeld gave a funeral oration for him at the Enlighteneds' Temple, the [ritual] judge Ehlenberg gave a funeral oration in front of the synagogue outside the town, and the teachers Michael Wolf and Bernhard Frankl – at the cemetery.[34] His body was interred next to the grave of Jakob Ornstein. As rumours spread that the Orthodox would remove his body from the grave, the grave was watched over by the management. Nevertheless, they said that the Orthodox had carried out their scheme.

During the funeral and after it several other suspects of Rabbi Kohn's poisoning were arrested by the police, including: Joel Schorr, Isaac Schramek, Gabryel Suchystaw [Gawril Suchestow], Abraham Weinreb, Motel Urich, Aron Mimelis, Meschulam Feibisz Schorr, Chaja Karpel, Mojzesz Chiger, Jossel Bubriki, Simche Piper and Abraham Atlas.

The Reformers established a special committee to protect the rights of Rabbi Kohn's family, headed by Dr. Blumenfeld and Dr. Menkes, who brought from Vienna the renowned defence lawyer Dr. Weissenstein, who took up their defence in March. Soon he realized that some behind the scenes had interest in blurring the incident. Under his initiative, the committee submitted a memorandum in German to the Governor, regarding those activities:

"Regarding the activities undertaken by the fanatic Jewish party, in order to thwart the success of the criminal investigation into Rabbi Kohn's murder."

The Governor sent the memorandum to the chairman of the criminal law–court. The investigation lasted several months, with the prosecutor eventually determining to cancel the trial against the suspects, with the exception of Pilpel, who in the first instance was sentenced to death. With the assistance of interested parties, however, he managed to escape from jail and, according to rumours which circulated through Lwów, the Orthodox furnished him with a false passport to escape to Eretz Israel, where he settled at Safed [Tsfat].

After a lengthy negotiation with the authorities who refused to grant the widow and children a fixed pension, the Vienna ministry of the interior allowed the community to pay Kohn's widow an annual pension of 400 Gulden for the rest of her life, and 200 gulden annually for the children's education until 1860.

Thus concluded the ignominious, sad affair of the malicious poisoning brought on Rabbi Abraham Kohn and his family by the Orthodox circles.

B.

On 3rd June 1848, as previously mentioned, Governor Stadion left Lwów and handed the civil authority to Agenor Gołuchowski, who was appointed head of the governorship, and the military authority to Galicia's military supreme commander, General Baron Hammerstein.

[Pages 265-266]

On his arrival at Vienna, Stadion Stadion proposed the partitioning of Galicia into two provinces. The plan was accepted by the government and its execution was set for 1st August 1848. Nevertheless, events in Hungary and Italy forced the government to postpone the undertaking. The Vienna authorities were liberal with the masses, hoping to succeed, in Italy under the command of [Joseph] Radetzky, and in Hungary with the help of the Croatians under General Jellachich [Josip Jelačić], which would enable them to annul the Constitution and subject the kingdom to an authoritarian regime.

On 30th July 1848, after the partitioning proposal was deferred, the Polish Wacław [Michał] Zaleski was appointed Galicia's Governor, replacing Stadion, and Gołuchowski remained as his deputy.

Prior to his appointment Zaleski set conditions as: no partitioning of Galicia; appointing Galician born Officers; strengthening the autonomous authorities; adopting Polish identity throughout the educational establishment and convening the Galician *Sejm*, at Lwów. During his two months' stay at Kraków, before arriving at Lwów on 25th October 1848, he had introduced significant changes to the administration and the educational establishment.

His efforts failed however. On 12th November 1848, a few days after the bombardment of Lwów, Zaleski left for Vienna at the behest of Hammerstein and never returned to his seat of Office. At Olmütz [Olomouc], the seat of government at the time, he failed due to the conspiracies of the radical military group, which paved the way for the Austrian reactionary regime with the assistance of Field Marshal [von] Windisch–Graetz.

The constituent assembly of the House of Representatives ("Konstituierender Reichstag") convened at Vienna; a parliamentary committee which processed the Constitution,[35] and determined the principle of civil and political equal rights for all faiths, including Jews, freedom of movement and of mixed marriages in the form of civil marriage.

On 26th September and 5th October 1848, in his speeches to the general assembly, Noah Mannheimer, the Brody delegate and deputy president of the parliament [Reichstag], demanded the abolition of the Kosher–meat tax and the candle tax, and under his influence it was decided by 243 votes against 20, to revoke the demand for the special Jewish taxes.[36] That established the principle of full equal rights of Jews and Christians. The 20th November [a] 1848 Imperial Decree (patent), made the decision legally and fully enforceable from 1st November 1848.

The Reichstag's decision to abolish the specific taxes was received with joy and great satisfaction by Galicia's Jews. The Jewish newspaper "Tsaitung [Zeitung]" published at Lwów, edited by Mohr, announced: "My dear brothers, 1st November is coming, remember that the candle and the meat tax was abolished, do not listen to the inciters' sayings trying to convince you that the taxes are still in force, since the Kaiser has not yet signed the decision. Know, that whatever the [Reichstag] has decided, the Kaiser is unable to alter. We know that the Kaiser himself does not wish such contemptible taxes." The announcement ended with the demand that the Jews should not be taken in by the officers' and lessees' threats, and avoid having the taxes docked.[37]

In their joy at the abolition of the taxes, and in their hatred for the lessees, Lwów's Jewish masses attacked them and their houses causing much damage. And it was only due to the intervention of the leaders that a serious clash was avoided.

The rest of the issues concerning the Jews' equal rights were not debated by the Reichstag since the following day, 6th October 1848, riots broke out at Vienna and the following Jews died: Adolph Kaliński, Emanuel Epstein, David Löb. The riots led to Vienna's siege and to a counter uprising, led by Field Marshal Prince Windisch–Graetz. The Reichstag relocated to Kremsier [Kroměříž] where it continued its work, but had no time to decide on the emancipation of the Jews. On 2nd December 1848, Franz Joseph I (1830–1916) became Emperor [Kaiser] and Prince Feliks Schwarzenberg was nominated Prime Minister.

Straight away, the government began to deal with the existing situation, and with preparing the new Constitution.

The 11th February 1849 session of the ministers' council[38] also dealt with the question of the Jews, and after an extensive deliberation it accepted Clause 1 of the basic law, in which each citizen was guaranteed freedom of faith and the enjoyment of civil and political rights, irrespective of faith.[39]

On 7th March 1849, the Kremsier parliament was dissolved and a new Constitution was provided, by force (*Oktroyierte Verfassung*), signed and approved by the Emperor on 4th March 1849. The Constitution, penned by the Minister of the Interior, Franz Stadion, was imbued with a liberal spirit and included the principle of equal rights for people of all faiths, with an emphasis that a difference in faith is no ground for discrimination in the enjoyment of political and civil rights.

That was the start of the reactionary regime. Following Windisch–Graetz's orders, Hammerstein was tasked with suppressing the riots which broke out at Lwów on 1st November 1848. The true reasons for those riots have not been settled, to date. Lwów's masses erected barricades. Two young Jews who took part in the fighting at the barricades, Nachman Sternklahr and Seidner, were mentioned in particular in the authorities' report.[40] The notables' companies tried to quell the unrest

[Pages 267-268]

but were unsuccessful. In the town's outskirts shots were fired, without knowing who started them Commander Hammerstein found a welcome excuse to intervene and surround the town centre with soldiers and cannons. Governor Zaleski and the notables' commander, General Wybranowski, lobbied Hammerstein to remove the soldiers. He agreed, with the proviso that the notables leave the town centre and the barricades be removed from the streets. The condition was met, but as the notables retreated the soldiers attacked them with beatings and shooting.

The events angered the masses and the riots resumed. Natan Hammerstein ordered the artillery companies to bomb the town from the "*Wysoki Zamek* [High Castle]." 648 canon shots were fired till noon. The municipality, the university, the technical college, the science high school, the theatre and many private houses were almost wholly destroyed. According to the government report 55 people (13 of whom were women) were killed, and 75 (19 of whom were women) were injured.

Among the Jewish fatalities were Grabscheid Bernhardt, Lipa Goldberg, the teacher Igulnizer and Ludwik Krasnopolski (a merchant from Brody, who had come for a wedding and in his "Angielski" hotel room was hit by bullets fired by grenadiers beyond the Governor's buildings.

A state of emergency was declared at Lwów, the national elite and all the organizations and clubs were dismantled, the newspapers shut down.

Thus ended at Lwów the spring of the Nations – 1848.

On 10th January 1849, a state of emergency was declared all over Galicia. On the 15th, Zaleski was called back to Vienna where he died six weeks later. Rumours spread throughout Lwów that he had been invited for a meal at Stadion's, and that while drinking black coffee the latter gave him a poisoned cigar.[41]

On 24th January 1849, Agenor Gołuchowski became Galicia's Governor which opened a new period in its history.

Despite the population's depressive condition, the Jews were joyful over the new Constitution which granted equal rights to all faiths including the Jews.

On 15th March 1849, the community held a festive prayer in the "Temple" and the preacher Dr. Moritz Löwenthal, Rabbi Abraham Kohn's successor, delivered a patriotic sermon which appeared in print.[42] But there was yet a long way from the promised emancipation to its implementation.

[Page 372]

Notes: – CHAPTER 16
All notes in square brackets [ ] were made by the translator.

1. Articles from Lwów in: *Orient* 1848, p. 118, 23/3; 24/3; *Allg. Ztg. d. Jt.* 1848, 24/3, No.16, p.241.

2. Even before the Constitution was passed, changes in the conditions of the Jews had been considered among the conservative circles. Graf Kasimir Stadnicki, member of the old *Sejm*–committee and advisor to the government, prepared a bill on the election to the Galician *Sejm*, and proposed that Lwów's town Rabbi should be the Jewish faith's representative for the forthcoming *Sejm*. Bronisław Łoziński: *Szkice z Hist. Gal. w. XIX w Lwów*, 1913, p. 81.

3. From the archive of the late Prof. Dr. Majer Bałaban. Also published in: " *Historische Schriften*, YIVO, II, pp. 634–638 (Dr. J. Shatzky [Szacki]; Archives).

4. In his memoirs, Ziemiałkowski recounts that Horowitz liaised between the Polish delegation and Count [von] Pereira, who was influential among Government circles, and the Court–advisor Kleyle, who draughted the Kaiser's reply to the Polish petition. (Ziemiałkowski vol. II, p. 146).

5. Dr. Ph[ilip] Friedman: *Die galizischen Juden im Kampfe um ihre Gleichberechtigung* (1848–1868). Frankfurt a/M. 1929, p. 55.
In his opinion, Dr. Oswald Menkes was also part of the delegation, as related in the

[Pages 373-374]

pamphlet published under the pseudonym "Malisz Karol." Dr. Friedman was however mistaken in his assumption, since the name "Malisz" was not a pseudonym of Dr. Menkes, but rather the name of another member of the Polish delegation, Dr. Karol Malisz, a Lwów lawyer. Stanislaw Schnür-Pepłowski: *Z. przeszlosci Galicyi (1772–1862)* Lwów 1895, p; 497. Stefan Kieniewicz: *Galicia w latach 1846–1848 Wiosna ludów* (1848) *na zemliach polskich*. Warszawa, 1948, p.292. Julius Starkel Rok 1848. Lwów 1899, p.35.

6. Floryan Ziemiałkowski: *Pamiętniki*. Kraków 1904, vol. II, pp. 48, 68, 73.

7. Seven representatives of the Polish intelligentsia (Piotr Gross, Albin Ruebenbauer, Franciszek Smolka, Robert Hefern, Jan Dobrzański, Dr. Aleksander Senkowski [Sękowski], Maurycy Srozinski [Sroczyński]), nine representatives of estate–owners, three townspeople, three Ruthenian priests, two Jews and one Polish priest.

8. *See* my article "On the Hebrew and Jewish press of Lwów" in volume II of this book. Before censorship was abolished, only two newspapers were published at Lwów "*Gazeta Lwowska*," and "*Dziennik Mód Paryskich.*" Seven months after censorship was abolished, 13 newspapers and weeklies were published. 1. *Dzienik narodowy*; 2. *Postep* (democratic in the extreme); 3. *Gazeta powszechna* (Magazine of the National Council), once the Council was recognized as a political body, the magazine was renamed: 4. *Rada Narodowa*; 5. *Polska Gazeta Narodowa* (magazine of the estate–owners, established by Gilbert Pawlikowski, in opposition to the National Council); 6. *Zoria Halycka* (the Ruthenians' magazine); 7, *Tygodnik polski* (a political. literary weekly edited by the renown historian Karol Szajnocha); 8. *Urzednik prywatny* (Magazine of the organization of private clerks, founded by the National Council); 9. *Kurjer lwowski* (an independent popular newspaper); 10. *Przyjaciel dzieci*; 11. *Przyjaciel ludu.* Five newspapers were published at Kraków, two at Tarnow, one at Stanislawow [Stanisławów], as well as a government paper *Gazeta lwowska*.

9. After a short while, when Anti–Semitic ideas pervaded the Polish public and fraudulent writings were published against the Jews, and "Anti–Semitism awoke" also among the notables, Johann Beiser published the poem: "Der Jude an die Christlieben Freiheits–kämpfer" ["From a Jew to the Christ–loving Freedom-fighters"], in which he addressed them with:
> "Extend the hand Christian brother
> Extend it to the Jew
> Let the sunny songs of Freedom
> Fire up the Jew's heart too
> Don't let him stand alone

10. Take it kindly I am a Pole
> A Pole and a Jew
> That is the double garland of adversity"

11. Busch [*Oesterreichisches*] *Central–Organ* [*für Glaubensfreiheit, Geschichte und Literatur der Juden*] 1848, p. 141.

12.   Following the proposal of the (Polish) commission official and member of the Council, Count Agenor Gołuchowski, a programme was prepared to establish a "Ruthenian Council" (Rada świętojurska [the Council of St. John}) headed by the Uniate Bishop Gregor Jachimowicz [Hryhorij Jachymowycz] (from 1859, Metropolitan of Lwów). The Ruthenian Council members sided with the Russians and advocated the partition of Galicia into two provinces: West and East, a programme already proposed by Metternich in 1846.

The Ruthenian intelligentsia led by Poznań, Antoni Dubkiewicz and Julian Horoszkiewicz, objected to the Council's actions, especially to the submission of the 19th April 1848 memorandum. They advocated a Ruthenian–Polish national–political merger, and countered the "świętojurska" Council by establishing the "Ruthenian" association (Sbod Ruski). On 15th June 1848, during the first session's programme–speech, Horoszkiewicz suggested that the role of "The Association" was to maintain the peace among Galicia's Nations: the Ruthenians, Poles, Armenians and Jews, and to fuse them into a single body that would face and support the demands of the government and of the Kaiser. "The Association" joined the National Council and sent four representatives. "The Association" published the newspaper "*Dnewnyk ruski*" countering the Council's magazine "*Zoria halytska*".

13.   Busch. *Central–Organ*, 1848, No. 5.

14.   Wiener Haus Hof und Staatsarchiv: Ministerratsprotokolle, 1848, Z 6281 ddo 5/5 1848.

15.   Ministerratsprotokolle, 1848, Z, ddo 22/v; Z 959 ddo 24/v, 1848.

16.   An anonymous (member of the grandees) pupil of Rabbi Kohn published an open letter against that pamphlet. Open Letter to the petitioners and the so–called supporters of Orthodox Judaism against the Regional Rabbi Mr. Abraham Kohn at Lemberg (1848). A second leaflet was also published:
A few words to the petition's signatories regarding the removal of the Regional Rabbi Abraham Kohn.

17.   Busch. [*Oesterreichisches*] *Central–Organ* [*für Glaubensfreiheit, Geschichte und Literatur der Juden*], 1848, No. 21.

18.   Busch. *Central–Organ*, 1848, No. 22.

19.   Dr. Majer Bałaban: *Dzieje Żydów w Galicji* p. 133.

20.   Dr. Ph. Friedman: *Die galizischen Juden im Kampfe um ihre Gleichberechtigung* 1929, p. 65.

21.   Allg. ztg. d. J. 1849, No. 3.

22.   Ever since the early forties the authorities deliberated on how to resolve peasants' serfdom. The issue was much aggravated after the 1846 massacres in Galicia during which many Polish noblemen were killed by peasants. After the massacres, Rudolph Stadion –the Governor's brother– was sent to Galicia in order to prepare reports and proposals. The committee appointed by the Kaiser and led by Hartig, inspected Stadion's reports which expressed doubt whether it was advisable to give land to the peasants who were burdened with debts, and whose lands were attached to Jewish lenders, and their farms were in danger of falling into the hands of the Jews. Hans Schlitter: *Aus Österreich Vormärz 1. Galizien und Krakau*, Zürich–Leipzig–Wien 1920, pp. 47; 109. For those reasons the Polish estate–owners also resisted a sudden solution to serfdom. Most Austrian officials considered that the 1846 riots were not triggered by the estate–owners' jurisdictions in the villages, but rather by the Jews, who as lenders exploited the peasants. One of Galicia's foremost officers reported that: "The Jew

[Pages 375-376]
is the peasants' prime cruel leech." "His deception and cunning confuse and stupefy him." That officer stressed however that the grim condition – the tax burden imposed on the Jews – as the cause for their action, and that consequently it was hard to determine that it was the Jew who caused the depletion, the immorality and the degeneration of Galicia's peasant. In towns, the Jews contributed adversely by holding back the development of the middle class. According to the report there was only one solution, "To eliminate the Jew and turn him into a Christian, or to forbid him from living in a Christian country." (Bronisław Łoziński: *Szkice z historji Galicji w XIX wielku*, pp. 317–319).

23.   Published in "*Historische Schriften*, I. pp. 744–748 (Dr. Majer Bałaban "from my archive").

24.   [*Oesterreichisches*] *Central–Organ* [*für Glaubensfreiheit, Geschichte und Literatur der Juden*]. 1848, pp. 138; 147.

25.   Central–Organ. 1848, No. 12, 12/vI; p. 170; No. 29, 22/VII, p.230.

26.   Against Münz a leaflet was also published by an anonymous, titled:
Wie gelangt man in den Himmel Deutscher Grammatik. Glossen zu der Scdhrift: Ein Wort zur Zeit von M...r M...tz Lemberg 1848. Gesamtertrag für die Nationalgarde. The leaflet accuses him of being the author of the memorandums and the petitions which the Orthodox had submitted to the authorities, and it advised him to avoid striving to become the people's representative. "Our sacred affairs will be represented with greater prestige and relevant understanding, by the renowned freedom fighters and supporters of Liberalism, Sanguszko, Lubomirski and Borkowski."

27.   Of the 383 National Diet delegates, 108 were from Galicia (including Bukowina) of whom 4 were Jews: the preacher Isaac Noah Mannheimer from Brody, Abraham Halpern from Stanislawow, Karmin from Ternopil and Rabbi Dov–Berisz Meisels from Kraków.

28. On 4.8.1848, *Tsaitung* [Zeitung], sheet 14 writes: "We Jews did not wish to say Jizkor [prayer in memory of the dead] in the Temple, because it was Rosh Chodesh [Start of the Month] but since the Rada Narodowa [National Council] demanded it, we assembled at the Temple, in the evening. There were many academics, a few companies of the National Guard, many Jews, more women. The reader at the synagogue, together with the choir, amended the afternoon prayer followed by three readings of El Maleh Rachamim [prayer in memory of the dead]; one for Wiśniowski, one for Kapuściński and one for Spitzer, a Jewish student who fell [died] during the Vienna Revolution, on 13th March, blessed by the Almighty. And to finish, a German prayer was delivered."

29. Central–Organ, 1848, p.104.

30. The full text was published by Dr. Majer Bałaban: "From my archive, in *Historische Schriften*, YIVO, vol. 1, Berlin 1909, pp. 741–765.

31. Gothilf Kohn: *Abraham Kohn* Lemberg 1898, p.174. On 15th August 1848, Rabbi Abraham Kohn's wife informed her brother–in–law, Bernhard Kohn, of his condition as follows:
"My dear Abraham has probably not informed you what those villains Bernstein, Ornstein, Münz and some others did; how they incited the commonality against him; promised money and gave it out, and wreaked total confusion within the community; how they even asked men of the most disreputable character to attack and manhandle him, which has happened once as he walked home from school. They even manhandled the children too, to spoil our life here." (Gothilf Kohn *op. cit.* p. 206) And Rabbi Kohn himself wrote to his brother on 14th August 1848:
"Finally I have also to report that our Orthodox villains have again raised their head during Cholhamoed [period within some Jewish holidays], provoked the mob against me and spread endless complaints and denunciations. The executive committee is long since demolished, devoid of esteem and meaning, yet the young who had only recently removed their traditional Jewish clothes, did and do hold themselves bravely and the community will be completely reorganized." Gothilf Kohn: *Abraham Kohn im Lichte der Geschichtsforschung*. Lemberg 1848, p. 196.

32. Gothilf Kohn: *op. cit.* p. 174.

33. Mohr's *Tsaitung* [Zeitung] wrote on 9.8.1848 (p. 147):
"Sad News I bring you now, my dear readers. A great calamity has now befallen us. Our regional rabbi, the wise Rabbi Abraham Kohn has died. But do not think that he died a natural death. No, he was poisoned. You might think him alone. But no, he with his wife, five children and two servants. Have you ever heard anything like that !" And the Newspaper warns: "Now see my dear friends what division leads to, and how dangerous it is."

34. Dr. Majer Bałaban: *Historja Lwowskiej Synagogi postępowej* Lwów 1937, pp. 58–59. The eulogies by Dr. Blumenfeld, Wolf and Frankl appeared in print:
–1. Dr. E. Blumentfeld: Words at the body of the blessed Rabbi Abraham Kohn, delivered at the Jewish Temple on 8th September of the year (1848) printed by Michael Poremba, Lemberg. Published also in: *Historja Lwowskiej Synagogi* pp. 59–60.
–2. Words of condolence at the grave of Abraham Kohn, the pious Rabbi of Lwów, in blessed memory of a righteous man, delivered by Michael Wolf. Teacher at the secondary school. Published in: Gothilf Kohn: [*op. cit.*] pp. 280–287.
–3. Commemorative address Lemberg, 8th Sept. 1848. Bernhard Frankl, Teacher at the Jewish secondary school. Dr. Majer Bałaban: *Historja Lwowskiej Synagogi* p. 279.
Apart from the eulogies, a poem in German by the notary Josef Blumentfeld was also published: "A tear on the grave of the deceased Rabbi Abraham Kohn." Published in *Historische schriften* [in Yiddish] I, pp. 748–751; and in Dr. Majer Bałaban: *Historja Lwowskiej Synagogi* pp. 280–281.
Abraham Kohn was made into the subject of a stage play in Polish:
Emil Roniecki: *Wielki Rabbi Abraham Tragedja w 5 aktach*. Lwów, 1875.

[Pages 377-378]

35. "Entwurf der Grundrechte des Österreichischen Volkes" [Clauses] 1–29. On the freedom of faith, and the civil and political equal rights debated under the proposal of the Parliament [Reichstag] [Clauses] 13–16.

36. The Galician delegates who spoke in favour of the abolition of the Jewish taxes were: Fedorowicz, Sierakowski, Dr. Dylewski, Count Borkowski, Popiel, and from among the other delegates– [von] Szábel, lecturer finance committee Lasser, Brauner (and he demanded to ask forgiveness of the Jews for the wrong done to them by those taxes). The Catholic priest Fuster from Vienna, Schuselka, Umlauft, Borrosch, and the finance minister Philipp Freiherr von Krauss (born at Lwów) also recommended the abolition of the taxes. Already at the session of 6th September 1848, when direct and indirect taxation was proposed for 1849, von Krauss suggested to revoke the Jewish taxes from 1st November 1848, since the Jewish taxes were contrary to the equal rights principle stated in the Constitution. Stenographische Berichte über die Verhandlungen des österreichischen konstituierenden Reichstages Band II, pp. 559, 615–618, 795, 806. [a] Seems to be a misspelling in original. Should read October.

37. Tsaitung [Zeitung] sheet 26; 27.10.1848.

38. Haus–Hof und Staatarchiv; Wien. Ministerratsprotokolle 1849; Ministerratsprotokil vom Februar p. 527, e.a. [year] 1849.

39. During this session a debate took place on the basic–laws proposed by the Constitution committee of the Kremsier Parliament. In the discussion over Clause 17 of the 25th April 1848 legislation, and Clause 16 of the Constitution committee of the

Kremsier Parliament, which determines that every Austrian citizen enjoys freedom of religion and conscience, and that the enjoyment of civil and political rights is independent of religion, inevitably extends equal rights to Jews. Thinnfeld, the minister of agriculture [however], expressed his concern that applying that clause would lead to riots in the provinces where till then Jews had been barred from living. He proposed to leave the decision to the National councils and the municipalities. The rest of the ministers expressed their opinion that it was inadvisable to restrict the Jews' rights in the constitution. The debate resumed again during the 20th February 1848 session (Protocol No. 533), when [von] Kübeck proposed an ambiguous version which was backed by Ministers Kolmer and Thinnfeld. The ministers Baron Krauss (who had been Lwów governorship's Officer) and Dr. Bach, on the other hand, recommended to grant the Jews full equal rights. Bach argued that were the Jews to be treated as "pariahs" (low rank) a dangerous situation would arise. "They have influence in the press, at public meetings and have large sums of money at their disposal." One has to grant them equal rights, but with the proviso: ["]To forbid them the purchase of real–estate and the right of residency in the provinces where no Jews are resident.["] This version was accepted after a debate.

40. Staatsarchiv Wien J.B. 8013, e. a. 1851. Report of Lemberg's head of the Empirical Criminal Court and the General Procurator of the province of Galicia (Pohlbaum) to the Minister of Justice von Krauss, about the political machinations as well as about the outbreak of the uprising which took place at Lemberg on 1st and 2nd November 1848.

41. Jabłonowski was member of the Galician *Sejm* and commander of the National management. Ludwik Jabłonowski: *Złote czasy i wywczasy*: Pamiętnik Szlachcica. Poznan p. 183.

42. Talk held at Lwów's Temple of the Progressive Jews on 15th March 1849 by Dr. Moritz Löwenthal, the Rabbi and preacher of Lemberg, on the occasion of the thanksgiving celebration for the Constitution conferred by His Majesty. Published by the Board of the Jewish Community as a call to all the country's other Jewish communities to register their joyous participation in the new homeland, through patriotic gifts on the day. Printed by Joseph Schnayder 1849.

[Pages 269-270]

Chapter 17: The Period of Transition to Constitutional Rule

Translated by Myra Yael Ecker
Edited by Dr. Rafael R. Manory

Annulment of the Law of equal rights in 4th March 1849 Legislation. Jewish craftsmen's problem with licences. The Jews' part in the development of Lwów's industry. The tradesmen and shopkeepers opposing the municipality. The community's administration in 1841–1854. The Torah scholar Jacob Isak Jütes successor to Jakob Ornstein. Lwów's *Maskilim*. Head of education, the teachers, the welfare institutions. The association "to promote agriculture among the Jews." Hersz Zipper. The question of acquiring real–estate by Jews. Lwów community's lobbying at Vienna the Minister of the interior Agenor Gołuchowski. Establishment of a crafts' school. The question over the rabbinical seminary. Meier Münz. Activity of "Association of the resourceful the good and the honourable." The Jews and the Galician *Sejm* elections 1861. Marek Dubs. The struggle against the town regulations. The Jews of Lwów and the 1863 uprising. The Jewish problem and the Galician *Sejm*.[1]

The nature of the civil rights granted by the 4th March 1849 Legislation was unclear to Galicia's authorities. In the absence of any statute to implement it, they continued to apply the regulations which had been in force before 1848. In particular, the authorities were unclear how to handle the Jewish–owned estates.

The opposition gathered among government circles under the influence of Minister Baron Kübeck and Archbishop Rauscher, tutor to the young Emperor. The kingdom was led by the State Council (Reichsrat), while the so called "liberal" cabinet ministers: Anton [von] Schmerling, Carl [von] Bruck and Philipp [von] Krauss resigned one by one. The Jews worried, with good reason, that the emancipation they had been granted would be revoked. The authorities believed that the issue of equal rights entered in the legislation document of 4th March 1849, had been agreed in principle, but that a specific Act was required in order to put it into practice. So long as such an Act had not been published, however, the earlier Regulation (✓) would prevail. After all, in a provision of 26th August 1849, the Minister of religious affairs Leo Graf [von] Thun, determined unequivocally, "there is a desire however that the equal rights granted by the Kaiser, should soon and in full be extended to all faiths."

Despite this, the 4th March 1849 Legislation also underwent considerable changes by the government. On 20th August 1851, Freiherr von Kübeck and Prime Minister Prince Schwarzenberg were assigned by the Kaiser to formulate the required changes to the Legislation. Although the committee established on 4thOctober 1851 had proposed a means of extending equal rights to all the kingdom's citizens, irrespective of their religion, the Kaiser did not endorse its proposals,[2] but rather just the law's principle of freedom of religion and the equality of all citizens. Consequently, the question arose whether the Jews were entitled to purchase property and to pursue businesses which they had acquired prior to 31st December 1851. The 3rd March 1852 session of the council of ministers addressed the question and appointed the Minister of the Interior, Dr. [von] Bach, to prepare appropriate instructions.[3]

During the 13th November 1852 government session,[4] Dr. [von] Bach determined that according to the 4th March 1849 Act all citizens had equal rights, and that consequently all the restrictions affecting the Jews were annulled. According to the Kaiser's 31st December 1851 order, however, no conclusion had been reached regarding the Jews, which gave rise to the question of what to do in their regard – a subject which embarrassed the authorities, with inter–ministerial debates taking place, the conclusion of which would be presented to the Kaiser for approval.

The state of affairs also affected the Jews of Lwów. The craftsmen's guilds submitted complaints to the authorities about the increased number of licences granted to Jews. For instance, the watchmakers' guild approached the ministry of commerce with the demand to publish a "good law" which would disallow them licences. The governorship stated that Lwów had 11 Christian, and only two Jewish watchmakers, and that the complaint over excessive number of licences granted to Jews, was baseless. Similar complaints were submitted by all craftsmen's guilds, apart from the goldsmiths', the furriers' and the tailors'.[5]

The municipality opposed the guilds' demands, stressing that for the good of the people the 7th May 1789 Regulations determined equal rights to Jews and Christians regarding crafts. "The Jew is enterprising and very capable, and the Christian guilds' complaints are founded on jealousy and stubbornness."[6]

In commerce the Jews held out. In 1850, the government established three offices of commerce and industry, at Brody, Kraków and Lwów, and was unable to overlook the Jews who were in control of the wholesale trade and of much of the industries. The Brody office elected as its president the renowned banker Majer

[Pages 271-272]

Kallier, and at Lwów seven out of the 15 office representative were Jews (Mejer Rachmiel Mieses, O. M. Goldbaum and Marcus Dubs of Lwów; O. H. Sluzker of Bolechow; Grabscheid of Sambor [Sambir], A. Kohn of Żurawno [Zhuravno]; and Weinberg of Grodek [Horodok]).

Meier Rachmiel Mieses

The Jews played a large role in the development of Lwów's industry. With the expansion of the crops trade in eastern Galicia, Jozef Tom and Marcus Dubs constructed Galicia's first steam–powered mills.

Lwów's Jews played also a prominent role in the manufacture of agricultural products, distilled wine and liquors, chicory, oil refining and matches. Galicia's two largest wine distilleries that belonged to Fischel and Dubs, were at Lwów.

Lwów's Jews were also at the forefront of advancements in banking. Dawid and Osias Horowitz who were in contact with the Vienna Rothschild Bank, Joseph Kolischer, A. Nirenstein and Osias Mieses put money into Galicia's economy. It was Joseph Kolischer who initiated the establishment of Lwów's Mortgage Bank (1867), he and A. Nirenstein were the branch managers of the Austrian National Bank, and Osias Mieses was Lwów's branch manager of the Austrian Credit Bank for Commerce and Industry.

Jewish shopkeepers on the other hand faced quite a different reality: every time they requested a relocation licence out of the Jewish Quarter they faced a struggle with the municipality. In 1851, based on the law which had promised equal rights to all the Monarchy's citizens, two distinguished merchants moved their stores out of the Jewish Quarter, but the municipal authorities closed down their stores. The merchants appealed to the municipality and the matter was debated during the municipality's session of 13th March 1851. The municipality members who were competitor merchants, tried to avoid any plenary discussion. [Karl] von Höpflingen–Bergendorf, the mayor and advisor to the governorship, who had initiated the debate, spoke in favour of the Jews; the wholesaler Floryan Singer also sided with them. A commotion broke out during the debate and the session had to be abandoned. The following day the two Jewish merchants received authorization to open their shops, but only in order to sell their existing stocks during the following three months, and they were forbidden from hanging any shop signs. The merchants appealed to the ministry, who transferred their appeal via the governorship to the municipality. This time, however, they were granted the right to remain outside the Jewish Quarter. Indeed, the rest of the Jewish traders who had moved outside the Quarter were ordered to vacate their shops by 1st November 1853. Nevertheless, the municipality approached the Christian house–owners and threatened them with fines up to 100 Florins were they to lease shops to a Jew.

Besides the issue of the houses, plots of land and estates purchased by Jews in 1848–1851, the grave question arose of overcoming the overcrowding within the Jewish Quarters where residential rent rose by 317% between 1821 and 1870, in contrast with the 85% rise in the town centre.[6] The municipality objected to the Jews' admission to the town's streets, despite the police administration's recommendation that the Jewish Quarter be abolished. Indeed, the entire matter rested on Governor Agenor Gołuchowski's attitude.

After his appointment as Governor, Gołuchowski expressed his opinion on the Jewish issue: ["]despite the fact that the Jews are cowards and greedy, it is worth noting that the abolition of taxes would inevitably drive them to side with the government. But the growing splits within the Jewish community should not ignore, and the efforts of the [Hebrew] Enlightened [*Maskilim*] who take care to instil education among the masses should be supported.["]

Dr. M. Beiser

Gołuchowski backed the emancipation of the Jews. In 1851, when the government sought the opinion of the Lands' representatives on the Jews' civil and political standing, Gołuchowski replied openly

[Pages 273-274]

that the Jews should be granted full emancipation. Their morals should be improved, and their abilities be put to good use in the state's economy, and their national isolation should be terminated. He noted that if a Jew could be the mayor of London, it was possible that in time a Jew might hold a similar position at Lwów. He showed interest in the communities' internal affairs and assisted the Lwów's Enlightened to control the communal activities.

The committee leading the community, elected by the regional Minister Millbacher in 1841, was made up of: Dr. Emanuel Blumenfeld, Dr. Oswald Menkes, Dawid Horowitz, Dr. Adam Barach-Rappaport, Marek Dubs, Dr. Leo Kolischer and I. A. Rosenstein. After the demise of I. A. Rosenstein in 1854, Abraham Mieses and Samuel Kohn, both active in the management of "The Temple of the Enlightened," joined the community committee.[6]

Bernhardt Pipes, who held the post of community–secretary (actuary) was replaced, after his demise during the cholera epidemic of 1855, by Dr. Ignatz Nossig (father of Dr. Alfred Nossig). The community leaders did much to improve the conditions, especially in the economic and cultural fields, and these achievements were commended by the authorities.

The situation remained unchanged till 1861, at which time new elections were held.

After the demise of Rabbi Jakob Ornstein in 1839, no new rabbi was appointed, but Rabbi Symcha Natan Ehlenberg was made acting rabbi. The community was unable to elect a rabbi in accordance with the 22nd May 1820 law, which determined that the rabbi had to be elected from among graduates in philosophy and ethics from an Austrian university. Apart from Rabbi Cwi [Tzvi] Hirsch Chajes at Żółkiew, no other Orthodox rabbi fulfilled the requirement.

Lwów had indeed a suitable candidate, but one who had no desire to join the rabbinate of Galicia, and of Lwów in particular. Born at Lwów on 30th April 1816, Rabbi Jacob Isak Jütes died on 20th April 1886; he was a wealthy individual who preferred to dedicate himself entirely to the Torah. His father was a great scholar who had a collection of valuable books and received traditional and secular education, at home. Without attending school he graduated privately [externally] and passed the Lwów university's philosophy exams. He studied the Torah, was head of a Yeshivah, and published the book *Ohalei Yaakov* ["Jacob's Tents"] (Lwów 1848) containing argumentation and responsa on the Laws of the Torah; the book *Mikruei Kodesch* ["Holy Scriptures"] on the [Hebrew] Bible (Lwów 1864) and sermons which were published in Rabbi Gawryel [ben Naftali Hirtz] Suchystaw's book *Maceweth Kodesz* [*Mazewes Kodesch*; "Sacred Memorial Monument"]. He was a son–in–law of Rabbi

Jehuda Samuel Rappoport, Rabbi Salomon Jehuda Rappoport's brother, with whom he corresponded. As representative of the Orthodox he was active in community life, but declined serving in the rabbinate.

Once Count [von] Thun was elected prime minister (1855), he supported the Orthodox and exempted candidates to the rabbinate from any prescribed exams, and then the Lwów community elected Rabbi Joseph Saul Nathansohn as its Rabbi. Rabbi Joseph Saul Nathansohn was backed by the *Maskilim* and the Enlightened who considered him an affable man, who also tolerated views contrary to his own. The Chassidim and the Orthodox supported his brother–in–law, Rabbi Mordoche–Zew Ettinger (1804–1863), a great scholar and head of the "Austrian Kollel" [Austria's advanced Judaic studies programme] in Eretz Israel, he also translated many books. Rabbi Joseph Saul Nathansohn won the election with the help of his sister Adele, who had convinced the Enlightened to vote for him.

At the same time, Dr. Szymon (Leon) Schwabacher[10] was elected preacher for the "Temple of the Enlightened," even though Lwów had other candidates: Dr. Lazar Elias Igel (1825–1892) and Dr. Efraim Israel Bleicher of Moravia (1813–1882).

Rabbi Dr. Szymon Schwabacher

Dr. Igel, the son of the renowned bookseller Samuel Igel, graduated from the rabbinical seminary at Padua and was a student of Samuel David Luzzatto [*SaDaL*]. In 1849, after returning to Lwów, he was appointed as teacher of religion at the secondary–school [gymnasium], and lecturer in Semitic languages at Lwów University. In 1854 Dr. Igel left Lwów and was appointed rabbi at Czernowitz [Czerniowce]. Also Dr. Bleicher who in 1850 was appointed lecturer at the university, was unsuccessful in being accepted as preacher and left Lwów in 1856.[11]

Apart from the professional intelligentsia, medical doctors and lawyers,[12] Lwów also had circles of educated individuals, such as, Hillel Lechner, Motel Braun, pupils and friends of Rabbi Nachman Krochmal [RaNaK] who at their own expense had published "Guide for the Perplexed of the Present Age," Jakub Bodek, A. M. Mohr, Izak Aron Rosenstein, Salomon Salman Bernard, an assistant to Joseph Csadek [Tsadek], Dubs, Abraham

[Pages 275-276]

Beiser, Samuel Modlinger, Jakob Bałaban,[13] Samuel Scheinblum, Mojzesz Dawid Lubich, Dawid Diamand, known for his book on Law, Aron Dornzweig, Jakub Bronik, Mojzesz Jakub Pordes, Heinrich D. Bernstein, David HaKohen Rappaport, Mejer Juda Maimon. The *Maskilim* took control over community life and endeavoured to steer it toward Enlightenment [*Haskala*] and education. The community management concentrated its efforts on the school, which had been established under the direction of Rabbi Abraham Kohn, in 1845. He was succeeded as headmaster by Dr. Bernhard Sternberg, who had previously been a teacher at Kolin (Bohemia). Dr. Sternberg expanded the curriculum and as the students' numbers rose he opened two branches and established evening classes for adults, in reading, writing and arithmetic. The education board that oversaw educational issues was made up of Dr. Barach–Rappaport, I. A. Rosenstein, and I. Kolischer.

The number of pupils at the Jewish schools rose above 1000.[14] Altogether there were eight classes in the [mixed] school for boys and girls. Apart from German, also Polish and Hebrew were taught there by experienced teaching staff such as: Akiba Lodner, Salomon Schlesinger, Leo Sekler and Michael Wolf. In addition to the community schools, two private Jewish schools were also founded.

Michael Wolf, was already offered a teaching post under Rabbi A. Kohn, in 1841. Born in 1807 at Gewitsch [Jevíčko] (Moravia), he died at Lwów in 1890. He studied at the Yeshivah of Rabbi Chaim Deutschmann at Trebitsch [Třebíč], and later at the technical colleges of Prague and Vienna. After graduating he taught at Prossnitz [Prostějov] and Lomnitz [Lomnice]. When in 1853 secondary schools and grammar schools started teaching Judaism, he was appointed teacher of religion and excelled in his method of lecturing and in his enthusiasm. In the years 1849–1857, he was also the preacher at the "The Temple of the Enlightened" where his sermons enticed the audience. Michael Wolf was also interested in social issues and prepared a plan for establishing Jewish agricultural settlements in Galicia.[15] In contrast to the settlements of poor Jews with no income, which were suggested during Joseph II's time, his plan proposed to involve wealthy Jews in those settlements and to form them primarily around the agricultural education for the young. Every community would select a boy aged 10–13 and a girl aged 8–12 and send them, at its expense, to an agricultural farm in the vicinity of Lwów for a six–years agricultural education. At the end of their studies they would have to be settled in a settlement and land allotted to them.

Wolf was also involved in publishing and writing, and he published his own textbooks. In partnership with the Christian printer Poremba he managed a printing house, and published the books of Rabbi Nachman, and Abraham Krochmal, Josef Perl, Samson Bloch, Isak Eichel, Natan Samuely, Ruben Aszer Braudes as well as the writings of Rabbi Jakob Emden against the cult of Sabbataj Cwi [Shabbtai Zevi] which had just sold out.

The abolition of the kosher meat tax caused the community difficulty in covering the schools' budget. The budget for each school amounted to 1200 Florin a year. When the school was first established the community was entitled to collect one Florin and 10 Kreuzer from every slaughtered beef cattle towards the expense of education. In 1853, the supplement was raised to one Florin and 40 Kreuzer.

The sudden abolition of the meat tax led also the rest of Austria's [Jewish] communities into grave financial embarrassment due to the inability to cover the budgets that were mainly drawn from that tax. The communities turned to the Minister of religion, Count [von] Thun, for his assistance. The rabbis also went to see him to explain the communities' financial situation. With the agreement of Treasurer Krauss, orders were issued to the affected regions –Bohemia, Moravia and Galicia– to continue collecting the tax.

During the government session of 13th February 1850,[16] the issue and discussed and it was decided to ask the regional governors for a list of rabbis and Jewish representatives in order to approach them for consultation. The consultation did not take place and the communities imposed a kosher meat supplement to cover their costs.

Lwów's community inevitably also struggled to cover the schools' costs.

The community collected an annual kosher meat tax in the sum of 3,733 Florin and 20 Kreuzer, 2,400 Florin of which were required for the maintenance of the two new schools, that with the increased number of pupils required parallel classes. The progress of the educational system at Lwów was recognised by the government, so much so that it expressed its willingness to cover the costs to support it –were the community unable to find means– so that the schools' activities should not suffer. The Ministry of Finance was even willing to increase the supplement on the kosher meat tax and also to permit the community to levy an additional tax on other goods.[17]

In 1855, for the following three years, the community was granted permission to raise the tax on slaughtered kosher meat from 1.74 to 2 Florins, on the grounds that "due to the known moral and cultural situation in which Galicia's Jews find themselves, [the community] will be unable to do enough for the youth's education."

Besides schools the community also maintained an orphanage, a children's care home, a hospital (with 170 beds, which treated

[Pages 277-278]

on average 2,300 patients annually), as well as a sanitorium for 30 people. In 1854, an "Association for financial assistance to impecunious Jewish students" was also established, to pay part of the tuition fees and the cost of books. The association was established by the first secondary schools [gymnasiums] graduates.

On 24th April 1854, the Kaiser's wedding day, the cornerstone was laid of the "workshop" for the poor, orphaned children. At the time 200 poor youths were given clothes.

In February 1851, under the influence of Rabbi Samuel Dajcz [Daitch] of Sambor, Majer Kallier established at Brody "The Society for the advancement of agriculture among the Jews of Galicia." To establish a

Meier Münz

branch of the society at the time, Lwów's community leaders created a temporary committee made up of: Dr. Blumenfeld, Dr. Kolischer, Meier Rachmiel Mieses, A. M. Goldbaum, S. Kellermann, R. Rosenstein and Meier Münz,[18] but this has never materialised.

The institutions were established and maintained with bequests and houses left by a few generous individuals, and through collected donations.

Particularly active in maintaining the institutions were Laura Losch (cousin of the Jewish statesman Gabriel Riesser of Hamburg),[19] who headed the orphanage, and Hersz Zipper (1796–1858) who was the police inspector in the Jewish Quarter since 1820, and founded the orphanage the funding of which he personally took care of for the rest of his life. In 1840, he was among the founders of "The Temple of the Enlightened" and was an active committee member. After the demise of Rabbi Abraham Kohn, he communicated with Rabbi Kohn at Rausnitz [Rousínov] about his election as a rabbi at Lwów, an appointment to which he did not agree. Zipper was well known and loved by the Jews of Lwów. There was no enterprise to which he had not contributed with energy and dedication. A memorial service was held at the "Temple" after his demise on 3rd September 1858, and the poet Heinrich Bernstein published an elegiac poem[20] in his memory.

The welfare issues were numerous due to the increased numbers of the poor and needy. The main question was how to centralise all the charitable activities. In 1854, Dr. Dawid Diamand (the father of Dr. Jakob Diamand) submitted a memorandum to the governorship,[21] suggesting that a charitable company be established at Lwów to sustain a Jewish fund for the poor that would maintain the charitable institutions, workplaces and crafts schools. It is not known whether the governorship took account of that comprehensive project. The conditions were not yet ripe for the execution of such a project.

The community took also care of the young children's religious Torah education, and at that time it also purchased a plot of land, for a new cemetery, on which L. Wixel built a synagogue for 6,000 Florin, at his own expense.

In the summer of 1855, a cholera epidemic broke out, gravely affecting Lwów's Jewish population. Among the renowned personalities who succumbed to that epidemic were: the writer Jakob Bodek, the physician A. Gussman, the teachers Salomon Singer and Leo Sekler as well as the community secretary Bernhard Pipes. Among the cholera victims was also Magdalena Kohn the widow of Rabbi Abraham Kohn.[22] The community was charged with taking care of the large number of widows and orphans who were left with no livelihood. To this end, the community spend 6,000 Florin, in 1857 alone.

One of the political issues that occupied the community, was the right of owning real estate. In 1851, the Ministry of the Interior adopted a principled position, that with the declaration of equal rights to all religions, all the limitations that had applied to the Jews, were abolished, as the limitations arose from regulations which had been revoked.[23] The Supreme Court's judgements of 19.10. 1852, 23.2.1853 and 19.4.1853, also determined that Jews were entitled to own land and houses even in states where they had previously been barred from purchasing land, plots and houses, from Christians. The 4th March 1849 abolition of the basic laws, brought to an end any renewal of these restrictions.

The Community Leader Dr. Emanuel Blumenfeld

Dr. [von] Bach, Minister of the Interior, Carl [von] Krauss Minister of Justice and [von] Bruck, Minister of Finance raised the matter for discussion, as mentioned previously, and because the government had not arrived at a

[Pages 279-280]

clear decision, on 2.10.1853, the Emperor ordered that until such time as no conclusive decision on all Jewish matters had been reached, in issues of property ownership (*Besitzfähigkeit*), each state should continue with the regulations that applied to the Jews prior to 1848.[25] This directive caused great confusion among the authorities' circles, most of whom believed that, politically too, the Jews should be treated according to the laws prior to 1848. The issue forced the Minister of the Interior, Dr. Bach, to send an explicit instruction on 7th November 1853, that the provisions in the 2.10.1853 decree applied only to property and real estate.

Throughout Galicia, excluding the Kraków district, only 46 farms had been purchased by Jews till 1848; from 1848 till October 1853, 1,389 land purchases from Christians took place, a third of which were farms.[26]

The decree spread fear among Austrian Jews. Joseph Wertheimer, Vienna's Jewish community leader, published a pamphlet on "The status of Austrian Jewry," in which he sharply protested the humiliation of Austria's 800,000 Jews.

Covertly, Vienna's community incited the communities throughout the kingdom to submit petitions to the Kaiser against the provision of that decree. The government was made aware of that action and immediately dispatched instructions to all the commissioners and district leaders to look out for that activity and consider it illegal. The authorities were ordered to guard and immediately report when community leaders set out to Vienna.[27]

Dawid Horowitz, a member of Lwów's community committee, was in Vienna at the time, attending to his business with the Rothschilds there. When he heard the proposal from Vienna's community, he immediately sent a letter to the community–elder, Dr. Menkes, in which he stressed the urgency of preparing a petition from Lwów's community, which should point out the special situation of Galicia, and should be delivered to the Kaiser by two messengers, Dr. Blumenfeld and Rachmiel Mieses. Horowitz instructed also to include in the petition statistical data, to show that in the previous five years few plots of land and farms have been purchased by Jews. Dr. Menkes replied that the community leadership had discussed the issue in depth and that Dr. Blumenfeld and Mieses were unwilling to go to Vienna. He added that he had spoken with Governor Gołuchowski who was uncomfortable with the action, and advised against sending empowered representatives to Vienna. Gołuchowski threatened that any empowered representatives who reached Vienna would immediately be expelled, even though he conceded that the community was entitled to submit petitions to the Kaiser. The Governor said that he would inform Vienna's higher police of the matter. After he met the Governor, the community council convened and decided to ask Horowitz, as he was unwilling to deliver the petition alone, whether he would be willing to do so together with two board members whom he would pick. Horowitz replied that he was unable to undertake the mission due to urgent business which called him to Köln.

On 21st October 1853, Governor Gołuchowski submitted to the Vienna authorities a detailed report of his conversation with Dr. Menkes. He also reported that Lwów's community had decided to forgo the submission of a petition, and to task Dr. Blumenfeld and Rachmiel Mieses who were travelling to Vienna for personal reasons, to contact the Vienna community and to report the results of the negotiation. Governor Gołuchowski drew Vienna police's attention to the need for keeping an eye on Mieses and Dr. Blumenfeld's moves.

The Vienna police made preparations to keep an eye on Dr. Blumenfeld and Mieses. It also summoned Dawid Horowitz for investigation; he informed them of the contents of his message to Lwów. He declared that in his opinion the petition would be sent by post, or the matter would be dropped altogether. Horowitz's assumption proved to be correct, as he was familiar with his friends and knew that they would not dare go against the Governor's wishes.

Indeed, Lwów's community did not send its representatives but posted its petition instead, while requesting to annul the regulations that restricted the Jews' right to property ownership. All the efforts were in vain. The restrictions were retained, and with them all the other pre–1848 restrictions were revived. The leasing of estates and land in villages, and of exempt farms faced no objections since Clause 34 of the 7th May 1789 regulations for Jews had permitted it, in addition to which and in conjunction with their estates, Jews were granted the right to lease in the provinces, and the right to mill.

The prohibition to purchase houses from Christians in Lwów proper, had greatly harmed the Jews however. The municipality and the governorship refused permission to expand the Jewish Quarter beyond its existing boundaries.[28]

The municipality's prohibition for Jewish bakers to keep market stalls outside the Jewish Quarter, in accordance with the pre–1848 regulation, led to grave economic damage. The community appealed, but the governorship objected, agreeing instead with the municipality under the assumption that lifting of the prohibition would harm the Christian bakers, and that Jewish sellers would affect the cleanliness of the non–Jewish areas.[29]

The municipality did not allow Jewish traders to keep shops in non–Jewish quarters. This issue also led to dispute between the Minister of the Interior Dr. Bach and the Lwów governorship. Bach held the view

[Pages 281-282]

that it was undesirable to sustain the dirty Jewish Quarters which held back their moral development, and exacerbated the hatred between Jews and Christians. Lwów's increased Jewish population was not to be ignored either, and sanitation was another reason for a larger Jewish Quarter.[30]

Governor Gołuchowski retorted that the Kaiser's decree forbidding the purchase of property outside the Jewish Quarter was still in effect, and that only special cases could be treated as exceptions.[31] In fact, Galicia's Governorship decided to maintain the Jewish Quarter.

On a different fundamental issue Governor Gołuchowski also followed the existing law:

The municipality demanded compensation from the community for the new Jewish cemetery land. On 31.3.1856, the community appealed the claim arguing that the Jews made up one third of Lwów's population, and that as tax payers they participated in the maintenance of all municipal property, and that it was dishonest to demand compensation for land which belonged to the whole town and its citizens. Nevertheless, based on clause 22, of the 7th May 1789 regulation regarding the Jews, Governor Gołuchowski determined that the community was liable for all costs associated with constructing the cemetery. Indeed, the municipality was not entitled to offer of its land without compensation, be it to an individual or the public. The claim that Jews shared in the municipal property was dismissed since the community was not united with the town but was managed independently and charged payment for the graves without sharing its income with the municipality.[32]

In 1858 and 1859 Lwów's community submitted memorandums, via Governor Gołuchowski, to the central government and the Kaiser about the restrictions on the right of property ownership,[33] the difficulties regarding marriage licences and the other severities which affected [their] economic life, and requested to have them annulled. During meetings of community representatives with the Governor, they again repeated the need and demanded to alter the legal status of the Jews.

Governor Gołuchowski was himself interested in supporting the Jewish *Maskilim* Circles. On 21ˢᵗ August 1859, when the community representatives congratulated him on the occasion of his appointment as Minister of the Interior, he asked to receive a memorandum and proposals on how to distinguish legally between Enlightened Jews dressed in European outfits, and the rest who wore traditional Jewish–Polish clothes.

On 28ᵗʰ October 1859, the community–committee submitted a comprehensive memorandum signed by Dr. Kolischer, Dr. Barach–Rappaport, M. Dubs and I. L. Kolischer.[34] It opened by stressing that it was advisable to grant all of the Jews of Austria, Galicia included, full equal rights similar to those granted to the non–Jewish population, without fear of customs, dress or education. The memorandum's authors refuted all of the authorities' and the Christian population's concerns, and pointed out that in other countries Jews on similar cultural level of Galician Jews also faced emancipation, and that only by putting them on a par with the rest of the population were they able to advance and evolve culturally and educationally. There was thus no reason to consider the Jews of Galicia, or some of them, unworthy of emancipation. The poverty, legal and political inequality, and the harsh conditions to which a large number of Galicia's Jews were subjected, were the principal stumbling blocks holding back their development, and granting them emancipation and annulling all existing restrictions would doubtlessly transform their lives and speed up the process of their progress. Consequently, one should not accept equal rights for the *Maskilim* alone, but rather, emancipation should be granted to all sections of the Jewish community. The memorandum delineated the complex limitations imposed on all economic life of the Jews, and the harm those limitations brought not only on the Jews but also on the Kingdom. The proposals stressed that to raise the cultural standing, schools similar to Lwów's Jewish community school, fully paid for or subsidised by the government, should be created. Preferably, they should be funded from the 1806 Jewish elementary schools' fund of 132,460 Gulden in banknotes, and 126,628 Gulden in government bonds (Obligations) which were transferred to the general schools, in 1806.

An effective means to advance the cultural status seemed the electing of educated individuals to the communal committees. The large number of uneducated community–elders was hindering cultural progress. As to the Jewish traditional dress, only education and reasoned propaganda would lead to positive results.

The memorandum expressed the hope of Lwów's elders that in his new role as Minister of the Interior, Governor Gołuchowski would successfully employ his talent, wisdom and humanitarian outlook, to promote the full emancipation of all Austrian Jews.

Lwów community's memorandums have probably influenced Governor Gołuchowski. Immediately he took up his role of Minister of the Interior, Gołuchowski tried to change the legal status of the Jews. At the council of ministers he recommended to annul the restrictive property ownership as well as the other restrictions. In his 11ᵗʰ January 1860 presentation,[35] in the presence of the Kaiser, Gołuchowski delivered

[Pages 283-284]

a comprehensive survey of the legal status and of the opinion, of the governorship in every individual state. In line with his proposals and by the Kaiser's order of 13ᵗʰ January 1860, restrictions were lifted in certain economic industries, in apothecary, as well as on the prohibition to settle in the villages of Galicia and Bukowina. The restrictions on Lwów's residency were not yet annulled because they had not been put forward by the governorship.

In December 1859, the council of ministers debated the annulment of restrictions on the right of property ownership. The Minister of Finance, Freiherr von Bruck (1798–1860), proposed that they be annulled in consideration of the Kingdom's financial situation, as these restrictions prevented the Jews' participation in Austria's financial affairs thus affecting the public credit. All the ministers agreed with him except for the Minister of Religion, Thun, and the Minister of the Interior, Gołuchowski who recommended that the restrictions in the districts of Styria, Carinthia and Carniola be maintained. In Galicia he proposed to exempt from limitations only certain categories, such as: 1. graduates secondary, and higher education; 2. holders of nobility titles; 3. officers; 4. franchisee wholesale traders and industrialists.

Despite the objection of most ministers to the Minister of the Interior's proposal, the Kaiser accepted his view, with mitigating changes,[36] and the decree annulling the restriction on the acquisition of property was issued on 18ᵗʰ February 1860. Having met the legal conditions, the Jews of Lwów have soon approached the authorities with requests for licences to purchase building plots, houses, land and even estates. From among the requests only 41 were approved.[37]

In the years 1860–1861:

1. Ignaz Lewkowicz, a wealthy wholesaler, active member on the "Temple" committee, licence to acquire estates. (1) 2. Emanuel Kohn, house owner and community elder. 3. Israel Schütz, surgeon. 4. Samuel Klärmann, merchant and censor for the Austrian National Bank, commercial expert, founder member of the Temple, son–in–law of Meier Rachmiel Mieses, community–elder. 5. Scheine Mendrichowitz. 6. Perle Mendrichowitz. 7. Meier Rachmiel Mieses, a leading *Maskil*, member of the municipality, a banks' and commercial institutions' management staff member since 1840. 8. Mendel Szochet, served

with the armed forces, clerk. 9. Osias M. Braun, branch censor for the National Bank, member of the chamber of commerce and industry. 10. Hermann Landes, restaurant owner. 11. Hirsch Mieses. 12. Aron Philipp, completed school education and passed the commerce and accountancy examinations. 13. Szalom Sanicki merchant. 14. Manis Rappoport.

In the years 1862–1866:

15. Salomon Haber. 16. Marcus Dubs, owner of houses, member of the municipality. (Lwów's police objected to granting his request "since Dubs had published books in Polish, and participated in the Polish committee's consultations during the Galician *Sejm* elections (1861), as a *Sejm* delegate he occupied a seat on the left side and voted with the Left, he wears Polish outfits and supports the Polish National Movement." The Vienna ministry rejected the police opinion since " there is no negative information about him"). 17. M. Ber Kozel. 18. Osias Mieses, wholesaler, branch manager of "The Credit Bank" and an administrator of the railways named after Carl Ludwig; member of the municipality. 19. Samuel Gall, owner of houses. 20. Emanuel Rotter. 21. D. Kohn. 22. L. H. Mett, in 1844 he still prepared for his secondary school examination to which the Governorship objected due to his age. 23. S. Poch. 24. N. Tepfer, served in the armed forces, held a residence and a restaurant licence outside the Jewish Quarter. 25. S. Mehler, lessee of an estate, wore European clothes. 26. Rachmiel Horowitz, branch censor for the "Austrian National Bank." 27. Landes, merchant. 28. L. Hirer. 29. S. Wahl, supplier to the armed forces. 30. S. Goldberg. 31. A. Nierenstein, "The National Bank" branch manager, member of the department of commerce and industry, municipality member. 32. M. Rosenfeld, a discharged soldier, a restaurant owner. 33. Klinghoffer, a non–believer. 34. K. Rapopport. 35. Goldstaub, builder. 36. Schnitzer, military supplier, member of the community committee. 37. Bernhard Czop, money changer and builder. 38. Sigmund Moritz Steiff, a wholesale shop owner. 39. Mojzesz Hescheles, government supplier, contractor and a member of the municipality. 40. Penzias. 41. Losch.

According to the regulation of the Jews of 7th May 1789, Jews were "members of the community" (*Gemeinde*), but devoid of the citizens' rights granted to the community's Christian members. According to the amendment of 14th July 1847, Jewish house owners in all of Galicia's towns were entitled to acquire citizen's rights, subject to the municipality's ruling, but in fact Jews were not granted citizen's rights. Joseph Kolischer, the branch manager of "the National Bank," was the first Jew to be granted citizen's rights at Lwów in 1866.

Nevertheless, although Jews had no citizen's rights, Lwów's Jews enjoyed the right to vote ever since 1848.

Dr. Jakob Rappaport

The community and the merchants objected to maintaining Lwów's Jewish Quarter, which they considered a negation of the Law, and they demanded its total abolition.[38]

Lwów's municipality issued strict instructions for the Jews to vacate the houses in the non–Jewish Quarters to which they had moved without the municipality's permission, and those refusing to vacate were to be punished in accordance with the Law.

The community's memorandums of 1864 obliged Galicia's governorship to deal with the conditions of habitation in the Jewish Quarter which had greatly worsened

[Pages 285-286]

due to congestion and to the danger from collapse of the old dilapidated houses, some of which had collapsed in 1863.

The municipality deferred the issue until the new municipal regulations were accepted. The governorship realized that the situation was unacceptable, but found no solution because the officers held diverse opinions about the issue. The minority recommended to demolish the Jewish Quarter while the Poles, hoping to attract the Jews to their political national cause, demonstrably approved of equal rights. As they preferred the issue to be neither offered nor decided by the higher authorities but rather by the municipal body, they proposed waiting till the new municipal regulations had been accepted.[39]

Although Governor Mensdorff recommended that things be speeded up due to the congestion in the Jewish Quarter, the authorities refrained from executing anything that countered the Polish public opinion, they decided to keep the Jewish Quarter as it was but allowed educated Jews to move to non–Jewish quarters. Among the first Jews permitted to settle in a non–Jewish quarter were Meier Rachmiel Mieses, Hermann Mieses and Osias M. Goldhaber, member of the municipality. In its decision the Governorship stressed that the time had not yet come to open the Christian quarters to the Jewish masses "who differ from the race (Stammesgenossen) in the rest of the Austrian states.[40] The Governorship stopped removing Jews who had moved to areas outside the [Jewish] Quarter, without authorisations.

Consequently, those Jews whom the authorities considered uneducated were forced to remain in the few overcrowded narrow streets and old houses of the Jewish Quarter for several years yet.

2.

The community faced the difficulty of organising elections for a new community committee.

No elections had taken place since 1840. Among the community elders appointed by the authorities, four had died, Dr. Barach Rappaport, Izak Kolischer, Samuel Kohn and Dr. Leo Kolischer whose death (3.3.1860) was a heavy loss.

Dr. Leo Kolischer (1792–1860) completed his studies as Doctor of Philosophy at Vienna University and returned to Lwów. A very wealthy man, he dedicated himself to public service, he headed the education committee and due to his boundless activities, he was known among the Jewish community as "Lwów's Josef Perl." He was one of the pillars of the Enlightenment movement.

Without a majority in the committee it became necessary to turn to the authorities for permission to call new elections. The community relied on the population growth since 1840. The Governorship consented to the request and ruled that all house owners and those who paid the community tax, were eligible to vote.[41] As the question of establishing a rabbinical seminary in Galicia was on the agenda at the time, the authorities were keen to have a full and qualified committee at the head of community.

As mentioned previously, Marek (Mordechai) Bernstein of Brody had already proposed in 1828 that a rabbinical seminary be established in Galicia. Nothing came of it as the Lwów community, led by the Orthodox, objected to it.

Marek Bernstein gave up his design to pay for establishing a rabbinical seminary, and left all his wealth for the construction of a crafts school in order to teach crafts to Jewish youths. Construction started in 1865. The fund was established in 1864.

Twenty years later, in 1884, the fund amounted to 75,000 Florins. The profits paid for 20–25 apprentices' maintenance and study fees with craftsmen and in workshops, at 600–800 Florins annually. After they had graduated, the apprentices were given clothes and a a sum of money. The fund spent on such causes between 1,000 and 1,500 Florins annually. There was also a preparatory crafts school with two classes which followed the elementary schools' curriculum. The classes took place in the evenings after the apprentices had finished their work at the workshops. They learned Polish, German, arithmetic, geography, physics, nature studies, draughtsmanship as well as religious studies and Hebrew.

In the years 1880–1900, the institute was managed by the board of directors led by Rabbi Bernard Löwenstein and after his death by Dr. Emil Byk. The board of directors included the community representatives, the craftsmen and the headmaster of the Jewish school.

In 1878, Dr. Teofil Gerstmann was the headmaster and among the teaching staff were Joseph Ahl, Bernard Bachus, Władysław Kłapkowski, Hipolit Parasiewicz, Nehemiasz Landes, Izydor Planer, Natan Ropschitz and Herman Rosenthal.

Of the 144 apprentices who were raised on the "Bernstein fund" during 1865–1885, those who finished their training included: 23 tailors, 6 shoemakers, 26 locksmiths, 13 carpenters, 9 tinsmiths, 11 engravers, 2 blacksmiths, 3 typesetters, 8 watchmakers, 3 bookbinders, 5 goldsmiths, 1 weaver, 13 signwriters, 1 wagoner, 3 saddlers, 2 painters (whitewash), 1 suitcase maker, 2 millers, 1 upholsterer, 134 apprentices all together.[42]

* *

The question of the rabbinical seminary arose in conjunction with the war–fine monies imposed in Hungary by General [von] Haynau, in 1849. In 1856, the government decided

[Pages 287-288]

to use part of the monies to establish a rabbinical seminary at Vienna.

The central government considered the issue during the days of Josef Perl, whose memorandums noted the importance of such an institution –modelled on the Padua seminary– to spread education among the youth and the Jewish population of Galicia.

Once the government council approved the rabbinical seminary, the Minister of the Interior, Gułochowski, gained the Kaiser's approval in the matter and on 21st February 1861 the government issued an ordinance to establish an accredited rabbinical seminary with public rights, and were the national sources not to suffice, it would be paid for by funds set aside for Jewish schools which supplemented the Catholic fund. Consequently, a decree was issued to separate from it the Jewish fund, to be dedicated to the needs of Jewish schools, from 1st November 1862.

It was stressed that the negotiation regarding the erection of the rabbinical seminary would proceed in such a fashion that it would be operational in the upcoming academic year. In the intervening period the candidates would have to present secondary school [gymnasium] qualification certificates.

The Austrian regime underwent great changes after the defeat in the Italian war (1859), including political and civil freedom to the Jews. The 29th November, 20th December 1859 and 10th January 1860 rules, abolished the restrictions on marriage, on craft and trade employment, on testimony collection, stressing the liberal spirit with which the government intended to approach its policy regarding the Jews. Unlike Minister [von] Bach who aimed to centralise power, the Vienna Prime Minister Agenor Gołuchowski (20th October 1859 – 15th December 1860), wished to form a federation in order to stabilise Austrian politics. His approach attracted the Poles, the Hungarians and the Czechs but he failed due to the stance of the Germans and the Imperial–Court circles, and a few months later he resigned to be replaced by the liberal statesman Schmerling who favoured a wholly centralised regime with a so–called liberal spirit.

The government believed that it would gain the approval of all Jewish circles, and the Orthodox in general, for the project to construct a rabbinical seminary. They were gravely mistaken, however, since on the initiative of Rabbi Szymon Schreiber who was elected Kraków's Rabbi in 1861, the Orthodox started a counteraction, and succeeded. The Enlightened objected to the proposal to model the school on the Pressburg [Bratislava] Yeshivah, as they doubted that it would fulfill its purpose to their satisfaction.

In December 1862, the Governorship appointed a special committee led by Court councillor [*Hofrat*] P. Vukassovich. The appointed committee members were expert clerks, and the Jews appointed Rabbi Kristianpoller of Brody, Majer Kallier of Brody, Perl (the son of Josef Perl) of Tarnopol, leaders from Lwów and representatives from several communities.

After lengthy negotiations and discussions with representatives from all the parties, the Governorship had reached the conclusion that the Jews did not approve of the project. And that, since they were split religiously and by sect, and were worried that establishing the school would thwart their aspirations. Consequently, the Governorship decided to defer the execution of the project indefinitely, and to wait with submitting the proposal until after the 16th November 1867 account by the director of the ministry of religion and education had been submitted for the Kaiser's approval.[43]

The rabbinical seminary was therefore not constructed at the time, nor any time later.

During the period in which Count Leo Thun–Hohenstein (1849–1860) was minister of education and religion, the Orthodox managed to divert his opinion to their cause to form a "separation of the God–fearing"

(Trennungs–orthodoxie) in Austria. Isak Dajcz [Daitch][44] drove events forward with his memorandums in which he informed on, and slandered the Enlightened as dangerous revolutionaries, and described the Orthodox as "the Emperor's most loyal servants, who opposed every revolutionary and liberal party." Count Leo Thun who had formed an alliance (concordat) with the Vatican, hoped also to form a "concordat" with the Jews, thus thwarting the intrusion of any liberalism among the Jews. For that reason he even agreed to prohibit, by law, the opening of Jewish shops on the Sabbath, and to extend the authority and the jurisdiction of the rabbis.

Accordingly, Count Thun agreed to acknowledge the Pressburg Yeshivah as a rabbinical seminary with public rights. During the 7th June 1860 cabinet session,[45] he proposed to establish in Galicia a school similar to the Pressburg Yeshivah, and to forgo the demand for secondary school and philosophy certificates from candidates for the rabbinate. The Minister of the Interior Gołuchowski concurred with his proposal, which was accepted by a large majority, and which the Kaiser confirmed on 4th July 1860.[46] Based on his acceptance, the statute was issued on 21st February 1861.

On 15th December 1860 Anton [von] Schmerling (1805–1893), known for his liberal views, was appointed Prime Minister. Despite the changes he had introduced on the religious and educational front, the favourable view of the Orthodox over the Enlightened remained in place; however, due to the impression that they presented no risk of "revolutionary intention" of which the educated [*Maskilim*] were suspected. That political stance was maintained till 1868.

The legislations of October 1859 and February 1860 stimulated political life. Parties were formed in Galicia, with a stance on

[Pages 289-290]

Galician politics and in particular on the Jewish issue. Those politicians who upheld the 1848 principles, such as Smolka and Ziemiałkowski, naturally favoured Jewish emancipation – so that they might assimilate and reinforce the Polish people. Podolia's conservative nobility opposed the emancipation. The Ruthenians took an anti–Jewish stand too, fearing that equal rights would tip the balance in favour of the Poles and Jews, who would subsequently occupy Galicia's major economic posts.

At the time an anti–Jewish struggle emerged at Warsaw, with the Galician Polish press as well as democratic writers such as the historian Henryk Schmitt[47] also objecting to Jewish emancipation. At Lwów the debate among the Jews was represented by Meier Münz who had published in German the booklet: "*Lelewel Kämpfer für Recht und Wahrheit und die Judenfrage* [Lelewel, fighter for law and truth and the Jewish question]" (Lemberg 1860), in which he attacked Henryk Schmitt and the Poles for opposing equal rights for the Jews. Meier Münz who distanced himself from the Orthodox after the poisoning of Rabbi Abraham Kohn, played an influential role among the Jewish intelligentsia. Galicia's Jews were just entering a period of serious conflict: the Chassidim and the Orthodox who considered emancipation a danger to Jewish existence, resisted all attempts to change the way of life of the Jewish masses in schools, or changes to the structure of the communities. The rabbis and leaders of the Orthodox objected to the establishment of any rabbinical seminaries. At the time, the best of Lwów's Jewish intelligentsia formed an "Association for the seekers of resourcefulness, the good and the honourable" or in German, "Verein für Bildung und Gesellligkeit," which aimed to spread education, awaken its members' interest in affairs of the Jewish community and cultivate social lives. Its home at 21 Sykstuska Street,[48] was a kind of "Jewish Casino" where physicians, lawyers and *Maskilim* gathered for lectures, conversations and discussions. As the association showed no sign of Polonisation, the Poles considered it an organ for the Germanisation of Galician Jews. The Polish immigrants at Paris also turned to "the Polish–Jews" with a call to attack the association and boycott it as an anti–Polish institution.

Dr. Jan Fried, Dr. Henryk Gottlieb, Dr. Filip Mansch and Dr. Braun who led the association, turned it into a cultural centre. Among its members and lecturers were the poet Dr. Henryk Gottlieb,[49] the Hebrew poet Jakob–Cwi [Tzvi] Sperling,[50] Abraham Krochmal (son of Rabbi Nachman Krochmal), Marek Dubs, Dr. Etroger, Rabbi Bernhard Löwenstein, David Rappaport,[51] Samuel Modlinger.[52]

The association was actively involved in investigating the problems facing Lwów's community, and it published a special pamphlet on the community's taxes (*Die besteuerungs frage der Israelitischen Kultusgemeinde in Lemberg*, 1863, p.31). It objected to the introduction of a Simple tax, suggesting instead to collect a kosher meat tax, two Gulden per oxen, which would bring an annual income of 12,000 Gulden (rather than 8,000 Gulden). They proposed to elect a five members' evaluation committee to assess, by area, those who owed tax according to reports from trustees' committees. According to their proposal, the community would annually publish accounts of income and expenditure.

In respect of Galicia's political issues, there was a difference of opinion among the Intelligentsia. Unlike the enlightened Jews of Kraków and their leaders Dr. Öttinger, Henryk Markusfeld and Abraham Gumplowicz, who supported the Poles, most of Lwów's Jewish intelligentsia favoured the Austrian centralised system and supported the "Party of the Constitution" (*Verfassungspartei*), with only a minority led by Marek Dubs, supporting the Poles. In respect of Jewish issues, the entire intelligentsia whose ambition was to retain the community's leadership and realise its educational and cultural programme, faced a difficult struggle with the Orthodox.

The Enlightened, who disapproved of the government's plan to establish a scholastic institute for rabbis, which they considered an Orthodox institute, aspired instead to a rabbinical seminary similar to the one at Breslau [Wroclaw].

Due to their disputes with the Orthodox, the *Maskilim's* standing declined to such an extent that in the May 1862 community committee's election, representatives of the Orthodox and of the moderates were also elected. The elected were Dr. Max Landesberger, Meier Rachmiel Mieses, Meier Münz, S. Kohn, Salomon Kellermann, Rachmiel Ornstein, Dr. Osias Hönigsmann and Marek Dubs.[53] Mejer Rachmiel Mieses was elected community chairman of the community council.

Based on the 26th February 1861 legislation, which redefined the "National Councils" (*Sejm*s) as authoritative over National issues, elections to the Galician *Sejm* were set for 15th April 1861. The Jews were however denied the right to vote. With Lwów's community led by the Enlightened at the time, its representatives were astonished and immediately gathered the representatives from Eastern Galicia's communities for consultation. Following the conference's decision, a delegation set out to Vienna for negotiation with the government, in contrast with the Kraków community whose representatives joined the Polish delegation. The Jewish delegation succeeded in lobbying [von] Schmerling

[Pages 291-292]

to accept the 1st March 1861 decree, which had granted Jews the right to vote.

The dispute over voting deepened among Lwów's Jews. Meier Münz, who was proposed by the Enlightened who followed centralisation, refused to support the Poles due to the Warsaw Lesznowski affair. The Enlightened who supported the Poles, on the other hand, put forward Marek Dubs. During [chol ha'moed] Passover, a voters' meeting was held at the "Temple for the Enlightened" in which Ziemiałkowski and Dubs spoke. Ziemiałkowski declared that the Jews' problem was a Polish issue and that he wished the Jews considered Poland their homeland, would integrate with the Poles and would be just like them.[54]

Münz lost, and Dubs was elected.

Among the 141 delegates elected to the first Galician *Sejm* 1861–1867, four Jews were selected from the whole of Galicia: Dr. Szymon Samelsohn from Kraków; Majer Kallier from Brody; Dr. Lazar Dubs from Kolomyia, who was replaced after his demise in 1865, by Dr. Maximilian Landesberger, a Lwów solicitor; and Marek Dubs from Lwów. Lwów's chamber of commerce and industry did not elect a Jew, but rather, the liberal Christian J. Brajer.

Marek (Mordechai) Dubs (1801–1874) who was born at Lwów, inherited a liquor factory, which he enlarged and held a prominent position in the Galician economy. In 1848 he became politically active and sided with the Poles, he was elected member of the municipality and remained so until 1870, he was also member of the Community Council. In 1850 he was elected member of Lwów's chamber of commerce and industry.

He was one of the earliest *Maskilim* who published his writings in Polish, and joined the Polish press. His book: *Historya narodu Synajskiego w polsce* ["History of the Sinaiticus nation in Poland"] made an impression at the time. He also published articles on the agricultural economy and the currency problems. Apart from his knowledge of rabbinical literature and Jewish wisdom, he also excelled in general education and was one of the renowned speakers in Polish and German. He was one of Abraham Krochmal's close friends, and supported Hebrew writers. He himself published articles in *Kerem Chemed*, in *Otzar Nechmad* and in *HeChaluts* published by Osias Heschel Schorr, and in *Sede Zofim*, a collection dedicated to Jewish wisdom, edited by Michael Wolf, published at Lwów (1860). He also exchanged letters with Samuel David Luzzatto. He played a very significant role in the Galician *Sejm*, defending Jewish interests.

The Jewish *Sejm* delegates represented in fact a tight circle of the Jewish intelligentsia, who sympathised with Polish assimilation, except for Majer Kallier who was inclined towards German assimilation and supported the Vienna–centralised government. In respect of all general issues, Marek Dubs, Dr. Lazar Dubs, Dr. Landesberger and Dr. Samelsohn supported the Polish national demands.

At the opening of the 26th April 1861 session, Dr. Samelsohn, Marek Dubs and Majer Kallier submitted the proposal for full equal rights to all Galician Jews. The same was also submitted to the *Sejm*'s presidency by Floryan Ziemiałkowski, but neither proposal made it to the discussion agenda.

The second session opened on 12th January 1863, and closed immediately due to the outbreak of the Polish uprising. It was only on 23rd November 1865 that the third session opened and lasted till 28.4.1866, and it was the fourth session, which ran from 29th November 1866 until 31st December 1866, in which the Jewish question was discussed.

The Jewish question was also debated by the town Council in conjunction with the new municipal regulations. Until 1861, 15 Jewish municipality members and five deputies, represented the Jews in Lwów's municipality. Among the Jewish representatives who distinguished themselves in their achievements at the municipality and in defending Jewish affairs during 1848–1861, were, Meier Münz, Meier Rachmiel Mieses, Osias Mieses, Salomon Kellermann, Osias Nirenstein, Dr. Hönigsmann, Dr. Landesberger, Kolischer and Marek Dubs.

In 1861, the government authorised new elections to the municipality. The above–mentioned members were again elected to represent the Jews. The municipality set out to prepare new municipal regulations, and the majority of the councilmen wanted to maintain the restriction on the number of Jewish representative which was 15, and to establish that all the municipal property belonged solely to the Christian population. The Jews' representatives objected to those proposals but were only supported by a small number of Polish Liberals such as Mieczysław Darowski, Robert Hefern, Stanisław Piłat, Zygmunt Rodakowski, and Floryan Ziemiałkowski. The stance taken by the Polish majority drove the Jewish representatives out from the town council.

Due to the 1861–1863 events –the Polish uprising in Congress Poland– the regulation was not confirmed. The events silenced the town council and deliberations only resumed in 1865.

3.

As known, part of Galicia's Jewish intelligentsia was impressed by the Warsaw in which "displays of Jewish–Polish fraternity" were prominent. The Austrian government viewed the events with concern, with apprehension that the Jews might join the Polish National movement. Jewish youths at the universities of Warsaw and Kraków spearheaded the notion of supporting

[Pages 293-294]

the Jews who joined the uprising. At Kraków propaganda for that aim was organised by Dr. Jakob Drobner, Dr. Jozef Öttinger, Bienenfeld, Adolf Aleksandrowicz, Henryk Markusfeld and the Gumplowicz family. The situation was quite different at Lwów, where the Jews were influenced by German culture and showed little interest in the Polish cause although some of the Jewish students had joined the Poles. The Law students Jozef Lewkowicz, Maurycy Jekeles and Fillip Zucker were the principal motivators for mobilising their friends in that direction, but were unsuccessful in attracting all the students. Many of them baulked at the Polish assimilation; their leader was the Lwów born Filip Mansch (born 17th March 1838). His father, Reb. Salomon Mansch, was a renowned merchant and *Maskil* who gave his son a secular education. In the years 1855–1861, Filip Mansch studied Law at Lwów university. Ever since his youth he had shown interest in Jewish matters and especially in the Yiddish language and grammar. Ludwik Gumplowicz, the leader of Kraków's assimilated youth, was his friend. In contrast to the assimilated, Mansch and his friends held the view that the Jewish People were a nation with a significant culture, who did not need assimilation. That idea drove Mansch to become active within "*Szomer Izrael* [The Guardian of Israel]." Consequently, Ludwik Gumplowicz protested that Lwów university's Jewish youth was not inclined towards the Polish national line.[55]

In June 1861, an announcement from Warsaw reached Lwów[60] stressing that the conflict between the peasants and the nobles had been led by the powers ruling over parts of Poland, who incited the Christians against the Jews, and the Ruthenians against the Poles, all of whom were of one country. The announcement noted that the Jews showed their sympathy for Poland and that "they are our brothers, and Poles like ourselves, although they adhere to a different religion. We are with them and they are with us, we shall work together in peace, in brotherhood and with joint efforts to free Poland." The leaflets were sold on Lwów's streets by Jews too.[61]

With the exception of a few students, the Jewish population was not much affected by the activities of the Polish movement. Filip Zucker, Jozef Lewkowicz and Maurycy Jekeles were the chief movers for the Polish cause, among the Jewish academic youth.

Filip Zucker, the son of Dr. Leon Zucker, the physician of Brody, collected uniforms for the rebels. A police search at his house revealed a large quantity of military uniforms. He was caught and sentenced to incarceration.

Jozef Lewkowicz, the son of Isak, a wholesale merchant who owned a house at No. 9, *Breite Gasse* (Plac Gołuchowski). Together with Jekeles he visited Rabbi Dow–Berisch Meisels during his stay at Lwów, a pretext under which the police searched his house on 11th March 1862, where they found material which seemed to implicate him in involvement with the Polish uprising movement. Sentenced to jail, he was released in 1867. Jekeles was jailed at the same time, and after his release he completed his studies and excelled as a lawyer in Lwów.

As mentioned, besides a small group of students the Jewish public showed no interest in the Polish revolt. The Jewish intelligentsia was mostly against supporting the Poles. The cool attitude toward the Poles arose from bitterness against the Poles who refused to grant Jews equal rights during the municipal regulations debate.

There were however a few individuals, including Dr. Moriz Rappaport and Marek Dubs, who sympathised with the Polish movement and expressed their national feelings. In his journal *Hamwasser*, the renowned Hebrew writer Joseph Kohn-Zedek adopted an anti–Polish stance and warned Galician Jews against joining the uprising, or extending active assistance to Poles who suppressed Galician Jews. He was well aware of the difficult situation in which Jews found themselves. The young Hebrew writer, Natan Samuely wrote openly that one could not rely on promises of "the Polish National government" that flattered the Jews in order to gain their support.

The bitterness and mistrust worsened when, on 26th July 1863, the Polish newspaper "*Goniec* [*Polski*; Polish Times]" published a notice that a Christian apprentice had been killed in the Jewish Quarter. The incidence led to attacks by Christians who rioted around Wałowa Street, even though it transpired that the rumour was false; order was only restored with the aid of the armed forces.

The following day, 27th July 1863, the uprising's town commander posted a flyer to the townspeople, stressing that the Polish people had announced to the world the principle of equality and fraternity among all classes and religions. Consequently, all Poles including Jews were fighting for the freedom of Poland. The Jews had equal rights in the homeland, and it was down to the Poles to convince the youth to oppose all outbursts against the Jews. A second flyer instructed the Polish craftsmen, merchants and pharmacists to accept Jewish apprentices. The theatres, too, were asked to avoid putting on plays that lampooned the Jews. As part of Poland and following the will of the people, Galicia's citizens had to be familiar with, and follow the directives of the secret national government, and no disregard for equal rights of any class or religion would be permitted. On

[Pages 295-296]

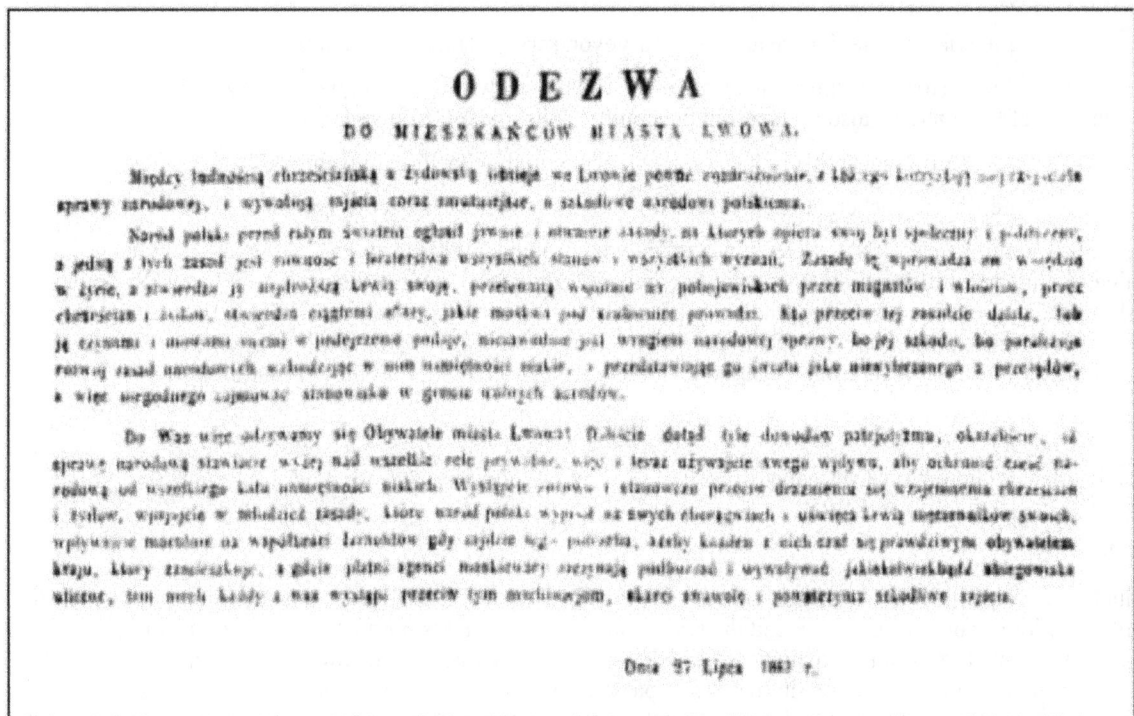

Appeal to Lwów's citizens, 1863

the other hand, the Jews had to demonstrate that they were good sons of the homeland, rather than joining the enemy and turning into its creature in the Germanisation of Poland. The Jews had to support the movement in blood and money, and join the fighting units.

To instil substance in the declarations the national government replaced Lwów's district manager, Tadeusz Skolimowski, by the Jewish manager, Eduard Weissmann, who was active in the movement and contributed to it financially. Under the existing conditions he knew full well that as a Jew he would face difficulties winning over the Poles, and initially he refused the post on the grounds that he was too young. After their repeated pleas, however, he agreed to the appointment.

To influence the communities of Lwów and Galicia, the leaders of the Warsaw uprising established Polish–Jewish committees, but to no avail, as apart from the small group of students headed by Zucker, the masses did not join the Polish movement. Only a few young men joined the rebels or helped the Poles at the border stations between Galicia and Russia. Lwów's community representatives stressed their loyalty to Austria on every occasion. On 21st August 1863, in an audience with commissioner Mensdorff, the community delegation thanked the government for extending the civil rights and easing the employment situation. On 14th November 1863, Lwów's national committee once more turned to the Jews in a call for unity and action for the uprising, but again in vain.

The names of Lwów's Jews who supported the Polish movement, were:

1.   Moritz Weber, one of the revolt fighters who joined the rebel unit in 1831. In 1882 he published his memoirs in the newspaper *Ojczyzna*, and died in the USA in 1884.

2.   Mojzesz Berger, member of Lwów's town council. Loyal to the national government, he managed the rebel army's finances and donated large sums to the purposes of the revolt. He died at Lwów in 1885.

3.   Dr. Mojzesz Beiser (1807–1880), concluded his medical studies at Vienna (1835), and was a surgeon at Gwoździec, Kolomyia and Lwów. In 1830–1831 he also assisted the revolt. In 1848, he was a member of the national council of Lwów. He was deported to Zólkiew as a political suspect and was under police supervision till 1850. In 1863 he returned to Lwów, where he was involved in planning the revolt. Due to his Polish patriotic conduct he was nominated an honorary citizen of Lwów, in 1876. He also took an active part in Jewish public life.

4.   Rittel, tailor (the father of Dr. Stanislaw Rittel, delegate to the Galician *Sejm*), who sewed army uniforms for the rebels.

5.   Ludwik Kunstfeld, born at Lwów, surveyor, served with a combat unit.

6.   Jozef–Noa Löwenherz, an estate owner, lived in Lwów (grandfather of the Zionist businessmen Dr. Henryk and Jozef Löwenherz), also took part in the combat units under Commander Miniewski.

7.   Jonas Löwenherz, his brother, student, active in the rebellion movement.

8.   Ferdinand Sacher, tailor, served with the units under Commander Wysocki, owner of a Lwów restaurant.

The Polish committee's efforts were however in vain, and in a record to the national government[62] the committee complained about the indifference shown by the Jews who refrained from joining the uprising. "From 1833 onwards –the report stressed– not a single Jew was among the accused in the political trials held in Galicia or Lwów, until recently." All the enlightened Jews (*zydzi postçpowi*) sympathise with the German intelligentsia that strives to obliterate the Polish character of Galicia. In the past years a small group began to assimilate among the Poles, but they are unreliable."[63]

4.

Shortly after the uprising which called for a Polish–Jewish solidarity, and for Jewish participation in the efforts to free Poland,

[Pages 297-298]

"the joint homeland," the difficult struggle started over the Jews' equal rights. The Jewish community led by Rachmiel Mieses, resubmitted petitions and requests to extend the real estate ownership rights for all Jewish citizens. On 11.1.1863, it submitted a comprehensive memorandum[64] to liquidate the Jewish Quarters due to the town's increased number of *Maskilim*. The municipality again referred to clauses in the municipal regulations and expressed an anti–Jewish stance. The Governorship sought the opinion of the police, which actually sided with the Jews. The police noted that the municipality's arguments contravened civilisation and the spirit of the age; the municipal regulations it cited belonged to an earlier era. The police also questioned the claim that the Jews segregated themselves from the Christian population. It was the restrictions which had forced them to be segregated, and lifting those would only be an advantage to the state, and granting the Jews equal rights should be recommended.

Not wishing to decide on its own, the Governorship left the decision to the ministry. On 25th January 1865, the ministry's response stated that Jews who had done away with the traditional Jewish dress and the side–locks, could live outside the Jewish Quarter. The majority of the Jews objected to the condition and preferred to remain within its streets.

Rabbi Izak Aron Ettinger

The town council renewed the debates about the municipal regulations which had been discontinued in 1863. Incidentally, the question arose of dividing the town into two communities (*Gemeinden*): Christian and Jewish. The Poles submitted a proposal to do away with the community altogether and instead to transfer all the Jewish affairs to the authority of the 20 Jewish members on the town council, while the Christian affairs would be settled by the Christian members on the town council.

The Pole, Gryziecki, suggested that were the Jews to insist on appointing 15 members on the council, they would need to appoint five Christians as members of the community committee. Despite the objection from members on the Jewish council who had rejoined the council after Dr. Hönigsmann had declared on their behalf, the regulations with all their restrictions on Jews, in accordance with Dr. Rayski presentation, were nevertheless accepted during the session of 9th October 1865. The 17th January 1866 session agreed to submit the regulations for the *Sejm*'s approval.

Unlike the 5th March 1862 government's proposed regulations submitted to the *Sejm*, which made no mention of restrictions on any religious community, it was decided to introduce fundamental changes, particularly in the chapter addressing issues specific to the Jewish and the Christian populations.

Chapter VI of the Regulations determined the precise differentiation

and the specific treatment of Christian and Jewish issues. The Christians' affairs would be settled by Christian members on the council without the participation of any Jewish members, while the Jewish affairs would be settled by the administrative committee of the 20–men Jewish council.

Lwów's regulation turned into a yardstick for other towns keen to retain a Polish character, for fear that in towns in which the Jews formed the majority, equal rights would secure a permanent Jewish rule. The *Sejm* submitted the municipal regulations to the scrutiny of a special committee. Most of the committee accepted all the restrictions, but the minority led by Dubs and Samelsohn wanted to omit all clauses dealing with the Christians' attitude towards the Jews. Their demand focused in particular on altering clause 34, which prescribed that the committee be made up of 80 Christian and 20 Jewish members; instead they proposed the committee be made up of 100 members without setting fixed numbers of Jewish and of Christian members. In addition, to leave out the restrictions, that the mayor and his deputy had to be Christian, as well as § 15 which determined that at least two thirds of the committee members and their deputies had to be Christian. They also demanded to leave out §§ 118–126 of chapter VI, which determined that all municipal property belonged to the Christian population and that the town was responsible for the Christian institutions and schools, as well as the matter of splitting the municipal council into two administrative committees, one Christian, one Jewish. All the amendments proposed by Dubs and Dr. Samelsohn were rejected. Only six Jewish delegates voted in favour of the proposal. The *Sejm*'s decision shocked Lwów's Jews and encouraged the community to approach the government with countermeasures. In April 1866, at Vienna, a memorandum was handed to the prime–minister by a delegation which comprised of

[Pages 299-300]

Dr. Emanuel Blumenfeld, Dr. Hönigsmann, Dr. Kolischer, M. Mieses, Dr. Nossig, Dr. Blumenfeld junior, Rabbi Bernhard Löwenstein–Lwów delegates; Majer Kallier and Dr. Schornstein–Brody delegates; Dr. Bardasch, Rabbi Rappoport–Tarnopol delegates; Pineles, Dr. Reiner and Garfinkel–delegates from the rest of the communities. The heading of the published memorandum read:

"Memorandum to His Excellency the Imperial and Royal Minister of State Count Belcredi presented by Lwów's Jewish cultural congregation on the occasion when Lwów's municipal status was decided by the Galician Diet (33 pages) Vienna 1866. [In German in the original]

In their memorandum the Jewish representatives of Galicia protested against Clause 34 of Lwów's municipal regulation, submitted to the Kaiser for approval, which contradicted the 5th March 1862 municipal law that did not distinguish a village or town population by religion. According to Lwów's municipal proposal the number of Jews on the town council was restricted to twenty members. The restriction demonstrated the segregational and discriminational stance held by the majority of Poles. Lwów's Jews made up around two fifths (or at least one third) of the population, and proportionately they were entitled to 33 seats on the town council, in particular considering that they were the town's main taxpayers. Clause 56 determined that the mayor and his first deputy had to be Christian. That restriction discredited and contravened the 5th March 1862 municipal law. Clauses 126–128, which determined that the municipal property belonged solely to Christians, rested on certificates granted to the Christian population by the kings of Poland, during the period when Jews had not yet been entitled to the town's citizenship. The community demonstrated that throughout the Polish and Austrian rules the income and profits from municipal property had been spent by the municipality on general causes enjoyed by both Christians and Jews. Ever since 1848 Jews had participated in the town administration, whereas the property was registered in the municipality's name only in 1849, at a time when Lwów's Jews had already been granted municipal voting rights. The community objected particularly to Clauses 124–125, which specified that Jewish issues be only decided by the twenty Jewish council members, thus leading to the dissolution of Lwów's Jewish community, in contravention of Clause 92 of the proposed municipal regulations in which a self–sufficient Jewish community was indeed acknowledged. As the entire regulation was against the interest of the Jews, the community opposed its approval. On 26th September 1866, the Kaiser received the delegation and promised to heed its request.

For the Poles, the community's petition to the Vienna central government was a hostile act, which the Polish press noted as "a provocative step."

On 28th October 1866, Belcredi handed the Kaiser a report regarding Lwów's regulations supplemented by comments that the representatives of Lwów's Jews had appealed against the regulations and that in his opinion part of their complaints were justified. The regulations contravened the general laws and constituted an insult to the Jews and consequently he suggested the Kaiser should not approve them; he also requested permission to submit his comments to Galicia's governor so that he might affect the removal of these flaws during the *Sejm* session.[65]

The Kaiser accepted the minister's view and refused to approve the regulations.[66] The regulations were sent back to Lwów's municipality to remove the blatant restrictions, and they were resubmitted with the alterations, in March 1867, for the Kaiser's approval. Despite the alterations, the regulations still contained clauses that contravened the law, such as: setting a single tribunal [curia] for all the voters (instead of three tribunals [curiæ]). By such means the municipality hoped to affect the results of elections, since the number of taxpayers among the Jews was disproportionately high. Viscount [von] Taaffe, the Minister of the Interior, disagreed with the municipality's stance and advised the Kaiser to defer the approval of the regulations.[67] Lwów's municipality received the regulations yet again, but after much effort succeeded in being granted approval for a single tribunal to hold elections, due to the town's special national circumstances. According to the regulations the town council was made up of 100 members elected by a single tribunal, an anomaly among the towns of Galicia and Austria, in which three tribunals picked the members. The council was elected for three years, and from 1909 for six years, in such a manner that every three years half the members departed,[68] to be replaced by others. In December 1865, during the Galician *Sejm*'s third sitting, the delegate Count Agenor Gołuchowski who had been Galicia's Governor, proposed granting all Jews, without exception, the right to purchase land, plots and houses throughout Galicia and the Grand Duchy of Kraków. His proposal surprised the entire *Sejm* and the Jews in particular, especially his address on 25th January 1866, in which he stressed that anti–Jewish laws had been abolished throughout European countries, with only Austria conspicuous in its handling of Jewish affairs entangled in archaic laws and mediaeval judgements, with just first steps taken to abolish the restrictions on Jews. The 18th February 1860 law did not directly increase Enlightenment among the Jews. Count Gołuchowski opposed the view that Jews had a bad effect on the rural population. The fact that regulations had been introduced in Russia forbidding

[Pages 301-302]

Catholic Poles from acquiring estates, to the indignation of the Polish people, obligated the *Sejm* to abolish the restrictions concerning the Jews. His proposal was however disputed by the Ruthenian delegate, Iwan Huszałewycz [Guszałewycz], and was referred to the administrative committee without being debated by the *Sejm*'s plenary session.

Count Gołuchowski 's demand reverberated throughout the Jewish communities, and the representatives of Lwów's community sent a delegation to express the Jews' gratitude. In his reply he noted his pleasure the Jews had realized that the rumours portraying him as a Jew hater, were false.

In September 1866, Count Gołuchowski was appointed Governor of Galicia, replacing Field Marshal [von] Paumgarten. In September 1868, in his post as Governor, he submitted to the *Sejm* the government's proposal to abolish all restrictions applied to the Jews that were in contravention of the new basic law of 21ˢᵗ December 1867.

During the sessions of the 30ᵗʰ September and 8ᵗʰ October 1868, after the address and arguments of Dr. Franciszek Smolka, the *Sejm* decided to approve the proposal and abolish all restrictions applied to the Jews. Based on that decision, Lwów's town council deleted from its regulations all restrictions regarding the Jews.

With the granting of full emancipation to the Jews, a new period in the history of Galicia's Jews has started. (*)

(*). To commemorate that struggle in the *Sejm*, Lwów's community published, in German and in Polish, the protocol of the *Sejm*'s debates about the Jewish issue,[69] and also the addresses of Franciszek Smolka.[70]

[Page 378]

Notes: – CHAPTER 17
All notes in square brackets [ ] were made by the translator or by the editor
[The spelling of most personal names were sourced from reference books by M. Bałaban.]

1. Archive of the Ministry of the Interior M.d.J. IV T. 8. 2447 e.a. 1851/1852.

2. Freiherr von Kübeck's diary of 30ᵗʰ and 31ˢᵗ December 1851, cited in: Joseph Redlich : *Kaiser Franz Joseph von Österreich*, Berlin 1928, p. 93.

3. Ministerkonferenzprotokolle 1852 z. 653 d.do 3/3 1852.

4. Ministerkonferenzprotokolle 1852 z. 3646 d.do 13/XI 1852.

5. Ministerkonferenzprotokolle 1853 z. 2761 d/do 11/VIII 1853.

6. The address of the Minister of Commerce and Finance, Baumgarten, IV T. 10 Z. 1549 ex/1861.

7. Dr. Stan. Hoszowski: *Ekonomiczny rozwoj Lwowa w latach 1772–1914*. Lwów 1937.

8. The bequest for charity institutions and for establishing an orphanage amounted to 50,000 Florins.

9. *Allgemeine Zeitung des Judenthums* 1854, 7/VI.

10. "After the death of Rabbi Abraham Kohn, Dr. Moritz Löwenthal was appointed as preacher, but the "Temple" management were dissatisfied with him as he was not an experienced preacher; was unfamiliar with "Lwów's stormy currents"; delivered lengthy speeches and addresses. The "Friends of Progress" published letters of complaints against him and demanded his resignation, in *Wiener Blätter* edited by Letteris (Addendum to Issue 15, pp.139, 141; Issue 23, pp. 213–214). Dr. Löwenthal accepted the demands, resigned his post and settled at Mosciska [Mościski] as an estate owner. In 1851, the preacher's post was offered to Rabbi Albert Kohn who was a rabbi at Radonice [Radonitz], Bohemia, but he declined the offer. On the recommendation of Salomon Jehudah Rappoport [*Shir*], Dr. Samuel Adler, who was rabbi at Alzey, Hessen (Germany) was accepted as preacher. For political reasons, the authorities refused to sanction his appointment as seen in the Vienna Ministry of the Interior's record: IV T. 14,799/1141 1855, 2. Juli. [in German; Editor's note: the following text is not edited]
["]The board of directors of Lwów's Jewish community has entered into a contract with Dr. Samuel Adler at Abzey in the Grand Duchy of Hessen, to fill the lifelong post, at Lwów, of learned teacher and actual preacher in the third religion, subject to subsequent official approval. The character reference testimonial by officials from the Grand Duchy of Hessen included however the remark that,

[Pages 379-380]

in 1848, whether from vanity or fear, he was seduced by the place of prayer of his Royal Highness Grand Duke, which had engaged for a while an intercessory of the "Leader of People," so the state officials immediately courteously approved the contract and only permitted Dr. Adler to act provisionally as preacher for Lwów's community, in order to be able to observe his behaviour more closely to decide whether he was worthy of a stable employment and of admission to the Austrian State.
Lwów's community appealed against the state officials' pronouncement. At the same time, however, it was noted in h.o. Note v.

4/III 1855, that the Ministry of the Interior had arrived at the same conclusion about Dr. Adler's admissibility for naturalization and that provisionally the data in hand against him needed to be taken into account at least for greater clarification of his political thoughts and actions. Due to the indication also stressed in the note, the Ministry of Education turned to the supreme Imperial–Royal Police authority to enquire whether it had any reservations to granting Dr. Adler permission to stay at Lwów. As a result, the Imperial–Royal Police authority revealed that after detailed enquiries, except for the above allegation, there had been no reason for a perception that his political convictions and tendencies should be considered in an unfavourable light, and that the responsibility for the incident lay more with the then democratic municipal councillor of Abzey than with Dr. Adler.

The Ministry of Education and Culture's unanimous decision was as follows:

Herewith one has the honour of conveying that with the present explanation of the supreme Imperial–Royal Police authority the above objections to Dr. Adler's political thoughts and actions are deemed to be resolved with no objection were the situation to arise regarding his admissibility to the Austrian State.

16th July 1855 ["] (Signature).

Dr. Adler probably declined Lwów community's offer, and in 1857 he was invited to officiate as Rabbi of the [Reform] synagogue, Emanuel, at New York. In 1886 he published a book on Hebrew literature "*Kobez al Jad*," and he died aged 87, in 1891.

Dr. Szymon Schwabacher was appointed as preacher at Lwów, instead of him.

11.   During 1856–1857, he was Rabbi at Oświęcim [Auschwitz]–Wadowice, later he established a secular secondary school [teaching math and technical subjects] at Vienna and after a period he settled at Budapest.

12.   Among the known Jewish lawyers were: Dr. Emanuel Blumenfeld, Dr. Leo Kolischer, Dr. Maximilian Landesberger, Dr. Oswald Menkes, Dr. Moriz Mahl.

13.   Jakob Bałaban was a well–known silk wholesaler in Lwów. The town's *Maskilim* gathered at his house. His daughter Rosalia (1803–1857) was known as "The Galician Madame [de] Staël" and was a friend of Rabbi Nachman Krochmal, Rabbi Salomon Jehudah Rappoport and Mejer Letteris. She married the banker Halferson at Odessa, and died at Vienna. Her daughter married the banker Efrati at Odessa. Letteris published her obituary in the newspaper *Wiener Blätter*, 1857, Issue 36.

14.   In 1856, there were 1053 pupils.
IV T 17, 11945/825 4/XI 1857.

15.   *Jutrzenka* [Morning Star] 1862, pp. 247–249.

16.   H. H. St. Archiv. Minrat. Prot. 1848 No. 647. ddo 23/XI.

17.   IV T. 11 23472/682 ddo 11/XI 1854; IV T. 7 14945/825 ddo 4/VII 1855.

18.   *Wiener Blätter* 1851 No. 26, p.176.

19.   *Wiener Blätter* 1851 No. 26.

20.   [in German] Graveside eulogy to the noble, deeply mourned philanthropist H. Zipper, imperial urban district supervisor. Promoter of Lwów's charitable institutions. Died on 3rd September 1858. Delivered by Heinrich D. Bernstein. Published by M. H. Poremba 1858; all proceeds dedicated to the institution providing meals for the poor.
Obituary in: *Wiener Mitteilungen* 1858, No. 38; pp.149–150.

21.   Diamand published the memorandum under the title: [in German:]
Memorandum concerning the authorisation of a charity – Lwów association for the establishment of a Jewish poor fund and endowment for the most essential benevolent institutions of the high imperial land of Galicia – executive committee submitted by Dawid Diamand, Lemberg 1854.

22.   *Wiener Blätter* 1855, p. 195. *Allgem. Ztg. d. Jtms* 1855, p.504.

23.   IV T 2 15925/629 e.a. 1851.

24.   IV T 2 1853.

25.   *Regierungsblatt* 1853, 190 V. 2/X 1853.

26.   Report by Gołuchowski of 11th January 1860, No. 1393/81.

27.   Wiener Staatsarchiv: Information Office 1853, No. 4574/B.M.

28.   IV T 2 fol.. 1–85, Galizia 22409/577
Report by Galicia's Governorship to the Ministry of the Interior, of 14/VIII 1855.

29.   IV T 10 26705/505 1859.

30.   IV T 2 fol. 1–85, Utterance by the Minister of the Interior, Freiherr von Bach 7883/166 ddo 4/IV 1856.

[Pages 381-382]

31.   Lwów Governor's report of 20/IV 1856, No. 10975, M.Z. 4916/116 ex 1876.

32. V T 3–7 22107/16112 e.a. 1857 30/7.

33. IV T 1 No. 1059 (13/VI 1859).

34. IV T 1 No. 1462 (10/VIII 1858).

35. IV T 1 30507/677 12/XI 1859.

36. [in German] The Minister of the Interior, Count Agenor Gołuchowski's most humble utterance regarding the Jews' rights of ownership, 11th January 1860. IV T 1 No. 1393/81 1860.

37. The annulment was granted to people who had graduated from a commercial school together with four years of secondary school [gymnasium] education.

38. According to the Ministry of the Interior's archive register. IV T 2

39. Memorandums of 21st February 1861 and 11th January 1863. IV T 6545/538 1864, 1863. *Allgem. Ztg. d. Judtms.* 1860, p. 625.

40. Governor Mensdorff's report, IV T 2 6545/538 1864.

41. IV T 1 e.a. 1864 Z 6545/538.

42. IV T 10 Fasz. 86 1149/1141 1861.

43. Reports of Bernstein–estate for 1865–1885. Lwów 1885.

44. [in German] House, Court and State Archives, Vienna, Conference protocols 1867. Z. 4427 ddo 15/XI 1867.

45. Dr. Gelber: *Aus zwei Jahrhunderten* 1924, pp. 162–169.

46. Conference protocols 1860 Z. 1906.

47. Henryk Schmitt: *Rzut oka na nowy projekt bezwarunkowego równouprawnienia Zydów, oraz odpowiedz na zarzuty z którymi dzisiejsi ich obroncy przeciw narodowi polskiemu wystepuja.* Lwów 1859.

48. In contrast to the nobles' casino which was termed "*Kasyno konskie*" [horse casino], the Jewish casino was termed "*Kasyno wołowe*" [beef casino], later the association was given the Polish name "*Towarszyskosc.*"

49. Dr. Henryk Gottlieb (1839–1905), a well known lawyer at Lwów with education in philosophy, was actively involved in community affairs on the side of the Enlightened. A founder member of "*Szomer Izrael*" ["The Guardian of Israel"], a friend of Abraham Krochmal, he published articles on philosophical questions, natural history, law and economics. Among historians' circles reverberated his article:
"Das jüdische Reich der Chasaren [The Jewish Empire of the Khazars]" published in: (*Österr. Wochenschrift* Jg. XI);
["]Schulbetrachtungen auch eine Todesstrafe["] (Wien 1872);
["]Der Weltuntergang, ein Gedicht["] (Hamburg 1888);
["]Die Ursache der allgemeinen Schwere["] (Lemberg 1902);
["]Juristische Untersuchungen: Der Kaufvertrag["] (Wien).
He edited the Polish periodical *Ekonomista*. His son, Dr. Bertold Gottlieb took an active part on the "Temple's" committee, while his wife, Sydonia *née* Sokal, was a well known activist.

50. Jakob Hirsch Sperling (1837–1901), *Shir's* Nephew, taught at the Jewish school and from 1877, taught religion at Lwów's German secondary school. He was an active member of "*Szomer Izrael.*" He published some 400 poems in *Kochbe Jizchak* ["Isaac's Stars"], *HaShachar* ["The Daybreak"], *HaBoker Or* ["The Morning Light"], *HaJbri* ["The Hebrew"] and *HaMagid* ["The Preacher"]. He also published books: *Chamisha K'tarim* ["Five Crowns"] (Lwów, 1873), *Sefer Chochmat Sh'lomo* ["Book of Solomon's Wisdom"] (Lwów, 1878).

51. Dawid Rappoport (1837–), the son of Jakub Samuel Rappoport (the brother of *Shir*). His father was a wholesale trader and a renowned scholar. He was one of Rabbi Abraham Kohn's opponents, although he was not affiliated with the Orthodox's faction. He resented his brother, *Shir*, for recommending Rabbi Kohn to Lwów's community–elders and to deputy Governor Krauss, who was one of his acquaintances. In his 2nd November 1847 letter to *Shir*, he wrote the following about Rabbi Kohn:["] He (Kohn) is a man of bad deeds who has slandered you in public and in private, more than once. He is ignorant of the Talmud and adjudicative literature, he also turns his back on all Jewish Laws, and I consider him akin to one of the local Gentiles."
Dr. M. Bałaban: *Historja lwowskiej Synag.* P. 74, note 23.
His son Dawid was a Maskil who participated in public life and was a founder member of "*Szomer Izrael.*" He published translations of Schiller's poems in *Kochbe Jizchak.*

52. Samuel Modlinger (1825–1898), was a researcher and author who came from a well–known Lwów family. He published: *Simoth Ajin oder Blicke in die Urgeschichte des israelitischen Volkes.* ["Historical Glimpses of the Jewish People"] (Lwów 1861);
"Reminiszenz an Munk (Ein Vortrag) ["Reminiscence of Munk" (a lecture)] Lemberg 1867;

Lessings Verdienste um das Judenthum. Eine Studie (Frankfurt am Main 1869).
As well as articles in *Le Libanon, Otzar HaChochmah*, and *HaSchachar*.

53.   *Allgem. Ztg. d. Just.* 1862, p. 289;
Ben–Chananja [Zeitschrift für jüdische Theologie; Magazine of Jewish theology] 1862, No. 15.
The Enlightened published a flyer in which they reminded the voters of their 20 years' work in the community, for the benefit of Lwów's Jews, and demanded that Enlightened candidates be elected.

54.   Published in: *Przeglad rzeczy polskich* Paris 1861, Vol. V, pp.57–58.

55.   See my article: "Filip Mansch und Ludwig Gumplowicz" in : *Fun noentn over*, Warsaw, 1938, II Pamphlet 1.

56.   *Jutrzenka* 1861, p.70.

57.   *Posłanie do wszystkich rodaków na ziemi polskiej.* [Call to all compatriots in Poland]
Published in: Józef Białynia Chołodecki : *Do dziejów powstania styczniowego.*

58.   *Obrazki z przeszłości Galicji*, Lwów 1912, p. 19;
Białynia Chołodecki p.32.

[Pages 383-384]

59.   In the poem: "Bajazzo, ein Gedicht," Leipzig 1866, Dr. Rapoport translated into German [Kornel] Ujejski's choral "Z dymem pozarów."

60.   See my book: *Die Juden und der polnische Aufstand 1863*, Wien 1923, p. 148.

61.   In the collected documents: *Ossolineum rekopis* 1884/11.

62.   *Ossolineum* 1884/II reports in the manuscript that Eastern Galicia sent to the front 35 companies with 14,000 combatants. Half a million Franks was collected towards the national tax fund, besides around one million Franks that was spent on the rebels' economy. Jewish lessees and estate owners were obliged to pay the national tax as well as to host and maintain rebels (Report for the Austrian authorities on the national movement of Eastern Galicia in 1863, by the Polish writer Kaczkowski, an Austrian government agent).
Dr. Eugeniusz Barwiński: *Zygmunt Kaczkowski w świetle prawdy (1863–1871)* Z tajnych aktów b. Austryjackiego ministerstwa policji. Lwów 1920, p. 74.

63.   Most of the Jewish intelligentsia rejected the Polish revolutionary movements. Such views were expressed in the Jewish newspaper *Tsaitung* [Zeitung], founded by Mendel Mohr. Once Mierosławski's emissaries started to establish revolutionary committees and collect a national tax, the newspaper appealed to the Jews not to respond, and "were wealthy Jews coerced into paying for Polish national goals, one has to stop the individual" and turn him to the police. (*Tsaitung* 1866, Issue 6).

64.   At the same time, Isak Dajcz [Daitch] of Vienna who considered himself the representative of Austro–Hungary's *Charedi* Jews, tried to stress the loyalty of the *Charedim* to the Empire and the revolutionary attitude of the Enlightened, and submitted a memorandum to Kaiser Franz–Joseph I in which he requested, in the name of Galicia's Jews, to annul the restrictions   on   property   ownership.
The Polish Press questioned how Dajcz came to represent half a million Galician Jews. The Polish newspaper *Praca* took particular exception to his assertion that it was not the *Charedim* but rather the Poles who had supported all the revolutionary movements of 1846, 1848, 1863 and 1864.
The board of directors of Lwów's community – Dr. M. Landesberger, Rachmiel Mieses, Samuel Kohn, Meier Münz, Salomon Kellermann and Rachmiel Ornstein published a strongly worded protest against Dajcz, and in March 1865 they pointed out in the Jewish and Polish press that while the Jews of Galicia aspired to see a rapid end to the restrictions on property ownership, it was not Dajcz's place to speak for them. They strongly opposed his assertions which conjoined the Jews' demands with their loyalty to the Empire and their anti–Polish stance.
Allgem. Ztg. d. Judems. 1865, pp.201–202.

65.   K.Z. 3374/66 Vortrag des Staatsminister Gf. Belcredi [Talk by government Minister Count Belcredi] v. 28/XI 1866.

66.   The Jews rejoiced at the news that the Kaiser had refused to confirm the Lwów regulations. "Tsaitung" (1866 Issue 5 dated 9/11) writes [in Yiddish]: We can bring pleasure to our readers with the good news that the Kaiser has rejected Lemberg's municipal regulations as determined by the State Diet, a law which would violently oppress us Jews. The Christian Council would control us completely, but our fair Kaiser would not succumb to that."

67.   K.Z. 1320 Vortrag des Leiters des Min. d. Innern Graf Taaffe v. 21/III 1867.

68.   The voting rights were granted in the following categories: **a.** Owners of real–estate or those enjoying their fruits, who pay land or house tax. **b.** Those paying Income tax in the sum of 8 Gulden, or other tax in the sum of 12 Gulden. **c.** Those who are educated. **d.** Those who pay tax in the sum of 250 Gulden. **e.** Industrial companies and associations paying annual tax in the sum of 50 Gulden. The Council elects the town's leader and his deputy, 3 deputies according to the 1909 regulations.

69.   *[Die] Debatten über die Judenfrage in der Session des galizischen Landtages vom Jahre 1868.* Lemberg.

70.   Mowy posła Fr. Smolki, wygłoszone[j] na posiedzeniach sejmu dnia 30 września i 8 pazdziernika 1868 w kwestyi
       zydowskiej Lwów 1899.

The *Sejm*'s resolution shocked Lwów's Jews and spurred the community into action against it. In April 1866, at the community's initiative, a memorandum was submitted at Vienna by the delegation made up of Dr. Emanuel Blumenfeld, Dr. Hönigsmann, Dr. Kolischer, M. Mieses, Dr. Nossig, Dr. Blumenfeld the younger, Rabbi Dr. Bernhard Löwenstein, Lwów's representatives; Majer Kallier and Dr. Schornstein, Brody's representatives; Dr. Barach and Rabbi Rapoport, Tarnopol's representatives; Pineles, Dr. Reiner and Karfunkel represented the rest of the communities. The memorandum was addressed as follows: [in German] Manuscript to His Excellency the Royal and Imperial Minister of State Count Belcredi handed by the Jewish community of Lemberg, following the adoption by Galicia's government, of the municipal statues for Lemberg. (33 pages. Vienna 1866).

The representatives of Galicia's Jews objected to clause 34 of Lwów's municipal regulation, which contravened the municipal law of 5th March 1862 that had not differentiated between religions. Clause 34 set the number of the Jewish members on the town council at 20. That restriction exemplified the prominent separatist and sectarian stance of the Polish majority. At Lwów the Jews made up almost two fifth, or at least one third of the population, which meant that they were entitled to 33 seats on the town council, especially since the high tax payers were mainly the Jews. Apart from that restriction, clause 56 determined that the mayor and his deputy had to be Christians. That restriction offended the Jews and contravened the municipal law of 3.5.1862. Clauses 127–128 regarding the municipal property, stated on the basis of gift certificates from the kings of Poland, that it belonged solely to the Christian population since it was granted to them during a period when the Jews had not yet been considered the town's citizens.

In contrast, Lwów's [Jewish] community attested that under both Polish and Austrian rule the income and profits from urban property were used for general purposes enjoyed by Christians and Jews. In addition, since 1848 the Jews made part of the municipal administration, while the town became the owner of the [urban] asset only in 1849, therefore, Lwów's Jews were already town members eligible to vote and to be elected.

In particular the community objected to clauses 124–125, which determined that the 20 Jewish council members would manage Jewish affairs. That is to say, they would constitute the community management, thus abolishing Lwów's Jewish community in contravention of clause 92 of the proposed municipal regulations.

[Pages 303-304]

Chapter 18: 1868 – 1918

Translated by Myra Yael Ecker

Edited by Dr. Rafael R. Manory

The standing of Lwów's Jews in the economy, in trade and in industry. The Jews within the general education system. The academic intelligentsia's involvement in the community's life. The 1868 community elections . The *Szomer Izrael* Association and its activities. Dr. Bernard Goldman and his drive toward Polonisation. The Jews and the Poles after the 1863 uprising. The 1874 municipal elections. The preacher Bernard Löwenstein. The 1878 communities' gathering and the resistance of the Orthodox. The community committee during 1883–1888. 1890 referendum. The *Machsike HaDas* Association. The Orthodox's struggle with the conduct at the "Temple." The 1890 parliamentary law of communities' regulation. The beginnings of the Zionist movement. Seminary for teachers of religion. The educational institutions. The beginnings of the workers' movement. Democratisation of the community and its institutions. At the outset of World War I. Lwów's occupation by Russia's armed forces. The Russian authorities' attitude towards the Jews. *Vaad HaHazala*. Collaboration with the "Committee of Russian Jews." Return of the Austrian armed forces. The resumption of public life. A commissioner in the community.

I.

The liberal policy, the development of the means of transport and of trade relations, placed Galician Jews in a significant role of economic life, and not only in trade and banking, but also in industry. However only limited strata of the community managed to improve their economic standing. The majority, who earned their living as retail traders, pedlars, craftsmen or employees, struggled for their existence and had to leave the small towns to seek employment in towns or in the capital. Due to the poverty and the difficulty in finding employment, many chose to leave Galicia and migrate to other parts of Austria or overseas. During 1870–1880 the move was to Vienna, Bukovina, Romania and Hungary, but from 1881 onwards the migration flowed toward the United States. The numbers of the Jews migrating from Galicia were as follows:

In the period 1881–1890   36,600 Jews

– " – 1891–1990   114,000 Jews

– " – 1901–1910.   88,000 Jews

Total   239,000 Jews [1]

The composition of the migrants by occupation was made up of: 34% craftsmen; 16% labourers, commercial assistants and salaried employees; 0.4% free professionals.

The lives of Lwów's Jews were improving. The town of Lwów, which had been neglected by the authorities who had no interest in its advancements and development, grew and progressed nonetheless since 1867, after the introduction of the Constitution and the integration of Galicia's administrative autonomy. The autonomous regime brought back the town's Polish character. The autonomous authorities and the town's administration introduced sanitary improvements and sewerage; roads and routes were laid around the town which improved the means of transport and the health of the population; the educational network was adapted to the needs of the population and buildings suitable for elementary and secondary schools were constructed.

For several years, Lwów was the cultural centre of the Polish people.

Considerable economic and cultural changes affected also the Jewish population. In 1869, the number of Jews who resided at Lwów was 26,694, and in 1880, there were 31,000 Jews (28.2% of the population); in 1890, their numbers reached 36,130 (28.2%); in 1900, 44,258 (27.7%); and in 1910 there were 57,000 (27.8%).

During the period of emancipation a particular phenomenon of conversion, previously very rare, appeared in the lives of Lwów's Jews. The integration into local life and the assimilation, drove unstable elements to abandon Judaism.[2]

In the years 1868–1877, the number of Lwów Jews who converted to Christianity was 55 (20 men, 35 women); since then, the number of converts grew: in the years 1878–1887, 157 (66 men, 91 women); 1888–1897, 245 (109 men, 136 women); 1898–1907, 256 (124 men, 132 women).

During the entire period 1868–1907, 713 Jews converted (319 men, 394 women), 486 of them (203 men, 283 women) became Catholics; 126 (46 men, 80 women) turned Greek Catholics; 73 (52 men, 21 women) became Greek Orthodox; 3 (1 man, 2 women) became Evangelicals; 25 (15 men, 10 women) became of no faith.

[Pages 305-306]

During the same period, 56 Christians converted to Judaism, (32 men, 24 women), 33 of them had been Catholics (21 men, 12 women), 7 had been Greek–Catholics (5 men, 4 women), 5 had professed no religion (3 men, 2 women).[3]

The establishment of the Vienna–Lwów–Chernowitz railway line, together with the rest of the routes within Galicia encouraged the economic growth of the town and drew Jews from provincial towns to find their livelihoods there.

Most of the export trade from eastern Galicia westwards, was in Jewish hands: wheat, cattle, horses, agricultural products and timber, as well as the import, eastwards and towards inner Galicia, of colonial goods, clothes, footwear, industrial products and agricultural machinery. In 1860–1870, the industrialists Schmelkes, Klein, Grüner and Schimer established beer breweries, the products of which were famous throughout Austria.

The industries of provincial–towns, such as: petroleum and timber products, had their managerial and commercial executive centres also at Lwów. Jews supplied railway sleepers to Austria and Germany; masts and construction timber for boats at Stettin [Szczecin], Danzig [Gdańsk], Trieste, Hamburg and England. Jews established transport companies, freight transportation, brokerage, insurance and agencies.[4] Hundreds of Jewish families made their living in these industries.

The vast majority of the wholesale trade, the large warehouses of textiles, leather goods, food, beverages, agricultural appliances, was also in Jewish hands and employed many clerks, assistants, labourers and salaried employees. Among the better known Jewish wholesalers were Natansohn, Aszkenazy, Kokris, Wahl, Klahrfeld, Beiser, Epstein, Kolischer, Sprecher, Glanz, Wixel, Stark and Halpern.

During 1866–1885, wealthy Jews also invested large amounts in the purchase of land and estates, giving rise to a class of Jewish estate owners that included the Jewish pioneers of Polonisation, who supported the Poles' policies in Galicia. The families Horowitz, Kolischer, Mieses, Löwenherz, Parnas, Lazarus, Baczes, Landesberger, Dubs, Wahl, Buber, Kellermann, Rozmaryn Frenkl, Tom, Neuwelt, were among Galicia's first Jewish estates owners, and many of them had their offices at Lwów. These estate owners employed Jews also as clerks and in agricultural work.

In the town proper, the Jews bought plots and built residential blocks in new quarters. In the field of building–construction were involved Sommerstein, who bought the Zamarstynów estate which for long was known as "Sommersteinhof," followed by Selzer, Jonas and Sprecher also constructing residential houses.

The flow of Jews from the provincial towns increased especially after the events of 1846, for fear of the peasants' revolt, and those who arrived were lessees, owners of spirits distilleries, middlemen estate owners engaged in trade, small scale industry and contract work or those who purchased houses and plots of land. Among these the known names were: Agis, Sokal, Klein, Beer, Parnas (who already in 1835 leased estates in Podolia),[5] Tenner, Landau, Kimmelman, Rochmis, Schönfeld, Blumenfeld, Pipes, Rohatin. They made a large donation to expand the town and its buildings and with their contacts they turned Lwów into a trade centre between East and West. They were especially successful in expanding the trade relations since Brody had lost its free–trade status, and many of its merchants, agents and wealthy citizens left and settled at Lwów where they continued to develop the economic contacts with Vienna, Germany and Russia.

Among the affluent Jews of Brody who moved to Lwów were: Löwenherz, Mieses, Inlender, Braunstein, Mendelsburg, Bernstein, Kornfeld, Trachtenberg, Margulies, Kellermann, Garfein, Haberman, Jekeles, Sobel, Byk and Reizes (who established a large bank at Vienna in 1879).

The launch of Lwów's stock exchange on 1st January 1867, did much to stabilise the town's trade. Of the eight inspectors appointed to oversee the stock exchange agents and commissioners, four were Jews: Jozef Kolischer (manager of Lwów's branch of the National Bank), Chaim Hochfeld, Majer Mieses and J. Wallach.

The Jews were active in banking too, whether as independent bankers or as branch–managers of Vienna's banks. Known among the independent bankers' names were: Horowitz, Jonasz, Lazarus, Mieses, Stroh, Kitz and Stoff.

The economic standing of Lwów's Jews was indeed much better than in any other town of Galicia, where only one percent of the families had an annual income of 20,000 Florin; 4% had an income of 10,000–20,000 Florin; 10% had an annual income of 200–500 Gulden; 25% earned less than 200 Gulden; about 60% of the Jews subsisted on an annuity.[5A]

The most marked change occurred within the academic professions. Once full emancipation had been granted, education of the Jewish youth entered a new era, in which they attended the general schools.

Till 1848 Jewish children required a special licence from the authorities in order to attend secondary school [Gymnasium]. In 1848,

[Pages 307-308]

that requirement was rescinded, leading to an increased number of Jewish secondary school pupils, and later of university students. Prior to 1848, the number of Jewish students who studied Law at the university of Lwów, was low: in 1825, 2 Jews; in 1826, 4; in 1827, 9; in 1828, 6; in 1829, 4; in 1830, 6. During the years 1831–1848 their numbers did not increase much.

The increased numbers of Jewish students at Lwów University during 1851–1870 can be ascertained from the numbers below; one needs to note that Jews from Lwów also studied at the universities of Kraków and Vienna, and as there was no faculty of Medicine at Lwów, many had to study medicine elsewhere.

The number of students at Lwów University was:
Law Faculty
1851. – 17 Jews, 285 non–Jews

1860. – 42 –"– 284 – " –

1870. – 38 –"– 484 – " –

Philosophy Faculty

1851. 25 Jews, 64 non–Jews

1860   6 Jews, 59 non-Jews

1870   13 Jews, 160 non-Jews

Technical Institute

1851. 46 Jews, 127 non–Jews

1860. 22 Jews, 207 non-Jews

1870. 35 Jews, 230 non-Jews

A different impression is conveyed by the figures of Jewish students at Lwów University and Technical Institute during 1881/2–1901/2

The number of students at Lwów University, by Faculty:[6]

	Law			Medicine			Philosophy							Technical Institute:		
Years	Non–Jews	Jews	%	Non–Jews	Jews	%	Non–Jews	Jews	%	Total	of whom Jews	%		Total	of whom Jews	%
1881/2–1885/6	532	88	16.5	–	–	–	127	15	11.8	762	103	10.4		199	33	16.6
1886/7–1890/1	650	139	21.4	–	–	–	145	28	19.3	762	103	10.4		199	33	16.6
1891/2–1895/6	814	208	25.6	33[a]	10	30.3	164	33	20.1	762	103	10.4		199	33	16.6
1896/7–1900/1	1162	276	23.8	134	44	32.8	206	41	19.9	1863	361	20		573	64	11.2
1901/2–1905/6	1307	415	31.8	89	42	47.2	761	104	13.7	2718	561	22.3		1045	234	22.4

Until 1894/5, Jews from eastern Galicia studied medicine at the universities of Kraków and Vienna. In 1905/6, the number of those studying philosophy increased markedly due to the profusion of secondary schools and because it was a requirement for teaching.

For 20 years (1870–1890), the numbers of university graduates increased and each year the numbers of lawyers and physicians grew markedly.

Lawyers:

In 1890, out of the 91 lawyers at Lwów, 33 were Jews (36.3%); in 1900, out of 168, 67 were Jews (39.9%); in 1910, out of 241, 137 were Jews (56.9%).

Physicians:

In 1890, out of 124, 30 were Jews (24.2%); in 1900, out of 242, 53 were Jews (21.9%); in 1910, out of 342, 103 were Jews (30.1%).

The academic intelligentsia played a very prominent role in Lwów's Jewish public life.

Despite the changes afforded by the constitution, however, the Orthodox began to demand rights in the community. They were prepared to take over the community's key positions. To begin with, they demanded that the civil registration books (of Births, Marriage and Deaths), be handed over to Rabbi Saul Natansohn. They objected that the Rabbi be required to obtain a marriage licence from the preacher, "the coordinating rabbi." The dispute was most acute within the community regulations' committee, during debates on the relations between the rabbi, the judge of the [rabbinical] court, and the preacher of the Temple [synagogue]. The lecturer Dr. Kolischer proposed the following wording: "The religious issues of Lwów's community are under the authority of the Rabbi and his two [religious] judges, one of whom is the Temple preacher." Dr. Filip Mansch proposed, on the other hand, that: "If the preacher were a Torah scholar, then he would be the judge of the [rabbinical] court." Members of the Orthodox community headed by Aron Ettinger, strongly objected to that, so in order to avoid any conflict with the Orthodox, the chairman of the committee Dr. Hönigsmann proposed accepting Dr. Kolischer's version. In respect of the civil registration books, it was decided that their administration be handed over to a specially qualified clerk rather than leaving them with the preacher. Dr. Ignacy Nossig, the community secretary, was appointed for the task.

That did not bring to an end the conflict between the Orthodox and the Enlightened, however. In 1868, a new community committee was elected that consisted mostly of enlightened members: Majer Rachmiel Mieses, Dr. Landesberger, Dr. Hönigsmann, Maurycy Kolischer, Dr. Juliusz Kolischer, Dr. A. Frenkel; (2A) and from the Orthodox: Ozjasz [Isaiah] Menkes.

Dr. Hönigsmann managed the welfare

[Pages 309-310]

and Charity[b] institutions; Maurycy Kolischer, education and school affairs. (3) The community affairs continued in the spirit of mutual tolerance, and the Enlightened attempted to expand the range of public institutions. The physicians who practised in the hospitals were Dr. Maurycy Rappaport, Dr. Silberstein and Dr. Witz. Great stress was laid on the issue of schools: already in September 1867, the community committee had unanimously decided to introduce the instruction of the Polish language at Jewish schools. Concurrently, an association was formed to spread the Polish language among the Jewish population. The association was headed by Dr. Hönigsmann, (4) Markus Dubs, M. Kolischer, Jozua Mieses, Rabbi Löwenstein, Dr. Juliusz Kolischer, Dr. Filip Zucker and Dr. J. Frenkel. The desire to publish a newspaper for the Jews was also realized with the establishment of *Szomer Izrael* [Shomer Israel; "The Guardian of Israel"] association.

Two contradictory political strands emerged among the Jewish intelligentsia: Centralists, supporters of the Austrian Liberal party, who were disappointed by the Poles and their anti–Jewish ploys at the Galician *Sejm*. Abraham Mendel Mohr's [Yiddish] newspaper *Tsaitung* (1869, Issue 9), openly objected to the Poles and their hypocritical friendship with the Jews, which they had solely cultivated in order to benefit from it. "The Poles wish to see the Jew as the 'Moszko' and 'Icko' of yesteryears. Times have moved on, however, and were the Poles to continue with their anti–Jewish policies, the Jews will know how to respond, and the Poles can forget any assistance from the Jews during the *Sejm* elections."

A contrary view was held by a small minority of Jews who supported the Poles and their aspirations against the centralist government.

The leaders of the centralist's group, Rubin Bierer, Dr. Filip Mansch and Dr. Josef Kohn initiated, in 1867, the idea of establishing the association *Szomer Izrael*. Its main purpose was to protect the Jews' human rights, to spur the [Jewish] masses to political public action in the community and the town, and to establish a Jewish representation at the *Sejm* and at the Austrian Parliament; to disseminate the ideas of the Enlightenment and of civilization; reconciliation and cooperation with the non–Jewish population; to develop Galicia in order to ensure that the emancipation be realized in practice. The Orthodox and the Chassidim considered *Szomer Izrael* an organ for the dissemination of Enlightenment. Members of *Szomer Izrael* were joined by the best of the *Maskilim*, the academic intelligentsia and the community, in attacking the Orthodox and the Chassidim for objecting to the expansion of schools.

The Association maintained a club with a library containing Jewish–studies books and newspapers in Hebrew and other languages. Lawyers, physicians, merchants, *Maskilim* and also observant Jews gathered at the club to read newspapers, listen to lectures and discussions on the issues of Judaism. Dr. Filip Mansch was the first chairman of the association. The association's German weekly *Der Israelit* edited by Jakub Klein, was at first printed in Hebrew script, but later also in German. Among the association's activists was the young lawyer Dr. Emil Byk (1845–1908), born at Janów he injected the centralist, anti–Polish bend into *Szomer Izrael*.

Szomer Izrael first entered the political arena in the October 1869 *Sejm* elections. At the voters' meeting on 20th October 1869 held at the Temple of the Enlightened, the leaders of the association (Dr. Mansch, Dr. Henryk Gottlieb, the preacher Löwenstein and Dr. Szymon Schaff) recommended the candidacy of Floryan Ziemiałkowski, Karol Wild and Abraham Mieses (the son of Majer Rachmiel Mieses). Ziemiałkowski was elected, but Abraham Mieses, the candidate of *Szomer Izrael* failed.

In the 1870 elections, Dr. Herman Frenkel,[7] the *Szomer Izrael* candidate was elected at Lwów with 2344 votes out of 3550. The elections were very turbulent. The Polish "Democratic Society" opposed the Jews and distributed anti–Jewish flyers to the crowds. Conflicts even broke out on the street, with windowpanes of Jewish homes being shattered. In Kraków Square events reached bloody blows and the military had to intervene.

In 1870, Dr. Bernard Goldman who had participated in the 1863 Polish uprising, settled at Lwów and gathered around him a group from among the Jewish intelligentsia who wished to be assimilated among the Poles, and started to fight against *Szomer Izrael*.

However, due to the Poles' stance against the Constitution and their demand for federalism, which the Jews considered a danger to their standing, the relations between the Jews and the Poles became adverse. The experience with the Galician *Sejm* convinced the Jews that it was best to rely on the Vienna centralist government rather than on the Poles. The slanderous speech of the *Sejm* delegates Krzeczunowicz and Zyblikiewicz (in 1870 he declared that the Vienna parliament was "Jewified" "Żydzali"), and the fact that the *Sejm* did not chose a single Jewish delegate as representative to the Vienna parliament, indicated to the Jews that most of the

[Pages 311-312]

Polish statesmen were anti–Jewish, and what the Jews of Galicia might expect were Austria to become a federal kingdom.

The Poles fiercely criticised *Szomer Izrael* for its opposition to the *Sejm*'s decision (1871) to Polonise the Germanic schools of Galicia,[10] and for its demand that the Kaiser not confirm that decision. *Szomer Izrael* demanded that parallel classes in German be formed at Lwów's secondary school.

The policies that *Szomer Izrael* followed, resulted from the Jew–hate that had spread within the circles of the nobility, the clergy and the Polish bureaucracy, whose propaganda was conducted under the slogan "Down with the Jews" (*Precz z zydami*). Immediately after the Constitution was declared, most of the Polish statesmen opposed equal rights. Consequently, the Jewish representatives were worried that if Galicia were to be granted autonomy, the Polish majority would annul the equal rights which the February 1867 Constitution had granted them. Thus, the representatives of the Jewish community, in particular the leaders of *Szomer Izrael*, sympathised with the centralist position which best suited Jewish life, and was similarly followed by Lwów's Jewish press.

In 1873 a new law was published which implemented the direct voting for the election of delegates to the Vienna parliament, rather than their election by the *Sejms*.

This change gave the Jews the opportunity to lead an autonomous policy.

On 28th May 1873, spurred by *Szomer Izrael*, the Jewish representatives from the towns of Galicia gathered and decided to stand in the elections as independent. At the gathering the "Central electoral committee of Galicia's Jews" was appointed, with Dr. Juliusz Kolischer its chairman, and Dr. Emil Byk its secretary. The committee announced no Jewish political programme, but declared its loyalty to the Constitution.[11] Dr. Szymon Samelsohn, chairman of the Kraków community who, while being member of the *Sejm* had voted with the Poles to boycott the Vienna Parliament, opposed the committee's stance. He advised the electoral committee even in writing, that the Jewish issues called for identification with Galicia's interests and that they were bound up with the destiny of the Polish nation for one hundred years. As a result, he refused to join the electoral committee. Dr. Byk retorted mockingly in an article in the weekly, *Der Israelit*, where he said that Samelsohn "goes around dressed in *Kontusz* and *Karabela*" (Polish national attire) with a curved Tatar sword on his belt.

In their desire to attract the Jewish vote, the Poles entered into negotiations with the Jewish electoral committee. The committee demanded assurance that six Jewish delegates be elected (at Lwów, Brody, Kolomyia, Stanisławów, Przemyśl and Drohobycz) and that in regions with a large Jewish minority, only Liberal candidates who opposed federalism would stand. The Polish electoral committee rejected the demands whereupon the Jewish electoral committee and the Ruthenian committee signed a technical elections agreement, but the Ruthenians who relied on the Jewish vote in the provinces, were obtained a disappointing result in the towns. Following Dr. Byk's proposal, at Lwów proper, the committee decided to recommend the Polish candidate Zbyszewski, rather than the federalist Czerkawski.

The elected Jews were: Dr. Hönigsmann (Kolomyia), Dr. Joachim Landau (Brody) and Hermann Mieses (Drohobycz), while the candidates, Rabbi Löwenstein (Przemyśl), Dr. H. Gottlieb (Stanisławów), Dr. Józef Kohn (Tarnopol) and Dr. Max Landesberger (Rzeszów [Reichshof]) failed to get elected. The elected representatives were also joined by Natan Kallier, who was selected by the Brody chamber of commerce, whereas Albert Mendelsburg, who was elected by the Kraków chamber of commerce, joined the "*Koło Polskie* [Polish Circle]." The four delegates from eastern Galicia together with the eight Jewish delegates from the rest of Austria's Lands (Vienna, Moravia, Bohemia and Bukovina) joined the Constitutional Party (*Verfassungspartei*) in parliament.

In January 1874, elections were held for the town council. *Szomer Izrael* together with the rest of the Jewish delegates formed an electoral committee and decided to form an independent Jewish list, because the Liberal citizens' committee had removed from its list of candidates, Rabbi Löwenstein and Dr. Józef Kohn, who during the parliamentary elections (1873) had recommended the Kingdom's Constitution over Federalism. A small number of members from *Szomer Izrael* (Rubin Bierer, Öhlenberg and Julius Hochfeld) proposed to abstain at the elections. Their proposal was however rejected and it was decided they stand for elections as an independent list.

The Poles, in particular Jan Dobrzański's newspaper, *Gazeta Narodowa*, conducted propaganda against the Jews depicting them as aspiring to Germanise Galicia. The newspaper called on the Poles to boycott the Jews economically. In 1874 their incitement had reached such levels that *Szomer Izrael* sent a memorandum to Dr. Glaser the Minister of Justice, with the request to order the government prosecutor at Lwów to act appropriately.[11A]

The new committee of *Szomer Izrael* elected on 29th September 1874, included Dr. Mansch as chairman, Dr. Byk, his deputy, Hilell Lechner as treasurer and Dr. Salomon Landesberg, as secretary.

Apart from the German language *Der Israelit*, there was also the Yiddish newspaper

[Pages 313-314]

Jüdische Presse, edited by Natan Samuely and Jakob Cwi [Tzvi] Sperling.

The community committee led by Dr. Juliusz Kolischer, expanded its charity and welfare work which included 53 societies and institutions at the cost of 75,000 Gulden, in 1873/4. Much attention was devoted to the system of religious education. In 1874 there were 69 *Cheders* at Lwów, where 955 children studied in gruesome sanitary conditions.

On the initiative of Rabbi Löwenstein, the community committee lobbied to introduce improvements to the *Cheders*, and to spent 7,731 Florins on Talmud Torah schools. His efforts were in vain however, as the Orthodox objected to the community's involvement in the internal affairs of the *Cheders* and the Talmud Torah schools. In 1874, the first soup kitchen was founded, and Rabbi Löwenstein was elected as its chairman and Dr. J. Fried as his deputy. The community's annual expenses rose to 57,960 Florins.

Dr. Kolischer worked in particular with regard to the two Jewish schools where 1,298 children studied, so that they be expanded to accommodate more children. Some 500 children attended the general schools. The spending budget for the Jewish schools was 36,000 Florins.

The "Marek Bernstein Foundation" used the interest it had accrued on children's craft training. Rabbi Löwenstein headed the fund's board of trustees. The community also supported the synagogues, the number of which had risen to 20.

The main activity of Dr. Kolischer and Dr. Mansch from 1871 onwards, involved compiling the community regulations. By the end of 1874, the regulations were submitted for the government's approval, which was granted by the Governorship on 13th October 1875 (No. 4464).

The Orthodox, who opposed the regulations, summoned the Jewish community at the Talmudic schools and the houses of worship and got their supporters to sign a written appeal, which was submitted to the Ministry of Religion at Vienna.

The appeal delayed the declaration of the new elections in 1876, and the authorities ordered to hold the elections according to the existing regulations of Joseph II. All the Orthodox candidates were elected. The elections were annulled, however, because the Minister of Religion also approved the regulations on 9[th]March 1877 with some minor changes. After the community had accepted the changes, the new regulations were approved on 11th July 1877 and the community called new elections, which were won by the Enlightened and *Szomer Izrael*. Those elected to the community committee were: Maks Epstein, Salomon Buber, Dr. Henryk Gottlieb, Dr. Filip Mansch, Majer Rachmiel Mieses and Dr. Juliusz Kolischer; from among the Orthodox were elected: Jozue Schmelkes, Ozjasz Horowitz. Dr. Majer Rachmiel Mieses was elected chair of the community committee. (11A)

The issue of electing a rabbi came up at that moment in time.

With the demise of Rabbi Saul Natansohn on 4th March 1875, the community committee advertised the rabbi's position. Two candidates presented themselves: Rabbi Isaak Aron Ettinger, member of the community committee, and his relative, Rabbi Cwi–Hirsch Ornstein. The Jews of Lwów were split into two camps. The Orthodox demanded the appointment of Rabbi Cwi–Hirsch Ornstein, grandson of the great scholar Rabbi Jakub Meszulam Ornstein who, together with Rabbi Naftali Herz Bernstein (1813–1873),[11B] had waged war against Rabbi Abraham Kohn. Rabbi Cwi–Hirsch Ornstein who had been rabbi at Brest–Litowsk [Brześć Litewski] from 1865 to 1873, but was forced to leave because he was a foreign national, and was elected to become rabbi at Rzeszów [Resche]. In March 1875, the Orthodox dignitaries assembled at the synagogue outside the town and decided to demand the appointment of Rabbi Cwi–Hirsz [Tzvi Hirsch] Ornstein. The community opposed his appointment because of the poisoning of Rabbi Kohn.[11C] The second candidate, Rabbi Isaak Aron Ettinger was particularly supported by the Chassidim who hated Rabbi Cwi–Hirsch Ornstein for being a "*misnaged*" [objector to the Chassidic movement].

Neither the community committee nor the delegates from *Szomer Izrael* objected to Rabbi Cwi–Hirsch Ornstein, apart from Hilel Lechner, a disciple of Reb. Nachman Krochmal, who openly opposed him.[12]

In the 9th and 10th May elections, Rabbi Cwi–Hirsch Ornstein was elected Lwów's Rabbi by a substantial majority, and he came to town on 22nd June 1875. He took up his community post with a solemn celebration attended by the community dignitaries.

Rabbi Cwi–Hirsch Ornstein, was a Torah scholar who had a broad education and was familiar with the German language and literature; he was tolerant and knew how to attract the *Maskilim* and the progressives. But he was hated by the Chassidim, with the Belz Chassidim led by the righteous Reb. Jozue Rokach, treating him with distrust.

The Jewish intelligentsia's views of Polonisation altered, which affected the policies of *Szomer Izrael* whom the Jewish public followed.

In 1870, Dr. Bernard Goldman, an active participant in the Polish uprising of 1863, settled at Lwów. In 1867 he arrived at Vienna and as a Congress Poland national he requested a licence to reside at Lwów to try and attain a lecturer position at the university.[12A] However, Governor Gułochowski

[Pages 315-316]

objected to his request, and Dr. Goldman remained at Vienna and became secretary to Rogowski, the Polish delegate to Parliament. Only in 1870 was he granted a licence to move to Lwów where he married the daughter of Rabbi Löwenstein.

Once at Lwów, he expressed his objection to *Szomer Izrael*, that considered him an instrument of Germanisation and an enemy of the Poles. In 1876, with the support of the Poles, he was elected a delegate to the Galician *Sejm*, and surrounded himself with those who favoured Polish assimilation. In 1878 he founded the Association "*Dorsze Szulom* ["Dorshe Shalom"; Peace Seekers], (*Zgoda*, in Polish), with the aim of improving the "social and political relation" with the Poles which had become unbearable due to the activities of *Szomer Izrael*. The Association which attracted members of the Jewish–Polish intelligentsia, was headed by Dr. Goldman, Maurycy Lazarus, Dr. Filip Zucker and Dr. I. Blumenfeld, a member of the town council. The Association published the Polish weekly *Zgoda*, with a bimonthly Yiddish supplement, but the supplement edition stopped after a few months.

Out of objection to *Szomer Izrael*, the Association even joined the extremists Orthodox in their battle against them. The Association was unable to attract a large number of friends and supporters however, because "the Jews of Galicia were unwilling to subject themselves to the mercy of the Poles,"[13] and six months later the Association dissolved and disappeared.[13A]

In contrast, the Association *Szomer Izrael* grew and its influence expanded. In 1868 it numbered 100 members, whereas by 1878 there were 650. In 1878, Dr. Emil Byk was elected its chairman. He started by preparing a conference of the delegates from the communities to debate the communities' work programme and how to unite them into an authorised and stable national organisation that would represent the entire Galician Jewry. To begin with, Dr. Byk attempted to attract Lwów's community committee to his programme. At first, the community leader Majer Rachmiel Mieses did not favour the proposal, but he eventually relented and the conference was scheduled for 18th June 1878 with the following agenda: 1. Regulations for the intercommunity organisation; 2. The establishment of a rabbinical seminary; 3. The question of the Jewish schools' fund from the period of Joseph II; 4. Sample regulations for the communities. The conference assembled at the Skarbek Hall and was opened by Dr. Emil Byk. Representing Lwów's community were: the chairman Mieses, Dr. Gottlieb, Dr. Mansch, the preacher Löwenstein and the secretary Dr. Ignacy Nossig. *Szomer Izrael* was represented by: Dr. Byk, Dr. Reizes, Mojzesz Buber, Rubin Bierer, Emanuel Frenkel, Hilel Lechner, Becalel Menkes, Öhlenberg, Jakub Stroh, Dr. Maksymilian Sokal and S. Zimels. Representatives from 25 communities attended the conference. The topics on the agenda were discussed by the general assembly and by committees over four days.

Dr. Emil Byk spoke of the need to establish an intercommunity organisation, *Brit–HaKehilot* ["The Communities' Alliance"], to represent Galician Jewry and its institutions. Until the establishment of *Brit–HaKehilot* the conference would act in its stead.

In his address, Dr. Filip Mansch offered an overview of the Jewish schools' fund and demanded that the authorities be actively approached to hand over the fund's monies, to the future–elected delegation of Galicia's Jews. The deliberations mostly focused on the founding of a rabbinical seminary. In the committee, Dr. Nossig and Lechner expressed their views against modelling the proposed rabbinical seminary on those in Germany, Italy or France, as it would provoke fierce objection from the Orthodox. Consequently, it was better to establish a seminary for the teachers of religion, the lack of which was noticeable in Galicia's schools.

Following heavy arguments the committee accepted preacher Löwenstein's suggestion to establish a Jewish studies seminary which would satisfy the country's requirements, with special consideration laid on the training of teachers of religion. The plenum rejected the committee's proposal. The extremist Enlightened maintained that one should not yield to the Orthodox, and that a decision be adopted for the establishment of a rabbinical seminary. During the debates young Chassidim burst into the conference hall, shouting: "Gentiles; Epicureans; 'Treifniacs' (those consuming non–Kosher food); a priests' seminary." The police were alerted and with difficulty they were removed from the hall. The intruders were led by Samuel Horowitz, the son of Ozjasz–Leib, the future leader of Lwów's assimilated Jews.

The committee decided to convene also a second "Communities Day" and to prepare the communities' regulations and a plan for the rabbinical seminary. A permanent committee was elected, which tasked Dr. Ringelheim (Tarnow) and Dr. Mansch (Lwów) to prepare the communities' regulations. Emanuel Frenkel submitted to the committee a plan for establishing a rabbinical seminary. According to his proposal, there needed to be established: a) a four–classes' preparatory school for 9–14 year–olds, where the Bible, Talmud and secular studies be taught at a low–level secondary school; b) a six–years advanced school of Talmud, Jewish studies and secular studies at advanced–level secondary school. After the matriculation examinations the students would attend the three–years course of the Talmud faculty. Upon completing the course, they would be accredited as rabbis.

[Pages 317-318]

The communities' conference decision with regard to the rabbinical seminary, alerted the Orthodox's camp. On 17th July (17 Tamuz) 1878, a rabbis' gathering led by Rabbi Cwi Hirsz Ornstein assembled at Lwów and decided to use any means to delay the realisation of the rabbinical seminary. According to the rabbis' gathering, a demand had also to be made that Jews should avoid the services of Jewish lawyers and physicians, so as not to "fall into the hands of those amending the [Jewish] religion." Rabbi Szymon Schreiber of Kraków was elected the convener of the rabbis' gathering, and with the aid of Isak Dajcz [Daitch] of Vienna, they hoped to succeed in lobbing circles of the Vienna government. Rabbi Szymon Schreiber, Rabbi Cwi–Hirsz [Tzvi] Hirsch Ornstein and the Belz Rabbi produced a proclamation to all the communities, in which they declared that the decision of the communities' conference was more damaging and dangerous than all the Spanish persecutions and Inquisition.

The rabbinical seminary thus led to a "cultural battle [*Kulturkampf*]" in Galicia, which the Orthodox conducted with extremism and exceptional fury.

The Orthodox established an organisation by the name of [*Kol*] *Machsike HaDas* [Upholders of the Faith] and published a lithographic newspaper in Yiddish: "[*Zeitung für*] *das wahre* [*Orthodoxische*] *Judentum* [(Newspaper for) the true (Orthodox) Judaism]" in which they disseminated articles of incitement against *Szomer Izrael*. Later on they published a weekly *Machsike HaDas* in Hebrew. In February–March 1879, a three curiæ [tribunals] election to the communities committee was held without any party war, as the Enlightened and the Orthodox had reached an agreement, and Majer Rachmiel Mieses was elected its chairman; those elected from among *Szomer Izrael* members were: Lazarus, Dr. Szymon Schaff, Dr. Filip Mansch, Dr. H. Gottlieb, Dr. Emil Byk, Jakub Stroh, Salomon Buber, Dr. Filip Zucker; those elected from among the Orthodox were: Jakub Jüttes, Rabbi Isaak Aron Ettinger, Samuel Schönblum, Jakub Diże. The elected deputies were: S. Landau, Mejer Bach, the pharmacist Dr. Zygmunt Rucker – all *Szomer Izrael* candidates.

In the same year, 1879, elections were also held for the Vienna parliament. On that occasion, the Jews sided with Poland. Most leaders of *Szomer Izrael* led by Dr. Emil Byk "took the view that the Jews' interest was best served by joining the Poles."

The Poles also preferred to add Jewish representatives to their list, to prevent the formation of a Jewish–Ruthenian agreement like the one of 1873, which had weakened the Poles' lists in Eastern Galicia.

The Poles' central electoral–committee of Eastern Galicia, offered four seats on the committee to the Jews, out of the Poles' 16.[14] After negotiation it was agreed on four Jewish representatives, as long as they joined the Polish faction in parliament (*Koło Polskie*).

Ever since 1879 the Jewish policy aligned itself with that of the Poles: support for the centralist government had passed, and its leaders were fully on the Polish side.

Government circles discussed the issue of the communities. The government was keen on bringing order to the communities by formulating approved regulations to which all the communities throughout Austria would have to adhere. The initiative came from the Galician *Sejm* in 1876, when it demanded to regulate the Jewish community in accordance with clause XV of the basic law.[16]

Regulating the communities in accordance with legal statutes, was a matter that also preoccupied the Jewish population.

In 1881 an enquiry was held into the issue of the rabbis and the communities, initiated by the Minister of Religion, Baron Conrad von Eybesfeld, and attended by rabbis, progressives and communities' representatives of the lands of Austria. The participants from Galicia were Natan Kallier and Rabbi Szymon Schreiber who had put forward the request to do away with the need for rabbis to present educational certificates, and to grant them the right to exclude from the community people who did not follow the faith. His demands were not answered, and so he decided to call Galicia's communities to act in the spirit of his proposals. On 15th February 1882 he held at Lwów a gathering of rabbis from Galicia and Bukovina, which was also attended by some representatives from small communities. Rabbi Szymon Schreiber, a follower of the Hungarian Orthodoxy, proposed community regulations, of which Clauses 2, 41, 58, 78 determined that the communities had the right to expel Jews who did not follow the *Shulchan Aruch* [abbreviated form of the Jewish ritual law]. Any community resolutions that contravened the *Shulchan Aruch* would be invalid. His actual intention was to give the rabbis absolute authority over the communities. The [his] entire set of regulations aimed at removing the progressives from the communities. He had in mind the example of Hungary where, after the "communities' congress" (14th December 1868–24th February 1869) the unified communities were split into three separate communities. Galicia's communities objected to the doings of Rabbi Szymon Schreiber, and sent telegrams of protest to Lwów's community, and many communities demanded that their rabbis quit the communities' gathering. Protest meetings against his proposals were also held in the towns. The rabbis' gathering, which was abandoned by many before it ended, accepted the proposed regulations.[17] Rabbi Szymon Schreiber, who was a parliamentary delegate, submitted the proposed regulations to the Minister of Religion. However, 51 of Galicia's foremost communities submitted to the government strong objections to the proposed regulations. In March 1883, Rabbi Szymon Schreiber died, and his proposal was also rescinded on his demise. Nevertheless, the Ministry of Religion

[Pages 319-320]

and Education could not remain indifferent to the many objections, and decided to reach a permanent arrangement regarding the communities. In 1880 Taaffe's government had already worked on the communities' regulations, but it took a long while for the right opportunity to submit it to the Council of Ministers for approval. On 19th January 1888, the Council of Ministers debated the proposed regulations brought by the Minister of Religious Affairs, Baron Gautsch [von Frankenthum]. On 21st March 1890, the communities' regulations for all of Austria's lands were published.[18]

In April 1882, after the Rabbis' gathering, new elections were held at Lwów for the community committee. Influenced by the previous gathering, only the progressives' list was elected, and no one from the Orthodox was elected.[19]

The Jewish intelligentsia espoused Polish assimilation. In 1880, Dr. Goldman and Dr. Filip Zucker established *Agudas Achim* [The Brotherhood Association] (*Przymierze Braci*) which led the assimilation movement till 1890, and published the Polish weekly *Ojczyzna* ["Homeland"] with a Hebrew supplement "A reminder of love for the homeland," edited by Isaak Aron Bernfeld. Dr. Emil Byk, one of *Szomer Izrael*'s leaders, also joined the group.

The Polish intelligentsia's stand was formed by the concepts of Aleksander Świętochowski, Elizia Orzeszkow and Henryk Rewakowicz, who viewed Poland's Jews favourably, and warmly welcomed the establishment of a group of assimilationists at Lwów, hoping to see the assimilation of Jews into Polish society.

Kol HaKore Davar BeIto
[a flyer in Yiddish; warning call about the current plight]

At Lwów and the provincial towns, the assimilated also launched cultural undertakings such as Polish language evening classes. They fought against the Lwów community which, according to them, followed the spirit of *Szomer Izrael* and the Austro-Germanic policy. However, the differences of opinion were smoothed over little by little through political integration with the Poles, and their aspiration to turn the community "into an institution imbibed in Polish spirit" was realized under the influence of its leaders, and with the assistance of the Polish authorities.

In the '80s, in contrast with the desire for the Jews' integration into Polish society, a prominent antiSemitic movement arose among the Polish people. During the 1880–1881 session of the Galician *Sejm*, the Polish delegate Teofil Merunowicz proposed to limit the Jews' equal rights. The committee which considered his proposal, included the amendment that the Jewish community's rights and authority be curtailed. The committee's proposal was unanimously accepted by the *Sejm*.

In the same year, the age–old conflict between the Polish and the Jewish merchants flared up again. The newspaper *Gazeta Narodowa* and its editor, Jan Dobrzański, known for his liberal and pro–Jewish publication in 1848 and 1863, called on the Poles to establish a Polish middle–class that the nation undeniably lacked. Although he did not call for the boycott of Jewish trade and its people, his call was interpreted as a call for war against the Jewish traders. A call to boycott Jewish trade and to displace them from all economic fields was openly declared by Galicia's *Sejm* delegate, Teofil Merunowicz, whose declarations turned him into a leader of Lwów's townspeople. His stance was also supported by Prince Adam Sapieha.

The Jews of Galicia and of Lwów in particular, underwent a serious crisis. And were it not for the assistance from organisations from foreign countries, Galicia's Jews would have been in a dire situation. Although in 1880–1890 there was talk of self–help, no attempt was undertaken due to the indifference of the few affluent strata within the Jewish population. The desire was also missing, to join forces to create congenial conditions to ameliorate the situation, as: professional education and strengthened trade, credit,[19A] expanding the crafts, establishing a cooperative network etc. Among Lwów's community, which was the centre of Jewish life and was suited to manage internal issues, there were only few individuals who sensed the situation and were able to conclude that it had to be changed.

[Pages 321-322]

In 1880–1882, tens of thousands of Jewish refugees from Russia passed though Lwów on their way to America. The community established an "aid committee for refugees." Representatives arrived also from welfare organisations from England and France, Sir Montague, Dr. Asher, [Emmanuel Felix] Veneziani, Karl [Charles] Netter as well as the British *Chovev Zion* [Lover of Zion, i.e. supporter of Jewish immigration to Palestine] Laurence Oliphant who was received by the community leader, Salomon Buber, who "stood by him."[c]

Despite the manifestation of anti–Semitism as a political movement, the leader and parliamentary delegate Dr. Emil Byk tried to convince Galician Jews that "anti–Semitism is a plant that sprouted only at Vienna, but not on Polish soil." The community espoused Polonisation. The 1883–1888 elected community committee, nominated as its chairman Dr. Filip Zucker, who was in the vanguard of the Polish assimilation. The committee members, Samuel Horowitz deputy chairman, and Dr. Emil Byk, had also abandoned the old policy of *Szomer Izrael*, the others on the board were Dr. Henryk Gottlieb and Samuel Kellermann. Dr. Zucker and Dr. Byk were on amicable terms with Galicia's governors, Count Alfred Potocki and his successor [Filip] Zaleski, as well as with other Polish statesmen, and they shaped Galicia's Jewish policy according to their desires.

The education of the *Charedi* youth was a subject that preoccupied the Jewish leadership in a significant measure. In 1885, the Viennese [*Israelitische*] *Allianz* embarked in Galicia on an intensified action in the field. They rented a house at Lwów, and 25 *Cheder* Torah–teachers declared publicly that they were willing to introduce secular studies at their *Cheders*. Nechemiasz Landes, headmaster of the school named after [Tadeusz] Czacki,[20] prepared the curriculum. A central *Cheder* was also established for youths under the age of 18.

In 1884, the preacher Löwenstein established the school "Ohel Moshe [Moses's Tent]" (named after Moses Montefiore) where children from poor families were given Jewish and secular education. 78 pupils enrolled straight away. The undertaking was supported by Szymon Landau. The preacher Löwenstein, a man with nationalist aspirations, wanted an education for the youth that was embedded in Jewish values and that prevented from being absorbed into the Polish assimilation that pervaded the general schools. However, the school and the *Cheders* supported by the *Allianz*, faced opposition from the Orthodox. In a meeting headed by Rabbi Cwi Hirsz Ornstein, he attempted to explain to the Orthodox that in view of the government's comprehensive educational requirement, soon to be imposed on the population, it was advisable to secure a suitably structured religious school. At the meeting, the leader of the Chassidim, Aron Piepes, declared that "religion and culture are at odds, like fire and water," and the meeting strongly objected to any change in the "*Cheder*" system and demanded to keep the educational system as it had been and as it was, despite Rabbi Cwi–Hirsz Ornstein's explanation. Rabbi Cwi–Hirsz Ornstein left the meeting in anger and continued to support efforts on that matter.

Dr. Ozjasz Thon

Under the community's initiative, in March 1885 an amended *Cheder*, initiated by the community, was opened at Lwów, in which 381 pupils enrolled. Six Torah teachers taught religious studies and eight teachers taught secular studies, in accordance with the elementary–schools' curriculum. The preachers Löwenstein and Nechemiasz Landes were involved in the matter. On preacher Löwenstein's initiative, holiday camps for Jewish school children were also established. Dr. Goldman and Jakub Stroh headed the board responsible for maintaining the holiday camps on behalf of the community.

Education and elementary schooling had preoccupied most members of the intelligentsia, who believed that with knowledge of the Polish language and with cultural integration, the Jews would gain the sympathy of the Poles, and that the pervading and growing anti–Jewish undercurrent would abate. On 16ᵗʰ March 1890, *Agudas Achim* whose primary aim was to exhort Polish assimilation, convened a referendum headed by Count Jan Tarnowski; among the Poles who attended were the renowned statesman Count Stanisław Badeni, Dr. Zdzisław Marchwicki, Tadeusz Romanowicz, Dr. Józef Wereszczyński, Dr. Zagórski, Dr. Ludmił German, Jan Franke; and from among the Jews, Dr. Emil Byk, Dr. Filip Fruchtmann, Dr. Natan Löwenstein (the son of the preacher Löwenstein). The issue debated was "what steps need to be taken in order to improve the situation of Galicia's Jews; how can one improve their education and what steps are required to ameliorate their economic condition."

After comprehensive deliberations it was concluded that it was desirable to increase

[Pages 323-324]

the number of Jewish pupils at state schools, under the compulsory education rule, by offering special terms to keep the [Jewish] holidays and the Sabbaths, and the teaching of religion to be undertaken by experienced teachers with a general education. Consequently, they proposed to establish at Lwów a seminary for teachers of religion as well as a rabbinical seminary. Lwów's community prepared a curriculum for a four–years seminary. The curriculum included the study of the Hebrew language and grammar, the Bible with commentaries, Talmud, *Shulchan Aruch*, dogmatics and its origins, ethics and Jewish philosophy, history of the Jewish people, history of Jewish literature as well as the methodology of religious studies.

Seminary students were also obliged to follow secular subjects at a state's seminary. The community attempted also to obtain funds from *Allianz* for the project, but to no avail.

In 1878 the community had already sent the *Sejm* a memorandum, based on the decision of the first community assembly, but the matter was transferred to the *Sejm*'s education committee only in 1884, after a fresh request from the community and from the general pedagogical association had been submitted.

The committee decided that by acknowledging the need to establish a specific course for Jewish teachers of religion, the *Sejm* had declared its willingness to allocate a set amount, with the proviso that Lwów's community on its own or together with other communities, would raise the majority of the expenses; tuition would be in Polish and the *Sejm* would have a say and appropriate supervision over the institution.

Adolf Stand

The *Sejm* accepted the resolution on the 28th November 1890.

In its attempt to secure the allocated sum, Lwów's community was prepared to shut the girls' school[21] and transfer its 6,000–Florin annual budget to the seminary. The community committee headed by Dr. Szymon Schaff, made this decision in its meeting on 5th December 1891.

The authorities delegated the settling of the matter to the town council, but the town council objected to the closure of the girls' school.[22] to avoid overburdening the municipality financially, as a result of the girls' transfer to a municipal school.

The rabbinical seminary and the Torah–study school never came to fruition. In 1902, after protracted negotiations with the national committee (wydział krajowy) and with the Vienna Ministry of Religion and Education, as well as on the opinion of the universities of Lwów and Kraków, Lwów's community decided to establish a private institution to train teachers of religion from amongst the Jewish pupils who were attending the state teachers' seminary.

Inevitably, the Orthodox objected to all the proposals and plans, and stood fast while continuing to attack the progressives, in their newspaper *Machsike HaDas*, which after the demise of Rabbi Szymon Schreiber became wholly reliant on the Rabbi of Belz's coterie.

The group of Lwów's Orthodox headed by Rabbi Cwi–Hirsz [Tzvi] Hirsch] Ornstein, who had changed his mind regarding the Jewish policy (during Rabbi Abraham Kohn's tenure he had been fanatically devout) but by and by reconciled himself to reality and to the requirements of his time. The transformation was also a result of Samuel Horowitz's leadership of the community, which he held from 1888 till 1903.

In 1888, when an organ was installed in the Temple, the Orthodox started another conflict with the community committee. Their representative, Jakub Ber Sokal, delivered a strong protestation to the community committee, but with Dr. Byk following Rabbi Löwenstein's view, the dispute was brought to an end once it was agreed that the organ would not be played on the Sabbath.

With the demise of several leaders, Lwów's community underwent changes. Young blood appeared on the horizon and took control.

After the demise of Rabbi Cwi–Hirsz Ornstein in 1888, Rabbi Izaak–Aron the son of Rabbi Mordche Zew Segal Ettinga [Ettinger], was elected to succeed him. Rabbi Izaak–Aron Ettinga was neither an extremist nor a fanatic, and contributed much to ground the community which had been unsettled by the Orthodox and the influence of the Rabbi of Belz's coterie.

On 15th March 1889, the preacher Isachar Ber Löwenstein died. Among the candidates to succeed him were Dr. Samuel Cwi Margulies (born at Brzeżany [Berezhany]) and Rabbi Dr. Isaiah Gelbhaus (born at Buczacz [Buchach]). The Polish authorities disqualified them both, as neither knew any Polish. Dr. Bernard Goldman proposed the candidacy of Nachum Sokołow, who had come to Lwów and held a sermon in Polish at the Temple of the Enlightened in the presence of the synagogue managers and a large crowd, which left a great impression on the listeners.

[Pages 325-326]

Sokołow returned to Warsaw, however, and his candidacy was annulled. It appeared that the authorities refused to accept a candidate proposed by Dr. Goldman.

In 1891, Rabbi Löwenstein's post was filled by Dr. Jecheskiel Caro, the son of Rabbi Józef Chaim Caro, the rabbi from Włocławek [Leslau] who officiated at Pilsen [Plzeň], Bohemia.

The community was led by Samuel Horowitz and Dr. Emil Byk, while the education committee's affairs were managed by Dr. Samuel Schaff. All three of them tried to expand the community's charitable and welfare activities. A women's committee was established, led by Dr. Adela Inlender to provide clothes, footwear and food for pupils of impecunious families. On 17th June 1888, following the community's petition, the government issued a regulation that the salaries of the teachers of religion be paid for by the government or the state. On 1st December 1889, a law was issued to determine the arrangement and grading of the teachers of religion at elementary schools. Dr. Pesz succeeded Dr. Ignacy Nossig as community secretary.

The communities' legal status underwent a marked change. On 1st March 1891, Baron Gautsch, the parliamentary and upper–house (Herrenhaus) Minister of Religion, submitted the regulation "regarding the religious community of Jewish faith" which was passed without objections, apart from some unrelated anti–Semitic speeches delivered in Parliament as pure propaganda.

The law only set the boundary that determined the scope and area of the community and its authority, the role of the holy servants (The rabbi, his deputy, *Dayanim* [Jewish ritual judges], caretakers), institutions and relations with the authorities. Clause 28 stated that the communities had to prepare a plan specifying the boundaries and area of the community, the composition of the administration, its election and the period of its tenure, its role and powers; regulations regarding the rabbi, his election, his authority, his rights and obligations; the rights and obligations of the community members, election regulations, the community institutions' maintenance and management; the regulations of synagogues and private Minyanim; the budget and taxes. The regulations and any alterations to them had to be submitted to the authorities for approval. A form for the communities of Galicia containing 93 sections was appended to the statute.[23]

During 1891–1892, Lwów's community worked on preparing sample regulations (Musterstatut) in accordance with the policy–form set by the government for all of Galicia's communities. The communities, apart from those in a few towns, had no existing regulations. The regulations were prepared by a committee made up of Lwów's community representatives, rabbis and governmental agents, and were unanimously accepted.[24]

In 1891 (16th January; 7th Shvat 5651), Rabbi Izaak–Aron Ettinga died and the community set about electing his successor. Among the candidates were Rabbi Izak Schmelkes of Przemyśl, Rabbi Arie–Leib Braude, Rabbi Weiss of Czernowitz [Czerniowce], Rabbi Rohatin of Złochów [Zolochiv] and Rabbi Izak Chajes of Brody. The rabbi's election by 80 adjudicators took place on 7th February 1892; 34 voted for Rabbi Izak Schmelkes, 25 for Rabbi Arie–Leib Braude and all the other candidates received 21 votes. The election of Izak Schmelkes was secured.[24A]

The community had also to elect the Jewish school's headmaster. On 15th July 1893, Dr. Bernard Sternberg (1823–1893) died; he had been headmaster for 45 years and contributed much to its educational progress and the increased number of its pupils and teachers. Dr. B. Sternberg was also active in the public life, and especially in the management of "The Temple of the Enlightened." Under his management, the school played an important role in the cultural life of the Jews of Lwów. He was followed as headmaster by the teacher Mendel, and in 1899 Dr. Samuel Gutmann (1864–1935) was appointed on an annual salary of 2,400 Crowns. On 14th February 1909, Dr. S. Gutmann left his post as headmaster after being appointed rabbi and preacher, and the school was managed by the teacher Samuel Szlagowski, and after his demise Herman Spet was appointed headmaster (till 1934).

During 1890–1895 the Zionist Organisation evolved at Lwów. The youth and the academic intelligentsia were instrumental in the movement *Chibat–Zion* and showed interest in Judaism, after the period of assimilation. The Zionist movement and the social, cultural and political impact on Jewish life, associated with the awakening of the Zionist concept will be discussed in the chapter "The History of the Zionist Movement["][d]

Attempts were made at Lwów and Galicia to provide economic assistance to craftsmen, retail salesmen and pedlars. In 1898, *JCA* [Jewish Colonisation Association; IKA] established "loan and saving funds" as well as a cooperative association for credit. Youths' training courses in crafts, and evening classes for general education were formed with the assistance of different institutions.

Intensive work was also undertaken to establish a hospital, founded by Maurycy Lazarus[24B] who donated the funds to erect a new hospital with 80 beds. In 1902, the hospital was expanded and its cost rose to reach 600,000 Crowns. His wife donated another 60,000 Crowns for internal furnishing. Lazarus handed the hospital, which was constructed

[Pages 327-328]

and fitted to suit modern medical practices, to the authority of the Jewish community.

In 1902, a new orphanage was opened as well; it was established by Dr. Szymon Schaff and his wife in memory of their daughter Otylia, who had died young. The community also constructed a new building – a home for incurable patients.

Following the publication of the 21st March 1890 community regulations, organising the rabbinate turned into an urgent issue. Since 1870, the community debated the integration of the preacher post at the "Temple of the Enlightened," together with the rabbinate. Due to the deep rift with the Orthodox over the community regulations and the rabbinical seminary, it became impossible to settle the matter. In 1891 when Dr. Jecheskiel Caro was appointed, he was assured that once his tenure had become permanent in 1895, his rabbinical appointment would also be settled. Nevertheless, all attempts to negotiate with the Orthodox resulted in their objection to the preacher being appointed community rabbi.

Dr. Dawid Schreiber

With the confirmation of new community regulations, the community committee wanted to implement the appointment even against the position of the Orthodox, because the regulations included a special clause on the maintenance of two rabbis at Lwów. The opportunity presented itself after the Governorship had approved the community regulations at Lwów, on 23rd December 1897.

In 1898, community elections were held in accordance with the regulations. Twenty–seven community elders were elected, out of which seven would form the management board, and twenty would form the council. To the board were elected: Dr. Emil Byk, Chairman; Dr. Szymon Schaff, deputy chairman; Salomon Buber, Dr. Józef Czeszer, Dr. Henryk Gottlieb, Jan Landau, and the engineer Emil de Mieses; to the council: Jakub Beiser, Dr. Salomon Bund, Dr. Jakub Diamand, Jakub Diże,

Mendel Feigenbaum, Dr. Wilhelm Holzer, Eliasz Hescheles, Samuel de Horowitz, Dr. Jakub Horowitz, Moritz Jonas, Dr. Maurycy Lazarus, Dr. Jakub Mahl, Dawid Maschler, Filip Natansohn, Samuel Nebenzahl, Leib Rosenfeld, Wilhelm Sakler, Maurycy Silberstein, Jakub Stroh, Mojzesz Dawid Wein.

One of first tasks of the new community committee was to settle the rabbinate issue.

Following clause 30 of the regulations submitted for approval, it was determined that the composition of Lwów's rabbinate should at least include two community rabbis, with equal status as the rabbis throughout the entire Lwów area: one Orthodox rabbi, and one progressive rabbi who was tasked, apart from his role as preacher and rabbi, also to supervise the religious studies in all the state schools.

Besides the two rabbis, the community had to maintain a rabbi for the synagogue and a rabbinical court.

Based on the above clause, it was possible to appoint Dr. Caro as community rabbi. Following clause 34 of the regulations, 30 arbitrators and nine deputies were elected from among members of the "Temple of the Enlightened," who, together with the community council (with 39 votes in favour against 15), appointed Dr. Caro as community Rabbi on 25th May 1898.

Although his appointment followed the regulations, the Orthodox submitted a written appeal to the municipality, signed by their leaders: Febus Ebner, Nachum Burstin, Mendel Margoszes, Lejzor Gutwirth, Abraham Juda Alter, Hersz Braser (known as Herszele Zorn) and Jakub Okin. The municipality did not respond to the appeal, but passed it to the Governorship.

On 11th June 1898, the community president Dr. Emil Byk swore in Dr. Caro as community rabbi together with Rabbi Izak Schmelkes and Aleksander Halpern. On 20th February 1899, the Governorship rejected the appeal by the Orthodox and confirmed the appointment.

The question of the religious education in primary and secondary school was also on the agenda. The 1899 regulations confirmed the primary and secondary schools' posts of teachers of religion. Due to the lack of teachers of religion with pedagogical qualification, the lessons were taught by general teachers who were seminary graduates.

In secondary schools the situation was much the same. Since 1883, Dr. Józef Kobak[25] taught the secondary schools' upper classes, while the lower classes of the fourth secondary school were taught by Jakób Klein, who had been the editor of *Der Israelit* since 1868 till his appointment as teacher of religion, in 1883.

As inspector of religious studies, the community tasked Dr. Caro to prepare the curriculum. Once Dr. Caro had submitted his curriculum, it was passed into law by the national educational council, on 30th August 1895.

[Pages 329-330]

In order to appoint the appropriate teachers for all schools, and secondary schools [gymnasiums] in particular, the community committee negotiated with Galicia–born graduates of Vienna's rabbinical seminary.

That led to the appointment of the following, as religious teachers: Dr. Mojzesz Schorr, Dr. Bernard Hausner,Dr. Spinner, Dr. Majer Bałaban, Hirsz Bad, Zygmunt Taubes–Sens, Dr. Majer Tauber, Dr. Lewi Freund and Dr. Samuel Gutmann.

At the same time, the community debated again the erection of a seminary for teachers of religion which had already been approved of by the *Sejm*. In 1894, the *Sejm* representative Dr. Bernard Goldman, brought the matter for discussion, and in 1898 the authorities accepted the opinion of the universities of Kraków and Lwów. On 19th October 1902, after a lengthy negotiation, the "Institute for teachers of religion" was opened, headed by Dr. Caro, who led the institute till 1913. The active lecturers were Dr. Gutmann and Dr. Hausner. Under Dr. Caro's initiative an "Association of Jewish teachers of religion" was also founded throughout Galicia. Dr. Caro did not sympathise with the teachers of religion who gravitated towards Zionism, but supported the leaders of assimilation, which led him to public conflict with the Zionists. When the assimilationists demanded to withdraw the teaching of the Hebrew language, he did not object, neither did he object when, in 1904, the Land's education committee under the influence of the assimilated, forbade the teaching of Hebrew during the lessons of religion. All the teachers of religion were willing to obey the order, except for Dr. Majer Bałaban who declared it impossible for him to teach religion by following the Polish translation of the Bible – Wujek translation; due to his objection, the Land's education committee annulled the prohibition.

In 1905, following Dr. Majer Bałaban's proposal, the convention of teachers of religion decided that religiously speaking it was necessary to teach also Hebrew, and Dr. Caro yielded to the teaching staff's wish.

In 1899, under the initiative of Dr. Majer Munk (of Hamburg, son–in–law of Samuel Rokach (a very wealthy man and among the leaders of the Orthodox) and with support from the community, the *Chinuch LaNoar* [Education for the Youth] school was established to teach the Hebrew language; in the afternoons, secondary–school pupils studied there Hebrew language, grammar. Bible, *Mishnah* and *Shulchan Aruch* [abbreviated form of the Jewish ritual law]. The studies lasted four years. The appointed headmaster was the pedagogue and Hebrew–Yiddish writer, Izak Ewen (1861–1925). Ewen was educated within a Chassidic home, but he "enlightened himself" and became a teacher. He published articles and stories from the lives of the Chassidim in *Machsike HaDas* and later in *HaMagid* (Kraków); at Borysław he established Galicia's first Hebrew school. In 1895 he moved to Lwów where he founded a modern school for teaching Hebrew, and in 1899 he accepted the role of headmaster of *Chinuch LaNoar* school.

Bernard Goldman

In 1902, Ewen left the school and Dr. Gutmann replaced him as headmaster.

In March 1899, the Jews of Lwów faced a difficult municipal council election struggle. The Poles' election slogan was "Delete" the Jews from all candidate lists, in order "to maintain the Christian character of the town of Lwów."

Of the 100 members on the municipal council, only 18 were Jews, even though they were entitled to 25% of the mandates

After a tough conflict, 18 Jewish members were again voted in: Rabbi Izak Schmelkes, Rabbi Dr. Caro, Dr. Emil Byk, Dr. Natan Löwenstein, Piepes-Poratyński, Dr. Bernard Goldman, the pharmacist Blumenfeld, the pharmacist Jonas Beiser, Dr. Mahl, Dr. Pisek, Dr. W. Holzer, Dr. A. Reiss, the merchant Fried, the banker Jonas, the industrialist N. Mayer, the pharmacist Dr. Rucker, the industrialist Sprecher, Dr. Edward Lilien.

During the ten years before the First World War, public life underwent big changes. The Zionist Movement kindled an interest in Judaism among Lwów's Jewish community and especially among the intelligentsia and the educated youth. Shoots of the Jewish Workers' Movement which spread from Lwów to the rest of Galicia, were also visible. Associations for workers, trading assistants and craftsmen were formed, and some joined the Polish Socialist Party (P.P.S. [Polska Partia Socjalistyczna]). Zionist workers' associations were also formed during the 1903 Kraków conference, such as *Poale Zion* [Workers of Zion].

Some of the Jewish workers who had joined the "P.P.S.," left and set up a Jewish association titled "Z.P.S." (Żydowska Partia Socjalistyczna), this was followed by the P.P.S. forming a "Jewish Section" which dissolved before the First World War, with some of its members

[Pages 331-332]

joining the Z.P.S. which formed associations that encouraged their national and social status recognition.

Although the assimilated were in charge of the community (In 1903, Dr. Emil Byk followed Samuel Horowitz as president of the community, and with support from the authorities they were elected to represent the Jews in the municipality, the *Sejm* and the Vienna parliament), their influence diminished within the Jewish population. Dr. Emil Byk's total control over the community aroused dissatisfaction also within the circles of the assimilated who were inclined towards democracy, and who took their revenge on him at the *Sejm* elections of 1898, by voting for Jakub Bojko, the leader of the Polish Peasants' Party, despite his inclination towards anti–Semitism.

While the committees of the welfare institutions *JCA, Baron Hirsch Fund* as well as the *B'nai B'rith* society, the Lwów branch of which was founded in 1899, were still controlled by the assimilated who influenced public life, nevertheless their hold diminished here too, as the influence of the Zionist Movement increased.

The community's activities included: 1) religious issues; 2) education; 3) welfare institutions; 4) monies and legacies. The community controlled an annual budget of 300,000 Crowns, in addition to the budgets of schools, hospitals, orphanages and soup–kitchens. The 1901 budget, for example, was made up as follows: 297,000 Crowns taxes, income and miscellaneous (of which 50,000 Crowns taxes; 247,000 ritual slaughter and legacies). The expenditure came to 308,000 [Crowns], made up of: the rabbinate – 17,980 Crowns; schools' maintenance[e] –10,334 Crowns ; kosher food for soldiers and the sick – 4,000 Crowns; professional training for orphans – 7000 Crowns; 9,620 Crowns to feed schoolchildren; 30,000 Crowns on support of cultural and welfare institutions; 1,000 Crowns for the Vienna rabbinical seminary; 400 Crowns for the *Chinuch LaNoar* school; 8,400 Crowns on pensions; 26,000 Crowns on administration. In 1904 the schools' budget rose to 82,190 Crowns, compared with the 73,256 in 1898; the hospitals' budget was 136,555 Crowns in 1904, compared with the 109,502 in 1898; the orphanage 35,543 Crowns in 1904, compared with 32,150 in 1898; the welfare fund 9,345 Crowns [in 1904] compared with 12,022 in 1898.

Apart from these budgets, the community had at its disposal the income from some 60 legacies of contributors and donors, the incomes which were largely allocated to the needs of the hospitals, the orphanage, welfare institutions and the granting of scholarships. The legacies came to 755,643 Crowns. In particular the 100,000 Crowns legacy donated by Samuel de Horowitz for the establishment of a loan fund for traders and tradesmen, needs to be mentioned. Its profits provided for 224 loans in the sum of 22,175 Crowns, in 1899 alone. The loan fund operated until the first world war.[26A]

In 1905 a plan to build a new "Temple" on a large plot in the town–centre facing the *Sejm* building, was discussed. However, objections from the state–governor to the construction of a synagogue near the *Sejm*, and the death of Dr. Byk (1906), put an end to the entire plan. The existing "Temple" was actually enlarged, two galleries were added and its interior was renovated.

The general economic crisis and the boycott by the Polish anti–Semitic parties ("the National Democrats" and their magazine *Słowo Polskie*) together with the Ukrainians, led to the dwindling economic life of Galicia's Jews. The decline also affected indirectly the lives of Lwów's Jews, despite the fact that the economic conditions there were much better than in other communities. The Jews held key positions in wholesale trade. Known are the textile wholesalers Abraham–Ber Ludmirer, Balsambaum, Spiegel on "Breitegasse [Wide alley]"; the import–fruits wholesaler Friedrich Schleicher; iron merchants Sprecher, Saul Birnbaum and Salomon Rappaport; wholesale furriers Gerszon Wolf and Singer; hat manufacturer Bernard Waldmann. The fruit trade was concentrated in the hands of Nachmann Luft, who travelled to Trieste to bring southern fruits including etrogs.

The "Agricultural Union" (*koła rolnicze*) at Lwów, tried to prise the trade in grains, cattle and agricultural produce, out of the hands of the Jews. Similar attempts were also made by the Ukrainian Cooperation, notwithstanding, the Jews held on firmly until 1914. In the hops trade Zygmunt Flecker was known, as was Leib Wahl in the timber trade.

The Jews advanced and did well, also in crafts. Among the well–known craftsmen, the artistic locksmith Führer; the tinsmith Müller; the joiner Fand; the mechanic Weich; the stone mason Judam; the fresco painter Falk; the house painter Staude; the engraver Szapira, need to be mentioned, who excelled not only in the quality but also in the artistry of their work, and who were also known outside the town of Lwów.[27] Best known was the carver (chiseller), the jeweller Baruch Dornhelm (1853–1928), who excelled in artistic work known abroad too. He learnt engraving

[Pages 333-334]

and carving from his father Salomon, who was known by his work throughout Lwów. His sons Boruch, Szymon and Jakob worked for him at his workshop, and produced precious works of art.[27A]

Boruch Dornhelm was a trained craftsman and his work was also in demand at Vienna, Berlin, [Saint] Petersburg, Budapest and London. He integrated Jewish motifs in his work, and his copper and silver openwork "the Exodus from Egypt," "Moses," "the Binding of Isaac," "David and Goliath" and "Samson," are well known. In 1907 he moved to Vienna, where he lived for the rest of his life.

Dr. Jan Piepes-Poratyński

Already in 1892, the Vienna *Allianz* and *Österreichisch– Israelitische* Union [Austrian–Jewish Association] had started on rehabilitation activities and founded the *Hilfsverein für die notleidende jüdische Bevölkerung in Galizien* [Association for the needy Jewish population of Galicia]. To that end, by developing home–industry the association created sources of income that occupied 4,000 people, including many from Lwów, whose annual income reached 300,000 Crowns.

Allianz also extended subsidies to schools and to students' welfare societies, and the German–Jewish association *Esra* supported kindergarten and orphanages. The community and its Lwów institutions were conducted in an orderly fashion. Vienna and foreign countries considered the Jewish Lwów "a town attached to Galicia by geography alone." The Zionists insisted on introducing democratic order in the community, and under pressure of their demands the community leaders began to look for constructive assistance.[29]

And then, amidst this process, the First World War broke out.

2.

The period of the First World War, 1914–1918, constituted one of the bleakest chapters in the history of Lwów's Jews.

Immediately with the declaration of the war, Lwów was flooded by streams of penniless refugees from the Austro–Russian border towns of Galicia, forced to leave their homes under the Russian occupation. It became necessary to care for the refugees, feed them, and provide them with lodgings.

Under the leadership of Samuel de Horowitz, the community established a "Rescue Committee [*Vaad Ha'Hazala*]" of 100 members from all the parties and strata of the Jewish population. In a flyer published by the "Rescue Committee," Jews were asked to donate clothes, food and money for the thousands of refugees arriving from the borders of Galicia.[30]

The "Rescue Committee" was very active and separated the aid to the refugees into different departments. Dr. Cecylia Klaften, Dr. Ada Reichenstein, Laura Olbert, Marja Mester, Marja Goldfarb, N. Mandel, Dr. Felicja Nossig, and C. Katz headed the "Women's Committee."

Apart from help to the refugees, the "Rescue Committee" was also engaged in forming a legion of Jewish volunteers. The undertaking was headed by Dr. Efroim [Ephraim] Waschitz, a veteran of Galicia's Zionist Movement, chairman of the Gymnastics Association "*Dror* [Liberty]" since 1913. Under the influence of Dr. Sterner and Arie Kroch, Dr. Waschitz became interested in the Scouts Movement and published an enthusiastic article about the Movement in the Viennese weekly "[Die] Welt." He was elected the Scoutmaster and held that function untill the outbreak of the World War.

In July 1914, a general recruitment was announced and the Jewish youth enlisted to fight against Russia – which they considered a source of anti Jewish sentiment. Dr. Waschitz sent a memorandum to the army headquarters at Lwów, offering the services of the Jewish scouts, for the purpose of reconnaissance and information. He was called to headquarters and in negotiation with Captain Rudolf Berger he proposed organising a brigade of Jewish volunteers. The headquarters accepted his proposal and put at his disposal, as a guide, the reserve officer Dr. Leon Rappaport.

But a few days later, as the Russians approached and the military headquarters left Lwów, Dr. Rappaport and Dr. Waschitz decided to leave the town together with the volunteers. On the way, the brigade dispersed and its men joined the regular military service.

Members of the "Rescue Committee" also left town. Only Jakub Stroh remained in town.

By the end of August 1914, the Russian had conquered most of Eastern Galicia and reached Lwów. On 30th August 1914, the Austrian authorities were given an order to leave the town and 16,000 Jews fled with them. Only

[Pages 335-336]

40,000 of the Jewish population (out of a population of 56,751 souls) remained in the town. (30) Over 40,000 Jewish refugees had actually arrived at Lwów from the border towns, all impecunious, because those who were well–off fled westward, to Bohemia, Moravia, Hungary, Vienna.

Confusion and fear of the Russians pervaded the Jewish Quarters. Once the Russian army had entered the town on 3rd September 1914, the Cossacks started attacking the Jews and robbing them of watches and jewellery. The Jewish shops were closed, and only after the Russian [military] headquarters announced strict prohibition of theft and expropriation of goods, did the owners who remained in town, open their shops. The shops of those who had fled were opened by relatives or acquaintances.

Opening the shops brought some economic relief since the Russians did much shopping. The situation did not last, however, as Russian merchants came to Lwów and the military personnel preferred buying from them. Particularly difficult was the situation of the craftsmen, except for barbers, tailors, shoemakers and bakers whose work did not stop.

Most of the local population and the refugees suffered hunger and had no income.

Apart from the grim economic situation, the political situation was further exacerbated. The Russian Governor general Count Bobrinsky in charge of the conquered Galicia, announced categorically that Galicia was legally a region of Russia and that the Russian laws would apply there. The Russian authorities started straight away with incitement against the Jews and "their arrogant authority" in Austria and in Galicia.

On 3rd September 1914, the Governor–General Bobrinsky received a delegation representing Lwów's population. The delegation included the mayor Tadeusz Rutowski, the cardinals, members of the municipality and Jewish representatives – Dr. Hausner and Rabbi Arie–Leib Braude. Count Bobrinsky spoke with them at length and enquired about their stance towards Russia and the occupying authorities. He ended his talk by asking Dr. Hausner to receive Colonel Drohomirecki at his home, and relate to him of the condition of the Jews. Drohomirecki visited Dr. Hausner several times and put to him his questions. The occupying authorities considered Dr. Hausner as the representative of the Jewish population. They did not stop the Jews from congregating at the synagogues and the "Temple" on the Sabbath.

On 11th September 1914, Dr. Jakub Diamand,[31] Dr. Filip Schleicher[32] (the Mayor's third Deputy),[33] Rabbi Arie–Leib Braude, Dr. Bernard Hausner Hausner–[34] and Dr. Herman Rabner were summoned by Lwów's military Commander Sheremetev. In his speech he blamed the Jews for sabotaging the Russian army and warned that he would have to take appropriate measures.

On 23rd September 1914, Rabbi Arie–Leib Braude and Dr. Hausner were received by the Governor General, Count Bobrinsky, who demanded that they keep order, otherwise he would have to resort to strict measures against the Jews; under the pretext that the Jews were enemies of Russia, many Jews were arrested and were robbed of the little assets they had. The secretary of "Okhrana" (the Russian secret police), Major Jacewicz, who was a Russian consulate officer at Lwów involved in an espionage trial, and was sentenced to return to Russia. He was familiar with Lwów and used his term in office to enrich himself. He was later also arrested by the Russians and was charged with embezzlement and fraud. Meanwhile he was in his post and his whole ambition was to incite riots against the Jews.

His plot was executed on 27th September 1914. Shots were suddenly heard in Rynek [Market] Square. The army was called. The inhabitants were ignorant of what was happening. Rumours spread that the Austrian army had arrived unexpectedly. Soon it became clear, however, that the Russians had shot into the houses in the Jewish Quarter; there were victims, the dead bodies were left on the streets. 42 people were killed that day, among them 40 Jews; 300 Jews were arrested; the Russians searched for weapons in the houses of Jews, under the pretext that a Jew had shot at Russian soldiers. The Polish newspaper *Słowo Polskie* also singled out the Jews as responsible for the shooting, and that "the foreign elements" (the Jews) had created provocations. The Russian–leaning press indicated clearly that the riots, based on well–practiced and known methods, were orchestrated by the Russians who found a pretext to persecute the Jews. The following day, 28th September 1914, Dr. Diamand, Dr. Rabner, Rabbi Arie–Leib Braude and Dr. Hausner as representatives of the Jews, were summoned to the town's commander, General [von] Eiche where the secretary Jacewicz informed them that on Sunday Jews had shot at the army, and he demanded that whoever shot, be handed in. The Jewish representatives maintained they were certain no Jew had done it and that there was no cause to hand in non–existent accused. The Parliamentary representative, Ernst Breiter, who remained at Lwów, and the Mayor Dr. Rutowski, lobbied Bobrinsky for the Jews, but in vain. On the eve of Yom Kippur rumours spread that the Russians were plotting trouble, whereupon the community committee debated whether the Yom Kippur prayers should be held at the Synagogues. During the debate, gendarmes entered the community and by order of the town–commander, arrested

[Pages 337-338]

the community–leader Dr. Diamand. As a result, it was decided to close the synagogues.

In the afternoon, Dr. Hausner and Rabbi Arie–Leib Braude, were summoned to General Eiche who again questioned them about the shooting. No prayers were held on the eve of Yom Kippur. The synagogues were shut. At night, Dr. Hausner and Rabbi Arie–Leib Braude were summoned to Count Bobrinsky, who informed them that shutting the synagogues appeared like a demonstration against the Russian authorities, and consequently he ordered that they opened the synagogues, the following day. His order was indeed followed, and prayers were held at the synagogues on Yom Kippur, and meanwhile Dr. Diamand was released from prison.

Only after the Jewish army physician Dr. Lander arrived at Lwów, and with his interest in the Jews' situation, did the condition improve somewhat. Dr. Hausner handed him a detailed memorandum about the Jews' situation at Lwów, and in occupied Galicia, and the memorandum was immediately sent to Saint Petersburg. With Dr. Lander's intervention, the secretary of *JCA* at St. Petersberg, Dawid Feinberg arrived at Lwów in December 1914. The community leaders avoided him and Jews from Russia in general, for fear of being accused of disloyalty by the Austrian authorities. Dr. Hausner swayed and convinced the community leaders that they were mistaken, and a meeting of Dawid Feinberg, Dr. Lander, Dr. Hausner Dr. Diamand and Jakub Stroh was held. After the meeting, D. Feinberg handed 14,500 Roubles to the community committee for charitable works.

Dawid Feinberg and Dr. Hausner visited Count Bobrinsky and obtained a licence for the operations of the "Rescue Committee." Notwithstanding, the authorities persisted in robbing, confiscations and thefts. A large number of Jews were arrested under the pretext that they were hiding Austrian captives in their homes, and most of them were exiled to inner Russia, as mixed descent.

With the Russian army's retreat on the front, the situation of the Jews worsened at Lwów. The Jews were also subject to a hostile attitude from the non–Jewish population, both Polish and Ruthenian, who accused them of charging exaggerated prices, lowering the value of the Rouble, and the concealment of food. After the Austrian had recaptured Lwów, the Poles, who did side with the Russians,[35] blamed the Jews for sympathising with the Russians; that they cheered the Tzar when he passed through Lwów in April 1915, and that they were pleased when the Cossack regiments entered and occupied Lwów (!)[36]

The Jews suffered in particular under the "Okhrana" (the [Russian] secret police), that also tried to recruit Jewish agents. In fact, among the 420 men in Okhrana's ranks, only 30 were Jewish (c. 7%), and those were men of the underworld and pimps. The Jewish population did not keep in contact with the Russian occupier. On the contrary, the Jews did everything they could to redeem the Austrian and German captives and help them.[37] They also helped Austrian officials who were left at Lwów and who suffered hunger, even though there was not sufficient food to sustain their own families.

The painter [Wilhelm] Wachtel

Ever since Galicia was occupied it was clear that the Russians had decided to annihilate the Jews whom they considered Austrian sympathisers, and knew that none of their promises would convince the Jews to betray Austria. Consequently, they considered every Jew a spy for Austria.

Under those circumstances it was hard to organise public life.

Once the Russians entered Lwów, all functions of the "Rescue–Committee" were handed over to the community headed by Dr. Jakub Diamand, as the leadership had quit town. In October 1914, a special committee that included Dawid Rubenzahl and Dr. Leo Auerbach, was established to deal with assistance and welfare. Apart from refugees,

Lwów's remaining population devoid of means of livelihood or income, also required urgent attention. 4,000 of Lwów's families and some 4,000 refugees from outside the town, needed help with food, dress, medicine etc. Tens of soup–kitchens opened in town, serving hot kosher food and bread to thousands of Jews arrested by the Russians, who needed looking after. Poverty rose and hardship increased throughout all strata of the population. The death rate also rose, due to poor nutrition and disease. From 1st August 1914 till 1st August 1915, the death rate among the Jewish population rose by a factor of around 11.5, compared with earlier years.

Once Dawid Feinberg had a licence from the

[Pages 339-340]

Governor general, the "Rescue Committee" (Żydowski Komitet Ratunkowy) was established, with its 20 members. The committee's president was Dr. Diamand, the principal secretary – Dr. Hausner,and the treasurer – Szymon Peller.[38] The nine members on the board of management were: Dr. Diamand, his deputy, Dr. Hulles, Szymon Peller, Dr. Hausner, his deputy, Professor Mandel and four other members.

Work was undertaken by the following nine departments: a. Finance dept., which dealt with raising funds and bookkeeping; b. Aid dept., for local citizens; c. Aid dept., for foreign refugees; d. Provincial dept., with two subsidiaries: 1. for teachers, rabbis and officers from provincial towns; 2. for towns and small towns. The "Provincial dept." organised local committees. Dawid Rubenzahl managed its operations on behalf of the "Rescue Committee"; e. Food dept.; f. Footwear and clothing dept.; g. Children's daycare and girls' workshops. In accordance with the Governor general's order, children were not allowed to be taught in workshops and daycares; h. Sanitary dept.; j. Przemyśl town dept.

Mrs. Dr. Cecylia Klaften was granted consent by the Mayor Tadeusz Rutowski, to open workshops for young women, for which she obtained ten rooms on 23 Sykstuska Street. Other active women obtained ten sewing machines, and the first courses in tailoring, underwear sewing and millinery opened on 19th April 1915. The organisation was managed by Mrs. Dr. Klaften, as well as by Paulina Schweber, C. Landes, Dresdner, Dr. Ada Reichenstein and C. Wechsler. 150 [female] students attended the courses.

The Russians continued in their usual practice: they exiled the mixed descent individuals to Russia, including the community–leader Dr. Diamand, and the deputy mayor Dr. Filip Schleicher, and members of the Rescue Committee, Leon Appel, Szymon Peller and Dr. Oswald Zion.

The community and the Rescue Committee did not halt their activities, and looked after the poor.

With the unexpected flight by the Russians after their decisive defeat near Gorlice[–Tarnow] in May 1915, they left behind men and goods except for 600 pianos. On 22nd June 1915, the Austrian army marched into the town.

After the liberation, the Rescue Committee reorganised. Jakub Stroh was elected president and his deputies were Professor Zygmunt Bromberg–Bytkowski and Leon Wahl; Dr. Bernard Hausner – principal secretary, and Dawid Rubenzahl – his deputy. New members supplemented the veteran members of the committee.

By and by Lwów's public life returned to normal; the daily newspaper [*Lemberger*} *Tugblat* edited by Dr. Cwi [Tzvi] Bikeles was published again. The community resumed its normal activities. Dr. Emil Parnas headed the community and did so till the beginning of 1917. Dr. Ozjasz Wasser (1866–1939) was appointed his deputy. At the beginning of 1917, Dr. Stesłowicz, the government commissioner of Lwów's municipality, handed the control of the community to Dr. Jakub Diamand (1856–1936) who, at the end of 1916, returned to Lwów from captivity in Russia where he had been exiled for being of mixed descent. Dr. Diamand served as the community commissioner till November 1924. During his tenure he appointed a community council of ten members, two of whom were Zionists (Dr. Ringel and Oransz). The Zionist Federation renewed its work.

On 5th November 1916, Kaisers Wilhelm II and Franz–Joseph I declared the establishment of a Polish state (in Congress Poland). At the time, in a special declaration, Franz–Joseph I advised his Minister–President Dr. von Körber that as a reward for separating from the Polish state, and for the heavy losses it had suffered during the war, it was advisable to grant Galicia full autonomy. The Ukrainians demanded to separate eastern Galicia together with Bukovina and northern Hungary, and to establish there a Ukrainian sector.

Although the president of the "*Koło Polskie*" in the Austrian Parliament, Dr. Leon Biliński, emphasised that the Poles would maintain equal rights for the Jews of Galicia, their policies were still rooted in the ancient Polish tradition of Tadeusz Czacki and Margrave Wielopolski (1861) that strove to integrate the Jews within the Polish people, which meant assimilation. On the other hand, Dr. Kost Levytsky, president of the Ukrainian club in parliament, stressed that the Jews were Galicia's third ethnicity and that consequently there was no option but to grant them cultural autonomy, in line with the other national minorities.

Galicia's Zionists also pointed out that as a national minority the Jews had to be granted autonomy, and focused their political activities in that direction. The assimilated, led by Dr. Natan Löwenstein, stressed that the Jews were just a religious community, but nationally they were associated with the Polish people.

Hand in hand with their political activity, the Zionists who made up the majority on the Rescue Committee improved the economic and cultural standing. Dr. Izrael Waldmann published the daily newspaper

[Pages 341-342]

Lemberger Zeitung, which supported the Jews' national demands. The youth movements renewed their activities and began to organise a pioneering movement [for Aliyah].

Politically, the existing tension between the Poles and the Jews erupted in October 1918, after Kaiser Karl [I] declared a federal Austria, and came to a head during the Polish–Ukrainian war.

Thus began a difficult period in the history of Lwów's Jews.

The acting committee of the Zionist Federation of East–Galicia in 1935 (including N. Sokolow)

[Pages 385-386]

Original Footnotes:

a.   From 1894/5.

b.   At the time there were 80 Jewish charity and welfare societies in Lwów.

c.   *HaMagid* [The Herald], 1882, pp. 128–129. The *Charedi*m circles took no part in the welfare undertaking, and stood quite at some distance away from him.

d.   In Vol. II of this book.

e.   There were three schools and three kindergarten.

Notes: – CHAPTER 18

All notes in square brackets [ ] were made by the translator, or by the editor.
[The spelling of most names was taken from different published works by Dr. Majer Bałaban; from Lwów registers and from other publications of the period.]

1.   Dr. Stan. Gruiński: *Materyały do kwestyi żydowskiej* [*w Galicyi*] Lwów 1910.

2.   Incidences of Jewish girls kidnapped by nuns who put them in convents and forced them to convert, took place also at Lwów:
Regina Philipp, who came from Prague to Lwów to visit her grandfather Wolf Kreps, was kidnapped by nuns of the Basilian Monastery (Stryiska Street), in 1884, and only the emperor's order saw her release from the monastery. Known are also the 1899 cases of Stiegliz and Michalina Araten. Despite the parents' protests, the law–courts and the authorities were unable the extricate the girls from the monastery.

3.   Dr. Stan. Gruiński: *Zmiana wyznania we Lwowie 1868–1908*. Lwów 1908.

4.   Jozue Schorr dealt with shipments of the railway named after [Archduke] Karl Ludwig

5.   The Parnas family hailed from Podolia, their previous name was Rafalowicz. In 1806, they settled at Janów, near Trembowla [Terebovlia].

A.   In May 1890, a memorandum by *Agudas Achim* was published in *Ojczyzna*.

6.   Dr. Gruiński: *Materyały*

7.   Dr. Herman Frenkel (1831–1872) was a lawyer, member of the municipality and the town of Lwów's *Sejm* representative. He was on the community committee for several years.

8.   *Allgemeine Zeitung des Judenthums* 1868, p. 170.

9.   *Allg. Ztg. d. Judt.* 1867, p. 267.

10.   *Allg. Ztg. d. Judt.* 1872, p.127.

11.   The principal of *Szomer Izrael*, Dr. Josef Kohn, defined the programme in four German words: "Festhalten an der Verfassung [sustain the Constitution]" (*Der Israelit*, Lemberg 1874, Nr. 18).

A.   *Die Neuzeit.* [*Wochenschrift für politische, religöse und Kultur–Interessen*] Vienna. 1877, p.276

B.   He was arrested, as previously mentioned, with regard to the poisoning of Rabbi Kohn, and released a year later. He numbered among the leaders of the Orthodox even after his release, and pursued a bitter struggle against the Enlightened, in which he was supported by the Polish Nobles. He died at Lwów in the month of Sh'vat [January] (1873).

C.   Supporters of Rabbi Ettinger, and opponents of Rabbi Ornstein, published a lampoon headed: [in Yiddish] "An anecdote of the powerful Rabbi and his entire entourage" (1875). It relates that Rabbi Ornstein's supporters were the Enlightened and the wealthy families of Mieses, Landau, Horowitz and Chajes, interested in "misleading Lwów ("but they only want to lead Lemberg by the nose").
The author uncovers the family secrets of Rabbi Ornstein's relatives, and reminds the progressives of Rabbi Kohn's affair: "But where are the Enlightened? Where are they, where is the old German [Ashkenazi] party?
Where are the old Germans [Ashkenazis], the forty–eight?
Who knows the story of the preacher Kohn? [end]
The Vienna Jewish newspaper *Die Neuzeit*, edited by Szántó and Rabbi Dr. Jellinek, retorted bitterly. Immediately after his election, the paper published a lead article "Lwów's choice of two rabbis" (Issue 23, pp. 181–182), that considered his election a decline and capitulation to the demand of the Chassidim. As long as "he has not been purged of suspicion of participating in Rabbi Kohn's poisoning" he should not be permitted to occupy the role of Lwów's rabbi. An article penned at Lwów (Issue 25; 18th June 1875) discusses his grandfather, Rabbi Jakub–Meszulam Ornstein and his fight with the early *Maskilim*, and his attitude to *Shir*. Rabbi Cwi–Hirsz Ornstein was a son–in–law of Rabbi Jechiel–Mechal son of Rabbi Majer Kristiampoler, Head of Brody community's [religious] law–court. Majer Kristiampoler was the son–in–law of Aron, the author of *Minchat Aron* about the Sanhedrin, one of Brest–Litowsk's great [scholars].

12.   An article from Lwów of 5th July 1875, *Die Neuzeit*, Issue 28.

A.   W[iene]r Staatsarchiv Informationsbüro No. 6096/1, 1867; 292/dep. II e. a. 1869.

13.   Article from Lwów; *Allg. Ztg. d. Judt.* 1878, p. 421.

A.   *Allg. Ztg. d. Judt.* 1879, pp. 103–104.

14.   *Allg. Ztg. d. Judt.* 1879, p. 345.

16.   The wording of clause XV is: "Every church and religious denomination recognised by law, is permitted to perform its worship;
organise and manage its internal affairs, independently; maintain institutions, funds and bequests designated for its worship; charity and education and derive enjoyment from them. Like every other association, however, it will be subject to the laws of the land."

17.   *Statuten–Entwurf für die Israelitischen Cultusgemeinden in Galizien*, verfasst von Rabbiner Schreiber et Consorten, vorgelegt der Lemberger Rabbiner Versamlung. Lemberg 1882, 77 prg.

18.   On the sequence of the communities' statutes in 1888–1890, see my article: "Ein vergessenes Jubiläum [A forgotten anniversary]," in *Die Stimme* [The Voice]. Vienna 1930, No. 121.

19.   Article from Lwów, *Allg. Ztg. d. Just.* 1882, p. 262.

A.   In 1882, Jakob Mendel Schütz (1805–1882), member of Lwów's hospital management committee died. He left 20,000 Gulden to establish a loan fund to offer loans at 2% a year.

20.   The school for Jewish children named after Tadeusz Czacki, was established by Lwów's municipality in 1878. In 1885, it catered for 800 girls and 500 boys. Most of the teachers, male and female, were Christian. The pupils were known as "Czacki's youth."

21.   In 1890, 280 girls studied at the school; 1916 Jewish girls studied at general schools.

22.   Dr. Majer Bałaban: *Historja projektu szkoły Rabinów i nauki religji mojz. na ziemiach polskich.* Lwów, 1907 pp. 40–43.

23.   Vorschriften betreffend die Verfassung der Israelitischen Religionsgenossenschaft of 21 March 1890, Regierungsblatt 1890, 57.
Was published with annotations, together with the law on bestowing names and managing the register of Jews, by Dr. Leo Geller, Vienna 1896.

[Pages 387-388]

24.   Der Israelit, Lemberg 1892.

A.   His grandfather, Rabbi Sander, who was not granted the right of residency at Lwów, accepted the surname of the Lwów Jew Schmelkes, who had died with no issue. In this manner he settled at Lwów.
Rabbi Izak [Judah] Schmelkes was born at Lwów in 1827. His father, Rabbi Chaim Samuel who died young in 1839, was a distinguished member of the community and lived on Boimów Street. His mother, née Wahl, gave both her sons a traditional upbringing. Rabbi Izak who was exceptionally talented, studied at Lwów and later under Rabbi Szlomo Klüger, the rabbi of Rawa Ruska. Rabbi Józef Saul Natansohn was particularly interested in his education. Rabbi Izak started his working life as a grains merchant, but when he went bankrupt after losing his entire fortune in the Crimean War he agreed, with influence of his wife's Allerhand family, to accept a post of rabbi at Żurawno, in 1855. As the Austrian statutes required him to pass an examinations in psychology, pedagogy and philosophy, he was exempted from the gymnasium studies and successfully passed the Lwów University exams. In 1857, at the recommendation of the *Maggid* [Jewish mystical preacher] Klüger, he was accepted as a rabbi at Brzeżany, where he served at the rabbinate till 1868. During 1868–1894 he officiated as rabbi at Przemyśl and had many disciples. Rabbi Izak Schmelkes was known as a great scholar, especially after writing [the Responsa] *Bet Yitchak*. As he did not sympathise with the *Chassidism*, their *Admorim* [Rebbes] objected to his election as a rabbi at Kraków, preferring instead Rabbi Szymon Schreiber. Unlike Rabbi Szymon Schreiber, Rabbi Izak did not get involved in politics, dedicating himself solely to the study of the Torah. He died on [*Yom Kippur*] the Day of Atonement (1904). His only son Rabbi Aron Schmelkes who excelled in his talent, died aged 23; the pamphlet he had written, *Minchat Aron*, was published inside his father's *Bet Yitchak*. His only daughter, Haddassa, married his disciple Rabbi Natan Lewin of Brody, the Rabbi of Rzeszów [Resche]

B.   Born in 1831, Maurycy Lazarus went to Vienna to study at the painting academy, but he arrived there during the March 1848 Revolution. Due to the closure of the institutions of higher academic education, and unable to study at the academy, he enrolled instead at the advanced school of commerce. Having concluded his studies and training at Vienna, he returned to Lwów and worked for a banking institution. He was a founder member of Lwów's Mortgage Bank, and was its manager for some 40 years.
Together with Samuel Horowitz and Dr. Szymon Schaff, he bought up Brody's estates and established there a vast timber industry. He was also involved in Lwów's public life. In 1886, he became a member on the board of the Jewish hospital.

25.   For biographical details see the Chapter "History of Zionism at Lwów," in volume II of this book.

26.   Later on he was appointed professor of Semitic languages at Lwów Univeristy. From 1920 onwards he was chief Rabbi of Warsaw.

A.   Tätigkeit des Cultusrates 1898–1904, report.

27.   [Die] Neuzeit. 1893, No. 26

A.   Maksymiljan Goldstein – Dr. Karol Dresdner: *Kultura i sztuka ludu zydowskiego na ziemiach polskich.* Lwów 1935, pp. 116–122.
Oskar Aleksandrowicz: *Z pod pyłu zapomnienia.*
Baruch Dornhelm: *Opinja.*

28.   Bertha Pappenheim – Dr. Sara Rabinowitsch: *Zur Lage der jüdischen Bevölkerung in Galizien.* Frankfurt am Main 1904, p.15.

29.   Regarding the political life, see my article "The history of Zionism at Lwów," Vol. II of this book.

30.   Prof. S. Bromberg–Witkowski [*or* Bytkowski]: *Die Juden Lembergs unter der Russenherrschaft* – Jüdisches Archiv; Wien 1917. Part 8–9; p. 33.

31.   Dr. Jakub Schall: *Zydostwo galicyjskie w czasie inwazji rosyjskiej 1 (1914–1916).* Nasza Opinia 1936, No. 19.

32.   Dr. Jakub Diamand (1856–1936), a lawyer who was deputy chairman of the "Rigorozants Association [*Rygorozantów Stowarzyszenie*]" and took an active part in the life of the academic youth. During 1898–1907, he was the head of the board of the Temple of the Enlightened. From 1907 onwards he was a member of the community's management committee. During the First World War (1915), he was exiled to Russia for being of mixed descent. After his return in 1917, he was elected the Jewish community's commissioner till 1924. From 1924 till 1936 he was in charge of the community's registry office. He was member of the municipality and of the municipal education council for some 25 years.

33.   Dr. Filip Schleicher (1870–1932), a lawyer who took an active part in Lwów's public life. During 1905–1927, he was a member of the municipality; in 1913 he was elected deputy–mayor. He excelled in administrative abilities, and particularly in the municipal supply. In June 1915 the Russians exiled him to Kiev for being of mixed descent. In August 1916 he returned to Lwów and was appointed the town's governmental deputy–commissioner. In that capacity he organised supply and established dozens of soup–kitchens for the poor. With the Ukrainians' capture of Lwów and the disintegration of the Austrian monarchy, he was offered the post of Minister of Supply in the government of western Ukraine. However, as a patriotic Pole he declined. Dr. Schleicher was a principled assimilate and the Poles appointed him member of the government committees. In 1919 he was elected deputy–mayor and held the post till 1927. Dr. Schleicher was also involved in Jewish undertakings: he was member of the board of trustees of the "*Baron Hirsch Fund*" educational system. In 1929, the non–Zionists elected him council–member of the Jewish Agency.

34.   Dr. Bernard Hausner (1874–1935), born at Czortków; Dr. of Philosophy and accredited by the Vienna rabbinical seminary and founder member of the Vienna academic association *Bar Kochba*. From 1903 onwards he was a teacher of religion at Lwów's second gymnasium. During the First World War he was a military rabbi on the Italian front; an organiser on the Aid Committee [*Vaad Ha'Ezra*]. After 1918, he was an active member of the Zionist Movement and a leader of *HaMizrachi* in eastern Galicia. During 1923–1927 he was a member of the Polish *Sejm*; in 1927 he was appointed Poland's consul to Haifa, and later to Tel Aviv. He took an active part in the public life of Eretz Israel; published scientific articles in Polish, German and Hebrew. He penned the book "Grammar of the Hebrew Language," and wrote about [Juliusz] Słowacki and his treatment of scripture, Job and the Greek drama.

35.   Bohdan Janusz: *293 dni Rzadów rosyjskich we Lwówie*. Lwów 1915.
Rossowski: *Lwów w czasie inwazji rosyjskiej*. Lwów 1916.

36.   Dr. Jan Hupka. *Czas* No. 393; 28/VII 1915.
The community committee immediately published an announcement in *Czas* and in the other newspapers, signed by Jakub Stroh, that he had spent the entire occupation at Lwów, that all his utterances were untrue and false. The Russians persecuted the Jews precisely for their loyalty to Austria.
The Austrian parliamentary delegate, Heinrich Reizes, published an open letter to Dr. Hupka, who was also a parliamentary delegate, stating the those who published the announcement had lied purposely.

[Pages 389-390]

37.   Prof. Siegmund Bromberg Bytkowski: *Lemberger Bericht* "Jüdisches Archiv," Wien 1916, Part 4–5; pp. 2–6.
One can also find there a poem by a German prisoner on the redemption of prisoners by Jews, and one of the verses follows:

Als man sie (Deutsche) dann hat gefangen genomen
Haben die Juden schnell die Nachricht vernommen
Kaum brachten die Russen hierher den Transport
So waren die Deutschen aus den Reihen schon fort.

38.   And these are the members: 1. Leon Appel, 2. Adolf Birnbaum (estate owner), 3. Maurycy Brandstädter (industrialist), 4. Rabbi Braude, 5. Prof. Dr. Zygmunt Bromberg–Bytkowski, 6. Dr. Jakub Diamand (Lawyer), 7. Dr. Emmanuel Dresdner (member of the supreme law–court), 8. Szymon Feld (merchant), 9. Lazar Goldberg (house owner), 10. Dr. Bernard Hausner (Prof.), 11. Eliasz [Eliyahu] Hescheles, 12. Dr. Maurycy Hulles (lawyer), 13. Adolf Lindenberger (merchant), 15. Norbert Lilien (physician), 16. Dr. Herman Rabner (lawyer), 17. Salomon Mandel (Prof.), 18. Rabbi Meszulam Salat, 19. Leon Wahl (merchant), 20. Dr. Oswald Zion (physician).

[Pages 391-392]

II
The Religious Life

Rabbis and Heads of Yeshivahs[1]

by Rabbi Reuven Margulies

Translated by Myra Yael Ecker

Edited by Karen Leon

Lwów's Jewish community is long standing. The "Lemberg *Chevra Kadisha* [Jewish burial society], May his creator preserve and revive him,"[2] was known throughout the diaspora as early as the end of the second century. However, the names of its spiritual leaders, teachers and children's Torah instructors, remain unknown. The first mention of a rabbi and head of the Beth Din [religious law-court] appeared in 5263 (1503), naming Rabbi Levy ben Rabbi Jakób Kikenes, but there are no details of his life or of his undertakings. The view of his contemporaries about him is inscribed on his gravestone: "Angels held the Holy Ark, angels soared the cliffs, and our crown, the crown of Israel, was removed from our head. The champion, the great scholar [*Gaon*], the centre of the diaspora, our teacher, Rabbi Levy son of the great scholar our teacher, Rabbi Jakób Kikenes, scion of the prophet Jonah, head of the rabbinical court and head of the Yeshivah of P... who dispense justice and charity, taught the Torah to Jewish children and created many disciples... Died on the first day of Passover 5263 [11.4.1503].["]

5282 (1522). R' Abraham ben Rabbi Jechiel of Cologne. "He is Abraham in his righteousness, from first to last. He gladly dispenses charity and justice. The great champion of the Torah, the great *Dayan* [Rabbinical judge], he was amongst those expelled from Portugal, and one of the Provence Sages [*Chachamim*]. He passed honourable sentences and taught the Torah all his life. He lived in the *Kollel* [advanced Judaic studies' college] and studied with his prestigious Yeshivah students. Ascended to heaven on the first day of Sukkot [Tabernacles] 5282 [16.9.1521]."

5316 (1556). Rabbi Juda Leibben R' Menachem. "A Lion ascended the mysteries of the Torah. Head of Yeshivah, who delved into the 1520

Halachah [Jewish law] and many imbibed his profusion, the source of wisdom... 3rd Av 5316 [10.7.1556].

5320 (1560). Rabbi Kalman of Worms. The first Rabbi to serve both communities [of Lwów]. In the preface to *Yam shel Shlomo* [Sea of Solomon] about the *Chulin* Tractate of the *Mishnah*, he is described as: "Aged and seated at the Yeshivah. The glory of Israel and its great scholar, its king, its master, the esteemed great scholar, our teacher and rabbi, Rabbi Kalman of Worms, the light of whose teaching shone over the holy community of Lwów, the great and important town, the centre of Jewish life." (Several of his responses, and those of his son-in-law, the great scholar, Rabbi Eleazar [Eliezer] ben R' Manoach, were published in the *Responsa* anthology of Rabbi Mojżesz Isserles).

In Rabbi Dovid [Solomon] Gans's chronicle, *Cemach Dawid* [*Tzemach David* = David's Scion (1592)], and in *Seder HaDorot* [The Generations Order] Part I, by Rabbi Jechiel Heilpern, under the entry for Rabbi [Szalom] Szachna [Shachna], three heads of Yeshivah are listed for Lwów, of that time: Rabbi Kalman of Worms, Rabbi Kalman [Kalonymus] Haberkasten, and Rabbi Juda Karowiec [Karowitz]. It is possible that Rabbi Kalman Haberkasten succeeded Rabbi Kalman of Worms, and that Rabbi Juda Karowiec followed him to the post. This last Rabbi Juda, is Rabbi Juda Karo [Caro], known in Poland as "Karowiec." For forty two years Rabbi Kalman of Worms taught the Torah within the town, as a quorum [*Minyan*]. "Who could praise and speak his glory. A man who dedicated his entire life to God. God's teaching was his expertise. He coveted no monetary gain. Saintly secrets were soon revealed to the Sage. He departed on 2 Iyar 5320 [28 March 1560]."

5332 (1572). Rabbi Juda Leibben R' Moses. Prominent in the Jewish community. Head of Yeshivah and head of rabbinical court. Died on 1 Elul 5332 [10 August 1572].

5340 (1580). Rabbi Benjamin ben R' Moses. "Held a sermon over every calligraphic embellishment in the bountiful *Halachah* [Jewish law]. He was said to be saintly. All great men of his generation trusted his word on questions about the Almighty. He wrote the book *Tav'nit HaBayit*, and *Ohel Shel Simcha*... [A Tent of Joy...]. 2 Nissan 5340 [18 March 1580]."
5340 (1580). Rabbi Mojżesz ben Mardochaj Askenazy [Aszkenazy]. First head of the rabbinical court outside the town. He was engaged in charitable giving and fair judgements. He taught the Torah to the community, from which many benefitted. He served God wholeheartedly, and enlightened Jews with his teaching... 7 Nissan 5340 [23 March 1580].

5342 (1582). R' Naftali Hirc [Hirtz] ben R' Nachman, head of Yeshivah. He taught many students, some of whom turned into great rabbis. He wrote a short commentary on *Midrash Rabba* on the Torah, the Song of Songs, Lamentations, Ecclesiastes and the Book of Esther. 18 Nissan 5342 [10 April 1582].

5342 (1582). R' Aszer ben Izak Kohn, head of rabbinical court and head of Yeshivah. Rabbi of both communities, succeeding Rabbi Kalman of Worms head of *Chevra Kadisha*. He was one of the synagogue treasurers, like R' Pinkas [Pinchas] ben Jair [Ya'ir]… 30 Nissan 5342 [22 April 1582]. His son, Rabbi Jakób Koppel, served as rabbi outside the town during 1620-1630.

5352 (1592). R' Eleazar [Eliezer] ben Mojżesz,

[Pages 393-394]

head of Yeshivah of a group of experts in the Torah and he was engaged in good deeds. A collector of charity and benevolence for the poor and needy. 1 Tamuz 5352 [11 June 1592].

5356 (1596). R' Józef ben R' Szmuel, was at Yeshivahs of several communities and especially of Lwów. Fought as a lion for the Torah. 30 Sivan 5356 [26 June 1596].

5359 (1599). Rabbi Izak Eizyk ben R' Jechiel the saintly. He was the last rabbi of both communities, succeeding Aszer [Asher] ben Izak Kohn. He was head of Yeshivah, and president the of rabbinical court. The large Tamarisk tree. The glory of Israel. 9 Tishrei 5359 [9 October 1598].

5369 (1609). Rabbi Mojżesz ben R' Aron. Mojżesz was a righteous man, steeped in the Torah and God-fearing. He had great powers of deducing the Torah through argumentation, and reasoned according to the *Halachah*. He was at Yeshivahs of various communities, settling at a Yeshivah where argument was settled according to the Torah… 2nd day of Sukkot, [16 Tishrei] 5369 [26 Sept. 1608].

5371 (1610). Rabbi Chanoch Hendel ben R' Shemarja [Szmarja], head of Yeshivah and leader of the diaspora's Jews. Mighty shepherd, his signals were great and his example, mighty. Brimming with every wisdom… 1st day of Rosh HaSahanna [1 Tishrei] 5371 [18 Sept. 1610]. 5373 (1613). Rabbi Jehuda [Juda] Leibben R' Mojżesz, expert in the secrets of the revealed and the concealed Torah. First head of rabbinical court at Podhajce [Pidhaitsi], and later head of Yeshivah at Lwów. 11 Cheshvan 5373 [6.10.1612].

5373 (1613). Rabbi Mojżesz ben R' Józef, head of Yeshivah in our great community, a town of *Chachamim* and writers. He drew spring-water out of a well, and answered his inquirers with the word of God, the Jewish law [*Halachah*]. 12 Sivan 5373 [1.6.1613].

5374 (1614). Rabbi Jozue Falk ben R' Aleksander HaKohen. A pupil of Mojżesz Isserles, and of Salomon Lurie, he married the daughter of Izrael Parnas of Lwów, who set aside a large house for him where he studied with great rabbis, whom he supported. He was appointed rabbi at Ludmir [Włodzimierz Wołyński], and he returned to Lwów as head of Yeshivah. Amongst his students were R' Jozue, the author of *Megine Schlomoh* [Defenders of Solomon], R. Abraham Schrenzel [Szrencel], author of *Ethan Haezrachi,* Rabbi Jesaja Halevy Horowitz [Hurwitz], author of *Shne Luchot HaBrit* [The Two Tablets of the Covenant] and others. Many regulations were issued, by the Council of The Four Lands, in his name. He dedicated twenty five years to the writing of his great works, *Sefer Meirat Enayim*, and *Drisha VePrisha* about the work *Arba'a-Turim* [Four-columns about the *Halachah*]. He also wrote other books, some of which were burnt, and some of which remained in manuscript form. "A great scholar [*gaon*] and God-fearing, crowned by all four crowns: Torah, leadership, sovereignty, and the good name he made for himself. He was at several Yeshivahs, he settled disputes, dispensed charity and generosity. He taught righteous and devout students, and before his light was extinguished, he made adjustments and amendments to regulations for his generation. Reached eternal life on 19 Nisan 5374 [25 March 1614].[A]

5376 (1616). Rabbi Majer ben Rabbi Gedalia of Lublin. Born in 5318 (1558), he was appointed head of Yeshivah in his home town Lublin at the age of twenty four. Aged twenty nine, he was accepted as head of the Yeshivah of Kraków, replacing his father-in-law, Rabbi Izak Schapira. At the age of thirty seven, he was appointed as head of the Yeshivah at Lwów, and head of the rabbinical court for the district of Lwów, a post which he held for eighteen years. In 5373 [1612/13], he returned to the town of his birth, Lublin, as rabbi, head of the rabbinical court and as head of Yeshivah. In one of his responses (Amendment 88), he states: "Glory be to God, I have taught many honest students about all the old great scholars, and most of my students are today heads of Yeshivah and teachers of Jewish studies."

His reputation among the scholars of his generation can be derived from the letter of Rabbi Jochanan of Halicz [Halych], where he describes him as "A holy righteous man, king of Israel. Ever since our holy Rabbi, no one has combined both Torah and greatness, in one and the same place. A great light, his support, a great scholar like our teacher and rabbi, Rabbi Majerhead of Yeshivah and leader of rabbinical court of the holy community of Lwów and its district." Of the books which he had written, the ones published were: *Meir Eynei Chachamim*, Tractate Innovations, and his *Responsa*. His soul rested on 16 Iyar 5376 [3 May 1616]. The Chariot of Israel, and his horsemen. He enlightens the people and its holy men. The light of wise and honest men. Unique in our generation among the Hebrews. Head of the committee of the elected… Speaker and judge of the difficult and serious. They responded to him in books. He showed his expertise in hidden wisdom… and an author for the last generation, level-headed like Moses and Ahron."

R' Józef (Kazi), headed the rabbinical court for the entire land of Podolia. When our teacher, the rabbi, Rabbi Majer of Lublin, recalled his dispute with one of the great scholars of his generation, who responded to a Jewish law [halachic] ruling which he had determined, the Rabbi said: "I repeated my initial answer and presented it to the great scholars [Chachamim] of our generation, and they consented with all I said. All the elder and great teachers, the great scholars [geonim] in Poland and Lithuania, who included the great scholar, our teacher, the rabbi, Rabbi Mardochaj [Mordechai] Jaffe, may the creator safeguard and give him a long life, head of the rabbinical court of the holy community of Poznań; the wondrous great scholar [gaon] our teacher and rabbi, Rabbi Mojżesz, head of the Kraków rabbinical court; the wondrous great scholar [gaon] in the Torah and devoutness, out teacher, the rabbi, Rabbi Leib, head of the rabbinical court of the holy community of Brisk and of the whole of Lithuania; the great scholar [gaon], our teacher and rabbi, Rabbi Józef, may the creator safeguard and give him a long life, head of the rabbinical court of Lwów and the entire land of Podolia." There are no further details about his life and undertakings. Later on he was a rabbi at Poznań, where he died. His son, Salomon Zelman, died at Lwów on 23 Tevet 5373 [16.1.1613].

5379 (1619). R' Izrael Eleazar [Eliezer] ben R' Mojżesz Abraham Graupen, an excellent rabbinical judge and head of the rabbinical court, taught

[Pages 395-396]

God's congregation, honest rules and laws. He taught and guided them in God's piety. 29 Sh'vat 5382 [11.1.1622]

5382 (1622). R' Natan ben R' Eleazer [Eliezer], physician. "He held a sermon over every thorn and mound in the *Halachah* [Jewish law]. Head of Yeshivah, he was one of the greatest rabbinical judges. He died on Chanukah 5382 [Dec. 1621].

5382 (1622). R' Abraham ben R' Dawid, "A righteous, holy and pure man, head of ritual court, leader of the wise, who wrote an interpretation of the works by [R' Isaac] Alfasi [al-Fasi]and by [R'] Mardochaj [Mordechai ben Hillel]. He also commented on the book *Akedat Yitzchak* [The binding of Isaac]. He taught students, great Jewish men, and responded to the inquirers into God's law. 5 Av 5382 [12.7.1622].

5389 (1629). R' Majer ben R' Naftali Hirc [Hirtz], head of Yeshivah. Like Abaye [Nachmani], R' Naftali Hirc ben R' Menachem wrote a commentary on *Midrash Rabba* [*Talmud*ic legends based on verses from the Torah]. He exerted himself in the Torah like a lion and a lioness. Exalted in Chassidism and with much knowledge in the occult. 2 Tevet 5389 [28.12.1628].

5389 (1629). R' Józef ben R' Jechiel, head of Yeshivah, and head of rabbinical court. Minister of the Torah, who knew the secrets of the Torah. He studied and amended interpretations and compositions on most parts of the *Mishnah* and the *Talmud*. 1 Av 5389 [21.7.1629].

5390 (1630). R' Jakób Koppel ben R' Aszer [Asher] Ansel HaKohen. One of those exiled from Spain, his lineage extended as far back as the priest [Kohen] Ezra. He taught and augmented the knowledge of the Torah amongst the Jewish People. In 5350 [1589/90], he signed the regulations at the *Gromnice* fair [the Candlemas, winter fair], as "Rabbi Koppel from the Lemberg allotment," and in 5380 (1620) he was made head of the rabbinical court outside the town (succeeding R' Mojżesz ben R' Mardochaj Askenasy [Aszkenazy]). Later on he was also promoted to leader of the rabbinical court within the town. A faithful shepherd who was invited to join the Yeshivah of heaven. Died 23 Tishrei 5380 [10.10.1629].

5390 (1630). R' Izrael ben Mojżesz Charif. A great Torah scholar [gaon], minister of the Torah, legislator for the Jewish People, a great Chassid, a charity collector. Died on 23 Av 5390 [1.8.1630]. R' Koppel Kalmankes (of the Lemberg [Lwów] suburb) is also mentioned as head of the rabbinical court and head of Yeshivah, at about the same time. He (Rabbi Koppel), together with 30 rabbis, signed a ban on payment for joining the rabbinate.

5391 (1631). R' Jakób ben Eleazer Kikenes, one of the descendants of the prophet Jonah. A holy and pure man, head of Yeshivah who wrote several essays. He died on *Hoshanah Raba* [the last day of Sukkot =Tabernacles] 5391 [28.9.1930].

5391 (1631). R' Mardochaj [Mordechai] ben R' Natan Neta HaKohen, was at first head of rabbinical court and head of Yeshivah at Brzeżany [Brzeziny]. Later on, he was head of Yeshivah at Lwów. A friend of Abraham Chaim Schorr, author of *Torat Chaim*, he collaborated with him on the writing of the book *Tzon Kodashim* [Sacrificial Lambs]. Dedicated to Chassidism, he was a righteous man. After the prayer of forgiveness for the charitable dowry of a needy bride, on 21 Tishrei 5391 [27.9.1630], he was swept up to heaven.

5391 (1631). R' Mardochaj [Mordechai] ben R' Dawid Katz, head of Yeshivah. A big man. Good in disputation over the *Mishnah* and the *G'marah*, in reasoned argumentation and hypotheses. He dived into the sea of the *Talmud* and retrieved jewels. An aged man who gained wisdom, day and night, through incessant reiterations. He attained old age. 1 Nissan 5391 [3.4.1631].

5391 (1631). R' Jekusiel Zelman [Jekutiel Zalman] ben R' Chanoch. A righteous man, devout and holy. Head of Yeshivah who pursued deep argumentation. 3 Tamuz 5391 [3.7.1631].

5391 (1631). R' Juda Löw ben R' Jakób Segal Epstein. A rabbinical judge [*Dayan*] and head of rabbinical court who kept a Yeshivah and taught the Torah. 1 Elul 5391 [29.8.1631].

5396 (1636). R' Elijah [Eliasz] ben R' Abraham Kalmankes, head of Yeshivah and head of rabbinical court. He was the first rabbi within the town, after the rabbinate had been split up. An active member in the Council of Four Lands. "As he approached the Holy Ark, holding a sermon and clarifying the departure of the bird released on the day of purification. While walking back and forth, imparting innovations of the Torah, his soul rose in holiness and purity out of the words of the Torah." 8 Nissan 5396 [13.4.1636].

5396 (1636). R' Mardochaj [Mordechai] ben Cwi [Tzvi Hirsz Askenazy [Aszkenazy]. During 1630-1636, he was rabbi of the community outside the town, succeeding R' Jakób Koppel ben R' Aszer [Asher] Kohen. "A great scholar [*gaon*] of his generation, wholly infused with God's law, who delved into disputation in greatness and wisdom. He passed fair judgements and taught the Torah to Jews and had many pupils. Died on the first day of Pessach 5396 [20.4.1636].

5397 (1637). R' Juda [Jehudah] ben R' Szmaja. A righteous and holy man. A kabbalist, expert in the Torah, head of rabbinical court and an excellent judge. He established a Yeshivah at home, and endlessly repeated the Talmud, out loud. 7 Nissan 5397 [1.4.1637].

5397 (1637). R' (Józef Jakób) Abraham ben R' Joel Aszkenazy Neustettel-Katzenellenbogen. He headed the rabbinical court for forty-four years, and for twenty three years he served as head of Yeshivah and teacher of Jewish law at Lwów. Leader of Sages [*Chachamin*]. Silver-tongued, scholarly speech, light of the brave, mild and severe invisible trends. Just like his greatness, so was his modesty throughout his entire life. His grandson, the author of *K'neset Jecheskiel*, described him as "The great eagle, one in a generation." 6 Iyar 5397 [30.4.1637].

5398 (1638). R' Majer ben R' Józef, head of rabbinical court and head of Yeshivah. The ultimate leader of his generation. Full of wisdom and learning, he wrote many essays. Second day of Rosh HaShana 5398 [20.9.1637].

5398 (1638). R' Salomon [Szloma] Charif ben R' Izak Abraham Halevy. Son-in-law of the author of *She'erit Yosef*, brother-in-law of Rabbi Mojżesz Isserles, he served at the rabbinate of Lwów (within the town, succeeding Rabbi Elijah [Eliasz] ben R' Abraham Kalmankes). During the period of the author of *Magine Shelomoh* [Defenders of Solomon; Jozue Heszel [Höschel], and of R' Abraham Schrenzel [Szrencel] , aged, he continued studying at Yeshivahs

[Pages 397-398]

of the great and glorious communities for forty years. He taught righteous students, many of whom lead Yeshivahs, and Solomon's wisdom rose over the ancients. He was exalted in his devotion and appealing attributes, and all his deeds were in the service of God. 26 Cheshvan 5398 [13.12.1637].

5399 (1639). R' Dawid Tebele ben R' Szmuel, master of the Torah and of piety. Head of Yeshivah and a great rabbinical judge [*Dayan* Second day Chol HaMoed Pessach 5399 [2.4.1638].

5400 (1640) R' Mojżeszben R' Dawid Halevy Horowitz, head of Yeshivah. His heart was full of wisdom, knowledge and science, and no reason or secrecy escaped him. 1 Elul 5400 [19.8.1640].

5401 (1641). R' Süsskind ben Elchanan Halevy. A leading educator, head of rabbinical court and head of Yeshivah. He delved deeply into disputation over the six parts of the *Mishnah*, dived into the sea of the Talmud, and taught students, many of whom turned into great men in the Torah. 13 Nissan 5401 [13.4.1642].

5402 (1642). R' Cwi [Tzvi] Hirsz ben R' Natan, holy scion. Champion in the Torah, a great rabbinical judge. He passed fair judgement and regularly taught the Torah at his renowned Yeshivah. 1 Nissan 5402 [1.4.1642].

5402 (1642). R' Jakób ben R' Eljakim [Eljakum] Heilpern, a scholar who reasoned according to the *Halachah* [Jewish law]. He was head of Yeshivah and taught many great students. 18 Elul between 5401-5405 [September 1641-45].

5403 (1643). R' Majer ben Abraham of the Levy family. An excellent rabbinical judge and head of Yeshivah. One of the leading teachers. 2 Kislev 5403 [24.11.1642].

5403 (1643). R' Aron Abba ben Jochanan Halevy. For 35 years rabbinical judge and head of Yeshivah, at Lwów. Master of the Torah, pillar of tuition. He taught men who became great Jewish scholars. 1 Tamuz 5403 [18.6.1643].

5405 (1645). R' Abraham ben R' Majer, holy scion. Son-in-law of R' Natan Schapira, author of *Megale Amukot* [Revealer of the Depths]. He was promoted to rabbi at Bar [Ukraine]. Later he was accepted as head of Yeshivah at Lwów, while his father, R' Majer, was the rabbi and head of rabbinical court within the town, 1638-1654. He did not last long, however, dying during his father's life. 16 Tishrei 5405 [16.10.1644].

5405 (1645). R' Izrael Isser ben R' Simcha Bunim. Grandson of Rabbi Mojżesz Isserles, disciple of R' Joel Sirkis,[Serkes] author of *Bayit Chadash*. Head of rabbinical court at Opatów, where he was appointed as head of Yeshivah at Lwów. The Torah pouch, leader of the herd... Second day of Sukkot 5405 [16.10.1644].

5405 (1645). R' Samson ben R' Kalonymus. One of the greatest teachers, head of rabbinical court. 13 Adar 5405 [13.3.1645].

5405 (1645). R' Meszulam ben R' Abraham Salzburg. Head of Yeshivah, leader of rabbinical court and teacher of Jewish law, outside the town, who succeeded R' Jozue [Joshua] ben Józef, author of *Magine Shelomoh* and *Pneh Jesua*. "He paid attention to the ancestral religion, ensuring that neither its body nor its roots were tempered with, and he led his People from banning, to allocating.["] 8 Iyar 5405 [4.5.1645].

5405 (1645). R' Abraham ben Azrjel [Azriel]. Head of Yeshivah, community trustee, head and leader of the Council of Four Lands. A *Magid Mesharim* [Preacher of righteousness] for the society *Shomrim LaBoker* [Chewra szomrim laboker]. A prominent preacher, head of the holy society, who was fluent in most parts of the *Talmud* with commentary by Rabbi Isaac Alfasi [al-Fasi; *Rif*], and by Rabbi Abraham ben David [*RaBad*]. Brother-in-law of the author of *Magine Shelomoh* [Jozue Heszel [Höschel]. 13 Elul 5405 [4.9.1645].

5408 (1648). R' Mojżesz ben R' Elijah [Eliasz]. Master of the Torah, he was head of Yeshivah for 24 years. Prominent among those pursuing disputations over the *Mishnah*, the *G'marah* and reasoned argumentation. *Shushan Purim* 5408 [9.3.1648].

5408 (1648). R' Isaiah [Izajasz] ben R' Jecheskiel. An exceptional and courageous rabbinical judge, who led his community with wisdom, reason and knowledge, and who reprimanded fairly. 13 Adar 5408 [7.3.1648].

5408 (1648). R' Jozue [Joshua] ben Józef. A disciple of our teacher Rabbi Majer of Lublin and the author of *Sefer Meirat Enayim* who was promoted to rabbi and head of Yeshivah at Tykocin [Tykotzin], Grodno, and was accepted as head of rabbinical court at Przemyśl. Later on, he served at the rabbinate of Lwów outside the town walls. From there he moved to Kraków to replace the [author of] *Megale Amukot*, as head of Yeshivah. When R' Jomtob [Yom Tov] Lipman Heller, author of *Tosafot Jomtob* arrived at Kraków, he was appointed as second head of Yeshivah to R' Jozue. As R' Jozue was wealthy and did not receive a salary from the community, while R' Jomtob had lost his assets, R' Jozue gave all his income to R' Jomtob. He was also appointed as rabbi at Kraków. R' Jozue taught the Torah to his disciples. These included R' Shabbatai Kohn, author of *Siftei Kohen*, the author of *Avodat HaGershuni* [R' Gerszon Ashkenazi], the author of *Ateret Zekenim* [R' Menachem Mendel Auerbach], and others. He wrote the book *Megine Schlomoh*, to clarify the contradictions in the *Tosafot* [annotations to the *Talmud*] about *Rashi*, and the responsa, *Pneh Josua*. He died in Kraków, 27 Av 5408 [16.8.1648].

5409 (1649). R' Abraham ben R' Mojżesz Askenazy [Aszkenazy]-Heilprin [Heilpron]. Brother-in-law of our great teacher Rabbi Samuel Eideles *MaHaRaSh*. He was born in 5338 [1577/8]. Head of the rabbinical court at Lwów, he wrote the book *Ahavat Tzion* about the entire Bible [*Tanach*], out of which the section about the Torah and the Scrolls [*Megilot*] was published (Lublin 5399 [1638-9]). He was exemplary in all aspects, in the Torah, in piety and in modesty. 19 Sh'vat 5409 [1.2.1649].

5409 (1649). R' Mojżesz Meisels [Meizels] ben R' Isak Askenazy who set a fence and prevented disaster. An excellent rabbinical judge, he enlightened the Jewish People with his teachings. 21 Tevet 5409 [5.1.1949].

5409 (1649). R' Samuel (Shmaria [Szmarja]) ben R' Eleazar [Eliezer]. He led the Yeshovahs of various communities, and taught many outstanding disciples. 27 Tevet 5409 [11.1.1649].

5409 (1649). R' Isaac, an Austrian man,

[Pages 399-400]

head of Yeshivah, and head of the rabbinical court. One of the great teachers who was a good speaker. 13 Av 3409 [22.7.1649].

5411 (1651). R' Matitjahu [Mattathias] ben R' Sinai. Head of Yeshivah and an influential rabbinical judge, he taught and guided his generation. Devout and humble, he was among the followers of Hillel. 7 Kislev 5411 [1.12.1650].

5411 (1651). R' Eleazar [Eliezer] Lipman ben R' Akiba. A leading figure, an exceptional great scholar [*gaon*] and a Kabbalist. Aged thirty-two, he immersed himself in the Torah, deeper than a veteran disciple. 7 Kislev 5411 [29.1.1651].

5411 (1651]. R' Abraham ben R' Izrael Jechiel Katz Rappoport-Schrenzel [Szrencel]. His father, R' Izrael Jechiel, was one of the greatest Torah scholars in Kraków. When his son, R' Abraham, turned thirteen, he held a sermon at the great synagogue of Kraków, and the biblical interpretation by this wise youth was later published in the book *Naki Kapayim* (Kraków 5411 [1597/8]). When he married the daughter of R' Mardochaj Szrencel of Lwów, R' Abraham also settled at Lwów and studied Torah under *Sefer Meirat Enayim* [Rabbi Jozue Falk Kohn]. He spent much time at the Yeshivah and used his fortune to provide for his disciples. He was appointed town rabbi and collector of dues [*Gabai*] for Eretz Israel. Minister and influential, father and benefactor, he wrote the book *Ethan HaEzrachi*, which, apart from its significance in the decision of the *Halachah* [Jewish law], it is an important source of Jewish history in his time, and of the history of the sages during his period. 18 Sivan 5411 [7.6.1651].

5411 (1651). R' Aron ben R' Pinkas. He was head of Yeshivah and an influential rabbinical Judge. Greatly devout, he prayed with his entire being. 28 Tamuz 5411 [17.7.1651].

5412 (1652). R' Józef ben R' Eljakim [Eliakim] Goetz [Giec], son-in-law of our teacher Rabbi Majer [MaHaRaM] of Lublin. He was head of the rabbinical court outside the town 1645-1652, head of Yeshivah for an extensive congregation. 17 Tishrei 5412 [2.10.1651].

5412 (1652). R' Jakób ben R' Józef Izrael of the house of Abraham Schrenzel [Szrencel]. Extreme in Chassidism, sanctity and purity. He was head of rabbinical court and an excellent rabbinical judge of the Council of Four Lands. 12 Av 5412 [17.7.1652].

5413 (1653). R' Jezajasz [Ishaiah] ben R' Józef. Head of Yeshivah and an influential rabbinical judge. He strengthened the status of the faith, and many followed him. First day of Chanukah 5413 [25.11.1653].

5413 (1653) R' Józef Jozue Heszel [Heschel] Ben R' Benjamin. Minister of the Torah, head of Yeshivah. Aged forty-two, he ascended to heaven. 24 Adar A, 5413 [21.2. 1653].

5414 (1654). R' Majer ben R' Abraham, holy scion. He succeeded R' Salomon [Szloma] Charif as Rabbi within the town (during 1638-1654). Eminent in every wisdom and Chassidism. Lighting mirror of the capital, head of Yeshivah and leader of rabbinical court. He assisted the needy, his righteousness contemplative as that of one who is aged. 20 Kislev 5414 [10.12.1653].

5414 (1654). R' Cwi Hirsz [Tzvi] Hirsch] ben R' Juda Leib Pfefferkorn. He enlightened the Jews with his teaching. He elucidated speculations, according to the *Halachah*. An excellent *Dayan*. First day of Chanukah 5414 [15.12.1653].

5417 (1657). R' Cwi Hirsz [Tzvi] Hirsch] ben Aron Szalom [Shalom] Segal. He was at Yeshivahs of several communities, studying day and night. 6 Tevet 5417 [16.12.1656].

5418 (1658). R' Naftali ben R' Cwi Hirsz [Tzvi Hirsch]]. A disciple of the author of *Sefer Meirat Enayim*. Fluent in the adjudicative literature, and in most parts of the *Mishnah* and of R' Isaac Alfasi

-Fasi; *Rif*]. He was one of the foremost rabbinical judges [*Dayanim*]. 22 Tishrei 5418 [29.9.1657].

5418 (1658). R' Józef ben R' Abraham Heinisch. He was head of the rabbinical court and head of Yeshivah. He engaged in deep debates on the Bible. 29 Tevet 5418 [4.1. 1658].

5419 (1659). R' Mordechaj Mendel ben R' Menachem Mendel. One of the greatest instructors, and excellent rabbinical judge who engaged in deep debates on the Bible. 7 Tevet 5419 [2.12.1658].

5419 (1659). R' Józef ben R' Natan Halevy Heller, the brother of R' Jomtob Lipman [Heller], author of *Tosafot Jomtow* [*Yomtov*]. Head of rabbinical court and head of Yeshivah. A man imbued with God's spirit to lead the community members and to stabilise the status of the faith. 29 Tevet 5419 [24.1.1659].

5420 (1660). R' Jakób ben Abraham Jakób, Josef Aschkenasi Katzenellenbogen [Kacenelenbogen], who filled his father's place in the Torah. Head of rabbinical court and head of Yeshivah, he was wise and devout and led his community, wisely. 13 Adar 5420 [25.2.1660].

5424 (1664). Thirty-six righteous and holy men. During the terrible massacre led by the oppressors between 8 Iyar and 24 Sivan 5424 [3.5.1664-17.6.1664], about one hundred men were murdered, among them the leading lights in the Torah and heads of Yeshivahs . Of these holy men we know the names: On 8th Iyar: R' Abraham ben Józef (head of Yeshivah at Kołomyja [Kolomyja; Kolomea]); R' Aron Jechiel ben R' Aszer (head of Yeshivah); R' Eleazar [Eliezer] ben R' Szmuel; R' Eleazar ben R' Avigdor; R' Baruch ben R' Mordechaj; R' Dawid ben R' Izak Nechamisch; R' Zacharyasz [Zecharia] ben R' Jakób; R'Chaim ben R' Baruch; R' Chaim ben R' Mojżesz Halevy; R' Juda Leib ben R' Szmul Katz Margulies (Rabbi at Przemyśl, one of the great *Dayanim* and head of Yeshivah at Lwów); R' Izak ben R' Jakób; R' Majer [Meir] ben R' Menachem Chazan Halevy; R' Menachem ben R' Izak (head of Yeshivah); R' Mordechaj Ben R' Jechiel (head and leader of the State); R' Mordechaj ben R'

Salomon (head of Yeshivah); R' Mojżesz ben Abraham; R' Mojżesz ben R' Szalom; R' Mojżesz Moszko ben R' Chaim (head of Yeshivah); R' Nachman ben R' Salomon; R' Ozer ben R' Salomon; R' Azriel ben R' Avigdor; R' Salomon ben R' Dawid; R' Salomon ben R' Szmuel; R' Szalom ben R' Nissan; R' Szmuel ben R' Juda (head and leader of the State); R' Szmuel ben Józef Chajes [Chajut] (cantor at the synagogue outside the town. He was murdered during his prayer); R' Simon ben R' Majer; R' Samson ben R' Becalel [Bezalel] (head of rabbinical court and head of Yeshivah of several communities). All were martyred for keeping their faith. 8 Iyar 5424 [3.5.1664].

[Pages 401-402]

On 10th Iyar: R' Cwi Hirsz [Tzvi] Hirsch ben R' Abraham Katz (the great author of the Jewish People. An outstanding rabbinical judge).

On 11th Iyar: R' Abraham ben R' Salomon (rabbinical judge and head of Yeshivah. A Chassidwith the mellifluous voice of the Levite poets at the Temple).

On 13th Iyar: R' Aron ben R' Lapides (An excellent rabbinical judge who was murdered, together with his wife, in their home, while in their beds).

On 14th Iyar: R' Eleazar [Eliezer] and R' Izak, sons of R' Eliasz [Elijah] (Exalted disciples who study regular lessons with their students).

On 8th Sivan: R' Izak ben R' Mordechaj (rabbinical judge and head of rabbinical court).

On 20th Sivan: R' Chaim ben R' Mordechaj (his life was cut short, he immersed himself in the study of the Torah like a hundred years' old scholar).

5424 (1664). R' Mojżesz ben R' Abraham. Leader of the rabbinical court at Byerazino [Berezyna; Berezin], and later head of the rabbinical court at Lwów. A pocket Torah, leader of the pack, cedar of Lebanon who wholeheartedly worshipped God through the Torah and in prayer. 29 Av 5424 [20.8.1664].

5425 (1665). R' Isaiah [Izajasz] ben R' Izak. Head of the rabbinical court at Żółkiew and later head of Yeshivah at Lwów, head of the *Chevra Kadisha* [burial society]. 1 Adar 5425 [16.2.1665].

5425 (1665). R' Mojżesz, head of Yeshivah, devout and saintly. He led his community in the worship of God and his laws. Day and night he studied the Torah with friends and students. 12 Adar 5425 [27.2.1665].

5426 (1666). R' Jekusiel Zelman [Jekutiel Zalman] ben R' Noah Jechiel. The light of Israel imbued with the divine spirit. Head of Yeshivah, pure and pious head of rabbinical court. He was charitable towards the living and the dead. 10 Tevet 5426 [18.12.1665]

5426 (1666). R' Isachar Ber ben R' Mojżesz. An excellent rabbinical judge, head of Yeshivah. Proficient in the revealed and the concealed. A holy light. Devout and exalted. A prominent Kabbalist, who knew to direct with his prayer, like Hezekiah. 13 Adar A' 5426 [18.2.1666].

5427 (1667). R' Dawid [David] ben R' Samuel Halevy. Stalwart of the Torah and of teaching. The light of his teachings enlightened generations. He was privileged to see his Jewish ritual [*Halachah*] established during his lifetime. He was the author of *Turei Zahav [Ture Zahaw]*. Born at Ludmir [Włodzimierz -Wołyński]; Volodymyr-Volyskyi] in the district of Wołyń [Volyn]. He was a son-in-law of R' Joel Sirkis [Serkes], the author of *Bayit Chadash*, an interpretation of *Arba'a Turim*. He was rabbi at Potylicz [Potelysch], head of Yeshivah at Kraków and at Poznań, head of rabbinical court and head of Yeshivah at Ostróg [Ostroh]. During the Khmelnytsky [Chmielnicki] massacres, he migrated to Moravia. Wherever he went, he revised useful religious regulations. After the turmoil had subsided, he returned to Poland and was appointed head of rabbinical court and head of Yeshivah at Lwów, succeeding Rabbi Jakób ben Eljakim [Eljakum] Goetz [Giec]. He wrote *Turei Zahav* about the *Shulchan Aruch* [an abbreviated form of the Jewish ritual law], and *Divrei David* [the Sayings of David] about the Torah. He ascended heaven on 26 Sh'vat 5427 [20.2.1667]. One of his contemporaries attested that when he died, he possessed no money to purchase his *Tachrichim* [shroud], because he had never accepted any money not honestly acquired, and he had not accepted any gifts.

5428 (1668). R' Gerschon Beck ben R' Beinisch. He ascended and transcended the study of the Torah. He fought back, hitting the target. Head of Yeshivah and a great rabbinical judge [*Dayan*]. 8th day of Hannukah, 5428 [18.12.1668].

5429 (1669). R' Naftali Hirc [Hirtz] ben R' Juda Zelki [Selki] was a descendant of Ashkenazi *conversos*. The forebears of the family, descendants of Jewish *conversos*, arrived in Poland from Germany. R' Juda Zelki was a son-in-law of R' Joel Sirkis [Serkes], the author of *Bayit Chadash*, and his son, Naftali, was taught the Torah by this grandfather. He acted in the rabbinate within the town of Lwów (1654-1669). He was a secret expert in the Torah, studying Torah to arrive at practical determinations rather than theoretical ordinances. 8th day of Hannukah 5429 [6.12.1669].

5429 (1669). R' Mojżesz ben R' Jakób Kikenes, a scion of the prophet Jonah, he was the author of *Kikayon* [*Kikayon deJonah* = Jonah's castor-oil plant]. Devout and trustworthy like Eithan and Heman. Head of Yeshivah and head of rabbinical court, his students became great scholars [*Geonim*] in their time. 2 Iyar 5429 [3.5.1669].

5430 (1670). R' Jakób ben R' Juda Leib. He acted as *Magid Mesharim* [a Preacher of Righteousness] at the Torah-study school outside the town. 19 Adar 5430 [11.3.1670].

5441 (1681). R' Aszer [Asher] Jakób Abraham ben R' Arje-Leib Kalmankes. A *Dayan* [rabbinical judge] and an instructor in Jewish law. He delved into vast expanse of the Torah, and wrote the book *Eshel Abraham* [Abraham's Tamarisk] about the Torah, and the book *Ma'ayan HaChochmah* [Well of Wisdom], a key and rules to the wisdom of the Kabbalah, and the mystery of the act of Genesis. Nisan 5441 [March/April 1681].

5445 (1685). R' Józef ben R' Abraham Chajes [Chajut]. Head of rabbinical court and preacher. He ruled and elucidated the Torah. A dear soul and pure spirit. He wrote the book *Ben Porat Josef*. 10 Adar 5445 [14.2.1685 *or* 16.3.1685].

5445 (1685). R' Juda Judel ben R' Mojżesz. Born at Kowel [Kovel], he was expelled from one exile to the next by the oppressor. He took part in the Council of Four Lands. After the demise of the author of *Turei Zahav* [Dawid Halevy], he was appointed to replace him at the rabbinate of Lwów outside the town. His soul rested at around the year 5445 (1685).

5451 (1691). R' Cwi Hirsz [Tzvi] Hirsch ben R' Zechariah Mendel Klausner. Born in Kraków, he studied under the author of *Bayit Chadash*, and under the author of *Megine Schlomoh*, and under the head of Yeshivah, author of *Zemach Zedek*, of Nikolsburg [Mikulov]. He succeeded Rabbi Naftali Hirc [Hirtz]; [Herz] ben R' Judah Zelki [Selki], as head of the rabbinical court and head of Yeshivah within the town (during that time Juda Judel was Rabbi outside the town). Later on, he was confirmed (1685) head of the rabbinical court of Lublin where he rests in peace. 17 Tishrei 5451 [20.9.1690].

5456 (1696). R' Simcha ben R' Mojżesz Izak. Aged in wisdom and tender in years, he was appointed head of the rabbinical court at Stryy [Stryj] and the region.

[Pages 403-404]

Later on he taught the Torah while he was head of Yeshivah and leader in Lwów. *Isru-chag Shavuot* [the day following the Weeks Holiday] 22 Nisan 5456 [24.4.1696].

5457 (1697). R' Juda Leib ben R' Jakób, son-in-law of the head of the rabbinical court, Rabbi Mojżesz Charif. Head of Yeshivah. 2 Tishrei 5457 [28.9.1696].

5457 (1697). R' Dawid from Lyda [Lida, Belarus] ben R' Arje Leib. Born around the year 5390 [1629/1630], to Arje Leib, head of the rabbinical court at Zwoleń, and to his wife, the sister of R' Mojżesz Riwkes author of *Be'er HaGolah* [Well of the Diaspora]. He was taught the Torah by his uncle and by Rabbi Heszel [Heschel], in Lublin. He married the daughter of R' Józefs of Lwów, the great-grandson of R' Abraham Horowitz [Hurwitz], author of *Yesh Nochlin*. In 5434 [1673/1674], he published his first book Divrei Dawid [the Sayings of David], the same year in which he was appointed head of the rabbinical court at Lyda in the Wilno [Vilna; Vilnius] region. With reference to this rabbinate, he was known as Dawid Lyda. From there he was appointed rabbi at Ostróg [Ostroh], and in 5437 [1676/1677], he was appointed as head of the rabbinical court for Mainz and the regions. On 1 Elul 5440 [26.8.1680], he was appointed head of the rabbinical court of Amsterdam's Ashkenazi community, where he published his books *Sod Adonai* [God's Secret], *Sharvit Hazahav* [The Golden Wand] and the book Migdal David [The Tower of David] and *Shomerei Shabbat* [upholders of the Sabbath]. He also started to print his big book *Ir David* [City of David].

At the time, a confrontation with him started, on the suspicion that in one of his sermons he hinted at the greatness of Sabbataj Cwi [Shabtai Tzvi]. The community-elders believed the rumour and he was dismissed from the rabbinate, as a result of which he left and returned to his family in Lwów. The dispute was brought before the Council of Four Lands. All the greats of the generation resolutely backed him, and boycotted those who conspired against him, including Amsterdam's community-elders. Rabbi Dawid returned to his post, but as the dispute within his community did not stop, he agreed with the community-elders to a compensation from the community. He resigned from the rabbinate, left the town, and returned to Lwów. Apart from the aforementioned books, he also wrote the book *Ir Miklat* [City of Refuge], about the 613 commandments mentioned in the Torah, (Dyhernfurth [Brzeg Dolny] 5450 [1689/1670]); *Chelkei Avanim* [Fragments of Stones] about the commentary by *Rashi* (Fürth–Prague 5453 [1692/1693]); *Tapuchei Zahav* [Oranges] (Fürth 5453 [1692/3]); and *Yad Kol Bo* (Frankfurt am Mein, 5487 [1726/1727]). His book *Ir David* was published posthumously, in (5479 [1718/1719]). His soul came to rest at Lwów, on 17 Cheshvan 5457 [1696/1697]).

5457 (1697). R' Izak ben R' Jakób Kikenes. The greatest of rabbinical judges and the greatest of leaders. A raiser of fences and preventer of disasters, who understood the secrets of the Torah. 1 Tevet 5457 [25.12.1696].

5460 (1700). R' Jozue [Yehoshua] Falk ben R' Juda Leib. A religious preacher, author of *Emek Yehoshua* [Joshua's Valley]. 5 Iyar 5400 [24.4.1700].

5462 (1702). R' Jakób ben R' Abraham. He exerted himself in the Torah like a lion and a lioness, and enlightened the Jews with his teachings. Head of Yeshivah. He was the son of R' Abraham, head of the rabbinical court at Rotterdam, and a son-in-law of Dawid Lyda. 1 Adar 5462 [1.3.1702].

5462 (1702). R' Józef ben R' Mojżesz Charif Segal. Head of Yeahivah, and later head of rabbinical court at Przemyśl [Pshemishel]. Son-in-law of R' Juda Leib Chassid head of rabbinical court at Lwów. 1 Iyar 5462 [29.4.1702].

5462 (1702). R' Mojżesz Pinkas ben R' Izrael Charif. Head of the rabbinical court of both communities, inside the town and outside the walls. He was a leading member among the Council of Four Lands. He wrote commentary and supplements to the section *Gett* [divorce certificate under Jewish law] of his grandfather Mojzesz Charif the First. 24 Elul 5462 [17.9.1702].

5463 (1703). R' Aszer [Asher] ben R' Ruben. An excellent rabbinical judge. He was killed in a bombardment sparked by an explosion in a gunpowder storage. 2 Kislev 5463 [22.11.1702].

5469 (1709). R' Mojżesz ben R' Dawid. He was extreme in his Chassidism, expert in the revealed and the concealed. An excellent rabbinical judge who studied regular classes with students. First day of Sukkot [Tabernacle] 16 Tishrei 5469 [29.8.1708].

5469 (1709). R' Benjamin Wolf ben R' Juda Kalmankes. Head of Yeshivah. He sat in his sack and in penance from one Sabbath to the next. He founded the pamphlet *Hanhagat HaBayit* [Guide to the Household]. 10 Sh'vat 5469 [21.1.1709].

5469 (1709). R' Izajasz [Isaiah] ben R' Menachem Mendel Kacenelenbogen [Katzenellenbogen]. He was a son-in-law of the head of the rabbinical court, R' Mojżesz Pinkas Charif. Excelled as a rabbinical judge and in his teachings of Jewish ritual. He led his community wisely, and taught many students. 1 Iyar 5469 [11.4.1709].

5470 (1710). R' Chanoch ben R' Mordechaj. Head of Yeshiva at Lwów for 34 years. 29 Tevet 5470 [1.1. 1710].

5472 (1712). R' Naftali Hirc [Hirtz] ben R' Izrael Aszkenazy [Askenazy]. In his day, he was known as "Rabbi Hirc [Hirtz]." He left no part of the Torah unattended. The leading holy treasurer was R' Pinkas ben Jair] [Ya'ir]. He succeeded his father-in-law, Rabbi Mojżesz Pinkas Charif, as head of the rabbinical court, and teacher of Jewish law [*Moreh Tzedek*], at Lwów and the district, during 1702-1712. A large number of his sayings are mentioned in the books of the greats of his time. 18 Cheshvan 5472 [31.10.1711].

5472 (1712). R' Samuel ben R' Chaim. Head of Yeshivah and preacher at the Torah study school outside the town. He followed his own preachings. 4 Av 5472 [6.8.1712].

5474 (1714). R' Joel ben R' Izak Eizik Heilpern. He was known by his generation as "*Der Grosser Rabbi, R' Joel*" (the Great Rabbi, R' Joel). At first he was head of the rabbinical court and head of Yeshivah at Łuck [Lutsk], and later at Pińsk [Pinsk]. When Rabbi Naftali Katz was appointed at Poznań, Rabbi Joel replaced him at Ostróg [Ostroh]. In 5474 [1714], after the demise of Rabbi Naftali Hirc [Hirtz] Askenazy [Aszkenazy], he was appointed as head of the rabbinical court and head of Yeshivah at Lwów. Notwithstanding, before he had reached Lwów, his soul came to rest at Ostróg. 4 Tishrei 5474 [24.9.1713].

5477 (1717). R' Menachem Mendel ben R' Aszer Potiker. He was rabbi and religious judge at Berezań. Later on he was head of the rabbinical court in the district

[Pages 405-406]

of Lwów and on the Council of Four Lands. He wrote many essays. 3 Tevet 5477 [17.12.1716].

5478 (1718). R' Cwi Hirsz [Tzvi Hirsh] Aszkenazy ben R' Jakób. He was known by the title of his book *Chacham Cwi [Sage Tzvi]*. His father, R' Jakób ben R' Benjamin, scion of holy lineage, was a son-in-law of R' Efraim, head of the rabbinical court in Wilno [Vilnius], the author of the book *Sha'ar Efraim*[Efraim's Gate]. In 5408 [1647/48], R' Jakób and his family wandered from his homeland and settled in Moravia. There, at Trebitsch [Třebíč] and Buda [Budin; Ofen], he served as head of the rabbinical court. Later on he settled in Ofen, and he was known as far away as Turkey and the lands of the east. Then, he fathered his son Cwi [Tzvi]. When the situation had quietened down in the country, his grandfather, the author of *Sha'ar Efraim*, and his father, R' Jakób, settled in Buda, Hungary. As a young boy, the grandson Cwi was taught the Torah by his grandfather and by his father. In his youth he went to Thessaloniki [Salonica] to familiarise himself with the Sephardi Sages' [*Chachamim*] ways of learning. There, he assisted R' Eliyahu Kobo in particular.

When he returned home, still in his youth, he was already considered amongst the revered, while he observed utmost Chassidism. There, he married the daughter of one of the wealthy members of the community, but when the Prussian armies laid siege to the town, firing cannons, a cannon-ball hit the house where he and his family lived. His young wife was killed together with their only daughter. R' Cwi [Tzvi] alone was saved. He left the town and moved to Sarajevo, where he was appointed rabbi. He left Sarajevo when he learnt that his parents were taken prisoners and brought to Berlin by the Brandenburg[-Prussians]. He moved to Venice, where he lodged in the house of R' Samuel Aboab, who welcomed him with great affection. From Venice he moved to Ansbach, Prague and Berlin. In Berlin he remarried, the daughter of R' Meschulam Zelman Neumark-Mirels, the rabbi and head of the rabbinical court of the three communities –Altona, Hamburg and Wandsbek. R' Cwi [Tzvi] settled at Altona and established a Yeshiva in a house founded by the well-to-do in these communities. There he focused on the revealed and the concealed until no secret of the Torah eluded him. He was faithful to the books of the Kabbalah, and was fluent in the writings of the holy Rabbi Izak Lurie Askenazy [*HaAri*]. During his wandering, he taught himself foreign languages, and was known to have spoken Spanish, Italian, Turkish, Hungarian and German. He was also familiar with all types of philosophy and other types of knowledge, and in his spare time he read secular books and world affairs.

Along his long and arduous road he never accepted a gift from anyone. He was never known to joke or jest, even though he had a convivial attitude and warmly welcomed everyone. He was respected and feared and at the same time loved and liked by all who knew him. He focused solely on Jewish law. He considered it by day and by night. Despite being a Torah scholar of growing stature, he was welcomed by his acquaintances who were aware that he was purely guided by the spirit devoid of any personal aspect.

For twenty years he taught the Torah at the Altona *Kloyz*. Learners and rabbis from Poland and Lithuania, expert in the Torah, assembled there to study with great diligence, the Talmud, *Rashi's* interpretations, annotations of the Talmud, the adjudicators, Jewish laws and rabbinical literature [*Aggadot*], together with other knowledge and grammar. His renown spread throughout the diaspora and he attracted, from far and wide, queries about instruction and on uncertainty that had arisen during their study. From him emanated the Torah to the Jewish People, and he was also responsible for the public wellbeing of the Ashkenazi and the Sephardi members of the three communities. Even during the lifetime of his father-in-law, R' Meschulam Zelman Neumark, as head of the rabbinical court, when R' Tzvi was officially only appointed head of Yeshivah at the *Kloyz*, he was nonetheless instrumental in all of the affairs of the community, because his father-in-law, Rabbi Meschulam Zelman, was old and frail for several years. R' Cwi [Tzvi] handled all the affairs of the communities without receiving any salary or reward from the management of the communities. For his income, he first joined someone with an understanding of commodities, to trade together and share the profits. Soon, however, the invested sum dissipated and the partner escaped to Amsterdam, leaving R' Tzvi without assets. A few benevolent individuals in Altona and Hamburg accepted however some money from him, to use in joint trading, and gave him his share of the profit, but he set the condition that they should not forego any of their share in his favour.

Burdened with sons and daughters, and lacking a large, permanent income, he was nevertheless generous, and helped the poor in his communities. He also took upon himself the responsibility as collector of alms for the poor in Eretz Israel. He sent the donations collected for the poor in Jerusalem, and he ensured that the shares were fairly distributed, so that each individual received their portion depending on their status, their needs and their dependents. He also introduced the practice that every individual signs an acknowledgement of the sum they received. Subsequently, the community in Eretz Israel grew stronger.

On 22 Tamuz 5447 [3.7.1687], R' Meschulam Zelman [Zalman] Neumark entered eternal life, and the post of head of the rabbinical court for the three communities was left vacant. R' Cwi [Tzvi] was then appointed as head of the rabbinical court for Hamburg and Wandsbek, but at Altona the post was shared between him and R' Mojżesz Süsskind Rottenberg, with each of them heading the presidency for half a year. In 5452 [1691/92], R' Cwi [Tzvi] published a manuscript of the section: "*Choshen HaMishpat*" from the *Shulchan Aruch* by [the author of] *Turei Zahav*, supplemented by his added innovations and commentary. Next to every comment, some of which clarified and expanded and some of which disagreed and replied, he noted "said the commentator." His name was not mentioned on the title page or in the introduction, but at the end of the book, at the insistence of his students, he agreed to enter his name with the saying: Who guards the Great Torah study school and the *Kloyz* at the holy community of Altona, in the year "in his Temple."

[Pages 407-408]

This situation persisted for over twenty years, until 5469 [1709/10], when R' Cwi [Tzvi] issued a decision which led to a controversy between him and his colleague at the rabbinate, R' Mojżesz Süsskind Rottenberg. This disagreement spilt out beyond the boundaries of town, with some of the great rabbis of the generation siding with R' Tzvi, and some rejecting his decision. The relations between these two presidents of the rabbinical court had escalated, until R' Cwi [Tzvi] removed himself from the rabbinate and returned to his previous post as head of Yeshivah at the *Kloyz*. Not much later he was appointed rabbi in Amsterdam. As soon as he had settled there, he rushed to publish *Chacham Cwi*, a collection of his responses, in which his responses to the disputed decision occupied the principal part. It seemed as if its frequent printing served purely to publish his reasons for that particular decision.

Both communities, the Ashkenazi and the Sephardi, honoured and admired him for his greatness in the Torah, his charitable characteristics and for the religious rulings he instituted in the rabbinate to improve the lot of the communities. Notwithstanding, a dispute erupted between him and the rabbi of the Sephardi community, Rabbi Solomon Ajalon [Ayalon], who had approved the book *Divrei Nechemya*, by Nehemiah Chaya Chayun, while R' Tzvi considered that book as one which aligned itself with the cult of Sabbataj Cwi's [Shabtai Tzvi]. R' Cwi [Tzvi] left once more the rabbinate of Amsterdam and travelled to London. There, he was welcomed with great honour and his stay was commemorated with a portrait by a professional artist. He did not remain there for long, however. He returned to Poland via Emden, Halberstadt, Berlin and Wrocław [Breslau], until 5474 [1714/15], when he was appointed head of the rabbinical court at Lwów. He led this presidency with great dignity. Even ministers of state treated him with such great honour as had never been bestowed on a Jewish rabbi. He was also licensed to judge capital cases, but he did not remain long on his seat, as he rose to heaven on the evening of 2 Iyar 5478 [3.5.1718].

5478 (1718). R' Simcha ben R' Nachman HaKohen Rappoport. After the demise of *Chacham Cwi* [Tzvi] R' Simcha was invited to succeed him. Previously he had been head of Yeshivah at Dubno, Grodno and Lublin, when he was invited to serve in the rabbinate of Lwów, but he did not occupy the seat for long. The wording on the tombstone of his son, Chaim HaKohen Rappoport, confirms that R' Simcha occupied the seat of Lwów's rabbinate for a while. It is possible that after his advancement, he returned in order to bring his family to Lwów. Midway, at Szczebrzeszyn [Shebreshin], he fell ill however, and died on 7. Av 5478 [4.7.1718]. A few of his homilies appear in his son, R' Chaim's book, *Zecher HaChaim* [The Recollection of Chaim = Life].

5479 (1719). R' Salomon Zelman [Zalman] ben R' Izak. A preacher and head of rabbinical court. A Chassidic great scholar [*gaon*] who taught many great Jewish scholars. 9 Cheshvan 5479 [3.11.1718].

5482 (1722). R' Cwi [Tzvi] ben R' Saul Landau of the Kikenes family. At first he was head of the rabbinical court at Żmigród [later Nowy Żmigród] [Schmiedeburg], and later he was one of the great rabbinical judges in Lwów. He saved the oppressed from the grasp of his oppressor. He taught men who turned into great rabbis and he composed shrewd essays. 1 Tamuz 5482 [16.6.1722].

5488 (1728). R' Chaim and his brother, R' Jozue [Jehoshua] Bnei R' Izak Halevy Reizes [Reices], the holy men who were martyred. R' Chaim (born 5447; 1687), was head of Yeshivah at Lwów. His brother, R' Jozue (born 5457; 1697), was also exalted in the Torah and in Chassidism. Affluent men, they were generous and philanthropic towards the poor and the down-and-outs. Then, a converted man arrived from afar, one who regretted what he had done, and reverted to Judaism. The head-priest heard of it and the convert was caught. When he was questioned about the person who had advised him to return to Judaism, he said that he did not know the community members, but that he would recognise the inciter, if he were to stand in front of him. The head-priest ordered the entire community, including the rabbis and heads of Yeshivah, to come and line up, because the leading members of the community were suspected in particular of influencing the convert to revert to Judaism. After the convert had considered all the members without picking out anyone, R' Chaim said to the head-priest in Latin: "You see, Sir, I am innocent of this event of which I was wrongly accused." When the convert heard these words, he turned to R' Chaim and to his brother and said: "Now I recognise them. They have tempted me." The two brothers were caught and suffered severe torture and on the eve of Shavuot [the festival of Weeks] 5488 [24.3.1728], these holy scholars underwent a severe death. They were murdered and burnt and stabbed.

5492 (1732). R' 'Jezi' [Jezaja] ben R' Abraham Halevy Horowitz [Hurwitz], a preacher and head of rabbinical court. He remained steadfast. He gave exceptional instructions. 29 Tevet 5492 [27.1.1732].

5493 (1733). R' 'Jezi' [Jezaja] ben R' Aron Meschulam from Łuck [Lutsk], head of Yeshivah, a great rabbinical judge and teacher of Jewish law. Died at Kolomyia [Kolomea]. 9 Tishrei 5493 [28.9.1732].

5500 (1740). R' Jakób from Kulików [Kulykiv]. At first he was rabbi at Kulików, and later he was preacher in Lwów. 23 Kislev 5500 [24.12.1739].

5506 (1746). R' Menachem Maneli ben R' Baruch Halevy. Rabbinical judge and teacher of Jewish law. He was the author of the book *Zera Baruch* [Scion of Baruch; *also*, Blessed Scion], new interpretation of *Mishnah* tractates, and of the book *Ta'am Man* [Taste of Manna] on the Torah portions. 7 Sivan 5506 [26.5.1746].

5510 (1750). R' Pinkas ben R' Jakób Kacenelenbogen [Katzenellenbogen]. Head of the rabbinical court at Krakówiec [Krakovets], and later, for 31 years, a *Magid Mesharim* preacher within the town [of Lwów]. 11 Adar 5510 [17.2.1750].

5514 (1754). R' Mojżesz Chaim ben R' Eleazar [Eliezer]. At first he was head of rabbinical court at Komárno [Komárom] and Złoczów [Zlochiv], and later, head of the rabbinical court at Lwów. During the dispute among the community management over the status of the author of *Pneh Jesua* [Jehoshua; Yehoshua] in the rabbinate, and when in 5488 (1728) the heads of Yeshivah, R' Chaim and R' Jozue Reizes [Reices], were falsely accused and brutally murdered,

[Pages 409-410]

the town rabbi was also accused together with them, but he succeeded in escaping Lwów. He crossed the border and got away. He reached the town of Khotyn [Chocin; Hotin] and remained there for the rest of his life, until approximately 5514 (1754), where his rest is honoured.

5515 (1755). R' Arje [Aryeh] Leibben R' Saul. His father was the son of the rabbi Rabbi Heszel [Heschel]. He was head of the rabbinical court at Łokacze [Lokatschi], Brest [Brześć; formerly Brześć-Litewski], Opatów, Kraków and Głogów [Glogau]. R' Arje Leib also served in the rabbinate of several significant communities, such as Rzeszów [Resche] and Głogów [Glogau]. Later, he was appointed to head the rabbinate of Lwów, the seat which his father-in-law, *Chacham Cwi*, had occupied. He served the rabbinate there, for a period. However, the lawsuits rift within the community over the author of *Pneh Josua* [Pnei Jehoshua], stopped him from settling in Lwów. He did not abandon his position at the rabbinate of Głogów until he was appointed to serve as rabbi in Amsterdam, where he died on the seventh day of Pessach 5515 [15.12.1754].

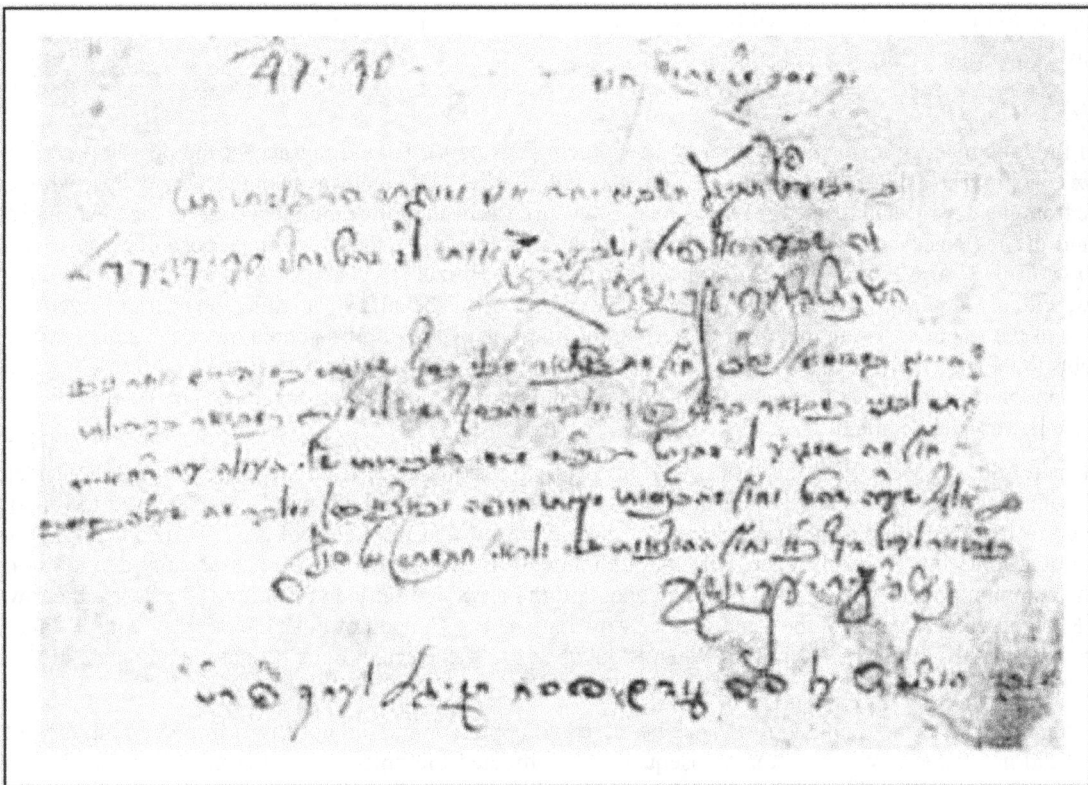

Manuscript of the great scholar [*gaon*] Rabbi Jakób Jozue [Josua], author of *Pneh Josua* [Pnei Jehoshua]

5516 (1756). R' Jakób Jozue ben R' Cwi [Tzvi] Hirsz [Hirsh]. Known for his book *Pneh Josua*, he was a grandson of the author of *Magine Shelomoh* [Jozue Heszel /Höschel], and was named after him. He was born in Kraków on 28 Kislev 5441 [19.12.1680]. In his youth he migrated to locations where the Torah was followed, and studied at various Yeshivot with his name spreading far and wide. He married the daughter of the head and leader of Lwów's community, R' Salomon Segal Landau, and settled in Lwów. There he taught the Torah to upright students and started to write the book of his innovations to the tractates of the *Mishnah*. Respected and revered by all the townspeople, he was elected elder and leader of the community.

One day, on 3 Kislev 5463 (1703), a barrel of gunpowder inside the military warehouse in the vicinity of the Jewish Street was set alight by a spark. An immense explosion ensued, destroying many houses and killing scores of people. Amongst these were also his young wife and their single daughter, as well as several members of their family. R' Jakób Jozue was also among the casualties. He lay covered by the heaped ruins, unable to move or breath. In this crisis, he vowed that if God were to save him from the collapse, he would increase the number of his students, he would persevere in the *Halachah*, and would follow in the footsteps of his grandfather, the author of *Megine Schlomoh*, including his teaching methods. Before he even concluded his prayer, God heard him and showed him steps through the heaps. He found a kind of path which led him to safely. After that, he concentrated his study primarily on clarifying the *Halachah* and on delving into questions on the Talmud, while excluding from his writings all irrelevancies, remote from the actual truth.

Even though he remarried the daughter of one of Lwów's prominent residents, the leader and magnet, Isachar Ber, R' Jakób Jozue was not inclined to settle in the town where his first wife's parents resided, to spare causing them any grief. He moved and settled in the small town of Kurów, in the Lublin district. In 5466 (1706), he was elected to serve the rabbinical court at Ryczywół, nevertheless, his solid character and his principle not to face a community-elder or leader, stopped him from sitting amongst them, and in 5469 (1709) he moved at Łuków. There again he found no rest and supplies to his Yeshivah. His resolute mother-in-law, lobbied to have him appointed to the rabbinical court at the village Tarłów near Ostrowiec, and built there a Torah study school for his Yeshivah. There, however, he also faced opposition from those who wanted to rule over the public. At the time, *Chacham Cwi* was in Poland, where he visited several small towns, and by chance he met R' Jakób Jozue, appreciated his character and his greatness in the Torah, and wondered that he was head of a rabbinical court, at a small town, and declared that he [Jakób Jozue] deserved a larger town. As the people of the town Lisko [Lesko] asked *Chacham Cwi* whom they should appoint as rabbi, he recommended R' Jakób Jozue.

Not long after, on 2 Elul 5474 [13.8.1714], R' Jakób Jozue

[Pages 411-412]

was elected to the rabbinical court of the community of Tykocin [Tykotzin]. He did not accept the post however, and that, since *Chacham Cwi* [Tzvi] Hirsh Aszkenazy] had died a few months earlier. With many acquaintances and those who respected R' Jakób Jozue from the days he had resided at Lwów, he was favoured as head of the rabbinical court of the town, and as Rabbi of the Land and the regions. There were also those who wished to appoint to these honorary posts the son-in-law of the revered *Chacham Cwi*, R' Arje Leib ben R' Saul [Shaul] the son of R' Heszel [Heschel] of Kraków. The family of R' Jakób Jozue in Lwów, with his mother-in-law in particular, lobbied however on his behalf. Meanwhile, the district Governor delayed the appointment of the Rabbi, insisting that prior to settling the question of the Rabbi's appointment, the community had first to pay their debts to the government, of over thirty thousand Gulden. The family of R' Jakób Jozue paid the debt and obtained authorisation to appoint the Rabbi for the town and the district, at which point R' Jakób Jozue became head of the rabbinical court of the town [Lwów] and of the district.

Still, the disputes did not cease, with the residents of the district breaking away from the townspeople. The leaders of the districts sided with R' Jakób Jozue, unlike those in the town proper. But R' Arje Leib ben R' Saul refused to relinquish his rabbinate and go to Lwów so long as a truce was not reached in Lwów, and the Rabbi of Złoczów [Zolochiv], R' Mojżesz Chaim, was brought to Lwów. R' Jakób Jozue, who did not renounce the rabbinate of Lwów, especially due to the financial claims from the community in respect of their debt payment, left the town and settled at Buczacz [Buchach], the town of his father-in-law, R' Arje Lejbusz, leader of the Land of the Lwów region. The Council of Four Lands sided with R' Jakób Jozue, and the dispute did not subside until 5490 [1730], when R' Jakób Jozue was elected to the post at the rabbinate of Berlin, and he left for Berlin.

Even in Berlin R' Jakób Jozue found no rest, since he feared no oppressor and did not flinch from a tyrant, did not turn to any officer and did not flatter any benefactor. Consequently he attracted the objection of the most adamant in Berlin, the community-elder and leader, Feiwel ben R' Efraim, who once stood trial before R' Jakób Jozue, together with the father of Mr. Daniel Jaffe. R' Jakób Jozue, who investigated the dispute between them, admonished Feiwel for his violence. He thus engendered the hatred of the adamant man. The head of the rabbinical court of Metz at the time, R' Jacob Reischer, author of *Chock Ja'akov*[Jacob's Law], and of *Sh'vut Ja'akov* [Jacob's Response], died, and R' Jakób Jozue acquiesced to the request of the Metz community and headed the rabbinate there, in 5494 [1733/34]. In 5499 [1738/39], R' Jakób Jozue travelled to Amsterdam to print his book *Pneh Josua* [Pnei Jehoshua; Yehoshua] on the *Mishnah*'s women tractate [about family life]. There he lobbied for the acceptance of the second candidate in Lwów, R' Arje Leib, the son-in-law of *Chacham Cwi*, as head of the rabbinical court in Amsterdam.

The resolute views of R' Jakób Jozue led at times to rulings that opposed the views of his predecessors at the Metz rabbinate. Many complained about him, especially about his instruction regarding priests [*Kohanim*] sitting in the street, neighbouring a deceased. R' Jakób Jozue ignored his detractors, but when the Sages of Eretz Israel approached him and appointed him their president, he left the Metz rabbinate and prepared to go to Eretz Israel. Then, the rabbi of Frankfurt-am-Main, Jacob HaKohen Popers, the author of *Lev Ya'akov*, [Jacob's Heart], died, and R' Jakób Jozue was asked to succeed him, thus delaying his departure to Eretz Israel. While he was in Frankfurt-am-Main, an emissary for Eretz Israel, R' Chaim Yosef David Azulai, visited him, and the impression R' Jakób Jozue made on Azulai, was noted by the latter: "I, the youth, was blessed to welcome the divine spirit for a few days, and he appeared like God's angel."

Just as in teaching, so also in all public issues, he would not budge from his set view, and always fought hard for everything he considered right and necessary to maintain Judaism and the Torah. In 5482 (1722), while still in Lwów, he headed the conference to boycott and ostracise the remainder of Sabbataj Cwi's [Shabtai Tzvi] cult. Ever since, he suspected anyone who diverted from the *Shulchan Aruch*, and followed the custom of the Kabbalists, and wondered if they were a kind of Sabbateans. When he heard that Rabbi Jonathan Eybeschütz had stopped laying [*tefillin*] phylacteries during *Chol Hamo'ed*, he ensured that the entire world heard of it. When the dispute broke out over the amulets, he again opposed him. However, with the town's majority siding with Rabbi Jonathan Eybeschütz, and the dispute escalating, R' Jakób Jozue gave up this rabbinate too. He left the town and settled at Mannheim. Meanwhile, Rabbi Moses Braude, the rabbi of Worms, died, and R' Jakób Jozue was accepted there. The government, however, would not confirm his rabbinate. He attempted to return to Frankfurt-am-Main, but the dispute had heated up even further, and so he left for Offenbach. On 14 Sh'vat 5516 [16.1.1756], before the start of Shabbat, he entered eternal life, and on Sunday his coffin was brought to Frankffurt-am-Main, where he rests in peace. It was said that he was born in righteousness and died in integrity.

5525 (1765). R' Menachem Manis ben R' Jokel Halevy, a Horowitz, brother-in-law of R' Jecheskiel [Ezechiel] Landau, author of *Noda BeJehuda* [Known in Judah]. Head of the rabbinical court and head of Yeshivah. 19 Sh'vat 5525 [10.2.1765].

5528 (1768). R' Izak Segal Landau. At first, he was head of the rabbinical court in his birth town of Opatów, and later at Żółkiew. From there he was elected rabbi to the Lwów region. Following the controversy over the rabbinate of *Pneh Jesua* [R' Jakób Jozue] which led to the severing of the district, from the town of Lwów, he was accepted as head of the rabbinical court and the head of Yeshivah at Kraków. Rabbi Jonathan Eybeschütz described him as "First amongst the prime Sages [*Geonim*] of the period. None was greater than him. Leader of the Levites in a generation replete with esteemed men, the Sage Izak Segal who had been head of the rabbinical court of the Lwów region, and now head of the rabbinical court and head of Yeshivah of the holy community of Kraków and of the district... entered eternal life at Kraków on *Simchat Torah* 5528 [23.12.1767]."

5530 (1770). R' Chaim Juda Leib ben R' Eleazar [Eliezer] Segal Ettinger [Ettinga]. He was the brother-in-law, and father-in-law of

[Pages 413-414]

R' Chaim Kohen Rappoport, head of Yeshivah during the rabbinate of *Chacham Cwi*, and *Pneh Jesua* [R' Jakób Jozue], and later, during the interregnum, he replaced them in the rabbinate of Lwów. He rests, honoured, at Jaryczów Nowy [Novyi Yarychiv]. 3 Sh'vat 5530 [29.1.1770].

5531 (1771) R' Chaim ben R' Simche HaKohen Rappoport. He was rabbi at Zitel, Słuck [Slutsk] and in 5501 (1741), he was appointed to replace his father and serve as head of the rabbinical court of Lwów and of the region. He was blessed with a long life, and occupied the seat for some thirty years. During his tenure at the town-rabbinate, his son, R' Arje Leib, served as head of Yeshivah, and died during his father's lifetime, in Sivan 5509 [May-June 1749]. R' Chaim Kohen was considered in his day as the noblest of Sages, and he was approached from near and far with many inquiries about the *Halachah* [Jewish law]. In 5519 (1759), he was forced to confront the followers of Jacob Frank's cult, and defend the *Talmud*. He was active in the Council of Four Lands. Part of his answers were published after a long time, under the title *Responsa of R' Chaim Kohen* (Lwów 5621 [1860/61]), and part of his sermons, under the title *Zecher Chaim* (Lwów 5626 [1865/66]). He entered eternal life on 13 Tamuz 5531 [25.6.1771].

5533 (1773). R' Majer ben R' Józef Teomim. He was at first head of the rabbinical court at Lubartów, and later a *Magid Mesharim* [Preacher of Righteousness] in Lwów. An influential preacher, who replied thoroughly to many. He wrote the book *Brachat Josef* [Joseph's Blessing], *Eliyahu Rabba*, and *Rav P'ninim veNofet Zufim*. He fathered R' Józef, author of *Peri Megadim* [Precious Fruit]. 19 Tamuz 5531 [1.7.1771]. 5539 (1779). R' Dov Berisz ben R' Arje Leib. His father, R' Arje Leib was rabbi at Zamość [Zamosch], and he officiated at the rabbinate of Kozienice [Kozhnits] (5505 [1744/5]), Kraśnik (5514 [1753/4]), and Rzeszów [Resche] (5518 [1757/8]). There, he was appointed as head of Yeshivah at Lwów, where he taught the Torah for fourteen years, until 3 Iyar 5539 [27.6.1779].

5545 (1785). R' Salomon ben R' Mojżesz of Chełm. Born at Zamość, he became head of the rabbinical court and head of Yeahivah at Chełm, rabbi at the Kollel [advanced Judaic studies programme] on the estates of Count Zamojski, on whose territory stood the towns of Zamość and Szczebrzeszyn [Shebreshin]. In 5531[1770/71], after the demise of R' Chaim Kohen Rappoport, he was appointed to take over his post at Lwów. A very great scholar in the Torah, who also had secular knowledge, he wrote *Merkewet HaMischna*, about Maimonides. *Atzeh Shulchan*, which followed the four parts of the *Shulchan Aruch* (out of which only the part on the Shabbath Laws, and the section *Even-HaEzer* from the *Shulchan Aruch*, were published). New interpretations about the Six Orders of the *Mishnah*, and responses, were left in manuscript form. In 5537 [1777/78], he left the rabbinate and moved to Eretz Israel. He remained there for a certain period, then left for Thessaloniki [Saloniki] in order to publish another volume of one of his books. There, his soul came to rest, around the year 5545 [1784/85].

5546 (1786). R' Mordechaj Zew [Ze'ev] ben R' Mojżesz. Known as "The great R' Mordechaj-Zew," he was said to be a holy man of God. He was head of the rabbinical court at Kamianka, Satanów [Sataniv] and Jampol [Yampil], and later at the two communities of Lwów, inside, and outside the town. He was the father of R' Jakób Ornstein, author of *Jeschies Jacow* [Yeshuot Ya'akov]. 2 Sh'vat 5544 [25.1.1784].

5550 (1790). R' Majer ben R' Cwi Hirsz [Tzvi] Hirsh] Margulies. He was rabbi at Jazłowiec [Yazlovets], and in 5515 [1754/55], he was appointed as head of the rabbinical court of the Lwów region. During his tenure, R' Chaim Kohen Rappoport and later R' Salomon of Chełm, were head of the rabbinical court within the town. A thorough adherent of R' Izrael Baal Shem Tov. In one of his books he writes: "Ever since childhood, from the day I got devotionally attached to my teacher, my friend, the rabbi, the Chassid, our teacher, Rabbi Izrael Baal Shem Tov, of blessed memory, I faithfully knew that his leadership was of sanctity and purity with great devotion and asceticism of a righteous man who lives within his faith. To whom the concealed and the mysterious was unveiled." From Lwów he moved to Ostróg [Ostroh] as rabbi, head of the rabbinical court. He wrote the *Responsa Meir Netivim, Or Olam* and *Sod Yachin VeBoaz*. 10 Iyar 5550 [24.4.1790].

5552 (1792). R' Józef ben R' Majer Teomim, the stalwart of education. Renowned for his compositions *Peri Megadim* about *Shulchan Aruch, Orach Chaim, Yore De'a* and others. Born at Szczerzec, near Lwów, his parents moved to Lwów in his childhood, where he grew up. He married the daughter of R' Eliakim [Elyakum] of Komárno [Komárom], where he taught children the Torah, and he signed his name *Makreh Dardakeh* [infants' teacher]. In 5526 [1765/66], at Komárno, he finished his book *Rosh Yosef* [Joseph's Head] about *Masechet Chulin* [Part of the *Mishnah*]. In 5532 [1771/72], he was appointed member of the Daniel Jaffe Torah study school, in Berlin. There, he found the books which he required to complete the books which he wrote himself. Subsequently, he finished his book *Peri Megadim*, to *Yore De'a*. From there he returned to Lwów and stood in for his father for seven years. In 5544 [1784/85], he was appointed head of the rabbinical court at Frankfurt-an-der-Oder. Apart from the above mentioned books, other books published by him were, *Ginat Veradim, Matan Secharan Shel Mitzvot, Noam Megadim, Notarikon, PoratYosef,* with *Masechet Yabamot* and *K'tovot, Rosh Yossef* with *Masechet P'sachim* and *Beyza, Shoshanat Ha'Amakim* and *Teyvat Gama*. Many of his writings remained in manuscript form. Died 4 Iyar 5552 [26.4.1792].

5553 (1793). R' Cwi Hirsz [Tzvi Hirsh] ben R' Mojżesz. At first, he was head of the rabbinical court at Biały Kamień [Bilyi Kamin`], later, he was head of the rabbinical court at Lwów. He was the father of R' Majer Kristianpoller, head of the rabbinical court at Brody. 19 Av 5553 [28.7.1793].

5554 (1794). R' Aszer Anszel [Asher Anshel] ben R' Mojżesz Askenazy [Aszkenassy]. Rabbi at Rozdól, later he was *Magid Mesharim* at Lwów, minister of the Torah and Wisdom. He kept and supported the poor, shored up the orphans and the widows. He was the father of R' Mojżesz Dawid Askenazy [Aszkenassy], of Tolcsva [Hungary], and later in France, author of the book *Toldot Adam* [History of Man]. 12 Cheshvan 5554 [12.10.1793].

5557 (1797). R' Schmuel Saler ben

[Pages 415-416]

R' Abraham Scheindlinger [Sheindlinger] was born at Dobromil. He was head of the rabbinical court at the town of Sale, and was named after it, R' Schmuel Saler. Later he was *Magid Mesharim, Moreh Tzedek* [teacher of Jewish law] and head of the rabbinical court within the town. He wrote the book *Schem Meschmiel* [Shem MiShmuel], *Bayit Chadash* about the Torah, the *Gmara* and *Halachah*. 3 Av 5557 [26.7.1797].

5565 (1805). R' Cwi Hirsz [Tzvi Hirsh] ben R' Isachar Dov-Berisz Rosanisch [Rosanes]. R' Isachar is the grandson[B] of the author of *Pneh Jesua* [Pnei Jehoszua; Yehoshua]. R' Cwi Hirsz was promoted to head of rabbinical court at Bolechów, and was later appointed head of rabbinical court and head of Yeshivah at Lwów. He wrote the book *Tesha Shitot* [Nine Methods]. 23 Kislev 5565 [26.11.1804].

5566 (1806). R' Izak ben R' Cwi Aszkenazy [Tzvi Ashkenazi]. Rabbi at Chodorów [Khodoriv], he was later *Magid Mesharim* and *Moreh Tzedek* in both communities, within, and outside the town. A profound great scholar. He wrote the book *Taharat HaKodesh* [The Purity of Sanctity] about *Masechet Zevachim* and *Masechet Menachot*. 28 Nissan 5566 [16.4.1806].

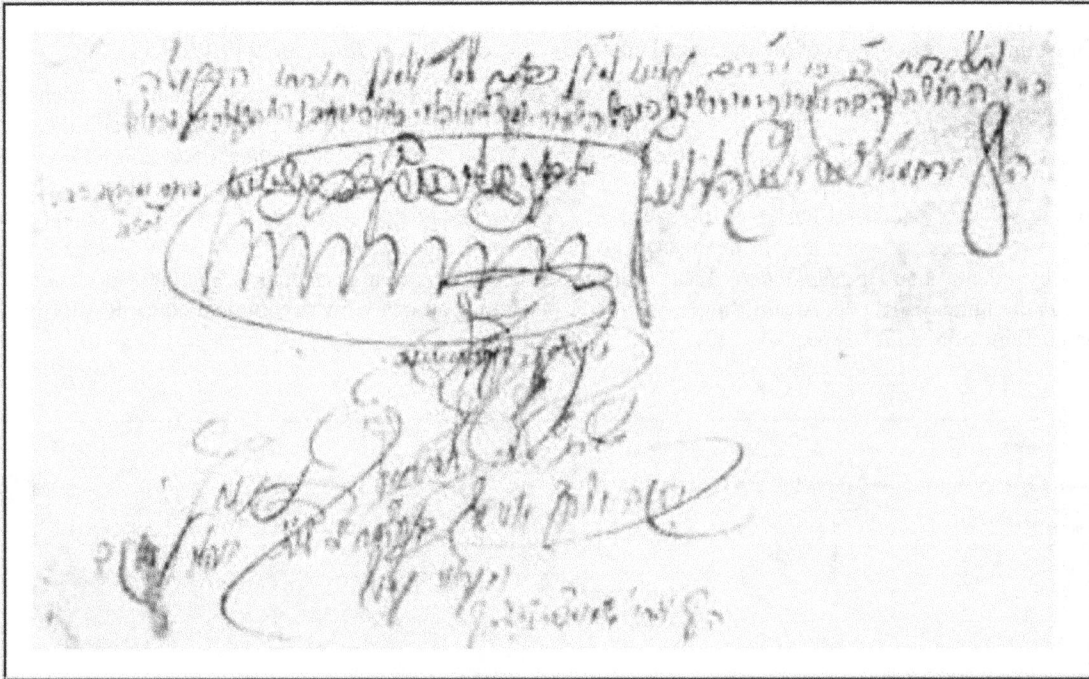

Handwriting of Rabbi Józef Saul Natansohn

5570 (1810). R' Meszulam [Meshulam] ben R' Joel HaKohen, brother of R' Izak Eizyk, head of the rabbinical court at Korzec [Korets] and Ostróg [Ostroh]. Author of *Brit Kehunat Olam*, he numbered amongst the privileged priesthood. R' Meszulam was promoted to head of the rabbinical court at Żurawno [Zhuravne], Korzec [Korets] and Bolechów [Bolekhiv]. Later on, he was head of the rabbinical court and teacher of Jewish law, at Lwów. He wrote the books *Pitcheh Neda* and *Gufeh Halachot*. First day of the festival of Sukkot [Tabernacle] 5570 [25.9.1809].

5570 (1810). R' Juda Leib ben R' Jechiel Michał, *Magid Mesharim* and *Moreh Tzedek* [teacher of Jewish law] within the town. A supreme saint. Conscientious and extraordinary as one of the Ancients. 25 Tishreh 5570 [5.10.1809].

5596 (1836). R' Naftali Hirc [Hirtz] ben R' Abraham Chaim Suchystaw [Suchestow]. Head of the rabbinical court, he was the father of Gabryel [Gawril], author of *Maceweth Kodesz* [Matzevet Kodesh]. 6 Nissan 5596 [23.3.1836].

5599 (1839) R' Jakób [Jakub] Meszulam Ornstein ben R' Mordechaj Zew [Ze'ev] Lwów, renowned for his book *Jeschies Jacow* [Yeshuot Ya'akov]. He was born in 5535 [1774/75]. When he was twelve years old, his father, R' Mordechaj Zew, head of Lwów's rabbinical court, died. In the same year, he married the daughter of R' Cwi Hirsz [Tzvi Hirsh] Meitlis from Jarosław [Yaroslav], in whose house he studied the Torah and wrote his book, part of the *Avoda Zara*. In 5563 [1802/3], he was appointed head of the rabbinical court at Żołkiew [Zhovkva], and in 5565 [1804/5], after the demise of R' Cwi Hirsz Rosanisch [Tzvi Hirsch Rosanes], head of the rabbinical court at Lwów, R' Jakób was appointed head of the rabbinical court, and for thirty five years he did his office proud. His book *Jeschies Jacow* [Yeshuot Ya'akov] spread his name throughout the Jewish diaspora. His sermons on the Torah and a collection of his responsa were also published. His son, R' Mordechaj Zew [Ze'ev], the father of Cwi Ornstein, died on 17 Cheshvan 5597 [28.10.1836], and R' Jakób, on 25 Av 5599 [4.8.1839].

5611 (1851). R' Jozue Izak Jair [Ya'ir] ben R' Jakób Horowitz. He was rabbi at Dukla, *Magid Mesharim* within the town of Lwów, and finally, rabbi at Żórawina. He published the book *Emunot VeDe'ot* [Beliefs and Opinions] (Lwów, 5618 [1858]) a clarification of all the commandments, the principles and the basics, and all shoots of faith and the articles. Died at Żórawina, 16 Kislev 5611 [20.11.1850].

5612 (1852). R' Aron Mojżesz ben R' Jakób Taubes. Born in Lwów in 5547 [1787], he was taught the Torah by R' Jakób Ornstein. He was rabbi at Śniatyn (5580 [1820]), and later at Iaşi [Jassy] (5601 [1840/41]. He composed the responsa *Tofa'ot Ra'am* and the rabbinical commentary *Karneh Ra'am*. Died at Iaşi [Jassy] 11 Tamuz 5612 [28.7.1852].

5619 (1859). R' Simcha Natan ben R' Arje Leib Öhlenberg, was head of the rabbinical court at Mościska [Mostyska], and later he was *Magid Mesharim* and teacher of Jewish law in Lwów. After the demise of

[Pages 417-418]

Rabbi Jakób Ornstein, he acted as head of the rabbinical court. He died on *Simchat Torah* 5619 [9.12.1858].

5623 (1863). R' Mordechaj Zew [Ze'ev] ben R' Izak Aron Segal Ettinga [Ettinger], the brother-in-law and friend of Rabbi Józef Saul Natansohn. Together they wrote *Mifraseh HaYam* [The Sea Sails] about the sea of the *Talmud,* and their uncle, R' Jozue Heschel of Tarnogród [Tarnegrod], the brother of Rabbi Jakób Ornstein the author of *Jeschies Jacob* [Yeshuot Ya'akov], *Magen Giborim, Meirat Enayim* -about *Halachot Trefat HaRe'a-, Ma'ase Alfas* (commentary about the pronouncements of R' Isaac Alfasi [al-Fasi]), *Masoret HaShisha Sedarim* and *Ner Ma'aravi* about the Jerusalem *Talmud.* A large collection of responses was also left, in manuscript form, *Shevet Achim,* which they had written together, in reply to questions posed by others about the *Halachah.* Apart from these books, his responsa book *Ma'amar Mordechaj* was also published. He was the father of R' Izak Aron Ettinger, who later became head of Lwów's rabbinical court. R' Mordechaj Zew [Ze'ev] died on 20 Tamuz 5623 [7.7.1853].

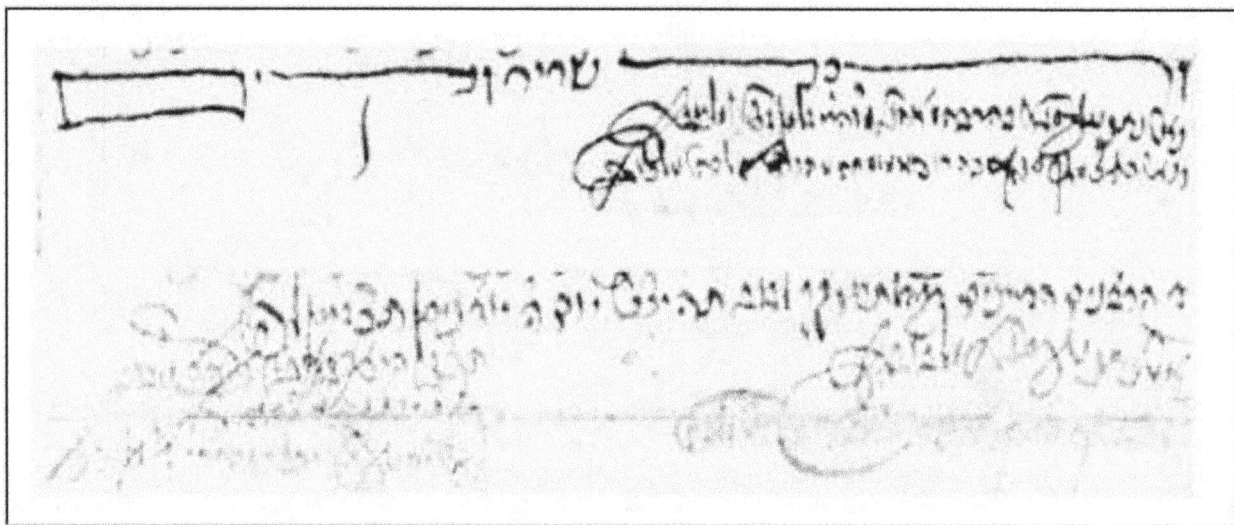

Verdicts by Lwów's rabbinical judges [*Dayanim*] – the signatures of R' Natan Neta ben R' Jekusiel Zelman [Jekutiel Zalman R' Cwi Hirsz [Tzvi Hirsh] son of head of the rabbinical court

5638 (1878). R' Józef Saul ben R' Arje Leibusz Halevy Natansohn, was born at Berezań in 5571 [1810/11]. He married the daughter of R' Izak Aron Halevy Ettinger of Lwów. In the home of his father-in-law he studied the Torah together with his brother-in-law, his wife's brother, R' Mordechaj Zew, and together they wrote the above mentioned books. On 17 Sh'vat 5617 [11.2.1857], R' Józef Saul was appointed head of Lwów's rabbinical court. He responded to every inquirer about Jewish law, and he wrote books about Jewish law and rabbinic literature. Amongst these, his *Sho'el VeMashiv* [Inquirer and Responder], appeared in five editions. *Yosif Da'at,* regarding Part II of *Yoreh De'a*; *Torat Moshe* on the teachings of R' Mojżesz Isserles on the laws that prohibit and those that allow; *Haga'hot Yad Sha'ul,* a new publication of *Shulchan Aruch*; *Beit Sha'ul* on the six Orders of the *Mishnah.* Page proofs of the book *Nachalat Shiv'a. Divreh Sha'ul,* on the Torah two editions *Divreh Sha'ul* sermons, and *Divreh Sha'ul* on the legends of the Babylonian Talmud. Several pamphlets explaining his rulings on the *Halachah,* which attracted his detractors, such as: the permission to knead Mazot by machine, and also a few sermons. He was appointed as head of the rabbinical court at Brześć-Litewski [Brest-Litovsk], but he did not leave Lwów. His soul came to rest on 27 Adar 5635 [4.3.1875].

5648 (1888). R' Cwi Hirsz [Tzvi Hirsh] ben R' Mordechaj Zew [Ze'ev] Ornstein. His father, Rabbi Moses Zacuto [*ReMeZ*], the sole son of R' Jakób Ornstein, died young, before his father, in 5597 (1837), when R' Cwi Hirsz was a youth. Later on, R' Cwi Hirsz married the daughter of R' Jechiel Mechel Kristianpoller, who was the son-in-law of R' Aron, one of Brześć-Litewski's great, author of the book *Minchat Aharon,* about the Sanhedrin tractate. In 5625 (1865), he was appointed head of the rabbinical court at Brześć-Litewski [Brest-Litovsk], where he served at the rabbinate for nine years, until the Russian government ordered him to leave Russia, as he was a national of a foreign country. In 5633 (1873), he was appointed as head of the rabbinical court at Rzeszów [Resche] and the region, and after the demise of Józef Saul Natansohn, head of the rabbinical court of Lwów, he was appointed to replace him. Many of his innovations and responses were published in the second edition of his grandfather's book, *Jeschies Jacow* [Yeshuot Ya'akov]. After his demise, his son-in-law, Arje-Leib Braude published a collection of his responses under the title *Birchat Rabbi Tzvi Hirsh* [*Blessing of Rabbi Cwi Hirsz*]. Died on 9 Nissan 5648 [21.3.1888].

5651 (1891). R' Isaak Aron ben R' Mordechaj Zew [Ze'ev] Halevy Ettinga [Ettinger], president for the whole of Galicia, to tend to the poor in Eretz Israel. He was appointed head of the rabbinical court at Przemyśl [Pshemishl], but as he was well to do, he did not need the income from a rabbinate, and he did not wish to uproot himself from his home in Lwów, his birth place. In 5648 [1888], after the demise of R' Cwi Hirsz Ornstein, he was appointed to replace him as head of Lwów's rabbinical court. Apart from [his] replies which were published in diverse books, two parts of his responses were also published

[Pages 419-420]

under the title *Responsa of Rabbi Isaak Aron Halevy*. His soul rested on 7 Sh'vat 5651 [18.1.1891].

5668 (1906). R' Izak-Juda [Yitzchak-Yehudah] ben R' Chaim Szmuel Szmelkes [Samuel Shmelkes], one of the giants of the Torah in the previous period. He was rabbi at Żurawno [Zhuravne], and later on at Brzeżany [Brzeziny], Przemyśl and finally at Lwów. He wrote the six-volumed responsa, Beit Yitzchak [Isaac's House], on the four sections of the *Shulchan Aruch*; the book *Si'ach-Yitzchak* [Isaac's Conversation], on R' Salomon Kluger; *Divreh Yitzchak* [Isaac's Sayings], homily for the appointment as head of the rabbinical court at Lwów. Died on the eve of Yom Kippur 5668 [8.10.1905].

5676 (1916). R' Mojżesz ben R' Izak, head of the rabbinical court. He was born in 5618 [1857/58] to his father, Rabbi Kalisz [Kalisch]. At the age of eighteen, he was appointed rabbi at Trembowla [Terembowla], and in 5668 [1907/08], as rabbi and head of the rabbinical court, within the town of Lwów. Died 26 Iyar 5676 [29.5.1916].

5688 (1928). R' Arje [Arye] Leib ben Chaim Braude, was the last head of the rabbinical court of Lwów. The son-in-law of Cwi Hirsz [Tzvi Hirsh] Ornstein, he published his *Responsa Bircat Rabbi Cwi Hirsz* together with the addition

Rabbi Izak-Juda [Yitzchak-Yehudah] Szmelkes

Milchement Arye [Arye's War]. He was a member of the rabbinical court of R' Izak Szmelkes, and later, head of the rabbinical court, and deputy within the town. After the demise of Rabbi Izak Szmelkes, he was appointed as rabbi of the rabbinical court. He wrote the *Responsa Mitzpe Arye*, Kama [First] (Lwów 5640 [1880]) and Tinyana [Second] (5672 [1912]), the book *Mukdam VeMe'uchar* Benevolence (5686 [1926]). Died in 5688 [1928].

Notes:

All notes in square brackets [ ] were made by the translator.

    1.   At the behest of Rabbi Margulies, his hand-written article was published, unaltered. The sources: *Klilath Jofi*, A guide to the book by Dembitzer; *Anshei Shem*, by Salomon Buber; Notes and addenda to *Anshei Shem*, which I have published in my book *Sinai* (Jerusalem 1950-1952); Most of the descriptions and acknowledgements follow the inscriptions on the gravestones that were copied in *Mazewes Kodesch* by R' Gabryel Suchystaw [Gawril Suchestow], with various corrections in my annotation.

    2.   See the *Responsa* of Rabbi Izrael Bruna [of Brno; Brünn] (Born approx. in 5160 [1400])

    A.   At the end of the book, *Mizbe'ach Adama* (Thesaloniki 5537 [1776/7]) [sections] 54-59, mention is made of the "Pamphlet of the great scholar [*gaon*], our teacher, the rabbi, Rabbi Alkabetz, of eternal memory, author of the book *Ma'or Enayim*."

    B.   His father was rabbi at Podhajce [Pidhaitsi], later he was head of Yeshivah at Frankfurt-am-Main. Died 22 Cheshvan 5505 [28.10.1744].

[Pages 421-422]

The Religious Life of the Jews of Lwów

by Tzvi [Cwi] Karl

Translated by Myra Yael Ecker

Edited by Dr. Rafael R. Manory

A. The *Charedim* [God–fearing; ultra–orthodox]

1.

The religious life of the Jews of Lwów was on the whole no different from that in the rest of the Lands of Poland and Germany, where Mediæval ways of life and customs still persisted.

Lwów's community was led by rabbis who were known as *Av Beth–Din* [Head of Rabbinical Court], or by Heads of Yeshivah who did not carry the title *Av Beth–Din*, such as Rabbi Jozue Falk [Kohn], author of *Sefer Me'irat Einayim*. From 1680 till 1780, two rabbis concurrently served Lwów as Heads of the Rabbinical Court. One within the town, the other outside it. Likewise, two teaching instructors called *Maggidim* [religious, itinerant preachers] were also appointed, one within the town, the other outside it, each of them acted as Head of the Rabbinical Court in his area, and both were subject to the authority of the overall Head of the Rabbinical court. Among the *Maggidim* outside the town were Rabbi Majer Teomim and his son Rabbi Jozef Teomim, author of *Peri Megadim* [Precious Fruit]. The custom of appointing *Maggidim* continued till 1859. When the *Maggid* Rabbi Symcha Natan Öhlenberg passed away, the community leaders decided not to appoint a *Maggid* outside the town. Instead, the head of the rabbinical court would sit outside the town and a single *Maggid* together with the rabbinical court would sit within the town.

At first, the authority of the rabbi of Lwów's *Beth–Din* within the town extended throughout the entire Land, and all the rabbis of the Land [of Reissen; Ruthenia] were under his supervision. Later on, the leaders of the Council of Four Lands split up the Land into two. One part remained under the authority of Lwów's town rabbi, who added to his signature: "Installed within the holy community of Lwów and the Land," for the town's second part a special rabbi was appointed, who was given the title "Head of the *Beth–Din* of the Land of Lwów" and he added to his signature "Installed in the Land of Lwów."

From the rules that set the rabbis' conditions, the following is worth noting: "The Land–Rabbis and the town–Rabbis are granted an apartment and a salary; the former ten Gulden a week and the latter eight Gulden. Every rabbi can accommodate on his premises one married son or a daughter with her husband. The Rabbi himself is exempt from all taxes, be they to the community or to the government, whether fixed or temporary. If a Rabbi or Rabbis conduct[s] any business, they are only liable to the *Berdonn* tax, and if there is a partner in that business, he has to pay from his share all the taxes levied on him as a community member. The Rabbi's married son or son–in–law, who is supported by him, are exempt, for three years after their marriage, from all taxes apart from the *Berdonn* due from the dowry. None of the Rabbi's relatives, as distant as great–great–grandchildren and those married to them, are permitted to apply for any honorary post on the community–committee or in the rabbinical court [*Beth–Din*].

"The communities' and Land's rabbis have to deliver a sermon twice a year (on Shabbat Hagadol and Shabbat T'shuva) for a fee: the community rabbi two Thalers from the community–committee, and the Land's rabbi five Thalers from the Land's committee.

"The Rabbi will receive one Gulden and 15 Groschen for every 100 Gulden dowry, from every wedding in the community; and four Gulden for every divorce [*Gett*]. The Rabbi and the [religious] judges will receive equal pay for the hearing, and for the certificate and signature–four Gulden.

"Apart from his regular income the rabbi will receive no other income for his incumbency, and he is not permitted to accept any presents from members of his community. The meal for guests following his sermons, is at his expense.

"The rabbi must be honourable, must conduct honest elections in the community and in particular he must oversee that the elections of the *shamayim* [community treasurers] be fair,[1] and he will himself swear in, individually, each and every *shamay*.

"For court hearings between the community–committee and one of its members or a member of another community, the rabbi receives no pay. The rabbi must forbid the eating of any meat slaughtered outside the community. As head of the rabbinical court he is not authorised to allow anyone to pay his debt on a home or plot, so long as the man has not [text missing]"

In respect of granting the titles *Chaver* [Friend] and *Morenu* [our Teacher], with which the rabbis

[Pages 423-424]

used to honour individuals, and the granting of such honours provided them with a source of income; the rabbis' regulations limited the annual number of honours they were entitled to grant: four titles of *Chaver* and two titles of *Morenu*; the title *Chaver*" was granted to individuals who had been married for more than three years, and the title *Morenu*, to those married for over six years. Over time, the rabbi could no longer grant titles to an individual, except on production of a certificate showing that he had paid into the community coffers the set amount demanded for such honours. The restrictions set for the communities' rabbis also applied to the Lands' rabbis.

The rabbi was entitled to excommunicate any offender in the community, subject to the elders' views and instruction. There were incidents in which a Land's rabbi intervened in a Land not under his jurisdiction. Such incidents led to disputes and to reciprocal boycotts. To safeguard against such incidents, King Sigismunt [Zygmunt] Augustus issued in 1551 an order, on pain of heavy financial penalties, forbidding the interference of those from one Land in matters outside their own Land, or a Rabbi calling for a boycott in a Land not under his jurisdiction. It was however possible to impose a preventative boycott; in case a person were to violate an obligation he could be subject to excommunication. At times the government took advantage of the Jews' boycott: when it wanted to impose payment on an individual who refused to comply, it then ordered the rabbi to excommunicate the individual.

The community rabbi was elected in the following manner: the community elders congregated and from among the highest tax payers to the community coffers they selected some [religious] scholars, and the latter, by majority vote, elected the rabbi. The manner of electing the Land's rabbi is not detailed in source records.

The number of rabbinical judges [*dayanim*] at Lwów was 12 inside the town, and 12 outside the town.

When the Austrians first ruled Galicia, a single rabbi was elected, in accordance with the Jewish regulation, for the entire region of Galicia and Lodomeria, and the Land of Zamość together with 12 community–elders and leaders (*Judendirektion*) managed all Jewish matters in the Land and the region. They acted as a kind of governmental consistory. In disputes between individuals and in questions of inheritance, the Land's *dayanim* acted in accordance with the Torah. In religious matters they had the authority to excommunicate the offender and separate him from the community and also to punish him by placing an iron yoke around his neck or placing him in jail. The rabbis' verdict, on financial issues, was not open to appeals. The sole option open was to submit a request to the Kaiser's court and to the upper legal department, the rabbinical judges would sanction the judgement by a seal stamped with a two–headed eagle and all other symbols of the Royal House.

The rabbi's election was in two stages: arbitrators were elected from among the Land's people, and the arbitrators elected the rabbi by majority vote. Three candidates were required, and were the votes even, then the decision was left to the Kaiser.

The fixed salary of the Land's rabbi amounted to 600 silver Florins. In addition, it was decided that any rabbi, cantor, [ritual] slaughterer, preacher and teacher of Jewish law at any of the Land's towns, would not be appointed without the authorisation of the Land's rabbi, who received a payment for granting the permission and the certificate. Moreover, the right to honour [an individual] with the title *Morenu* was granted to the Land's Rabbi alone, which formed a source of income for him.

The 7th May 1789 Jewish statute of Kaiser Joseph II, ruled that rabbis needed to be appointed just for the Lands (*Kreisrabbiner*), in towns only cantors (*Schul–sänger*) had to be assigned. The rabbi had no authority over the Jews in legal matters, and he was not permitted to excommunicate other than when so instructed by the authorities. Six years after the unveiling of the Jewish statute (*Toleranzedikt*), secular secondary–school level examination certificates were required from rabbis. Over and above such a certificate, a certificate demonstrating knowledge of the principles of religion in accordance with the official text (*Bne–Zion* by Herz Homberg) was in fact also required. The rabbi would be elected by the members of the community entitled to vote, depending on payments of the candle–tax – (seven candles in Lwów) – during the year prior to the elections. At Lwów the district–rabbi was paid an annual salary of 400 Florins from the community purse. Following the 1836 government order, the rabbinical candidate was required to present proof he had passed an Austrian University examination in philosophy and ethics. On the whole, no candidate for the rabbinate had such proof. In 1855, the *Charedim* managed to convince the Minister Graf [von] Thun to waive this requirement, and he provided certificates for candidates to the rabbinate, exempting them from this requirement. Due to such certificates, Rabbi Józef Saul Natansohn was appointed in Lwów, as did others who followed him.

2.

During the peak of the conflict between the Chassidim and the opposers, Lwów's rabbis played a significant role. Rabbi Hirsz Rosanes (1787–1806), imposed a boycott on the Chassidim, forbidding to employ Chassidim as replacement slaughterers

[Pages 425-426]

and the Chassidim were forbidden from setting up prayer houses and from following their unique version of prayer. During the days of Rabbi Jakub Meszulam [Ornstein], author of *Jeschies Jacow* [*Yeshu'ot Ja'akov*] (1805–1839), opposition to the Chassidim had waned however. At that time, the Chassidim reverted from the path of resistance to the Talmud and set regular times for the Talmud and were known as *Chadaszim* [New]. The name *Kloyz Chadaszim* [house of worship of the New] was given to the synagogue that the *Chassid* Jakob Glanzer [Jankiel Jancer] constructed on the site of Saint Theodore's church, Lwów.

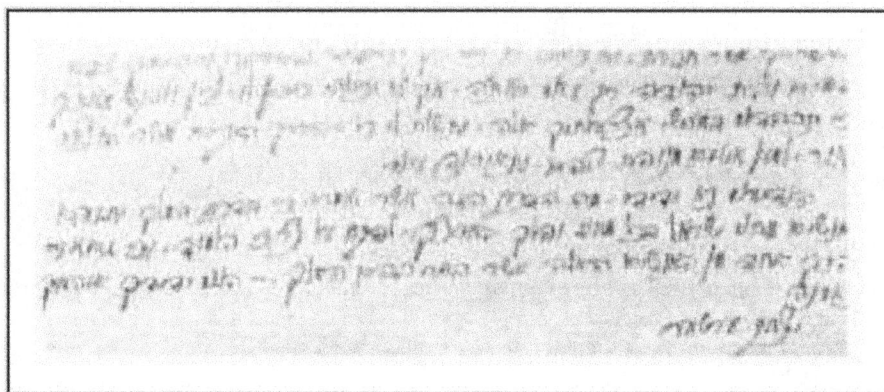

Handwriting of [Dr.] I. Erter

Rabbi Jakub fought the representatives of the *Haskala* [Enlightenment] with greater vigour, and in 1816 he excommunicated *Shir* [Salomon Jehudah Rappoport], Erter and others who were considered the disseminators of the *Haskala*. Subsequently, the authorities obliged him to revoke the excommunication in public.

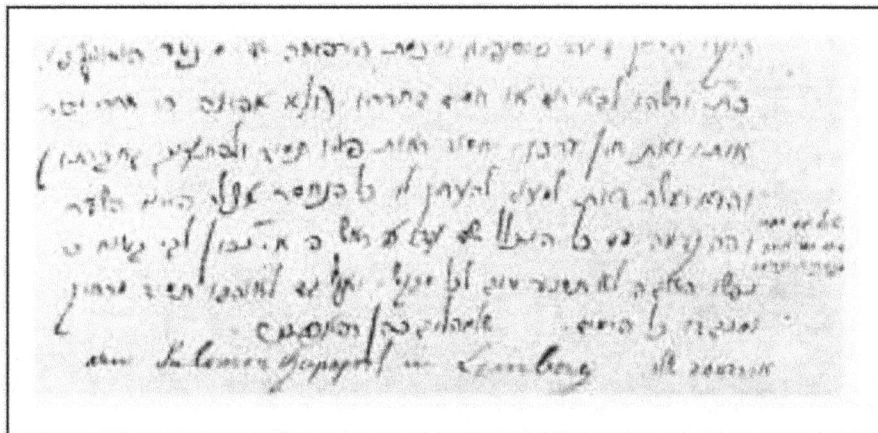

Handwriting of SHIR

The period after the demise of Rabbi Jakub Meszulam Ornstein, was filled with conflict and controversy between the *Charedim* and the Enlightened [*Maskilim*].

As the conflict escalated, one of the community leaders, Natan Sokal, in an attempt of reconciliation, held a consultation at his home to which he invited moderate *Charedim*. No compromise was reached however, because the *Charedim* insisted that Rabbi Abraham Kohn relinquish his post. Not wishing to show any sign of surrender, the progressives did not let Rabbi Kohn leave Lwów.

During the funeral of Modal, the cantor of the synagogue outside the town, a severe clash erupted at the cemetery when the Temple's cantor, Ozjasz Abras, attempted to deliver a eulogy for the deceased. Beaten and wounded the people escaped the cemetery; even the "National Guard" had to get involved to bring the conflict to an end. The dispute was also published in the Jewish press outside Galicia, such as the Leipzig *Allgemeine Zeitung des Judenthums*, and the Vienna *Central–Organ* [*für Glaubensfreiheit, Geschichte und Literatur der Juden*]. The dispute ended with the poisoning of Rabbi Abraham Kohn, his daughter and son on 6th September 1848 (by one of the fanatics, Berl Pilpel).

After the tragedy, Rabbi Symcha Natan Öhlenberg served as the acting rabbi for the *Charedim*. The *Charedim* feared to have a rabbi appointed from among the progressives, and were stumped by the 1836 decree that obliged a candidate to the rabbinate to provide proof he had passed the university examination. Rabbi Hirsz Chajes at Zólkiew was the sole candidate to the Galician rabbinate who had passed this examination. Only later was Rabbi Józef Saul Natansohn appointed (1857), (the son of Rabbi Leibusz of Brzeżany [Brezhan], author of the book *Bet El* [House of God], and son–in–law of Isaak Aron Ettinger of Lwów). Rabbi Józef Saul wrote many books, and it was he who had sanctioned the baking of *matzot* in a machine [a recently invented machine], contrary to the view of others. The relationship between Rabbi Józef Saul and the preachers at the "Temple of the Enlightened," Dr. Schwabacher and Dr. Löwenstein, was amicable.

In 1861, the Kaiser approved the founding of a Rabbinical seminary at Lwów, and granted it official rights. The Kaiser

[Pages 427-428]

also determined that candidates for the rabbinate would not be required to provide proof of gymnasium education or studies in philosophy, but solely proof of knowledge of specific subjects. The *Charedim* objected to the establishment of the Rabbinical seminary and took steps to thwart its execution. They were successful and the seminary did not open, even after 1907 when its opening was approved by the Galician *Sejm*.

In the sixties [1860s] Lwów's *Charedim* submitted appeals to the Ministry, requesting to penalise Jews whose shops were open on the Sabbath or on religious Holidays, and further, that the right to elect the community committees be granted solely to Jews who upheld all the laws noted in the *Shulchan Aruch* [an abbreviated form of the Jewish ritual law]. The Ministry investigated the issue and came to no conclusions.

Rabbi Józef Saul Natansohn died in 1875, and at the head of the rabbinate was Rabbi Tzvi [Cwi] Hirsz Ornstein, the ardent opponent of Rabbi Kohn.

In 1882, a gathering of rabbis took place at Lwów, that was also attended by Rabbi Szymon Sofer [Schreiber] of Kraków (son of Rabbi Moses Sofer [Schreiber], author of *Chatam Sofer* [Scribe's Seal]). At the meeting, the *Charedim* decided on a plan to withdraw the voting rights from a Jew who did not adhere to the laws of *Shulchan Aruch*. Notwithstanding, he would be obliged to pay taxes to the community coffers. Rabbi Cwi Ornstein objected however to the plan and left the gathering. Concurrently, the weekly magazine *Machsike Hadas* [*Zeitung für das wahre Orthodoxische Judenthum*; Upholders of the Faith] made its first appearance.

Of his reservations about the rabbis' gathering, Rabbi Cwi [Tzvi] Ornstein wrote to Rabbi Meszulam Halevi Horowitz, the Rabbi of Stanislawów, in the following letter:

"With God's help, Lwów, Sunday *Shavuot* [the Festival of Weeks, celebrating the Giving of the Torah, seven Weeks after Passover] eve, 1882.

To the all knowledge and my fervent comrade, the outstanding, renowned great scholar, the sage who acquired wisdom in Israel, great is the name of my teacher, Meszulam Halevi Horowitz, light of the Jewish People, Head of the *Beth–Din* of Stanislawów and its quarters, May the Lord's grace be on him.

After wishing well to him, whose honourable teaching is like law, a great man may the like of him multiply in Israel, his dearest letter has reached me on time, in reply I herewith express to the honourable teacher that I withdrew without intervening in matters concerning *Machsike Hadas*, after noting during the Rabbis' assembly of last year, that they would not listen to a whispering voice and directness, but they persisted and I called after them, destroyers and wreckers you will beget destroyers, called destroyers on purpose and wreckers are those who wreck everything, mindlessly. Their common ground to go and harm as experience has taught me, and they still hold on to their stupidity, let them have whatever they have and innocently I go, that is what I found to respond to his honoured teaching and will remain a kin who blesses him with the joy of *Yom Tov* [Jewish Holy day], his admirer who esteems his merit, the Rabbi Cwi Hirsz Ornstein."

Rabbi Cwi [Tzvi] Hirsz Ornstein was succeeded, as Lwów's Head of the Rabbinical Court, by Rabbi Isaak Aron Ettinger. He did not subscribe to the views of Rabbi Józef Saul Natansohn, who held that Lwów could be considered "private–domain," where one could carry items from place to place on the Sabbath. And consequently he lobbied to have fixed *Eruvs* [wires that form the physical boundary of an urban space within which the Orthodox can carry items on the Sabbath & Holidays] installed in the town, to allow supervising the integrity of the wires and the *Eruvs*.

Rabbi Isaak Aron Ettinger did not live long; and died in 1891.

Rabbi Izak Schmelkes of Przemyśl was appointed his successor. During his tenure the Governorship approved the new regulations for the community that determined to have two rabbis for Lwów: a community–rabbi for the *Charedim* and a community–rabbi for the progressives. According to the regulations, 30 voters were appointed who, together with the managers of the "Temple" and members of the community committee, elected Dr. Jecheskiel Caro as community–Rabbi (39 votes, against 15), on 25th May 1898. The *Charedim* submitted a petition against this selection. Among the *Charedim* signatory to the petition were Nachum Burstin, Mendel Margoszes, Lejzor Gutwirth and others. The Governorship rejected the petition. On 1st January 1898, the swearing–in ceremony of the community's three rabbis took place: Rabbi Izak Schmelkes, Rabbi Halpern and Rabbi Dr. Caro.

After the demise of Rabbi Izak Schmelkes, Rabbi Leib Braude, the son–in–law of Rabbi Hirsz Ornstein who had been preacher within the town, was appointed Rabbi for the community's *Charedim*. The relation between the progressives and the *Charedim* improved, as they too realised the need for knowledge of secular studies. Many of the *Charedim* provided their sons and daughters also with a secular education. Indeed, when the question arose about nominating Rabbi Leib Braude to the rabbinate, many objected to his nomination, and when he was elected they showed their objection by bringing to Lwów Rabbi Mojzesz Rappoport[2] from America, and received him as the town's Rabbi. His flock concentrated largely at the *Chadaszim* synagogue.

[Pages 429-430]

The *Chibat Zion* Movement [Affection for Zion] that sprang up in Galicia, started to make waves and even permeated the *Charedim* circles. The *Charedim* at Lwów founded the society *Dorsze Szlom Zion* which was later renamed *Tikwat Zion* [The Hope of Zion].

The national movement led the *Charedim* to collaborate with the progressives, while notwithstanding, the relations between some of the *Charedim* and the progressives had improved. *HaMizrachi* Union, formed from the ranks of the Zionists with the aim of cooperating with all circles, and with the Progressives in particular on matters of non–religious nature, rejected a section of the *Charedim* who found fault in all contact with the Progressives, which led to the formation of *Agudas Yisroel* (in Congress Poland, the association was known as *Shlomey Emuney Yisroel* [Stalwarts of the Jewish Faith]), that also operated in Lwów.

However, *Agudas Yisroel* did not encompass all those *Charedim* who did not cooperate with Lwów's Zionists. Those who did not join *Agudas Yisroel* were largely the Belz–Chassidim who congregated around the [*Kloyz*] *Chadaszim*. The *Achdus Yisroel* Association also had a presence in the town. During the twenties, the appointed community–committee was made up of the assimilated, the Zionists, as well as representatives of *HaMizrachi* and *Agudas Yisroel*. Concurrently, the society *Machsikey Limmud* was founded, which offered evening classes in Judaism.

B. The Progressives

1.

In the 1830s, Joseph Perl of Tarnopol spurred Lwów's intelligentsia to emulate, in their town his Tarnopol undertakings in the field of education and in improving religious life. This concept did not however come into fruition before 1840, when two advocate, Dr. Emanuel Blumenfeld and Dr. Leo Kolischer had decided to get involved in the creation of a prayer house for the Progressives, in Lwów. They approached Dr. Jakob Rappaport[3] with the request that he join them to turn their idea into reality, and sign with them an invitation to the Yeshivah to discuss the undertaking. Dr. Rappaport consented to their request, and a meeting was held at Dr. Emanuel Blumenfeld's home on 4th October 1840. Among the invited were: Dr. Moritz Rappoport, a German poet and relative of *Shir*; Dr. Natkis, the son of Rabbi Benjamin Cwi [Zvi] Hirsz Natkis, member of the *Maskilim* [Enlightened] group, whom Rabbi Jakub Meszulam Ornstein had boycotted; Dr. Maksymilian Landesberger who later became a delegate to the Galician *Sejm*; his son–in–law Dr. J. Rappoport; Dr. Oswald Menkes; Keller; Dr. Adam Barach-Rappaport; the meeting was also attended by Majer Rachmiel Mieses, and his son–in–law Samuel Kellermann and his brother–in–law Meier Münz and others. The issues debated at the meeting were:

1. Should a prayer–house be constructed for the Progressives?
2. What would be the source of the funds?
3. Should the fundraising and management be for Lwów alone?
4. The organisation of the new prayer–house, its ritual service etc.
5. Elections for the committee.

All the assembled agreed to establish a German–Jewish prayer–house. The question remained however whether a large hall should be constructed straight away, a choir assembled and a cantor and preacher appointed, or whether the more modest steps of hiring a hall should be settled for. It was eventually decided to start the building of a "Temple" suited for Lwów's Jewish community. The appointed community–committee included Jakub Rappoport, Epstein, Kolischer, Blumenfeld, Dubs and Rosenstein. Mendel Schorr was appointed treasury, Dr. Grünberg as secretary, Natan Kolischer as supervisor and Majer Baczeles, director (who some years later converted to Christianity and changed his name to Baczewski). At this meeting the participants committed themselves to partake in the undertaking to collect 1,800 Gulden. Of that sum, Fischel Dubs and his sons donated 200 Gulden. The order of prayer was debated at the meeting, but it was decided to get the advice of the preacher Mannheimer of Vienna, and Dr. Sachs of Prague. An annual budget was set at 1,800 Gulden.

After the meeting they began collecting funds, and when they reached 4,000 Gulden they decided to elect a construction committee and to inaugurate the

[Pages 431-432]

"Temple of the Enlightened" in a great ceremony. At the meeting held in Dr. Blumenfeld's home, in October 1840, Dr. Jakub Rappoport delivered a speech, saying: "Today, with the Lord's workings, we inaugurate a Temple and we have to be mindful that most of our brethren who are unable, or are still unwilling to attend this Temple, should not turn against us. That will certainly happen were we not to use the old, Hebrew language but rather use German in our prayers, and we would provoke the anger of the *Charedim* were we to omit some of the prayers. We need not be ashamed of our nationalism. As a man involved with people, I assert that the peoples do not hate us as much as some of us claim. Furthermore, we need not be ashamed of our religious practices, be it the language or the ritual. There is however a section of the Holidays' prayers that can easily be omitted, as the Chassidim have already done (i.e. liturgical poems). Nevertheless, the basic prayers must be maintained. Personally, for as long as there is breath in me, I shall resist any adulteration of the prayer sequence, or the inclusion of prayers in the German language. I fear however that after my death you will be prepared to do so, for that reason I implore you and make you take an oath that you will not do so." Some of those who heard the address shed tears, but all rose as one from their seats and took the oath to remain faithful to the traditional synagogue, without any alterations to the language or the religious practice in the new prayer–house. After every detail of their sworn commitment was entered in the minutes, they elected Dr. Jakub Rappoport as chairman of the "Temple's" committee. He was succeeded by his son–in–law Dr. Adam Barach-Rappaport. Donations kept coming, and the fund–collectors did not avoid the doors of the *Charedim*, and one of them, Jakob Glanzer, a wealthy *Chassid,* donated 60 Gulden. On the whole, the donations trickled in slowly, and it took a long time before the vision could be materialised.

1842 saw a marked change in the political status of Lwów's community. Initially the authorities did not involve themselves in the conflicts between the *Charedim* and the progressives, but suddenly they sided with the progressives, delayed the elections that were due and introduced a "supervising committee" in lieu of the elected community committee. Nearly all the supervisors were from among the progressive circles.

The appointment of the commission also advanced the actual construction of the "Temple." In June 1842, a planning application was submitted to the authorities for the construction of a modern prayer–house, like the synagogues of Vienna and Prague, to which a school for Jewish youth would be attached. The authorities demanded from the applicants to justify the need for such a prayer–house, and to supply information about the financing of its construction and maintenance. The founders replied that the intelligentsia found the old synagogues unsatisfactory, because the prayer in them was loud, they had no preacher and offered no moral instruction, no cantor and no choir to sweeten the prayer for the youth to commune with their God.

Committee of the "Temple of the Enlightened" (1910)

[Pages 433-434]

"The Temple of the Enlightened"

Also, because all the seats in Lwów's synagogues were sold in perpetuity, it was impossible to obtain additional seats in them. It was also impossible to hold in them patriotic parties, and this adversely affected the youth's education. In respect of the finance, they mentioned the 4,000 Gulden legacy left by Isak Rosenberg for the purpose of constructing a new prayer–house. A positive reply was received from the authorities and the only question was where to erect the prayer–house. After an extensive debate they chose a site on Rybia Street that they had purchased from Lwów's municipality for 1,434 Gulden. The land was entered at the land–registry office under the title "Deutsch–Israelitisches Bethaus [German–Jewish prayer–house]." At the end of the 19th century, its name was revised to "Synagoga postępowa" (Synagogue of the Progressives).

Among the donors to the appeal was Graf Saryusz Zamojski, who donated a large number of trees, and Kaiser Franz–Joseph I's father donated 100 Gulden, and these facts were published in all the newspapers.

The construction of the "Temple" began to the discontent of the *Charedim*. It is said that at the beginning whatever was built during the daytime was demolished at night by unknowns, so that guards had to be posted to protect the construction from being destroyed. The building plan emulated that of the prayer–house on Seitenstettengasse, Vienna (as noted by Dr. Bałaban in his book: *Historia Lwowskiej synagogi Postępowej* [History of the Lwów's Progressive Synagogue]. As a child I heard told that the building was constructed according to a plan that followed the template of the cross of the Catholic Church, and that only later by adding buildings on the sides of the edifice, the form of the cross was disguised.). While the building was under construction, those engaged in its undertaking turned their attention to inviting those who might officiate in it. For the post of cantor, the proposal of Ozjasz Abras of Tarnopol was accepted. It was harder to find a preacher. On the advice of cantor Sulzer of Vienna, Dr. Emanuel Blumenfeld approached Rabbi Abraham Kohn, who was rabbi at Hohenems, Vorarlberg (Austria) and invited him to come and deliver two trial sermons at Lwów, and promised to pay his travel expenses.

Rabbi Abraham Kohn was born at Zalužany [Saluschean], Jungbunzlau district of Bohemia. His father, Salomon Kohn, was a peddler. The son studied the Bible [Tanach] and Talmud with great interest. At the age of twelve he moved to Jungbunzlau where he concluded his humanistic education, and concurrently studied Talmud with Rabbi Izak Spitz. He was employed by a wealthy Jew, but was dismissed after being caught reading a French book. He moved to Pisek and earned his living as a private teacher. It was here that he delivered his first sermon at the inauguration of the new prayer–house. He spent some time in Prague and befriended Rabbi Samuel Landau, who furnished him with a teaching permit. Rabbi Samuel Kauders at Kaladay, Hungary, also granted him an ordination certificate. Herz Homberg granted him a pedagogical certificate for teaching [the Jewish] religion. In 1833, he was given the post of Rabbi at Hohenems; he taught at two schools: the German school and the religious school where he was headmaster, taught religion and the Hebrew language. At the prayer–house he introduced some reforms: he shortened the prayer, introduced a choir, introduced the calling to the Torah by the use of first name and surname, and on *Simchat Torah* calling just nine individuals to the Torah.

[Pages 435-436]

Apart from these functions he also founded societies, "*Gemilus–Chesed*" and others. His sermons were published in print and he contributed to various magazines and published a book on the grammar of the Hebrew language.

Rabbi Kohn was asked to serve as preacher in Lwów. He delivered his sermon at the Synagogue outside the town, on the Sabbath of the weekly Torah portion (*Parashat*) *Ekev*. The progressives who congregated in the Synagogue, listened to the preacher's words with satisfaction, and did not wait

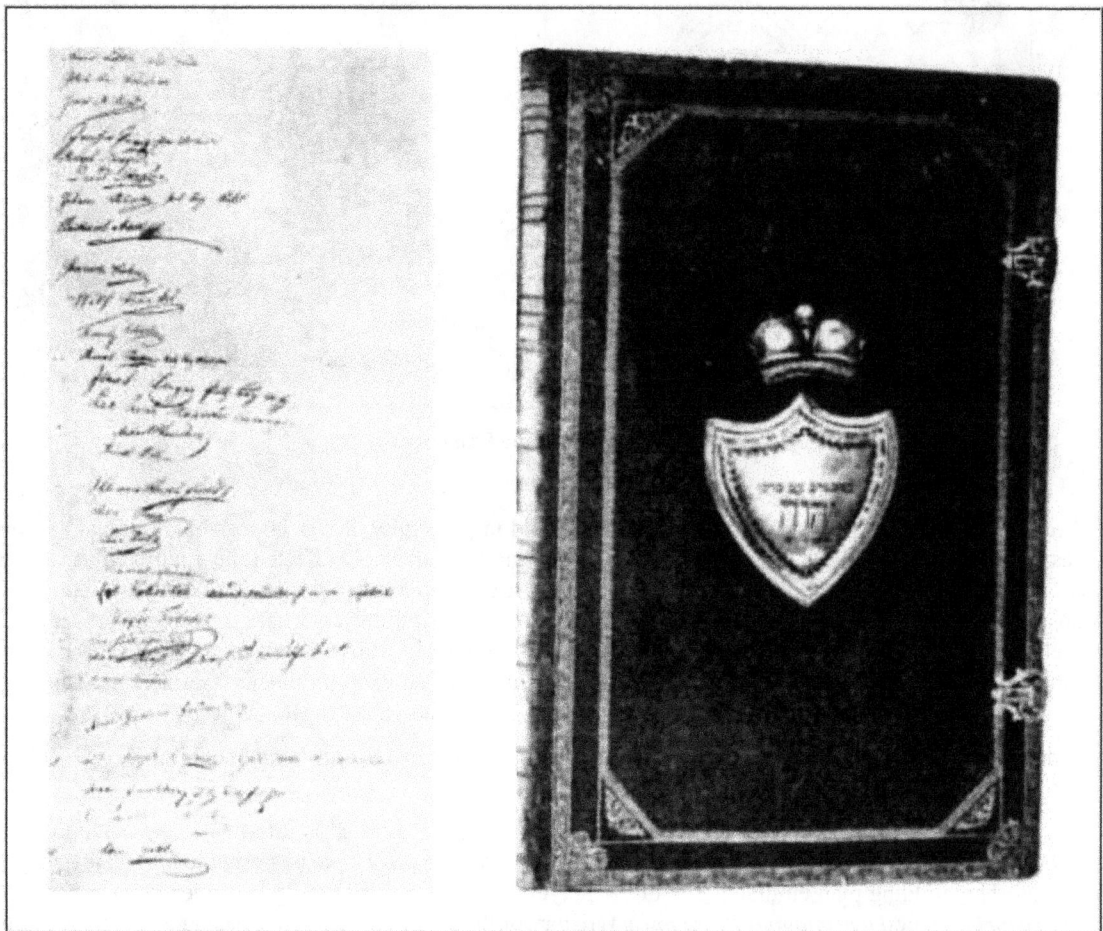

[(Title missing) Title should be:
Register from 1840 created by the Committee for the Construction of the Progressive Synagogue at Lwów]

for his second sermon, but immediately made a contract with him and submitted it to the authorities for their approval, and the approval was received.

According to the contract, he was given the post of instructor of religion (religionsweiser) and he was obligated to officiate as preacher at the yet to be constructed "Temple," wearing the official preacher's garments that were decided for him. Once the question of the religious instruction was set, he would be entrusted the teaching of [the Jewish] religion at gymnasiums [secondary schools] and at the state school planned to be built locally, at which he would become headmaster and would oversee the religious instruction. Were he not to be granted the authorities' licence as instructor of religion, he was promised the Lwów's rabbinate with all its privileges and duties. Rabbi Kohn returned to Hohenems, resigned his post there, returned to Lwów and reached it on 5ᵗʰ May 1844.

His first sermon on the first Shabbath after his arrival at Lwów to officiate as preacher, was also delivered at the synagogue outside the town, in the presence of the Jewish intelligentsia and the government representative, [Franz] Ferdinand Archduke of Austria–Este, the regional Head, von Millbacher, and the Mayor Festenburg with his entourage. Rabbi Kohn wore a preacher's attire. The following day, according to the Rabbi's brother, the Orthodox tore their clothes over the desecration of the holy building with quotes from the Bible, in German. To enrage the *Charedim*'s even further, an anonymous writer told in *"Mefer Ezat Reshaim* [Breach the advice of the wicked"], that during the prayer the *"Parochet"* [ornamental curtain in front of the holy ark in a synagogue] was placed on the floor and Rabbi Kohn stepped on it. Once the general school opened, Kohn became its headmaster.

In 1844, the cantor Ozjasz Abras of Tarnopol who took on himself the task to form a choir at "the Temple" and train its members in their roles, was also engaged. Abras who was born at Brody, studied to be a cantor while serving as assistant to Cantor Model, at the

[Pages 437-438]

synagogue outside the town, as well as with Cantor Bezalel of Odessa. He also studied with Sulzer, and according to him even with Liszt. During 1842–1860 he was cantor at the Tarnopol "Temple" founded by Josef Perl. Being unsuccessful in training the choir, the Italian Józef Ernesti, and the German Pollak, were brought in to assist him, and to train the choir. Michał Wolf was appointed reader of the Torah at the synagogue. The first caretakers of the "Temple" were Juda Samuel Kantor and Salomon Blumenfeld. On Friday 18ᵗʰ September 1846, the inauguration of "The Temple of the Enlightened" was celebrated in the presence of the government representatives and under the protection of the armed forces. Rabbi Abraham Kohn gave his address after the opening words of Dr. Blumenfeld.

Abraham Kohn held the title of "Instructor of religion and preacher" (*Religionsweiser und Prediger*), but he aspired to be Lwów's Rabbi, replacing the author of *Jeschies Jacow*, Jakob Ornstein, who died in 1839. The issue was in the hands of the authorities, and once the *Charedim* heard of it, they submitted an objection to the authorities, describing Abraham Kohn as a peasant and an outlaw; their protestation was in vain and Kohn was confirmed by the authorities as Lwów's town Rabbi.

In his sermons he strongly criticised the behaviour of the *Charedim*, and in "Letters from Galicia" which he published in the board of shame; he mocked superstitions and mystery, the custom of *Kaparot* and the *"Tashlich,"* as well as women's head shaving and their wearing of wigs, and adornment with jewellery that gave rise to the envy of the gentiles. He also organised "confirmations" (Bar–Mitzvah celebrations unlike the traditional custom) for boys and girls, which the Orthodox considered a step towards religious conversion.

After the 1848 March Revolution in Vienna, the *Charedim* decided to submit a petition to the Kaiser or to the government, to dismiss Abraham Kohn from his post, because he was the cause of all evil, and furthermore to remove from their status the leaders of the progressive community of Lwów and the other towns; it was that which they considered a prerequisite for equal rights. The petition which was signed by a large number of people, reached the community officer Bernard Piepes, who confiscated it, and Grünfeld who had collected the signatures, was jailed and the *Charedim*'s recommendation was opposed. The hot–headed among the crowd surrounded Rabbi Kohn's home, threw stones at its window–panes and tried to force themselves into the house that was closed to them. The army was alerted, and was hard put to disperse the attackers. A consultation of the community leaders and the *Charedim* ended in deadlock because the *Charedim* insisted on their demand that Kohn leave Lwów, and they even agreed to provide him with a large compensation, for his livelihood until he found another job. The progressives opposed the condition and the schism between the two sides widened. Ever since then, Rabbi Kohn could not walk the streets in safety. Eventually he was maliciously poisoned to death.

Dr. Moritz Löwenthal replaced him as rabbi for a short period only, followed by candidates for the post of preacher: Dr. Eleazer [Łazarz] Igel, who studied at the Padua rabbinical seminary directed by *SaDaL* [Samuel David Luzzatto] and was lecturer at Lwów University; and Dr. Efraim Izrael Blücher. Dr. Igel was originally from Lwów and on his return from Padua he got a post as teacher of religion at the gymnasium and a licence to teach Oriental–languages. Unable to manage as a preacher nor as a University lecturer, however, he left Lwów and became the rabbi of the progressives at Czernowitz. Dr. Blücher also left Lwów. Michał Wolf held the post of preacher at "The Temple of the Enlightened," first on a temporary basis but he was later permanently appointed.

The "Temple" synagogue managers in those days were Dr. Emil Blumenfeld, Marek Dubs and Hersz Zipper. In 1850, they were succeeded by Kolischer and Ozjasz Jolles, and in 1852, the appointed managers were Izak Aron Rosenstein, Ignac Lewkowicz, Abraham Beiser, Dr. Leo Kolischer and Berisz Hescheles. The managers in 1858, were: Dr. Bernard Sternberg, the advocate Dr. Dawid Diamand, Hilel Lechner (from among the *Maskilim* circles, and council leader at Zniesienie) and Motel Braun. Lechter was said to occupy himself with the Sabbath laws, in order to know how to transgress them; he was a "Temple" manager for over twenty years.

For years no preacher had replaced Rabbi Abraham Kohn at the "Temple." The progressives had their eyes on Dr. Leopold Lŏw, the Rabbi of the Szeged community in Hungary, who came to Lwów and delivered a sermon and a scientific lecture at the Temple, and to the community, but was not appointed. In 1857, Dr. Szymon (Leon) Schwabacher was appointed preacher. He was born at Obernsdorf, [Baden–]Württemberg, in 1817. He gained rabbinical ordination [S×³michut] and in addition, a doctor of philosophy from the University of Tübingen. He served as preacher in Prague and later as Rabbi and preached at Homburg, Schwerin and Landsberg. When he arrived in Lwów as candidate for the post of preacher at the "Temple," the community did not take to him because of the arrogance he showed towards them, receiving them dressed in the official clothes. Even to weddings and funerals he arrived in his official clothing, thus provoking the *Charedim* and probably also the Catholic clergy, on appearing in front of Governor Gułochowski in a garment that enraged him. After a short period he left for Odessa where he was appointed community Rabbi and preacher (1859). In that capacity he served there for 25 years. When elections to the Odessa rabbinate were held in accordance with Czar Alexander III's orders,

[Pages 439-440]

however, Dr. Schwabacher was unsuccessful, and aged seventy he was left without an income. He died on 25th December 1888 [10 Tevet 5648].

Together with Dr. Schwabacher, the cantor Abras also left Lwów for Odessa, where he had been accepted as cantor.

Sixteen candidates vied for the post of preacher for the Lwów community, of whom only four had passed the examination: Dr. Duschak, Rabbi at Gaya in Mähren [Kyjov]; Dr. Hajjim Jolowicz, of Kŏnigsberg [today Kaliningrad, Russia]; Moritz Hirschfeld, of Gross Meseritsch [Velk*Tashlich* MeziŘíčí]; Bernard (Isachar Berusz) Lŏwenstein, Rabbi at Buczowice. Dr. Lŏwenstein won the election with a large majority (1862). In addition to his post as preacher, he was also charged with teaching religion at the secondary schools, and managing the population register (births, deaths and marriages). As registrar, the Rabbi of the *Charedim* required his approval for arranging marriages, an approval that he was not permitted to delay except when the marriage was illegal.

After cantor Abras had left Lwów, his deputy Mojzesz Roman replaced him and only in 1862 was the scholar and *Maskil* Oswald Weiss of Szeged appointed cantor. Dr. Lŏwenstein and the cantor Weiss managed to gain the favour of the praying public at the "Temple." Dr. Lŏwenstein who was born at Międzyrzec [Podlaski] in 1821, was a scion of the Rabbi who wrote *Pnei Jehoschua* [Yehoshua], and was related to the families Herc Bernstein and Horowitz. He studied in Amsterdam and Hanover (at the Yeshivah of Rabbi Natan Adler, who later became a Rabbi in London), at Prague University and with Rabbi *Shir*, Jakub Józef Ettinger and others. He was preacher and headmaster of the school at Lipto St. Miklosz and Rabbi at Buczowice, and from there he was invited to Lwów.

Dr. Lŏwenstein's sermons aroused much interest, and even non–Jews, among them Governor Mensdorff, came to hear his speeches. He held his sermons on special events such as, on the 70–th anniversary of Lipman [Leopold] Zunz, the eulogy for *SaDaL*, etc. and further at the 1878 opening of the first congress of Galicia's communities, which was instigated by *Szomer Izrael* [The Guardian of Israel], and at the congress of the "Fire Brigade" he held prayers at the "Temple." The prayers on State occasions, were generally accompanied by music played by a military orchestra.

Dr. Lŏwenstein often lectured to the "Association for the resourceful the Good and the Honest" (*Verein für Bildung und Geselligkeit*) and also to the *Szomer Izrael* society, which for a while formed the hub of political activity.

Dr. Lŏwenstein taught religious studies at two gymnasiums and also acted as the prison's preacher. In 1883, together with Szymon Landau, he opened a *Talmud–Torah* [Torah–Study school] named *Ohel Mosze* [Moses' Tent] where Jewish and secular studies were taught. This *Talmud–Torah* lasted only two years because of disputes with the *Charedim*. Apart from his educational work, he was also much involved in charity and was even elected to the town–council. He received the "Gold Cross for Merit" and in 1885, the Kaiser Franz Joseph I's Medal. He died in 1889. His only son, Natan, married Miriam the daughter of Samuel Horowitz, one of the well–to–do, the community leader and among the leading assimilators.

During his time, the managers of the "Temple" were Dr. Sternberg, Lechner, Leib Russman, the pharmacist Jonas Beiser and the pharmacist Zygmunt Rucker. In 1870, the anniversary of the "Temple" was celebrated in the presence of the *Sejm*'s Christian delegates: Smolka and Ziemiałkowski as well as representatives from the municipality and the armed forces. Dr. Lŏwenstein gave a celebratory address and cantor Weiss showed his prowess in musical renditions. At the festive reception that followed, Hilel Lechner also spoke, warning of the culture–war that threatened Lwów's Jewish community at the time. Hilel Lechner was the chairman of the Temple's management, and his colleagues were Jonas Beiser, Emnuel Gall, Zygmunt Rucker, Dr. Szymon Schaff who later became chairman of the community committee. In 1882–3, of the earlier managers [of the Temple] only Lechner and Beiser remained, and new ones were appointed: Dr. Salomon Landesberg, Natan Mayer and Henryk Jolles. Natan Mayer, who joined the community committee after some time, was a member of the chamber of commerce and of the municipality as well as chairman of the "Temple's" management board. Under his management a foot pedal harmonium (Fussharmonium), and later an organ were introduced into the "Temple." In 1883 there were elections to the management, but most of the elected withdrew from their posts; the community committee then appointed Lechner as management–commissioner, and Dr. Schaff and Dr. Landesberg, his assistants. Shortly afterwards new elections were held and Beiser, Mayer and Landesberg, Emil de–Mieses and Eliasz Zabludowski formed the management.

After the death of Dr. Löwenstein (March 1889) the preacher's post was offered by tender. Part of the candidates' requirements was the knowledge of German and Polish. Of the candidates, three were invited to the examination: Dr. Szymon Dankowicz, Dr. Herman Klüger and Dr. Jecheskiel Caro. Of the three, Dr. Caro was accepted as preacher and the supervision of religious studies was also given to him. The title of "Rabbi" which he requested to be granted, was declined until the regulations were changed.

Dr. Jecheskiel Caro was born in 1844 at Pniewy where his father, Józef–Chaim was rabbi. His family lineage extended back to Rabbi Józef Caro, author of *Shulchan Aruch*. Rabbi Józef–Chaim wrote books and was also rabbi at Fordon and Włocławek [Leslau], he contributed to [Nachum] Sokolow's periodical *HaAsif* [The Harvest] and was a sympathiser of *Ahavat Zion* [Love of Zion] Movement. His eldest son Jakub was

[Pages 441-442]

a lecturer in general history in Vienna University and was appointed professor at Breslau [Wrocław] University. Dr. Jecheskiel Caro attended the gymnasium at Bydgoszcz [Bromberg], studied at the Breslau rabbinical seminary, as well as philosophy and eastern–sciences at the University. He received his doctoral degree at Heidelberg, was a teacher at Lodz [Łódź] and rabbi to the joint communities of Tczew and Gniew, and [later] at Erfurt. He contributed to *Jüdisches Literaturblatt* by Dr. Rahmer of Hamburg, and published researches about Jewish studies. In 1882 he was appointed as teacher of religion at Pilsen [Plzeň], and in 1891 he moved to Lwów. In his handwritten submission he noted that he had been a preacher at Lodz, knew Polish but was not fluent in it, as for twenty years he had served the communities of Germany. He looked forward, however, to renewing his knowledge of Polish and that it would be possible for him to deliver sermons and speeches also in this language. His declaration led at first to doubt about his appointment, but his candidacy was accepted nevertheless. This was probably due to the strong recommendation by Rabbi Dr. Jellinek of Vienna.

At the start of the 1891–1900 decade, the "Temple" management consisted of: Beiser, Mayer, Wohlfeld, Emil de–Mieses and Nechemiasz Landes. Mieses and Landes who had resigned, were replaced by Salomon Rosenzweig (formerly a school teacher), Ephraim Appel and Dr. Jakub Diamand (advocate). In 1894, the community–committee's representative, the advocate Dr. Salomon Landesdberger joined the management. The 1898 elections replaced Beiser, Mayer and Rosenzweig by Dr. Adolf Menkes and Jakub Rubinstein. During that decade, the "Temple" building was renovated, an organ was installed in it and even women were admitted to the choir. Prof. Wojnowski (a Christian), was appointed organ player, and it was decided to use it even on the Sabbath and religious Holidays.

Once the authorities had confirmed the new community regulations, elections were held and Dr. Caro was appointed community Rabbi. He was also appointed member of the municipality. To teach religion he prepared a syllabus for school–classes at all level, and a biblical writing for schools, "History of Lwów's Jews" [*Geschichte der Juden in Lemberg*].

As deputy–preacher, Dr. Samuel Gutmann was appointed to deliver sermons in Polish. Born in 1864 to a poor family, his parents married him young, and when he reached the age of 27 he divorced his wife and went to the gymnasium at Radowce [in Bukowina] and Lwów and passed his matriculation examinations (1893). He went to Vienna where he studied at the rabbinical seminary and gained a doctorate and a rabbinical ordination before returning to Lwów. Here he was appointed prison's preacher as well as headmaster and teacher of religion at the community school. While exercising his undertaking he had the opportunity to deliver sermons to the youth and the worshipers at the "Temple." With his sermons he tried to inject a Jewish spirit into the education of the youth. The assimilated complained to the national schools' council about the teachers of religion and of Hebrew, and the council issued a ban on the teaching of the Bible in its original form, demanding instead that teachers use the priest Wujek's translation in their teaching. Consequently, in his sermons Dr. Gutmann vigorously voiced the demand to teach the youth to read the Book of Books in its original form, so that they understood the language of the prophets, and that it was necessary to tell the youth the history of its People, its greatness and its glory. In 1905, the community committee confirmed Dr. Gutmann's status and he was appointed preacher in Polish. In time he was released of his duties as school teacher, and Samuel Szlagowski was appointed in his place. Initially, Dr. Gutmann served as "The synagogue's Rabbi," but in 1920 he was given the title of "Lwów's community Rabbi." Dr. Lewi Freund was appointed the synagogue's acting Rabbi.

In addition to his roles as community Rabbi, Dr. Gutmann was also tasked with the management of "The Institute of Education for Teachers of the Mosaic Religion," and the supervision of religious studies, at first at the general and secondary schools. In 1903, he organised together with Prof. Taubes a Jewish–studies course. In due course, Prof. Allerhand, Prof. Schorr, E. M. Lifshitz, Cwi Karl, Gerszon Bader, Dr. Hausner, Dr. Freund, Hendel, Dr. Braude, Dr. Bałaban, Dr. Samuel Rappoport and Dr. Goldstein joined the "course." In 1905 the [Jewish] "Association of Teachers of Religion" was established and issued the magazine "*HaOr* [The light]." Dr. Gutmann was invited to manage its homiletic section.

During 1901–4, Dr. Maksymilian Fried and Jonasz Ehrlich joined the Temple's management board. During 1904–7 Jakub Rochmis replaced Maurycy Wohlfeld. And during 1907–10 Dr. Diamand who had been elected to the community committee, left the management, as did Dr. Fried, while Herman Dattner, Wiktor Mendrochowicz and Leon Hescheles joined. Dr. Menkes who had been elected to the community committee, was replaced by Dr. Wasser as chairman of the board, a post he held during the First World War and later.

In time the "Temple" was too small to contain all members of the intelligentsia who wished to pray there, especially during the High Holidays, so that prayers had to be held at the community–committee's hall, where the cantor was an assistant from among the community officials and the role of preacher was filled by one of the religion–teachers. Some of the intelligentsia prayed at the synagogue of the orphanage, where the cantor was the religion–teacher Wein, and the preacher was Dr. Bałaban. Once the idea to construct a new synagogue for the progressives was mooted, it reverberated around the community with the chair of

[Pages 443-444]

the community committee, Dr. Emil Byk, who was also a delegate to the Austrian parliament, supporting the proposal and taking deliberate steps to see it through. The chosen building plot was in the vicinity of the *Sejm*, within Kościuszko Park, but the plan was shelved for political reasons. Changes to the "Temple" were however undertaken, the building was extended, electric lighting and gas heating were installed. Its official name "The German–Jewish Prayerhouse" was also changed, to the Polish "Gmina Synagoga postępowa" (The Community's Progressive Synagogue). With Dr. Jakub Diamand's endeavour an archive was established both at the "Temple" and at the "community committee."

A custom was introduced at the "Temple" to hold a prayer for the youth, at the start and at the end of the academic year, as well as on Polish and Austrian national holidays. On the Festival of *Shavuot* [Weeks] 5602 (1902) a "festive confirmation" of Jewish girls took place conducted by the religion–teacher from the state school, Natan Schipper. At the ceremony the young girls donated a *Parochet* they had embroidered themselves. Prayers outside the authorised prayers were also conducted, on the national Polish, Austrian and Jewish Holidays, and on special memorial days, such as the 700–th anniversary of Maimonides's demise, memorial celebrations for Rabbi Saadia Gaon, Rashi, Herzl's memorial, etc.

During Rabbi Dr. Caro's incumbency, the custom of whispered praying was replaced by the cantor praying aloud while the community listened and responded with Amen; furthermore, [the prayers] *Yakum Purkan* and *Av–Harachamim* were dropped from the Sabbath service. In 1911, the cantor Halpern left the post and was succeeded by Jehoszua Seitz, cantor at Berdyczów [Berdychiv]. The composition of the last management board of the "Temple" before the outbreak of the First World War, was: chairman, Dr. Wasser; deputy, Jonasz Ehrlich; secretary, Dr. Sofer, deputy secretary, Karol Stand[4]; member "without–portfolio," Wiktor Mendrochowicz.

With the outbreak of the war in 1914, the "Temple" board members, together with Dr. Caro and members of the community committee, were away from Lwów. Only Dr. Jakub Diamand had remained in town. Dr. Gutmann joined the armed forces as a military rabbi and was sent to Bukovina. Dr. Diamand gave the role of rabbi and preacher to Dr. Hausner. In his role he officially performed marriages for many couples who had no marriage certificate, in order that the wives of those joining the forces would receive the assistance they were due by law.[**]

In November 1914 a temporary "Temple" management board was put together, made up of: Dr. Maurycy Kahane (chairman), Rubin Kroch, Adolf Lindenberger, Prof. Salomon Mandel, Mikołaj Weinreb, Józef Hausmann. Prayers were held as usual and the new management tried to assist the home workers. Despite the quiet and order, the Jews were not oblivious to the fact that special caution was required at such times. There was an instance on 19th December 1914, Tzar Nikolai's birthday, that Jews from Russia who were visiting Lwów on trade business asked Dr. Hauser to hold a festive prayer for the Tzar's wellbeing. Margolin, a Jew from Kiew, offered a large sum to the Temple coffers. The General Governor Bobrinsky also approached Dr. Hausner supporting this request. However, having considered the danger that the Jews of Lwów might face from the Austrian authorities as a consequence, Dr. Hausner refused their request.

On 22nd June 1915, Lwów was liberated from the occupier, and on 28th Dr. Gutmann returned to Lwów and took up his old post. Rabbi Dr. Caro did not return from Vienna and died there, aged 70. Other members of the "Temple" management board who had settled in Vienna during the war, and who died there, were: Jonasz Ehrlich, Herman Dattner and Wiktor Mendrochowicz. The board members who returned to Lwów were: Rochmis, Appel, Aszkenazy, Karol Stand and Dr. Wasser.

The chairman of the community committee, Dr. Diamand, was deported to Russia by the occupying authorities, and Jakub Stroh, who stood in for him, was elderly. The authorities then handed the community committee's management to Emil Parnas and appointed Dr. Wasser as his deputy. Dr. Wasser did not give up his post on the board of the "Temple," however, and regained all the roles, which he shared with the colleagues who returned to Lwów.

Even before the end of the war, Rabbi Dr. Caro's coffin was dispatched from Vienna to Lwów and Dr. Gutmann delivered a eulogy during his burial.

Homes were searched for weapons, and in one operation a Polish company headed by the officer Łos went to the "Temple" and demanded to search it. Dr. Wasser was informed and he came immediately. When he saw the officer smoking a cigarette, he ordered him to throw it away before entering the house of God. The officer refused and Dr. Wasser blocked the building's entrance with his body and declared: "I shall not permit the desecration of a holy place; you will only enter smoking, over my dead body." His words made their mark and the officer dropped the cigarette from his mouth and began his search. Dr. Wasser followed him throughout, and when the officer finished his work he arrested Dr. Wasser

[Pages 445-446]

and led him to headquarters. Many accompanied him on the way including Dr. Gutmann. The commissioner at headquarters asked his pardon and expressed his regret over the incident, and the searches in general, and apologised, blaming the state of war for the incident.

It seems that the incident gave rise to an anti–Semitic myth. Some years later, Prof. Jakubski in his book "Defence of Lwów" [*Obrona Lwowa*] told the following: "On the 23rd (November) –I don't recall the exact time– my room was entered by three strange characters, presumably due to the absence of Mączyńskie [Manczynski]. Two respectable elderly Jews slowly led an old man who could hardly stand on his feet, propping him all the while by his arms. The old man appeared like a biblical figure… I rose in deference and invited the guests to sit down. But the old man said in a whisper: Sir! the "Temple" was destroyed, the holy of holiest place was desecrated. Help!

Letter of Rabbi Kohn to his brother, 1848

I immediately reached for the telephone and contacted the Cavalry minister, Mączyńskie… and ordered: Sir, let the Cavalry minister immediately send a company under the command of an able officer to the "Temple" to defend it. Let me know immediately the reply, I am waiting on the line. Mączyńskie repeated my order and a company was sent straight away. The three old men waited for the response and I calmed them that order would be restored… A quarter of an hour later the phone rang and Mączyńskie sent a message that is hard to believe: 'The company sent found the "Temple's" vicinity completely quiet, but assuming that robbers hid inside, it opened the gate and carried out a search, and behind the *Parochet*, in place of the holy ark, was a machine gun and some boxes with bullet, and more than ten hand grenades'. I was enraged and reproached these distinguished people who tried to secure for themselves an arsenal, by relying on our naivety. 'Begone, I called, or else I shall order an arrest!'. They immediately vanished into thin air."

When these words were published in Prof. Jakubski's book, Dr. Wasser wrote in the newspaper *Gazeta Poranna* an open letter published on 27th February 1933, in which he detailed the facts of the search as carried out by Officer Łos, and its outcome, and he accused Prof. Jakubski of misrepresenting history and instilling hatred in the citizens of one country. Prof. Jakubski's riposte to Dr. Wasser was impolite, but as to the issue itself he tried to backtrack on his statement, when Christian witnesses also confirmed Dr. Wasser's version. As known, the Jews were accused that when the Polish army had marched into Lwów, they showered it with boiling water, from their windows. When Lwów's Jewish delegation, with Dr. Wasser among them, appeared before Piłsudski at Castle Belvedere, he reminded him, by–the–way, of this accusation. The delegation, and Dr. Wasser in particular, protested against his words and declared that it amounted to nothing other than a hoax fabricated by Jew–haters, to cover–up for the pogroms they had inflicted on the Jews in November 1918.

After World War I and the subsequent wars between the Poles and the Ukrainians, and between the Poles and the Russians, the "Temple of the Enlightened" was renovated and the fire damage inflicted on it during the pogroms was repaired.

In 1920, Dr. Lewi Freund was appointed acting Rabbi of the synagogue, to assist Dr. Gutmann in his many roles, and because of his weak health from a disease that he caught.

Dr. Freund was born at Przysietnica in 1920, he received a *Cheder* education, studied with Rabbi Szulim Gabel at Brzozów, Rabbi Gedalja Schmelkes at Przemyśl and others. In 1903, he graduated

[Pages 447-448]

Rabbi Bernard Lõwenstein

from the national gymnasium at Sanok, and entered the rabbinical seminary in Vienna where he also studied philosophy at the University. After concluding his studies he came to Lwów and was employed as teacher of religion at the gymnasium. During the years 1914–1915 he remained at Lwów and later joined the teaching staff of Lwów's Torah study school for teachers. During 1917–1918 he was a military rabbi with the Austrian army. After the war he returned to Lwów and taught at gymnasiums. When the "Association of primary and secondary schools" was formed in Lwów in 1919, chaired by Prof. Mojz Tashlichsz Schorr, Dr. Freund joined its committee together with Dr. Tauber, Cwi [Tzvi] Karl and others.

In 1920, the Jewish Pedagogical Institution was founded in Lwów by the "Association of primary and secondary schools." Prof. Schorr taught Arabic there, while Dr. Freund was involved there too, together with Rabbi Gutmann, Dr. Tauber and Cwi Karl.

Dr. Szymon Schaff

In 1921 Dr. Freund was given the title "The Synagogue's Rabbi," and in 1928 he was elected the community–Rabbi. Apart from the rabbinical function he was also tasked with the supervision of religious study at the state and the secondary schools. When Prof. Schorr left Lwów and was appointed rabbi at Warsaw, Dr. Freund took over the post of headmaster of the Pedagogical Institution; in 1943, Cwi Karl took over this role.

During the *Shavuot* Holiday of 1925, a celebration was held in honour of Dr. Gutmann's work for the past half–jubilee. The "Temple" management–board consisted of Prof. Schorr, Karol Stand, Józef Hausmann, Jakub Mund, Izak Melzer and others.

The rabbinical post underwent change too. Rabbi Dr. Gutmann fell ill, and Dr. Freund replaced him. The work was so extensive that a second rabbi was required to share the load. Dr. Jecheskiel Lewin (son of Rabbi Natan Lewin, and grandson of Rabbi Izak Schmelkes) was then appointed to the role.

Dr. Ozjasz Wasser

Dr. Jecheskiel Lewin was born at Rohatyn in 1897, he concluded his gymnasium schooling at Rzeszów [Resche] and studied history, philology and philosophy at Kraków University. He received his doctorate in philosophy as well as a teaching certificate from Rabbi Pinkas Dembitzer and the Rabbis of Brody and Tarnopol. He was appointed rabbi at Katowice, and was later invited to serve in Lwów (1928). Besides his role of rabbi, he was also tasked with the supervision of religious studies at the state schools, and he was also part of the Jewish Pedagogical Institution.

These roles did not suffice for Rabbi Lewin, and he was also drawn to political and Zionist involvement. He was even appointed as delegate to the Zionist Congress, and as president of the Keren Kayemet LeIsrael [Jewish National Fund] for Eastern Galicia.

At the request of Dr. Lewin, it was decided to play the organ only during the prayers on the three High Holidays [*Regalim*] and on Friday evening prayer up to *Barchu*.

In 1934 and 1936, Jubilee celebrations were held at the "Temple" for Dr. Ozjasz Wasser, chairman of the management; on the 20–th anniversary of his service, and on his 70–th birthday.

In 1935, Rabbi Dr. Gutmann died and his collected sermons were published by a group of friends.

On the outbreak of the WWII and the occupation of [Eastern] Poland by the Russians, religious studies were prohibited at Lwów's schools and the rabbis were forced to officiate in Yiddish. Rabbi Dr. Freund died (1941) during the Russian rule. In town, Dr. Lewin was left, and he regarded his role as a mission; he gathered large crowds at the "Temple" and refused to renounce his position as Rabbi

[Pages 449-450]

Dr. Jecheskiel Lewin   Dr. Jecheskiel Caro   Dr. Lewi Freund   Rabbi Dr. Samuel–Wolf Gutmann

despite offers from the authorities of important posts in the public and scientific fields.

On 30th June 1941, the first Nazi battalions marched into Lwów. The following day the Ukrainians rampaged and attacked the Jews. Friends of Dr. Lewin asked him to hide from the peril, but he was determined to approach the Metropolitan [Greek Catholic Archbishop] Sheptytsky and ask him to influence the Ukrainians to stop the massacre. Dr. Lewin composed an address to the Metropolitan that his son Isaac translated into Ukrainian. He put on his rabbinical garment and the black gloves that he wore solely to funerals, and walked to the Metropolitan's Palace. The latter asked him to stay at his Palace till the riot had subsided. Rabbi Dr. Lewin replied: "My mission is over. I came to ask on behalf of the community, and I return to the community where I belong, and may God be with me," then he left the Palace.

His son Izak describes his death in the following words:

"At that moment, there was a Ukrainian militia in our house that dragged Jews to Brygidki (the large jail on Kazimierowska Street), one of our neighbours waited specially to warn my father, but he said to her: "All the same." And white as a sheet he climbed the stairs. Near the door of our apartment the Ukrainians got hold of him and marched him to Brygidki, where he died a martyr to God. Beaten by Germans and Ukrainians, he walked proud, his head held high and his expression peaceful, the face of a man whose mission had been discharged and whose conscience was singularly pure. When he came among the many Jews in the jail, he recited the prayer prior to death and turned to his co–sufferers and in a loud voice called out: "Sh'ma Israel, Adonai…" and did not finish his words as a machine gun put an end to his words and his life."[5]

Thousands of Lwów's Jews were murdered together with him, and the "Temple" was totally destroyed by the Nazis.

Notes: All notes in square brackets [ ] were made by the translator or by the editor.
[The spelling of names was mainly derived from publications by Dr. M. Bałaban, other names/titles were added as they were spelt in Lwów at the time.]

Original footnotes:

1.   Who set the amount of tax every member of the community had to pay.

2.   R' Mojzesz HaKohen Rappoport (BRZ"P) [son of R' Zalman Perles] was known as "The Rabbi of Leżajsk." He was born at Lwów in 1827. His father, R' Mordchaj'le, together with Wolf Schönblum, had established the house of worship [*Kloyz*] "R' Schönblums Schiehlechel" on Szajnochy Street, in the courtyard of the Sykstuska synagogue. His mother was the daughter of Rabbi Szymon Natansohn of Brody. Taube, the wife of Rabbi Mojzesz Rappoport, was the daughter of Reb. Szmuel Babad, the brother of Rabbi Józef ben Mojzesz Babad (1800–1875), the rabbi of Tarnopol, author of the book *Minchat Chinuch* (1869). In 1890 he travelled with his wife and son Simcha to Eretz Israel; but due to the Turkish Empire's sanction on Jewish immigration, he was unable to disembark [in Israel], despite the efforts made by the Jewish population to acquire an entrance licence for him, and he was obliged to return. When knowledge of this had reached Galicia, they telegraphed him to sail to America. In 1893, he returned to Galicia and became Rabbi at Leżajsk. When the question arose about the rabbinate of Lwów's "suburb," a group of *Charedim* nominated him to stand against the candidate Rabbi Leib Braude, but Rabbi Leib was the appointed Rabbi. In

contravention of the law, the group of *Charedim* appointed Rabbi Mojzesz Rappoport as Rabbi of the *Chadaszim Schul* of R' Jakob Glanzer who held his post till his death in 1911, despite protestation by the community and by the authorities who did not recognise him. Rabbi Majer Schapira, head of the "*Chachame Lublin Yeshivah*," was his disciple.

  3.   *See* Article by Dr. N. M. Gelber *History of the Jews of Lwów* Chap. 15.

  4.   His brother Adolf cooperated in the publication of the newspapers *Przyszłość* and [the weekly] *Wschód* and was a member on the board of the Jewish hospital.

  5.   Isaac Lewin *Aliti MeSpezia*, Tel–Aviv 1947, p.26.

  6.   In this undertaking he was assisted by Dr. Bałaban who had been given power of attorney by Dr. Diamand, in this matter., Tel–Aviv 1947, p.26.

[Pages 451-452]

Synagogues and *Kloyzes*

by Ze'ev [Zew] Zohar

Translated by Myra Yael Ecker

Edited by Karen Leon

I. Synagogues

Some four–hundred synagogues and Torah–study schools were recorded in Lwów's community register [*Pinkas*], besides the many *Minyanim* of the "Rebbes" and "the Grandsons," such as: Reb. Zyndel Neuhaus of Sambor, R' Beril of Stratyn, R' Leibisch Efrati of Strzelisk [Strzeliska Nowe] and the *Admorim* of Gliniany [Galina], Krotoszyn, Mikołów [Nikolai] etc.

Over many generations of splendour and grandeur the royal town of Lwów was an "important Jewish town," with its hundred–thousand Jewish inhabitants, its rabbis, great scholars, Chassidim and its "opposers." The Enlightened and the progressives, the common people, the craftsmen and those in trade, dedicated to Judaism and the Jewish people, its doctrine and its country – all of whom hard–working to maintain their homes and economic status, felt nonetheless obligated to engage in acts of charity and benevolence, providing assistance to others via the societies associated with the town's synagogues.

Through all the unbending decrees and the tortures over hundreds of years and their sufferings under the rule of Poland, Austria, and the New–Poland, the Jews found consolation in their faith in God and their yearning for redemption. Great Jewish scholars and leaders instilled pure faith and confidence in the hearts of the masses by teaching them the Torah and guiding them to virtue and charity.

The diaspora Jews assembled at the synagogues to pray to their creator and the Jewish prayers filled their hearts with hope and bolstered their desire to perpetuate the generations. Lwów's prominent rabbi, the great scholar Rabbi Józef Saul Natansohn, encouraged, and was lovingly engaged in establishing a large number of the town's synagogues. He steered the craftsmen, each trade individually, to establish for themselves Torah and prayer houses, benevolence and good deeds. An air of sanctity and modest life pervaded Lwów's Jewish street in those days.

The rest on Shabbat was absolute: no buyer nor seller and the shops were shut. The Shabbat candles shone in every house. Labourers and merchants sat peacefully. On the Sabbath morning a hush fell, the street–traffic came to a halt and Jews were seen walking slowly and relaxed to the synagogues. On the Sabbath afternoons, the singing of Psalms was heard at the Great Synagogue. Before the stars appeared in the sky, cantor R' Berl's animated and mellifluous voice erupted and the cantillation filled the hearts of the assembled. They answered him in praise and thanksgiving: "Unto the end, in hymns, a Psalm of a canticle: May God have mercy on us, and bless us: may he cause the light of his countenance to shine upon us, and may he have mercy on us; Selah." It was customary at the synagogues for the congregation to recite the first canticle standing outside the locked doors of the synagogue, and once they ended the canticle "Bring to the Lord, O ye children of God," the beadle or the cantor approached the locked door, knocked three times with the round copper knocker on the door, then the congregation entered the hall and began the canticle "Unto the end, in hymns."

In this fashion our innocent and honest Jewish brethren passed their days at Lwów, in Synagogues and Torah–studies, and *Kloyzes* and the Rabbes' *Minyanim*, wrapped in sanctity.

I shall endeavour, herewith, to perpetuate the names of the synagogues.

1.   **The Great Torah–study School** outside the town, on Bożnicza Street. A Torah and prayer house where the town's scholars found their place. The building consisted of three floors: First floor – the Great Torah–study school; Second floor – women's section; Third floor – two small synagogues and an apartment for the beadles. On the First floor, opposite the entrance to the Torah–study, there was a small narrow room where, in his time, lived the great scholar Rabbi Jozef Teomim, author of *Peri Megadim* [Precious Fruit], a *Maggid* [religious, itinerant preacher] at Lwów who barely made an income. On the wall of his room was engraved "I set the Lord always in my sight." His renowned artless awe was noted by the fact that: the author of *Peri Megadim* was appointed *Av Beth–Din* [Head of Rabbinical Court] and head of Yeshivah at Frankfurt an der Oder, for which purpose he ordered a new *kapotah* (black garment). Since he was engaged in the Torah and worked at the Torah–study school, till the late hours, he gave the Rebbetzin a sum of money to pay the tailor when he arrived. The great scholar returned home late at night, his wife had already gone to sleep and he noticed the new *kapotah* on the table. The great scholar worried

[Pages 453-454]

that the tailor had not been paid, and that the Torah transgression "the wages of him that is hired shall not abide with thee all night until the morning," had been committed in respect of the tailor. Out of respect he did not wish to wake the Rebbetzin, so he shut the door behind him and in the night's darkness he went looking for the tailor. When he found the house, he woke the tailor, and the latter who shook with concern, asked: "What is our Rabbi doing in my house at such a late hour of the night?" The great scholar calmed him and explained his concern. When he heard that the Rebbetzin had paid in full, the Rabbi's face lit up.

This Torah–study attracted also the town's "Men of status" who sat and studied there. The building was a relic from the days when the *Shulchan Aruch* [abbreviated form of the Jewish ritual law] was practiced in its severest, "*Ashkenazi* style." All the liturgical poems introduced in the Middle Ages were recited here in their unique melody; liturgical poems from the days of "Rabbeinu Tam" and the crusades; here they practiced the *Ashmoret*, a form of *Tikun–chazot* [midnight prayer] on Mondays and Thursdays.

In later years the place unfortunately turned into a source of blasphemy. This house, where the Torah was studied for its own sake, also attracted in winter the poor, who came to warm themselves. Men of the "underworld" abused the place. Saying that they came to warm themselves, they hid and secreted "stolen goods" there instead, and the frequent searches undertaken revealed legally prohibited goods, which amounted to actual blasphemy.

2.   **Chassidim Schul.** Chassidim outraged at the strict *Ashkenazi* customs practiced at the Great Torah–study school, constructed directly opposite it on the same street, a synagogue in the custom of the Chassidim and named it "Chassidim Schul." For a long time prayers there followed the Sephardi style and the customs were those of the Chassidim. Over the years the two sides "cooled off" and the "Chassidim Schul" turned into a meeting place for simple Jews who altered the style of prayer by introducing the *Ashkenazi* style.

3.   **"Kove'a Itim LeTorah** [Time setter for Torah]." With encouragement from the great scholar Rabbi Józef Saul Natansohn, some prominent homeowners purchased a site on Szpitalna street corner Kazimierzowska Street, to erect a synagogue. Due to a lack of funds they sold two shops at the end of the building facing the street. The magnificent building had two floors: Floor 1 – a beautiful, large synagogue; Floor 2 – Torah–study school, a fine *Sukkah* and an apartment for the beadle. "A special aspect existed at this synagogue, not found at any other of Lwów's synagogues. The Holy Ark was not placed facing East, but facing South–East, and that was because the architect who constructed the synagogue had discovered, by calculation, that Eretz–Israel was due South–East. This took place in the days of the great scholar Rabbi Józef Saul Natansohn, and led to a great controversy with the desire to demolish the building straight away and to make changes, but nevertheless everything remained as built. The prayer at the synagogue followed the *Ashkenazi* style, and it served as a place of prayer for the masses and for the professionals. They appointed their particular *Maggidei Shiur* to teach them every morning and every evening, a chapter from the *Mishnah*, *Eyn Jakuw* and *Shulchan Aruch – Orach Chaim*, and an extra lesson of *Talmud*. At times they recounted tales from the *Agada*. In the Torah–study school upstairs, prayer followed the Sephardi style. Among the *Maggidei Shiur* one recalls R' Mendel Buber and R' Hersz Hammer. R' Natanel Lichter acted as their private assistant and as an outstanding Torah–reader who later became one of the town's renowned *Mohels*. His brother–in–law, R' Jakub, served as his deputy. Located at the centre of town, the building served among other, all benevolent public meetings of political parties, national foundations, preachers, *Maggidim*, and cantors. The lesson at the Torah–study school was followed by honouring their rabbi with an invitation to the –nearby– "wine cellar" of R' Mendel Weinstein, for "a glass of honey water" (mead). The synagogue managers in the latter years were: Szmelke Barach, Jesaja [Isaiah] Wirklich and Chaim Perlmutter.

4. **"Koryte Schul."** Named after the nearby *Poltva* [Pełtew] river, or *Koryto* [trough] in Polish, situated at the edge of town, the large magnificent synagogue termed "Zólkiewer Schrank [Żółkiew cupboard]," to which a certain legend was attached. Before his death, an heirless Jew donated a plot to erect a synagogue. This took place during the days of the Jesuits, and it was claimed that the Jew had donated the plot to build a synagogue as well as a church. The dispute ended in a court of law where it was concluded that it was impossible to construct both buildings on one site; that the plot would have to be sold at auction and the money divided between the two parties. The auction date was set for Yom Kippur [Day of Atonement], in full knowledge that the Jews would not attend on that day. Lewkowicz, a member of the family that had donated the Lewkowicz school, an assimilated and open–minded Jew, appeared specially on Yom Kippur with a cigar in his mouth to remain undetected. He took part in the sale and procured it. At dusk, before the *Ne'illa* prayer, the Jewish purchaser arrived at the synagogue within the town, approached Lwów's Rabbi, author of *Jeschies Jacow* [*Yeshu'ot Ja'akov*; Jacob's Salvations], and told him what he had done. The Rabbi shook his hand and told him that he had secured for himself a place in paradise. On that site was built the magnificent synagogue that for years was a prayer and teaching place for the Jews of the neighbourhood.

5. **Synagogue "Ma'or VeSzemesz [Light and Sun]."** The donation of Mr. Czop, on Miodowa Street, was named after him "Czop Schul." A wonderful building maintained by wealthy people of the neighbourhood who kept a special cantor and holy vessels.

[Pages 455-456]

6. **Retirement Home Synagogue.** Adjoining the old [Jewish] cemetery on Rappaporta Street. Its worshippers were largely from the retirement home, but also visitors to the cemetery and patients of the neighbouring hospital in memory of Lazarus [Elazar]. The building was a centre for charitable and benevolent undertakings.

7. **"Express" Synagogue** on Źródlana Street. Built by prominent porters, particularly by Mordechai Weiser, one of the town's wealthy, renowned "Expressists." They built the synagogue for the "Express" porters registered with the municipality, who used to gather near "The Deposit Bank." Prominent homeowners living in the vicinity prayed here too. They were noted for their charity and good deeds, and built a large hall next to the synagogue where *chuppot* and weddings could be held for poor and orphaned brides unable to afford a suitable hall, and where the dignity of the wedding was ensured. They also established a *Hachnasat Kala* [Dowry] fund and they generously assisted orphans and poor brides. In the latter years a Yeshivah "Machzikei Lomdei Torah [Torah Scholars]" was also located there.

8. **"Orchei Shulchan veMan'imey Zimrah** [Table Setters and Music Captivators]" **Synagogue.** At 1 Plac Teodora, a group of "servers" (waiters) and musical instrumentalists who earned their living from serving at weddings and *Mitzvah* celebrations in town, established this synagogue, they prayed together, studied [religious] lessons together and maintained mutual assistance. At the head of this synagogue stood the renowned "server" R' Joel Weitz.

9. **"Kizru lefi Chessed** [Reap in Mercy]" **Synagogue** on Teodora Plac [Square]. A synagogue of labourers, small traders who kept trade kiosks and stalls. They banded together for the purpose of praying and for lessons in the Torah and for mutual help, to maintain good standards, especially just measure for the buyer, following the instruction of Rabbi Natansohn, who coined the synagogue's name, as said: "Let your sextary [be] equal and the bushel just; Do no unjust thing in judgment, in rule, in weight, or in measure" "Reap in mercy."

10. **"Zovchei Zedek** [Honourable Sacrificers]" **Butchers Synagogue**, incorporated within the Great Synagogue outside the town. Apart from prayer and lessons, its worshipers were known in town for their acts of charity.

11. **Big Tailors' Synagogue**, incorporated within the Great Synagogue outside the town.

12. **Small Tailors' Synagogue**, also incorporated within the Great Synagogue outside the town (there was also a Small Tailors' Synagogue within the town).

13. **"Marki'eh Pachim** [Metal Beaters]" **Synagogue** on Bożnicza Street, for tinsmiths.

14. **"Melamdim** [Torah Teachers] **Schul"** – Initially it was designated for all the children's instructors of religion, but later on for all Jews who distinguished themselves in their piety, and a religious instructor as well as a "*Maggid* were appointed for them, and they concentrated on the Torah, prayer and good deeds.

15. **"Noseh Katef** [Shoulder Bearers]" **Synagogue**, for actual porters, who after a hard day's work came in the evenings to study a chapter of the *Mishnah* and the weekly Torah portion with its *Rashi* interpretation, guided by a special "Rabbi"; they prepared themselves a cup of tea and listened to their rabbi's rabbinic literature.

16. Shmoklerim [Lace–makers] **Synagogue** or **"Szniek Schul"** on Blacharska Street within the town, established by craftsmen who made this the meeting place of their Society, but after a while the place turned into a sacred place for homeowners and Chassidim dissatisfied with the rituals at the "Lubliner *Kloyz*" with its strict discipline. Here, the Sephardi–style prayer was introduced. The leaders of the synagogue included: R' Eliezer Drimer (died 1953 in Tel–Aviv) and his brother–in–law R' Abisz Roth. In 1921, when the Russians invaded Poland, he spent some months at Lwów. The Rabbi of Gliniany [Galina], the great scholar Rabbi Majer Schapira who at the time resided near the synagogue, gave there a daily lesson for six months, to a group of *Agudas Jisroel* youths, on Maimonides' *Laws of the Temple*.

17. "Melechet Chanoch [Enoch's handicraft]" **Synagogue**, for the shoemakers, was named after the *Midrash*: "Chanoch–was a shoes sewer." This synagogue was situated within the Great Synagogue outside the town. Maintaining their own synagogue, entitled the shoemakers also to attain "honorary roles," such as collector of dues and second cantor; they also maintained Torah lessons and charitable activities.

18. "Menakrim" [Meat trainers] **Synagogue.** Also housed inside the building of the Great Synagogue outside the town, was one of the much praised synagogues.

19. "Bikur Cholim [Visiting the Infirm]" **Synagogue.** Besides prayer and lessons, the worshipers dedicated themselves primarily to the kindness of visiting the sick and helping them.

20. "Chevrat Bnei Levaya [Society of the Attendants]" **Synagogue.** They too set for themselves a specific act of kindness, one which they kept to – the funerals of the town's dead. In time the society evolved into several branches of important work in the field.

21. "Sifteh Ranenot [Words of Exultation]" **Synagogue** of the "Psalms" Society within the town. They concentrated particularly on daily reciting the Psalms, in addition to prayer and lessons.

22. "Ahavat Re'im [Friendship]" **Synagogue** on Żółkiewska Street. Among the regular worshippers at a certain period, was R' Majer Gerszon with his *Minyan*, that was customarily late with his prayers.

[Pages 457-458]

23. "*Kloyz* of R' Meszulam Zusia," on Tkacka Street. R' Meszulam Zusia was a *Maggid Mesharim* [Preacher of Righteousness] at Lwów, who had a large number of followers and Chassidim; he died in (5615) 1854–5. One of the worshippers at his *Bet Midrash* [Torah–study], a Jewish man who had no sons, pleaded with R' Meszulam Zusia to bless him with a viable seed. The *Tzadik* acceded to his request and blessed him, and subsequently the man fathered a son. As a mark of gratitude, when the son grew up he built within the town another synagogue named after Rabbi Meszulam Zusia.

24. "*Maggid Mesharim*," R' Meszulam Zusia's second synagogue at Lwów was situated on Strzelecka Street according to the aforementioned.

25. "Filip" Synagogue on Hermana Jakóba Street, a large synagogue donated by the philanthropist Józef–Filip, a Jewish scholar, member of Lwów's community council. The synagogue was situated on the site of his flour mills. The synagogue offered evening classes in Torah subjects, and a large library. Prayer was in the Sephardi style and Chassidim came to pray there. The president of the synagogue was Józef–Filip, and his deputy was Rabbi Menachem Hager (died at Tel–Aviv in 1954).

26. *Kloyz* R' Eliezer Lubitscher, at 14 Rzeźnicka Street. Rabbi Eliezer was a grandson of the old Belz *Admor* and led a congregation of Chassidim. Some 150 worshippers attended the *Kloyz*. With the demise of R' Eliezer, the Chassidim installed his son–in–law, Rabbi Menachem Hager, on the seat of *Admor* (see 25). This *Kloyz* existed until 1915.

27. "The Israeli Waiter" Waiters' Synagogue. A large and spacious synagogue for waiters at 1. Furmańska Street. In the evenings Torah lessons were also held there.

28. "Jeszareh Lew [Upright in heart]" **Synagogue** on Rzeźnicka Street.

29. "Agudas Jeszurim [Association of the Righteous]" **Synagogue**, on Rzeźnicka Street.

30. "Tze'irim [Youth]" **Synagogue** situated on the upper floor of the Great Synagogue outside the town.

31. The Old Synagogue within the new cemetery. A large and attractive building that also served as a place of prayer for the residents on Janowska Street and those in the vicinity of the cemetery.

32. **"Beis Lechem** [House of Bread]" **Synagogue** of the bakers, on Starozakonna Street. It served as a place of prayer for many grandsons and scholars who influenced its members and organised lessons there. On the upper floor of the synagogue were housed infants' Torah teachers.

33. **"Raff" Synagogue** at 11 Berka Joselowicza Street. R' Abraham Raff founded the synagogue, a beautiful, unique building that was named after him.

34. **"Barach" Synagogue** on Piniński Street, a large magnificent building.

35. **"Gilod** [Gilead; Gal–Ed; monument]" **Synagogue** on Królowej Jadwigi Street, near Gródecka, a large and magnificent synagogue with a special cantor. A place of prayer for the entire neighbourhood. The synagogue was constructed in 1905 as the private property for the industrialist and estates owner, Gall of Tarnopol, who was a delegate to the Austrian parliament during the years 1907–1918. After a time Gall converted to Christianity and he planned to sell the synagogue to Christians to use as a factory. In 1919, worshippers at the synagogue, headed by Wittlin, Marek Feierstein, Queller and Natan Weinreb – who was president of the synagogue (today at Tel–Aviv), paid the converted Gall for the synagogue, in full, and they served as part of the management until the end. The neighbourhood rabbi, Dayan Rabbi Mojzesz Ehrenpreis, was both the synagogue's rabbi and among its principal worshipers. Some 300 Jews prayed there and among the synagogue managers were Abraham Hirschfeld and Chaim Locker. Its serving cantors were Mojzesz Patrontasch, Leibisch Schorr, Kruszewski, Richter, Jakub Kusewicki, Idelson, the choir conductor – Izak Hillman and the preacher –Dr. Zew Waschitz.

36. The Great Synagogue **"Cori Gilod** [Tzori Gil'ad; Gil'ad's Balm]." In 1922 a magnificent new building was erected on Króla Leszczyńskiego Street, where hundreds of Jews prayed. The ethos of the synagogue was more "Orthodox" than that at the "Gilead" Synagogue. It was larger and served as a place of worship for the widely dispersed Jewish population of the wider surroundings. Dr. Weiser was the synagogue preacher.

37. **"Szowtej Szabat** [Shovte Shabat; Those resting on the Sabbath]" **Synagogue**, on Bożnicza Street, opposite the Great Synagogue. The synagogue distinguished itself in particular by its acts of "hospitality." Every Sabbath impoverished Jews rushed there for the Sabbath meals. The synagogue–worshippers went past the yards of the town's Jewish residents, calling out, "Good Shabbes, Jews" – the windows would open and they would hand food that was immediately brought to the synagogue in order to set the tables for the poor.

38. **"Szomrej Szabat** [upholders of the Sabbath]" **Synagogue** for hairdressers on Berka Joselowicza Street, was established for the hairdressers to prevent them from desecrating the Sabbath.

39. **"Pe'er Migba'ot** [Brimmed–hats' Grandeur]" on Słoneczna Street. A small hatters' synagogue.

40. **"Mecapim LeJeszua** [Metzapim LeYeshua; Anticipating Salvation]" **Synagogue** for butchers on Słoneczna Street. Its worshippers – ordinary Jews who studied a chapter of *Mishnayot* and *Ein–Yaakov*, in addition to prayer and lessons. A class of the urban "Etz Chaim Yeshivah" was housed within the synagogue, where

[Pages 459-460]

one of the best heads of Yeshivah, R' Pinkas Schwarz studied with his disciples.

41. **"Chevra–Kadisha** [Holy Society – or funeral Soc.]" **Synagogue** on Sieniawska Street, was situated at the home of the rich and devout R' Szmuel Kalisz, who offered his home to the Yeshivah "Etz Chaim." The Yeshivah's classroom was at the synagogue where teaching was by the most dedicated head of Yeshivah, Rabbi Izrael Zipper. The synagogue was founded by members of "Chevra Kadisha." Over time, however, once the Society moved to a designated office, the synagogue was used by the neighbouring residents.

42. **"Likuteh Shemot** [Compilation of Names]" **Synagogue**, at 5 Furmańska Street, where in addition to prayer and Torah study they also collected "Names" (pages and torn sacred books), prayer–books and Pentateuchs that were brought from every part of the town. The worshippers placed special boxes at many synagogues to collect the "Names" which they later transferred to their synagogue. Twice a year they held a special ceremony to bury the Names at Lwów's old cemetery. The synagogue was first located on Kazimierzowska Street in an old shack that was destroyed, and was later replaced by the large Poltorak building.

43. **"Kulikower** *Kloyz*" on Starotandetna Street. A small synagogue where young men had daily Torah lessons. The 12–13 year–old boys had a wide knowledge of the *Gmara* and the annotations to the *Talmud,* and they studied with a Torah instructor. The pupils included the poet Uri–Hirsch [Tzvi] Grünberg. The founders of the *Kloyz* are not known, nor after whom it was named. It appears that one of the *Admorim* who resided at Kulików had Chassidim at Lwów and they were the founders.

44. **"Choresz Etzim [Grove]" Synagogue**, on 55 Żródlana Street, was a synagogue of simple carpenters who prayed and had regular lessons.

45. **The Great Synagogue** outside the town.

46. **The Great Synagogue** inside the town.[1]

47. **"Oskim BeMelechet HaKodesz [Engaged in Sacred Work]" Synagogue**, at 12 Bożnica Street. Established by a group of print workers, setters, and binders of sacred books, led by R' Jossel Schwabel, an ardent Jewish scholar, devout and modest, the author of the book *Jad Josef*, brother of R' Icckel Żólkower. R' Jossel who led his flock, died young. His work was subsequently kept up by another great Jewish scholar, the synagogue manager, R' Icckel, who continued for the rest of his life. The synagogue served small traders who attended the lessons and the talks by R' Icckel.

48. **"Yig'al Yaakov Yi'smach Israel** [Jacob shall rejoice, and Israel shall be glad]" **Synagogue**, in the middle of Żółkiewska Street, a prayer house designated for passersby and for a section of the community residing in the vicinity.

49. **The Great Synagogue at Zniesienie**, a Lwów suburb that was a kind of community all its own, with its own slaughterer, rabbinical judge, cantor and also a separate cemetery. The Jewish community at the edge of town expanded and developed during WWI, when refugees arrived there and found cheap accommodation and means of income. The suburb's residents excelled in their hospitality and helped refugees settle. The synagogue managers were Lazar Rotter, Turnscher, Szalom–Wolf Vogel, Izrael Sobel, Berl Löb, the cantor was R' Rachmiel Schächter.

50. *Kloyz* **Zniesienie**. Near the Great Synagogue there was a Chassidim *Kloyz* where hundreds of Jews prayed. The *Kloyz* was not dedicated to Chassidim who followed a single Rabbi, but rather a "joint *kloyz*" for every type of Chassidim: Belz, Husiatyn, Czortków [Chortkov], Sącz [Sanz] etc. The *Kloyz*'s worshippers espoused Jewish unity and lived in brotherhood and companionship with never a cross word between them. From time to time there were indeed some stormy discussions, but never in division, rather in debate of logical argument among scholars locking horns over the practice of the *Mishnah*[religious doctrine] and Jewish law. Daily before dawn, throughout the year, summer and winter, one could find at the *Kloyz* Jewish businessmen studying a lesson be it of *Gmarah* or *Mishnah*, before their morning prayer. Scores of young men sat day and night at the *Kloyz* and regularly attended lessons and became exalted in the Torah, one of them, Rabbi Mojzesz Katz, later became a Dayan in town. Among the homeowners there were also exalted learners, such as: R' Fischel Lojar, Samuel Landau and Rabbi Cwi Rosenfeld, who was a rabbinical judge at Zniesienie. Among the *kloyz* managers was the renowned Mojzesz Löw, owner of a mead (honey–water) manufacture, R' Neta–Jonah Teomim, R' Zew–Wolf Neubauer (now at Bnei–Brak), all of them strove to expand and enhance the local community–life, they created a *Mikveh* [ritual cleansing pool] and built a children's Torah school etc. Best remembered was the manager and Torah reader at the synagogue, R' Matityah Weintraub who, while bringing people together, he was strict in the extreme towards women, and did not let them cross the threshold of the *Kloyz*.

51. **Bet Ha***Midrash* **HaGadol** [The Great Torah–study School] of Zniesienie, was built by Hugo Ulrich in 1913.

52. **Bet Ha***Midrash* **HaChadash** [The New Torah–study School] of Zniesienie. The manager of the Torah study was Michał Steiger.

53. **Craftsmen's Synagogue**, Zniesienie. The synagogue served a group of craftsmen not only for prayer and lessons, but also for meetings and charitable activities.

54. **"***Spadkes* [Hatters]" **Synagogue**. In the mansion at 11–12

[Pages 461-462]

Gołuchowski Square, the "Craftsmen's Association" of *Spadkes* [fabric head wraps] and *Shtraimlech* [rabbis' fur hats] established a prayer house in the first half of the 19th century. The synagogue served also residents from the vicinity [Breite Gasse] including: R' Iszaja–Becalel Menkes who for years represented the Charedim in the association "*Szomer Izrael*" (the father of Dr. Bertold Merwin, among the leading assimilators and among the editors of the weekly *Jedność* who later converted to Christianity); and also the grandfather and the father of Prof. Dr. Majer Bałaban. At the start of the 20th century the hat–merchant Mojzesz Reiss purchased the two buildings (No.s 11–12), where he built two large halls, one he gave to the "*Spadkes*" and the second to the Zydaczów Chassidim who maintained their *Kloyz* there.

55. **Rabbi Bezalel Maggid** *Kloyz*, on Objazdowa Street. Rabbi Bezalel Maggid was the son the renowned great scholar Rabbi Naftali HaKohen [Katz] of Poznan, author of "*Semichat Chachamim* [Ordination of Sages]" (Frankfurt a/M; 5464; 1703–1704). The year the *Kloyz* was founded is not known, and its worshippers were Chassidim who lived in the Zamarstynów–Żółkiewska neighbourhood and were followers of diverse Rebbes. Many of the Husiatyn

Chassidim worshiped at the *Kloyz*, which also served as a Torah study for young Lwów Chassidim. During the *Kidush* receptions on every Shabbath they recounted tales on *Tzadikim* and biblical exegesis and engaged in song, music and dance. Among its managers are known: Aron Lutwak, the father of the rabbinical judge Rabbi Mordechai Zew Lutwak, and also Mojzesz Simon.

56. "The Sea Sails" Synagogue, on Lwia Street, was named after the owner of "The Sea Sails." Its worshippers were Jewish students and homeowners from the neighbourhood.

57. *Kloyz* Rabbi Jossele, a disciple of the "Seer of Lublin," on Lwia Street. A place of prayer for Chassidim and businessmen, and also a place of study for youths.

58. Great Synagogue, on Bogdanowska Street.

59. The Orphanage Synagogue, on Janowska Street, where apart from the orphans, residents from the neighbourhood also prayed.

60. The Great Synagogue, known as "Sykstuska Schul" on Szajnochy street [Sykstuska's side–St.]. It was founded in the 1840s by the wealthy, respected and philanthropic Jew, R' Salomon Pelz, at the same time as the "Temple" was built on Żółkiewska Street. The reason for founding the synagogue on Sykstuska Street, apart from creating a prayer–house for the residents in the neighbourhood, was to provide the *Ashkenazi* [German speaking] homeowners within the town with a counterbalance to the "Temple." Until the First World War in 1914, the offsprings of R' Salomon Pelz prayed there.

The principal manager of the synagogue was one of the Mund brothers on Sykstuska Street. Among those who prayed there were the town's prominent and wealthy, such as Rabbi Schmelke Horowitz, the community leader and others. The community rabbi, Rabbi Leib Braude, and the head of the *Beth–Din*, the great scholar Rabbi Meszulam Salat, were among its worshippers for a certain period.

In addition to the daily prayers, Torah lessons by *Maggideh Shiur* [Torah lecturers] were daily delivered to groups at the synagogue. On Friday nights in winter, and on summer evenings, they studied a *Midrash* [interpretation] of the week's Torah portion. The last *Maggid Shiur* was Jakle Grill. Latterly amendments were introduced at the synagogue, that many considered to be a departure from the tradition for which the synagogue had been constructed. Rabbi Dr. Dawid Kahane preached at the synagogue till 1939.

61. The Great *Bet Midrash* [Torah study school] on Boimów Street within the town. At the time, Lwów's dignitaries, Torah–sages and its rabbis prayed there. It was the centre for learners and eminent scholars. Young men studied there day and night. One of the great libraries of Torah literature was housed there, together with the library of the great scholar Józef Saul Natansohn, including his hand–written sheets of elucidation.

62. Turei Zahaw [Golden columns] **Synagogue**. One of the places consecrated for generations, about which much is said in this book. In this hallowed place prayed, sat and taught the author of *Turei Zahaw*, after which the synagogue was named. Built in 1582, and considered even by the government as a treasured museum. Its building – a magnificent work of art, was registered as an arts national–property. Here, every detail of the Ashkenazi style was followed to the letter, in the tradition of *Turei Zahaw*. As known, the author of *Turei Zahaw* [Dawid Halevy] was the son–in–law of the renowned great scholar [Joel ben Samuel Sirkis], the author of *Bayit Chadash* who lived at Kraków. One Shabbat, the author of *Turei Zahaw* visited Kraków and stayed with Joel ben Samuel Sirkis. On Friday before sunset, Rabbi Dawid Halevy handed his purse to his father–in–law for safekeeping till the end of the Sabbath. As a result, *Bayit Chadash* abstained from speaking with his son–in–law for several days. Later, *Turei Zahaw* asked *Bayit Chadash* about what and how he had saddened him. *Bayit Chadash* responded that a rabbi who had money in his pocket seemed suspect in his eyes, and as a result he was saddened and was unable to talk with him. The author of *Turei Zahaw* apologised to his father–in–law, saying that he had received the money from prominent house–owners who implored him to have his eyes treated. Only then did *Bayit Chadash* rest.

63. Agudat Benjamin [Benjamin's Association] **Synagogue** on Łyczakowska Street, close to the town's periphery. Founded in (5664) 1903–4 by R' Benjamin Weinitz and his wife Breindel. R' Benjamin Weinitz was an imperial supplier (Kaiserlicher–lieferant) of gravel and stones for roads, with a profitable and respectable income. An affluent Jew who was a Żydaczów [Zhydachiv] Chassid, he built himself a house at the edge of town and in his garden he created a synagogue

[Pages 463–464]

where some ten *Minyanim* prayed, where Torah lessons were held and charitable activities were undertaken. The prayer was in the Sephardi style and *Jahr–zeit* [annual memorial] of *Tzadikim* was celebrated communally with meals and song [*Melave Malka*] etc. Adjacent to the synagogue were two large rooms, one for men and one for women, offering hospitality to the poor who came to visit their sick relatives at the state hospital on Łyczakowska Street. Breindel Weinitz saw to the visitors, and offered them a hot meal in addition to providing Kosher food for the hospital patients. On top of the synagogue, the visitors constructed a large *Sukkah* that served as the women's section of the synagogue. R' Berl Toper was the synagogue's cantor.

In 1914, with the invasion of the Russians and Lwów's first pogrom, the rampagers entered his garden and killed 11 Jews from Winniki near Lwów, destroyed and burnt down the synagogue and the visitors' hospitality quarters. R' Benjamin Weinitz managed to save his family and flee into town, to his son Majer Weinitz–Karmi (now in Tel–Aviv). The Żydachów Chassid, R' Majer Weinitz–Karmi, changed his name still at Lwów, and migrated with his family to Eretz Israel. His sons are maklers for the "Histadrut HaOvdim HaKlallit."

64. Achi'ezer Synagogue for the Płoskirów [now, Khmelnitskyi] people, in the Weissman Passage. It was founded when some 300 families arrived from Płoskirów during the year 1920–1921. With the demise of their rabbi, Rabbi Izrael Sandruf, they maintained the family and appointed, as rabbi and preacher, his youngest son Rabbi Sanhedrai (now manager of *Ezrat Torah* at Tel–Aviv). Rabbi Sanhedrai conducted lectures and lessons in Torah and Jewish studies. The synagogue managers headed by Lisowoder, Grünstein and Betlin, were particularly engaged in the rehabilitation and settling of the refugee–families and assisted them in their immigration to Eretz Israel, USA etc.

**

Most of Lwów's synagogues were founded by Rabbi Józef Saul Natansohn. The smaller synagogues were situated on the upper floors of the Great Synagogue within the town and of the Great Synagogue outside the town, and in the large Torah Study schools. They were established as mentioned in the writings of our Sages (Tractate Sukkot, folio 51) "One who did not see the *deyofloston* [great synagogue] of Alexandria in Egypt never saw the glory of Israel. etc." "And they [members of the various crafts] would not sit mingled. Rather, the goldsmiths would sit among themselves, and the silversmiths among themselves, and the blacksmiths among themselves, etc."

Lwów's great rabbis and leaders followed the same practice. All the craftsmen established their synagogues according to their trades: goldsmiths and blacksmiths, butchers and tinsmiths and so on. The common people longed to pray, lead the prayer and listen to a lesson out of *Eyn Jakuw* and a chapter from *Mishnayot*, or to study a section of the Torah with *Rashi* interpretation, seasoned with *Agada* or Talmudic legends etc., on Friday evenings.

Every synagogue had a special Shabbat assigned to it: The Shabbat of the *Lech Lecha* Torah portion, was the Shabbat of the tailors and the shoemakers, since it says in this portion "From a thread even to a shoelatchet"; the portion *Mishpatim* was the Shabbat of the Bikur Cholim Society, for it says "and shall cause him to be thoroughly healed"; the portion *VeShalach* was that of the Bnei–Levaya [Funeral] Society, on account of the phrase "And Moses took Josef's bones with him"; etc.

II. *Kloyzes*

1. *Kloyz* Lublin. In 1811, during the lifetime of the *Admor* Rabbi Jakub Izak Horowitz, the "Seer of Lublin," the "Lubliner *Kloyz*" was established on the second floor of the Great *Bet Midrash* [Torah study school] within the town, on Boimów Street, by the Lublin Chassidim among whom was the brother–in–law of the "Seer," the affluent Chassid and scholar, R' Arie–Leib Mimeles.

With the demise of the "Seer," the number of the Lublin Chassidim at Lwów diminished, but the Kloyz remained a respected place in town.

Among the principal worshipers were Chassidim sages and authors, and businessmen: Rabbi Iccke Ettinger, R' Herzl Rappaport and his son R' Mojzesz Rappaport, R' Jakub Babad the son of the Rabbi of Kalisz – all members of the *Beth–Din* under the great scholar R' Aleksander Heilpern, including R' Berisch Modlinger, the renowned, affluent R' Hersz Rokach, R' Abraham Anschel head of the *Beth–Din* of Tomaszów, a disciple of Rabbi Józef Saul Natansohn, the renowned philanthropist R' Alter Chassid, R' Simche Rappoport, Rabbi Szymon Klüger and R' Mojzesz Piepes (who was the *Kloyz* manager for some 40 years), as well as R' Szmelke de Horowitz, leader of Lwów's community.

After WWI, the place became a branch of the "Belz Chassidim" within the town. Latterly, the *Kloyz* leader was Rabbi Abraham–Juda Alter, a descendant of the author of *Turei Zahaw*. Although he himself followed the Ashkenazi style, his sons found their way to the Belz Chassidic sect, especially his son Rabbi Mojzesz–Elchanan Alter who was a rabbinical judge, and also the rabbinical judge Rabbi Anschel Schreiber.

Among the *Kloyz* leaders were also Pinkas Klüger, manager of the Great *Bet Midrash* outside the town, Rabbi Aron Fisch and the philanthropist R' Abraham Penzer.

Among the worshippers at *Kloyz* Lublin was also Rabbi Józef Saul Natansohn, as was a group of Sieniawa, Ropczyce and Stratyn Chassidim. The *Kloyz* was practically the only prayer house within the town, where prayers were in the Sephardi style. On every Shemini–

[Pages 465-466]

Atzeret, the managers of all the synagogues within the town arrived wearing "Top hats," to participate in the Chassidim's "*Hakafot.*"

Lwów's rabbi, the "Lithuanian" Rabbi Arie–Leib Braude, who followed the *Ashkenazi* prayer style and worshiped at the *Turei Zahaw* Synagogue, honoured the "Lubliner *Kloyz*" with visits, and on the eve of Yom Kippur he used to pray there *Kol Nidrei.*

Once the "Lublin *Kloyz*" had turned into the bastion of the Belz Chassidim, Rabbi Abraham–Juda Alter introduced strict discipline. These were Jews who held a consistently unyielding radical stance.

2.   *Kloyz* Asiri [10th]. Adjacent to the "Lublin *Kloyz*" on the second floor of the Great *Bet Midrash* on Boimoów Street, was found the "Tenth *Kloyz*," be it a *Kloyz* or just an ordinary synagogue. It too was one of the town's oldest. There are no clear records of its founder nor of the year in which it was founded.

The *Kloyz*'s purpose: A particular *Minyan* made up of ten Jews most of whom were Torah scholars and intensely God–fearing, who set for themselves a fast every tenth day, said *Slichot* and special liturgical poetry, lit a wax candle and exercised self–denial. They were exceptionally God–fearing and always acted modestly, inconspicuously "the Tenth shall be Holy."

Among the *Kloyz* worshippers and leaders was R' Jozef Stand, the father of Adolf Stand, one of the most distinguished and wealthy in town.

In latter years the custom was maintained by ordinary Jews, and among the worshipers were also elderly Jews with trimmed beards, a group of *Maskilim*, who studied the Torah with interpretation by Ibn–Ezra, grammar and "exegesis," a kind of "competition" and also "to spite" the neighbouring Chassidim.

3.   Strelisk *Kloyz*. Around (5585) 1824–5, the Chassidim of Strelisk [Strzeliska Nowe] established the *Kloyz* on Starozakonna Street, in a small dilapidated house, in the style of Poland's "Przysucha," abandoned and shabby. Inside the house, however, inside the *Kloyz*, prevailed an air of brotherly love, inner happiness and exalted joy of life – as in "Divine spirit is among them."

Their rabbi, Rabbi Uri of Strelisk [Strzeliska], the "*Seraph*, [Angel]" a disciple of R' Salomon Karlinger, taught them a deep love for all Jews, a heartfelt joy, a venerable devotion to the Creator and content in moderation or even in actual poverty, and a true piety.

They were among the earliest Chassidim at Lwów who excelled in the ways of Chassidism, in wit and endless enthusiasm. Most of them were paupers, nevertheless they were always full of joy. In the early days they suffered much from their opposers, but they never responded to any persecutions, with the exception of one, when the *Admor* of Strelisk was personally summoned by the State investigator. After spending several hours with him in a closed room, the investigator turned –as the Chassidim tell it– into a great admirer of the Strelisk Rabbi.

The *Kloyz* leaders were the "*Seraph*'s" remaining Chassidim, Rabbi Uri of Strelisk, and later, of his successor, the *Admor* Rabbi Juda Cwi [Tzvi] of Stratyn, a quintessential disciple of the "*Seraph*," Rabbi Wolff Schönblum, who headed the *Kloyz* up to the construction of his own Torah Study school on Sykstuska [Street].

With the demise of the *Admor* Rabbi Juda–Cwi of Stratyn, the Strelisk Chassidism declined markedly and its veteran Chassidim went in search of a new rabbi.

Latterly, the *Kloyz* leaders included: Samuel Riss, Michael Kitower and Jakob–Meszulam Nick.

When the last of the veteran Strelisk Chassidim, Rabbi Berl Stratyner, the son–in–law of Rabbi Juda–Cwi of Stratyn arrived at Lwów, he gathered at his home and at his Torah Study school the remaining Stratyn–Strelisk Chassidim, and the *Kloyz* remained a prayer–house for the residents of the neighbourhood and for visitors. Latterly, the building disintegrated with age. Among the followers of Rabbi Berl of Stratyn were the remaining Chassidim, such as: Saul Grünberg (the owner of Lwów's renowned Kosher restaurant), Samuel Birnfeld, Samuel Krausz, Mojzesz Puder, Kalman Ehrenpreis, Juda Parnas and others.

The son of Rabbi Juda and grandson of Rabbi Berl of Stratyn, Rabbi Samuel Seinwel, published the Charedi monthly *Jiwne* for several years. Rabbi Uri of Strelisk's second grandson, Rabbi Leibisch Strelisker, moved to Lwów and established his own *Minyan*.

4.   Belz *Chadaszim* [New] ***Kloyz***. The *Chadaszim* synagogue was founded in (5616) 1855–56 by the well to do Jakob Glanzer [reb. Jankiel Jancer], one of R' Izak Iccik of Zydaczów's Chassidim. The title *Chadaszim* was coined by the Rabbi of Zydaczów after the verse "They are new every morning; great is thy faithfulness" (Lamentations 3; 23). At first, the worshippers were not exclusively Chassidim but included home–owners who had abandoned the synagogues where prayer was in the Ashkenazi style, and transferred to the *Chadaszim* synagogue because a larger number of the *Maskilim* wished their sons to be educated in the spirit of the tradition. In time, the *Kloyz* and the synagogue turned into a bastion of strength for the "Belz Chassidim" whose practice followed the renowned Belz discipline. The Belz–Chassimdim's onslaught started with a dispute over the style of "liturgical poems." At the *Chadaszim* synagogue it was the custom to say the poems in the style of Zydaczów. The Belz Chassidim objected to this and introduced their own style. As they

[Pages 467-468]

formed the majority among the worshippers, they forcefully overcame the Zydaczów Chassidim and R' Jakob Glanzer, and took over the synagogue.

All of Lwów's large synagogues were entered at the land registry either as the property of, or under the guardianship of Lwów's Jewish community, apart from the *Chadaszim* synagogue for which R' Jakob Glanzer had paid the community a very large sum to ensure its freedom from all external influence. As at the time the community was led by the Enlightened, he aimed to prevent any secular influence. The *Chadaszim Kloyz* was registered in the name of three appointed guardians, with the proviso that on the demise of one of them, the two remaining would appoint a third guardian in his place, and in this manner the access or intervention by any company or institution would be prevented.

When the number of the Belz Chassidim rose to form the majority of the worshippers, they wanted to establish a study place inside the synagogue, but the sanctity of the synagogue made them build adjacent to it a spacious *kloyz* that was inaugurated by Rabbi Jozue of Belz and was known as the *Chadaszim Kloyz* or *Belzer Kloyz*. The *Kloyz* was always bustling with worshippers and Torah students, Yeshivah students, Chassidim and ordinary home–owners.

Every scholar who came to town held a sermon at the *Chadaszim*. Every renowned rabbi who came to town set his "bench" at the *Chadaszim Kloyz* thus turning the place into a significant centre for the town and the surroundings.

The *Kloyz* was led by R' Hersz Braser (Zorn), a veteran Chassid who followed the Belz customs to the letter; Rabbi Muses Wolf Mesuse, author of *Chidusze RaMaZ* (Lwów 1935), who was blind towards the end of his life; Naftali Hersz Rappoport; Mordche Pelz, a friend of the Belz *Admor*, who managed the Belzer coterie in town; R' Febus Ebner, editor of the newspaper *Kol Machsike HaDas*, and his son, R' Jozef; Jozue Heller, a Chassidic Yeshivah student who was influential with the youth; and the businessman Mojzesz Lustig.

When the community board accepted Rabbi Leib Braude as Rabbi and head of Yeshivah, the Belzer Chassidim objected to him, unequivocally, because his sons "do not follow the righteous path."

On the Sabbath following the session that decided to appoint Rabbi Leib Braude, a heated meeting took place at the Synagogue followed by a demonstrative procession to the home of the community leader, Dr. Emil Byk, led by a delegation vigorously protesting against the election of the rabbi. After weeks of dispute and struggle to no avail, the Belz Chassidim appointed as rabbi the great scholar Rabbi Mojzesz son of Rabbi Zalman Perles [BRZ"P] Rappoport from Lezajsk, in opposition to the majority who chose Rabbi Leib Braude. The first difference of opinion between the two Rabbis regarded the issue of Eruv [wires that signify the physical boundary of an urban space within which the Orthodox can carry items on the Sabbath & Holidays] within the town; whereas Rabbi Leib Braude ruled that it was permissible to carry [items] throughout the town, Rabbi BRZ"P, on the other hand, forbade carrying generally. The *Kloyz*–Belz Chassidim forbade conflict over anything novel – "novel is forbidden from the Torah." As zealots and extremists they conducted a fight to the death against any organisation, and any Zionist organisation in particular. For years they sided with Lwów's assimilated and supported the State's policies. Any Jew entering the *Kloyz* in an ironed white collar was instantly removed from their company. Any garment that was even slightly modern, was strictly forbidden. A tie was on a par with – "Not to be seen nor to be found." It was forbidden to use electricity or gas at the *Kloyz* and the Synagogue, on the grounds that the electric installation also passed through Christian churches, [to distinguish holy from profane]. The tougher the strictness – the greater the excellence.

The Belz Chassidim did not restrict their resoluteness to themselves alone, but instead tried to impose it on others too. The Belz *Admor*, Rabbi Issachar–Dov Rokach, of blessed memory, who was a great scholar, great in the Torah and in the fear of God, bore his presidency with esteem and was unwavering in his thought and action. Under him, the Belz Chassidism expanded to number thousands and tens of thousands. He led his Chassidim not only in Chassidism but also in strategy. The Belz Chassidim headed all public activities at Lwów. In the Austrian parliamentary elections the Belz Chassidim contributed much to the success of the government party, and defeated the Jewish list. The Belz strategy was to do anything at all except for joining the Zionist cause. They dedicated their entire beings to that end, which was followed by the masses of Chassidim.

As previously said, the *Belz– Chadaszim–Kloyz* was a meeting place for all their activities. In the early years, summer 1878, a gathering was held there of rabbis against the "communities' conference," at which it was decided to establish the organisation *Machsike HaDas* and they also started to publish the weekly *Machsike HaDas* [*Zeitung für das wahre Orthodoxische Judenthum*] as well as *Kol Machsike HaDas*, edited by Mendel Margoszes, one of the leading Belz Chassidim (the father of [Samuel] Margoszes, the editor of the [*Yiddishes*] *Tageblatt*, New York). At the instigation of the Belz–Chassidim's leaders, the organisation *Machsike HaDas* waged a bitter war against every innovation in Jewish life.

Rabbi Tzvi [Cwi Hersz] Ornstein of Lwów and a number of other rabbis did not join *Machsike HaDas*. Lwów's *Chadaszim Kloyz* was chosen as the *Machsike HaDas* operation centre, and the Belz Chassidim resorted to any means in their fight.

5.   Chabad–Breslau *Kloyz*, at No. 4 Pełtewna street, not far from the bustling fishmarket at the heart of the Jewish Quarter and behind the *Chadaszim* synagogue,

[Pages 469-470]

the Chassidim's deep devotional song and dance were heard at midday – verses from Psalms, liturgical song and praises. Such was the Torah–Study school of R' Icikel Żólkower, known as *Kloyz* "Chabad–Breslau"

For Jews who crossed the Russian–Galician border on their way to prostrate themselves on the grave of the rabbi, Rabbi Nachman of Breslau [Wrocław], at Uman [Humań], Lwów was a principal junction, and their hostelry was the home of R' Icikel of Żólkiew, where they prepared themselves for the trip and where they returned.

This was the sole Galician *Kloyz* where hardly any of the Lyubavitsh or Breslau Chassidim could be found, and so their gatherings at the Torah–study school of R' Icikel Żólkower was an interesting event.

R' Izak Schwebel, known as R' Icikel Żólkower, was an exceptional man, an entrepreneur and thinker, knowledgeable in the teaching of the revealed and the occult. He was born at Żólkiew in 1840, into a family of religious scholars descended from the family of the Baal Shem Tov. Little is known of his method of study. As a young man he crossed the Russian border, travelled to Kopys and for three years studied Torah and Chassidism with the *Admor* R' [Menachem] Mendel of Lyubavitsh [Lubawicze] the author of [the responsa] *Tzemach Tzedek* [Righteous Sprout], excelled in the Torah and was one of his favoured pupil. Having received as a mark of affection from the author of *Tzemach Tzedek* some of his own manuscripts and many other books, R' Icikel returned home. He got the manuscripts and the books across the Russian border, a precarious undertaking fraught with difficulty and mortal danger.

R' Icikel spent his days in Torah study and work, repeating to himself and his friends the saying: this world is but a corridor to the next, therefore man needs to reflect on his deeds and prepare himself for entering the living–room.

At his Torah study school he held sermons on every Sabbath, Holy Day and festivity. On memorial days to *Admorim* and to Chabad, he preached and studied chapters from Tanya [basic text of Chabad philosophy] and Chabad Chassidism, paying heed to affairs between man and man. He helped every man, be he Charedi or secular, Gentile or Jew, rich or poor. He did not look at the face of a woman, not even the faces of his granddaughters, yet he did help women, and once when walking down the street a woman laden with baskets fell on the ice, he immediately turned to help her.

When at Żólkiew as a young man, he met Rabbi Natan, the faithful disciple of Rabbi Nachman, who disseminated his teaching and came to Żólkiew to print *Likute Halachot, Etz Chajim Yoré–De'a* together with MoHaRaN's [Rabbi Nachman] anthology, and it was there that he encountered him [Rabbi Natan]. The Breslau chassid, R' Izrael Halpern of Tarnopol, also resided at Lwów for a long period and printed the books of Rabbi Nachman of Breslau. He frequented R' Icikel's home, befriended him and turned into an ardent admirer of the Chabad doctrine. He died at Lwów in the month of Adar (5686) 1925. With his demise the honour of the *Kloyz* waned and the singing of the travellers to Uman ceased.

In his will, R' Icikel instructed to move all his books and manuscripts to the central library of the Lyubavitsh Yeshivah at Warsaw, and to consult the great Chassidim whether his own writings deserved to be published... and were they to consent, then they were to publish his books, and furthermore they were to deliver the late *Tzemach Tzedek*'s manuscripts to the Lyubavitsh Rabbi, because he was their beneficiary.

He was unsuccessful in having his books published. Apparently there was no one to deal with it. And thus his books together with the Yeshivah's library were lost during the Second World War.

His yearning for Eretz Israel ran deep. He regretted his entire life not being able to travel to the Holyland. In 1918 he made preparations to travel to Eretz Israel, but his migration was unsuccessful.

6.   **Żydaczów** *Kloyz*. The synagogue "Zichron Yitzchak [Isaac's Memorial]," named after the late *Admor* of Żydaczów, Rabbi Izaak Izik of blessed memory, was inside the home of the community elder R' Mojzesz Reiss in Gołuchowski Sq. There is no information of the date it was established, but it was probably during the years (5640–5650) 1879–1889, by Jakob Glanzer.

Lwów's veteran Chassidim congregated at the Żydaczów *Kloyz*; dedicated great scholars, Kabbalists distinguished by their piety and acuity, of noble spirit and refined soul. They followed a distinct intellectual line of enquiry into the Torah. Study was pursued there continuously, day and night. The outstanding and privileged young men studied there, be it singly or in groups. The lessons for mature young men were conducted by the Chassid and confirmed great scholar, R' Dawid Kulikower. The *Kloyz* held set nighttime lessons in the Talmud, *Eyn Jakuw*, *Midrash* and research books for permanent learners. The lesson *Maggidim* were Jews who worked hard all day and at dusk and on the Sabbath were in the habit of delivering lessons, including: the elderly R' Szmuel "cake Jew" with his passionate words and explanation, and R' Abraham Leiwand with his pleasant speech.

The great scholar Rabbi Uri–Wolf Salat, leader of Lwów's *Beth–Din*, was among the first ten men at the *Kloyz* who prayed in the Żydaczów style. R' Zisza Stand, R' Michael Preminger and R' Szmaja Halpern, infused vitality and enthusiasm into the prayers that they led. And when the upright, great learned Jew R' Lipa–Menle Kunst stood up to pray, those around him were all excited. The prayers of the Żydaczów Chassidim pierced hearts in their innocence and affability – among them R' Mojzesz Hibl, R' Feiwel Rosner, R' Mojzesz

[Pages 471-472]

Sokolower, R' Aron Mojzesz Kawa, R' Abszalom, R' Jankiel Goldberg, the holy and pure R' Tewel Leiwand, R' Chaim Leib Paps and R' Judele Kimel, the modest R' Mojzesz Wolf and R' Jossele Kurz, the great scholar and author R' Hersz Philipp, the gentle R' Szulim Halpern, R' Pinkas Lewer and R' Judel Atlas, R' Samuel Leib Landau and his son R' Nachman, the noble and modest R' Szulim Eybeschütz, the zealots R' Mendel Schwarzwald and R' Izak Brendler, the progressives, so to speak, R' Jozef Klarberg and R' Chaim Moses Schreiber [Sofer],. R' Mardochaj Liskowter studied a lesson with the best students, the sharp and knowledgeable R' Gerschon Heiselbach, the researcher and philosopher R' Lipa Gerschon, and R' Mardochaj Baumel may he live, rabbi at New–York, and the author and historian Dr. Hilel Seidmann. A true Judaism of pure faith, kindness to others, pure prayer and Jewish study, with yearning for salvation and life's poetry that suddenly came to a halt. Żydaczów *Kloyz* gathered the best of Lwów's Chassidic intelligentsia, where lessons were guided and studied by the sage, the great scholar R' Reuben Margulies, who lives among us at Tel–Aviv, whose prominent personality stood out within this company.

Torah and greatness, Chassidism and Kabbalah, research and science, kindness and charity –Chassidic Torah education and respect– such was Lwów's Żydaczów *Kloyz*.

7.   **Stepaner** *Kloyz* at 5 Furmańska Street. According to tradition, the *Kloyz* was founded by the *Maggid* of Stepań, a disciple of the *Maggid* of Międzybóż [Medzhybizh], during his stay at Lwów on his way to Brody after his battle with the "opposers."

There is no data about the early days of the *Kloyz* that was situated inside the large courtyard of the wealthy Chassid R' Lazar Gutwirth's house. The *Kloyz* building remained in his courtyard and underwent repairs and in the large hall the walls were covered in books up to the ceiling. The *Kloyz* bustled with worshippers from daybreak till noon and was always filled to capacity. Chassidim from every "Court [Rebbe's circle]" gathered at the *Kloyz*. The town's dignitaries prayed there regularly, including R' Herzle Rappoport, member of Lwów's Rabbinical law–court. Among the *Kloyz*'s grandees and managers were the philanthropist R' Jona Rosenfeld, Izrael Liberman, Lazar Gottlieb, Majer Schein, Szmuel–Jossel Mohel (Harth), Mojzesz Alster. Until his demise R' Mendele the *Admor* of Olesko [Alesk] worshipped regularly at the *Kloyz*.

The *Kloyz* members excelled in acts of charity and kindness, and did much during the First World War to best assist Galician and Russian refugees. The principal motivator was R' Meszulam Altstater and his circle of friends.

The Stepań *Kloyz* was a meeting place for the *Admorim* who came to Lwów. They set up their "tables" there for hundreds and thousands of Chassidim.

Among the managers were: R' Hersch Schrenzel [Szrencel], Schmelke Barach, Samuel Kraus, Judel Frensler and Mojzesz Puder.

8.   Sykstuska *Kloyz*. One of Lwów's magnificent and ancient buildings was the Sykstusta synagogue on Szajnochy Street – a payer house for the aristocracy residing in the area: the wealthy, titleholders, community–leaders, "the town" and scholars; among them the distinguished families Landau and Sussmann. Inside the courtyard stood the Torah Study school for the distinguished learners, such as: R' Schmelke Rokach, Schmelke Horowitz the community president, R' Leibisch Wahl a community–leader, his brother Isser Wahl, the esteemed businessman R' Wolf Kahane, son–in–law of R' Jossele Popers of Brody, Rabbi Jakub Wittels president of *HaMizrachi* and later president of Eastern Galicia's *Agudas Jisroel* and more.

Around (5603) 1843, the *Kloyz* was established with the assistance of the philanthropist R' Aleksander Zisza Pfau, in honour of, and with the generosity of R' Benjamin Zev (Wolf) Schönblum, the firm disciple of the righteous "*Seraph*" Rabbi Uri of Strelisk and his son Samuel, author of *Shlosha S'farim Niftachim* [Three books are being opened]. The *Kloyz* was the centre for the "learners" with some of the Strelisk, Czortków and Zydaczów Chassidim who lived in the vicinity and young, perpetual learners arrived the entire week. Among the *Kloyz* leaders and worshippers were R' Wolf and his son R' Samuel, R' Icche–Majer Ettinger (who was later elected head of Yeshivah at Lwów), Mardochaj BRZ"P –Rappoport, family Weksler, Noah and Saul Pfirna, Nachum Burstein (who was appointed head of Yeshivah at Chodorów and at Bursztyn). By and by the *Kloyz*'s glory waned so that in the years before the war it was quite unnoticeable. New life breathed through the building of the Sykstuska Synagogue that was oriented towards emulating the "Temple" to some extent.

9.   Sasów–Pomorzany *Kloyz*. At the outbreak of WWI in 1914, hordes of people from Galicia's small towns fled to the towns, and those who had not succeeded in reaching Vienna, Prague or Hungary, arrived at Lwów. Among the refugees who came to Lwów was the *Admor* R' Szlome of Sasów with his large family: sons and daughters, sons–in–law, grandchildren and great–grandchildren. He resided in the house of Landau, one of his Chassidim, on Kotlarska Street.

A few years later the old rabbi died at Lwów and his dynasty, his sons and sons–in–law, dispersed and joined several [Chassidic] "courts." These included one of his sons–in–law, the *Admor* R' Szalom Taub, head of Yeshivah of the holy community of Pomorzany [Pomoriany] near Sasów [Sasiv], who had joined his father–in–law in the move to Lwów at the beginning of the war. At his apartment

[Pages 473-474]
on Legionów Street opposite the Polish Opera, the *Kloyz* was immediately established.

Rabbi Szalom Taub was noted for his pleasant voice and as a talented composer. A great many people came to hear him pray and his wonderful songs that he sang backed by his son–in–law R' Jankele and his son R' Judel, who subsequently replaced him at the rabbinate of Pomoriany. R' Szalom Taub managed "tables" that were attended by all sorts of Chassidim, especially by young men who came to listen to his teaching and renditions. Jewish cantors, artists and "theatre stars" also came to hear him sing.

In the years before the second World War, the Rabbi moved to Sasów and replaced his father–in–law as ritual judge and *Admor* of Sasów.

10.   "*Kloyz* Czortków" was established on Berka Joselowicza Street in 1910. After the outbreak of the war in 1914, the Czortków refugees and a group of Chassidim who were at Lwów, moved the "*Kloyz* Czortków" to a spacious apartment on Szpitalna Street, opposite the Jewish hospital. Hundreds of Czortków Chassidim occupied a very prominent place in town. The *Kloyz* acted as a magnet for the Charedi youth. Regular Torah lessons were held there and it was a centre for Charedi traders and especially for *Agudas Jisroel*. The best of the *Kloyz*'s youth became leaders of the Young *Agudas Jisroel* in Galicia and Poland, as: Cwi [Zvi] Hirschorn (Chairman of the union of Poland's Young *Agudas Jisroel*, and later rabbi at Jaworzno and at Biała Podlaska), R' Szlome Schikler (rabbinical judge at Kalisz), Rabbi Winkler, R' Mojzesz Hirszsprung (member of Lwów's community management board), Bracy Horn, Alter Lipa and others.

The Czortków Chassidim at Lwów were on a permanent war footing with the Belz Chassidim. It was a silent war between the methods of Belz and Czortków. The fight of the Belz Chassidim was very loud and full of "boycotts" against any innovation, since "New is prohibited by the Torah," indeed, the Czortków *Kloyz* members took all precautions to prevent blasphemy by following the instructions of the Czortków *Admor*, who resided at Vienna during the war, and whom they consulted by mail or via special messengers. This distressed the Belz Chassidim who were unable to come to terms with the style of "war" of the Czortków Chassidim, whose politeness and moderation was polar opposite to their own style.

"Belz" opposed the creation of Israel, while "Czortków" was involved in settling Eretz Israel and in its construction. This formed the basis for a silent and passionate war. Lwów's Czortków Chassidim supported Galicia's first pioneers' training–farms for the religious youth, while the Belz adherents opposed them. The Czortków Chassidim decided to disregard the provocation in silence and continue in their own way.

Chassidic celebrations at *Kloyz*–Czortków were noted for their inner joy. The Rabbi of Czortków's talks on the Sabbath, Holidays and on students' breaks – repeated and taught over a glass of "*LeChaim* [wine]" according to tradition; at *Mitzva* meal, or *Third–meal* on the Sabbath, instructive tales were told, of R' Izrael of Ruzhyn and of the first *Admor* of the House of Czortków, and about R' Izrael's leadership at Lwów and details of his life at Vienna. In 1923, on his way to Czortków, Rabbi Izrael arrived at Lwów for the first time after the World War. Thousands of his Chassidim and admirers flocked to Galicia from all corners of Poland to welcome their Rabbi, and formed a huge manifestation. The aged, gentle and noble Rabbi made an impression on all who saw him. On Legionów Street, in the large hall of the factory belonging to his Chassid R' Mojzesz Griffel his Chassidim assembled and approached him, one by one, with notes (*Kvitels* [small messages]) in their hands, to relate to him their joy and troubles. He received them with love and delight, read and studied every detail, and asked and replied and blessed every single one. Later, the Rabbi received representatives of the town's different organisations: The Zionist Federation, *HaMizrachi*, *HaAgudah*, the community's management etc. On his departure from Lwów he was accompanied by crowds in an impressive farewell ceremony.

11. "*Kloyz* Husiatyn." A group of Chassidim, old men and yeshivah students devoted to their rabbi, Rabbi Izrael son of Mardochaj–Feibisch of Husiatyn, established in 1910 the *Kloyz* at 11 Pełtewna street. With the outbreak of the First World War the Rabbi of Husiatyn was obliged to leave his magnificent hall and court and he moved to Vienna. Many of his Chassidim came to Lwów. The *Kloyz* on Pełtewna Street was too small to contain them all, and the accommodations were also far, and so a new *Kloyz* was established at 3 Kotlarska Street.

In 1938, R' Nachum Munia, the son–in–law of the *Admor* of Husiatyn settled at Lwów and assembled Galicia's Husiatyn Chassidim. The *Admor* of Husiatyn, as known, lived in Vienna till his migration to Eretz Israel in 1939.

Among the the founders and heads of *Kloyzes* were: Rabbi Mendel Laszczower of Leypun, Mojzesz Laszczower, Feivel Polturak, Samuel Liebling, Abraham Zamora, Eli Polturak, and the very last, the elderly R' Izrael Brikenstein who passed away last year at Tel–Aviv.

12. "*Kloyz* Komárno [Komárom]" In (5673) 1913 the *Kloyz* of the Komárno Chassidim was established at Lwów on Alembeków Street. A multitude of Komárno Chassidim and also righteous women travelled to see Rabbi Jakob Mojzesz Safrin to "achieve salvation." Chassidism spread among the artless and the believing masses.

[Pages 475-476]

The *Admor* of Komárno, with pedigree and handsome appearance he bore his presidency with esteem and had the reputation of a *Tzadik*. In 1914, the Rabbi of Komárno arrived at Lwów and was received with enthusiasm. During his stay a Torah Book was written in his honour, and the *Kloyz* moved to 28 Słoneczna Street. With the outbreak of war, it moved to his house at 37 Kazimierzowska Street and was followed there by men and women who came to his open house. After his demise the seat of *Admor* was occupied by his son, and later by his grandson. Until the Holocaust the *Kloyz* remained a Chassidic house for the residents in the neighbourhood who prayed there. Among the early founders of the *Kloyz* were: Izrael Lubin Frankfurter (who moved to Paris after the demise of the *Admor* Rabbi Jakob Mojzesz, where he led his own flock); Mardochaj Deutscher one of the Rabbi's confidants; Rabbi Kalman Ehrenpreis and Jona Löb.

13. "*Kloyz* Alesk [Olesko]" was established in 1913, on Rzeźnicka Street, at the home of Rabbi Arie Leib Braude. The *Kloyz* had no distinguishing aspects and its Chassidim did not frequent it much either, because the *Admor* of Olesko who all the years resided at Lwów, had his Torah study school at his home on Legionów Street. The Chassidim attended his Torah Study school every Sabbath. The *Kloyz*, as mentioned, was quite unnoticed in town. The worshippers who attended it were the residents of the neighbourhood and visitors to the hotel and restaurant of Saul Grünberg, in an adjoining building of the same courtyard. Rabbi Leib Braude also prayed there, daily.

Rabbi Mojzesz–Dawid Aszkenazi, the grandson of the *Admor* Rabbi Izak of Olesko, also assembled part of the Olesko Chassidim at his Torah study school on Furmańska Street, and they did not attend the *Kloyz*. Rabbi Mojzesz–Dawid left Lwów at the start of the First World War and settled at Grosswardein [Oradea] (Transylvania).

14. *"Kloyz* **Boyan** [Boiany]." In 1917, during WWI, the *Admor* Rabbi Abraham Jakob son of Rabbi Izak of Boyan arrived at Lwów as a war asylum–seeker and settled at 29 Legionów Street. The Boyan Chassidim, headed by Szalom Wallach, Icche–Majer and Abraham–Jozef Münz, established the "Boyan Chassidim's *Kloyz*" adjacent to the apartment of the Rabbi who gathered amongst his worshippers and visiting Chassidim from the houses of Ruzhyn, Czortkov, Husiatyn, Sadigura, Vizhnitz, Kosov etc. Among the *Kloyz* leaders was Majer Gerszon, one of the biggest merchants in town, a philanthropist who kept an open house. Some twenty men regularly sat at his table as "guests." A regular *Minyan* was held at his home, attended by Jews who prayed with him till the late hours.

Kloyz Boyan constituted a meeting–house for Chassidim. Crowds flocked to the Rabbi's "tables" to listen to his teachings and to the singing of the renowned Boyan renditions by the Gur–Arie Hornstein family, and other Chassidic musicians. The Boyan Rabbi's demeanour excelled in modesty. He showed interest in everyone who turned to him. He instructed his colleagues to involve themselves in the town's and the national public endeavour. Prominent among his Chassidim were: Chanoch Aszkenazi, under whose initiative the "Boycott Committee" against the black market was established after the War and the Lwów Riots, and it was he who saved the Jewish masses from actual hunger at the time. He himself was a very firm "Boycott Rabbi," was a member of the community board and a leading member of *Agudas Jisroel*, he also served as manager of the centre for Eretz–Israel issues under *Agudas Jisroel* in Galicia; R' Cwi Elster, Benjamin Schreiber, Juda–Hersz Wittmann, Mojzesz Zwik. The Rabbi instructed them in particular to engage in charity, and he himself set them an example. The Rabbi of Boyan was an ardent admirer of Eretz Israel, and he guided his Chassidim along this path. He was filled with much joy over every emigrant heading there, among whom was Rabbi Szmuel–Cwi Weiss, an active member of Lwów's *HaMizrachi*, and Abraham–Jozef Münzer who later, at his own expense, invited the Rabbi to come to Israel for the housewarming of his home at Tel–Aviv. In 1932, the *Admor* of Boyan visited the Holy Land and cantor R' Jossele Rosenblatt heartened his reception with ritual songs.

*

Until the First World War, except for the assimilated [Jews], Lwów was distinguished for its traditional way of life. The synagogues also served as "*Cheders*" and as Torah study schools where thousands of young children were taught the Torah by Torah teachers, who never stopped quoting the Torah and who formed a screen against the assimilation that started to take giant strides in this town.

The synagogues also served as dormitories for *Mettibtot* [colleges] and Yeshivahs managed by their rabbis, heads of Jewish colleges, who conducted the classes there. The great scholar, the sage, described the town of Lwów in this way: "The great and magnificent town, full of sages and authors and deputies. It is the source of wisdom and the spring of knowledge the cornerstone of the Faith." And the great scholar our teacher Rabbi Petachiah Lida, head and leader of the holy community of Lwów, asserted: "And this is what they will say of this town of perfect beauty, joy of everyone, full of sages and writers, great in the Torah and in good deeds, in justice and charity, and their honour lit up the land."

May the list of synagogues, those mentioned and those left out, be a sacred–memorial to Lwów's crowning Judaism and eternal memory to its Greats and to its honest and innocent masses who gave their souls for the sanctification of God.

Note: All notes in square brackets [ ] were made by the translator

[The spelling of a large number of individuals' names in this chapter could not be verified in other sources and are spelt as closely as possible to the author's spelling.]

Original footnote:

    1.   *see* Article by Z Karl.

[Pages 477-478]

Architecture and Art of the Synagogues

by Jacob Pinkerfeld

Translated by Myra Yael Ecker

Edited by Karen Leon

The ancient synagogues of Lwów, both "within" and "outside the town," were constructed in timber. Not one of them remained standing after going up in flames in the frequent fires that swept through the town. The sole remains of an ancient synagogue, a single timber beam, was uncovered when digging the foundations of a building on "The Tinsmiths" (Blacharska) Street, some fifty years ago. The beam was decorated in geometric motifs superimposed by ornamental Hebrew text. The synagogues generally were very small and belonged to craftsmen's associations, such as: tinsmiths, goldsmiths, upholsterers, purgers [of kosher meat] etc., or to the diverse charitable societies. In the first half of the nineteenth century, the last of the ancient buildings were abandoned and their worshippers moved to *Cheders* on the upper floors of the new *Batei Midrash* [Torah–study schools] that were constructed during this period.

Among the synagogues that remained until the town was invaded by the Nazis in the Second World War, the oldest was the synagogue *Turei Zahav* [Golden Columns] or "Golden Rose" named after the wife of Nachman ben Izak (of the Nachmanowicz family who founded the building). The synagogue *Turei Zahav* superseded a much earlier building, constructed in the second half of the 15th century after the great fire of 1352. When the "old synagogue" became too small to contain the worshippers of the growing community, R' Izak ben Nachman appointed the Italian architect, Paolo Romano [Paulus Romanus], engaged in the construction of buildings in the town, to erect the new synagogue.

The building constructed in 1582, consisted of a hall with a single–colonnade, almost square – measuring around 11x9 meters – with an additional corridor, due west, and two rooms situated off it. After some years, R' Izak was granted a licence to enlarge the building, but he died, and the second stage of the building was undertaken by his son, Nachman, executed by the architect Paolo Romano, in 1595.

The partitions between the corridor and the two rooms were removed and the entire space was added to the hall of the synagogue by means of three wide openings that were pierced into the western wall. On the south side, a corridor was added to the hall, replacing the deleted entrance. Part of the corridor was allocated to a prison–cell, where delinquents were locked up following the judgement by the community's law–court, that held its sessions inside the synagogue hall.

A women's section that did not exist in the earlier period of the building, was constructed over the corridor and the lower wing, due west, annexed to the hall.

In front of the synagogue lay a spacious courtyard, connected by a passage from the street through the residence of family Nachmanowicz. The entrance from the courtyard was via the southern corridor that led to the lower wing of the hall. From here the hall was visible through the three wide openings that formed a kind of frame. The roof of the hall was made up of a series of Gothic domes. Along the symmetrical axes of all four walls, windows were pierced in their upper half, two on every side that spread magnificent light into the inner space. The high windows that terminated in pointed arches, were also in the Gothic style. The surprising aspect about this building constructed by an Italian architect during the period of the Renaissance, was that the other buildings he had constructed in town followed the style of the period. In my view, the deviation from convention rested on the instructions that the architect was given, to maintain the tradition and the architectural details of the old synagogue that the initiators still had in their mind's eye.

The hall's splendour rested on its wide *Bimah* [raised platform in the synagogue for reading from the Torah] situated at its centre. The *Bimah's* balustrades and its upper structure were made of beaten sheet–metal decorated in motifs of lions, ornamental plants and geometry. The stairs' banister leading up to the Holy Ark was also crafted of similar sheet metal.

Entirely different was the appearance of the two "great" synagogues, the one in the Kraków suburb, and the one in town – both from the seventeenth century. The period between the mid sixteenth century and the end of the eighteenth, was generally fertile for progression in the architecture of synagogues. Because of the improved economic condition in Poland and the wider autonomy of the Council of Four Lands during

[Pages 479-480]

this period, independent architectural styles shaped the internal space of the synagogue. The most interesting among the stone built synagogues was the type with a centralized form, square on plan, with four columns that supported nine domed "areas." In the central area bound by the four columns, was placed the *Bimah*, the dominant element in the space.

Among the oldest synagogues was the synagogue "outside the town" of Lwów, which was constructed in 1632. Its four heavy pillars, 1.13 meters thick, were built in ashlar. The flank of the square hall measured 20 meters, and its height almost 11 meters. Along all walls – at mid height – was a frieze of false arches, a motif very common to this type of synagogue in Poland.

Almost one of a kind (a second known example is the synagogue of Zamość [Zamoshtsh]) was the construction of the high gallery for the boys' choir, supported by the south facing wall. A ladder with 15 steep risers and a single handrail near the wall, led up there. The galleries of the women's section were built above the entrance area, along the entire western wall, and the two sides of the hall.

After the synagogue "outside the town" was constructed, the synagogue within the town–walls was built at 54 Boimów Street. In 1797, the building was demolished by order of the authorities, for fear of collapse, and was re–erected in 1801. The internal space of this synagogue mirrored almost exactly the form of the old synagogue outside the town–walls.

Besides these three synagogues, there were scores of small synagogues, prayer *Cheders* and [*Batei Midrash*] Torah–study schools. Architecturally noteworthy among these are two large Torah–study schools built in the 18th century; one within the town and the other in the Kraków suburb. Both had large domed halls with heavy vaults on the ground floor, that also contained great libraries. On the upper floors were the prayer rooms of craftsmen's societies and associations that had moved there from the old timber buildings that had been vacated during the previous era.

In 1848, as assimilation started to spread among certain circles of Lwów's Jews, the synagogue of the "Enlightened" known as "the Temple," was constructed. Its building illustrated the gradual severance from the architectural tradition of synagogues from earlier periods. This is evident in the layout of the space. Although the large, domed building had a centralized form, externally, this was not followed consistently inside the hall. The *Bimah* was not in its natural place at the centre of the hall underneath the dome, instead, it was placed in front of the Holy Ark's dais,

Dr. Oswald Hönigsmann

and was reduced to a set table. The influence of Christian church architecture was further evident with the introduction of the preacher's dais in the form of a small high balcony [pulpit] near the northern wall. From the pulpit the rabbis delivered their sermons on the Sabbaths and holidays, intermittently in Polish and German. The women's section stretched along three sides of the wide hall, on two upper galleries. The top level, facing the Holy Ark, was occupied by the mixed choir and the organ.

Lwów's synagogues were distinguished by the abundance of Torah–scrolls and their decorations – crowns, salvers and *Yads* [pointers for Torah–scroll reading] *Parochets* [ornamental curtain in front of the Holy Ark in a synagogue] etc. An idea of the extent of the treasures in past centuries, can be deduced from the list of items of which the synagogues had been robbed during the riots of 1664: from the synagogue outside the town, 72 Torah–scrolls; 24 *Keters* [crowns], 60 *Parochets*, and from Nachmanowicz's synagogue, 65 Torah–scrolls, 34 *Keters*, 12 *Parochets* and 136 Torah–scrolls coats etc.

A large number of magnificent copper chandeliers hung from the vaults; light reflectors adorned with flora and fauna ornaments and even human figures decorated the walls. It is worth noting that two of the large, shallow copper and silver bowls at the Nachmanowicz synagogue, illustrated the spies carrying bunches of grapes, and another bowl illustrated Adam and Eve next to the tree of knowledge.

The bibliographical list offers extensive historical and illustrative material about Lwów's synagogues.

All notes in square brackets [ ] were made by the translator.

[Bibliography]

Dr. Majer Bałaban: *Zydzi lwowscy na przelomie XVI go i XVII go wieku.* Lwów 1906.
Dr. Majer Bałaban: *Dzielnica zydowska, jej dzieje i zabytki.* (Biblioteka Lwowska V/VI), Lwów 1909.
Dr. Alfred Grotte: *Deutsche böhmische und polnische Synagogentypen vom XI. bis Anfangs des XIX. Jahrhunderts.* (Mitteilungen der Gesellschaft zur Erforschung jüdischer Kunstdenkmäler in Frankfurt am Main VII/VIII 1915. *Rocznik Architektoniczny Uczniow prof. Szyszko–Bohusza w Szkole Politechnicznej Lwowskiej.* 1913–14.
Dr. Jan Sas–Zubrzycki: *Zabytki Miasta Lwowa.* Lwów 1928.

[Pages 481-482]

Chassidism and Lwów's Community

by M. S. Geshuri [Bruckner]

Translated by Myra Yael Ecker

Edited by Karen Leon

A.

What role did the Jewish Lwów play in the dissemination of Chassidism, and in its conquest struggles? Writers on the history of the Baal Shem Tov hardly mentioned whether he had visited Lwów, and only legend relates his participation in the (1759) Lwów debate between the Rabbis and the Frankists in front of Lwów's Archbishop, which, according to the pamphlet by R' Abraham of Szarogród, "A terrible incident in Podolia" (in the collected anthology from ancient books, Altona, 1769), was attended by the Land's rabbi, R' Chaim Rappoport, by R' Ber of Jazlowiec [Yazlovets] and by R' Izrael of Miedzybóz [Medschybisch], blessed be his name. Based on the minutes from the official meetings, Majer Bałaban determined that none of the Polish sources made any mention of the Baal Shem Tov at this debate.

For scores of years, in the days of the Baal Shem Tov and the Podolia centre, Chassidism spread through Galicia and captivated most of the small communities and even spread into the larger communities of east-Galicia. Burgeoning Chassidism was noted at Lwów and Brody in the days of the *Maggid* of Mezeritch [Miedzyrzec Korecki], when his Galician disciples returned home.

R' Juda-Leib "The *Mochiach* [preacher] of Polonnoye [Polonne]" (died 1770), as the Chassidim termed the disciple of the Baal Shem Tov, purposely chose for his first outing as a Chassidic *Mochiach*, Lwów, which was full of scholars and rabbis who at the time ruled it with no restrictions, and precisely at the great synagogue, where not every preacher and *Mochiach* was granted the privilege to stand on the *Bimah* [raised platform in a synagogue, used when reading from the Torah]. The Chassidic legend [*Aggadah*] recounts at length the *Mochiach's* endeavours to hold a sermon at Lwów's Great Synagogue in the presence of the community elders headed by the Rabbi. The sermon that focused on the sayings of the Baal Shem Tov, "greatly pleased them." He managed to win the community's affections for Chassidism, and the Rabbi invited him into his home, to have him as a guest for three weeks. But it did not come to pass: the Rabbi died shortly after.

The objection of Lwów's rabbis to Chassidism, continued even after it had made great strides in Galicia. The Kraków community's decision of 10th October 1784 against the Chassidim, forbade any deviation from the instructions of Rabbi Mojzesz Isserles, or to change the style of prayer, or alter the customary tunes and pray while shaking, included among its signatories, Rabbi Izak ben Mardechaij Halewi of Lwów,[1] who led the rabbinate of Kraków in 1776-1798. Still, the Kraków decision could not change the facts on the ground, and victory was with Chassidism.

But the objection of Galicia's rabbis to Chassidism was as nothing compared to the fight against it by the rabbis of Lithuania. The rift between them and Chassidism was not so deep, as most of Galicia's Chassidim and *Tzadikim* were engaged in the Torah. When the *Tzadik* R' Izrael of Rużyn [Ruzhyn came to Galicia, the scholars marvelled at him: Is this the man who does not read and does not study, who arouses the realm of Chassidism? They watched him and his followers with ridicule and derision. They wished to hear him elaborate on the Torah and to follow his doing as they were ready to watch and listen to the Galician *Tzadikim*. They were not satisfied with expressions derived purely from internal faith. This treatment of R' Izrael was expressed in the widespread legend: Once, R' Izrael came to Lwów and visited the Head of the *Beth-Din*, the renowned great scholar Rabbi Jakub Meszulam Ornstein. The Rabbi was convinced that they would discuss new Torah interpretations. However, the first words of R' Izrael were: What do they use for roofing, in Lwów? The great scholar replied: iron bars. The man from Ruzhyn responded: why? after all bricks are strong too, and aren't affected by fire? After R' Izrael left him, the Rabbi chuckled and said: Is this the man who spurs the world and its inhabitants and attracts flocks of Chassidim? The *Tzadik* Majer of Przemyślany [Peremyshliany], who at the time was at Lwów and was told of the conversation, said: The great scholar missed the meaning when the *Tzadik* of Ruzhyn wisely asked: Just as the roof covering protects the entire house, so the Rabbi has to defend the entire town, and he requires a breakable heart, just like bricks that break easily, rather than the toughness of iron bars. .

The great scholar, Rabbi Jakub Meszulam Ornstein (author of *Jeschies Jacow* [Yeshu'ot Ja'akov]) himself, was an ardent opposer of Chassidism, while his only son, R' Mardechaj Zew joined Chassidism. R' Mardechaj Zew

[Pages 483-484]

invoked fear in the public, and although he grew closer to the Chassidim, he detested the *Tzadik* R' Izrael of Ruzhyn.

The great scholar Rabbi Józef Saul Natansohn who served on Lwów's rabbinate, proclaimed everywhere that he opposed Chassidism and hated the Chassidim, and protested that Chassidism underestimated the Torah.

During the time of Rabbi Józef Saul Natansohn, the *Tzadik* of Belz did not dare come to Lwów, following the Rabbi's warning that he should not enter the town. And although the Rabbi had no authority to withhold entry from Lwów, the *Tzadik* of Belz took heed in order not to provoke him. When he was in the vicinity of Lwów he stayed outside the town, and his well-wishers went to welcome him. The Chassidim did not dare cross the Rabbi, and in their conversations they referred to him as "The Rabbi, long may he live." And in respect of the dispute between him and the R' of Belz, they said with humility: Best not to put our heads in between two big mountains.

Apart from Lwów's rabbis who detested Chassidism and objected to it, opponents also came to Lwów from elsewhere, further inflaming the fight. The preacher of the opposers, Israel Löbel, author of *Sepher Vikuach* [Book of Polemics], caused outrage with his sermons and his books, and he mockingly critiqued the Chassidism's books *Tzava'at HaRabbi Yisroel Baal Shem Tov* [The Testament of the Baal Shem Tov] and *Keser Schem Tow* [Crown of Shem Tov]. He arrived in Galicia from Warsaw, to disseminate his books against Chassidism. Because his activities had failed at Rzeszów [Resche], where the authorities disrupted the distribution of his books, at Lwów he was on his guard not to disseminate his books among the Chassidim, and even in his sermons he avoided mentioning them, preaching instead on morals in general. Nevertheless, his stratagems were to no avail. Lwów's government officials removed his books and kept them. The preacher Israel Löbel submitted a written protest to the authorities and dared submit a petition to Kaiser Franz, and was even granted an audience with the Kaiser to hand him his petition in person. The results of the enquiry were severe for the Chassidim: a total ban on the public meetings of Chassidim was enacted throughout the lands of Poland under Austrian rule, and several leaders of the Chassidim left their abodes and moved to districts of Poland and Warsaw "Until the wrath had passed."

In those days, the fight of the Chassidim with the opposers, and of the Enlightened with the Charedim [ulta-Orthodox], took place within *Bet HaMidrash* [Torah-study school], the community hall or the Street of the Jews. However, the differences between the Charedim and Lwów's rabbis had subsided, and in the fight against the *Maskilim* [Enlightened], they joined forces and reconciled in order to form a united front against their joint foe – *Haskalah* [Enlightenment]. Rabbi Szymon Sofer [Schreiber], head of Kraków's rabbinical court, son of the great scholar Rabbi Moses Sofer (*Chatam Sofer* [Scribe's Seal]) of

Pressburg [Bratislava], came and united the Orthodox with the Chassidim. The rabbis, who did not acknowledge *Tzadikim,* and always pitied the honour of their teachings, joined them so that the Orthodox and the Chassidim formed a single alliance.

B.

With the blurring of the boundaries between Chassidism and the rabbinate, and after the differences between them waned, the Chassidim and the rabbis vowed a joint war against the *Haskalah*, which they considered a movement set to slay the soul of the Jewish People and wipe it out. Enlightenment and Chassidism could not coexist, despite the fact that the Hebrew Enlightened aspired to "combine wisdom with faith." Chassidism clung to the love of the Jewish People and to the affection for Zion and Jerusalem, and it drew its strength from the *Kabbalah*, while the *Haskalah* demanded a scientific-critical approach to everything. Lwów was one of the towns where the conflict between Chassidism and the *Haskalah* had led to boycotts on both sides, the religious fanaticism increased in the Chassidic camp, and the fight reached the peak.

The *Maskilim* viewed Chassidism externally, without comprehending its social roots. They despised Chassidism which formed a stumbling block to the spread of the *Haskalah*, and hatred blinded them from seeing the positive aspect of Chassidism.

The *Maskilim* triumphed as the Austrian Kaiser, Joseph II, and with his authorisation – the school headmaster, Naftali Herz [Herc] Homberg, implemented coercive means to instil Enlightenment among the Jews and turn them into so called "useful" citizens.

Lwów had a *Maskilim* circle. The wealthy and freethinking Juda Leib Mieses [Miezes]; Tzvi [Cwi] Natkes, known by the Orthodox as "the false prophet" because he brought examples from the Books of Prophets to substantiate his preaching about Enlightenment; Izak Erter; Salomon Jehudah Rappoport [*Shir*] etc. In the custom of the *Maskilim*, they used to meet and criticise, the delusions of the Chassidim whose numbers rose in Galicia at the time, and the ignorance of the rabbis and the Torah teachers, and they attracted the young men who crowded the Torah-study school and spurred them to research wisely, to study the Bible and grammar, foreign languages and read Enlightenment books. They educated, free of charge, all those craving for wisdom.

Juda Leib Mieses, born at Lwów in 1798, was one of the extreme polemicists who fought Chassidism with excessive severity. In his book *Kinath Haemeth* [Kin'at HaEmet; The True Zealousness] (Vienna 1828), he attacked the bastion of Chassidim that he despised, by expressing his opinions on reforming the religion, and he spoke much on the need to reform the Jewish prayer and the need to do away with the reciting of liturgical poems and so on. He preached for war against the belief in spirits, devils

[Pages 485-486]

and witchcraft that had gathered strength among the people, with the spread of the "Baal Shem Tovist sect." The book made a great impression among the circles of the *Maskilim* and the *Charedim*, and enraged most of the Chassidim. However they feared him and did not harm him even though he fought them furiously, and specifically forbade any fight against the rabbis. He published Dawid Caro's book, *Techunath HaRabanim* [The Rabbis' Trait], with supplements and corrections. This book started the war of the *Maskilim* against the rabbis, and it besmirched them with such expressions as "the rejectors of wisdom and the contemptuous of reason," whose language "is wild, spent and distorted," and who only know how to further tighten restrictions.

Salomon Jehudah Rappoport, who hailed from Lwów, also wrote a pamphlet, *Ner Mitzvah* [Mitzvah Candle], that he intended to publish, but for fear of the "sanctimonious" it remained in manuscript form and was only published after his death (*Nachlat Jehudah* [Yehudah's Legacy] 1863). *Shir* served as treasurer and trustee for the leasing of the [Kosher] meat tax, it provided him with an income for some 25 years, at Lwów, until receiving the position with the Tarnopol rabbinate. Joseph Perl of Tarnopol used to visit the towns of Galicia for the purpose of trade, including Lwów, and here he was negatively affected by the *Haskalah*. Born into an Orthodox family, he adhered to Chassidism which led to his extensive knowledge of Chassidic literature and of the Chassidim's lives. And this Chassid turned into a *Maskil*, who hated Chassidism and even wrote a couple of satires about it: *Megaleh Tamirin* [Detector of Secrets] and *Bochen Zadik* [Tzadik Examiner], choosing satire as his fighting weapon against Chassidism and fanaticism, and against ignorance and the declining standards that had permeated the Jewish population. Perl aimed his spears of satire at the Chassidim and the fanatics whom he considered to be "walking in darkness and fighting the light." He published his books at Lwów.

Dr. Izak Erter (1791-1851), a cousin of Joseph Perl, even surpassed him in the field of satire. In one of his satires, *Chassidut VeChochmah* [Chassidism and Wisdom], he joked about the Chassidim who, "like the beast in the field," will follow and be attracted by the "Rebbes" and the "*Tzadikim*" who deceived with their cunning and mischief. Perl found the remedy for Chassidism in the sciences. He did not spare his tongue-lashing from the assimilating *Maskilim*, however. Izak Erter also joked about the cantors, who, without harmony, produced a mixture of voices, roaring like lions while supporting their windpipes with their fingertips, cheating the people in their fictitious righteousness, while drinking spirits with hollow, rash people and with actresses and also "spiced wine they slake and delicacies sate them at the honour of every wedding and every circumcision." This criticism was not levelled at the simple, popular prayer leader who, in a voice that choked back tears and with a pure heart and devotion to God, begged for mercy on his senders, nor was it levelled at the cantor who was familiar with the music, who sang with a choir accompanied by an organ, but at the cantor who was not a "prayer leader" nor was he even able to read music, a passing individual common in Galicia at the time, was the subject of his wrath.

The ire of fanaticism attacked Erter and his colleagues. Rabbi Jakob Ornstein published a warning that the *Maskilim: Shir*, Erter and so on, were inciters and agitators, and that one had to distance oneself from them because they were to be considered banned and ostracised. The boycott was soon annulled due to the Austrian government's intervention. Meanwhile however, Erter was deprived of his livelihood when parents stopped sending their children to "the inciting and agitating" teacher, and he was obliged to leave Lwów.

Salomon Jehudah Rappoport had a friend and helper in a high ranking officer at the Lwów bureau of the Kaiser's Governor. He was a righteous among the nations, and without any prompting, he assisted the *Maskilim* and charged their persecuting fanatics for the insults. In time, he was appointed the Tarnopol Land-Minister, and he protected Salomon Jehudah Rappoport for as long as he served as rabbi in that town. So when *Shir* was boycotted at Lwów, he went to demand satisfaction for the insult at the *Maskilim*. Rabbi Jakub Ornstein was forced to proclaim the boycott annulled, by order of the government, which forced the Rabbi to hold a sermon at the synagogue and say that there was no boycott and no ban, but rather, that *Shir* and his colleagues had to be treated with respect. It was said that Rabbi Jakub Ornstein fell ill with grief. The *Maskilim* won the "boycott," but were on the losing side in their fight against the Chassidim.

R' Nachman Krochmal who resided at Żółkiew but frequently visited Lwów and influenced his *Maskilim* colleagues, was also subject to the zealots' anger. They declared that as he was on friendly terms with the Karaites' "Chacham," he had abandoned the ways of the Torah. R' Nachman Krochmal published an "apology" in which he refuted the accusations of his opponents from the "sect of the sanctimonious," who were themselves persecuted, and "having attained power their courage rose to the point of corruption, and may the Lord save us from a persecuted who has turned persecutor." But only few had R' Nachman Krochmal's moral courage, as many among the *Maskilim* were affected by the Charedim's persecutions and rejoined the circles of the Chassidim, with their joy-filled homes: The chassidic students rejoiced, told miraculous anecdotes, imbibed "Tikun," danced and sang because "the Rebbe ordered to be happy." Those *Maskilim* unable to withstand the pressure, retraced their steps and rejoined the Chassidim circles. Even one of Salomon Jehudah Rappoport's loyal relations, Samuel Byk, abandoned the *Haskalah* and declared his sympathy for the "sanctimonious," he spoke with reverence about the *Tzadikim* and the Chassidim. Byk concluded that love of the Jewish People took precedence over the *Haskalah*, and that it was preferable to join the Chassidim in their ardent,

[Pages 487-488]

communal faith, and to write in Yiddish for the community, than to copy the Gentiles and engage in their wisdom and remove oneself from the Jewish People. The move by Byk, one of the greatest *Maskilim* and writers, threw confusion among the helpless *Maskilim* in face of the Chassidim who started to make demands everywhere. There were many reasons why the Enlightenment backslid in Galicia in face of Chassidism, only at Lwów did it hold fast.

In (5600) 1839-40, Lwów's Enlightened built the new "Temple." The Chassidim did much, however, to disrupt its construction. Every night, Belz and Sacz [Sanz] Chassidim demolished whatever had been built, smashing the stones, splitting the quicklime and shattering the building tools so that eventually the building constructors had to appoint soldiers for security. Only when the zealots realised that they would be unable to attack the building, did they decide to take revenge on its principal promoter, Rabbi Abraham Kohn.

At the end of the nineteenth century the struggle between the *Maskilim* –or the "Germans"– and between the Chassidim, over the governing of the community, gathered force.

For long, the leadership was in the hands of the *Maskilim*. And then the Chassidim attempted to wrestle it out of their hands. The *Maskilim* noticed that the majority of the community was attracted to R' Szymon Sofer [Schreiber] and to the *Tzadik* of Belz. So they made changes to the community rules in order to keep hold of the leadership. It did not work, however. The Chassidim won the elections. The *Maskilim* found fault with the elections, declared them invalid, and the fight started again, leading to the *Maskilim*'s victory with help from the satirical pamphlets written by a young *Maskil*, member of the *Szomer Izrael*Association. The *Maskilim* attributed the defeat of the Chassidim to this young man's messages.

C

Lwów was acclaimed for the printing houses where Bibles and books of scholarly literature were published, thus greatly enriching Jewish literature. The printing houses quietly pursued their "sacred work" without a tremor.

In (5548) 1787, a year after the demise of the *Tzadik* of Lizhensk [Lezajsk], R' Elimelech [Weisblum], his son R' Eliezer published at Lwów the book *Noam Alimelech* [Elimelech's Grace] that caused quite a stir among the opposers. The Chassidim, on the other hand, received the book with much joy, and for several years the book was published numerous times and was found in almost every house, turning it into a masterpiece of Chassidism.

After the publication of the book *Noam Alimelech,* there was a ten years' lull in the publication of Chassidic books at Lwów, and the list of the published Chassidic books, by subject, were as follows:

1. **Books of Legend**, or **Righteous Lives of the Chassidim**: *Vikucha Rabba* [*–ben HaChassid LaMitnaged*; Great polemics–between the Chassid and the opposer] (5627) 1866-7; *Maggid Sichot* [Jewish mystical preacher of discourse] (Chassidic Discourses of MoHaRaN [R' Nachman] of Braclaw [Bratslav]), Lwów (5622) 1861-2; *Sichot MoHaran* [R' Nachman's Discourses], Lwów (5620) 1859-60; *Schewuche Huran* [Praises of HuRan, *probably* MoHaRaN] (5624) 1863-4; *Jeme Mahrnat* [The days of Mahrnat; MoHaRaN] Lwów (5636) 1875-6; *Seider HaDores MiTalmideh HaBaal Shem Tov* [Genealogy by the Disciples of the Baal Shem Tov] Lwów (5625) 1864-5; *Shivchei HaRav* [The Rabbi's Praise] [published] by Michael Levi [Rodkinson] Frumkin, Lwów (5624) 1863-4; *Adas Zadikim* [Edat Tzadikim; Congregation of the Righteous] by the above mentioned, Lwów (5625) 1864-5; *Sipurei Zadikim* [Tzadikim's Tales] by the above mentioned, Lwów (5624) 1863-4; *Maseh Zadikim* [Tzadikim's Events], Lwów (5625) 1864-5; *Kahal Chassidim* [Chassidic community], Lwów (5626) 1865-6.M.

2. **Books of Chassidic Theory**: The righteous' anthology by four of the close followers in God's true path: the Baal Shem Tov; the *Maggid* [R'' Dov Ber] of Mezhirichi [Miedzyrzecz Korecki]; R' Menachem Mendel of Przemyślany; and R' Jechiel Michal of Jampol [Yampol, Lwów (5552) 1791-2; *Tzavaat HaRiBaSh* [Testament of R' Israel Baal Shem Tov], Lwów (5622) 1861-2; *Tanya* [fundamental text of Chabad Chassidic philosophy] by R' Schneur Zalman of Lyady, Lwów (5624) 1863-4; *Darke Cejdek* [Darchei Tzedek VeHanhagot Yesharot; Righteous Ways and Honest Leadership] written by R' Zecharjasz Mendel of Jaroslaw, Lwów, (5556) 1795-6; *Keduschas Lewi* [Kedushat Levy; The Sanctity of Levy] by R' Lewi Izak of Berdyczów [Barditchev] about "Pirkei Avot," Lwów (5623) 1862-3; *Yismach Lev* [Gladdened Heart] by R' Nachum of Chernobyl, Lwów, 1848; *Or HaMair* [The Shining Light] by R' Zeev Wolf of Zytomierz [Zhytomyr], Lwów (5620) 1859-60; *Mevaser Zedek* [Herald of righteousness], by R' Issachar-Bär of Zloczów [Zolochiv, Lwów (5610) 1849-50; *Or HaGanuz* [Light of the Secreted] (Elucidation of the *Tanya* Book), Lwów (5611) 1850-51; *Or Torah or Mze Torah* [Torah Light] by the *Maggid* of Mezeritch, Lwów (5623) 1862-3; *Darke Jescharim* [The Ways of the Righteous] (The Guidance of R' Mendel of Przemyślany), Lwów (5622) 1861-2; *Likute MoHuRaN,* Lwów (5636) 1876; *Likute T'philos* [Prayers Compilation] by R' Nachman of Niemirów [Nemyriv], Lwów 1876; *Sipirei Masioth* [Fairytales] by R' Nachman of Braclaw, in Hebrew and Yiddish, Lwów (5662) 1902; *Ner Mizwe veToras Or* [Candle of Good-Deed and Torah of Light] by the "Middle" Admor of Lyubavitsh, Lwów (5620) 1860; *Avodas Halewi* [Work of Halewi] by Ahron Halewi of Stashelye, Lwów (5602) 1842; *Kle HaRoim* [The Seers' Tools] by R' Zevi Elimelech Szapira of Dinów [Dinov], Lwów (5609) 1848-9; *Igereth Hakodesch* [Sacred Episle] Lwów (5619) 1858; *Likute Remal MeSasów* [Anthology of Rebbe Mojzesz Leib of Sasów] (5633) 1873; *Muer Weschumesch* [Maor veShemesb; Light and Sun] by Kalonymus Kalman Epstein of Kraków, Lwów (5620) 1859; *Kesones Pasim* [Kutonet Passim; Striped Gown] by R' Izak Jozef HaKohen from Polonnoye, Lwów 1866 (5626); *Likutei Schoschanim* [Anthology of Roses] R' Mojzesz Cwi [Tzvi] of Sawran [Savran], Lwów 1874; *Derech Chasidim* [Chassidic Path] An Anthology arranged alphabetically, Lwów (5636) 1876; *Scheiret Israel* [The Remainder of Israel] by R' [of] Wieledniki [Novi Velidnyky] with consent of the great scholar Rabbi Jozef Saul Natansohn and an introduction by the publisher and arranger Michael Lewi, Lwów (5624) 1864; *Bozina Dinhora* by R' Boruch of Miedzybóz, Lwów (5640) 1879.

Lwów became the prime source for the dissemination of Chassidism books to Russia and Poland.

The *Maskilim,* however, did not sit idly either, and from time to time they printed at Lwów a polemic book or pamphlet, such as *Megalle Temirin* by Joseph Perl, Lwów, 1864; *Kinath HaEmeth* by Juda Leib Mieses, Lwów, 1879; *Orot MeOfel* [Lights from darkness] (about R' DovBer Friedman of Sadagura [Sadigura; Sadhora]) by M. Ornstein, Lwów, (5642) 1882.

At a certain point, the printing of Chassidic books at Lwów was confronted with a serious obstacle in the form Tarla, a one-time *Maskil*, later converted to Christianity, who was appointed principal censor over the publication of Hebrew language books in Galicia, and he avenged himself on the Chassidim for the dispute he had had with the Rabbi of Belz. For as long as the publication of [Hebrew] books

[Pages 489-490]

required his approbation, he did not permit the printing of Chassidic books in Galicia, and he even ensured that books printed abroad be confiscated. Tarla had belonged to the circle of *Shir*'s *Maskilim* and his friends, having converted to Christianity he nonetheless continued to frequent *Shir*'s home and spend time with the *Maskilim*.

Most of Lwów's Jews were God fearing and observant, but there were also Enlightened Jews who had given up the encumbrance of the *Mitzvot*, not overtly, but privately. Very few at Lwów belonged to the faction of the Chassidim. Within the town there was just one *Kloyz*, prayer-house of the Chassidim, where prayer followed the Sephardi style, however its worshippers were not disciples of a particular "Rebbe," and as most of them were merchants who regularly travelled to the capital, Vienna, they were referred to as: They are not Sadigura Chassidim nor Belz Chassidim, but Vienna Chassidim… These Chassidim were congenial, and did not envy anyone. Outside the town there were one or two *Kloyzes* too, and their Chassidim were largely disciples of the Belz Rebbe, and they held no sway.[2]

On the Sabbaths, High days and holidays the prayer-houses were filled with loud Chassidic chants in the style of their respective *Tzadikim*'s houses. And they nurtured first rate "prayer leaders" who filled an important role in the town's religious life.[3]

Notes:

All notes in square brackets [ ] were made by the translator.
[The spelling of names was mainly taken from publications by Dr. M. Bałaban, names/titles were added as they were spelt at Lwów at the time.
The spelling of printed works were taken from the title page of the actual publication, where ever possible.]

Original footnotes:

1. Grandson of Jozue [Joshua] Reizes [Reices] who was executed by fire at Lwów in 1728
2. For Chassidic *Kloyzes* and prayerhouses– see article by Z. Zohar.
3. See article on *Cantoring*.

[Pages 491-492]

Lwów's *Chazanim* [Cantors]

by M. S. Geshuri [Bruckner]

Translated by Myra Yael Ecker

Edited by Karen Leon

Over the hundreds of years of Lwów's existence, many cantors and composers were associated with the town. Although some of them were renowned for their singing and for the substance of their compositions, their names fell into oblivion.

The name of one cantor was connected with the massacres at Lwów. During Lwów's 1664 conflict between the Jews and the Ruthenians, it is said that the cantor Jozef Chajes [Chajut] was killed while standing in prayer. One of the sources also recorded that the Jews of Lwów and its suburbs had a cantor who also was a children's Torah teacher. He did not receive a regular salary, but earned his living from Purim's *Mishloach manot* [sent offerings], gifts on Simchat Torah as well as receiving pay for performing at every celebration, wedding etc. This bears witness to the fact that the financial situation of cantors, and of other holders of public posts, was not a bed of roses. They were, at times, referred to as "enslaved."

The typical eastern–European cantorial singing [*Chazanut*], known as "the Polish cantorial singing," was also practised at Lwów. This style of Polish cantorial singing lacks the European musical meter and form. The scales follow the Gypsy scale and the soft eastern scale. Apart from the Torah reading of Song of Songs, Ruth, Ecclesiastes and *Lecha Dodi* [part of the Friday evening prayer] that follow the firm eastern scale, the Polish Jews did not employ the firm scale. Situated remotely from European culture and untouched by other nations or their spiritual resources, they clung to their native musical tradition. Little is known about the cantors and the *Chazanut* before the eighteenth century, not only at Lwów but also in all the other communities.

Jewish Lwów, steeped in tradition and nationalism, was one of the significant centres for Jewish liturgy in eastern–Europe. Cantorial singing and the fondness for emotional melodies by the greatest prayer leaders, were an integral part of this community's customs. As one of the oldest Jewish communities it upheld the traditional, devotional and spiritually uplifting ancient cantillation, in contrast to the innovation in musical arrangements adopted primarily by western European communities who introduced musical Enlightenment into Jewish liturgy.

Only 11 synagogues kept a cantor, including:

1. The Great Synagogue within the town.

i. Baruch Schorr (1823–1904)

Baruch Schorr's name is still respected and admired by Galician Jews, especially those from Lwów. Whoever heard Baruch Schorr and saw him lead the communal prayer, felt that his yearning and devotional prayer touched the Jewish heart. His pleasant renditions perfectly reflected his prayers. His composition "As Jeremiah walked on the graves of the fathers" encapsulated the destruction of Jerusalem and brought many of its listeners to bitter tears.

Among the great *Chazanim* who served Lwów, Baruch Schorr was the only one born at Lwów. He grew up, and was educated in Torah and the commandments among Orthodox and ultra–Orthodox Jews in the districts of Galicia, during the rise of Chassidism. He was taught Torah by his father, the fervent chassidic scholar of the Różhin [Ruzhyn] Chassidim, grandson of the *Tevuot Schorr* [Schorr's Crops], who served from youth till advanced age as cantor in synagogues of ultra–Orthodox Jews. In accordance with the *Shulchan Aruch* [abbreviated form of the Jewish ritual law], he was a most suitable prayer leader, punctiliously following the commandments, be they light or severe, while playing and composing with excellence and brilliant talent. Most of his compositions were not designed solely for his age, but for future generations too. His creativity, knowledge and talent will always surprise the listener. He adapted his accompaniment for choir renditions, and incorporated the Jewish spirit into every movement and tune. Renowned musicians, ministers and lords came to hear his singing and music, especially the *Kol Nidreh* prayer on the eve of Yom Kippur.

At the age of nine, he accompanied the cantor R' Bezalel Schulsinger of Odessa on his "travels." Later, he sang with Little Jerucham [Jerucham Blinderman], and at the age of thirteen, he led the prayer and became a cantor. He was married at Iaşi [Jassy] (Romenia), and his well to do father–in–law sent him to Bucharest to study music. Even at that time, he was known as a composer of prayers for the Jewish High Holidays, and in particular for his sequence of prayers on Yom Kippur. In 1859 he was invited by Lwów's town synagogue.

[Pages 493-494]

Lwów's Cantors

Cantor Jakub Bachman

Cantor R' Baruch Künstler

Cantor R' Baruch Schorr

Cantor Zeidel Rovner (Maragowski)
the elder of the cantors

Cantor Izak Halpern   Cantor Jakob Kahane   Cantor Izrael Alter

[Pages 495-496]

During the thirty years' he served there, he continued to compose prayers that were distinguished by original liturgical melodies and simple structure. A selection of his prayers were published by his son, the cantor Izrael Schorr, in a prayer book for the High Holidays, titled *N'ginot Baruch Schorr* [Cantillations by Baruch Schorr]. He was also expert in the Torah, and wrote essays on the Torah and on the book of Ecclesiastes. The one book he published was titled *Bechor Schorr* [Firstborn Schorr].

An incident led to a dispute between Baruch Schorr and Lwów's community leaders. In 1890, he composed an operetta titled *Shimshon HaGibor* [The Mighty Samson]. He attended the operetta's performance, and in response to the enthusiastic audience he stepped onto the stage and took a bow of gratitude in acknowledgement of the cheers. For this misdemeanour, the synagogue's managers fined him and stopped him from leading the communal prayer for four weeks. Unable to bear the shame, the cantor left his town and went to the United States. With his departure, there was a cantorial void in Lwów. There was no *Chazan* whose prayer was accepted by the community. Eventually, a special delegation went to New York to appease him and bring him back to Lwów. From then on, and for the rest of his life, he again served his home town. He enjoyed a good life that lasted eighty–one years. He died while conducting the community prayer on the last day of Pessach. During the *Mussaf* prayer he began to sing in reverence "*veMipney Chataenu*" and when he reached the verse "*Avinu Malkhenu Gale,*" he fell full height to the ground. His soul departed pure, and he died a painless death.

ii. Mordechaj (Motel) Schorr

After the demise of Baruch Schorr, his son Mordechaj (nicknamed Motel) replaced him as cantor. He was the opposite of his great father. He lacked personal musical authority, his voice was not exalted, he did not compose works and he was unable to sing solo as his father did. R' Abraham Meisels, a renowned Lwów music lover used to say: Three things Gentiles are unable to understand about Jews: a. A school that did not teach writing (*Cheder*) ; b. A singer without a voice (many among the known *Chazanim* had no voice, such as Nissim Belzer with his hoarse voice, the hoarse R' Jankel etc.); c. A trader without capital. Motel's voice was not a pure tenor, it only resembled a tenor. He was cantor due to ancestral merit, having received this inheritance from his father. He sang his father's compositions. Many who remembered the pleasant prayer and the compositions of his father, came to hear him for his father's best compositions: the Lamentations on Tish'a B'Av [day on which the First and the Second Temples were destroyed] and the sequence of prayers on Yom Kippur. His choirmaster was Hellman (now in Haifa). Motel's strength lay primarily in the choir's performance. He served as acting cantor for his father at the town's [Great] Synagogue until the outbreak of the Second World War. His whereabouts are unknown since that time.

2. The Great Synagogue outside the town (the suburb's Schul)

iii. R' Zeidel Rovner (Jacob Samuel Maragowsky)

R' Zeidel Rovner was born in 1856 at Radomyśl [Radomyshl] (Russia). In 1904, on his journey from England to Russia for Pessach, he stopped at Lwów and was appointed cantor at the synagogue outside the town, where he stayed until 1911. He returned to Równe (and was thus known as "Równer [Rovner]") where he remained for three years. Later he left for the United States where he lived for the rest of his life.

During the seven years R' Zeidel officiated at Lwów he was well liked by the community, especially by the Great Synagogue's regular worshippers. Many among the congregation outside the town were music lovers. The post of community prayer–leader suited R' Zeidel well. He was an ultra–Orthodox upright Jew, learned, of advanced age and accommodating, and his teaching was fine and tempered with wisdom. He was aware of the importance of his mission and was an expert in his art. He is one of the few great cantors [*Chazanim*] whose name will always be mourned.

R' Zeidel stepped into the cantorial world by chance, or miracle. He became cantor by authorisation of the *Tzadik* R' Jakob–Izak of Makarov [Makariv], after the latter had prophetically detected that he was born for it, and he ordered him to become a cantor. At the "Makarov" *Kloyz* he absorbed the lugubrious tune of the Torah study, on the one hand, and the cantillation of the *Tzadik*'s yard, on the other. Whether it was the tune that expressed the outpouring of the excess spirit at "*Bnei Hechla*" [twilight] during the Shabbat's third meal, or the excitement of the joyful Chassidic dances, his cantillation melded with the Chassidic prayer styles. The Rabbi's gentle and pleasant rendition at the Shabbat table, High Holidays and holidays, as well as Jewish wedding tunes, especially the playing of the then renowned violinist Aron Mojzesz Podhorcer of Berdyczów [Barditchev], were merged and blended in his soul. All of these elements were given expression by his talent in his personal style. His lengthy compositions excelled in rich Jewish melodies combined with Chassidic lyrical motives accompanied by major scale overtone. R' Zeidel sang his compositions and performed them with a band of performers, in addition to his choir. These concerts were known throughout the diaspora. At Lwów he had a great many admirers who, following the prayers at their prayerhouses, flocked to delight in his "truth and faith" of the evening prayer, or the morning prayer of "*Mizmor Shir leYom HaShabbat*," or the "*Malchuyot*" on Rosh HaShana [Jewish New Year]

[Pages 497-498]

that lasted hours. His renditions had a wide spread influence on his generation's Chassidic music. The length of his compositions was not a drawback in those days; on the contrary, it marked the measure of a *Chazan*.

His pleasant alto solo singing of the chant "*veYehi Noam*" during the *Omer* [the seven weeks leading to the Festival of Weeks], or of his compositions for the Holidays and the High Holidays, were well known. By combining the movements and altering the scales, then returning to the original scale, his performances were wonderful.

He became a renowned conductor through his work with singers and musicians. His choir was made up of singers of all ages: children, youths and adults who were arranged by the colour of the tones: sopranos, altos, tenors and basses. Their singing was faithful to the utmost precision, and the singing was performed perfectly and on key. Only a talented conductor such as R' Zeidel could have shaped them all into such a wonderful ensemble. The period of his tenure at Lwów, and his synagogue service are well described by the Lwów born S. Z. Javetz (*Beit Haknesset*, Tel–Aviv, pamphlet 3–4, Kislev–Tevet 5707 [Dec.1946–Jan.1947]). He too focused on R' Zeidel's choir that gladdened the heart. As a *Chazanut* enthusiast he depicted, in the words of an amateur, the impression the choir had made on him.

R' Zeidel's compositions were created in a specific style, independent fashion and typical form. Most of the compositions he created during his tenure at Lwów, were enjoyed by most Jewish communities in eastern and western Europe as well as in the United States. Even though he had not attended an art institute or conservatoire, and had not been taught musical arrangement or code, his compositions successfully combined features, characteristics and outlines, full of beauty and grace, splendour and goodness.

He officiated for seven years at Lwów before leaving for Równe, and from there to the United States. Observations and memories from his life story and his revelation in the *Chazanut* are consigned to folktales.

iv. R' Baruch Künstler (Konstantiner)

Two cantors were known as Künstler. One officiated as *Chazan* at Karlin–Pinsk, and the other came from Konstantin in Russia to Lwów, and was accepted to serve at the synagogue outside the town, following R' Zeidel Rovner. The period when he officiated at Lwów was exceptional in the history of cantorial singing in the town. Three great cantors officiated at Lwów:

Baruch Schorr at the synagogue inside the town, Baruch Künstler at the synagogue outside the town, and Izak Halpern at the *Temple*.

Künstler, who composed cantorial works, performed only his own compositions. As a conductor, he closely observed the purity of the choir's sound, to which he dedicated his best efforts. The choir rehearsed each of his compositions for three to six months. His singers excelled and some of them became world renowned cantors. Baruch Künstler officiated as *Chazan* at Lwów until he lost his voice. He remained at Lwów until his demise a few years later. He was treated with respect in his advanced age. His choir's grace was not forgotten.

v. R' Zysza Harer

He was followed by Zysza Harer who officiated at the synagogue outside the town from 1918. In just a few years he reached his peak as cantor, along with his choir, composed of exceptionally talented singers. Harer excelled particularly as a composer and choirmaster, notwithstanding his pleasant tenor voice. He succeeded in attracting Lwów's best singers to his choir. The notes flowed as calm waters or poured like an agitated and stormy cascade. Once the troupe of exceptional singers dispersed, and he was unable to replace them with singers of the same calibre, the status of the choir declined in the public's mind. Harer was familiar with musical literature and harmonic theory. Professors from the conservatoire used to consult him. Among the singers in his choir were Zew [Zeev] Richter (now a cantor at Haifa), tenor; Izak Schrager (nicknamed *Icchele*); a youth named Alter Kimmer, a child prodigy with an alto voice. The cantor wrote many solo scores for him, and he was much admired by the community. He wrote and composed works for the entire year, for the Shabbath, Holidays and the High Holidays, and introduced his own compositions into prayers. All of his compositions were traditional in spirit, but he never published any of his great works with their charm and beauty. Zysza Harer became a "byword" for Lwów's *Chazanut*. He employed all of his inborn musical gifts for "prayer and glory," and his name is remembered with reverence and delight even today.

vi. Aron Szalom Schierman

Aron Szalom Schierman served as second cantor at the synagogue outside the town. Born in Russia, he was a great music–player and a good musician. He wrote many excellent scores for Jewish compositions, and he was much admired by his audiences. He died in Lwów, aged 54.

vii. Izrael Hakohen Schorr

Izrael Hakohen Schorr (who was not related to Baruch Schorr) was born at Chyrów [Khyriv], Galicia, to a well to do and prominent family. He received an ultra–Orthodox education and even in his youth he was granted the honour

[Pages 499-500]

of singing at the tables of the great *Admorim*, and conducting part of the prayers [*Mussaf*] on the High Holidays at the *Admor* of Rymanów and Czortków. At the age of eighteen, he married a woman from Bircza, Galicia. Starting in 1909, he officiated as the town cantor of Przemyśl [Pshemishl], but did not remain there for a long time. Lwów's synagogue, outside the town, invited him to serve as cantor, where he officiated until the outbreak of the First World War, in 1914. He went to Brno, Moravia's capital, where he was engaged as cantor at the great synagogue, and then he returned to Lwów, where he remained until the end of the war. He moved to Kraków and was accepted as cantor at the old synagogue in place of the well known cantor Leisor Goldberg. He became ill, there, and convalesced at the summer–resort PiešÅ¥any [Pieszczany; Pistyan], where he served as cantor. From there he travelled on a concert tour throughout Austria and Hungary and reached Zurich, Switzerland, and then to the United States. In 1923, he served as cantor and led prayers at Chicago, Boston and other cities. Schorr was also learned in the Torah [*Talmid Chacham*], was deeply god–fearing, and like a family member he frequented the houses of the *Admorim* and the Rabbis who greatly appreciated him. He recorded many of his cantorial songs, in the United States, and his records were much appreciated. He died aged 50 from a heart disorder.

3. "Gal–Ed [Gil'ad; Monument]" Synagogue

viii. Dov Ber Lejbowicz

Dov Ber Lejbowicz arrived at Lwów from Congress Poland. Earlier, during 1923–1930, he officiated at the *Temple*. He had a slight tenor, with a thin voice of two octaves. "Quality over quantity" characterised his singing with his excellent soft and pleasant voice. He was fluent in all the branches of music. His praying embraced and excited his listeners. As a *Maskil* he also wrote articles in Hebrew on the issues of Jewish music. However he did not want to remain in one place for long. A strained relationship between him and the preaching rabbi at the *Temple* led to his resignation, after which he officiated as cantor at the Gal–Ed synagogue for two years. Here too, disputes between him and the synagogue manager resulted in his dismissal. He moved to Łódź [Lodz] to the Great Synagogue. During the two years Lejbowicz officiated at the Łódź Great Synagogue he created the right atmosphere for quiet prayer, and the Jews of Łódź flocked to the Great Synagogue every Sabbath and Holiday to hear his musical interpretations. Here again, he quarrelled with the synagogue manager and eventually left this post as well.

ix. Mendel Pinster–Rokach

The cantor Mendel Pinster–Rokach, a grandson of the *Admor* of Belz, was born in Galicia in 1906. Together with the cantor Izrael Meisels of Lwów, he studied at Vienna under the renowned cantor, Juda Leib Miller. With his lyric baritone voice he officiated as cantor at Stanisławów [Stanislau], received a stipend and studied at the conservatoire. Learned in the Torah and secularly educated, he officiated as cantor at Lwów's Gal–Ed synagogue during 1935–1937. From there he moved to Rotterdam. When the Nazis occupied the town, he, his wife and their two children were sent to Poland's extermination crematoria.

x. Dawid Kacman [Katzman]

Dawid Kacman was born into an Orthodox family in Ukraine. His father was a great Torah scholar, well educated and a renowned prayer leader. Due to the 1920 pogroms he left Russia for Lwów, where he was accepted as cantor at the synagogue known as the "Beautiful Schul" or Sykstuska Synagogue. He had a lyric tenor voice and received a musical education. The renowned cantors Gershon Sirota and Yossele Rosenblatt who came to Lwów as visiting cantors and led the prayer, did not overshadow him. Kacman's pleasing prayer attracted many worshippers. He officiated as cantor at Lwów until 1926. From there he moved to Vilnius [Vilna], to the Great Town Synagogue, to Białystok and wandered farther to Canada and the United States. There he has officiated as cantor till now [The date of this article is not clear. He died in 1959].

xi. Jakob Koussevitzky

Jakob Koussevitzky, one of the Koussevitzky cantorial brothers, was born at Vilnius and came to Lwów in 1926, to replace Kacman at the Sykstuska synagogue. After some time, he arranged for his brother David, to be choirmaster. Jakob was a second rate tenor and a good lecturer. From there he moved to the Gal–Ed Synagogue, and later to London.

xii. Jozef Idelson

Jozef Idelson, born at Vilnius, had a tenor voice, officiated at Lwów's Gal–Ed Synagogue during 1930–1939, was much loved by the public. He is now in the United States.

xiii. Cantor Kruszewski

Cantor Kruszewski officiated as cantor at the Gal–Ed Synagogue. From Lwów, to moved to the United States.

xiv. Zeev Richter

Zeev Richter sang in the choir of Zysza Harer who wrote works suited to his tenor voice. After

[Pages 501-502]

leaving Lwów he went to Australia, and from there to Haifa, where he officiates as cantor at the synagogue on Josef Street.

4. Sykstuska Synagogue.
xv. Cantor Dawid Packer

5. *Turei Zahav* [Golden Columns] Synagogue

xvi. Samuel Kantorof

Samuel Kantorof was born at Kremeńczug [Kremenchuk], Poltva province. His father was head of the town's rabbinical court and he received a religious education, studied at the *Chofetz Chaim* Yeshivah of Raduń [Radin] and of Lyubavitsh [Lubawicze] and was ordained rabbi. He had a beautiful lyric tenor voice. His first post as cantor was at Lwów's *Turei Zahav* Synagogue, the oldest of Lwów's synagogues. He went on to officiate at *Beit Shlomo* Synagogue, Tel–Aviv, and emigrated to the United States.

6. *Or HaYashar Mefarsheh Yam* Synagogue.

xvii. Chaim Wallfisch

Chaim Wallfisch was born at Brody in 1886. His father, R' Mojzesz was an ardent Torah scholar. His passion for *Chazanut* was so great that he walked on foot to Lwów in order to see, and to learn in the shadow of the great cantor, Baruch Schorr. At the age of ten, he was accepted by Schorr and sang with his choir for eight years. His first post as cantor was at Lwów's *Or HaYashar Mefarsheh Yam* where he remained for two years. He moved to Budapest and officiated as cantor for two years. At the *G'milut Chassadim* Synagogue of Vienna's 17th district, he officiated for eight years. He had a beautiful lyric tenor voice and a good musical knowledge, having absorbed a great many renditions from others in the pulpit. In July 1921, he left Europe and settled in the United States.

7. At the *Temple of the Enlightened*

xviii. Ozjasz Heszel (Pitzi) Abras (1820–1896)

Pitzi Abras was a great cantor and composer. At the age of six, he already showed a strong inclination for music and singing at the synagogue of Joseph Perl. During 1837–1844, he was a cantor at Tarnopol. He studied a few years at Vienna under Sulzer, at Lwów with the renowned cantor Model and with Bezalel Odesser. He wrote compositions in the style of the Italian old masters. While in Lwów, he was able to develop his musical–cantorial talent. Abras wrote a string of compositions and recitatives, and his name was known worldwide. His baritone, solo voice, like a magical bass, was exceptionally noticeable. At times, his voice reached the lowest tones, or rose up the coloratura with his clear and polished embellishments, thus exciting and astounding his audience. The renowned cantor Pinkas Minkowski said of him: "I was more than once moved by Abras's singing. With a moderate temperament, without fervour, but with the power of a marvellous voice and a strong larynx reaching to heaven, he soared like an eagle and from his throat trills of pure silver and gold surged effortlessly."

His book *Zimrat Yah* [God's Music] was used by many communities in Russia and Poland. During 1844–1860 Pitzi officiated as cantor at Lwów. From there he moved to Odessa and reached old age (over eighty years), and unlike other cantors he was also wealthy. He had a daughter who was a first–rate opera singer.

He was followed at the *Temple* by the cantor Mojzesz Roman (1860–1862), and Oswald Weiss of Szegedyn [Szeged] (1862–1873).

xix. Jacob Bachman (1846–1905)

Jacob Bachman, one of nineteenth–century's renowned cantors, was known throughout Europe as a "star" of song and prayer, and for his wonderful voice and vocal range. He was born at Lugin (Wołyń). His musical talents were already evident in his childhood, and he sang under the town cantor Pasternak, at the Berdyczów Synagogue. On the advice of a friend, he travelled to Saint Petersburg and studied under the great musician Anton Rubinstein, who was at the time director of the conservatoire. He excelled in his studies and became the top student. He even gave concerts in Russian towns, accompanied by his teacher Rubinstein. But he was drawn to cantorial singing rather than to Opera and secular music. He left the capital and officiated as cantor at Rostov–on–Don and at Berdyczów. In 1873 he was appointed the cantor of Lwów's *Temple*. In 1879 he moved to Odessa, where he founded a mixed choir, and started to compose his famous works that he published in 1884 in the book *Schirath Jacob* [Jacob's Song]. He became a professor of music. He composed a cantata celebrating the crowning of the Russian Tsar, and was rewarded with a letter of thanks signed by the Tsar.

Bachman published articles on cantorial singing and on music, and he wrote words of appreciation about Sulzer, Nowakowski, Löwenstein and others. He was an educated man, with knowledge of language and books.

xx. Izak Hirsch Halevi Halpern

Izak Hirsch Halevi Halpern was born at Żytomierz [Zhytomyr] in 1854. He was accepted as singer, while still a child, under the cantor, Jecheskiel Feinsinger, and was third in line in traditional liturgy, after Little Jerucham and Nissim Belzer. Halpern was taught Torah by the renowned cantor, Wolf Spitzberg, who had learnt

[Pages 503-504]

traditional singing under Little Jerucham, the master of ancient song, and later, the prayer chants by Sulzer. With his baritone voice and his warm temperament, he resembled his mentor Sulzer, and the singers termed him "the Russian Sulzer." Halpern was appointed cantor at the Nikolayev *Temple* of Cherson [Kherson].

Halpern came from Cherson to Lwów and on 18 August 1886, he was accepted as the *Temple's* cantor, where he officiated for some twenty–five years, and was greatly respected and loved by the community and his friends. Halpern knew Hebrew, German and French, provided musical notations, and wrote Yiddish lyrics with renditions. He was a classical cantor, and published a collection of songs *Der Liederkranz* [Wreath of Songs], Odessa, 1889.

After serving at Lwów for 25 years, he quarrelled with one of the *Temple's* managers, left Lwów and returned to Russia. In 1891, he came back to Lwów and was again appointed chief cantor and officiated until 1911. Due to family disputes, he submitted his resignation in the summer of 1911, with the proviso that he would receive 6,000 Crowns as compensation. During the dispute, Halpern printed a lampoon in Yiddish, titled: "The secrets of the Voltaver *Kloyz*, formulated by Choglah, daughter of Zelophehad, a weak woman who wants to bring before the prayer leader, Shalmiel, to manage all the evil people seeking sins with their rabbi, R' Katriel: you had a blindfolded Rabbi in all the land that is under you and all present here at Voltaver in (5672)" (Lwów 1911).

From Lwów he moved to Vienna. During the first World War he suffered hardship and was supported by the community. He died in Vienna in 1927.

xxi. Pinkas Minkowski

Pinkas Minkowski came to Lwów in 1885 and was accepted as cantor at the *Temple*. He had heard of the available post while in Odessa. However, his wife refused to remain in Lwów and so he left.

xxii. Cantor Darewski (Kowner)

The Cantor Darewski officiated at the *Temple*. He was born in Lithuania and was well versed in the Torah. He studied opera singing in Italy, and dubbed himself "Prince of Singing," "Prime Italian Tenor" etc. He had a pleasant voice, but despite his good–looks, and big talk, he remained a singer unable to properly read a line of musical notation.

xxiii. Mojzesz Jehoszua Seitz

Mojzesz Jehoszua Seitz was accepted as cantor at the *Temple*, on 19 May 1912. He was one of the cantors who excelled in the Torah and in secular knowledge, in music and in the art of singing. He was born to Chassidic parents, at Savran, district of Podolia, in (5640) 1880. At the age of eight, he began to sing, and at thirteen he led the prayers for the first time. Until he was twenty–two, he sang under different cantors, such as Zeidel Rovner, Schneor, Schalom Grünspan and others. He officiated as cantor in the Russian towns: Ekaterinoslav [now Dnipro], Zvihil [actually Novograd Volynsk], Boryslaw, Warsaw, and Berdyczów.

At the *Temple* he officiated for nine years, and in 1921 he moved to the United States.

xxiv. Hermann Bornstein

Hermann Bornstein, who came from Warsaw to Lwów to replace Dov Ber Lejbowicz, officiated as the *Temple's* cantor during 1922–1932. Born at Kalisz, Poland, he sang under the renowned cantor, Noach Lieder (Zaludkowski), and studied music at Berlin. He also performed an international, classical repertoire with his dramatic tenor, but not cantorial renditions. He was much admired by the public that always filled the synagogue to hear him pray and sing.

The much reduced financial situation of Lwów's community in his day, forced it to decrease the salaries of synagogue assistants. Consequently, he resigned and moved to Budapest where he was accepted as cantor at the Rumbach Synagogue. He was much appreciated there and served until 1937. When he received a deportation order from the authorities, he moved to Liverpool, England, where he remains to date.

xxv. Azriel Samuel Schneider

Cantor Schneider did not have a big voice. He remained in his role until the outbreak of the Second World War and was probably murdered in the Holocaust.

xxvi. Eliasz Körner

One principal cantor and three deputies served at Lwów's *Temple*. Eliasz Körner, who during 1879–1929 served as a deputy cantor at the Temple, was familiar with all the styles of *Chazanut*, had a good Torah reading voice and was much appreciated by the public.

xxvii. Mendel Schein

Another native of Lwów, he officiated as deputy cantor at Lwów's *Temple* since 1920. He was very accomplished in praying with a choir and knew his way around the cantorial renditions. He was very knowledgeable in the field of music.

[Pages 505-506]

xxviii. Salomon Edelstein

Salomon Edelstein had previously been a singer under Zysza Harer, a status that conferred a badge of honour on its bearer. He had a low voice, but he prayed tastefully and with feeling, and those who heard him enjoyed his warm prayer. He was appointed deputy cantor in 1931.

xxix. Alter Kimmer

Alter Kimmer, a native of Lwów, was a child prodigy and was accepted as an alto singer under the cantor Zysza Harer. When his voice change to that of a tenor, its quality was not he same. He studied at Vienna, and moved to Yugoslavia where he officiated as cantor. He vanished during the Holocaust.

8. Various Synagogues

xxx. Mejer Körner

Mejer Körner was invited to Lwów to officiate as cantor, and after the demise of Baruch Schorr he was asked to replace him. His trial prayer filled everyone with delight, but Körner declined to manage a choir and to take the place of such a great and renowned musical cantor as Baruch Schorr. He served as cantor for a short while and left for the United States. His compositions for synagogue prayers were novel in style and traditional in their structure.

xxxi. Mardojai Schnurmacher

Mardojai Schnurmacher was born at Drohobycz [Drohobych] in 1882. At ten years of age, he started to sing under different cantors. He moved to Lwów and for three years he sang under the cantor Alter Baumann (later, his father–in–law). He spent several years at Tarnopol, where he studied music with the great musician Markus Wolfsthal. He returned to Lwów, studied harmony, orchestration and different branches of music with Bernstein, the conductor of Lwów's town orchestra. He studied in Germany and moved to the United States.

9. Lwów–born Cantors.

xxxii. Jakub Warmann

He served in Lwów as a singer without officiating as cantor. He studied cantorial singing with the renowned cantor Juda leib Müller, at Vienna, and sang there. Müller wrote a special composition titled *Ribono Shel Olam* [The Almighty] for the *Yom Kipur Hakatan* [Lesser Day of Atonement] prayer, to suit Warmann's voice.

xxxiii. Izrael Meisels

Abraham, his father, was also from a family of cantors, and was a tenor in Baruch Schorr's choir. He was a cantor in Hungary. He returned to Lwów, but not as cantor. A great Torah scholar and significant music lover, his opinion was consulted in the examinations of Lwów's cantors.

In his youth he sang alto under Zysza Harer, but his voice broke and turned into a tenor. He studied music at Lwów's conservatoire. In 1929 he moved to Vienna where he continued his music studies at the conservatoire, and cantorial singing under Müller. He officiated as cantor at the small synagogue *Mikdash Katan*[small Sanctuary] in Vienna's second district, and later at Pressburg [Bratislava] and Debrecen. In 1937 he received an expulsion order issued by the state authorities. He moved to England and officiated as cantor at Southport for three years and was invited to the Great Synagogue in Manchester. From there, he moved to Eretz Israel and is officiating as cantor at the *Yeshurun* Synagogue, Jerusalem.

xxxiv. Izrael Alter

Izrael Alter, a great–grandson and grandson of a distinguished Lwów family (associated with *Turei Zahaw*), was born in 1901 (5661). He sang as cantor at Lwów, and at the age of seventeen he moved to Vienna and studied cantorial rendition under the renowned cantor Müller. His first post as cantor was at the *Talmud Torah* Synagogue on Vienna's Malzstrasse, and later at the *Temple* in the 20th district of the same town. During 1925–1936, he officiated with honour as cantor at the Great Synagogue of Hanover, Germany. He visited the community centres of western and eastern Europe, and sang not only cantorial songs, but also Jewish folk songs. On his visits, Alter appeared together with the renowned cantor Mosze Kusewicki, who said at the time that both sang in accordance with the laws of Moses and Israel (Mosze Kusewicki and Izrael Alter). From 1936, Alter officiated as principal cantor at Johannesburg, South Africa. He composed many cantorial pieces, including the famous work: *Akavia ben Mahalal El omer, Ribono shel Olam* for the Lesser Day of Atonement, that were published and recorded by the cantor Mosze Kusewicki. Alter is busy publishing all his works, at present.

xxxv. Moses Morgenstern

He sang under Lwów's cantors, but never officiated there as cantor.

xxxvi. Jakob Kahane

He was educated in the spirit of the Torah and tradition at his parents' home. He had a pleasant voice and sang with a dramatic lyric tenor under cantors. He counted among the Husiatyn Chassidim and Lwów's young

[Pages 507-508]

cantors. He went to Vienna where he studied at the conservatoire, and in 1938 he arrived in Canada. He was accepted as cantor at the *Young Israel* Synagogue, Montreal, Canada.

10. *Ceirej Gilead* [Tzeirei Gilead; Young Gilead] Synagogue

The cantors who officiated at this synagogue were: a. Cantor Szerman, who came to Lwów from Harbin, Manchuria; b. Cantor Chemalnicki, of Równe [Rovno], Poland; c. Cantor Sunikantz, a kabbalist from Wołyń [Volhynia]. There are however no details of their works.

11. *Kove'a Itim LeTorah* [Time setter for Torah] Synagogue

Cantor R' Oswald [Issachar] Weiss who came to Lwów from Szegedyn, Poland, officiated at this synagogue.

12. Choirmasters

The choirmasters at the traditional synagogues were: a. Icchak Heilaman (nowadays choirmaster at the Haifa synagogue); b. Schwarzmann; c. Landman.

On the other hand, at the *Temple* the choirmasters who officiated were: a. Abraham Kaplan (1874–1916); b. Mojzesz Schneider (1916–1920); c. Feiwisz (1920–1924); d. Becalel Kinstler, the son of the cantor R' Zeidel Rovner at the town synagogue (1924–1932); I. B. Gimpel (1932–1939).

Most of the cantors and choirmasters who officiated at Lwów at the outbreak of the war, were murdered by the Nazis during the Holocaust.

The cantor Samuel Schneider

The choirmaster Adolf Gimpel

The cantor Eliasz Körner

The cantor Mendel Schein

The cantor Salomon Edelstein

Note:

All notes in square brackets [ ] were made by the translator.

[Pages 509-510]

The Jewish neighbourhoods
(Topography)

by Dr. N. M. Gelber

Translated by Myra Yael Ecker

Edited by Karen Leon

When Lwów was first settled, the town extended between Wały Hetmańska [Hetman's Embankments] and Żółkiewska Street. At its heart was the old market, *Stary Rynek*, and the boundary of the town wall was close to the Castle Mound (góra zamkowa). At the crossroads of Żółkiewska Street and Bożnicza Street, was a ditch that stretched as far as the town square with a bridge above it, known colloquially as: *Auf der Brück* [on the bridge]. West of the ditch, in the direction of the Poltva [Pełtew] River (prior to 1939, between Solski Square and Poltva [Pełtewna] Street), lay the suburban ghetto (ghetto przedmiejskie).

After the great fire of 1350, the affluent Jews resided in the south–eastern part of the new town, in a trapezoid formed by the Hetmańska Embankments, [ulica] Sobieskiego Street, the Austrian Governor's Embankments and [ulica] Skarbkowska Street.

This is where the community hall inside the town stood. *Communitas infidelium Judaeorum intra moenia civitatis habitantium.*

The majority of the population remained in the suburb and had their own community, *Communitas infidelium Judaeorum in suburbio a Cracovia dicto.*

Lwów was the only town with two independent [Jewish] communities, each with its institutions and rights. One community lay within the town and the second was located in the suburb. In time, the two communities separated completely. The residents of the community within the town considered themselves superior to the residents of the suburb. Nevertheless, despite their differences they assisted one another in the hour of need.

I. The community within the Town

The Jewish Street [ulica Żydowska], founded in 1387, that was named Blacharska Street from 1871, lay to the right of the market (rynek). This street narrowed at its end. In between the two facing rows of houses, propped up on the two corner–houses, the Korkes house on the right and the Michalewicz house on the left, rested the Jews' Gate (Porta judaeorum) or *Der Tojr* in Yiddish. The second gate was located at the other end, at Halicka Street (Haliczer Gasse), which faced the town. One could enter the ghetto only through these gates. The gates were locked in the evenings and in times of danger and onslaught, such as threatening peasants leaving the nearby church, or menacing soldiers or students.

The Jewish Street connected to Boimów Street, was also called Jewish Street. After the Austrian occupation in 1772, it was known as The New Jewish Street (Żydowska Nowa; [*Neue Judengasse*, in German]). Later, it was named ulica Wekslarska [*Wechslergasse*] (Money–changers' Street) as well as Boimów. The Boimów and Serbska crossroad, was a dead end known as *Dus Roisenlükel*, surrounded by the town–wall. At the corner stood a tower that was generally leased to a Jew. Adjacent to the wall, in the vicinity of the arsenal (*Zbrojownia*) built in 1555, stood two timber houses leased to Jews for dwellings and trade. Most of those who owned the houses were Ruthenians.

The houses of the Jews were connected to one another by joint yards and party–walls, a situation that led to continuous disputes and litigations amongst the residents.

Due south–east lay the ghetto surrounded by the town–wall, superimposed by turrets, one of which was occupied by the town's hangman and his assistants, neighbours who could cause much harm. The Jews lobbied the municipality to remove him from this dwelling. In 1619, the municipality accepted this request.

The high housing density, the narrow streets and the population growth, led to an appalling state of hygiene, a situation that the poet [Sebastjan] Klonowic described, in 1584, in a special verse.[1]

The fires of 1571 and 1616 almost destroyed the entire ghetto and the Ruthenians' neighbourhood.

At the time, a large number of building plots owned by Christians were abandoned after the houses were destroyed by fires. The Jews were able to overcome difficulties in obtaining municipal building permissions, as many homeless, affluent buyers were willing to pay any price for the plots.

[Pages 511-512]

In the 15th century, the Jews could purchase plots and houses as long as they were in the permitted quarters. The townspeople, the nobles and also the leading clergy, such as Archbishop Grzegorz [Gregory of Sanok], sold houses to the Jews. The nobles even offered residences to Jews outside the specified quarters. They sold houses to the Jews and leased apartments to them in their dwellings in town, at high prices.

The Christian tradesmen's approach to the issue was entirely different. When they sold a house to a Jew, they would set an explicit condition that no trade could be undertaken in it.

As the municipality, was laden with debt and needed money, it was quite content to sell vacant plots to Jews, especially those plots close to the town wall, including the turrets and fortresses.

Jews also bought the plot on which a brothel had stood before the fire. After the fire, the brothel was moved to the torture tower (Wieza Tortur). The community elder, Rabbi Izak ben Nachman (Nachmanowicz), put all his efforts into lobbying to acquire the tower and move the brothel away from the ghetto. They succeeded in leasing the tower, in perpetuity, for a one time payment of 200 Gulden and an annual fee of two Grzywny.

By and by the entire ghetto area was owned by Jews, particularly by the family of Izak ben Nachman. Inside the area they erected three–story buildings, and also constructed buildings inside the courtyards.

Nevertheless, overcrowding increased daily. The Jews even filled apartments on Ruska Street which bordered the ghetto and ran parallel to *Żydowska nowa*, on Szkocka Square (later Serbska Street), on Zarwańska Street, on the lower part of Boimów Street and on Różana Street. There were shops throughout the Jewish Quarter, but the congestion drove these also beyond its boundaries, though not fronting the street (Rynek), but at the back of houses. This angered the Christian traders and led to legal actions. There were instances in the 17th century when the nobles and the townspeople flouted the restriction and sold houses to Jews. In 1660, for example, Jakób Leszczyński sold the house at the corner of Serbańska Street and Szkocka Square–Boimów No. 23–25. The Jews rented apartments under the jurisdiction of the Benedictine Order, on plots of land that belonged to the Jabłonowski family. Leasing shops outside the Quarter was more difficult as the Christian traders and craftsmen considered every Jewish shop as competition and a threat to their livelihoods. They resorted to all means to obtain an explicit prohibition, and their efforts worked. On 27 May 1656, King Jan Kazimierz issued an edict that forbade the renting and leasing of Catholic houses to Jews, as the issue was "an insult to God and a legal transgression." In case the prohibition were violated, the Jews would be removed from the house and the house–owner would be fined.

The prohibition was to no avail, however. Twenty one years after its publication, a municipal agent protested that Jews did not only lease Christian plots and houses, but even purchased properties. After disputes and an attempt ot force eviction, all the town's Classes and Nations issued a regulation in 1909, declaring that Christian citizens were forbidden from leasing apartments and shops to Jews. The regulation was approved by King Augustus II, on 11 April 1710.

King Sobieski's House, Rynek No. 10

An explosion at the arsenal near the town wall inside the ghetto, on 23 November 1703, and the Swedish invasion of 1704, destroyed several houses in the ghetto and the Jews had simply no place to live. Jewish trade increased and there was a need for warehouses and shops. Indeed, in 1708, the authorities' assessment concluded that the town market (Rynek), including the King's house (No. 10), were fully occupied by Jewish shops, not only the ones in the courtyards but also those facing the street. Jews occupied apartments and workshops in every house on Ruska Street.

It just so happened, that the majority of the house–owners were members of the town council, and they defied the regulation and leased houses to Jews, who were ready to pay as much rent as was asked of them.

The Jews continued to occupy the shops despite the prohibition and the threat of fines. As their numbers grew, there were 71 Jewish shops without a licence, in 1738 .

In the year 1738, the King appointed a special committee to investigate the situation. On 21 June 1740, an agreement was signed in which the Jews committed themselves to conduct their business in the spirit of the 1592 agreement. The issue of vacating the shops was not raised.

In 1757, however,

[Pages 513-514]

under pressure from the poorer townspeople, the municipality restarted its pursuit to remove the Jews and return them to the ghetto. On 12 February 1759, they were successfully granted the decree of King Augustus III, to expel the Jews from all Christian Quarters. The debate with Jakób Frank [the "messiah"] was held at Lwów in the same year, and in the atmosphere that ensued, the masses led pogroms against the Jews. The *Szlachta*, that so far had sided with the Jews, also turned against them.

The Jews' housing difficulty in the town continued also under the Austrian rule. On 20 November 1772, the Governor issued a ruling according to which, as of 1 December 1772, each week six Jewish families had to vacate apartments from Christians houses, the house–owner had to reimburse the tenants with the rent they had prepaid.

The Jews appealed to the Vienna authorities and the matter dragged on until 1793. The Vienna central authorities issued two rulings, on 12 December 1793, and on 1 May 1797: i. The Jews are permitted to reside inside the town only on the Jewish Street, Zarwańska and Ruska, and in the Krakówski and Żółkiewski suburbs. ii. Well–to–do Jews who sold goods from Austria, were entitled to reside outside the ghetto, but only with approval from the royal–court (*Hofkanzlei*). The rulings were reissued in 1804 and in 1811, and eventually the Jews were evicted from the prohibited streets.[2]

The community administration continued in its struggle with the Vienna authorities. The municipality persisted in its objection to enlarge the ghetto. During the years 1846–1855, the ministry of the interior tasked Lwów's governorship with resolving the matter. A vote on the matter resulted in an equal number of those cast for, and against changing the ghetto. The Governor, Agenor Gołuchowski, ruled against the Jews. On 11 January 1863, the community submitted a new appeal, but it was in vain.[3]

Indeed, as the 1868 Constitution granted Jews equal rights, there was a ruling in their favour. The ghetto was abolished and since then the Jews resided in every part of the town with no hindrance. Nevertheless, most of them crowded together on Sykstuska and Kopernika streets, colloquially known as *Die Neue breite Gasse* [The New Broad Street], parallel to *Breite Gasse* in the town centre.

The houses on the Jewish Street were as follows:

1.   The building nearest the gate of the ghetto was Michalewiczowska house, as previously mentioned. The first house owner was the Ruthenian, Stefan Chomic, and his wife Helena. From 1617 until 1706, the house belonged to the community–elder Mardochaj [Marek] ben Izak (Izakowicz). From 1706 until the end of the 19th century, it was owned by the Sternbach family. In 1907, a new building was erected in its place.

2.   Adjacent to this building stood the house of King Jan Sobieski's physician, Dr. Simche–Menachem ben Johanan–Baruch de-Jonah, known as "Kamienica Doktorowska [the Doctor's house]," a three–stories building with a narrow, Renaissance facade. It was one of the most beautiful and magnificent buildings in the ghetto. In 1767, it passed to the lessee of the community's tax–collector, Izrael ben Józef. During the Austrian rule, the building was under the conservation of the inspector of ancient monuments. However, during works to realign the road a few years before the outbreak of the First World War, the house–owner, Mrs. Sassow, had it demolished and a new building was erected in its place.

3.   The adjoining house, built in the 16th century, was acquired by Szlome Krochmal (it was consequently termed "Kamienica Krochmalowska"). In the 19th Century, the building was owned by Mrs. Schönblum. After a grave dispute with the inspector of ancient monuments, she had the house demolished and built a new one in its stead.

4.   No. 28, Leyzor [Eliezer] house, "Kamienica Leyzorowska." In the 18th century the house passed to the community and served as the law–court of the deputy–Voivode [deputy district governor]. The house was then known as "Kamienica Podwojewodzinska," and by the people as *Dem Schofetshaus* [the judge's house]. At the end of the 18th century, the Austrian authorities sold the house to Leyzor [Eliezer] Boruchowicz.

5.   No. 25, Krywes House, was built by the Ruthenian, Kost. In 1601, the building was acquired by Aron ben Rubin. After 1704, the house was sold to the community leader, Zelman ben Pinkas.

6.   No. 27, the community committee's house, contained the community's offices and its courtyard was a passage to the *Turei Zahaw* synagogue. According to Rabbi Dawid Halewy, author of *Turei Zahaw* [commentary on the *Shulchan Aruch*] and the community Rabbi, during 1652–1667, weddings were held in the courtyard, and during the pogroms it served as shelter from the rioters.

In 1704, the Swedes placed a gallows in the courtyard. The community elders were threatened with hanging unless the Jews filled the baskets placed under the gallows with gold and silver. The synagogue was erected in 1582 by Rabbi Izak ben Nachman, who was the head of the community, and in 1589 served as chairman of the Council of Four Lands, at Lublin. A women's section was added to the building in 1594. The synagogue was constructed in the Gothic style by the architect Paulus Italus [Paolo Romano] who also built the Woloska [Wallachian] church on Ruska Street. There is a story about the synagogue. In 1603, King Sigismunt III granted the plots and the entire area to the Order of the Jesuits. After debates and legal trials, the Jews were forced to hand over the synagogue and its surroundings, practically the entire Jewish Street, to the Jesuits. However, access to the synagogue was available only through Mardochaj [Marek] ben Izak's house, and he did not permit such access. The Jesuits had to forgo the synagogue and all the surrounding houses, and return them to the Jews.

The synagogue was inaugurated on the Sabbath after the Purim festival (5369) 1639, and Izak Halewi composed the *Shir HaGeula* [Song of Redemption] that was annually recited on the Sabbath after Purim.

At this very synagogue, in the middle of the 18th century, the Catholic Clergy held a debate with the Jews, forcing them to attend

[Pages 515-516]

the clergymen's sermons, and it was here that Poland's rabbis declared a boycott on Jakob Frank and his faction. In the courtyard stood The *Turei Zahaw* Synagogue was located in the courtyard.

7.   On the right hand side, near the synagogue, stands the Sokołowski house. Before 1571, it belonged to the municipality. In 1604, the community elder, Mardochaj ben Izak, purchased the plot and established the *Hekdesh* that was later moved to the last building on Boimów Street. At the end of the 1th century, the community leader, Józef Cymeles [Zimeles] bought the house.

8.   In 1588, the Jews purchased the house on the "Płaczek" plot (No. 31) from the municipality. In the 18th century, the house was bought by Chaim Czopownik (alcoholic drinks' tax–collector). In the 19th century, the house belonged to the community's hospital.

1.   Across the road, opposite Nos. 1–7, at the corner of Ruska Street (Blacharska 20), stood the first building, the "Kamienica Korkesów [Korkes House]." In the 17th century the house belonged to the Nachmanowicz family, and in the mid–18th century until 1914, to the Ablowicz family. During the Austrian rule it was named Korkes.

2.   The adjacent house (No. 22), was separated from the Korkes house by a courtyard at the front. In the 18th century the building belonged to Mardochaj ben Abraham Feigels. Later, the Korkes family purchased the house and also constructed the facade.

3.   The house at 24 Blacharska Street was the home of R' Nachman ben Izak, the husband of *die goldene Rojze* [the Golden Rose]. On their demise, the house passed to their son Izak ben Nachman, and his heirs.

4.   The house at 26 Blacharska Street was the house of Awner Celnik [Zelnik].

5.   The house at 28 Blacharska Street was the property of the Żółkiewski family. In 1590, the building was bought by Izrael ben Józef Eideles, where he established a Yeshivah. The Yeshivah was led by R' Jozue Falk ben Aleksander HaKohen. Ever since, the house was known as the Rabbi's house (Kamienica Rabinowska). In the 18th century, the house was in the hands of the Carmelite Order, but in 1788 it was bought from them by the community leader, Süssman Leib Bałaban. The house burnt down in 1837.

6.   After the fire in the 18th century, the house at 30 Blacharska Street was owned by the Dominicans. Izrael ben Pinkas bought it from them and built a new house on the plot.[4]

There is history behind the houses on Zerwańska (Serbańska) Street. From 1871, the street was named [ulica] Wekslarska [*Wechslergasse*; Money–changers' street], or The New Jewish Street (*Żydowska nowa* [*Neue Judengasse*]), and from 1888 until 1939, the street was known as Boimów, and it the oldest street in the Jewish Quarter. There, in the south–eastern corner, the Jews settled after the 1552 fire, and founded the synagogue that was the heart of the community until 1604. Its importance waned after Rabbi Izak ben Nachman's synagogue was constructed. During 1799–1801, the community erected the Great Synagogue.

Until nearly the end of the 19th century, most of the houses in the street were still standing. After the town walls were demolished, four houses were also demolished in order to pave the square named after Nowa, later Plac Sobieskiego.

1.   Next to the synagogue stood the house at 52 Boimów Street. According to a register from 1767, it belonged to the goldsmith Boruch ben Wolf [Ze'ev].

2.   The neighbouring house, No. 50 (Kamienica Koplowska), belonged to the wife of the goldsmith Mojżesz Kopel. Later on the house passed to the ownership of the community.

3.   No. 48 was the house of Moszke Ber ben Zelman.

4.   No. 46 belonged to the Mizes [Mizys] family, "Reb Majer Miżys Haus." In 1767, it was purchased by Szlome Pinkas, the father of Rachmiel Mizes. At the start of the 19th century, the Mizes family moved to No. 18, Rynek, and the house passed to Rabbi Józef Saul Natansohn.

5.   No. 44, the house on the corner of Plac Wekslarski [Square], belonged during 1730–1750 to Icek Brodzki, and was later passed to his heirs.

6.   The houses Nos. 40 and 38 (Lapidea Gdalowska) belonged in the 18th century to the tailor Hersz and to Fiszl ben Wolf.

The Fish Market in the Jewish Quarter

7. The adjoining house, No. 36, was the house of Landys [or Landes], one of the wealthiest men in the community. It was purchased by the Carmelites in the mid–18th century.

8. Houses Nos. 34, 32, 30 were urban shacks that around 1632 were sold by the municipality to the community elder, Jakób Gombrycht. He demolished the shacks and constructed a large house in its stead. In 1648, Gombrycht's heirs sold the house No. 32 to the Jew, Zelman. The house No. 34 belonged to Salomon Frydman.

In the 18th century the municipality filed legal actions against the house owners, under the pretext that the plot had never been sold. In 1708, the town's financial management sold all three houses to Dawid ben Szmerl, for the sum of 600 Gulden. In the 19th century, the house No. 34 belonged to Jakób Mendel Schütz and to S. Bernstein. The house No. 30 was acquired in the mid–18th century by Izak and Dawid Markowicz. Until 1939, the house was known as *dem Parnas Haus* [the elder's house](in memory of the community–elder Gombrycht).

[Pages 517-518]

In Różana Alley (*Roisenlükel*) that separated the Jewish Street from Serbska Street, stood the "Kłopotowski" house (No. 28). In 1648 it was leased to Lewko, who was killed during the 1664 pogroms. The house was damaged. In 1691 after undergoing repairs, it was leased to Hersz Lewkowicz, Samuel Lejzor and to Hersz Chaimowicz. In 1788, the house was owned by Mendel Futernika, who was a furrier.

The opposite side of the New Jewish Street starts with the house on Serbska Street [corner] Boimów 23. The house collapsed in 1862, and after it was rebuilt, it was purchased by Joel Todros and the heirs of Schwarzwald.

The adjacent house, No. 27, belonged to Berko [Berek] Monyszowicz, and in the 19th century it belonged to L. Nossig. Next to it stood the houses (29, 31, 33) that belonged to Mendel ben Joel, Berek Danczes and to the renowned community leader Süssman Lew (Lewko) Bałaban.

The block of houses Nos. 35–45 underwent different fates. In 1788, timber houses stood on that spot, among them a Torah–study school at No. 41, prayer–houses, and craftsmen's organisations (tinsmiths, upholsterers, weavers). In addition to the residential houses there were 17 butcher shops, a bathhouse, a prison and other shops. This street bordered on the Alley Za Zbrojownia [behind the armoury], where there were three houses that belonged to Eizyk the manager, Majer [Szkolnik] the caretaker, and to the community prison.

This timber block of houses was in a very dilapidated state by the end of the 18th century, and the Governor ordered to have them demolished, including the Torah–study school.

They were replaced by the building No. 39 and by a new Torah–study school at No. 41. The end building, No. 43, was a school for girls named after the preacher Abraham Kohn. After the Jewish schools' educational network was reorganised in 1860, No. 43 was used as a general elementary school, and in 1899 as a girls' elementary school. This school was led by the renowned, scholarly headmaster, Dr. Henryk Biegeleisen (grandson of Nachman Krochmal), and later, until 1914, by the headmistress Mrs. Joanna Planerow.[5]

Before 1914, the building also contained a state institute for the training of Jewish teachers of religion.

The last house on Za Zbrojownia Alley was the community prison. Later, a bathhouse and a *Mikveh* were erected there.

Around the First World War, the neighbouring houses were demolished and were replaced by the building of the Ukrainian insurance company, *Dnister*.

II. The community in the Krakówski suburb

The Kraków suburb, to the north of the town, was the location of the community outside the town. A few Jews, spirits merchants and other shop owners, also lived in the Haliczki (Gliniański) suburb. Jewish and Christian houses leased to Jewish tenants sprawled from the Krakówski Gate and the fortress embankment in the direction of Żółkiewska Street. The Jews termed these streets, "*in front of the gate.*" The suburb proper extended from Kleparowska Street and St. Anna Church, at the one end, to the bridge over the Poltva River, at the other. The river split the suburb in two, both administratively and judicially. The area on the Poltva's right bank was under the jurisdiction of the castle, and that on the left bank, under the jurisdiction of the municipality. The Jewish residents were subject to the Starosta's jurisdiction. As subjects to his rule, they also benefitted from his protection, and were permitted to reside in the vicinity of his castle. Lwów's Jewish community had its roots in the first synagogue in the area from the Poltva to the old market (*Stary Rynek*), and later on from Żółkiewska Street, Bożnicza [*Sinagogen Gasse*], and between Zbożowy Square and Krakówski Square. The first cemetery was situated at Podzamcze, and the second (1300–1855) in the area between Szpitalna and Rappaporta Streets, part of which was the Karaites' cemetery.

In the 16th century, the overcrowding and squalor inside this Quarter increased. In his epic poem *Roxolania*, written in Latin, the Polish poet Sebastian Fabian Klonowic, who was a municipality clerk, depicted the Jewish Quarter in the town's suburbs as follows:[6]

"Tu na przedmiejskich kałużach się wioda

"Chałupy Zydów obdartych nędzarzy

"Kazdy jak kozieł aszpecony broda

"Z wieczna bladoscia na usciech i twarzy."

The Jewish community congregated on the right bank of the Poltva, from the Krakówski Gate to the Ruthenian Church named after Mikołaj. The few Jews who resided on the left bank were of the lower strata of society, such as horse thieves and other adventurers. The heart of the community was the synagogue outside the town (*die vorstädtische Schul*) situated in between the streets Bożnicza, Cehulna and Owocowa, near the town walls. A square with shops and small huts faced the synagogue. Near the stone–built synagogue was a house with a courtyard and gardens that had belonged to a Jewish family ever since 1462. To the East of the building stood houses that were either let or sold to Jews. Here, the Jews were allowed to construct and to purchase

[Pages 519-520]

plots and houses. They were granted that right after the 1623 great fire that began in the synagogue and destroyed 1,200 houses, including all of the Jews' houses (according to Józef Bartłomiej Zimorowic).

In 1632, the synagogue was rebuilt close to the Poznański yard. The entire area was referred to by the people as "*far der Schul* [in front of the synagogue]."

In 1640, a fire again broke out almost destroying the entire suburb. The synagogue and the houses were rebuilt, but they were damaged during the wars in the 1640s. During the period of peace and quiet, the Jewish community and its houses expanded. A Torah–study school was constructed next to the Great Synagogue , that included a great library and prayer–houses for the craftsmen's organisations. A Chassidim Synagogue (Chassidim Schul) stood at the junction of Bożnicza and Łazienna Streets. Next to the synagogue was the Jewish market.

During the Austrian rule, the area expanded in the direction of [Tzebulna] Cebulna[7] – Plac Strzelecki, as far as Żółkiewska Street– Podzamcze, [św.]Marcina [St. Martin] Street at one end, in the direction of Kleparowska, to Kazimierzowska Street and Janowska, at the other end.

Early in the 19th century, the Jewish community expanded particularly on Kazimierzowska [street], known by the Jews as *Die Brejte Gass*. Here, families Berger, Birnbaum, Mittelmann, Hescheles built large residential houses, the earliest in the Jewish Quarter.

The printer Abraham Józef Madfes, who came from Holland, Salomom Buber, Dr. Ehrenpreis, Dr. Braude and Lejbowicz who participated in the 1863 uprising, lived on Kazimierzowska.[8]

Despite the freedom to live in any part of the town, which was granted under the 1868 Constitution, most of the Jews kept to their streets and did not move from their apartments in the suburb.

Notes:

All notes in square brackets [ ] were made by the translator.
[The spelling of names was taken from publications by Dr. M. Bałaban]

1.   See Chapter 2 of my articles: *History of the Jews of Lwów*

2.   [Michael] Stöger: [*Darstellung der gesetzlichen Verfassung der galizischen Judenschaft* (1833)] Vol. I, p. 32.

3.   G[erschon] Wolf: "Zur Lage der Juden in Galizien" [*Monatsschrift für Geschichte und Wissenschaft des Judentums*] 1867; p. 203.

4.   Dr. M. Bałaban: *Dzielnica Żydowska*, Lwów 1909; pp. 55–57.

5.   Dr. M. Bałaban: *Dzielnica Żydowska*, Lwów 1909; pp. 73–87.

6.   Polish translation by W. Syrokomla, Vilnius 1851, pp. 70–77.

7.   The house of Rabbi Izak Rappoport, the brother of *Shir* [Salomon Jehudah Rappoport], and son–in–law of the great scholar R' Jakub Jüttes, stood at the beginning of the street. The house was known as "*Leben Gitalen.*" Also living in the house were his nephew Izak, R' Dawid and the poet Dr. Moritz Rappoport.
After 1920, the house belonged to Róża Melcer [Melzer].

8.   Dr. Jakób Schall: *Przewodnik po zabytkach* [*Żydowskich miasta*] *Lwowa*. Lwów 1935.
Deborah Vogel: "Lwowska Juderia" *Almanach i leksykon*. Lwów 1937 pp. 89–98.
Dr. M. Bałaban: "Die brejte Gass" *Chwila* [Zionist daily], Lwów 1925, 1926.

[Pages 525-526]

III
The Cultural Life

Characters and Personalities

by Dr. Zeev Pinot-Finkelstein

Translated by Myra Yael Ecker

Edited by Karen Leon

I.

During the entire 19th century, and up to the outbreak of the Second World War, a Jewish aristocracy had formed at Lwów. This aristocracy distanced itself from the extensive Jewish masses and withdrew to its own quarters. Jewish aristocracy was attained by three means. There were old families that had resided at Lwów for hundreds of years. There were families with lineage related to rabbis and to great Torah scholars, and there were families of Jewish magnates that had accumulated great wealth, especially from the grain trade, in the free town Brody and Tarnopol. However, once Brody's status of a free town was rescinded, they moved to Lwów.

Among the first category were the families that came to Poland from Germany and Italy and settled at Lwów after lengthy wanderings. These included the families of Rappoport, Löwenherz, Blumenfeld, Sokal, Reizes [Reices], Parnas, Tenner, Schönfeld, Aszkenazy, Ehrenpreis, Rokach and others.

Among the second category were the families of Horowitz, Löwenstein, Landau, Chajes [Chajut], Margulies, Braude, Natansohn and others.

The third category included the families of Mieses, Schaff, Byk, Kolischer, Garfein, Trachtenberg, Rohatyn, Lilien, Kimmelman, Diamand, Buber and others.

Dr. Bernard Tenner, Dr. Jakub Horowitz, Dr. Emil Byk, Dr. Natan Löwenstein, Dr. Emil and Józef Parnas, Dr. Tobiasz Aszkenazy and others were among some of the renowned advocates among this group. Dr. Aszkenazy was also Lwów's deputy-Mayor.

Dr. Inlender from one of Lwów's old families, was greatly respected, and his son, Adolf Władysław, was a renowned journalist in Poland.

The Mieses family that consisted of bankers and grain merchants, held a special place in Jewish life. The family had close contact with Count Gołuchowski, and the banker, Rachmiel Mieses, was able to obtain important political information from his close contact with the Austrian Minister of Finance. Consequently, Rachmiel was held in high regard by the members of Lwów's stock market. In the 1860s, Jozue Mieses, was the branch manager of Lwów's Mortgage Bank. Hermann Mieses, another son, was elected to the Austrian Parliament by the district of Drohobycz. Although his Polish rival gained most of the votes, the latter's election was annulled after the voting procedure was investigated. Mieses received the mandate with no further elections (an unheard of incident in the history of the Austrian Parliament). Hermann Mieses held this post until 1879. After losing his entire fortune, he went into newspaper publishing, where his comprehensive knowledge brought him great success. Emil Mieses, served for years as vice-chairman of Lwów's community committee.

Included among the elite Jewish aristocracy was the Rappoport family, whose status derive from its lineage of renowned rabbis, and not from wealth or public engagement. There were two Rappoport families: the priests [Cohanim], and those who were not priests. The priestly family arrived at Lwów as far back as the 17th century, and filled key roles in the community. The family's significance increased during the life of the great scholar [Gaon] R' Chaim Rappoport. The community did not like him, and disputes broke out between the community and himself that even came to the attention of the authorities. Nevertheless, his scholarship and especially his participation in the 1759 debate with the "Frankists," increased his prestige amongst both Jews and Christians. The grandson of his brother, R' Benjamin who was rabbi at Oleśnica [Oels], was the renowned Lwów physician, Dr. Jakubka Rappaport, one of the founders of the *Temple*. A Rappoport descendant, R' Simche Rappoport was known for having established a brewery on Janowska Street, and for being among the largest of the estate lessees in eastern Galicia. His son, R' Majer, was a prodigy in his youth as a pupil of Rabbi Ehlenberg and R' Jüttes. He clandestinely studied secular subjects and acquired extensive knowledge of Greek and Latin, attaining a fluency in classical literature and the ability to recite Homer and Virgil. His father's fierce objection and concern with the family's honour, made him forgo his desire to study at university. R' Majer participated, as a "self-taught"

[Pages 527-528]

(autodidact) in Austrian Law, and chose to follow an unusual profession. He "bought" cases of unsuccessful lawsuits, and appealed them at the Vienna Upper Law-court. He appeared in court without an advocate, but with his knowledge of jurisprudence, he succeeded in winning most of the cases. The Vienna Upper Law-court's chairman once asked him, "Where do you have your knowledge from?" R' Majer replied, *dank dem Talmud* (thanks to the Talmud and to sophistry). While R' Majer had not fulfilled his desire to study at a university, the son of his brother R' Izak, Dr. Artur Rappaport, did achieve a university education and was appointed lecturer in Classical Languages at Lwów University.

The brother of Salomon Jehudah Rappoport (*Shir*), R' Jakub Samuel Rappoport, also lived at Lwów, and opposed the election of Abraham Kohn as preacher. In a letter to his brother *Shir*, who by then was a Rabbi in Prague, he asked for his influence with Lwów's *Maskilim* [Enlightened] to avoid electing the preacher. His son, Dawid, a great scholar and a *Maskil* who published poetry and articles, held a different view.

Among the Rappoport family members who were not priests, was the wealthy iron merchant, the Chassid R' Salomon Rappoport. He had a large family. One of his sons fled to Brody, the "Jerusalem of Galicia," where he studied at the *gymnasium*. He was Dr. Samuel Rappoport, one of Galicia's early members of the Zionist Movement, known as a renowned scholar in Jewish Folklore studies.

Jan Skarbek-Kruszewski: Caricatures of Lwów's Jewish Characters

Among the "distinguished" was the Kolischer family, that originated from Kalisz. At the end of the 18th century they moved to Lwów, and in 1785 the family adopted the name Kaliszer (later altered to Kolischer). They were known as merchants, as well as house and plot owners. The first of them to "be Enlightened" was Leo. He concluded his university studies as a Doctor of Law and numbered among the renowned advocates. He was a founding member of the *Temple* and a leading community committee member, for decades. He was also an active member on the committee of *Szomer Izrael*.

Other scions of this family included, the very wealthy Natan and Ignacy Kolischer, Dr. Józef Kolischer, who was Branch Manager of Lwów's National Bank, and also member of the municipality, and Dr. Juliusz Kolischer, the community chairman in 1876.

Dr. Heinrich Kolischer, a well known personality, was a delegate to the Austrian Parliament, and to the Galician and Polish *Sejm* (1907-1919). He was among the wealthiest men in Galicia, owner of a paper mill at Czerlany [Tscherljany], near Lwów, a renowned economist and a trade and industry expert. Due to his special talents, he headed the Organisation of Galician Industries, at a young age. While he was considered among the renowned economists in the Polish club of the Austrian Parliament, he was not elected minister because he was Jewish. As a realist and a businessman, he considered his political rise only in relation to the Polish nobles, irrespective of whether its effect on the Jewish masses was positive or negative. The Zionists fought him vigorously, and he received no thanks from the Jewish masses, either. Because he held no clear view about Polish independence, he also angered the Poles during the war years. Consequently, he did not settle in Warsaw, but chose to spend his later years in Vienna, in his magnificent palace on Reisnerstrasse. His palace turned into the committee house for the Austrian-Polish nobility, and his nobly spirited wife, from the houses of Klärmann and Mieses, hosted the invited guests.

Among the typical Kolischer family members were the brother of Dr. Leo Kolischer, Janek and his wife Babte-Breindel, and their sons Hermann, an executive officer at the Mortgage Bank, and Friedrich, known in town by his name "Fredzio." He studied medicine in Vienna, but did not have the time to conclude his studies. He spent most of his days at *Café Wien* engaged in reading *Neue Freie Presse*, and was living on the income from their house on *Breite Gasse*. His son Janek, who was also not interested in studying, went to Vienna, appeared in Cabarets and made a name for himself as a comic actor. The Kolischer coterie also included the wealthy families of Leiblinger and Mohrenberg.

Leora, the daughter of Janek and Babte Kolischer, was married to Dr. Wilhelm Holzer.

The Löwenherz family that owned estates and mills around Krystynopol [Kristianopol], Sokal and Brody, was among the privileged families that moved to Lwów in the mid-19th century.

Best known among the heads of the family was Józef Noah, a handsome man who behaved like a Polish nobleman. Noah Löwenherz played a prominent role in the agriculture of Galicia. He was one of the first to assimilate and was a Polish sympathiser. In 1848, he worked with the Polish revolutionaries and in 1863, he joined the Polish uprising.

He established a rebels' centre on his Ohladow estate, where

[Pages 529-530]

they kept stores of weapons and food. As the Austrian authorities trusted him, he was able to support the revolt without endangering himself. The National Polish government in Warsaw, fully appreciated his assistance and his name was sometimes mentioned in the headquarters' commands.

His brother, Jona, also joined in the battles. Noah Löwenherz moved to Lwów and was publicly involved in the assimilation movement. However his grandsons, Dr. Henryk and Dr. Józef Löwenherz, followed different paths. They joined the Zionist Movement while still at secondary school.

2.

Among Brody's wealthy residents, who moved to Lwów after its status of a free town was abolished, was the Reices [Reizes Reitzes] family. They claimed to be descended from Spanish survivors, but this claim is historically unproven. The family was not descended from the Reices brothers who died as martyrs in 1728.

They were wholesalers and were involved in leasing at Lwów. The head of one branch of the family, Kasriel Reizes, was among the founders of the *Temple* and donated generously towards its building.

The branch of the family headed by Jan Reices, moved

Dr. Leon Reich

to Vienna in the 1870s and was successful in banking. They purchased the majority shares in Vienna's horse-drawn tram-company [Wiener Pferdetramway], and made a large fortune. Kaiser Franz Joseph I granted the title of Baron to Jan Reices, for the improvement to the urban transport system.

His son Maximilian married an Austrian aristocrat, Maria Korper von Marienwert.

Apart from families that arrived from provincial towns, were also the families of Blumenfeld, descendants of the martyred Reices; Schönfeld, in-laws of the Löwenherz family; Tenner, Margulies, Landau and Sokal, relatives of the Reizes family.

The Parnas family, originally from southern Russia where their name was Rafalowicz, carved out its own special. They held important posts in Russia's financial economy and assisted the Russian treasury.

One branch of the family settled at Dubna, and excelled in managing the community, which gave rise to the origin of their name, Parnas [community-leader], Marszałkiewicz in Polish. At the end of the 18th century they moved to Tarnopol, where they were engaged in leasing estates. Like other Jewish families of estate lessees, they were wary of peasants' riots and chose to leave Podolia and move to Lwów. The Parnas family members attended university and worked in the State Attorney's Office. Dr. Emil Parnas and Dr. Józef Parnas, among the leading assimilated, played a pivotal role in the community. In time, they took a positive approach to the establishment of Eretz Israel, and joined the "Extended Jewish Agency," and were also involved with *Keren Hayesod*.

The Byk family was from Podolia. They had been engaged in the export of grain and in leasing estates, and joined the wave of wealthy families that moved to Lwów. After the 1846 peasant revolts in the villages, they preferred to leave Podolia and move to the Land's capital. At Lwów they engaged in export-trade.

The younger generation became "Enlightened" in the years 1840-1860, and favoured German assimilation. Dr. Emil Byk received a German eduction at home. After his studies he led the Jewish intelligentsia which supported Austrian centralisation.

After a while he changed his view, and joined the circle of Polish sympathisers.

He was, by nature, stubborn regarding political issues that affected him personally. His ambition led him to a lifetime, key position in the leadership of Galicia's Jews.

He fought his opponents ferociously. In fighting elections, Byk did not recoil from any means, including bribery, harassment by the authorities etc. Memorable struggles took place between Dr. Byk and Dr. Józef Bloch over the 1885 elections to the Austrian Parliament, and over the 1906 elections against the Zionist candidate Adolf Stand.

His right-hand man in this strategy was Samuel Horowitz. Samuel's father, R' Ozjasz Arie Horowitz, and his mother, Rivke of the Aszkenazy family, owned a bank in Lwów. Samuel Horowitz received a complete religious education in his father's home. In his youth he was known for being a religious fanatic, and he led demonstrators against the *Maskilim* and the Enlightened. By and by, however, he abandoned the customs of

[Pages 531-532]

Chassidism, and began to learn secular studies and languages, and his occupation at the bank, and in trade led him to joined the faction of the Enlightened. He had an outstanding financial business-acumen and was known in banking circles. While still young, he was offered the job of managing the Mortgage Bank. He declined as his father stopped him from wearing European style clothes.

From 1875, he managed his father's Bank and expanded the business. Besides the Brody estates, he also established industries.

Under the influence of Dr. Byk, he publicly supported assimilation and was a leading figure in the fight against the

Dr. G. Blatt

Zionist Movement. While he led the community in the years 1887-1897, he suppressed all Zionist influence. He exploited his status as the community president, even to the detriment of the interest of the Jewish community.

He was prominent among the privileged strata of Lwów. He was stubborn and politically uncompromising. As leader of the assimilated, he fought all his life for the concept of Jewish-Polish integration, and was instrumental in all of Galicia's Jewish undertakings. He never denied his Jewishness, but did wish to loyally merge it with the Polish culture. Despite his vigorous fight against Zionism, he openly donated a large sum of money to the Jewish *gymnasium* in Jerusalem, and he supported the crafts school named after Korkis.

He also paved the way for the political stance of his son-in-law, Dr. Natan Löwenstein, son of the preacher, Bernard Löwenstein. Natan inherited his father's talent for public speaking, and with his father-in-law's assistance, he joined Lwów's Jewish aristocracy. When he was appointed delegate to the Austrian parliament in 1907, he became known as one of its illustrious speakers. Dr. Löwenstein was a realistic and critical statesman. As a young man he had already joined the circle of his assimilated brother-in-law, Bernard Goldman, that aimed to integrate the Jews into Polish culture. He stood for the Polish Party in the Austrian parliament and only supported Jewish interests when they advanced Polish Nationalism. Löwenstein considered Zionism his arch-enemy, injurious both to Galicia's aim for Polish nationalism, to which he was devoted, and to his political standing. Nevertheless, he knew how to maintain his influence among the Jewish masses that elected him to the Austrian parliament. In 1911, he submitted his candidacy for the Drohobycz district, and his election led to bloodshed in which several Jews of the nationalistic faction were killed.

Löwenstein dared to attack Polish chauvinism only one time, and that was during the trial of [Stanisław] Steiger. Dr. Löwenstein defended him together with the advocates Dr. Lajb Landau, Dr. Michał Ringel and Lwów's eldest Polish defence advocate, Dr. Grek.

Dr. Löwenstein attempted to bolster the assimilation movement among the youth too, but with little success. Only a few individuals among the younger generation were involved in the Polish Movements.

From 1880, Dr. Stanisław Ruff and Wiktor Chajes, were active in the Polish underground movements. In 1897, when Professor Michał Bobrzyński, chairman of Galicia's educational committee, introduced the compulsory wearing of a uniform to students at secondary schools, *Gymnasiums* and *Realschule*, the Polish students decided to wear the national headgear, *Batorówka* [-*magierka*; named after the Hungarian born, King Stefan Batory to accentuate the uniform's national character. Wiktor Chajes, who was part of the organising committee, was consequently expelled from school.

During 1902-1904, Maksymilian Landau of Brody organised a Polish underground organisation. The organisation published an illegal magazine titled *Wolne polskie słowo* (Free Polish Word). In 1892, when Kaiser Franz Joseph visited Lwów, Landau and his underground cell defaced the town-governor's posters calling on the townspeople to welcome the Kaiser. Landau was arrested by the police.

Many young assimilated Jews, led by Chajes, participated in all the actions of the underground organisations such as *Promień* [Ray] and *Teka* [Portfolio]. And from 1905 onwards, also in the defence organisations *Sokół* [Falcon], *Drużyny Bartoszowe* [Bartosze Troops], *Kuźnią* [Forge], *Zjet* and others, that managed underground actions for national freedom.

[Pages 533-534]

The Jewish Club at the Austrian Parliament 1907-1911:
Dr. I. Schalit, Adolf Stand, B. Straucher, Dr. H. Gabel, Dr. Mahler, Dr. M. Braude

In 1903, the weekly *Jedność* [Unity], edited by Dr. Bertold Menkes-Merwin, appeared as a rival to the Zionist weekly *Wschód* [East]. In 1907, under the management of Jakob Herman and Emil Goetz, the first society of assimilated students, *Zjednoczenie* [Unification], was established to promote the assimilation and merger of the Jews into Polish culture, and to boycott Zionism. The organisation joined in the activities of the assimilated, "Jews of the Mosaic Faith," who mingled among the Polish students as representatives of the Jews. They published the monthly magazine *Zjednoczenie* to rival the monthly Zionist youth magazine, Moriah. In 1912, an underground organisation of secondary-school students was established, named after [Berl] Berek Joselowicz, with the aim of attacking the Zionist students' organisation *Tzeirey Zion* [Young Zion].

Most prominent among the assimilated, involved in the Polish underground were: Maksymilian Landau (teacher at Brody's German *gymnasium*, and from 1918, Colonel in the Polish armed forces, and Commander of the officers' school at Toruń [Thorn]. He died at Katyn in 1940); Dr. Izidor Schenker; Dr. Ignacy Weinfeld (deputy Minister of Finance in 1918); Dr. Herman Diamand, leader of the Polish Socialist Party P.P.S.; Dr. Rafael Buber; Dr. Stanisław Löwenstein; Dawid Salamander; Dr. Zertbaum; Dr. Salomon Perlmutter; Karl Nacher and Kornelia Parnas (a renowned collector of Chopin memorabilia); Dr. Presser (biographer of [Stanisław] Przybyszewski, who was much admired by Lwów's Jewish circles); as well as Wiktor Chajes, chairman of the community council. Many young men from this circle joined the Polish legions as soldiers and as officers, during World War I.

3.

Lwów's Jewry established an extensive network of charitable institutions for its poor, such as soup-kitchens, shelter-houses, hospitals and children's care homes. The institutions were established and maintained by a few philanthropists. The philanthropist Maurycy Lazarus established the Jewish hospital before World War I.

Among the many Jewish philanthropists, two charitable businessmen sacrificed their fortune and power for the town's poor, the banker Jakub Stroh, and the advocate Dr. Wilhelm Holzer. Both of them forsook their professions and immersed themselves in social activism, such as the establishment and the financing of soup-kitchens, medical clinics etc. for the poor.

Jakub Stroh was a self-made-man, and self-taught. A few successful stock-exchange transactions made him very wealthy. In his private life he was thoroughly mean. He skimped on his family but distributed his fortune among charitable institutions, soup-kitchens, shelter-houses, medical clinics and charitable welfare funds. Notwithstanding, he refused alms to beggars in the street. During the First World War, he headed the *Jewish Rescue Committee*. For his philanthropic undertakings he was awarded the title *Kaiserlicher Berater* [imperial advisor]. He left his entire fortune to charitable institutions, leaving none of it to his wife and only son.

Dr. Wilhelm Holzer was cast in the same mold. Born at Rzeszów [Resche], he married the niece of the advocate Leo Kolischer, for whom he worked, and whose practice he subsequently inherited. Dr. Holzer was not blessed

[Pages 535-536]

with a normal family life. He was a warm hearted Jew interested in the circumstances of the poor, while his wife distanced herself from it. He sought solace in synagogues and charitable institutions. In his old age he also started to learn Hebrew. He was revered by Lwów's poor. From the early hours of the day, he was imposed upon by every distressed and embittered man. Queues of poor, sick, men, women and children dressed in torn and worn rags lined the doors of his office to ask for his help. The short-statured man with a top hat, was often found among the paupers as he rushed from one office to the next to settle their affairs for no financial consideration. He visited the soup-kitchens and the charitable institutions daily, to ascertain the progress of work. He also received people at the offices of the Jewish community, where he managed the department of social welfare.

He died penniless, after spending his entire fortune on social welfare institutions. Dr. Holzer was among the early proponents of the national concept. Together with Dr. Kobak, Dr. Rubin Bierer and Rohatyn, he organised Lwów's first Zionist Association, *Mikra Kodesz* [Mikra Kodesh].

Among Lwów's well known characters was Saul Birnbaum, an ultra-Orthodox [Charedi] Jew, a wholesale steel merchant (competitor of his neighbour, R' Salomom Rappaport), who owned the house No. 12 *Brejte Gass*. His account manager, R' Naftali Perlmutter, a renowned *shofar* blower, was another interesting person.

In the second half of the 19th century, "the lady, Mrs. Bessel Bałaban" maintained a bookshop in R' Saul Birnbaum's house. The bookshop was renowned for its *Mishnayot* publications that were also widely available in Lithuania.

The landlord and Mrs. esel fought and quarreled for years, with shouts filling the house. Pesel complained that a bookshop required silence and an appropriate atmosphere for the publication of *Mishnayot*, but R' Birnbaum refused to accept this. As a steel merchant he was used to laud noises and he would not take notice of a woman who uttered "women's nonsense."

Pesel was not the only one with complaints about him. The chief inspector of the horse-drawn trams, the Jewish Bernfeld, also claimed that it was hard to pass there because of the crates and goods that blocked the thoroughfare. The struggle ceased only with the demise of R' Saul Birnbaum. His heirs were involved in litigation for scores of years, until the house collapsed.

4.

Among Lwów's typical personalities, two Jewish scientists, Prof. Dr. Gerson Blatt (1858-1916) and Prof. Dr. Henryk Biegeleisen, need to be mentioned. Dr. Blatt, was the first Jewish lecturer in Classical and in Hindo-European linguistics at Lwów University, and he published comprehensive essays, in Latin, that laid the foundation for the science of linguistics, especially that of Sanskrit.

Dr. Blatt was born at Jarosław to a poor family. He struggled to support himself during his *gymnasium* studies. Even after he finished his education, he was not able to obtain a *gymnasium* teaching post at Lwów. He worked in Brody until 1896, at which time he went to Leipzig to study at the Institute of Linguistics. He was appointed lecturer at the University of Lwów, in 1902. During his whole life he remained a modest, reclusive scholar engaged solely in his scientific work. Blatt never denied his Jewish origin, and in his comparative study he delved into the origins of the Hebrew language.

Dr. Henryk Biegeleisen (1856-1934) was a similarly reclusive academic. His father was a physician at Tłuste [Touste], a small township in eastern Galicia, and his mother, Rozalia, was the daughter of R' Nachman Krochmal (RaNaK). He received a Polish education in his father's house, against the wishes of his mother (in 1848 his father was part of the National Guard, and in 1863, he was a physician during the Polish revolt). Although Henryk Biegeleisen always considered himself a Pole, he was proud to mention that he was the grandson of the renowned Jewish philosopher, R' Nachmman Krochmal, and he displayed his grandfather's picture in his room. He studied philosophy at Lwów University, and dedicated himself to the research of Polish literature and history. He was awarded the title of Doctor of Philosophy by the University of Leipzig. When he returned to Lwów from Leipzig, he published papers on the history of Polish literature. Adam Mickiewicz was a main subject. Readers appreciated his books, but he faced harsh criticism from Polish experts who did not forgive his democratic stance on political issues. Biegeleisen was also interested in folklore, and wrote books on this subject. He was also interested in Jewish Folklore about which he published studies in *Zeitschrift für Volkskunde* and was a member of the society for the research into Jewish Folklore founded by Benjamin Segel, J. Landau and Dr. Malz. Despite his extensive knowledge, he was not accepted as a teacher at any *gymnasium*. At the behest of his friends, the community offered him the post of headmaster at the boys' school named after Abraham Kohn.

[Pages 537-538]

The democratic Biegeleisen argued with the leading assimilators, Dr. Bernardß Goldman and others, in whom he saw bourgeois leaders concerned only with their private affairs.

Dr. Goldman, a *Sejm* delegate, took revenge on Biegeleisen and sought to close the school. Nevertheless, Biegeleisen found many supporters in his conflict with Dr. Goldman and the unrelenting members of the community. He was triumphed, as the school was not closed down. Later, petitions from supporters led to his appointment as professor at Lwów's *gymnasium*.

Biegeleisen's interest in Judaism and in Eretz Israel grew out of an appreciation that he was RaNaK's grandson and that he owed loyalty to his people.

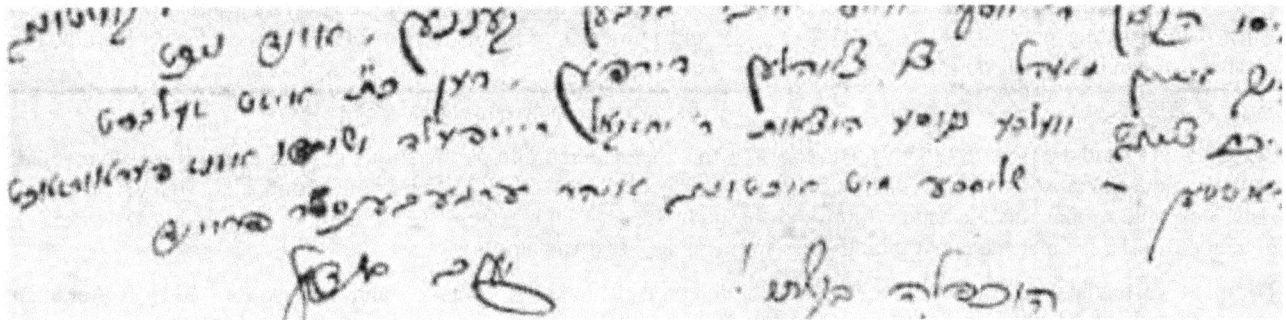

Jakub Bodek's handwriting

Notes:

All notes in square brackets [ ] were made by the translator.
[The spelling of names was taken from publications by Dr. M. Bałaban]

[Pages 539-540]

The Hebrew Printing Presses at Lwów

by Chaim Dov Friedberg

Translated by Myra Yael Ecker

Edited by Karen Leon

The Jewish community of Lwów was among the oldest and most populated, in Eastern Europe. Due to the town's location, however, its trade connections with the communities in Central Europe, was tenuous. This constituted the principal reason why Lwów did not have a Hebrew language printing house capable of satisfying the demand for Hebrew books from its residents, and from those of the neighbouring towns. As a result, book merchants and collectors were obliged to import books, including prayer books, from towns in central Poland, including Kraków and Lublin.[1]

In 1569 (5329), when Rabbi Naftali Hirtz ben R' Menachem of Lwów, the author of an interpretation of the *Midrash Rabbah* on the Torah and the five *Megilot* [Scrolls], heard that the printer R' Izak [Iccek] ben R' Aron established a new printing house in Kraków, he brought his book there to be published. This book was the first work produced by the printer, in that year.[2]

150 years later, a Hebrew printing house was established by the printer Uri Schrage Feibusch Halewy of Amsterdam, in the town of Żółkiew near Lwów, on King Jan Sobieski III estate. This printer was supported by the King, and was able to provide the community with religious texts.[3] After his demise, the printing house passed to his family who followed in his footsteps.

In 1782 (5542), the Austrian government created an office for the censorship of Hebrew books, in Lwów, the capital town of Galicia at that time. In order to make the censor's task easier, the government ordered the printers of Żółkiew to move their printing houses to Lwów, where they were subject to the censor's censorship. In addition, the government levied an annual 20 Gulden tax, on every printing press.[4]

The first censor appointed by the government was the learned Innocens Fessler,[5] who was replaced by Aron Friedenthal of Jarosław, in 1788 (5548).[6] The post was filled again in March 1789 (5549) by R' Herc [Herz] Homberg, who was permitted to print his book *Neima Kdosza*, (Lwów 1789). He was replaced by the learned Haan, who held the post until 1806 (5566), when the censor's bureau was moved to the royal town Vienna.[7] The censors scrutinised all aspects of the Hebrew printing presses, to ensure nothing was concealed from them.

Those who established printing presses at Lwów, were as follows:

I. R' Ze'ew Wolf Letteris, moved his press from Żółkiew, and worked until 1806. After his demise, the operation of the press passed to his son R' Gerszon who managed it together with his mother, Mrs. Tscherne, until 1793. In that year, his mother returned to Żółkiew, where she moved her press with the government's consent. However, her son remained at Lwów for another year, before he also returned to his birth town.

II. R' Chaim Dawid ben R' Aron Halewi Madfes, was a descendant of the founder of the Żółkiew printing press. He also established his printing press at Lwów, in 1782 (5542), and immediately published books. He was accused of producing counterfeit Russian banknotes, during his years at Lwów, but

[Pages 541-542]

was exonerated,[8] and died in 1789 (5549). His son, R' Aron, then entered into partnership with Mordechaj Rubinstein,[9] and their press produced many books. In 1792 (5552), the two partners parted, and R' Aron became betrothed to Mrs. Chaja Taube. She was a capable woman, her husband's pride, and she tirelessly assisted him in his work, until he died around 1821 (5581). From then onwards, she managed the printing press alone, under her own name.

For many years, the proofreader at the press was the religious, R' Juda Leib Reiss,[10] and he was followed by R' Abraham Edel [or Edil], son of the author of the book *Afike Jehuda.*

Around 1848 (5608), Mrs. Chaja Taube gave her printing press to her son, R' Abraham Józef Madfes. He improved and expanded the enterprise in accordance with the spirit of the age, in good taste and understanding, and undertook to enrich the biblical literature with literary works. In 1858/9 (5619), he planned to republish the *Babylonian Talmud*. After making the necessary preparations, he received consent from the renowned Rabbi Józef Saul Natansohn, to prohibit anyone else from entering into competition with him, on the work, such as the printer R' Abraham Izak Menkes. Rabbi Isaiah Schorr, head of the Rabbinical court of the Łaşi [Jassy] community, said in his consent: "A great *Mitzvah* to assist the elder, R' Abraham Józef Madfes, may his light shine. Buy the *Mishnah* Books from him, and anyone who purchases the great *Mishnah* books from any other printers, does so against the laws of the Torah." The printing of the Talmud started in 1860 (5620), and the task was completed in all its glory, in 1868 (5628). Subsequently, he also published the four parts of the *Shulchan Aruch* [an abbreviated form of the Jewish ritual law] with all its early commentators, the five Books of the Torah with various commentaries, and others.

R' Abraham Józef Madfes managed his enterprise for over sixty years. I met him toward the end of his life, when he was still full of vigour. He worked with vitality until his last day.

Another wonderful man in Lwów managed a printing press named after R' Aron ben Chaim Dawid Madfes, until the start of the sixth hundredth year in our count 1840 (5600).

III. R' Juda Salomon son of the late R' Naftali Hirtz, known as R' Salomon Jurisch, was later named R' Salomon Rappoport,[11] established his new printing press at Lwów, in 1784/5 (5545), where he printed diverse books. In time, he also cast German letters. In 1802 (5562), he printed booklets in German, probably without the censor's license. Consequently, he was fined 8 Gulden, and the German letters were confiscated from his printing press, by order of the prosecutor.[12]

In 1405 (5165), the printer began to print a fine edition of Maimonides's *Mishneh Torah*, and of the Bible in three translations, the full and the shortened version of the traditional text, *Rashi's* interpretation, *HaMizrachi* [Rabbi Elijahu Mizrachi's elucidation of *Rashi's* interpretation of the Torah], Gur Aryeh's annotation of *Rashi's* interpretation of the Torah, interpretation of RaDaK [Rabbi David Kimchi] and Rabbi [Moses] Alshech's interpretation of The Prophets, [Dawid Altschuler's] *Metzudat David* and *Metzudat Tzion* [interpretations of The Prophets and of The Chronicles]. The printer assembled Torah scholars at his house, including R' Abraham Edel, R' Aron ben R' Naftali Hirtz and R' Meszulam Salman ben R' Chaim Segal, who examined the texts to ensure that the books leaving the press were completely accurate. Two books in particular were the masterpieces of the printer's production. Work on the first book, published by R' Joseph Schmelke Reischer and his two partners, was completed in 1811 (5571). The second book, concluded in 1805 (5565), was published by the printer together with his son-in-law, R' Aszer [Ascher] Lemel[13] our teacher R' Majer Dawid Schrenzel [Szrencel]. Many more books were printed under the printer's supervision until 1820 (5580). In addition, he also kept a bookshop at Lwów, near the synagogue in the Kraków suburb.

IV. Mrs. Judit, the daughter of the printer R' Aron, and who was married to R' Dawid ben R' Menachem Mann, established and managed a printing press, on her own, at Żółkiew.[14] After her husband's demise, she married R' Cwi Hirsz [Tzvi Hirsch] Rosanes [Rosanisch], and moved the printing press to Lwów. Her son, R' Naftali Hirc [Hirtz] Grossmann, was in charge of her printing business in 1782/3 (5543). He assisted his mother until 1805 (5565).[15]

The proofreaders at the press in the early period, included R' Tzadok ben R' Salomon Salman, son-in-law of R' Dawid Bardach of Lwów,

[Pages 543-544]

who was replaced by R' Gabryel Halevy ben Naftali Goldenberg, of Zlozitz, and R' Izrael ben Isaiahof blessed memory.

V. R' Naftali Hirc [Hirtz] Grossmann, above mentioned, began his printing business in 1793 (5553). He enriched the available Torah literature until his demise in 1826/7 (5587). After his death, the printing press passed to his widow, Mrs. Chawe, and in 1848/9 (5609) to her daughter, Mrs. Feige Grossmann. The printing press and all printing matters were managed by R' Dawid Cwi Hersch Schrenzel [Szrencel] until 1857/8 (5618).

VI. The bookseller, R' Aron Jozef HaKohen[16] printed the book *Zewed Tow*, in 1795 (5555). This printing business did not last long after printing only a few books.

VII. In 1807 (5567), the Torah sage R' Uri,[17] son of the previously mentioned R' Mordechaj Rubinstein, requested from the government a licence to establish a printing press based upon his earlier study of the art of printing and typesetting, at Breslau [Wrocław]. The printers already established in Lwów, R' Aron Madfes and R' Naftali Herz Grossmann, submitted a complaint against R' Uri's request, stating that his assertion was fundamentally untrue, that he had never studied printing at Breslau. Nevertheless, R' Uri knew how to successfully present his petition, and the government accepted his request. On 7th February 1808 (5568), he was granted a licence. A few months later he printed tractates and other books. A year later, he realised that the location was to small, perhaps due to the competition from the other printers, and asked to move his printing press to Żółkiew. The authorities refused his request, but he was ultimately able to accomplish his move. During the short period at the end of 1809 (5569), when the town of Lwów was under Polish rule, he moved his printing press to the town of Żółkiew. His early work there consisted of printing scholarly books. He intentionally left out the location of the press from the inscription on the title page.

When Austrian armed forces returned to Lwów, they intended to prosecute R' Uri, perhaps for libel. When the rumour reached him, he quickly returned to Lwów and urgently printed there the book *Lashon Limudim* [on the language of the Torah], in 1810 (5570). He died before the authorities could prosecute him. After his death, a petition in his widow's name, Mrs. Chaje Rubinstein, was submitted to the government to allow the press left in her husband's estate to move to the town of Żółkiew, and be managed by her bother-in-law, her husband's brother R' Izak Rubinstein. Mrs. Chaje Rubinstein filed legal proceedings against her brother-in-law, R' Izak. She died however on 3rd January 1813 (5573), and her printing press was closed down by the government.[18]

VIII. The printing press of the religious R' Judah Leib Bałaban of Brody, was inaugurated in 1839 (5590), and passed to his son R' Pinkas Mojzesz, in 1851 (5601).[19] Twenty years later, the renowned Mrs. Bessel Bałaban was the owner of this printing press. This industrious woman very sensibly managed her printing press. She enlarged and expanded it, and over time she published a fine edition of the four parts of *Shulchan Aruch* [an abbreviated form of the Jewish ritual law] supplemented by many important commentaries; the Pentateuch; *Chok l'Yisrael* [compendium of Jewish texts for weekly study]; the six sections of the *Mishnah*; prayer books and many other reference books. Around 1885 (5645), the printing press was in the hands of her son, Leibusz Bałaban who followed in his parents' footsteps.

[Pages 545-546]

IX. R' Józef Schneider's printing press was established in 1844 (5604), with assistance of the letter-engraver Issachar Beck,[20] and it operated for several years, publishing a variety of books.

X. In 1850 (5610), Michał Franz Poremba opened his general printing press, and also printed Hebrew-language books from time to time. Around 1879 (5639), the entire printing press with all of its tools and appliances, in all its different departments, passed to A. Wajdowicz and his wife Anna, who operated it at 18 Ringplatz. In 1886 (5646), Feliks [Szczęsny] Bednarski acquired the printing press together with its typographical content, and he continued to print until 1902 (5662).

The Hebrew department of this printing press was under the management of different publishers, including R' Dov Berisz Lurie 1850 (5610), R' Cwi [Tzvi] Schreiber 1856 (5616), R' Cwi Hirsch Sperling 1858 (5618), R' Abraham Jozue Heschel Druker, ben R' Juda Gerson 1860 (5620), R' Abraham Nissan Süss 1861-74 (5621-5634), R' Michał Wolf[21] 1874-1879 (5634-5640) and R' Eliezer Margulies 1883 (5644).

XI. In 1840 (5610), Franz Galiński established his printing press and printed a variety of books. In 1859 (5619), R' Salman Leib Flecker, known as "R' Leibusz Madfes," established a printing press at Żółkiew, together with R' Dov Berisz Lurie, who parted from him in 1861 (5621).

XII. The printer Edward Winiarz established his printing press in 1851/2 (5612), and for some years he greatly enriched the book market with useful compositions.

XIII. R' Dawid Cwi [Hersch] Schrenzel [Szrencel], who previously managed Mrs. Grossmann's printing-press (*see* V.), established his own printing-press in 1858 (5618), after leaving Mrs. Grossmann's employ. He shared his enterprise with R' Abraham Jozue Heschel Druker and R' Abraham Nissan Süss (*see* X.). Both were experienced in the field of printing and publishing books, and they published many books together.

XIV. In 1858/9 (5619), the previously mentioned letter-engraver R' Issachar Beck, established a printing press together with R' Abraham Izak Menkes,[22] in order to publish a new edition of the *Babylonian Talmud*. In 1859/60 (5620), tractate *Brachot*, sequence *Zeraim* was prepared, and proofread by the Torah scholar R' Jakub Jona Maimon ben R' Dawid Cwi. After its completion, Beck left the partnership. Menkes continued to print all six sequences on his own, with the accreditation of R' Salomon Kluger and others of the generation's greats who supported his undertaking, until 1864/5 (5625).

In 1863 (5623), he was joined by his brother-in-law, the renowned officer R' Salomon Spercher, and by his father-in-law, R' Nissan Margulies, and they concluded the six sequences, in folio format. Meanwhile, his brother-in-law R' Salomon Spercher, together with R' Issachar Beck, printed the entire *Talmud* in octavo format,[23] through 1866/7 (5627). R' Abraham Izak Menkes's printing press operated until 1876/7 (5637).

XV. R' Abraham Jozue Heszel Drucker founded a printing press with Salman Leib Flecker, in 1859/60 (5620). After some time, R' Abraham Jozue Drucker parted, and R' Salman Leib Flecker continued on his own until 1861/2 (5622), and

[Pages 547-548]

then continued with other partners, Rabbi Uri Zew [Wolf] Salat, R' Szmuel Goldberg and R' Izrael Elimelech Stand. These religious partners printed countless books by *Posskim* [adjudicators], Responsas etc., in all the branches of Talmudic literature.

XVI. R' Berl Lejb ben R' Hersz Nechles,[24] who in 1847 (5607) was a typesetter at Mrs. Chaja Taube Madfes's printing press, established his own printing press in 1861 (5621), and published many books together with R' Szymon Jakub ben R' Mojżesz who was the proofreader. Beginning in 1891/2 (5652), his son, R' Hersz Nechles, managed his father's printing press for some years.

XVII. The printing press of the partners R' Szmuel Elazar Lejb ben R' Majer Kugel, Natan Michael Lewin[25] & Comp., was established in 1861 (5621) and was responsible for the publication of many books. Beginning in 1861/2 (5622), R' Szmuel Elazar Lejb Kugel, operated this press on his own.

XVIII. The partners R' Dov Berisch Lurie and R' Cwi Hirsch ben R' Wolf Sperling, mentioned in (X.) established a printing press in 1861 (5621), and printed a large number of books.

XIX. Rabbi Uri Zew Wolf Salat ben R' Jecheskiel, inaugurated his printing press in 1863/4 (5621). About ten years later, he shared his undertaking with the industrious bookseller R' Jakob Meschulam Nyk. They only printed Torah and Chassidic books. From 1892/3 (5653) on his widow, Mrs. Esther, managed the printing press and later, it passed to R' Jozue Wolf. In 1903/4 (5664), it was purchased by the author R' Jona Karpel, son-in-law of the printer, R' Jozef Fiszer of Kraków, who published the Hebrew newspaper, *HaJom* [Today], that only appeared for a few days. Later, he published different newspapers in Yiddish.

XX. The printing press of R' Izrael Elimelech Stand [26] was established in 1864/5 (5625) and functioned until around 1879/80 (5640).

XXI. In 1871/2 (5632), Karl Budweiser moved his printing press from Kraków to Lwów, where the renowned bookseller Jakob Ehrenpreis [27] printed a large number of books in its Hebrew language department.

XXII. R' Chaim Rohatyn established his printing press in 1882/3 (5643) in order to print the *Charedi* [ultra-orthodox] religious newspaper *Machsike HaDas* [Upholders of the Faith]. In 1895/6 (5656), the press passed to R' Fajbus Awner. After his demise, his sons inherited the printing press and it functioned at 23 Słoneczna Street.

XXIII. R' Izrael Dawid Süss, the son of R' Abraham Nissan Süss, continued his father's work, starting in 1894/5 (5655). He and his brother-in-law, the renowned bookseller R' Ehrenpreis, published a large number of books.

At the end of the First World War in 1918, the *HaAvoda* printing press was established at No. 17 Bernstein Street. R'Altstadt established his press in 1927/8 (5688). The *Alpha* printing press began at No. 8 Blacharska Street. The printing press of the partners R' Jecheskiel Seif and R' Zelig Langstein, was at No. 4 Starozakonna Street.

Lwów gained worldwide recognition for the important books published there. It became the principal provider of books for the communities of the Balkan Peninsula, and its spirit affected all Jews who resided in those countries. That was the splendour of Lwów.

**

The following are the names of the books published by Lwów's printing presses until 1840 (5600), according to bibliographical lexicon *Beit Eked Sepharim*

[Pages 549-550]

Not included are the multitude of the prayer books, the *Machzorim* [festivals' prayerbooks], *Haggadahs* etc.: *Pirkei Elijah* (5543) 1782/3, *Keshet Jonatan, Tachana Imahot* (5544) 1784; *Chidushei HaRabbi Shlomo ben Avraham Even Aderet al Shavuot, Amudei Shesh, P'ri HaAretz, Shulchan Aruch HaRabbi Izak ben Shlomo Lurja* (5545) 1784/5; *Birkat Ya'akov, Etz Chaim, Shem Tov Katan, Safa B'rura* (5546) 1785/6; *VeCherev Pifiyot* (5546) 1786; *Igerret, Bechinat Olam, Chok Le Yisroel, Noam Elimelech* [Elimelech's Grace], *Etz Chaim, Ketsot HaChoshen, Rimonei Zahav Sfas Emes*; *Shulchan Aruch HaRabbi Izak ben Shlomo Lurja* (5548) 1787/8; *Arba'a Ture Even, Gevulas Benyamin, Ma'amar HaRabbi Moshe ben Jacob Corodovero, Ne'imah Kedoshah* (5549) 1788/9; *Beis Ya'akov, HaChochmah, LaYesharim Tehilah, Mishnat Chachamim, Nefesh David, Sha'ar HaMelech* (5550) 1789/90; *Chovat HaLevavot, Milot HaHegayon, Kav Hayashar, Rasa Mehemna, Sha'arei Kedusha,* (5551) 1790/1; *Avkat Rochel, HaGan, Ginze Yosef, Yesod Emuna, Likutei Amarim, Likutei Yekarim, Menorah Tehorah, Mitzvat HaShem, Poel Tzedek, Kitzur Shnei Luchot HaBrit* (5552) 1791/2; *Ahavat Dodim, Taharat Hakodesh, HaYashar, Mesilan Yesharim, Oneg Shabbat, Kehilat Moshe, Shem Tov Katan, Shearei Teshuvah* (5553) 1792/3; *Ohel Ya'akov, Hagadah Chelkat Benjamin, Keter Malchut, Nachlat Tzvi Naim Zemirot Yisroel, Sha'ar HaHachanah, Sha'ar HaMelech, Tochelet Tzadikim* (5554) 1793/4; *Hagadah* [shel Pessach Afikoman al pi] *Yafeh Nof, Tzeved Tov, HaYakar, Megaleh Amukot, Pnei Yitzchak* (5555) 1794/5; *Brit Kehunat Olam, Darchei Tzedek, Hagadah,Taamei HaMsora, Maaseh Choshev, Mitzvat HaShem, Lev Tov, Nefesh David, Kitzur Chowat Halevavot, K'tzot HaChoshen, Tikun HaT'chuva* (5556) 1795/6; *Binah LeItim, D'rashot HaRaN, Kulam Ahuvim, Likutei Amarim, Netivot Olam, System Shel HaYehudim, Pitchei Neda, Tzava'at HaRabbi Israel Baal Shem Tov Shivchei HaRabbi Yitzchak Lurja, Tokef HaNess* (5557) 1796/7; *Ya'arot D'vash, Mivchar HaP'ninim, Modaa VeOnes, Kitzur Reshit Chochma, Shnem Asar Drashot, She'elot VeTchuvot HaRabbi Josef Colon* [Trabotto], *Tomer Devora, Targum Sheni* (5558) 1797/8; *Or HaChaim Al HaTorah, Halacha LeMoshe, Hilchot Talmud Torah, Chavat Da'at, Yefeh Enayim, Ma'avar Yabok, Pitchei Ya, Tzenah Ure'enah, Kinot LeTish'a B'Av, Sh'not Eliyahu, Tola'at Ya'akov, Talmud Torah, Tana Debi Eliyahu* (5559) 1798/9; *HaBrit, Zichron Yitzchak, Choker Umekubal, Yad HaKtana, Mesilot Chochmah, Reshit Chochmah, Tesha Shitot* (5560) 1799/1800; *Ahavat David VeYonatan, Benayot BaRama, G'vul Benyamin, Yosifon, Midrash Emanuel, Revid HaZahav, Shevilei Emunah* (5561) 1800/1; *HaZohar, Peri Kodesh Halulim, Iyov* [Job] (5562) 1801/2; *Afikei Yehudah, Midrash Rabbah, Shev Shmatta* [Sheva Sugiot]*, Shulchan Aruch Orach Chaim* (5563) 1802/3; *Even Pinah, Ahavat Shalom, Eldad HaDeni, Imrei Yosher, Hagadah Al Pi Hilula Depas'cha, Hachayim, Nofat Tzofim, Sipur HaChalomot, Ateret Tzvi, Pirkei Moshe, Tzenah Ure'enah, Tzel HaOlam, Kol Ya'akov, Reshit Chochmah, She'erit Israel* (5564) 1803/4; *Iggeret Baalei Chaim, Orach Mishor, Berech Avraham, Hagadah, Chochmat Shlomo, HaYir'ah, Mivchar HaPninim, Midrash Tanchuma, S'lichot, Itur Sofrim, Etz Chaim, She'elot Vetshuvot Bar Sheshet, Tana Debi Eliyahu* (5565) 1804/5; *Gan Na'ul, Mitzvat HaShem, Etz Chaim* (5566) 1805/6; *Hagadah, HaYashar, Midash Rabbah Al Eichah, Midrash Tanchuma, Noam Megadim, Sivuv Rabenu Peretz, Shem Shmuel, Kontres Rabbi Chaim Jona Teomim* (5567) 1806/7; *Beur Al HaTorah MeRav Ovadiah Sforno, Midrash Rabbah, Ma'aneh Lashon, Mishneh Torah,* [28] *Eyn Ya'akov, Emek B'Racha, Emek HaMelech, Akedat Yitzchak, The Bible* with extensive interpretations in folio format (concluded in /5575/ 1814/5), *Torat Moshe Elimelech* (5568) 1807/8; *Igrot HaRabbi Shlomo ben Avraham Even, Beit Ephraim, Divrei Chachamim, HaBor Yafe MehaYeshuah, Chidushei HaRabbi Yosef Halevi*

Iben Migash, Cheshbon HaNefesh, Melechet HaMispar, Pnei Yehoshua,[29] *Rosh Ephraim, Masechet Megilah* (5569) 1808/9; *Binah LeItim, Beit Ephraim, Binyan Habait, Lashon Limudim, Seyag LaTorah, Peri Megadim, Kitzur Chovat HaLevavot, Takfu Kohen* (5570) 1809/10; *Beur Rabbi Bahya ben Asher, Midrash Rabbah, Midrash Shmuel, She'elot VeTchuvot HaRabbi Josef Even HaEzer, Shnem Asar Drashot, Toldot Adam* (5571) 1810/11; *Menorat HaMaor, Emek B'Racha, T'mim Deim,*[30] (5572) 1811/12; *LaYesharim Tehilah* (5573) 1812/13; *Meir Eynei Chachamim, Tiferet Tzvi, Taryag* [613] *Mitzvot* (5574) 1813/14; *Birkat David, HaYashar, Nachlat Shimon, Itur Sofrim, Masechet Beytza* (5575) 1814/15; *Avnei Miluim, Orach LeChaim, Binah LeItim* (5576) 1815/16; *Shem MeShmuel, Masechet Yevamot* (5577) 1816/17; *Beit Ephraim, Hagadah, Eyn Ya'akov* (5578) 1817/18; *Ohel Yitzchak* (5579) 1818/19; *Lev Arie, Nofet Tzofim, Kwutzat HaGeonim* (5580) 1819/20; *Meluchat Sha'ul* (5582) 1821/2; *Dema'ot Lezikaron Yashar* (5583) 1822/3; *Likutei Tzvi, Palgei Mayim, Peri Megadim, Pirkei Moshe* (5584) 1823/4; *Har Evel, LaYesharim Tehilah, HaMidot, Kitzur Evronot* (5585) 1824/5; *HaPliah, Tana Debi Eliyahu* (5586) 1825/6; *Eshkol Anavim, Yam HaTalmud, HaRo'eh, Shitah Mekutzevet* (5587) 1826/7; *Peri Megadim, Shalosh Shitot* (5588) 1827/8; *Afikei Yehudah,* (5589) 1828/9; *Michtavim Shonim, Masechet Ketuvot* (5590) 1829/30; *Beit Yehudah, Dover Mesharim, Segulah Nifla'ah, Kehilat Ya'akov*(5591) 1830/1; *Chamishah Shitot, Nishmat Chaim* (5592) 1831/2; *Divrei Torah, Derech Tevunot* (5593) 1832/3; *Beit Israel, Zichron Aharon, Chavat Da'at, Magen Giborim, Torah, Tchunat Ir Paris* (5594) 1833/4; *Hagadah, Mivchar HaPninim, HaNefesh, Netivot HaMishpat, Kol Ya'akov* (5595) 1834/5; *Beit Meir, Nachlat Shivah, Sidreh Taharah, Ateret Tzvi, Shevet Yehudah* (5596) 1835/6; *Ginat Veradim, Zichron Avraham, Chidushei Rabbi Meir Ben Ya'akov Shiff, Chovot HaLevavot, Levushei Srad, Rav Pninim, Shitah Mekuvetzet, Masechen Baba Kama* (5597) 1836/7; *Ohel Yitzchak, Givat Pinchas, Mesilat Yesharim, Ma'aneh Lashon, Netivot LeShabbat, Shev Shmatta* (5598) 1837/8; *Darchei Yesharim* (5599) 1838/9; *Or Pnei Moshe, Urim VeTumim, Gaon Tzvi, Haggadah, Ma'ayane Yeshuot, Ateret Tzvi, Shulchan Aruch Even HaEzer* (5600) 1839/40.

This list indicates that book printing in Lwów almost ceased twice. Both times resulted in a considerable rupture in production. The first interruption

[Pages 551-552]

was due to Napoleon's journey across Poland on his way to Russia from 1812 (5572), to 1813/4 (5574).[31] The second pause occurred during the Cholera epidemic of 1830-32 (5591-92) that spread throughout Poland. After 1832/3 (5593), however, Lwów's printing presses were active again. Output surpassed that of other countries, and Lwów attained worldwide recognition for its publishing.

The following are the names of the typesetters and printers (*pressenzieher*) who worked at the printing presses of Lwów:

The Typesetters:

R' Elijahu Menachem ben Abraham and his son, R' Mordechaj Tempelsmann; R' Menachem Cwi [Tzvi] ben R' Jozef (5543-5569) 1782-1808; R' Juda Leib ben Menachem Mendel (5546-5550) 1785-1790; R' Majer ben R' Becalel Arie (5548) 1787/8; R' Szalom Zelik ben R' Chaim Katz (5551-5565) 1790-1805; R' Majer ben Mordechaj (5551- 5556) 1790-1796; R' Abraham Dov ben R' Jozef Mojzesz Katz[32]; R' Abraham Izak ben Aszer[33] Zelik; R' Szlomo ben R' Majer Katz (5555) 1795 and later; R' Izak ben R' Cwi Hirsch (5555-5568) 1794-1808; R' Szymszon Cwi Hirsch ben Izak (5555-5556) 1794-1796; R' Pinkas ben Cwi Hirsz (5555-5563) 1794-1803; R' Becalel Naftali Hirc [Hirtz] ben Salomon Jungerer (5557-5575) 1796-1815; R' Mordechaj Elimelech ben Szmarie (5559) 1798/9; R' Izrael ben Izak (5559-5562) 1798-1802; R' Naftali Hirc [Hirtz] ben R' Jozef Margulies (5559-5561) 1798-1801; R' Azriel Juda ben R' Cwi; R' Chaim Simcha ben R' Szmuel Katz (5568-5569) 1807-1809; R' Zew Wolf ben R' Dov Ber; R' Izrael ben Chanoch Hennig (5569) 1808/9; R' Mordechaj Szmuel ben Izak Iccik of Lubartów, R' Chaim ben Eliezer of Józefów (5570-5607) 1809-1847; R' Mojzesz ben R' Izak (5594) 1833/4; R' Eljakim Götzel ben Majer; R' Alter ben Boruch Katz; R' Abraham ben Izak Frenkel; R' Berl Leib ben Cwi [Tzvi Hirsch (5607) 1846/7; R' Izrael Nachman ben Majer and R' Simcha Eljakim ben Chaim Juda (5620) 1859/60.

Printers:

R' Joel ben Abraham Segal Horowitz; R'Mojzesz Cwi Hirsch Margulies (5545-5550) 1784-1790; R' Szymon ben R' Juda Judel (5548) 1787/8; R' Jechiel Michael ben Abraham; R' Jakob ben Cwi Hirsz; R' Mojzesz Pinkas ben Szalom Friedl (5551) 1790- onwards; R' Nissan ben Mordechaj (5551) 1790- onwards; R' Ruben ben Szymon (5552-5553) 1791-1793; R' Aszer Anszel son of the holy R' Eljakim (5551) 1791-onwards; R' Abraham ben R' Aszer (5548-5556) 1787-1796; R' Jozef ben R' Jozef Katz Grünberg (5552-) 1791/2 onwards; R' Abi Ezra ben Juda (5552-) 1791- onwards; R' Aleksander Sander ben Izak; R' Majer ben Szmuel Zeinwel (5552-5553) 1791-1793; R' Jozef ben Josue Heszel (5557-) 1796-onwards; R' Dawid ben R' Cwi Hirsch (5557-) 1796-onwards; R' Mojzesz Jakob ben Zew Wolf (5555-) 1794-onwards; R' Majer ben Juda (5558-) 1797-

onwards; Szymon Segal (5563-) 1802-onwards; R' Cwi Hirsch ben Szmuel (5564-) 1803-onwards; R' Boruch Juda ben Jozef Segal (5568-9) 1807-9; R' Jakob ben Baruch (5569) 1808-onwards; R' Jakob Isser ben Izak; R' Salomon ben Isser (5575) 1814/5; R' Menachem Mendel (5588) 1827/8; R' Mojzesz ben Juda Leb; R' Izak ben Jozef; R' Mojzesz ben R' Izak; R' Izrael ben R' Jerucham (5594) 1833/4; R' Jakob ben Arie Hilel; R' Chaim ben Elijahu Zew (5608) 1847/8; R' Jakob ben Chaim Mojzesz; R' Jakob Leb ben Dawid Cwi and R' Jakob Salomon ben Mojzesz Abraham (5611) 1850/51.

Notes:

All notes in square brackets [ ] were made by the translator. [The spelling of names and titles in this chapter was partly taken from publications of the period, and partly translated phonetically.]

1.   In my book: *The History of Hebrew Printing Presses in Poland*, I demonstrated that the motivation to establish the printing houses at Kraków and Lublin, came from abroad (compare *op. cit.* pp. 1; 45

2.   About the events triggered by the appearance of the book, compare *ibid.* p. 6.

3.   Compare [Salomon] Buber: *Kirja Nisgaba* [Sublime Town - Żółkiew] p. 3.

4.   *HaMazkir* [*Hebraeische Bibliographie - Blätter für neuere und ältere Literatur des Judenthums.* ed. M. Steinschneider], Eighth year, p. 59;
Dr. Majer Bałaban: *Soncino Blätter* [Beiträge zur Kunde des jüdischen Buches], Third year, p. 18.

5.   [Gerson] Wolf: *Kleine Historische Schriften*, [Wien 1892], p. 14.

6.   [Majer] Bałaban: *Rocznik Żydowski* (1906), p.141.

7.   compare: [Bernhard] Wachstein: *Minchas Shlomo* - [*Katalog der Salo Cohn'schen Schenkungen*], p. 14.

8.   Compare: Dr. Majer Bałaban: *Soncino Blätter* [Beiträge zur Kunde des jüdischen Buches], Third year, p. 20.

9.   Compare, *ibid.* Clause 7.

10.   He was the son of R' Izrael Reiss, leader of Lwów's community (compare: Buber, *Anshei Shem* [*Men of Renown*], Section 302).

11.   He printed these words on the title pages of the books he published.

12.   Bałaban, *op. cit.* p. 19.

13.   R' Aszer Lemel Schrenzel [Szrencel] was also involved in the publishing of such books as *Eyn Jakuw*, that was published at Lwów in 1806 (5566), together with R' Eliezer Zew [Wolf] ben R' Cwi [Tzvi], nephew of the wealthy R' Jakob Koppel Batczisz, a Lwów money exchanger, R' Elimelech ben Jakob Chus, and R' Benjamin-Zew ben R' Pinkas Schwarz, son-in-law of Rabbi Abraham Abli Pineles. Moreover, in 1809 (5569), together with his two partners, he printed a new, folio edition, of *Midrash Rabbah* with interpretations.
The Schrenzel [Szrencel] Family was one of the old, Lwów families. (compare: Buber, *Anshei Shem*, Section 304.

14.   Compare: [Bernhard Friedberg] *History of Hebrew Typography in Poland*, p. 65.

15.   Compare: *Kiryat Sefer*, 17th Year, p. 96.

16.   In 1815, Aron Kohn of Lwów submitted an application for permission to establish a Hebrew printing press at Lwów. In June 1816, the Vienna central authorities consented, and granted the licence to him. He was authorised to print books of the *Talmud*. Archive of the Vienna Ministry of the Interior, IV T 7 Carton 62627, 121 ex. Juni 1816.
For some unknown reason however, he did not make use of the licence nor did he establish the printing press (Dr. G.).

17.   He abbreviated *Ruach Chen* [Spirit of Grace], an interpretation of *Chochmat Sh'lomo* [Solomon's Wisdom], by R' Naftali Hirc [Hirtz] Wiesel [Hartwig Wessely] (Lwów 1805; 5565). He also added supplements and corrections to the book [*Dovev*] *Sifteh Jeshenim* [Stimulated Drowsy Lips] by R' Szabbatai Bass (Żółkiew 1809; 5566). In (1809; 5569), he published at Lwów the book *Melechet HaMispar* [The Numbers' Craft] by Rabbi Elijah Mizrachi, with his supplements *Limudim BeDarkei S'chok HaIskoki* [Lessons in the Game of Chess].
R' Uri had a brother, Salomon, who printed a new edition of *HaFluah* [HaPliah; The Wonder] (Ketubbah) at Lwów, in 1826 (5617).

18.   Bałaban: *Soncino-Blätte*, Third year, p. 20.
Also M. Bałaban: *Z historji Żydow w Polsce*. Warszawa 1920, pp. 81-82.

19.   The Responsa *Shoel veMashiv* (Third Edition; Part 3, Section 160) [by Jozef Saul Natansohn] states: "In 1857 (5617), we sat in judgement here, Lwów... The printer, R' Pinkas Mojzesz Bałaban and his brother-in-law, R' Zusia, sued R' Abraham Jozef Madfes... printed the prayer book *Korban Minchah* [Grain Sacrifice] also in fluent foreign language, that he copied... Because they did not want to allow the previously printed Hebrew-German language, he purchased the copy, from this copier, in perpetuity." (Till here. R' Eliyahu-Moshe Ganhovsky).

20.   He studied the craft of letter-engraving, in his home town Berdyczów [Barditchev], at the printing press of his brother Israel Beck, the founder of the Hebrew press in our land. In (5600) 1839/40, he took part in a publication of the *Babylonian Talmud* at Czerniowce [Chernowitz], but after the printing of several tractates he left the partnership and settled at Lwów.

21.   The renowned, learned Moses Schulbaum was his proofreader. Moreover, R' Michał Wolf advised him on the choice of books he should print.
R' Moses Schulbaum was born at Jezierzany [Ozeryany] in 1828. He was an erudite author who published a progressive Hebrew language weekly, *HaEth* and *Kol HaEth*, in 1871/72 at Lwów. He also translated Friedrich Schiller's *Die Räuber* [The Robbers] and a few of his poems. In 1877, he published a translation of Aristotle's *Ethics*, with commentary, under the title, *Sepher HaMidoth*. His principal output, however, was the adaptation of [Judah Leib] Ben-Zew's *Otzar HaShorashim* [The Treasure of Roots], that was published at Lwów by Hirsch Schlag. In 1898, a second edition appeared. In 1904, Schulbaum published a Hebrew-German dictionary *Otzar HaMilim HaKlali* [The General Vocabulary; *Neues, vollständiges deutsch-hebräisches Handwörterbuch*], that included many renewed words. He was amongst the first to attempt to write precise and clear Hebrew, unencumbered by the declamatory style adopted by the Maskilim [Enlightened]. As a progressive, he was attacked by the Orthodox who claimed that he "laid *Tefillin* [phylacteries] on the head of a dog" and smoked on the Sabbath. He died at Vienna in 1918 (for further details about him, see: Jacob Knaani "Moses Schulbaum" in *Leshonenu* 1932/1933 (5693). Dr. G.

22.   His sister's son, R' Joseph Kohn-Zedek, helped publish the newspaper *HaMevaser* [The Messanger]. (compare: *Beit Eked Sefarim* [Bibliograpgical Lexicon] 2nd Edition Letter M. No. 390).

23.   R' Lazar [El'azar] Halevi Horowitz, head of the Vienna community's rabbinical court, states in his approval of this edition: "We have to praise and exalt these printer rabbis for their fine enterprise, blessed be they who were privileged to honour the masses with the printing of the *Talmud* in a small format, which many have yearned for… And I concede herewith to their request to set a bar to stop others from making use of their formats and templates, as the great scholarly rabbis, my predecessors, have done before me."

24.   The name and fame of the Nechles family was well known at Lwów (compare: Buber *Anshei Shem* [*Men of Renown*], sections 234, 258). R' Jakub Isaiah ben Aron Nechles was the community leader in 1743, and R' Józef-Josles ben Aron Nechles was one of the leaders of the community outside the town, in 1770.

25.   One of his grandsons is the historian in Jerusalem, Dr. Nathan Michael Gelber.

26.   The renowned veteran Zionist, Dr. Adolf Stand, member of Vienna's House of Representatives, was the son of R' Izrael Elimelech.

27.   The father of Dr. Mordechaj Ehrenpreis, who was the chief rabbi of Sweden. R' Jakob Ehrenpreis married the daughter of the printer R' Abraham Nissan Süss, mentioned above. Around 1871 (5631), he started his trade in books from his home, on the street opposite the Great Synagogue in front of the well, and most of the books published by him were printed at the press of the above mentioned Karl Budweiser.

28.   Printed by Joseph Schmelke of Rzeszów [Resche] and his two partners.

29.   Was published by the partners R' Juda Leib P"B of Lwów, R' Natan Porusch of Lwów, R' Juda Leib Adler of Sambor, R' Cwi Hirsz Sakler of Chelm and with the assistance of the wealthy R' Abraham Lieber and R' Salomon Holisch Deina of a Lwów privileged family. (Compare: *Anshei Shem* by R' Samuel Buber section).

30.   Published by R' Samuel ben R' Joel Halevi Rotenberg, head of the Rabbinical court of Tartaków, with the assistance of R' Dov Berisz Halberthal and R' Abraham Babad.

31.   In 1812, Napoleon marched through Poland on the way to Russia. Like a surge of floodwater, Napoleon's armies burst onto this country's roads swamping them as they progressed, and took wherever they could lay their hands on. The country and its inhabitants were ruined and consequently, most of the printing presses closed down. Several years passed before the printers gathered the resources to redevelop their presses and restart their work.

32.   At the end of the book *Maggid Devarav LeYa'akov*, he signed his name as Catz, but in the second edition of (5556) 1795/6, he already corrected the spelling of his name, to Katz.

33.   At the end of the above mentioned book, this uneducated individual, a friend of the typesetter, signed his name "ben R' Aszir [Wealthy]," but at the end of the second edition of (5557) 1797, he corrected it and wrote "Aszer."

[Pages 553-554]

The Historians of Lwów's Jews

by Dr. N. M. Gelber

Translated by Myra Yael Ecker

Edited by Karen Leon

The earliest information about the history of Lwów's Jews, was presented by the Polish writer [Dyonizy] Zubrzycki, in his book *Kronika miasta Lwowa* [The Chronicles of Lwów],[1] where a large number of details appeared about the private life of Jews, especially about their struggle with the municipality. Zubrzycki relied on records held at the municipal offices in his day. The "Accounts" of the priests [Ignacy] Chodyniecki,[2] and [Tomasz] Józefewicz,[3] dedicate sections to the history of Lwów's Jews. The Polish poet, Józef Bartłomiej Zimorowic, depicted details in his letters about Lwów's Jews, written in an anti-Jewish vein.[4]

The first Jew to concentrate his activity on assembling the historical records of Lwów's Jews, was Gabryel Suchystaw [Gawril Suchestow]. He reproduced the tombstone inscriptions from the cemetery, and made also use of the notebook [*pinkas*] of the synagogue outside the town. He also collected and printed the legends and tales about Lwów's personalities and dignitaries. Later on, Rabbi Dr. Jecheskiel Caro attempted to present us with a brief history of Lwów's Jews. At the same time, the eminent scholar, Salomon Buber, published his work *Anshei Shem* [*Men of Renown*], which includes biographical data on Lwów's Rabbis and community-elders. In addition, Chaim Natan Dembitzer published the first part of *Sefer Kelilat Yofi* about Lwów's Rabbis.

The first person to write the history of Lwów's Jewry from an historical-scientific aspect, was Dr. Majer Bałaban.

The following are biographical summaries of the authors who depicted the history of Lwów's Jewry:

I. Gabryel Suchystaw [Gawril Suchestow]

Born at Lwów, Gabryel Suchystaw [or Gawril Suchestow] was the son of Rabbi Hirc [Hirtz Suchystaw, known as the *Black Maggid*] the rabbi of the community outside the town. In his youth he studied Torah under great scholars, and became a prodigy. Despite his profound knowledge he was unable to earn a living. He taught, and later became a preacher and a *Maggid* [religious, itinerant preacher] at the synagogue on Boimów Street. Every Saturday, his supporters assembled there to hear his biblical exegesis. He spoke at length and presented references from our sages of blessed memory, from *Midrashim* [interpretations] and from scholars' sayings. On weekdays he visited his followers to collect alms for his livelihood. He remained a pauper his entire life and failed to find employment that suited his personality. To his misfortune, he broke his arm and it had to be amputated.

His narration was filled with vivid imagination and rich vernacular language, however, his learning consisted only of Judaic religious studies. He did not know other languages and he did not have a secular education. However, he was always drawn to historical research. He visited cemeteries and reproduced the inscriptions found on the tombstones. He was drawn to the ancient stones and the inscriptions, and to the legends told about the personalities buried there.

The printing cost of his research was funded by Mendel Schütz, a wealthy hospital administrator, who helped Suchystaw publish the reproductions of the tombstone epitaphs. The first printed booklet, *Maceweth Kodesz* [Mazewet Kodesch; Matzevet Kodesh; Holy Memorial] - a memorial to the *Tzadikim*, appeared in 1860. It was "a book of remembrance to all the great scholars and holy men who are on the Lord's duty at this ancient cemetery in the town of Lwów. The tombstones' epitaphs and comments shed light on their lives. Also, the history of the great scholar, light of the diaspora, our Rabbi *Chacham* Cwi [Sage Tzvi], may his memory live on. (by the printing press of D. H. Schrenzel [Szrencel])."

Booklet I, included 62 tombstones from (5338) 1577 until (5398) 1638, together with the history of the great scholar, *Chacham* Cwi, reproduced from the book *Eidut Ya'akov* [Jacob's Testimony]. The prayer, "*El Maleh Rachamim* [God full of Mercy], for the souls of the Rabbis Chanoch and Jozue Reizes [Reices]," from the notebook of the small Synagogue, was also included.

One-hundred-twenty-two epitaphs were reproduced from the tombstones dating from (5340) 1580 until (5479) 1719, in the second booklet which was published in 1862 (printing press of L. Madfes). The *Maskil* [Enlightened] author, Mendel Mohr, wrote an introduction to Booklet II, in which he expressed "Praise and Glory to the precious book *Maceweth Kodesz*, a memorial to the righteous."

[Pages 555-556]

R' Joseph Kohn-Zedek, one of the Galicia's leading *Maskilim* and Hebrew language news press writers in those days, wrote a poetic introduction on the importance of Suchystaw's endeavour.

This booklet also included *Shir Geula* [Song of Redemption] by R' Izak Halevi, together with "A Pleasant Interpretation and A Dreadful Event which occurred at Prague in (5374) 1613/4."

Suchystaw offered a new booklet in 1864, published by the Lwów printers Kugel and Lewin, which included 57 headstones of rabbis from the period (5320) 1560 – (5477) 1717. This booklet also included the prayer *El Maleh Rachamim* from the notebook of the Great Synagogue within the town, for the holy people murdered outside the town on 3rd May 1664 (5424), and inside the town, from 3rd May until 13th June 1664.

His third booklet was published in 1865, by Kugel and Lewin. It contained an introduction by Mendel Mohr and Dawid Rappoport, supplemented with an article by Gabriel Falk on the character of Amsterdam's *Beit-Chaim* [cemetery], and *Imrei Noam* [Pleasant Sayings] by the renowned Lwów scholar, Jacob [Isak] Jütes.

In 1869, Lwów's Poremba press printed a new booklet, 352 pages long, that contained new tombstone inscriptions as well as those presented in the earlier booklets. Suchystaw's booklets also included a variety of tales and legends, reproductions of writings from the Rabbis' responsa notebooks, and rabbinical articles such as articles by R' Jozue Falk on Interest Law, etc. Suchystaw's books were confusing, unstructured and poorly organised. Suchystaw died in poverty, at Lwów, at the age of seventy.

II. R' Chaim Natan, ben Jekutiel Salman, Dembitzer (1821-1893)

R' Chaim Natan was born at Kraków, where he served as *Dayan* [rabbinical judge] from 1856. He was influenced by the writings of R' Cwi [Tzvi] Hirsch Chajes [Chajut] and R' Salomon Jehudah Rappoport [*Shir*], and he dedicated his work to researching Jewish history.

His book *Kelilat Yofi*, which provided a history of Poland's rabbis, was considered to be an important work. Part I of the book (Kraków, 1888), was dedicated to the history of Lwów's rabbis from the origin of the community until the present.[5]

This book, which forms the basis for Lwów's rabbinic history, also contains comprehensive historical material about the community's inner life. The book is based on primary sources from the rabbinical literature and the communities' notebooks. Even in its great meticulousness, the book lacks a true scientific and historical method of research. A major drawback of his book lies in the confused mass of quotes and facts that are difficult for the reader to wade through.

II [III]. Salomon Buber (1827-1906)

Salomon Buber's investigations were largely influenced by R' Nachman Krochmal and R' Salomon Jehudah Rappoport, as well as by critical publications of manuscripts and prints. His book *Anshei Shem* (Kraków, 5655; 1894/5), published in a lexicographical fashion, was based on surviving community notebooks, biographical data on 564 scholars, rabbis, heads of Yeshivah and Lwów's community-elders. At the end of his bibliographical book he also entered several reproductions from the notebook. His prime source was Suchystaw's book.

Salomon Buber's book does not constitute a history of Lwów's community.

IV. Dr. Jecheskiel Caro (1844-1915)

Dr. Jecheskiel Caro was the son of Rabbi Józef Chaim (1800-1895), the Rabbi of Włocławek [Leslau], and brother of the renowned historian Prof. Dr. Jacob Caro (1835-1904). In 1891, he was appointed preacher at Lwów's *Temple* of the Enlightened. His teacher, the historian Prof. Dr. Tzvi [Hirsch; Heinrich] Graetz, demanded that his students research the history of the communities in which they served as rabbis and preachers. Dr. Caro, who had already published the history of the Jewish communities of Erfurt before arriving at Lwów, decided to dedicate his time researching the history of Lwów's Jews, based on the information in Lwów's archives.

Dr. Caro, made use of the publications by Suchystaw and the recordings of Salomon Buber, and was the first [Jewish] researcher who also studied Polish sources and data from Lwów's municipal archives, under the directorship of the Polish historian Dr. Aleksander Czołowski.

The first part of Dr. Caro's book[6] describes the history of Lwów's Jews until 1772. It is largely comprised of German translations of entire sections about Jews, from the *Chronicles* of Zubrzycki, Józefewicz and Zimorowic. Part II, which focuses on the cultural life, relied on Suchystaw's book, but unlike the original text, Caro arranged the content chronologically, including the lineage of the rabbis, scholars and community-elders. However, Caro's book still lacks historical research, and does not provide the actual process of development of Lwów's Jewish community during the early reign of Poland. Despite the many shortcomings of

[Pages 557-558]

Dr. Caro's book, it is the first history book about Lwów's Jews, on which later historians greatly relied.

V. Prof. Dr. Majer Samuel Bałaban (1877-1941)

Professor Bałaban was the first historian to research the history of Lwów's Jews, using modern historiographical methods. He was not self-taught, but had acquired the scientific method of historical research at university.

As a student of the renowned Polish historian, Prof. Dr. Ludwik Finkel, he had the opportunity to systematically hone his research method.

Dr. Majer Samuel Bałaban

Dr. Bałaban, was engaged in the field of Jewish historiography for over 45 years. He was one of its main founders and exponents. In addition to his proficiency as a scientific researcher, he was a significant personality in the Jewish life of Galicia, and later of the whole of Poland. He charmed his friends and acquaintances with his good company, interesting talk, and pleasant personality.

He was also one of the few researchers of Jewish history who succeeded in establishing a particular system of historical research. He had many students who carried on his work and taught Jewish children in Polish schools, about the history of our People. This was accomplished from novel, historiographical perspective and not as a dry "religious study."

Dr. Majer Samuel Bałaban was a great-grandson, and grandson of a well known Lwów family whose members were community-elders, and leaders, as far back as the 17th century. One of them, Lewko Bałaban, from the middle of the 18th century, did much for Lwów's communities, and was known for his fair judgement. His son, Zusman (Zyskind), led the community for years. He was active in the fight of the Objectors against the Chassidim. He detested the Chassidism and led his family on an anti-Chassidic route. His grandfather, Majer Bałaban, supported Rabbi Jakob Ornstein in his fight against Chassidism.

Prof. Bałaban was born in 1877 and received a traditional, Jewish education at his parents' home. He attended secular schools, and studied Torah in the afternoons with Torah teachers. He began to study law at Lwów University in 1895. Due to his father's financial situation, however, he was obliged to abandon his studies and turn to teaching to earn his living.

He started a life of wandering from job to job. He began as a teacher at the first elementary school established by Baron Hirsch in Gliniany [Hlyniany], one of Galicia's towns known for its Zionist-national organisation and way of life. Later, he continued at Gołogóry [Holohory], a remote small town in eastern Galicia. During all his hardships he never gave up his plans to pursue historiographical research. Immersing himself in it, he realised that his mission was to dedicate himself to historical research. In 1900, after extraordinary tribulations he was transferred to Lwów's primary school named after Tadeusz Czacki, that was in the Jewish Quarter.

A couple of years later he returned to university, but not to the study of law, despite his father's desire to see him as renowned advocate. Instead, he immersed himself in the study of philosophy, and especially of history, and began working in his field of research while he was still a university student.

In 1903, he published the first bibliography written in Polish on the history of the Jews in Poland. He earned the degree of Doctor of Philosophy in 1904, became qualified as a teacher, and was appointed as instructor of history and geography at *gymnasium*s. After a short time, he was obliged to teach the "Jewish Religion," because it was deemed unacceptable for a Jew to teach History, at *gymnasium* level. The Vienna Ministry of Education considered history to be fundamental to patriotic education, and could not, in its opinion, be entrusted to a Jew.

Bałaban's difficult economic conditions left him no other option but to accept the post of "Teacher of Religion," even though he had already been awarded two premium scientific prizes: [Hipolit] Wawelberg Prize by the University of Lwów, and [Probus] Barczewski by the

[Pages 559-560]

Polish Academy [of Fine Arts] in Kraków, with the recommendation of the leading Polish historian, and Galicia's governor, Prof. Dr. Michał Bobrzyński. The prizes made no difference in Bałaban's status. He was a proud Jew and had to manage with the post of "Teacher of Religion."

From time to time Bałaban travelled abroad for his research, to Berlin, Breslaw [Wrocław], Vienna etc. He spent the First World War, as a refugee in Vienna, and in 1915, he was appointed a military rabbi to the Austrian armed forces. He served in 1915-1918, during the Austrian occupation of Lublin, and did his best to improve the situation of the Jews.

After the war, he settled at Częstochowa [Tschenstochau] where he managed the Jewish *gymnasium*, and one and a half years later he moved to Warsaw. Ten years after that he directed the *Tachkemoni* rabbinical seminary, and the *Ascola gymnasium*. In 1928, he was appointed lecturer of the History of the Jews at Warsaw University, and in 1929, lecturer at the Free [Polish] University (Wolna Wszechnica Polska). In 1936, he was appointed full-time Professor. In 1928, together with Prof. Dr. Mojżész Schorr, and Dr. Markus Braude, he established The Institute of Judaic Sciences [Instytut Nauk Judaistycznych w Warszawie], that during the years 1928-1939 occupied a very important role in the cultural life of Poland's Jewery.

Bałaban's historical undertakings were derived from his Zionist-national conviction. Beginning in the 1820s, the Zionist movement took root amongst secularly educated youth and attracted a large number of supporters, whom it encouraged to cultivate the Jewish culture. Young men from the Torah-study school gave up the world of the *Halachah* [Jewish law], and put their faith in secular education at the universities of Vienna and Berlin. Zionist movement facilitated the return to Judaism amongst the youth. Students studied Hebrew in secret circles, along with the history and culture of the Jewish people. Apart from the interest in a Jewish national organisation, the romanticism of the Zionist movement also encouraged the Jewish youth to delve deeper into the sources of Judaism and its history.

Galicia's Jewry, a fount of great Judaic scholars, including Rabbi Nachman Krochmal [RaNaK], Salomon Jehudah Rappoport [*Shir*], Salomon Buber, Salomon Rubin, Abraham Krochmal, Tzvi Hirsch Chajes, Dr. Moses Ehrenreich, Jozue Heszel Schorr, author of *Hechaluc* [HeChalutz], Faybus Mieses, Dr. Józef Kobak and others, fell silent for several years. With the waning of the *Haskalah* [Enlightenment], it could no longer offer the youth a suitable fresh life-plan in this period. Although

Galician [Jewish] Enlightenment stayed clear of the spiritual assimilation noted in Germany, it was unable to halt the cultural assimilation that took hold of Galicia's youth.

Then, in the 'eighties, the national Zionist movement appeared, imbued with many elements of the *Haskalah*, especially with the teaching of Rabbi Nachman Krochmal, which refreshed the [Jewish] cultural life, rescued the youth from the clutches of assimilation and invested in it a positive life-purpose and faith in its People's future. It played a vital role in the revival of Jewish science in Galicia. It was this period that also influenced Bałaban, who joined the earliest circle of Lwów's Zionist Students, under the spiritual leadership of Dr. Mordechaj [Markus] Ehrenpreis, Dr. [Jozue] Ozjasz Thon and their associates.

Dr. Bałaban's literary work began with journalism. In *Przyszłość* [Future], the first Zionist Weekly of Galicia, he wrote articles about the problem of Jewish life, under the fictitious name *Emet* [Truth]. The Weekly's editor, Adolf Stand, one of the first Zionist leaders in Galicia, relates in one of his letters the literary beginnings of Bałaban: "It was in 1897, in the good old days. A young student worked for us, naturally not proofreading the *Przyszłość*. Once he approached me embarrassed, blushing, and handed me an envelope containing a manuscript. I corrected it and informed its author that in a few days he would proofread his article. That must have been the happiest day of his life. After this article he wrote other articles. I realised that the young man was less suited to journalism that to history. And so I steered him in that direction. The man is the author of comprehensive books on the history of the Jews of Lwów and of Kraków. And were he not a Jew, he would certainly have been a full-time professor by now, at one of the Polish universities."

Bałaban published his first research on the history of Lwów's Jews in *Rocznik Żydowski* [Jewish Yearbook] edited by Stand, in 1902-1906. Incidentally, he inherited the "desire to tell stories" from his father, Zusman, who was a renowned Lwów "Objector," and left his vividly written memoirs in manuscript form, which Bałaban intended to publish.

Before delving into the history of Poland's Jewry, Bałaban tried his hand at the history of the Jews in the days of the Second *Temple*, and presented his findings in articles on Josephus Flavius and the Hasmoneans. Bałaban abandoned that field of investigation once he started his archaeological research. He and Mojżesz Schorr were the first to make use of the significant treasures found at the Bernardine Archives [at the Bernardine Monastery, Sorbona Sq.], and at the municipal archives, in

[Pages 561-562]

search for the Jews' history. Most of the monographs on the history of Poland's Jewry published earlier than theirs, such as those by Samuel Joseph Fuenn (*Kiriya Ne'emana*, Wilno [Vilna; Vilnius]), Arieh Löb Feinstein (*Ir Tehilah Brisk-Delita*), Szymon Eliezer Friedenstein (*Ir Giborim*, Grodno [Hrodna]), Salomon Buber (*Kiriya Nisgavah*, Żółkiew; *Anshei Shem*, Lwów), Jechiel Matityahu Zunz (*Ir HaTzedek*, Kraków), Chaim Natan Dembitzer (*Kelilat Yofi*), were based on informations from Jewish sources. They rarely used non-Jewish documents. Consequently, the historical depiction of the Jewish past, lacked definition, due to its one-sided aspect.

Mojżész Schorr, is notable for conducting researches

Dr. Mojżész Schorr

in the Polish archives, and thus expanding the historical framework. But Schorr abandoned historiography, and dedicated himself to Oriental Studies. Bałaban, who continued Schorr's undertaking, established the research into the history of Poland's Jewry.

His early writings: *Żydzi lwowscy na przełomie XVI i XVII wieku* [Lwów's Jews at the turn of the 16th and the 17th centuries] (in Polish), for which he received the Wawelberg and the Barczewski prizes; "Herz Hombergi szkoły Józefińskie dla Żydów w Galicyi: (1787-1806)" ["Herz Homberg and the Josephine Schools in Galicia (1787-1806)"] (in Polish, Lwów 1906); *Dzieinica żydowska we Lwowie* [Lwów's Jewish Quarter] (in Polish, Lwów 1906), already demonstrated his fundamental lines of scientific enquiry that was quite different from the methods of the earlier mentioned Jewish historians, who considered that the history of the Jews was that of the rabbis, the *Dayanim* [rabbinical judges] the *Mohels*, cantors etc. Bałaban's method also differed from another type of historians, who applied an apologia or an aspiration for assimilation, to the history of Poland's Jews. This type of historians, such as Hilary Nussbaum, Aleksander Kraushar and Dr. Ludwig Gumplowicz, also failed to provide a true depiction of the Jewish past, in Poland.

Bałaban, pursued entirely different avenues. His primary ambition was to provide an investigative research of the Jews' history in a specific town. In his opinion, it is impossible to write a synthetic history of Poland's Jews, without having detailed knowledge of their lives, throughout the country and from every aspect.

The historian's mission is to delve into all aspects of life comprehend the fundamentals and nuances, in order to provide a full view. It is possible that at times Bałaban provided too many details in his research, but his aim was to assemble these details in order to weave the canvas required for his painting. This he did with endless devotion and artistry. The writing of history was always poised between science and art, and the debate whether historiography is a science, is yet to be resolved. Bałaban's particular historical narration was the key to his greatness. His work was based on actual documents without embellishments or concealment. His creative talent highlighted the past in all the aspects of life. The individuals mentioned in his accounts are no heroes, but human-beings who just stepped out of the crowd and remained part of it. In Bałaban's opinion, it was the Jewish People, their origins, customs and manners but above all the pinnacle, their spiritual culture, that were the deciding factors in history's power-struggles. This clarifies why in his classic monographs on the history of the Jews of Lwów, Kraków and Lublin,

Bałaban wrote lengthy descriptions of the lives of common people, their pleasures [*simches*], weddings, pain, hardships and even conflicts that appeared at times unfair and quite rough.

With the flair of an artist-author, Bałaban depicts the conflicts and intrigues between the community masses and its elders, and even amongst the community-leaders themselves, in all their unsightliness and sordidness which set his concept apart from those of the apologists, who wished only to portray the attractive facet of the Jews. Bałaban did no flinch from recounting the plunder and theft by the elders of the Holy Communities, and by the elders of the Council of Four Lands, who ruthlessly deprived the Jewish people of their rights and who looted as much as they could.

Bałaban's descriptions of the informers are noteworthy. There was Szlome Rabinowicz, part of the privileged Jekeles family from Kraków. There was Feibisch Abrahamowicz, Kraków's community leader at the end of the 18th century, who took part in the theft and embezzlement perpetrated by the community's tax-lessees. His partner, Herschel Stobnicki, organised an entire gang in 1780-1792, that did not recoil from committing

[Pages 563-564]

detestable deeds. There was the heinous act by Zalman Wolfowicz, Drohobycz's community leader, about whom a Ukrainian folksong was written. Bałaban knew how to engage the reader by skilfully describing the hardships, trembling and horror of the masses. He did so irrespective of the opinions of his detractors, historians and apologists, who were very careful not to divulge any evil events amongst our people, to the Gentiles. To Bałaban's great credit, he did present Jewish history as a separate entity, but introduced it within the framework of general history. He strove to unravel all causal connections between the outside world and the Jews, and he examined how, and how far, the general events affected the lives of Jews.

In his monographs on Lwów, Lublin and Kraków, Bałaban created a model of historical monograph, *par excellence*, both in the precision of the archaeological research, and in the organisation and process. His books occupy a prime position in Jewish historiography, where they will remain as eternal memorial stones. Not satisfied with regional or local research alone, Bałaban also delved into the problems of communal governance among Poland's Jewry, and into the history of the spiritual-psychological factors. His study on the Sabbateans in Poland, that formed the introduction to his book *History of Jewish Mysticism in Poland* (which was left in manuscript form, and was lost); his book in Hebrew, *LeToldot HaTnua HaFrankit* [The History of the Frankist Movement]; and his short but invaluable research written in German: *Studien und Quellen zur Geschichte der frankistischen Bewegung in Polen* [Studies and Sources on the History of the Frankist Movement in Poland], based on new archival sources and unknown manuscripts, show Sabbateanism and Frankism in Poland, in an entirely new light and reveal unknown, general facts instrumental in the formation of these movements and in their conceptual foundations. His studies of the management and governance of the community were important. He published his research into the community's legislation in 16th- and 17th-century Poland in *Jewrejskaja Starina* [Jewish Antiquity magazine], as early as 1910-1911.

In 1913, Bałaban published "Die Krakauer Judengemeinde-Ordnung von 1595 und ihre Nachträge" [*Jahrbuch der Jüdisch-literarischen Gesellschaft*; The Kraków Jewish Community's Regulation of 1595, with its Amendments], which contained his research about the autonomous Jewish institutions in Poland. He studied the community, the Jewish *Sejm*, and the Council of Four Lands (published in Russian, in *Istorja jewrejskog Naroda* [History of the Jewish People], Vol. XI, St. Petersburg 1914), and published his small book *Polish Jewry's governance Problems*, provide focused description of these genetic developments.

Much of his scientific work concernec the history of the cultural life and its leaders, such as R' Samson Wertheimer, Jakób Pollak, Jozue-Jonas Teomim-Frenkel, histories of physicians, pharmacists, printers and pioneers of the *Haskalah*. His investigations uncovered new material on the history of blood libel in Poland. He unveiled the mysterious world of the Jewish ghetto in Poland, in a sequence of studies. Beyond collecting and processing material, Bałaban largely occupied himself with the questions of historiographical-investigation. An example was his study into conceptual conclusions, which he derived from sources and facts, to resolve the historical question "When and whence did the Jews arrive in Poland" ["*Kiedy i skąd przybyli Żydzi do Polski*"] (in Polish; Warsaw 1931). Another was the lecture on the evolution of the "Cultural Elements from the river Rhine to the Vistula-Dnieper" ["*Elementach kul–turalnych od Renu po Wisłę i Dniepr*"] which he delivered at the [7th] International Congress of Historical Sciences in Warsaw, in 1933. He also gave significant lectures at the Fifth Congress of Polish Historians in Warsaw [28.11-4.12] 1930, on the "Tasks and Requirements of the Historiography of the Jews in Poland [*Zadania i potrzeby historjografji Żydów w Polsce*]." In these lectures, he specifically stressed the national character of Poland's Jewry, which required its own historiography rather than being included in the general Polish historiography, because the concept of national priority constitutes the driving force of historical reality.

In his research "Questions about Jewish historiography in relation to the history of the Jews in Poland," he touched upon issues which had troubled Jewish historiography as far back as Rabbi Nachman Krochmal and [Isaak Markus] Jost: How to determine the typical periods of our People's history, and, to what extent should our history reflect the historical framework of the nation amongst whom we reside at any particular time.

Dr. Markus Braude

This was not a new dilemma. Bałaban just wanted to inject his own contribution, although he was well aware that reaching a true conclusion was well-nigh impossible. The main questions, in his view, were: should Jewish history follow the generally accepted historiographical periods (Ancient Period; Middle-Ages; Modern Period), and should our history follow the dynamics of every particular period.

[Pages 565-566]

According to Bałaban, the turning point from the Ancient Period to the Middle Ages in our history did not occur in 375, which was the start of nations' migration, but rather in 135 CE, the year of Bar Kochba's revolt, the last attempt to liberate the Jewish State. Consequently, the turn from the Middle Ages to the Modern Period in 1492 CE is not compatible with our history either, since our Middle Ages lasted until after the French Revolution.

The conventional view holds that Bałaban was a purely local historian, but his studies lead to a different conclusion.

There is no field in the history of Poland's Jewry which was not advanced by Bałaban in some way. He presented a quantity of new material on the history of Jewish art and crafts in his extensive and comprehensive study of "The historical remains of Poland's Jewry," and rich material on blood libel, in his legally and psychologically important article on "Hugo Grotius und die Ritualmordprozesse in Lublin 1636 [Hugo Grotius and the blood libel trials in Lublin 1636]" (in *Festschrift zu Simon Dubnows siebzigstem Geburtstag*, Berlin 1930). He extensively researched the history of Galicia's Jews, a topic on which he published several articles, including the book *Historja Zydów Galicji i Rzpltej Krakówskiej (1772-1868)*, Lwów 1912 (History of the Jews in Galicia and in the Kraków republic 1772-1868, Lwów 1912). His last book *Historja Lwowskiej synagogi Postępowej*, [History of Lwów's synagogue of the progressives], contains a great deal of information on the history of the cultural life of Galicia, and particularly of Lwów, at the end of the 19th and the beginning of the 20th century.

Bałaban started his work in the field of bibliography, and his final work was also in this field. He gathered all the material over many years, and hoped to publish it as an extensive bibliographical sequence, arranged in 25 sections, that followed a new system. His students also assisted him in this work. The first volume was published which introduced the sections list. The fate of the manuscript that was not yet published, is unknown.

He told me that he had four monographs: i) The history of blood libel trials in Poland; ii) History of the Council of Four Lands; iii) History of the Jews in Poznań; iv) A volume of historical investigations, that included his articles about "Lwów's Jewish Street," all of which had been published in *Chwila* [Zionist daily], and made a great impression at the time. His work over 45 years amounted to 300 books, studies, articles and reviews.

It took a lot for Bałaban to attain this position in his own lifetime. From his youth on, he experienced hardships that required him to pave his own way, both materially and socially. Poverty forced him to give up this university studies and take up teaching at Baron Hirsch's primary schools, where he faced a struggle with the assimilated managers. After he eventually returned to Lwów and finished his university education, a new episode of difficulties and conflicts began.

Bałaban refused to succumb to political demands and betray his Zionist views. He never made any concessions and always stressed his Jewish heritage, despite the fact that he could have held a professorship at university if he were willing to declare his affiliation to the Polish nation.

Although he confronted many struggles throughout his life, he never lost his passion for the scientific work to which he tirelessly dedicated his time and effort.

Bałaban was also successfully involved in the field of Hebrew education. He prepared teachers to provide Jewish education in Poland for many years. His three-volumed textbook on the history of the Jewish People to the end of the 18th century, is one of the best. As an academic instructor, he was perhaps the first and only among Jewish researchers of the pre-1939 generation, who successfully established an historical system.

Over a hundred scientific works and dissertations were completed at his seminary, with all the archival references appended to each one of them. Those communities under particular study, divulging a variety of subjects on the history of the Jews in Poland between the 16th and the 19th centuries, included, Zamosz [Zamość], Tykocin, Brody, Opatów, Kołomyja, Przemyśl, Łuck [Lutsk], Sandomierz, and Lublin. This invaluable material, especially now that most of the Polish archives were destroyed, is kept today in Warsaw. Who knows, perhaps one day it will find its way to Israel.

As a creative historian, Bałaban knew how to guide his students because he understood the essence of history. Besides expanding the material and the summaries of the information in his monographs, he also outlined the morphology of Jewish history in Poland. He highlighted their problems and their roles based on European methodology, and he created a bridge between Jewish historiography and the historical science in Poland. His last works were marked by a desire to end his analytical research, process the rich material he had collected, and turn his hand to the writing of a concise and comprehensive book on the history and lives of Polish Jewry. Fate, however, decided differently.

[Pages 567-568]

The loyal historian of Poland's and Lwów's Jewry, fell victim together with his beloved brethren, to the depiction of whose histories he had dedicated his brilliant writing, his life's vigour.

The Jews of Poland and their chronicler did not part in life nor in death.

Notes:
All notes in square brackets [ ] were made by the translator.

1.   [Dyonizy Zubrzycki]: *Kronika miasta Lwowa*. Lwów 1841.

2.   [Ignacy Chodyniecki]: *Historya miasta Lwowa*. Lwów 1829.

3.   [Tomasz Józefewicz]: *Kronika miasta Lwowa [od roku] 1634 do 1690*, translated [into Polish] by M. Piwocki, Lwów 1854.

4.   [Zimorowic]: *Pisma do dziejów Lwowa [odnoszące się]* (ed. K. Heck Lwów 1899).
The Polish translation by Piwocki, was published at Lwów in 1835

5.   Part II (Kraków, 1896), includes the history of Kraków's rabbis.
In *Otzar HaSifrut* [Literature's Treasure] 1892, he published letters of criticism about the Council of Four Lands.

6.   *Geschichte der Juden in Lemberg von den ältesten Zeiten bis zur Teilung Polens 1772*. Kraków, 1897.

[Pages 569-570]

Lwów's Old Jewish Cemetery

by Rabbi Dr. David Kahana

Translated by Myra Yael Ecker

Edited by Karen Leon

The origin of the Jewish cemetery in Lwów probably goes back to the beginning of the 14th century and possibly even to the end of the 13th century. To date, it is not known if there was another Jewish cemetery, nor were traces of any other found within the boundaries of the old town and suburbs of Lwów. Presumably, therefore, from the time the Jewish community of Lwów was first established until 1855, that is to say until it closed, the old cemetery near Szpitalna Street served as cemetery for all the Jewish residents of Lwów, with its two communities: the Holy Community within the town, located in the Kraków suburb, formed Lwów's principal and the earliest Jewish community, and the Holy Community outside the town, which was established at a later date.

The cemetery is first mentioned in the municipal records of Lwów in 1414.[1]

These records mention the long established Jewish cemetery that bordered on the field that belonged to a Christian who lived near the Jewish Quarter. As Lwów's official documents first mention the Jewish Street in 1383-84,[2] and as no other cemetery existed in the town proper nor in its vicinity, one can safely assume that at the end of the 13th century there was already a Jewish cemetery in Lwów.

The perimeter of the cemetery, before the Holocaust, formed a square flanked by Rappaporta, Szpitalna, Meiselsa and Kleparowska streets. Flanking Szpitalna Street, was the hospital established by [Maurycy] Lazarus, the Jewish retirement home, and the storerooms of the Jewish burial society [Chevra Kadisha]. Beyond these buildings sprawled a thick forest, its thickets littered with thousands of grey stones, holy headstones leaning against one another with age.

The early days of the cemetery, like that of the community itself, was wretched. In time, with the development of the community within the town and outside it, and as the small communities surrounding the town had no other cemetery, it was a matter of urgency to expand the cemetery.

According to the land purchase register of the municipal archive, eminent members of the town purchased land from their Polish or Ruthenian neighbours, piece by piece, in full payment, until they acquired this plot land.

The cemetery was enclosed in part by a fence, and in part by a wall. A tent stood at the entrance gate, where memorial services were held, where eulogies for the deceased were read out, and from where the funeral processions set off. It is hard to tell whether a synagogue existed there, too, as was generally customary. The synagogue on Szpitalna Street, known as the "Cemetery *Shul*" was only constructed in the nineteenth century. At the centre of the plot, where the paths crossed, stood the Jewish *Pantheon*. Here were buried the rabbis, heads of Yeshivas and the leaders of the communities, as well as important personalities and leading rabbis from other communities who died in Lwów. This practice was followed by Lwów's Jews until the old cemetery was closed. Consequently, a concentration of headstones from different periods amassed in one place. Next to the tombstones of R' Nachman ben Izak and his wife Rózà (*die goldene Rojze* [the Golden Rose]), of Mordechaj [Marek] ben Izak, of the community-elders from the seventeenth century, are found tombstones of community-elders from the nineteenth century. Next to the tombstone of Rabbi Jozue Falk from the seventeenth century, is interred Rabbi Chaim Kohn Rappoport of the eighteenth. The tomb of Rabbi Jakób Ornstein from the nineteenth century is next to the tomb of Rabbi Abraham Kohn. Adjacent to this group are the graves of the holy Reizes [Reices] brothers, who were martyred in 1728. The place was over crowded. In time, the cemetery was practically in the middle of the town.

It is believed that the dead of the Karaite community, which left Lwów in the fifteenth century to establish new communities in eastern Galicia, in Halicz, Dawidów [Dawydiw] and Kukizów [Krasny Ostrow], are also buried in this cemetery. Lwów's elders referred to a narrow strip near the wall which bordered Szpitalna Street, as the burial area of the Karaite sect. Although there were no graves in the area, it was full of broken stones and smashed headstones. I heard the same assumption from Dr. Ananiasz Zajaczkowski, professor at

[Pages 571-572]

Warsaw University, head of Poland's Karaite sect after WWII.

The cemetery was full of trees and bushes, and from afar it looked like a grove. The trees were planted in the sixteenth century. It wasn't until the seventeenth century that their branches and leaves shaded the tombstones and paths, so that the priests [*Kohanim*] were forbidden from entering the grove for fear of entering a "tent of impurity." The debate on this issue between Rabbi Jakób Koppel ben R' Aszer Kohn, head of the Rabbinical court, and head of the Yeshivah outside the town (1620-1630), and the great rabbis of his day, is interesting.[3]

As mentioned earlier, the topography indicates that the cemetery was almost at the centre of town, and it was surrounded by houses and gardens that belonged to Christians. Prof. Majer Bałaban, of blessed memory, found after extensive search, that in 1588, 63 Christian houses and courtyards surrounded the Jewish cemetery.

The question is, how did the Jewish funerals arrive at the cemetery through the Christian neighbourhood? The issue was complicated in those days.

From all the data and assessments it is possible to deduce that the funerals arriving from any direction had to pass through two danger spots: via the Dominicans-Square (*Plac Dominikański*), and via the Kraków-Gate (*Brama Krakówska*). At times, the funerals met with processions of the clergy, near the Dominicans-Square, while at the Kraków-Gate (at the crossroad of Krakówska and Skarbkowska Streets), a riotous mob and the Christian poor congregated.

I will mention two incidents as examples. On Sunday, 10 August 1631, a large, celebrating crowd blocked the way of a Jewish funeral which passed the Kraków Gate on its way to the cemetery. The mob was led by two students from the religious Metropolitan [Greek Catholic Archbishopric] school, Jan Czech and Stanisław Wiszomorski. They were joined by apprentices and craftsmen who chased the funeral procession, caught up with it near the gate, attacked the escorts, beat them up, robbed them, and destroyed the buildings inside the cemetery. The town police put an end to the outrage. They caught the two leaders while the rest ran away. The second incident took place near the Dominicans' yard, on 26 May 1636. The funeral met with a Christian procession that ended in a fight between the Christians and the Jews. According to the official complaint submitted by the Dominicans, the Jews attending the funeral pushed the priest, who held the sacrament in his hand, and the Christians drew their swords. Many Jews were injured on their heads, many ears were chopped off and many remained disabled for the rest of their lives. These two incidents, which surely were not the only ones, clearly illustrate the pain and torture the Jews suffered on their way to the cemetery to pay their last respects to their relatives.

Among the tombstones in the cemetery, it is worth mentioning,[4] in particular:

I.

1. Tombstone of Jakób Bachor

יעקב בחור לו יה כ"ב אלול ,
בכה אליל אף וחרונה
ויעקב הלך לדרכו חריף ושננא
בן חמש עשרה למד וקרא ושנה
מה"ר הרבו לו כי שם טוב קנה
א"הר"ן נשא עליו נה"י וקינה
הוי בני הודה זיוה והדרה פנה
תנצב"ה

Jakób Bachor with God 22 Elul
God cried with rage
And Jakob departed bright and witty
Fifteen years old he studied read and iterated
Often called teacher rabbi having made a name for himself
Rabbi Aron Juda Leib delivered eternal majesty and lamentation
Woe my son departed making an impression
May his Soul be Bound in the Bond of Everlasting Life

According to the Lwów folklore, the gravestone of Jakób Bachor was the most ancient in the old cemetery.

The stress on the letters ק-ה, points to the date in the sixth millennium [of the Jewish calendar], that is, 1348. The style of the gravestone indicates a measure of Biblical knowledge, which is improbable at that time. There were no Yeshivahs in Poland in the mid-14th century, and the level of Torah knowledge was very poor. Perhaps there was an additional detail or indication which Suchystaw missed, or which in time had fallen off or had been erased from the gravestone.

In contrast, the inscription on the second gravestone from the 14th century is undoubtedly faithful, that of:

2. The woman Miriam-Marisza

> Here is interred the honest hearted and modest
> M[rs] Miriam Marisza bat our teacher Rabbi Szmuel
> Who passed away on Sunday, 2nd Tamuz 5140 [6 June 1380]
> May her Soul be Bound in the Bond of Everlasting Life.

One hundred and forty of the sixth millennium, that is to say 1378. If one compares the date 1378 on Marisza bat Szmuel's tombstone, with 1414, the first mention of the Jewish cemetery near Szpitalna Street, as it appears in the official records of the municipality, one can conclude with certainty that the old cemetery of Lwów was established at the end of the 14th century.

Incidentally, the name Miriam-Marisza calls for deeper investigation. It points to the spoken language, probably affected by a Slav language, which was used by the Jews of Lwów in those days, before the migration of the Ashkenazi Jews.

[Pages 573-574]

3. Tombstones of the brothers Nachman and Mordechaj bnei R' Izak

The Nachmanite family ruled Lwów's community in the second half of the 16th- and in the beginning of the 17th-century.

The family's forebear was Izak ben Nachman, a wholesale merchant, community leader and elder, who built a synagogue at his own expense in (5342) 1582. The researchers refer to it as Nachman's synagogue, but it was popularly known as the *Synagogue named after Turei Zahaw* (*Die Turei Zahaw Schul*) or *die goldene Rojze* [the Golden Rose] Schul.

The inscription on their gravestones read as follows:

i) Tombstone of R' Nachman ben Izak

> Lamentation in memory of the here resting jar of manna, the
> splendour of time, a faithful shepherd, holy, generous and
> merciful man, the great champion, our teacher R' Nachman ben
> our teacher R' Izak, the revered local Rabbi, chief, angel, leader
> and prime speaker against kings, rulers and ministers. His mouth
> and tongue speaks noble wisdom and innocent, honest reason.
> Great in the Torah, in his standing, will raise his reputation, his
> large charitable giving from his fortune bears witness to his
> principled distribution. He is also hospitable in his house. For
> all this May his Soul be Bound in the Bond of Everlasting Life. Amen.

ii) Tombstone of R' Mordechaj ben Izak

> Here is interred the affable Rabbi, our Teacher Rabbi Mordechaj
> ben the leading Rabbi, our Teacher Rabbi Izak who turned his
> teaching into a regular law. As stuart he also dispensed his
> wealth among relatives and strangers. A champion in the Torah,
> head and leader of the community and of the Land, he faithfully
> handled the public's needs and founded Yeshivot as of old. He
> was engaged in the redemption of captives, according to custom
> and law, he donated his money to the poor in Eretz Israel. As
> stuart he regularly fasted for long periods and he also donated a
> building for the hospital and also donated the roof to enlarge the
> synagogue that he, his father and his brother had built. His
> goodness was boundless, he built a hostel for guests and donated
> a great deal of money to brides' doweries. His benevolence and
> righteousness is immeasurable. For this May his soul be Bound
> in the Bond of Everlasting Life and his spirit and soul abide

under the shadow of the Almighty. May his good deeds stand in
good stead for us and all Jews. Amen.

The version of the inscriptions on the gravestones indicates communal involvement and engagement. The attitude toward Eretz Israel needs a mention. Nachman ben Izak was termed "revered local Rabbi" and it was said of Mordechaj ben Izak that he "sent his coins to the poor in Eretz Israel." Both of them were "presidents of the Holy Land," and they transferred the donations to the appropriate destinations. As known, from the early days, the donations from the whole of Poland were sent to the town of Lwów, to the safekeeping of a faithful man who was given the title "President of Eretz Israel," who then transferred the donations to Eretz Israel.

iii) Rózà bat R' Jakób - the wife of Nachman ben Izak

She was known as *die goldene Rojze* [the Golden Rose]. She took part in the fight against the confiscation of the synagogue built by the Nachmanowicz family. She was an energetic, enterprising woman. A bouquet of legends was created around this woman.[5] The text on her tombstone reads as follows:

> Here is interred an honest, standard-bearing lady Mrs. Rózà
> bat Rabbi Jakób. Tuesday – 4 Tishrei (5395) [26 September
> 1634]. I deeply lament the grave loss of the daughter of Jakób.
> The crown fell off his head, his resourcefulness was displaced
> and the branches of the pure candelabra broke off. A more
> wonderful woman could not be found. Angels and clerics saw
> her, rose and bowed.
> May her Soul be Bound in the Bond of Everlasting Life.

The style of the gravestone inscription bears witness to the fact that Rózà, the wife of Nachman ben Izak, died a natural death in 5395 (1635), with no hint of a murder or martyrdom. The absence of the customary phrase "God will avenge her blood," lays to rest any doubt that these were founded on fiction.

The love and admiration of the masses created these myths about her. It is possible, and according to Dr. Jecheskiel Caro,[6] over time, the masses introduced the name Rózà in place of another woman who was actually martyred, Adel of Drohobych.

And this is the wording of her tombstone:

iv) Adel of Drohobych

> On Friday, 27 Elul 5470 [22 September 1710], the holy and pure
> lady, Mrs. Adel, daughter of the great head and leader our
> Teacher and Rabbi Mojzesz Kikenes, was sentenced consecrated
> and gave her soul for all the Jewish People. God will avenge her
> blood and for this May her Soul be Bound in the Bond of
> Everlasting Life.

Adel daughter of Mojzesz Kikenes was sentenced and martyred in 1710.

v) Tombstone of the holy Reices brothers

> And the entire Jewish People will mourn the fire burnt by God.
> Like a blade, the flame set out to separate the parts into pieces,
> the head and the fat for fragrant scent. The day of judgement is
> upon us on that massacre day, the eve of *Shavuot* [Festival of
> Weeks]. The evening shadow darkened our countenances in the
> year 1728 as woe betide us. The fire started and consumed the
> foundations of the sacred brothers. The Rabbi, the light the great
> scholar, our teacher Rabbi Chaim head of Yeshivah of the two
> communities, crown and jewel of Israel was brutally killed, burnt
> at the stake, and his young brother *Pneh*

[Pages 575-576]

> *Josua* observed the moon for several years, sat fasting and died
> of thirst and bitterness, our teacher, the great scholar, Rabbi
> Jozue. The sons of our teacher Izak Halevy who courageously

sacrificed their souls and were martyred for the sanctity of the special God. They both departed terribly, burnt to death in the fire, unwilling to convert. Their souls departed sacred and pure, and their ashes saved from the fire were interred here and it was collected and placed like the ashes of Izak in perpetual memory of the martyrs. For this May their Souls be Bound in the Bond of Everlasting Life.

Adel of Drohobych and the Reices brothers bear clear witness to the method of persecution of the Spanish Inquisition. The Latin Archbishop of Lwów, who headed the Inquisition's tribunal in the district of Lwów, sentenced to death Adel of Drohobych and the Reices brothers.[7]

II. Rabbis and Heads of Yeshivah

i) Avenging God, come and avenge the spilt blood of your servant, revenge of our teacher **The head of Yeshivah, light of Israel the Rabbi, the great scholar, holy and pure Menachem ben Rabbi Izak of blessed memory** who sanctified the great and awesome God and who gave his life for the Jewish community and suffered a brutal, grave death by the hands of the reckless who congregated on the holy Shabbath (8 Iyar 5424) 3rd May 1664, here at Lwów outside the town. May his Soul be Bound in the Bond of Everlasting Life, and God soon avenge his blood and may his virtue stand all the Jewish People in good stead.

ii) Woe betide that our teacher light of Israel, head of Yeshivah, the **great scholar [gaon] Eliezer ben our teacher Aszer** was taken for our sins and suffered a brutal and grave death by the reckless on the holy Shabbath (8 Iyar 5424) 3rd May 1664, here in the holy community of Lwów outside the town. For teaching Torah and raised many disciples, May his Soul be Bound in the Bond of Everlasting Life, God be his inheritance. May he rest in peace and God avenge his blood.

iii) The crown fell off our head, the pride of our generation, the great scholar our teacher light of Israel Rabbi **Simon ben Rabbi our teacher Bezalel** who suffered a brutal and grave death by the reckless, on the holy Shabbath (8 Iyar 5424) 3rd May 1664, here, outside the town of Lwów. For teaching Torah to the Jewish People, being the head of the rabbinical court and head of Yeshivah in several important, concealed communities, for this the Merciful will ensconce him under his wings for eternity and will bind his soul in the bond of Everlasting Life. God be his inheritance and soon avenge his spilt blood.

iv) Our eyes darkened as, for our sins, **our teacher head of Yeshivah, Light of Israel, the great scholar Rabbi Izak ben our teacher Rabbi Samuel** was taken from us. He sanctified the special God and was martyred for God's divinity and for our holy Torah and was killed by the accursed reckless who gathered on the Sabbath (8 Iyar 5424) 3rd May 1664, here, outside the town of Lwów. May his soul be bound in the bond of Everlasting Life, and may God soon avenge his blood.

v) Here is interred the great scholar [gaon] head of Yeshivah, may his light shine, our teacher and rabbi, Rabbi **Maszka son of our late rabbi, Rabbi Chaim**, who was martyred and forsook his soul, and underwent a harsh and difficult death on the Sabbath (8 Iyar 5424) 3rd May 1664, outside the town of Lwów. As he taught Jews the Torah, and for this may his soul be bound in the bond of Everlasting Life, and may God soon avenge his blood.

vi) Here rests the Torah pouch and our precious vessel, the holy and the pure great scholar, **our revered teacher Mordechaj ben Rabbi Salomon head of Yeshivah** who was martyred, forsaking his soul for the Almighty, he underwent a harsh and difficult death on the Sabbath (8 Iyar 5424) 3rd May 1664, in the holy community of Lwów outside the town. For this, May his soul be bound in the bond of Everlasting Life, and may God soon avenge his blood. Amen.

vii) Woe to us for our loss of our precious, beautiful and glorious agent. Avenging God, avenge the blood of your servant, the soul of our teacher and rabbi, the great scholar, **our teacher, Rabbi Aron Jechiel son of our teacher, Rabbi Jozef the blessed head of Yeshivah and excellent *Dayan*** [religious judge] who passes honest judgements, young in years but a leader of wisdom who was murdered by four parts death and his blood spilt like that of a common bovine. May the ground not hide his blood. Killed by a gruesome four part death of stoning, burning, slaying and suffocation on the Sabbath (8 Iyar 5424) 3rd May 1664. For this, the Merciful will eternally shield him under his wings and preserve his memory as the ashes of Izak or others murdered for their Jewish faith. May his soul be bound in the bond of Everlasting Life.

viii) Avenging God, come and avenge the spilt blood of your servant by the good-for-nothings who in rage and anger murdered **the holy and pure great scholar, our splendour and glory, the great *Dayan* and head of Rabbinical court, our teacher Rabbi Judah Leib ben our teacher the priest Rabbi Szmuel Margulies head of the Rabbinical court in the community of Przemyślany where he wielded an exalted presidency** and taught the Jewish community Torah, which he also avidly studied day and night. But alas, he who delved into the Torah was penalised with a harsh and frightful death and for this, the Merciful will protect him under his wings for eternity and bind his soul in the bond in everlasting life. God is his domain. May he rest in peace and God soon avenge his blood. His good deed will reflect on all the Jewish People.

ix) **Sons of Turei Zahaw** ([*Turei Zahav*]; Golden Columns) Almighty, the most esteemed, avenge the spilt blood of your servants, the soul of the beloved, affable brothers. The special one, leader of the group, the ultimate champion, our teacher and rabbi, Rabbi **Mordechaj**

[Pages 577-578]

and the second, the ultimate rabbi our pious teacher **Rabbi Slomon, sons of our teacher and rabbi the great Rabbi Dawid Halevy** who were day and night engrossed in the Torah (two lines were erased) for that avenging God soon avenge their blood. May their souls be bound in the bond of Everlasting Life

x) Gravestone of the great Scholar, Cwi [Tzvi] Hirsch Aszkenazi author of *Chacham Tzvi*.

Under a brilliant moon the splendour of the Torah was plucked, and its glory dissipated during the season of the first grapes when a bunch is insignificant. Asceticism and purity have perished, the mood was stored. Holy light, a once in a generation wonder. What of a generation that has lost its leader, commander of angels, man of God in the capital, our master, teacher and rabbi. The quintessential rabbi the renowned great scholar [*gaon*] as our Teacher Cwi Hirsch ben the quintessential Rabbi Jakób who presented the light of his teaching to the holy community of Amsterdam and that of Hamburg, and was confirmed as head of the Rabbinical court and head of Yeshivah of the holy community of Lwów and of the district. Died on the eve of the second day of Iyar (5478) [2.5.1718]

The reverse of the gravestone reads: The generation was left orphaned without a comparable in wisdom and pure God-fearing, reliable biblical teaching. His instruction was disseminated as a clear ritual law and he wrote responsa books and innovations of religious tracts and shining articles like sapphires and jewel, his divine wisdom mesmerised. A great and strict traditionalist, minister of God's army who in order to uphold the religious practice, he extricated senses and artfully commented on death. He stood at the fissure to defend the rampart of faith and fence it in. May he safely dwell in heaven and rest in peace. May his soul be bound with his God and his spirit preserved in heaven and his soul in the Bond of Everlasting Life.

III. Community Leaders

xi) Here was interred the holy and virtuous, the head and leader of the Land, our teacher and rabbi, Rabbi Szmuel ben our teacher Rabbi Juda who was sentenced to a severe death and was murdered by an accursed hand, in Lwów outside the town, on the Holy Sabbath, 8 Iyar 5424 [3rd May 1664]. May his Soul be Bound in the Bond of Everlasting Life, and God soon avenge him.

xiv) Here is interred the trusting, holy and virtuous head and leader of the Land, the rabbi, the eminent sage [*Chacham*], the overseer our teacher, Rabbi Mordechaj ben the great scholar, our teacher, Rabbi Jechiel HaKohen who was martyred for the sanctity of the special and awesome God. For this, may his Soul be Bound in the Bond of Everlasting Life, and may God soon avenge him. Amen.

xv) Here is interred the trusting, holy and virtuous eminent and dear charity collector of the new synagogue outside the town, our teacher and rabbi, Rabbi Dawid ben our teacher and rabbi, Rabbi Daniel. As he was martyred for the sanctity of the special God, and was murdered harsh deaths , in Lwów outside the town by the accursed hands of the reckless, on the Holy Sabbath, 8 Iyar 5424 [3rd May 1664]. For this may his Soul be Bound in the Bond of Everlasting Life, and God soon avenge his blood.

xvi) And Samuel who lovingly and with awe followed God and who prepared himself to face the holy sacrament and the pure candelabrum and who focused his prayer, was suddenly punished with a harsh, severe death. He was murdered during payer by the accursed hands on the Holy Sabbath, 8 Iyar 5424 [3rd May

1664]. **The quintessential Torah scholar, our teacher
and rabbi, Rabbi Samuel ben the teacher and rabbi, Rabbi
Jozef Chajes** [Chajut], he was the prayer leader outside the town,
and honoured God with his larynxes. For this, God will soon
avenge his blood and bind his Soul in the Bond of Everlasting
Life, and may he rest in peace.

IV. The Saintly

xvii) Here is interred the exalted worshipper, our learned, holy and
pure teacher and rabbi **Juda ben the great scholar** [*gaon*] **our
teacher Salomon**, of blessed memory, who was martyred and
underwent a harsh death, in Lwów outside the town, by the
accursed reckless on the Holy Sabbath, 8 Iyar 5424 [3rd May
1664]. For this, may his Soul be Bound in the Bond of
Everlasting Life together with the souls of Abraham Isaac and
Jakob and with the ten royal martyrs and God will avenge his
blood.

xviii) Avenging God, avenge the spilt blood of your worshipper, **our
teacher the great scholar and rabbi, Rabbi Nachman ben our
teacher Salomon**, of blessed memory, who was martyred and
was murdered in Lwów, by the accursed reckless, on the Holy
Sabbath, 8 Iyar 5424 [3rd May 1664]. For this may his Soul be
Bound in the Bond of Everlasting Life.

xix) Here is interred our trusting, holy and the virtuous **teacher,
Jakob**, may he rest in peace, who was martyred in Lwów, for the
sanctity of his People, on the Holy Sabbath, 8 Iyar 5424 [3rd
May 1664]. For this, may his Soul be Bound in the Bond of
Everlasting Life, and God avenge his blood.

xx) Here is interred our holy and virtuous **teacher, Majer ben our
teacher Menachem Chazan Halevy** for the harsh death and
was martyred for the sanctity of God on the Holy Sabbath, 8 Iyar
5424 [3rd May 1664]. May his Soul be Bound in the Bond of
Everlasting Life, and God avenge his blood.

[Pages 579-580]

xxi) Here is interred our holy and virtuous **teacher, Izak ben our
teacher and rabbi, Rabbi Jakob**, whose blood was spilt like the
blood of a bull, and who was murdered a harsh death, on the
Holy Sabbath, 8 Iyar 5424 [3rd May 1664]. For this may his
Soul be Bound in the Bond of Everlasting Life, and God avenge
his blood.

xxii) Here is interred our holy and virtuous **teacher and rabbi, Rabbi
Juda ben our teacher Szmuel** who was martyred, murdered in
Lwów, on the Holy Sabbath, 8 Iyar 5424 [3rd May 1664].
May his Soul be Bound in the Bond of Everlasting Life,
and God soon avenge his blood.

xxiii-xxiv) Here is gathered and interred our holy and virtuous **teacher and
rabbi, Rabbi Juda ben our teacher Szmuel** who was martyred,
harshly murdered, set on fire like wood, on the Holy Sabbath,
8 Iyar 5424 [3rd May 1664]. May his Soul be Bound in the Bond
of Everlasting Life, and may God soon avenge his blood.
Also his holy and virtuous brother, our teacher **Salomon ben our
teacher and rabbi, Rabbi Szmuel** who was martyred, murdered

on the Holy Sabbath, 8 Iyar 5424 [3rd May 1664]. May his Soul be Bound in the Bond of Everlasting Life.

xxv) Here is interred and gathered the body of our holy and virtuous teacher **Ozer ben our teacher and rabbi, Rabbi Salomon**, who was martyred and was murdered outside the town of Lwów, by the accursed reckless, on the Holy Sabbath, 8 Iyar 5424 [3rd May 1664]. For this may God avenge his blood and bind his Soul be in the Bond of Everlasting Life.

xxvi) Here is interred our holy and virtuous **teacher, Shimon ben our teacher and rabbi, Rabbi Majer**, who was martyred, murdered in Lwów by accursed hands on the Holy Sabbath, 8 Iyar 5424 [3rd May 1664]. May his Soul be Bound in the Bond of Everlasting Life, and may God soon avenge his blood.

xxvii) Here is interred our holy and virtuous **teacher and rabbi, Rabbi Mzes ben our teacher and rabbi, Rabbi Salomon** who was martyred outside the town of Lwów, murdered a harsh and severe death for the special and awesome God. For this, may God bind his Soul in the Bond of Everlasting Life and avenge him.

xxviii-xxix) Here is gathered and interred our holy and virtuous **teacher and rabbi, Rabbi Izak ben the teacher and rabbi, Rabbi Jakob**, who was martyred for the great and awesome God, who was murdered in Lwów by an accursed hand on the Sabbath, 8 Iyar 5424 [3rd May 1664]. For this reason, may his Soul be Bound in the Bond of Everlasting Life. His holy and virtuous brother, our teacher Zecharija, ben our teacher **Jakob**, who was martyred for the special God, and whose blood was spilt like the blood of a bull. For this, may his Soul be Bound in the Bond of Everlasting Life, and may God soon avenge his blood.

xxx) Here is interred our holy and virtuous **teacher Eliezer ben our teacher Avigdor**. For worshiping the great and awesome God, and being martyred on the Holy Sabbath, 8 Iyar 5424 [3rd May 1664]], may his Soul be Bound in the Bond of Everlasting Life, and God avenge him.

xxxi) Here is interred the trusting, judicious, holy and virtuous **head and leader of the Land, the quintessential *Chacham*, influential man, our teacher Mordechaj ben our teacher Jechiel HaKohen**, who was martyred for the special and awesome God. For this may his Soul be Bound in the Bond of Everlasting Life, and may God soon avenge his blood, Amen.

xxxii) Here is interred our holy and virtuous **teacher Eliezer ben our teacher and rabbi, Rabbi Abraham**. In Lwów, outside the town, he was martyred for God, murdered a harsh and severe death, on the Holy Sabbath, 8 Iyar 5424 [3rd May 1664]. For this, may his Soul be Bound in the Bond of Everlasting Life, and God avenge his blood.

xxxiii) Here is interred our holy and virtuous **teacher Baruch ben our teacher Mordechaj**, who was martyred. He was murdered outside the town of Lwów by the hands of the accursed reckless, on the Holy Sabbath, 8 Iyar 5424 [3rd May 1664]. For this, may his Soul be Bound in the Bond of Everlasting Life, and God avenge him.

xxxiv) Here is buried and gathered the body of our righteous, holy and virtuous **teacher and rabbi, Rabbi Szulem ben our teacher and rabbi, Rabbi Nissim**, who gave his soul for the sanctity of God. Full of love and fear, he was murdered by an accursed hand on the Holy Sabbath, 8 Iyar 5424 [3rd May 1664]. For this may God bind his Soul in the Bond of Everlasting Life, may he rest in peace and God avenge his blood.

xxxv) Here is buried and gathered the body of our righteous, holy and virtuous **teacher and rabbi, Rabbi Izak ben our teacher and rabbi, Jakob** who was martyred for the special and awesome God, and was murdered outside the town of Lwów, on the Holy Sabbath, 8 Iyar 5424 [3rd May 1664]. For this, may his Soul be Bound in the Bond of Everlasting Life, and may God avenge him.

xxxvi) Here is interred our trusting, holy and virtuous **teacher, Azriel ben our teacher and rabbi, Rabbi Avigdor**, who was martyred for the special God, and was murdered a harsh and severe death, by the accursed reckless, in Lwów outside the town, on the Sabbath, 8 Iyar 5424 [3rdMay 1664]. For this, may his Soul be Bound in the Bond of Everlasting Life, and may God avenge him.

xxxvii) Here is buried and gathered the body of the righteous, holy and virtuous great man, **our teacher and rabbi, Rabbi Shimon ben our late teacher and rabbi, Rabbi Majer**, who was martyred for God's sanctity, murdered, in Lwów outside the town, by the hands of the accursed reckless on 8 Iyar 5424 [3rd May 1664]. For this, may his Soul be Bound in the Bond of Everlasting Life, and may God avenge him.

xxxviii) Here is interred the holy remains of the holy and virtuous rabbi, **our teacher Eliezer ben our teacher and rabbi, Rabbi Reuben HaKohen**, who was martyred for the sanctity of the special God, and was sentenced to harsh deaths and his body set alight on the

[Pages 581-582]

Holy Sabbath, 8 Iyar 5424 [3rd May 1664]. For this the merciful will bind his Soul in the Bond of Everlasting Life, and his memory will ascend with the ashes of Isaac, and like the ten royal martyrs, may God avenge his blood like and the blood of his disciples spilt like a fragrant scent, Amen.

xxxix) Avenging God, dressed in avenging garments, avenge the spilt blood of your worshippers, spilt like water. The young and wise wait for sweets from a larger and more sprawling family. He was always very astute in his studies, displaying great proficiency, his heart as wide open as a hall entrance. He devoured the Torah like a lion and his notable leadership was like that of a seventy-years old. He mastered the Torah as no student of a hundred years or more could. Scripture says of someone like him: the sleep of the worker is sweet, if short, and the satiety of the rich is in the wealth of the Torah. By an accursed hand, here in Lwów, outside the town, on the Holy Sabbath, 8 Iyar 5424 [3rd May 1664], **our teacher and rabbi, Rabbi Dawid ben R' Izak Nachmisz** was murdered in his youth, kicked by a snake. For this, may his Soul be bound in Bond of Everlasting Life, Amen.

xl) Regard his origin, the sign marking his cave represents the cornerstone. How such excellence turned into ashes, he, who aged fifteen, wrote and read a great deal. The astute and proficient **Mr. Chaim ben our teacher and rabbi, Rabbi Baruch**, who was murdered by accursed reckless hands and by those good-for-nothings. For this, the all merciful will bind his soul in the bond of Everlasting Life, and will avenge his blood. God is his patrimony and may he rest in peace.

The Martyrs of 10-11 Iyar 5424 [5-6 May 1664]

xli) Our eyes darkened as our dear, youthful light, **our teacher, Cwi [Tzvi] Hirsch ben our teacher and rabbi, Rabbi Abraham Katz**, was snatched from us. Here, in the town of Lwów, on 10 Iyar 5424 [5-6 May 1664], the great scholar [*Gaon*], champion in the Torah and Chassidism, in sanctity and purity, in the great Jewish literature and a foremost Rabbinical judge [*Dayan*], was murdered and stabbed a severe death. For this, the all merciful will shield him under his wings, and bind his soul in the bond of Everlasting Life. God is his patrimony and will soon avenge his blood and the blood of the virtuous, may their souls be bound in the bond of Everlasting Life.

xlii) Exhausted, Abraham died prematurely and without trial. Judgement is in the hand of the avenging God. Protecting and avenging God, avenge the spilt blood of your disciples, our champions and our virtuous, the great champion in the Torah and in the fear of God, an instructor of the Torah who taught many students. **The *Dayan* and head of Yeshivah, our teacher and rabbi, Rabbi Abraham ben our teacher and rabbi, Rabbi Salomon**, the great Chassid who poured his troubles and prayers, body and soul, and his mellifluous voice as that of the Leviates in the Temple, was martyred by those good-for-nothing who together murdered and stabbed him. Martyred for the love and fear of God, and the sanctity of his great name, he was murdered in the town of Lwów on 11 Iyar 5424 [6 May 1664]. For this, may his death serve as atonement for the entire Jewish People, and God avenge his blood, and bind his soul in the bond of Everlasting Life.

The Martyrs of 13-14 Iyar 5424 [8-9 May 1664]

xliii-xliv) Protective and avenging God, dressed in avenging garb… Avenging God, avenge the spilt blood of your disciples, blood spilt like water by a group of good-for-nothing, who murdered them on 13 Iyar 5424 [8 May 1664], in their homes in their beds. The champion, pure light, proficient in the Torah, our holy, great scholar and pride, **our teacher Aron ben our teacher Lapidot** who spent all his days studying the Torah, he also taught many disciples. He was a great and excellent rabbinical judge and greatly devout, who followed God wholeheartedly and prayed **with his entire being.** He extolled the great and awesome God, and his modest and devout wife, the Holy and pure **Mrs. Reisel bat our teacher and rabbi, Rabbi Jakob of blessed memory.**

For this, God will soon avenge their blood, may their soul be
bound in the bond of Everlasting Life.

xlv-xlvi) Avenging God, avenge the spilt blood of your disciples, and the
blood of the Holy who were martyred for the sanctity of the
special and awesome God. For alas, men of the covenant were
lost, and no one blocks the fissure or protects the boundary.
These two brethren of mine among the Holy, exalted, pure the
devout, steeped in the Torah and sanctity, our teacher and rabbi
Rabbi Izak and our teacher and rabbi, Rabbi Eliezer bnei the
champion and great scholar, our teacher, Elijahu used to sit
and study Torah lessons with disciples in an orderly fashion.
They were sharp and refined, but were alas murdered severe
deaths by an accursed hand, on 14 Iyar 5424 [9 May 1664], and
God will soon avenge their blood and bind their souls in the bond
of Everlasting Life. God is their domain, and may they rest in
peace.

The Martyrs of 20 Sivan 5424 [13 June 1664]

xlvii) Lament and howl for the tree of life cut short in its short years.
Like the holy fruit of an edible tree of life, he was heavily
laden with the Torah. He exerted himself in the Torah, like a
one-hundred years old student. A harsh and difficult death was
suddenly inflicted on him. The great rabbi, the quintessential
scholar [Chacham], our teacher and rabbi, Rabbi Chaim ben
the rabbi our teacher, Rabbi Mordechaj, was murdered on 20
Sivan 5424 [13 June 1664]. God will avenge his blood and
bind his Soul in the Bond of Everlasting Life, and may he rest in peace, Amen.

xlviii) Our heart ached, our eyes darkened at God's blows of removing
off our heads our crown and splendour, the great scholar, our
teacher, Rabbi Abraham ben the champion great scholar, our
teacher, Rabbi **Josef Katz**, head of Yeshivah of the Kolomiya
community, who was removed, for our sins, and was murdered
harshly by an accursed hand. He was martyred for the sanctity of
God in his special awesomeness.

[Pages 583-584]

As he taught Torah and raised many disciples, the Merciful will
ensconce him for eternity under his wings and will soon avenge
his blood. May his soul be bound in the bond of Everlasting
Life.

The holy men, within the town, were not mentioned in the book by Gabryel Suchystaw [Gawril Suchestow], apart from the holy man Chaim ben Mordechaj, who was murdered on 20 Sivan 5424 [13 June 1664]. They were probably buried in a separate, unknown area of the cemetery.

The Decorations and Symbols

In the manner of religious art designated to serve as the memory of generations, the tombstones in Lwów's ancient cemetery are noted for their decorative wealth, their diverse ornamentation and their complex forms and clues.

On the whole, they are made of an upright stone with a semicircular or a triangular top. The prevalent stone here is the sandstone (*Sandstein*). The ornamentation of some tombstones consists largely of their epitaph. Their motives are reminiscent of ancient *Prochets* [ornamental curtains in front of the holy ark in a synagogue] with two columns on either side. Fauna and flora motifs, or symbols, primarily bedeck the semicircular or triangular portion, but appear also along the borders.

Among the symbols engraved on the tombstones of Lwów's ancient cemetery were these that were common and well-known to the Jews of Poland: Raised hands of a priest - symbol of a Kohen's grave; a washbasin, jag or musical instrument – symbol of a Levite's grave; charity box on the grave of a philanthropist; parchment covered in a goose feather - symbol of a scribe of Jewish religious texts; a lion on the grave of an "Arie, Leib"; a deer on the grave of "Hirsch [Hirsz; Cwi; Tzvi]"; candelabrum [*Menorah*] or lit candles on the grave of a modest woman; a tree that was cut down - a symbol of a young man whose life cut short; Keter-Torah [crown shaped ornament set on top of a Torah scroll] on the grave of great scholar; an open book engraved with the title of an essay - symbol of a great rabbi and an author; an open Ark with a Keter-Torah above it - symbol of a rabbi or head of Yeshivah.

Besides the aforementioned symbols, a unique heraldic motif is used in Lwów's ancient cemetery. Drawings of fish decorate the tombstones of members of the Kikenes[8] family, referred to as the descendants of the prophet Jonah. A magnificent drawing of two fish is carved into the top, semicircular or triangular portion of the tombstone.

The following are a few examples:

i) Levy ben Izak Kikenes

Angels seized the Holy Ark. The angels conquered the cliffs and off our heads was removed the crown and splendour, the great scholar, the eye of the diaspora, our teacher, Rabbi Levy ben the great scholar, our teacher, Jakób Kikenes, scion of the prophet Jonah, head of the rabbinical court and head of Yeshivah at Lwów. Woe betide us for losing a righteous man who dispensed justice and charity among the Jews, taught them the Torah and raised many disciples. Woe for this adornment which will wither in the dust. For this, may his Soul be bound in the Bond of Everlasting Life.

Died on the first day of Pesach [Passover] 5263 [11.4.1503].

An interesting tombstone, according to Suchystaw but for which unfortunately we have no other source, is an ancient tombstone, the first of an official rabbi who served as head of the rabbinical law-court, and head of Yeshiva at Lwów in 5263, that is, in 1503. According to the wording on the tombstone he taught Torah and raised many disciples. He was presumably one of the refugees who came from the west and brought with them a deep knowledge of the Talmud and laid the foundation for the teaching of the Torah in Poland. Nathan Dembitzer writes in his work *Klilat Yofi* [*Klilath Jofi*] (Part I, 5648 [1888 ; pp. 37; 38) "nor did the decorated saying conceal that even earlier than the great scholar, our teacher (Kalman of Worms), at Lwów there were already in the middle of the third hundred [Jewish calendar] a head of yeshivah and head of rabbinical law-court, such as the champion, our teacher Rabbi Levy ben the great scholar, our teacher, Jakób Kikenes of blessed memory, who was known as R' Levy the physician, who died on the first day of Pesach 5263 [11.4.1503]. The name of this rabbi was not mentioned, however, in any other place, nor was it mentioned in any verses [*P'sukimi*], unlike the great scholar, our teacher, Kalman of blessed memory, whose name was well known throughout the Jewish diaspora."

ii) Abraham ben Jechiel of Kolomiya [Kołomyja]

(Two fish at the top of the tombstone)
And Abraham returned to his place and God made a covenant with Abraham, to say, this righteous man, Abraham, who comes to my hostelry, is charity from beginning to end. Those in heaven rejoiced in his proximity and those on earth wept over his departure. He rejoiced and dispensed charity and justice, he was a great champion in the Torah. Our teacher, R' Abraham of Kolomiya ben our teacher R' Jechiel, the great *Dayan* at Lwów, who was "one of those exiled from Portugal, and of the provincial Chassidim, and a descendent of the prophet Jonah, dispensed honest sentences and taught the Torah all his life,. He studied the Torah with is Yeshivah and rose to heaven on the first day of the Tabernacles [Suckot] Holiday 5282 [16.9.1521]. For this, may his Soul be Bound in the Bond of Everlasting Life.

Abraham ben Jechiel of Kolomiya "Among the exiled from Portugal and the provincial Chasidim" also arrived in Lwów from the west. He established Yeshivot and raised the knowledge of the Talmud in Poland to a level similar to that in France during the days of the Commentators on the Talmud. He died in 5282, 1522.

iii) Jochanan Baruch ben Simcha-physician

Here a great dark terror befell us on the day when

[Pages 585-586]

the crown was removed from our heads. Our lord, great scholar [*Chacham*], our father with whom there was a covenant of the Torah and the commandments, the honour of his name, our teacher R' Jochanan Baruch de-Jonah. The specialist doctor ben Simcha, died on 14 Sivan 5429 [13.6.1669]. May his Soul be Bound in the Bond of Everlasting Life.

iv) Simcha Menachem ben Jochanan Baruch-physician

Here is interred the Rabbi the leader and the community-elder renowned in his day, the specialist doctor to many, generous to the poor and weak, charity collector and the rabbi of Jerusalem. He was the minister, our teacher, R' Simcha Menachem ben our teacher R' Jochanan Baruch *de-Jonah*. In memory of a righteous man, blessings for the afterlife. May his Soul be Bound in the Bond of Everlasting Life.

v) Eliezer ben Jochanan Baruch-physician

Our teacher, R' Eliezer ben our teacher R' Jochanan Baruch *de-Jonah*, who was a specialist physician to many. Died young, on 1 Elul 5432 [24.8.1672].

The family of physicians, Baruch and his two sons, Simcha-Menachem and Eliezer *de-Jonah*, was a well-known and distinguished family which did much for the benefit of their brethren in Poland, at the end of the seventeenth century.

They and their deeds towards their brethren were favourably mentioned by all the luminaries of the sixteenth century and others. Simcha-Menachem (Emanuel), known by the people as "Simcha Doctor," who was physician to the Sultan, and later until 1696, physician to the King of Poland, Jan Sobieski [III]. In 1689, he donated a large, attractive bronze candelabrum [*Menorah*] to the synagogue within the town named after *Turei Zahav* [Golden Columns]. It was hand-made by a Breslau [Wroclaw] artist whose name was engraved on it. [In 1942, when the accursed Nazis destroyed this synagogue, they removed the candelabrum]. Dr. Simcha-Menachem was twice president of the Council of the Four Lands in the years 1697-1702.

G[abryel] Suchystaw as well as the researcher [Rabbi Elyakim] Carmoly, in his book *HaOrvim uB'ney Yona* [The Crows and the sons of Yonah], tried to prove that all of these were descendants of the prophet Jonah. To prove this concept they put forward the fish (fish Jonah) on their tombstones, with the name Kikenes, probably derived from *Kikayon deJonah* [Kikayon of Jonah = Jonah's Castor-oil plant]. Scientifically, it is hard to seriously accept the assumption. Since in the sixteenth century most members of this family were physicians, there is reason to assume that the fish on their tombstones were an heraldic, family symbol which over time turned into a professional sign, as in the case of crows on the tombstones of the members of the Rappoport family.

I have found no appropriate answer with regard to the actual name Kikenes. I do not agree with the assumption presented by Dr. Jecheskiel Caro in his book *Geschichte der Juden in Lemberg* [History of the Jews of Lwów] p. 178, that the name Kikenes was derived from the female name Kika, in the same way as was Reizels from Reize, Chanals from Chana, and Friedelsch from Frieda. According to this, their surname should have been *Kikels* rather than *Kikenes*. In my opinion, the forebears of the Kikenes family brought their name to Poland from the East, and one needs to search its meaning in the country of their origin.

The sole source of information on the history of the old Jewish cemetery in Lwów is the book by G. Suchystaw *Macewet Kodesch*, pamphlets that appeared in Lwów in 1860, 1863, 1865, 1869, which are not based on scientific method. Unfamiliar with original, scientific investigation, Suchystaw copied the wording on the different tombstones, and combined it with anecdotes, sermons and eulogies. His book is the work of an amateur, a Lwów Jew who held dear his native town's past and the memory of the eminent personalities of his generation. Unfortunately one cannot always rely on him. He added whatever the spirit moved him. He omitted and garbled things without knowing or noticing mistakes and distortions. Despite the fact that he had no knowledge of historical research, Suchystaw's work was extensive and a very important one. [Salomon] Buber, Caro, Bałaban and Reuven Margulies have highlighted his mistakes, distortions and the defects, yet they all rely on his work. Despite all his mistakes, he offers us the only remaining source that provides information about Lwów's ancient cemetery. In the preface to his work *Anshei Shem* [*Men of Renown*], Buber declared that he dedicated all the income from this book to establish a special commission that would concentrate on copying the wording on the gravestones of the ancient cemetery. On several occasions Lwów's community committee proposed to carry out Salomon Buber's plan, even setting a special budget for the task, but it never happened. Eventually in January 1942, since the Germans had already started to destroy the cemetery, the *Judenrat* of Lwów decided to undertake the task of copying of the gravestones. A joint commission was established, made up of representatives from the department of religious affairs and from the department of cultural affairs, and it started to deal with the issue very seriously. The work continued intermittently until the well known *Grossaktion* of August 1942. In the autumn of 1942, the Germans, with their renowned thoroughness, began to destroy the cemetery. Part of the tombstones were taken to the Concentration Camp on Janowska Street, and part were taken to Kadecka Street, to the former cadets' school [K. und K. infanterie Kadettenschule in Lemberg]. In both locations, the Jewish prisoners sentenced to death paved the streets with the ancient tombstones. And ["]I am the man that hath seen affliction by the rod of his wrath["]. When I was a prisoner at the Concentration Camp on

[Pages 587-588]

Janowska Street, I was personally engaged in laying the paving of Kadecka Street with my own hands. I do not know what happened to the documents collected by the commission to copy the tombstones. No doubt they were exterminated together with the last Jews of Lwów during the liquidation of the ghetto on the 5th June 1943, and what sorrow over those who were lost and are no longer here.

Bibliography

A. Hebrew

Gabryel Suchystaw [Gawril Suchestow]: *Maceweth Kodesz* [Matzevet Kodesh], Lwów 1860-1869.
Salomon Buber: *Anshei Shem*, Kraków 1903.
Natan Dembitzer: *Klilat Yofi*, Kraków 1893, Part I.
Tzvi [Cwi] Karl: *Lwów* (Jewish Towns and Communities; Rabbi Kook Institute, Jerusalem 1946.)
Rabbi Reuven Margulies: *LeToldot Anshei Shem* [History of Anshei Shem] printed in *Sinai* Vol. 26-31; 1950-52' Jerusalem. Published by Rabbi Kook Institute.

B. Foreign Languages

Aleksander Czołowski: *Pomniki dziejowe*, Lwowa, t. III.
Aleksander Czołowski: *Najstarsza kręga miejska*, [1382-1389].
M[ajer]. Bałaban: *Żydzi lwowscy na przełomie XVI i XVII wieku*. Lwów 1906.
J[echeskiel]. Caro: *Geschichte der Juden in Lemberg*. Kraków 1894.

All notes in square brackets [ ] were made by the translator.All notes in square brackets [ ] were made by the translator.

1.   Aleksander Czołowski: *Pomniki dziejowe Lwowa [z archiwum miasta; Księga przychodów i rozchodów miasta, 1414-1426 / wyd.]* Vol. 3.
[Dyonizy] Zubrzycki: *Kronika miasta Lwowa*. [Lwów 1841.

2.   A. Czołowski: [*Pomniki dziejowe Lwowa z archiwum miasta] Najstarsza księga miejska,[1382-1389 / wyd.,* 1892].

3.   In the month of Elul [August-September] of (5380) 1620, he went to the cemetery to say private prayers, and when he got there he noted there were many trees with their branches in such close proximity as to form a kind of Tabernacle with some of them screening over the graves. As a result, priests [*Kohanim*] are forbidden to meet in the shade of these trees, as they form a tent of sin. At that very moment, the dues collectors were collecting for the blind, and when he remarked about it to them, they answered that Rabbi Jozue Falk [Kohn], author of *Sefer Meirat Enayim* who was a *Kohen* [priest], used to walk under the branches with no compunction. The issue led to a disputation which involved the author of *Ethan HaEzrachi* [Ethan the Civilian] [R' Abraham ben Izrael Jechiel Rappoport-

Schrenzel [Szrencel], and the author of *Tosafot Yom Tov* [Rabbi Saul ; Lipman Heller Wallerstein]. However, R' Jakób Koppel forbade the *Kohanim* in his community from walking under these trees, or passing along a corridor shaded by these trees, and he installed a special entrance for the priests. The result of the controversy was that the priests outside the town followed the severe interpretation of their rabbi, and the priests inside the town, ignored it.

4.   The wording on the tombstone, according to Gabryel m,,: *Maceweth Kodesz* [Mazewet Kodesch; Matzevet Kodesh], Lwów 1860, 1864, 1869.

5.   See: Dr. N. M. Gelber's article: *History of the Jews of Lwów*.

6.   Dr. J. Caro: *Geschichte der Juden in Lemberg*.

7.   See: Dr. N. M. Gelber's article: *History of the Jews of Lwów*.

8.   In the introduction to his book: *Maceweth Kodesz*, Gabryel Suchystaw introduces eleven tombstones of Lwów's renowned men from the Kikenes family.

[Pages 589-590]

IV
The Destruction and the Holocaust

The Period
of Destruction and the Holocaust

[Pages 591-592]

[Blank page]

[Pages 593-594]

Annihilation of the Jews of Lwów
During 1941-1944
by Dr. P. Friedman
Translated by Myra Yael Ecker
Edited by Karen Leon

[Pages 595-596]

[Blank page]

[Pages 597-598]

Table of Contents

[Pages 599-600]

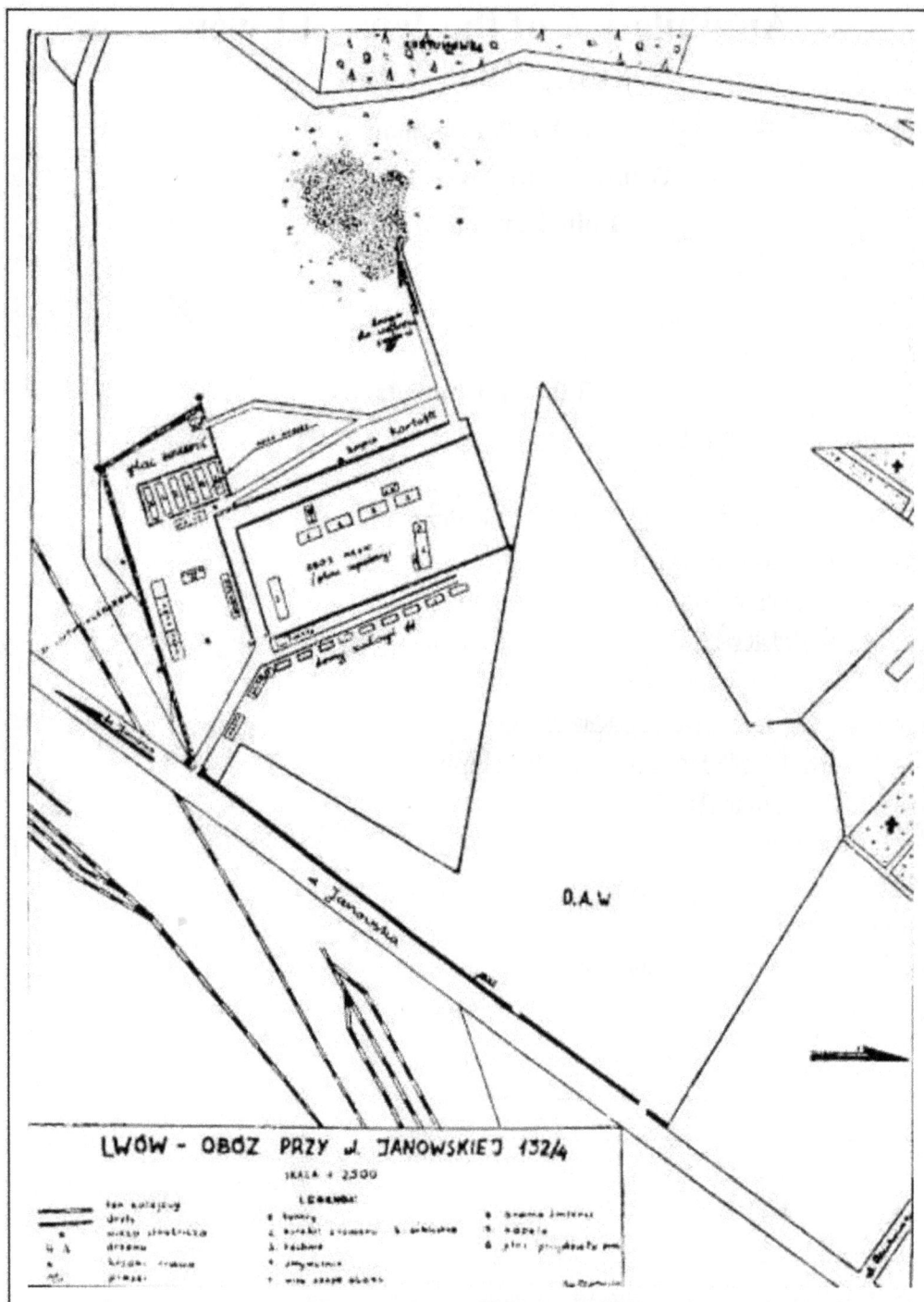

Plan of Lwów's Ghetto

[Pages 601-602]

Chapter 1. The German invasion and the *Blitzkriege*

At dawn of 22nd June 1941, the residents of Lwów awoke to the thunder of bombs that rained down onto the quiet town from German aeroplanes. The Nazi strategy of surprise worked perfectly. Because of the sudden onslaught by the Germans, the Soviet Minister of Foreign Affairs declared that very morning that war had begun between Russia and Germany.

Lwów's Jewish population numbered between 150,000 and 160,000 at the time, although the exact number is not known. The last official census was carried out on 9th December 1931, at which time 99,595 Jews were counted. From 1931 until 1939, the number of Jews increased by at least 10,000. At the start of the Polish-German war in September 1939, many Jews hastily moved from the western districts of Poland, to escape the Nazi armed forces, and many of them settled at Lwów. After the military operations in Galicia (at the end of September 1939), a new wave of migration moved from western Poland, that was in the hands of the Nazis, toward the eastern part that was under the administration of the Soviet Union. Some Jews fleeing Nazi persecution chose to illegally cross the borders between the zones occupied by the Germans and the Russians. Some were forced to cross the border when the Nazis expelled them. In any event, a very large number of Jews crossed the border during the autumn and winter months of 1939-1940. Most of the refugees who settled at Lwów were from Kraków, Lodz [Łódź], Warsaw and Kielce. At the beginning of 1940, the number of Lwów's inhabitants was more than double that of pre-war. (In addition to Jews, many Polish refugees also came to Lwów). At the time, the town's inhabitants were generally estimated to number 700,000, 180,000 of whom were Jews.

In 1941, a fear of death gripped Lwów's Jews. They agonised about the German invasion and its perils for the Jewish population. The Soviet authorities decided to remove the Russian population from Lwów, but they only managed to move a small number of officials and army recruits. Due to the sudden German attack, even the partial removal created great complications. The means of transport and transportation were not adequate for such a vast transfer that already faced disruptions by German aeroplane attacks. Consequently, the Russian authorities did not help the escape-frenzied Jews, and even obstructed the success of escapees fleeing westward on their own. At Tarnopol, Podwołoczyska and other towns along the old border between Galicia and Russia, the refugees were stopped and ordered to return to their homes. As a result, only a meagre number of Lwów's Jews managed to evade the Nazis. A few thousand youths (mostly those with connection to the left wing movements and to the Communists), specialist officials and a few thousands of the Russian army, escaped to the Soviet Union.

At the time of the German invasion of Lwów, the Jewish community committee estimated its population to be around 150,000 on 28th August 1941. According to general [Fritz, Friedrich] Katzmann, *SS Gruppenführer* of the Lwów district, the estimated number of Jews in July-August 1941, was 160,000.

The last Russian army companies left Lwów on 29th June 1941. The first German troops entered the town on the following day and were jubilantly greeted by the Ukrainian masses. The Ukrainians hoped that the Germans would help to sever the eastern Ukraine from the Soviet Union, and unite the two parts of the Ukraine into a single, independent country. When Stepan Bandera, Ukrainian's National Party leader arrived at Lwów, he called for war against the Bolsheviks and spoke venomously and hatefully against the Jews. Concurrently, the Ukrainian militia was established, and from the first moment of its existence

[Pages 603-604]

it attacked the Jews. Andrey Szeptycki [Sheptytsky], the Metropolitan (the Greek Catholic) [Ruthenian] Uniate archbishop [of Lwów], on the other hand, appealed publicly to his Ukrainian followers, warning them against bloodshed and acts of violence.

The Germans, however, did not wait for the Ukrainians to start attacking the Jews. Their destructive plan was prepared several months earlier, before the outbreak of the German-Soviet war. The plan was created and sanctioned in meetings with Hitler and his associates, and in joint consultation with agents of the SS, the Gestapo and the upper military echelons. It was decided that four "extermination companies" (*Einsatzgruppen*) were to be tasked with eliminating the Jews in all territories that would be seized from the Soviet Union. "Company C" (*Einsatzgruppe C*), led by Dr. [Emil Otto] Rasch, operated in east Galicia. Erwin Schultz, one of the company's officers, and an SS and Gestapo official, submitted under oath, at the International Court of Justice in Nürnberg/Nuremberg, the following supportive evidence regarding the actions at Lwów:

"On 23rd of July 1941 or there about, the extermination company C, made up of special companies *Sonderkommando* 4A and 4B, and extermination companies (*Einsatzgruppen*) 5 and 6, set out for Gleiwitz [Gliwice], on its way to Lwów. At the beginning of July, we reached Lwów, and here we were told that some of Lwów's residents had been killed before the Russian armies retreated from the town. Shortly after we arrived at Lwów, we were told by Dr. Rasch, the *Einsatzgruppe C* officer, that Jewish clerks, and Jewish residents were among the perpetrators of the killings. The military headquarters had already organised a local Ukrainian militia. Dr. Rasch who worked closely with the militia, ordered the *Sonderkommando*s to support it. Those who participated in, together with those suspected of the mentioned killings, were incarcerated that very day and the next. In addition to that, the special company of [Karl Eberhard] Schöngarth was also brought to Lwów from Kraków."

The meaning of this euphemistic evidence is clear: The Germans sent the extermination company C to Lwów in order to incite the residents against the Jews. They spread rumours that the bodies found at Lwów's prison, found after the departure of the Russians, had been killed by the Jews. In this way the Nazis encouraged the non-Jewish residents of Lwów to take revenge on the Jews, without exposing German supervision. Thus, in the early days, the Ukrainian militia was used to execute the Germans' evil deeds. The Germans inflamed the hatred of the masses against the Jews with inciting proclamations, flyers and oral propaganda. Pogroms and attacks against the Jews started immediately after the arrival of the German army. From 30th June until 3rd July, German soldiers circulated throughout the town, accompanied by Ukrainian nationalists and hordes of residents. They attacked Jews in the streets, beat them brutally, and dragged them to "work," especially to clean the jails that were littered with dead bodies and blood. Thousands of Jews were caught and taken to the prisons on Zamarstynowska Street, Jachowicza Street and on [Ulica Eliasza Łąckiego] Łącki Street, to *Brygidki* prison [formerly a Bridgettine convent] on Kazimierzowska Street and to the gestapo building at 59 Pełczyńska Street. The Jews feared imminent death. They hid in basements and avoided going outside. Consequently, the terrorists, especially members of the Ukrainian militia, entered Jewish homes and dragged out the men, and at times even women, for "purifying work." Most of the Jews were held in the jail yards, and they never left alive. They were murdered after severe torture or they were shot. Eye-witnesses who escaped the thugs during the days of rage, reported that the walls of the *Brygidki* jail were soaked in fresh blood and speckled with human brain, up to the second floor.

One of the eye-witnesses who escaped the slaughter in *Brygidki*, surmised that thousands of Jews were tortured to death there, and that about eighty were saved and let free.[1] Among the saints murdered in the yard of *Brygidki* prison, was Dr. Jecheskiel Lewin. This Rabbi of Lwów's synagogue of the Enlightened, and lead editor of the Jewish-Polish weekly *Opinja*, died a hero's death. When the abuse started and the first Jewish victims died, Dr. Lewin approached the Metropolitan Sheptytsky, to ask him to convince the Ukrainian masses to leave the Jews alone. And so he did. His opening words were as follows:

"I came to Your Grace, to plead on behalf of Lwów's Jewish community and on behalf of half a million Jews living in western Ukraine. You once said to me 'I am a friend of the Jewish People.' You have always stressed your sympathy for us. I beg of you during this terrible danger, to prove your friendship, to influence also the rampaging masses attacking us. I beg in order to save hundred of thousands of Jews, and the Almsighty will repay your endeavours."[2]

[Pages 605-606]

Sheptytsky probably promised Dr. Lewin that he would fulfil his request, and did indeed publish a proclamation to the Ukrainians, which did little to influence them. He also offered refuge in his Palace to Dr. Lewin until the rage had subsided, but Lewin replied: "My mission is done. I came to plead for the community and I return to the community among whom I belong, and may God be with me." After leaving the Palace and crossing Plac sw. Jura [St. Jura Square] where the Metropolitan's Palace stood, and on his way to his apartment on Kołłątaja Street close to *Brygidki*, some people came to warn him that Ukrainian detectives were in the vicinity of his home, dragging Jews to jail. Dr. Lewin did not turn back. When he reached his home the Ukrainian police caught him and led him to the courtyard of the jail. His son Izak, who was also in the *Brygidki* death courtyard at the time, describes his father's last moments:

"At ten I saw my father. Two Germans pushed him and hit him with gun butts. White as a sheet, dressed in his priest's outfit, he marched toward death... When my father came among the group of Jews, he recited the prayer prior to death, and said in a loud voice: *Sh'ma Israel*. At that moment the Germans started firing in that direction. All those engaged in removing the bodies, heard his prayer... and joined in, and the sound of their prayer "*Sh'ma Israel*!" drowned the sound of the firing. The threats and beatings did not stop our prayer that gave us superhuman power."

Those martyred at the beginning of July, included the brother of Dr. Jecheskiel Lewin, the renowned Rabbi Aron Lewin, head of the rabbinical court at Rzeszów [Resche], leader of *Agudas Yisroel* and delegate to the Polish *Sejm*, Henryk Hescheles, principal editor of the daily newspaper in Polish *Chwila*, and also the editor, Dr. Igel.

It is difficult to estimate the number of Jews murdered in all the jails and in the streets, during these pogroms. According to an eye witness,4,000 were murdered.[3] The Germans, on the other hand, estimated a very much larger number of victims. The official report recorded at the main German police station by the "Special Service," *Chef der Sicherheitspolizei und des F.S.D.* in Berlin, on 16th July 1941, stamped "highly Secret" (*Streng geheim*), summed up this *Aktion* as follows:

"In the hours after the Bolsheviks had left, the Ukrainian population took a laudable action against the Jews. By abusing Lwów's Jewish residents they caught about thousand people and brought them to prison that previously belonged to the GPU [Soviet; State Political Directorate], and that now housed the German army. Some seven thousand Jews were caught and shot by the police for the cruel and inhuman acts {that were supposedly perpetrated by the Jews prior to the departure of the

Russians}. Seventy three people {Jews} were appointed by the NKVD [Soviet, People's Commissariat for Internal Affairs] as clerks and spies, and were also shot. Forty people were liquidated based on proven reports from {Lwów's} residents. The age of most of the Jews who were caught, was between 20 and 40 years. The craftsmen and specialists among them were let free as far as possible."

The report continues in this vein, to disclose similar "reprisals" and "laudable" murders that took place in other parts of eastern Galicia, such as Dobromyl, Jaworów [Yavoriv], Tarnopol, Złoczów, Sambor etc.

[Pages 607-608]

Chapter 2. Other *Aktionen* in Summer 1941

Even after the "spontaneous pogroms" of July 1941, the Germans were not yet satisfied. Their method was not to allow the Jews to breath air, to gain strength, to have mortal danger removed from their consciousness. Jews in a state of permanent fear would have no time to consider covert propaganda, to spread rumours that would damage German prestige, or to trade in the black market, that would cause a loss to the German economy. This was the official explanation issued daily by the Berlin offices of the Ministry of Propaganda. These slogans served as camouflage for the plan worked out in Berlin, to annihilate the Jewry of eastern Europe. The goal of total eradication was unattainable by sporadic pogroms or by other destructive stratagems such as those adopted by the tzarist authorities. The Germans replaced the pogrom by a new concept which symbolised their novel strategy, with the strategic military term *Aktion* (action, act, undertaking). Its essence: a systematic, deliberate and planned action.

Throughout the whole of July 1941, the *Aktion* consisted of searches and arrests of Jewish leftist businessmen, and in particular of young Jews who were, or were reported to belong to the Komsomol. Without investigation or further requirement, all the suspects caught were put to death at Lesienice [Lysynychi] Forest near Lwów. Concurrently, a second *Aktion*, kidnapping for "work," was underway. This *Aktion* gathered force on 25, 26 and 27 of July. Hundreds and thousands of Jewish men and women were abducted by the Ukrainian trackers, and were taken to a "place of work." These wretched people were most often taken to the courtyard of the jail on Łącki Street. The Ukrainian mobs burst into the courtyard, time after time, screaming wildly: "Revenge for Petliura, our Hetman," and beat many of the Jews to death. Many of the abducted disappeared without a trace. Very few managed to save their lives. This *Aktion* was known as *Aktion Petliura*. Rumours spread around town that the Germans gave the Ukrainian Nationalists three "days off," to do with the Jews as they wished, to avenge the blood of Hetman Symon Petliura, who had been killed in Paris on 26th May 1926 by the Jewish Sholem Schwarzbard. According to a tentative estimate of those days, *Aktion Petliura* led to the murder of at least two thousand Jews.

A continuous chain of bloodshed continued on a smaller scale for the entire summer of 1941. One of the atrocities in particular shook Lwów's Jews. A German military hospital was housed in the school named after Saint Anna (on St. Anna [św. Anny] Street). At a certain point the German soldiers complained that a shot was fired into the surgery from one of the houses opposite the hospital. Without any investigation or inspection, or a search for the culprit, the German hobnailed soldiers burst into the houses of Jews on St. Anna Street (houses No. 1; 3; 5; 7) and on [Rappaporta] Jakóba Street (Nos. 11; 18) at dawn. They removed all the Jewish men without touching any Christian residents, and shot almost all of them. Some eighty souls in total.

[Pages 609-610]

Chapter 3. The Economic War, varied Acts of Robbery and Brutality;

"Official" and "Private" Larcenies

Hand in hand with the murders, an "economic war" was also started against the Jews, primarily executed through violence and plunder. There were official and private thefts. The private robberies were very simple. A German intruded into a Jewish house, raided anything that took his fancy, and often demanded that the ransacked Jew wrap the items and deliver them to the German's house. The Jew was glad if he were lucky enough to return home safely after his "mission".

The official theft started by imposing ransom (*Kontribution* [contribution]) on the Jews, in the sum of 20,000,000 Roubles (or 22,000,000 Roubles, according to other witnesses). The *Kontribution* announcement, signed by the General of the Infantry [Karl] von Roques, was declared at the beginning of August 1941.

The pretexts for imposing this penalty were, "Since the town suffered greatly from the war operations {i.e. from the explosions and bullets rained down on it by the Germans during their attacks. P.F.} it stands to reason and is just, that the Jews who were the cause of this war, should contribute financially to rebuilding the ruins." The rest of the residents were naturally not asked to contribute. The Jews received the ransom demand with a sense of relief. They considered it a sign signalling the end to the reckless pogroms of the invasion period, and the start of a new, civil government that would be appeased by using them as a source of extortion. The Jews hoped it would be possible to negotiate and save lives with future payments. That period's slogan read "*Kontribution* will save from death." In every town quarter, Jewish committees were formed under their own initiative to collect the required sums. The Jews rushed to pay their contribution. In the early days long queues formed in front of the offices of the committees by those who came to pay their large sum or a symbolic 18 Roubles. From those unable to pay in cash, the committees accepted gold and silver items, watches, jewellery, candle sticks, wedding rings etc. Christian Poles also contributed, although mostly anonymously.

Despite the willingness to pay, the Germans took Jewish hostages. When the announcement was first issued, small groups of German and Ukrainian police entered the homes of Jewish dignitaries and removed them under the pretext that "hostages" were required. This particular *Aktion* focused on members of the Jewish professional intelligentsia, physicians, advocates, engineers etc. and also large scale merchants, factory owners, bankers, communal representatives etc. Through this *Aktion* over one thousand people (closer to two thousand, according to a different estimate) were arrested. This event affected the ransom payment. The Jews believed that if the *Kontribution* were paid in full and on time, the hostages would be released, and consequently they sold the remainder of their possessions to contribute to the "soul-saving" *Kontribution* collection box. They guarded vouchers they received for their contributions with their lives.

The ransom money was paid on time. The first instalment was made on 8th August 1941. Besides the cash, the Jews brought a great deal of jewellery and gold, and about 1,400 kg. of silver. However, the hostages were not returned. They disappeared without a trace.

This cynic deception was the first encounter of the Jews of Lwów with "the new institution" of Nazi Germany. The Germans adopted the same deceptive ploy of "hostage" taking also in other towns. The outcome repeated itself everywhere. As a result, the lives of a large number of the communal and cultural leaders were cut short. The Germans employed the strategy of eliminating the leading strata when dealing also with other nations, such as the Poles, Czechs and others, but they avoided a similar heinous implementation with them.

While the *Kontribution* and the hostages *Aktion* "evolved," a new edict was issued. The Germans started systematically burning down synagogues: the old Synagogue of the author of *Turei Zahaw* (known as the Golden Rose Synagogue, *die goldene Rojze*), and the rest of the synagogues on Sobieski, Boimów, and Blacharska Streets, the synagogue on Szajnochy street, and also the synagogue of the Enlightened (the *Temple* prayer house) on Żółkiewska Street (its ruins and burnt walls were only removed in the summer of 1942). This arson *Aktion* was led

[Pages 611-612]

by the SS Officer Wollenberg. The remaining synagogues were later demolished by the Germans, especially during the period when the Ghetto was liquidated in 1943.

The Germans also practiced an "economic exploitation" of the Jewish cemeteries. They removed tombstones from the cemeteries and used them to pave the streets and roads (some of the tombstones were later used as floor tiles at the Concentration Camp for Jews, on Janowska Street).

We don't have precise information about the extent of this "economic *Aktion*," however, a report submitted by General [Fritz] Katzmann indicates that the Germans removed about 2,000 square meters of material (stones) from a cemetery near Lwów, which was used for paving roads. Those engaged in the arduous physical labour of uprooting the commemorative stones, breaking them up and transporting them, were the Jewish labourers who had been abducted by the Germans, and were forced to carry out the work.

[Pages 613-614]

Chapter 4. The Jewish Council (*Judenrat*)

The Jewish committee was formed during the *Kontributions Aktion*. Its first official act was to collect the donations and pay ransom to the Germans. The Jewish community committees in eastern Galicia were abolished by the Soviet authorities during their period of occupation. It was the policy of the Germans to organise a Jewish Council wherever Jews lived, and to turn it into an apparatus to execute their own commands. The German military headquarters summoned diverse Jewish businessmen to negotiated the formation of a new Jewish committee. These negotiations took place at the beginning of

July1941. The Germans suggested to Maurycy Allerhand, a renowned scholar in jurisprudence and Professor at Lwów University who for some years before the war was a government appointed manager of Lwów's community, that he should accept the leadership of the Jewish Council. He refused, citing his age and ill health. Others (Dr. Juda Ehrlich among them) also declined the positions of council members. The Germans eventually gave up on their tricks of negotiating with the important, the best and the good of the town and when they realised that none volunteered. They appointed the Council members from their own list of candidates. At first only five members were appointed, which was augmented after a few days (until 29th July 1941). By the autumn of 1941, after all the appointments and additions, the composition of the Jewish Council consisted of: Dr. Oswald Kimmelman, Dr. Edmund Scherzer, the engineer Naftali Landau, Dr. Henryk Ginsberg, Chiger, Seidenfrau, Józef Hoch, Szymon Ulam, Dr. Marceli Buber, Dr. Żarnicer and others. By late autumn 1941, the composition of the Council had changed. Dr. Józef Parnas, who was seventy years old by then and one of the assimilated representatives, was unable to adjust to the Germans' ways and methods of work. He was an advocate from a wealthy, estate-owning family and had been a cavalry officer (*Reitmeister*) in the Austrian army. He had a strong character, he displayed no signs of submission towards the German authorities, and even refused some of their demands. In October or November 1941, Dr. Parnas was arrested by the Germans. According to the chroniclers and to rumours that spread at the time in town, he was arrested because he refused to supply the Germans with the amount of forced-labourers the Germans demanded. Dr. Parnas was led to the jail on Łącki [Lantzki] Street and was shot dead in the jail courtyard. He was replaced by Dr. Rothfeld, a Zionist activist and member of east Galicia's Zionist executive committee, but he died of a fatal disease in February 1942. He was followed as president by Dr. Henryk Landesberg, a renowned advocate, an active businessman and member of *Bnei Brith*, before the war. He also did not hold his post for long. He was murdered by the Germans in September 1942. The fourth president, Dr. Ebersohn, an honest, helpless man with no influence, held the post until the Germans murdered him together with the rest of the Council members, in February 1943.

The authority of the Jewish Council was very broad and surprised even the most optimistic amongst the Jewish public. On the face of it, the Germans granted the Jews a very wide range of "self governance". The Jewish Council had to manage its administration in accordance with German orders. After the Ghetto was erected, the Council administered a territorial self governance. It organised a financial and taxation department that relied on various, independent income sources. It opened social aid institutions including clinics, hospitals, orphanages, old-age-homes, soup-kitchens and inexpensive restaurants. It managed economic issues, industrial and commercial enterprises, consumer markets, etc. It organised work preformed by Jews through its employment agency. It oversaw nutrition in the ghetto through the distribution of food-cards, the acquisition of food, and the establishment of bread bakeries. The Council allocated apartments through its housing department. It managed the Jewish post-office. Finally, the Jewish Council was granted jurisdiction of the legal department and the Jewish police.

The activities of the Jewish Council branched into many fields and required a very large structure. From the start, the community employed around 1,000 clerks. That number increased to 4,000 in 1942. According to some members (Farber,

[Pages 615-616]

Maltiel), there were up to 5,000 clerks and labourers, in addition to craftsmen and the employees of financial enterprises near the community. The Council was composed of the following departments: i) Personnel Dept., headed by Józef Hoch, an energetic individual with much influence within the Jewish Council, was responsible for hiring and supervising clerks and workers. (In a cynical song about the Lwów *Judenrat*, the entire Jewish Council system was termed *Organisation Hoch* {parallel to *Organisation Todt*, after the Germans' [military] work organisation}). ii). Provision Dept., led by Agid and his deputy Beno Teichholz. iii). Housing Dept., led by Dr. Schutzmann of Prsemyśl, and after his death, by Dr. Jaffe of Bilsko [Bielitz], Silesia. One of the clerks and managers within the housing department was Szmuel Pacanowski of Łódż, a leading member of the *Zionist Youth* movement, and who was murdered by the Nazis in August 1942. iv). Finance Dept., led by Dr. Zarnicer, Stanisław Rothfeld, Dr. Bardach and others. v). Employment Dept. vi). Taxation Dept. vii). Health Dept., managed by Dr. Ginsberg, followed by Aleksander Blaustein. viii). Dept. of Care and Social Assistance, headed by Dr. Jozef Kohn, a veteran social worker. ix). Legal Dept., led by Dr. Hirschsprung and others. x). Dept. of Statistics, managed by Dr. Fryderyk Katz. xi). Building Dept. xii). *Chevra-Kadisha* [Holy Society - or funeral Soc.]. xiii). Education Dept., managed by Abraham Roth, who had been the headmaster of the Jewish commercial *gymnasium*, and Mrs. Dr. Cecylja Klaften, who had been very active in the field of vocational education before the war. Since the Germans prohibited Jewish schools from opening, the education department was impotent. xiv). Culture Dept., principally engaged in the administration of religious issues. Among the Orthodox rabbis employed in this dept., were, R' Izrael Wolfsberg, R' Mojzesz-Elchanan Alter, R' Natan Leiter, from among the progressive rabbis, Dr. Kalman Chameides, who had been R' at Katowice [Katowitz] and Dr. Dawid Kahana. There were also six *Dayanim* [religious judges]. The function of this department was very restricted since the Germans prohibited public prayer. Almost all the synagogues were burnt down and the *Midraashim* [Torah study schools] and the *Kloyses* were closed, and turned into dormitories for Jewish refugees displaced from their homes by the Germans, who came to Lwów. Praying in private *Minyanim* was also forbidden. Soon after the start of their rule, the Germans burst into such *Minyanim* and arrested the worshippers, who disappeared without a trace. Secular, cultural activities were completely forbidden in Lwów.

The Jewish Council was allotted an old building near the scraps market, not far from the old synagogue *far der Schul* at 2 Starotandetna Street, but the building was too confined to contain all the community departments. Later, the old community building at 12 Bernstein Street was given back to the Council, and the Statistics and Religious Affairs Departments were relocated there. On the lower level was the "Jewish self-help" (*Jüdische soziale Selbsthilfe*) that was not directly reliant on the community system. This was the sole independent institution managed outside the Jewish Council, a branch of the Jewish "social aid" that was managed by the "General Government [*Allgemeine Regierung*]" (a term the Germans used for occupied Poland). The head-quarters of the "social aid" was in Kraków, led by the Jewish writer and theologian, Dr. Michał Weichert. The manager, of Galicia's branch located at Lwów, was the renowned advocate, Dr. Leib Landau, and the manager of the Lwów branch was Dr. Maks Schaff. The Jewish Council also had a social aid department, which to a large extent, paralleled the work of the "social self-help." This department was situated in a synagogue the Germans had not destroyed, on Jagiellońska Street. The taxation department operated from the synagogue at 2 Rappaporta Street. The *Chevra-Kadisha* was located nearby on the Schleichera Street. The housing department was first located in the Great Synagogue on Bożnicza Street, and later moved to the school named after Abraham Kohn, on św [St.] Stanislawa Street. The office for the distribution of food-coupons, which functioned under the financial department that employed a large number of clerks, was on Żółkiewska Street and contained an enormous ticketing machine. The Jewish police, known by its official title "The Jewish security-service [*Jüdisches Ordnungsdienst*]" filled a special place within the "self governance." The police were organised during August-September 1941. According to one chronicler of those days,[4] Warsaw's Jewish chief of police was brought to Lwów to instruct and organise the force. The 100 workers who first formed this police, soon increased to 500, and later to 750 men. The Jewish Police operated in four commissariats (districts) The police of the first district, together with the headquarters and the criminal department (*Kripo*), were at "Yad

[Pages 617-618]

Charuzim [the diligents']" house at 11 Bernstein Street. The police of the second district was situated at 112 Zamarstynowska Street, the third district was at the Kleparów suburb, and the police of the fourth district was in the Zniesienie suburb. The criminal department (*Kripo = Kriminalpolizai*) and the "special service" (*Sonderdienst*) occupied a specific section within the Jewish police, that closely collaborated with the Gestapo [*Geheime Staatspolizei*]. The managers of this section (Goliger-Schapiro and his deputy Krumholz) were considered a disgrace by the Jewish community, because of their evil deeds. In general, the role of the Jewish police and their stature steadily declined in the eyes of the Jewish public. The militia was formed to assist the Jewish Council in maintaining order and cleanliness in the Jewish neighbourhoods. By and by, however, the police collaborated with the Germans. Eventually, these Jewish police divisions became part of German control while loosing all connection with the Jewish Council. The composition of the police also changed over time. At the start, mostly young men from among the Jewish intelligentsia joined the police, but when its function turned into another oppressive German tool, the Jews, those with a sense of public responsibility abandoned it. They fled to the Aryan neighbourhoods, or were expelled by the Germans. A mob of greedy, self-serving thugs replaced them amidst a dreadful scandal. And these new recruits were ready to execute the orders of their German masters.

The activities of the Jewish Council also moved in a direction that was more harmful than helpful. The Germans intended to create a tool to execute their schemes against the Jews, operated by the Jews themselves. By employing their tricks, they succeeded in disguising their stratagem from most of the Jews. While this scheme was only uncovered at a later stage of the Nazi occupation, it was plain from the start that the Germans used the community as a means to extort money, objects and work from the Jews. One of the important departments of the Council was the provisions department. One would be mistaken, however, to think that its purpose was to assist the Jews. This department was tasked with to satisfying the lists of demands that emanated daily from the Germans. One day they demanded 100 Persian rugs, the next a dozen porcelain dinner sets, silverware, kitchenware. and luxury furniture, crystal vessels, jewellery and diamonds, fancy clothes, works of art and paintings, or barrels of coffee, salmon roe and other delicacies that had long vanished from the market. And although officially the provisions office had only to fulfil the demands of German offices or their representatives, woe betide the clerk who did not quickly fulfil the wishes of private Germans, especially those of the clerks for the secret-police and the SS. The provisions department leader, Agid, once refused to supply the German police clerks with some private "invitations." The following day he was invited to the secret police under a pretext of a meeting, where he was shot. The Germans justified their demands from the Jews under the "legal" pretence that the Jewish wealth in the occupied countries was confiscated by Germany. It was only in Jewish hands temporarily. The Jews were permitted to use their resources only until the Germans decided to remove them.[4a] This law, following the edict of 7th August 1941, was extended to include the area of eastern Galicia.

The provisions department employed many clerks whose sole task was to go to the houses of the Jews to confiscate those items that the Germans. Besides these regular "orders," it was also necessary to offer special presents to the German officials, to soften their hearts to "forgo" some of the "exaggerated orders." Other clerks, specialised in using "gentle" bribery in their negotiation with the Germans, and were able at times to lobby for the good of the community or for specific individuals. This led to frequent contacts that eventually created a class of panderers and mediators who knew how to "organise" things, and who earned a great deal of money in their lobbying. This resulted in corruption to the malaise of the Jewish public.

The extent of the German "legal" robbery was immense. According to one of the Jewish Council clerks, the value of the items seized in August-September 1941, was 30% greater than the (*Kontribution*) ransom payment made to the Germans in the July *Aktion*.[5]

Apart from the legal robbery that was perpetrated via the departments of provisions, taxation and labour (whose task was to supply the Germans with free-labour), the Germans used the Jewish Council to create division amongst the Jews themselves. The strategy of sowing a chasm between the community clerks and the rest of the Jewish population, the policy of "divide

[Pages 619-620]

and rule," was also practiced by the Germans with regard to interactions among Jews and Poles, Jews and Ukrainians, Poles and Ukrainians, etc. Members of the Jewish police, and to a certain extent clerks of the Jewish Council (members of the *Judenrat*, the provisions department clerks and others), were granted privileges, such as protected living quarters, free movement in the streets without fear of being picked for forced-labour, additional food rations, etc. The police and the community clerks, on the other hand, did not receive a fixed salary for their work, and the cost of living rose daily. Consequently, some of the clerks exploited their official position out of greed and to oppress. The work documents carried a minor protection from abduction for forced labour while wandering in town, and other accessibility. Indeed, even among the community clerks, graded "privileges" led to "class differences." Those of the upper stratum were members of the Council and department managers. The middle stratum was made up of the high officials who held "stiff" work-certificates (a stiff paper-card, or bound certificates), while the labourers and the provisional workers held "soft" work-certificates (ordinary paper slips, not printed but written with a typewriter or a pen). Other privileged strata were those of the professionals, expert workers, technicians, engineers, surgeons and medics, who mainly worked for German offices or enterprises. The least privileged were the hordes of tradespeople and shopkeepers, panderers, ordinary house owners, teachers, advocates, those in religious-service, and synagogue staff. Last of all were the masses, the unemployed, the poor, the "impoverished" and those who "lost" their jobs, who were not protected by work-certificates or lobbying, and were consequently objects of plunder by the Germans. The lower classes were destroyed and wiped out without mercy from the very start.

The class segregation among the Jewish community was entirely different from the professional and social structure before the war, as if the world had turned upside down. The chasm was sharper and more pronounced than before the war, when class difference did not only deprive a man of his livelihood, but also literally of his life. A man with no means, privileges or a profession that benefitted the Germans, had one destiny, to die, be it by "a kiss of death" (starvation or ill health), or by "fast death" as forced-labour, in a camp or in an *Aktion*.

Eventually it became clear to all that the *Miniature Jewish State* granted by the German authorities, was nothing but a sham, a vicious caricature of self rule, with the one aim – to be an instrument of convenience for the Germans.

[Pages 621-622]

Chapter 5. Legal Restrictions and anti-Semitic Incitement; the Ukrainians' attitude towards the Jews

From the early months of their rule, the Germans made housing subject to racial principles. They intended to segregate the town's residents of different nationalities into different geographic zones. In particular, they intended to separate the Jews, Slav nations (Poles and Ukrainians) and the Germans (including those of German culture, *Volksdeutsche*). The Germans chose the most attractive part of town for themselves, where the mansions and grand houses stood. This was where Poles and many Jews, mostly wealthy and professionals, lived. The Jews, who resided on the streets in the vicinity of Listopada, Potockiego, Wulecka, Kadecka, and the streets that surrounded the Stryjski [Kiliński] Parc, Dwernickiego Street, św Zofii [St. Sofia], Snopkowska and Żyżyńska Street, were issued an order to vacate their residences without delay. They were allowed a few hours to vacate, and allowed to remove only whatever they could carry. At times they were ordered to leave their homes behind, empty handed and destitute. This *Aktion* was accompanied by terror and resulted in approximately 200 murdered Jews.

The Jews residing in the *Aryan* parts of town were fearful, and took preventative measures before the order to vacate reach them. Every day, people looking for a residence in the Jewish neighbourhoods formed long queues in front of the accommodation department of the Jewish Council. However the *Aktion* that uprooted people from their residences came to a halt in the late summer, only to be followed by new calamities.

On 1st August 1941, a new edict was issued that annexed eastern Galicia as part of the *Generalgouvernement* (*Distrikt Galizien*). The Ukrainians were greatly disappointed by this law. They had believed the Nazi propaganda that promised the Germans would help them found a "single, undivided, free and sovereign" Ukrainian country. The Germans seized the Ukrainian nationalists and locked them up. Among them was the leader of the extreme Ukrainian nationalists, Hetman Stepan [Andriyovych] Bandera, who was held in a concentration camp and only released after the defeat of Germany. His followers (known as *Banderowcy* [Banderites]) formed underground battalions of partisans to fight the Germans. Eastern Galicia was full of these partisans. In their fight against the Germans, however, they also massacred Jews. A large section of the Ukrainian mob, the peasants in particular, were Bandera supporters, snd the Ukrainian intelligentsia fell into different factions. One part collaborated with the Germans, another part followed Bandera, and the democratic faction kept out of politics. But even the democratic intelligentsia circles did not help the Jews, nor did they try to restrain the Ukrainian mob. An exception which deserves mention, was the Metropolitan [Andrey] Szeptycki [Sheptytsky] and his rescue operation. He provided refuge to a large number of Jews, especially children, whom he sheltered at his home, in prayer houses and Catholic monasteries under his jurisdiction. He saved 150 Jews[6] in this way. No one from among Metropolitan Sheptytsky's flock of worshipers followed his example.

After the Galicia district was annexed to the *Generalgouvernement*, the Jews of Galicia and those of Lwów in particular, were subject to the Anti-Semitic [Nazi] law that had been issued two years earlier. One of the decrees that was issued as early as 15th July 1940, stated that all Jews over the age of ten, including anyone of Jewish extraction to the third generation, had to wear a white ribbon with a blue Star of David on their left arm. This identifying symbol increased the danger of wandering in the town's streets, and acted as magnet for attacks. A Jew caught in the street with a ribbon improperly fastened, or soiled ribbon, was arrested by the police, thoroughly beaten, and released, or taken to a place from which he never returned. A ribbon-fear seized the Jews. Warning notes appeared on walls and house entrances: "Remember the Ribbon!," "Mortal danger! Do not forget to wear your ribbon!" There were also illustrations of a skull with a ribbon next to it, a self-explanatory symbol.

While the ribbon was meant to segregate the Jews from the non-Jews, the purpose of the rest of the restrictions was to limit the possible movement from place to place, pursuing a livelihood, finding food, etc. A curfew, imposed on non-German Christians that began at 9 p.m. (there were no such restriction on the Germans), restricted the Jews by 8 p.m. Whoever was found in the street, even a few minutes after 8 p.m., was shot or sent to a concentration camp. On the trams, a special compartment was designated for Jews (*Nur für Juden*). In time, they were even deprived of the right to ride a tram, and had to walk to their places of work, often several kilometres at a times. The long route was exhausting and full of danger. Train riding was proscribed, as was the right to leave the town. Buying provisions in the town's markets

[Pages 623-624] was permitted only between 2p.m. and 4p.m. Employment in many professions was forbidden, and Jews were compelled to provide forced-labour. Their possessions, including their worldly goods, real-estate, and money in amounts over 2,000 Gulden were confiscated. (The Germans were unable to execute the law regarding money.).

Dr. Karl Lasch was the first governor of the Galicia district. On 24th January 1942, Lasch was arrested for embezzlement from the state. He was charged with forging accounts, the theft of "countless carpets, furs, artworks etc.," and bribing the wife of Governor-General Hans [Michael] Frank. He was also suspected of "incest" (desecration of the race) and betrayal of the fatherland. He was replaced by Dr. [Baron Otto Gustav von] Wächter, who had been the governor of Kraków. The head of the German administration was assisted at Lwów by the head of the secret police and the SS [*Schutzstaffel*] for the district of Galicia, Major-General [Fritz] Katzmann, and the head of the regular police, Dr. Robert Ulrich from Graz, Austria. In the early days of the German occupation the Ukrainian scholar, Professor [Jurij] Polanśkyj (a geographer), served as Lwów's mayor. When Galicia was annexed to the *Generalgouvernement*, the Germans dropped all vestiges of Ukrainian "autonomy," and appointed the German clerk [Hans] Kujath, who was succeeded by another German, Dr. [Egon Ambros] Höller.

By means of restrictions, outdoor attacks, insults, beatings and abductions, the Germans wanted to instil fear among the non-Jewish, Christian inhabitants, and even more so among the Jews. The Germans planned to prevent any sense of solidarity and joint fate from forming among the victims, through strategic levels of privileges and discriminations. The Ukrainian slave felt superior to the Polish slave who was more oppressed and abject than himself, and both considered themselves aristocratic *Aryans*, compared to the Jews. The Germans constantly inflamed the feeling of contempt for the Jews, in newspapers, advertisements and placards, in plays and exhibitions, in songs and on the radio. The Nazi Ministry of Propaganda poured out endless, unfounded accusations and false allegations, without sparing the converted [to Christianity] through Lwów's newspapers, that had shrunk to two dailies, one Polish and one Ukrainian, and the official German newspaper. The article "They forgot their origins" in *Gazeta Lwowska* of 22nd October 1941, expressed the view that those who had converted were also obliged to wear the white ribbon, as was every Christian related to Jews by marriage. It seems that in the early stages of the German invasion, many of the converted innocently assumed that conversion would save them from the restrictions that befell the Jews (a similar mass process took place in Slovakia and Hungary). According to *Gazeta Lwowska* of 8.11.1941, in September 1942[a] there were about 4,000 Jews who wished to convert. Although the information in this newspaper was not necessarily reliable, as it counted Jews and the converted together, the numbers of those ready to convert were presumably quite large. Consequently, Lwów's Catholic bishop's office organised special lectures for them, and set a six months' trial period for the converting candidates. The monk A. Paulo, at the church of St. Vincent [de Paul], whom *Gazeta Lwowska* (9th and 11th November 1941) vigorously attacked, was particularly active in the Jewish conversions. It did not take long for the converted and the would-be converted to realise that conversion would not be their salvation. The precise definition of the term "Jew," in German law, was based on a racial rather than a religious notion. The converted Jews were also subject to the restrictions. Only a small portion of them, with Christian relatives or friends, were concealed or acquired false *Aryan* papers that saved them.

Dr. Henryk Hescheles

[Pages 625-626]

Chapter 6. The "Work" Penalties and Work-Gifts

Among the *Generalgouvernement* laws was that of Jewish forced-labour [*jüdische Zwangsarbeit*], which forced every male and female Jew between the ages of 14 and 60, to work for the Germans. After the annexation of Galicia, the Jews of Lwów were also subject to that law. The Germans established a labour-office that had a special section for Jews (*Judeneinsatz*). The office for Jewish employment was first located in a school on Zamknięta Street (in a side alley off Gródecka Street). Later, it was moved to the school named after Mikołaj Rej, on Misjonarski Square. The department was led by Heinz Weber, an extremely cruel, uncultured and uneducated man. The department clerks were Jews. Some of these clerks were reviled among the Jewish community for being servile to the Germans, and for their wicked deeds against other Jews. The new office conducted a roll-call of all the Jews of forced-labour age. Those who did not present a work-permit from an institution that performed useful work for the Germans, had to do the forced-labour assigned to them. The Jews were not used to this physically demanding hard labour. Many evaded registering with the German labour-office which led the Germans to use a new strategy. They employed Jewish "kidnappers" (*Chappers*) to hunt Jews without work-permits. The kidnapped people were locked up in the office until the next "transport" left for the place of work.

The work of the German labour-office ran parallel with that of the Jewish community's labour-office. This type of duplication was common and typical of the Nazi strategy, for two reasons. First, they did not trust the Jews, and second, it was wilfully done to create confusion in the labour market. The actual work accomplished by the Jews was not important, but rather the accompanying persecution and accessibility. The labour-office of the Jewish Council tried, in vain, to come to an agreement with the Germans in order to introduce a work recruitment or a quota system for obtaining Jewish workers. Even when an agreement had been reached after great efforts, the Germans took no notice of it, dismissed the workers sent by the community, and again they sent out the kidnappers who led their captives to places whence no one returned.

"Work" was a pretext for any German who wished to abuse Jews. In addition to the two employment offices, military cars and the secret-police wagons, drove through the streets almost daily, seizing Jews for work. The snatching for work was often undertaken by German individuals, in uniform or not. Not only was the work unpaid, it was also mostly fruitless work, aimed solely to deride the Jews. It general, it was gruelling and beyond mortal strength. For instance, the elderly

Street attacks by Ukrainians in *Aktion Petliura*

were ordered to carry cement bags weighing 100 kg, and then carry them back. The young were forced to transport 200 kg. or greater weight, iron bars. At times, the Jews were compelled to carry such heavy burden while running. Those who lagged behind or fell down were slapped, beaten, wounded and even murdered.

At most of the army's work places, the Jews received a paltry salary of 2-4 Gulden per day. On occasion they were even given food provisions depending on the generosity of the oppressor overseeing their work. The Jews working for enterprises organised by the German trust-offices [*Treuhand Ämte*], also received pay in money or food. During the Soviet rule (1939-1941), the private factories and stores owned by Jews or Christians, had been nationalised. At the start of their occupation, the Germans declared that they would reinstate their private owners, but the promises were not kept, and all the industrial enterprises

[Pages 627-628]

and the consumer unions established by the Russians were handed over to German "trust-offices." The Jews who had been factory owners and merchants, were glad to get a labourer's job in these establishments. Stone houses that had been confiscated by the Russians, were also not returned to their rightful owners, and some among the past house-owners succeeded in getting the post of gatekeeper of their own homes.

Most of the Jews who worked in German institutions did so not for the paltry salary, but to have a work-permit, trusting that it would shield them from a worse fate, especially from being sent to labour-camps.

The Germans referred to labour-camps for Jews, by the fraudulent title "Educational institutions [*Erziehungsinstitutionen*]." The need for such institutions, according to the head of the secret-police and of the SS, General [Fritz] Katzmann, was as follows:

"Our (the German secret-police) obligation was first of all to fight the widespread, black market activities of the Jews throughout Galicia, especially that of the self-serving, the unemployed and the idlers. The most effective means was establishing forced-labour camps by the leader of the secret-police and the SS. Our best opportunity arose when it was necessary to repair the Thoroughfare [*Durchgangsstrasse*] DG IV, which was of great significance for the entire southern front, and was in a very poor state of repair..." "On 15th October 1941, we started to establish the camps at the side of the Thoroughfare DG IV, and despite the many obstacles, we established seven new camps within a few weeks, so that we could say in our report that there were 15 such camps, where some 20,000 Jews worked.["][7]

It appears from the report that education was not the sole purpose of the Germans for moving the Jews to the camps, and that these were not the first camps established at Lwów and its surroundings. Several were created even before 15th September 1941. A small labour-camp (for 30 to 60 labourers) was formed on Herburtów Street, as early as July 1941. A larger camp existed on an urban farm at Sokolniki near Lwów. The Jews worked there in boggy soil and water pools. The camp was organised in mid July 1941, and there were always 200 to 400 Jewish labourers there. The Ukrainian police who oversaw their work were led by the Ukrainian Czubak [Tchubak] and his deputy Jaworski. The Jewish labourers were forced to stand in the middle of the pool, with water reaching up to their knees and above, to uproot the bulrush and hydrophyte, and move them to dry areas. In the winter months, with the increased cold, the work that lasted 12 hours a day, led to serious diseases and a great many deaths. On a monthly basis some 70-80 percent of the labourers were lost to sickness from cold, lack of food and the inhuman conditions of living. Many died from their wounds that were inflicted by the Ukrainians on the "malingerers." Some were shot by the supervisors. The Jewish Council's labour-office was obliged to supply "replacements" for the dead and the sick. On average, every fortnight about 100 men were sent to fill the gap. The camp policemen stopped all contact between the imprisoned and their families, and with the Jewish community. The camp was tightly closed. No one went in, nor out, except for replacing labourers and the dead. The total secrecy surrounding the Sokolniki camp was maintained throughout its existence. The number of the Jewish victims swallowed up by this camp is not clear, nor is the date of its liquidation. Some say the camp was closed down in December 1941, and others claim that it still functioned during 1942.

The Jews of Lwów were also sent to other labour-camps, such as: Lacki Murowany; Hermanów, west of Lwów; Winniki - Weinbergen and Ostrów; Medike; Unterbergen; Kurowice; Kozaki - near Złoczów [Zolochiv]; Jaktorów - Złoczów district, and others. Most of the Jews did not leave these camps alive, and of the few who did, a large percentage of them were maimed and sick.

The secret police and the SS also established two camps in town. An SS labour-camp, on Czwartaków Street in the SS neighbourhood (between Listopada Street and Potockiego Street), and Janowska Street camp (Janowska Street camp is discussed later on). The camp on Czwartaków Street was renowned for the rough behaviour of the SS men, and their cruel abuse of the Jews. The camp was liquidated in the spring of 1943, after most of the Jews there had been murdered by the SS.

[Pages 629-630]

Chapter 7. The Jewish Ghetto and new *Aktionen*

In October 1941, the Germans announced the establishment of a Ghetto in Lwów, and allocated the suburbs of Zamarstynów and Kleparów to the north-west of the town, as a specific living district for the Jews, *Jüdischer Wohnbezirk*. These areas were slums without sewers, water, and generally no electricity. There were only a few large houses there, so most of the accommodations were in decrepit hovels and mud huts, in an area that typically housed paupers, prostitutes and thieves. Here, the raised barrier of the railway separated the suburbs from the town of Lwów. Only four streets joined the suburbs to the town via culverts or tunnels under railway bridges. These streets were Kleparowska, Żródlana, Pełtewna and Zamarstynowska. The topography made the neighbourhoods of Kleparów and Zamarstynów ideal for the ghetto. It was simple to separate them from the town, and supervise the connecting routes. On 15th November 1941, an announcement appeared in the official German Newspaper, *Lemberger Zeitung*, stating that within one month, from 16th November until 15th December (1941), the Jews had to vacate their homes in all parts of the town, and move to the new ghetto. Pełtewna Street was the one route out of the four that the Jews were permitted to use enroute to the ghetto. Ukrainian police guards and SS men were posted under the railway bridge to check the last few possession the Jews moved to their new abodes. The inspection centre was an old bathhouse turned into a barrack of the German-Ukrainian "garrison." The inspectors closely checked the continuous stream of Jews carrying their meagre possessions. From morning till dusk convoys of Jews flocked via Pełtewna Street, under the railway bridge, all laden with sacks and packages, or pushing their chattel in a cart or wheelbarrow. Under the railway bridge, known by the Jews as "the bridge of death," stood patrols of Jew-haters. Anyone whom they considered gaunt, hungry, dressed shoddily, sick or old, was immediately dragged over the fence of the old bathhouse. There he was confronted by supervisors and guards who slapped him and beat him to death. The supervisors included a few Jews who served the Germans. A tall Jewish woman named Malkale was particularly notorious. Anyone whom the guards and checkers did not like, was arrested, beaten up and later moved

Ukrainians' onslaught: "A Jews' hunt"

to the jail on Łącki Street. From there, the victims were victims were flung into freight-wagons, taken to the forest and murdered. In this way the lives of many Jews, including a large number of women, were ended in "the bridge of death" *Aktion*. This was the first mass *Aktion* against Jewish women, in Lwów.

It seems that at the time the ghetto was intended to extinguish the lives of thousands of Lwów's Jews, to uproot them and move them from place to place, to create confusion and instil a fear of death among them. For a while the Germans stopped at that, and once the set date for closing the ghetto had passed, 15[th]December 1941, nothing happened. Most of the Jews had not yet managed to find accommodation "beyond the bridge," and were left with no choice but to remain in their apartments in the centre of town, waiting in fear for the severe retribution. Although the Germans pretended to have forgotten their order, they nevertheless did not officially annul the ghetto decree. The Jewish Council was therefore forced to manage a protracted negotiation. The community representatives seem to have tried to soften the Germans' intentions with bribes and suitable gifts, but we have no documents or proof of such actions. Clearly, the Germans paid no heed to the ghetto issue, and this "neither here nor there" situation of living with fear in the "forbidden" neighbourhoods continued for almost a year until September 1942.

The number of Jewish residents in Lwów decreased each month

[Pages 631-632]

as a result of he recurring *Aktionen*, the work recruitment and the movement of people to labour-camps. In addition, people simply chose to leave the town. Many refugees had arrived at Lwów from western Poland during the Soviet rule, but now, it was rumoured that despite the persecution and restrictions, Jewish life was quieter and more settled in the western regions of the *Generalgouvernement*, than in the areas the Germans had conquered from the Russians. The rumours were indeed true, since at that point the Germans schemed to annihilate only those Jews "infected by Communist propaganda," seemingly those who had previously lived in areas under Soviet occupation. Refugees who had relatives in the western districts moved there from Lwów. Many of Lwów's residents also decided to leave their big home town and settle in the quieter, small provincial towns. In this way several thousands left Lwów despite the German prohibition. But as their departure was illegal and clandestinely undertaken, their exact number is impossible to determine.

Abuse of Jews

In January-February 1942, the town of Lwów experienced a short, quiet spell, even if not a total calm. Although large murder *Aktionen* did not take place at the time, "minor-*Attionen*" continued. One minor *Aktion* involved the eviction of Jews from Żołkiewska Street and its surroundings, in the middle of winter, from December 1941 to January 1942. The Jews who lived on these streets were suddenly forced to move to the Zniesienie suburb, which was a semi-rural settlement and a longstanding refuge for bandits and robbers. The new residents suffered greatly in their new surrounding that lacked any amenities and personal security. One of Lwów's Jews described his new accommodation as follows:

"A new apartment. Two rooms like mouse-holes. Small hatches embedded in the soil, peek out. Nine souls now reside in this shack. The mustiness is putrid. Years of little air dazes the head. Here we have something the wealthy are proud of: a WC right next to the table… and the stench rises like a bloom. The shack lacks a cellar, but has a potato pit, and the drinking-water well is tens of yards away.

During our stay at Zniesienie, robbers broke in at least 30 times. Every two or three days we were paid another visit by the guests from neighbourhood. They stole anything at hand, including food, heating logs, coal, pieces of furniture, fence posts, etc. Everything was suitable for stealing.["][8]

During December [1941]-January 1942, the "fur *Aktion*" also took place. The Germans demanded that the Jews hand over all leather clothing, women's furs, fur-collars, woollen textiles and woollen clothes. All of it was needed for the soldiers fighting for the "fourth Reich in the cold parts of Russia. Only the Jews were recruited for this "patriotic *Aktion*," and any Jew transgressing the order would face death. Not all the collected furs and fabrics were sent to the fighting soldiers. The administration and the German secret police kept a large quantity of furs, especially luxury furs, for their own use, and for commercial plunder which they sold on the black market. (As previously mentioned, even Dr. Lasch, the Governor of Galicia, was caught personally profiting from the plunder). According to General Katzmann's official report, even after all of the personal plunder, the Germans sent the army 35 rail-carriages filled with furs, from all parts of Galicia. The report does not specify how much of the loot was taken from the Jews of Lwów, and how much from the provincial towns). Those Jews who were caught with secreted furs, were murdered.

Despite everything, the "fur *Aktion*" was one of the quietest. It caused financial damage, but led to few deaths. There were, however, other minor *Aktionen* that resulted in a much greater number of deaths. On one occasion the Germans decided to rid the town of its Jewish beggars. Another time they caught orphaned children. Then, they hunted old men and women, for days. The victims of the *Aktionen* were taken to an undisclosed place, never to be seen again. The kidnap *Aktionen* did not stop even for a day. Every day 50-100 Jews disappeared without a trace. After the massacres and slaughter of the previous months, the Jews of Lwów treated them with equanimity - a sacrifice to the devil.

[Pages 633-634]

Chapter 8. The Plights of Livelihood, Hunger and Sickness

The German regime completely revolutionised the economic life of the Jews. This was the second economic upheaval the Jewish population underwent since the outbreak of World War II. The first occurred during the Soviet occupation, when, in the socialist manner, all the property and assets of house-owners, industrialists and tradesmen, were confiscated. Other groups, such as clerks, advocates, teachers of religion, etc., had practically lost their livelihoods through the changes in the social order. Many Jews, on the other hand, found employment as labourers, clerks, teachers, etc., within the new trade and industry of the collective regime. The great capitalists, bankers, industrialists and merchants, the functionaries and the former officers, as well as the unemployed (among them many refugees) were considered with suspicion by the Russian regime. Many of these were moved from Lwów to the provincial towns of eastern Galicia or to Russia in 1940-1941. During the Soviet period, the Jewish community in Lwów existed in a state of instability and ever-changing standards. Now, the community

Ukrainian police working the Jews in the destruction of graves in the cemetery

that had previously endured the unsettlement of its economic life, was again faced with far-reaching crises.

Suddenly, most of the clerks, employees, professionals and self-employed professionals were left without a means of livelihood. All of the collective economic institutions automatically passed to the Ukrainian and German authorities, and they laid off all the Jews. The sole remaining avenue open to the Jews was hard physical labour, mostly forced-labour that did not pay enough to sustain the workers. Even where Jews were paid for their labour, it was purely symbolic, too meagre to sustain life. The remaining Jewish capital, on the other hand, was eroded by the contribution [*Kontribution*] payment and other extortions. The expulsions and transfers between living quarters resulted in grave financial damage to most families, many of whom lost their breadwinners when sons and fathers were taken as forced-labour and to camps. There was no steady source of financial income open to Jews. Most of them were left to follow a makeshift existence dependent on the sale of chattel still in their possession. They sold furniture, clothes, underwear, gold and silver items and anything they managed to conceal from their persecutors. Once their "merchandise" had run out, they were reduced to the level of beggars and relied on public or private charity. Others, under mortal danger, tried to earn a living through temporary, covert dealings in the blackmarket, etc. (Such an "economic strategy" was naturally unsustainable, and short-lived.).

This however, was not the end of the Jews' economic tribulations. The Germans introduced the use of grocery-card which rationed the supply of food to the population. The food portions varied according to their nation status. The Jews received only 10% of the ingredients provided for the Germans, that was 50% of the portion which the Poles or the Ukrainians received.

The food ration allotted to the Jews consisted of, 1,400 gm. bread per week, an amount that was later reduced to 1,050, then to 700, and eventually to 500 gm. Sugar as allocated at 250 gm. and later 100 gm. per month, and there was half a kg. of black salt ("salt for animals") once in two or three months. Rations included 200-400 gm. of mouldy flour (black flour known by the Germans as

[Pages 635-636]

"Proof" how the Jews evade deportation
(from the documents folder of the oppressor [Fritz] Katzmann)

"Jews' flour" *Judenmehl*), or alternatively the same quantity of groats, only once in two months. Other items included half a litre vinegar, sometimes 200 gm. red beetroot jam, a box of matches, a small quantity of mustard, and rarely a small quantity of other groceries devoid of nutritional value. In the winter of 1941, the Jews received 25 kg. potatoes per person. The Jews were not given any wood or coal for heating, and were obliged to purchase these from the grocery shops intended only for Jews, established by the Jewish Council. Jews were permitted to buy unrestricted amount of vegetables from the markets in the town, but their shopping time was restricted to two hours in the afternoon, by which time most of the market produce had been sold. Since the official provision did not satisfy the needs, a section of the Jewish population who could still afford to, purchased groceries on the black market. The prices on the black market shot up without control. In 1941, the price of a loaf of bread (1400gm.) cost 30 to 40 Gulden, 1 kg. butter was 200 Gulden, a box of matches 1.50 Gulden, etc. Apart from the high costs, buying on the black market also involved mortal danger as the Germans ruthlessly pursued offenders. The Poles caught with goods or buying on the black market, were sent to jail or a camp. Jews caught for the same transgression were murdered. One woman, Mrs. Barabasz (a Latin teacher at the Jewish gymnasium, wife of the renowned Polonist, Dr. Barabasz) attempted to purchase several kilograms of potatoes from a Christian gatekeeper, and she was caught redhanded by the Gestapo. She was immediately taken to jail, never to return. Similar incidents are known about other Jews.

However, as the Jews' funds ran out, they had to contend with the official food portion. They suffered from, and became worn down by hunger, lack of decent accommodations, the cold, their thin, worn clothes, the endless moving and the physical and moral torments. Fatal diseases spread among the children, particularly among the poor, wretched orphans who had lost their parents in *Aktionen*. Everything was stolen from them; they had no home or possessions. They roamed the streets, naked and destitute, as they tried to earn some meagre amount through begging "trade" and even theft. Many people dropped dead in the streets. A member of the Jewish Council calculated, on the basis of the statistics of deaths from hunger, sickness and suicide, and taking into account of the low birth rate, that also without the *Aktionen*, no Jew would be left in Lwów within five years.[9] However, even this pessimistic calculation was wrong as the natural growth had come to a complete halt during 1942-1943. According to an estimate by Jewish physicians

[Pages 637-638]

at Lwów, more than 50% (others suggested 90%) of women no longer menstruated. Sixty to eighty per cent of the ghetto inhabitants in 1942-1943 were swollen from hunger. Many fell victim to typhoid, tuberculosis and scurvy.

No organised public aid could alleviate

Aktion Petliura **near the cathedral of the Metropolitan [Andrey] Sheptytsky**

this mass disaster. The "Jewish social assistance" and the community's welfare department, had a very limited budget. The employees of these institutions were helpless, and despite their dedication, they could only help a few individuals. They were also powerless to halt the overall catastrophe, as the German policy of extermination and extortion eliminated any possibility of effective assistance. Even the fight to cure the sick was unsuccessful under these conditions. The Jewish hospital named after [Maurycy] Lazarus on Rappaporta Street, was confiscated by the Germans immediately after their arrival, and they did not permit the Jews to transfer furniture or medical equipment to the new hospital. Yet, the Jews managed to establish three small medical clinics. These included the hospital in the school named after Tadeusz Czacki [Tzatzki], on Alembeków Street, a second hospital in a school on Kuszewicza Street, and a hospital for infectious diseases at 112 Zamarstynowska Street. Each day, the injured and disabled, the seriously ill, the dying and the starving were brought to the clinics from their places of "work" and the camps.

Notes:

All notes in square brackets [ ] were made by the translator.
Notes framed in the brackets { } contain comments provided by the author.
The spelling of most individuals' names in Pt. IV; Chapter 4, were taken from a local directory of Lwów from 1935/6.

Translator's note:

      a.   A misprint in the original. Should say Sept. 1941

Original notes:

1.   Izak Lewin *Aliti MeSpezia* [Tel-Aviv, 1947] p. 61.

2.   Quoted in the above mentioned book by Izak Lewin, the son of Dr. Jecheskiel Lewin. Izak Lewin translated his father's speech from Polish to Ukrainian.

3.   Isaac Farber, "*Cronika Shel Ish Lwów* [Chronicle of a Lwów man - the Community's Sufferings during the Nazi Occupation]" *Reshumot* Vol. I, New series, [Tel-Aviv, 1946,] p. 7.

4.   Maltiel [-Gerstenfeld, Jacob. *Be'ain Nakam...* Tel-Aviv Am Oved, 1947], p. 53.

      a.   The law regarding the occupied territories of Poland, dated 17th September 1940, *Reichsgesetzblatt*, Vol. 1, 1910, Chapter 6, Clause 2, p. 1270.

5.   Maltiel [-Gerstenfeld], *op.cit.* p. 29.

6.   About his activity, see: Izak Lewin *Aliti MeSpezia* [Tel-Aviv 1947]. (the writer was one of these saved by Sheptytsky).

7.   [Fritz] Katzmann's report of 30th June 1943 to General [Friedrich Wilhelm] Krüger, head of the secret police and the SS at the *Generalgouvernement*.

8.   Maltiel, [-Gerstenfeld, Jacob. *Be'ain Nakam...* Tel-Aviv Am Oved, 1947], pp. 63; 64.

9.   Maltiel, *op. cit.* p. 143.

10.   Maltiel [-Gerstenfeld, Jacob], *op. cit.* p. 245.

11.   **Szlojme Mayer**: *Der Untergang fun Zloczów* [Munich 1947]. pp. 21-2.

12.   J. Blitz, a Yiddish writer who was among the Tarnopol refugees, and who survived, recounted the shocking event in detail in his testimony that was published in the newspaper *Dos naje Lebn, Łódź*, in 1945.

13.   E. Unger: *Zechor* [Massada, Tel Aviv 1944/5] pp. 190-191.

14.   *Warszawski Dziennik Narodowy* 1937, 36.

Annihilation of the Jews of Lwów (cont'd)

Translated by Myra Yael Ecker

Edited by Karen Leon

[Pages 639-640]

Chapter 9. "Despite everything" - First deportation from Lwów

Despite all their sufferings, the Jews in Lwów did not lose heart. They had confidence, and they adopted an optimistic philosophy that looked forward to a better future "despite everything." They formed their views on the assumptions that the Germans had already engaged most of the Jews in hard physical work, and that Lwów's trade and industry, which depended on Jewish labour and professionals, was vital for the army at the front. Consequently, they believed, the Germans would not want to unsettle these important economic foundations and eliminate the Jews. Although they understood that in future they would still face a great deal of personal violation and wild persecutions, they hoped that eventually Germany would be defeated, which would end their sufferings.

These calculations, based on normal human rationale, did not match the policies of the centralised German authorities. From records and documents in our possession today, we now know that the Jews under the Nazi regime were unaware that the policy to annihilate the entire European Jewry had been decided in Berlin by the end of 1941. At the end of 1941 and at the beginning of 1942, the Germans launched the great extermination (*liquidierung*) *Aktionen* in the parts of Poland annexed to Germany (the provinces of Poznań, Śląsk [Silesia], Łódż). On 20th January 1942, a big committee of significant Nazis in the German government and of the Berlin Nazi party convened, and confirmed the programme to annihilate Europe's Jewry. In March 1942, Mielec [Mieletz] was the first town in western Galicia to experience the great deportation [disgorging a town of all its Jews]. It was followed by similar deportations from other towns of Poland, Brzesko, Rzeszów [Resche], Nowy Sącz [Neu-Sandez], Kielce [Kjelzy], Zamość. The great *Aktion* at Lublin took place from 17th March till 20th April, etc. In March, 1942, it was Lwów's turn.

The Nazis deployed the same strategies of subterfuge they had used everywhere else, and on every occasion, throughout their rule. They informed the Jewish Council that they wanted to move some of the Jews to other locations as the overcrowding in the town adversely affected supplies and health. Indeed, to spare the Council the unbearably heavy burden of social assistance, they proposed to remove the "antisocial" elements, in particular, such as prostitutes, beggars, and criminals listed by the secret police, and all those subsisting on social assistance. To further increase the illusion that it was not a question of an "evacuation" (*Aussiedlung*), but rather a move from one residence to another, they issued a very detailed decree listing the items that every "emigrant" was permitted to take with them. 200 Gulden in cash, provision for the trip, clothes, pillows and blankets up to 25 kg. The Germans also wanted to induce the Jewish Council to execute the execution of the evictions. They demanded that organised groups of community officials and the Jewish police use pre-prepared lists to expel people from their homes

Gravestones of Lwów's cemetery

and bring them to the assembly-point. To impart an impression that the evacuation would be conducted honestly and judiciously, they appointed a scrutinising-committee at the main assembling-point (the school on Zamarstynowska Street, named after Sobieski), in the presence of representatives from the secret police (head of the *Schupo* [*Schutzpolizei*; normal police] Dr. Ulrich), Work dept. (head of dept., Weber), representatives from the town's finance department, representatives from the SS and the Gestapo, and lastly also administrators of the Jewish Council (intermittently representing the committee were: Dr. Jaffe, Hader, Seidenfrau, Natan Buchsbaum, Szmuel Pacanowski and others). The Jewish administrators on the committee were in a difficult situation. The decisions were purely in the hands of representatives from the German departments, who treated with contempt the Jewish administrators who tried to save at least a few individuals with contempt.

Even before the "deportation *Aktion*,"

[Pages 641-642]

Dr. Adolf Rothfeld

Dr. Leib Landau

Dr. Michał Ringel

Dr. Landesberg

Isaac Jaeger

Dr. Gerszon Zipper

Dr. Abraham Korkis   Jakób Bodek   Dr. Natan Löwenstein

[Pages 643-644]

the Jews held different opinions about the question of participating in this act. It seems that several unions and parties were against the community's participation, and they informed the Jewish Council of their opposing stance. We do not have actual knowledge about the debates and meetings that took place, apart from one intervention which was probably one of many. Rabbi Dawid Kahane (who after Poland's liberation became Chief Rabbi of the Polish army), recounts that before the deportation, a delegation made up of the rabbis Israel Leib Wolfsberg, Mojzesz-Elchanan Alter, Dr. Kalman Chameides and Dr. Dawid Kahane, went to Dr. Landesberg, the leader of the Jewish Council, to warn him not to agree to involve the Jewish officials in the deportation project. Dr. Kahane related that they did not receive a clear answer from Dr. Landesberg. He only complained that the Jewish Council was not free to choose, as its acts and functions were wholly dependent on the German authorities. It appears that the community leaders hoped to moderate the evil predicament by involving the officials and the police, to save as many as they could from deportation. A few days later they realised, however, that the Germans wanted the Jews to undertake the entire operation, and that they did not select only the "antisocial elements," but also took anyone unemployed, old, children, sick and disabled, and those whose occupations were "unproductive," such as pimps, touts, etc. On occasion even work-permits were of no use. In the words of one of the high ranking German officials to his Jewish acquaintance: "A decent hiding-place is the best certificate."

Jewish officials who were tasked with the deportation project were not anxious to carry out the job. Jewish scouting groups found only a few individuals to start with, so after three days the Germans gave up on Jewish assistance and took over the entire operation. The *Aktion* took about three weeks. At times the German strategy was one of a "Blockade" of certain neighbourhoods, which they then thoroughly searched. At daybreak of 4th Nissan (1st April 1942), the *Aktion* came to an end. On the eve of Passover, the last victims were removed.

The destruction of Lwów's Jewry was considerable. Over 15,000 souls were transferred to an unknown destination. Rumours first hinted that the Jews were settled in provincial towns. Only some months later, following the earliest information they received, was it clear that they had been sent to the Bełżec extermination camp, close to Rawa-Ruska, where they were murdered by electric current or in gas-chambers. Jewish Lwów sank into mourning and a deathly silence. There was hardly a Jewish family that did not weep over its devoured sons. Even children stopped their laughter and games, and at the sight of an Ukrainian or German policeman, they fled in fear of their lives.

The people began to explore new schemes to save themselves from the danger of extermination that hovered over them.

Dr. H. Kolischer

Filip Schleicher

Dr. Emil Byk

Dr. B. Hausner

Notes:

All notes in square brackets [ ] were made by the translator.
Notes framed in the brackets { } contain comments provided by the author.
The spelling of most individuals' names were taken from a local directory of Lwów from 1935/6.

Annihilation of the Jews of Lwów (cont'd)

Translated by Myra Yael Ecker

Edited by Karen Leon

[Pages 645-646]

Chapter 10. "Work will save from Death"

Immediately after the deportation *Aktion*, the Germans carried out a roll-call of the Jewish workers. They issued new identity cards, and this time the workers received special cards and special ribbons, different from those "revoked." Every working Jew received a registration-card (*Meldekarte*) with his photograph and very detailed personal description. The registration-card also bore a very typical warning, aimed to "protect" the Jews with the following message: "It is forbidden to abduct the card-bearer, within the town." The workers' large, white ribbons were bore the letter "A" (*Arbeiter*; worker), with a personal, consecutive, number stitched on it. Every worker was also entitled to a special registration-card for one woman (his wife, mother or sister) who kept his household. These women, who supposedly were also under the protection of the Works Department, were given the letter "H" (*Haushalt*; household). Some 50,000 men and 25,000 women were given the revised registration-cards and the ribbons.

A new spirit filled the Jews after the roll-call. They clutched on to the ray of hope that the deceitful Germans conveyed. Again the Nazis managed to drive a wedge between the Jews who were "armed" with registration-cards and ribbons, and those without any protection, who faced death. The Jews believed that everyone with an "A" ribbon, and a registration-card was safe, and all the others tried to get work by any means. The Germans continued to issue cards and ribbons to every Jew accepted for work at an approved German enterprise

Removing the Dead

by the department of Work. The Jews continued to storm the new work places, since "Work will save from Death."
The new workplaces,

"The Valley of Death" where tens of thousands of Lwów's Jews were murdered

resulted in a great, bogus "prosperity." A massive production plant "the municipal workshops," was created at the time, but had a very turbulent existence in its short duration.

As late as January 1942, Dorfman, a German national (*Volksdeutsche*), arrived at Lwów to establish a tailoring and knitting workshop for the German air-force (*Luftwaffe*) and to employ Jewish workers. The German contractors and industrialists earned large sums by engaging very low paid Jewish workers. Dorfman set out to exploit this scheme. With that in mind, he negotiated with the German authorities, but did not receive a response until after the March 1941 *Aktion*. D. Greiwer, a Jewish merchant from Kraków who came to Lwów at that time, had already established "municipal workshops" at Bochnia [Salzberg] in western Galicia with great success. His workshops at Bochnia employed several hundreds of Jews, and he boasted that this saved them from deportation. When he arrived at Lwów, it seems that he acted in collaboration with Dorfman, and with several of Lwów's public-activists who sought the means to save thousands of unemployed Jews. The matter was discussed with the town's governor (*Stadthauptmann*), Dr. Heller, and his economic adjutant, Dr. Reisp, on the one hand, and with Greiwer and Dorfman, on the other. The public-activists were, the industrialist Tremski, the advocate Dr. Izydor Reisler[1] (Known after the [2nd World] War, under the name Jerzy Sawicki, and as Prosecutor at the Supreme Court of Poland, and as Prosecutor at the Criminal War Crimes Trials against the German perpetrators of Majdanek, Lublin and Nürnberg [Nuremberg]), and the young merchant, advocate Dawid Schechter. These three

[Pages 647-648]

were appointed managers of "the municipal workshops" that were established in April 1942, while Greiwer was the principal manager. This new institution was actively supported by Dr. Leib Landau, the leader of the "Jewish self-help," and by Dr. Mehrer, well known for his involvement with Lwów's Jewish craftsmen's association. The founders of the workshops hoped that the industrial undertakings would save thousands of unemployed Jews, not only workers and craftsmen, but also those from among the Jewish intelligentsia. Small-industry departments, such as haberdashery, luxury items, baskets, brushes, bookbinding, lingerie, millinery, paper boxes, small leather goods, etc., were opened at the "municipal workshops." Most of these crafts were easily learnt, and were open to free professions such as advocates, the influential, teachers, merchants, etc. It was hoped that they would acquire these in a short time. They were also accepted for other work in the workshops, work that did not require "professional" preparation. Thus, the gatekeepers and night-watchmen of the workshops included the renowned pianist, Leopold Mincer, the advocate Dr. Julius Menkes, the journalist Dr. Adolf Friedman, and others.

Dr. Reisp, a Viennese advocate and theatre-man, appointed by the German town governance, was said to be an amenable and thoughtful person, but lacked economic experience. He promised one of the Jewish managers, that in case of deportation or other danger, the "municipal workshops" would be "an oasis of peace and calm" for their workers. The Jews rushed to this place of work and salvation, and soon 3,000 Jews found work and refuge there. The management of the workshops demanded that they bring their own machines and equipment to work, as the Germans only provided bare halls and rooms (at 17, 20-22 Kazimierzowska Street; and at 9 Furmańska Street). The labourers brought the last of their money, their remaining sewing machines, or other machines and even the furniture needed in the halls. But despite the enthusiasm and energy that the managers had invested in organising the undertaking, the workshops did not turn out to be the safe haven they had hoped.

The fundamental flaw lay in establishing the workshops in agreement with the civilian town governance (Dr. Heller and Dr. Reisp) and not with the army and the SS. The agreed upon plan had stipulated that all the workshops would supply civilian provisions for the Germans (tailoring, haberdashery etc.). Representatives from the armed forces, especially those of the SS (Dr. Wagner head of the economic department, [Ernst] Inquart, and General [Fritz, Friedrich] Katzmann), claimed that such production plants were irrelevant in wartime. Throughout Germany in 1942, the competition grew much tighter between the industries of the civil administration and those of the SS. The disputes between [Hugo] Schäffer, the German Reich's Minister of war provisions, and the SS, are well known, as was the dispute between [Ernst Otto Emil] Zörner, the governmental administrative commissioner of Lublin, and General Odilo [Lothar Ludwig] Globocnik, of the SS. Similar disputes undoubtedly took place at Lwów. However, the workshops were a bone of contention not just between the municipal governance and the SS, but rather, a state of permanent dispute existed between Greiwer and the Jewish Council and between Greiwer and Weber, head of the Labour office. Weber believed that Greiwer's actions took away Weber's own supervision over thousands of Jews. The Jewish Council had more fundamental arguments against Greiwer. Although very energetic, Greiwer was a vulgar and uneducated man, whose ego would not even endure the opinions of his close friends with regard to his governance. The Council said that he aspired to great wealth in a short time, irrespective of the means, and even in partnership with Dorfman. The Jewish Council had no say in the management of the "municipal workshops," and the community members feared that the institution would eventually be in the hands of one man. Consequently, they planned to establish new workshops, under the guardianship and supervision of the Jewish Council.

The "municipal workshops" were also found ineffective and uneconomical. Most of the machines brought there, were not suited for actual production, and the abundance of untrained workers slowed down the production. The greatest obstacle, however, was the total lack of raw materials, which restricted large scale production. As a consequence, the workshops limited their manufacture to small haberdashery products and to the repair of shoes, tailored clothes, furs, etc., and all the management could do was to produce nice statistics and hold exhibitions to reassure the Germans.

Private German companies also began to show interest in Lwów's cheap Jewish labour, and established branches, there. The largest workshop was established by Schwarz, the Berlin firm, that included a large block of houses on [St.; św] Marcina Street (Nos. 3, 5, 7, 9, 11). Some 3,000 Jews worked there, in three shifts. One of the prime "productions" of this establishment was the repair and adaptation of clothes sent there by the SS from all of eastern Galicia. The clothes had belonged to Jews who were murdered by the Germans during the *Mordaktion* [murder *Aktion*]. The restored, cleansed and repaired suits were later sent to German charities in Germany, especially to WHW, *Winterhilfswerk* (Winter Relief Organisation).

[Pages 649-650]

The work at the "acquisition of raw materials" enterprise of Victor Karmin, was hard and depressing. The labourers there roamed the streets like pedlars, gathering rags and trash from rubbish heaps. Other shifts of labourers cleaned and repaired the collected material. In addition, torn and worn military uniforms from the front, covered in lice, contaminated with blood and pus, arrived there to be cleaned and repaired. Worst of all was to work with clothes of the Jews murdered in *Aktionen*.

Not only did these private companies profit handsomely from the Jewish labour, which they had for next to nothing, or free of charge, but they also charged the Jews entry fee that generally amounted to thousands of Polish Gulden. Mediators, Jews and non-Jews, arranged such workplaces and extorted large sums brokerage fees.

The Jews soon realised that even the protection of work for German institutions was a false hope, and that they were living under the sword of Damocles.

[Pages 651-652]

Chapter 11. The Imminent Disaster

This laborious "prosperity" was suddenly shattered, shocking the Jews of Lwów, with a new *Aktion*, known by the Germans as *Blitzkrieg* [flash war]. In the middle of summer, on a Wednesday, probably 24th June or 8th July 1942, an SS brigade designated to murder (a brigade termed by the Jews *Realkommando*, or *Vernichtungskommando* [extermination squad]), burst into the town and carried out a sudden and brutal *Aktion*, lasting only twelve hours, from 2pm till 2am. The *Aktion* was organised by two of Lwów's SS Officers, [Erich] Engels, [Friedrich] Katzmann's deputy and one of Lwów's Gestapo leaders, and his deputy, [Carl] Wöbke. The soldiers burst into Jewish houses and removed the "unemployed," that is to say, the elderly, women and children. The victims (numbered between 6,000 and 8,000), were taken to a transit camp (*Durchgangslager*, "*Dulag*"), near the Janowska camp, where they were murdered in terrible tortured ways. There were rumours that among the grotesque deaths, common during that dreadful slaughter, the Germans used trained hounds to attack the victims and devour them alive. The new *Aktion* left deep marks on the Jews of Lwów.

Several other small *Aktionen* took place during the summer. One night, all the Jewish veterinarian surgeons were removed from their houses and led to Janowska camp, where most of them died shortly after. On another occasion, the Germans seized all the Jews who worked for insurance companies (the Assurance agents) before the war had, and led them away somewhere. Once, an inspection parade of the Jewish police was held and about 200-250 policemen were moved to Janowska camp to serve as camp policemen. Their end, like that of all the camp's dwellers was murder.

In July 1942, another penalty (*Kontribution*) payment was demanded from the Jews. It was the third payment of this kind. As early as April 1942, the Germans declared that the second *Kontribution* did not turn out well. The third *Kontribution* did not bring them much money either. After the murder of tens of thousands of Jews, the remaining thinned out and impoverished slaughter-fodder, could not provide the desired extortion. The few optimists amongst the Jews still believed that that *Kontribution* was an indication that the Germans had changed their mind and that the ransom would serve in lieu of blood. They were wrong again.

After the total annihilation of the Jewish population had been decided upon at the meeting of the central German authorities in Berlin (2nd January 1942), fundamental changes took place within the administration. Earlier, the Jews were subject to two authorities, and two separate offices dealt with every issue. There were the civil administration (the Governor, the mayor, etc.) and the armed forces, and then there were the SS and the Gestapo which was part of the SS. At the hight of summer 1942, all issues relating to Jews passed to the SS. It was a victory for the fanatic Nazis over those considered "moderate" economic circles, who preferred to delay the extermination of the Jews until after the war. The objection of the economic and military circles, to the annihilation, was not grounded in humanitarian welfare but in sheer profitability. High officials of the civil administration (such as [Wilhelm] Kube, Governor of White Ruthenia, and Prof. [Peter-Heinz] Seraphim a specialist in the economy and population of Poland and Ukraine) and German generals, sent protest letters to the central German authorities, warning of the dangers of annihilating the Jews "prematurely." The German civil administration of Lwów also voiced its opinion on the subject in an official report dated 29th August 1942 (this document is available at the Archives of the Institute for Jewish Research, YIVO, New York). The representative of Lwów's German administration stated:

"The workforce in the district of Galicia is stretched to the limit, on top of which the removal of the Jewish work-force from the labour market was done in a most radical way. Galicia's administration only had one year to plan for the elimination of the Jewish labour force. The Aryan population of Galicia is much less agile in crafts and industry, than in other districts. Consequently, the war economy will also suffer much more than in other parts of the *Generalgouvernement*.

"It seems that the fundamental question regarding the annihilation of the Jews, was either the priority of the political reasons or those of the war-needs. The question was decided by the supreme government in favour of the political momentum, while accepting the fact that the economic production in these areas would drastically decline. I have to stress in particular that this policy will lead to very difficult results in the district of Galicia."

[Pages 653-654]

General [Fritz] Katzmann, on the other hand, made a victorious declaration in his report delivered to the head of Kraków's secret police, and the SS:

"The (civil) administration did not gather strength and was too weak to control the chaos in this area (forced Jewish labour). Consequently, the head of the secret police and the SS (General Katzmann) took over the entire operation of Jewish labour. All the Jewish labour offices (of Galicia district), where hundreds of Jews had worked, were dismantled. All the work-certificates that had been given to the Jews by different companies and offices were revoked. All the work-cards which the work departments had issued to the Jews were invalidated if not renewed by a new stamp of the Gestapo. During this inspection roll-call, thousands of Jews with false identity-cards, or who had obtained work-certificates by deceit or under other pretexts, were abducted. All of them were handed over for "special treatment" (*Sonderbehandlung* – for killing)."

Katzmann's report describes precisely what happened in Lwów and the entire district of Galicia. Lwów's Jewish labour office was liquidated in August 1942. In the farewell speech to his sacked Jewish clerks, Heinz Weber advised them how to survive in the future: "It will be better for you to be rags (labourers "collecting raw materials") than bookkeepers and clerks."

In conversation with the Jewish Council's representative, Weber also let slip: "Henceforth, issues concerning the Jews will not be settled on the basis of economy, but on that of politics."

The new SS masters immediately initiated an inspection of the Jewish workplaces. In each one, a "patrol" examined the location and dismissed Jewish workers. The dismissed workers were not sent home, they were arrested by the SS. The sick men and women were sent to "*Schmelzen*" (to smelt used iron – that is to say, killing), and the stronger ones were sent to Janowska camp. The work-cards of the survivors were marked by a new stamp during the inspection, but even they realised that it was only a temporary rescue, and that no safety lay in the new work-cards and the "A" ribbons. Katzmann was said to regularly express his disdain for the sham "protection" with these cynical words: "The ribbon imparts no shame whatsoever, the ribbon is a "death" sentence.

Katzmann's aids in the "Jewish employment" department were SS officers: Hildebrandt, for the district of Galicia, and Lenart, for the town of Lwów.

As in all other production factories, an inspection roll-call was also held in the "municipal workshops," only here, those who "deserved to be saved," had their card stamped by the SS in purple (red), rather than the black stamp given in other institutions. No one paid attention to this slight detail which seemed like a minor error. It was only during the *Grossaktion* [big action] of August 1942, that the disaster of that "error" came to light.

The situation of the 5,000 Jewish Council's clerks was quite unique. The SS refused to stamp their work-cards. This did not bode well for them.

[Pages 655-656]

Chapter 12. The *Grossaktion* of August 1942

The *Aktion* started at dawn, on Monday, 10th August 1942. It was the biggest murder action that the Germans committed in Lwów. It was systematically planned in advance by military and political experts. The *Aktion*, overseen by [Friedrich] Katzmann, was carried out by a battalion made up of the SS, the Gestapo and the German and Ukrainian secret police specialised in the extermination of human beings (*Vernichtung Komando*) [death squad]. According to German army officers, Katzmann deferred the operation several times. For every delay he received a bribe of half a million Gulden from the Jews. At the start of this *Aktion*, Katzmann remarked to Greiner, a German army officer: "Katyn? How does it apply to our operation (in Lwów)! Katyn was just a one day's job, in comparison." (evidence of Alfred Greiner, a German soldier from Munich). The *Aktion* was executed by the Germans and the Ukrainians with great precision, sanguinity and satisfaction. They blockaded specific houses, streets and neighbourhoods, one after the other, and conducted methodical searchers. After all the residents had been removed from their homes, they conducted a second inspection, and later a final inspection which they termed "fine combing" (*auskämmen*). They removed several thousand victims to Janowska camp, daily, as a result of this meticulous detections.

The Jews were unprepared for the *Aktion* that caught them unawares. Only a few protested. The Jews sought endless hiding places in cellars, tunnels and ditches, but they were mostly unsuccessful. The hiding places that were hurriedly prepared at the last minute were easily uncovered, especially with the aid of detection hounds. The Gentile children frequently divulged the hiding places to the police. The number of suicides increased, as did personal resistance and attempts to evade transport. Hundreds of such "criminals" were immediately shot by the police.

In general the Germans took the work-certificates marked during the previous inspection with the SS stamp into consideration. However, they showed exceptional cruelty towards the "municipal workshops," the old bone of contention between the

"The Killings Valley" - beside the gravestones

civil administration and the SS. On 13th August 1942, they burst into the institution with wild shouts and conducted an "inspection." At this point, as a result of the "inspection," the sordid deception of the Germans came to light. At the time, "workshops" workers were given a purple stamps. Now, the Germans claimed that only the black stamps were valid. At the time, about 3,500 labourers worked at the "municipal workshops." Since the German, Dr. Reisp, had claimed that these would be "an oasis of peace and quiet during the storm," the workers brought along also their families, to protect them during the calamity, adding another 2,000 people. The Germans transported over 4,000 Jews to Janowska camp, and left behind only 1,000 people at the institution.

The *Aktion* at the hospitals and orphanages was also terrible and cruel. The Germans removed not only the sick, but also the physicians and all the sanitary staff. Unable to move from their beds, the sick were shot on the spot. The children were thrown into the wagons like sacks, with one on top of the other.

All the victims were brought to Janowska camp where they were made to stand for hours in a large courtyard, and ordered to wait for another inspection. Meanwhile, the policemen beat them to death, and examined

[Pages 657-658]

their clothes and bodies, in search for silver, gold, precious stones, foreign coins, etc. A very small number of those imprisoned were released after the additional inspection. The *Grossaktion* ended on 23rd August 1942, during which over 50,000 people were murdered.

During the first days of the *Aktion*, the Germans still attempted to give it a "cultural" appearance. Such an appearance could not be maintained about such an undertaking of murder and killing. Soon Lwów turned into a nightmarish, bloody town. Things had gone so far that even the German civil administration, which generally concurred with the SS about the "final goal" regarding the Jews, objected to the execution of that "goal." In a report of 16th October 1942, a representative of the civil administration wrote:

"The transferral of the Jews (*Umsiedlung*) is an operation which at times appears incompatible with a cultured nation, so much so that they bring to mind a comparison between the methods of the Gestapo and those of the GPU [Soviet State security service]. It is said that the carriages used in these transportations are so dilapidated that it is impossible to stop the Jews who want to escape from the transport, from doing so. Consequently, from time to time at the railway stations en route, wild firing is heard and human hunt… Although the German and the other non-Jewish population is convinced of the need to annihilate the Jews, it would nevertheless be worthwhile for such acts of annihilation to be executed in a way that would not cause so much confusion and discontent." (from the Archives of YIVO, New York).

Order of Lwów's town *Kommandant* of 8th July 1941
regarding the Star of David badges for Jews

[Pages 659-660]

Governor of Galicia's announcement about the Lwów's Jewish Ghetto

[Pages 661-662]

Chapter 13. Establishment of Lwów's Ghetto

After the *Aktion* of August 1942, the establishment of the ghetto was announced. This announcement was not made by the civil administration which no longer had any control over the Jews. Instead, it was signed by the SS commander General [Fritz] Katzmann. The end date for the establishment of the ghetto was set for 7th September 1942. The fate of any Jew found outside the ghetto after that date, was death. This fate would also befall any Christian who sheltered a Jew outside the ghetto walls.

The establishment of the ghetto constituted another of General Katzmann's victories over the German civil administration regarding the Jews. In a report to the chief of police of the "General Government [*Generalgouvernement*]," Katzmann blamed the civil administration for lacking the required talent and mettle to "resolve the question of the Jews," and presented the reasons that led him to establish the ghetto. Even in this SS internal report, Katzmann produced false excuses and phantasies for establishing the ghetto, or in his words:

"Over time it gradually became clear that the civil administration does not possess the ability to solve the Jewish question, not even partially and unsatisfactorily. The civil administration tried, for example, to limit the number of Jews in an enclosed Jewish district, but unsuccessfully. The issue was therefore resolved by the commandeer of the secret police and the SS (i.e. Katzmann himself) and his officers, without hesitation. The order could not bear any delay because during the winter of 1941 several typhus cases were recorded in different parts of the town of Lwów. The situation was not only very dangerous to the local population, but moreover to the army, whether stationed at Lwów or passing through on the way to the front. During the transfer of the Jews from the town to the ghetto, several gates (*Schleusen*) were created for the purpose of finely sifting out all the antisocial and work-shy Jewish mob. All such elements were caught and taken for "special treatment" (*Sonderbehandlung*, that is to say, slaughter)."

Katzmann's words reveal that during the transfer from the town to the ghetto, the German secret police planned a new means of "purification" of the Jews, which they then carried out. Many Jews were murdered during the new examination, in addition to the many who fell victim to the different wild *Aktionen*, the cruellest of which took place in early September (probably 1st September 1942), within the new ghetto area.

After the order to establish the ghetto was issued, the offices of the Jewish community moved from Starotandetna Street (which remained outside the ghetto, in accordance with the new order), to the building at the corner of 15 Jakóba Hermana Street and 2 Łokieteka Street. Both the main office of the Jewish Council [*Judenrat*] and the housing office were moved there. Groups of fear stricken and homeless Jews huddled around the housing office, begging to be given a corner somewhere in the new ghetto. Suddenly, tens of hobnailed soldiers of the SS and Gestapo emerged out of their cars, tore into the people and rioted. According to rumours that spread around town, it was a "retaliation *Aktion*" [*Verwaltungsaktion*] for an incident in the town the previous day. A Jew tried to defend himself against a German clerk, during which the German was wounded and died. At the time, the leader of the Jewish Council was not in the community building, because he had been imprisoned in the jail on Łącki [Lantzki] Street, a few days earlier. It was said in town that Dr. Landesberg was jailed because he had conducted secret negotiations with the Polish underground organisations, and that he was accused of financially supporting these organisations. The German officer who managed the *Aktion* (eyewitnesses provided different names for the officer. Some said Engels, others gave the name Wöbke or Gustav Willhaus), sent a special car to bring Dr. Landesberg to the slaughtering area in the Jewish Council building. Meanwhile, the Germans managed to abduct and shoot tens of men and women in the crowd, fleeing in panic. The murdered corpses were piled into a big mound, opposite the Jewish Council building. After that deed, the Germans continued with the second act of their nightmare. They picked twelve Jewish clerks and policemen in order to publicly execute them, hanging from balconies and lamp posts. As the Germans did not have ropes, they sent for strong new ropes from the town. (The Germans later sent the receipt for the ropes to the Jewish Council, with the demand that the community reimburse the cost of the purchase. Dr. Jaffe, head of the housing office, retained the original voucher). Notwithstanding, the ropes

[Pages 663-664]

that tied several of the wretched victims, unravelled. They fell off the balconies onto the pavement below and were injured. Still, the Germans beat them, and forced those injured and bleeding to climb back to the house, where they were tied up a second time. Among those murdered were the Jewish-Polish writer, Ludwik Roth, the physician Dr. Taffet and Dr. Tunis, the community's director of the department for assistance to the Jews in the camps. Dr. Tunis, who had been an Austrian army officer, was "pardoned" from a public execution. His fate was changed to the honourable death by shooting. The rest of the victims were hung from the first floor balconies, and the street lamp posts. The Germans organised a special spectacle of ridicule for Dr. Landesberg. The Germans decided that in recognition of his status as the leader of the Jewish Council, his condemnation had to be greater than that of his clerks. His death was to be from the second floor.

Dr. Landesberg was first hanged by very thin ropes that broke immediately and he fell to the ground. Then the Germans took him back to the second floor, and the spectacle was repeated three times. Shocked, wounded and bleeding, his courage gone, Dr. Landesberg begged for mercy from his executioners. He based his plea on the legal custom that a convicted person is pardoned from the death sentence if his life was not extinguished during the execution. The Germans disregarded his request and hanged him.

ПОСТАНОВА
Управи м. Львова з 22. 7. 1941

§ 1.

Зорганізувати жидівську громаду м. Львова.

§ 2.

Затвердити ТИМЧАСОВЕ ПРАВЛІННЯ жидівської віроісповідної громади в такому складі:

Голова: Д-р Парнас Йосиф, адвокат, вул. Пекарська, 1 ц.

Заступник голови: Д-р Ротфельд Адольф, адвокат, вул. Пан-ська, 2.

Члени Управи: Д-р Гінсберг Ісидор, лікар, вул. Ягайлонська, 15; Д-р Зеравнізер Хаїм, адвокат, вул. Сикстуська, 12; Ерліх Йозуа, купець, вул. Офіцерська, 14; Зайденфрау Ізак, купець, Краківська площа, 2; Хірер Якіз, ремісник вул. Різницька, 3; Ландав Нафталі інженер, вул. Асника, 11.

§ 3.

Для потреб віроісповідної жидівської громади призначити будинок при вул. Старотандитній, 2а, що сперш був призначений для нової полікліники.

Водночас зобов'язати Відділ Здоров'я м. Львова і Житлове Управління підшукати для жидівської полікліники інший відповідний будинок.

§ 4.

Дозволити жидівській громаді наложити на членів громади податок, який призначується на цілі організації громади та фінансування установ.

§ 5.

Встановити такий тимчасовий обсяг діяння жидівської громади: 1) Ведення метрик. 2) Ведення евіденції жидівського населення. 3) Ведення шпиталів, полікліник і санітарних установ для потреб жидівського населення. 4) Організація соціальної забезпеки, дешевих кухонь і апровізації.

Голова Управи м. Львова

Д-р Ю. Полянський

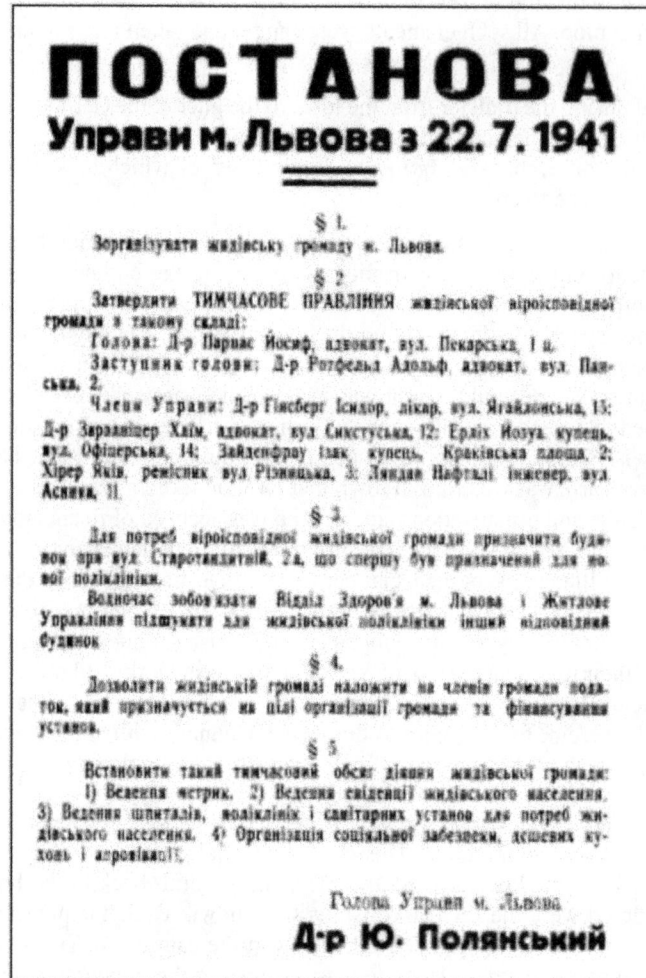

The Mayor's Notice regarding the Appointment of a Jewish Council at Lwów

[Pages 665-666]

After this event, the Germans ordered that the hanged bodies should remain on display for a day (or, two days, according to other eyewitnesses), for the Germans and the local population to see.

One of the ghetto survivors recounts the atrocity as follows:

"I went with my mother to the community about accommodation. On the balcony above, the hanged bodies swayed in the light wind, their faces turning blue. Faces of horror, their heads hung backwards and their tongues out stretched and black. Impressive cars raced from the centre of town as German citizens with their wives and children, came to view the spectacle. As usual, even here the visitors enthusiastically photographed the view. Others arrived more modestly, by tram, Ukrainians and Poles…".

Notes:

All notes in square brackets [ ] were made by the translator.
Notes framed in the brackets { } contain comments provided by the author.
The spelling of most individuals' names were taken from a local directory of Lwów from 1935/6.

Translator's note:

    a.   The son-in-law of Dr. Leib Landau.

[Pages 667-667]

Chapter 14. The Organisation and Inner Life in the Ghetto

The size of the ghetto established in accordance with [Fritz] Katzmann's order, was considerably smaller than the area which the urban administration had allocated for it, the previous year. Indeed, due to continuous murder, there were at least 70,000 fewer Jews. The new ghetto encompassed part of Kleparów and Zamarstynów suburbs (excluding that of Zniesienie). Due south, the natural boundary of the ghetto was formed by the railway tracks. To the west, from the bridge under the railway tracks up to the house number 105, lay Zamarstynowska Street. The Poltva [Peltew] River flowed on the north side, and the border to the east was delineated by Tetmajera and Warszawska Streets. Even for the one-third, remaining Jewish population after the *Aktionen* and the deportations, the area of the ghetto with its diminutive clay and wooden houses, was too small to contain them all. A large building as a rare sight in these parts. Unfortunately, the newcomers had to find accommodation among the densely packed dwellings within a fortnight between the proclamation order and the closure of the ghetto. The Jewish Council, and especially its housing department, tasked with this arduous undertaking, were put into a state of turmoil and confusion due to the *Grossaktion* [big action] and the calamity of 1st September 1942.

The public and the family life, the customs of every Jewish home, were wrecked and broken, with not a single family remaining intact after the devastation. The uprooting from the previous home to relocate in the ghetto, the accessibility, the checks and persecution foreseen on the way, resembled a new form of *Aktion*, at the end of which Jewish families found no shelter for themselves. They camped for many weeks in the streets or in gardens behind the houses, in corridors in stables and in a variety of sheds. It was late autumn, and the approaching cold and the heavy rains affected their health and greatly damaged their meagre possessions and food. The sole open space in the ghetto, Kleparów square, was full of those "who left Egypt," parked in tents, sheds, or under the open sky, bereft and destitute. In their desire to aggravate even that kind of life of the Jews, the Germans had not made the necessary preparations for the *Aryan* families to leave the ghetto before the arrival of the Jews. It was only after the Jews had arrived in the ghetto that the *Aryan* residents began to leave, whether to swap their meagre lair for a spacious Jewish apartment in town (for these exchanges the Jews were obliged to pay a large ransom), or, in order to leave the Jewish area to avoid being inflicted with the suffering of the Jews. A few months later, most of the Gentile families had left the ghetto, thereby allowing the Jews more space. The overcrowding was also reduced as a result of the large number of deaths among the Jews, in part from diseases and in part as victims of the incessant *Adktionen*. Nevertheless, the space was inadequate. Legally, every Jew was entitled to living quarters of three meters square, but such "luxury accommodation" was only theoretical. In practice, every small room with a hatch, was occupied by at least ten people, that is to say, by two, three and even four families. As there were not enough sleeping places for all, at one time, different schemes were contrived. Some opted for sleeping in two shifts, one group during the daytime and one at night (especially where day-workers and night-workers occupied the same living space). There were those who divided the sleeping time into three shifts. Others constructed ledges on two levels, and one had to climb onto these wooden tiers at night for a short sleep. The beds were of course only made for sleeping. During the daytime they had to be removed outside, in order to be able to move in the room, sweep and prepare food. A ghetto resident described the way of living as follows:

"There were very few houses in the normal sense. On the whole there were ruins, disintegrating shacks that were ready for demolition even before the outbreak of war. The ruins had previously been occupied by the lower strata of all types. Such a ruin deserves to be described: Its tiny hatches, mostly without panes, are patched and sealed with rags, sheets of paper, filthy cushions and as a measure of luxury also plywood and boards. The external walls are a grey-brown stained in rough slime and mud splashed by the wheels of wagons that slowly wove their way through the putrid puddles with their standing slush through summer and winter. All the walls are just covered in green… the north facing walls are rotten and damp up to the roof slopes. The roof is covered in shingles and the gutters are rotten and disintegrating… The passage (to the house) paved in wood planks, forms a minefield… for the feet of a stranger who might break bones and fall on his face… An apartment with "amenities" has a broken tap with a decomposing sink… hard to be taken as a tap for drinking water. The rooms… not whitewashed and not tidied, the walls and the floors are in disrepair, and in every room and dark corner, a mud stove and a rusting, sooty pipe to the chimney."[8]

[Pages 669-670]

Metropolitan Andrey Szeptycki [Sheptytsky]

The Germans introduced several types of ghettos in Polish towns. There were open ghettos (for example at Częstochowa [Chenstochowa]) and there were ghettos enclosed by walls, surrounded by a wood fence or an electrified wire. The ghetto at Lwów was surrounded by a wooden fence. The task of constructing the fence was handed to the engineer Naftali Landau, member of the Jewish Council, and the Council was responsible for the cost of the construction. N. Landau fell behind with his construction work. He explained that the work took longer due to the lack of the required wooden boards. Eventually the work came to an end, and the Jews could only enter and leave through the gate of the ghetto. Jewish policemen stood on the inside of the gate, and German and Ukrainian secret police were outside. The Jews passed through the gate on their way to work outside the ghetto. At first, everyone was entitled to go out, but later, the inspection for departure was restricted to clusters of companies

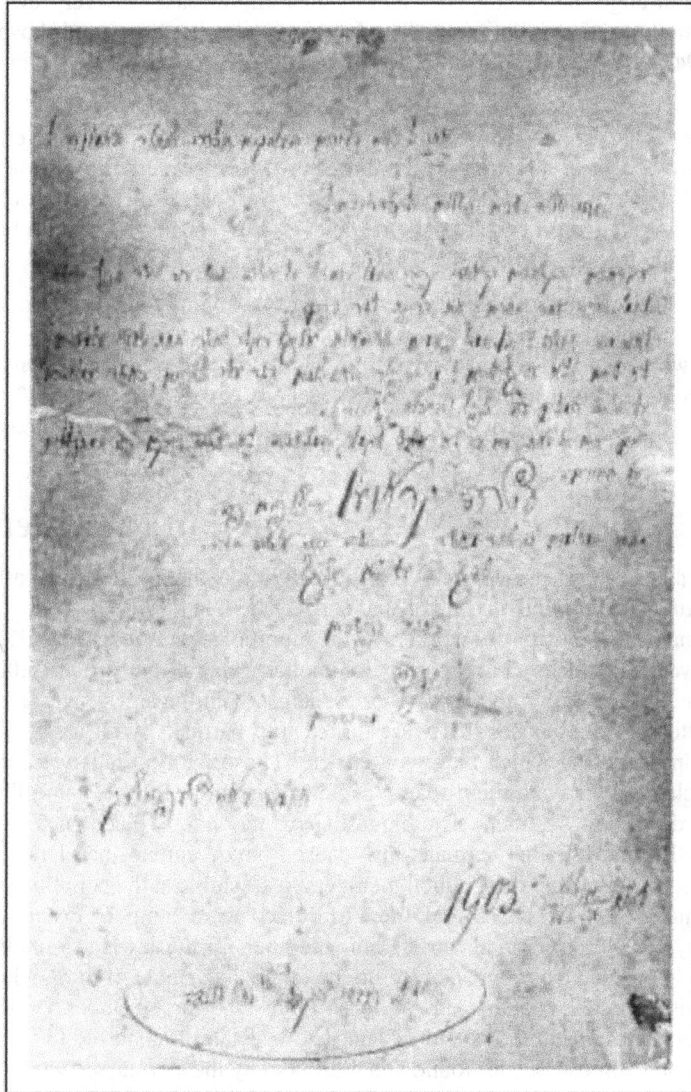

Letter of the Metropolitan Szeptycki [Sheptytsky] to the community elders (in Hebrew) 1903

[Pages 671-672]

and present work-cards. The secret police thoroughly checked the workers to ensure they did not take anything with them on their way out, nor smuggle any food into the ghetto.

Generally, the food supply for the Jewish population worsened from the moment the ghetto was created. Commercial contact and negotiation with the Christians and with the black-market was suspended. The Jewish and Christian mediators who smuggled goods into the ghetto under mortal danger, demanded exorbitant prices, at times 300%-400% of the prices on the *Aryan* black market. The official amount of food supplied to Jews was nominal, and its quality was well below standard. The main meal of a person in the ghetto (the main meal was at noon or evening, depending on the work schedule of the family members), was extremely limited, consisting of soup made of beans, potatoes or coarse groats, turnip and bread. Coffee was replaced by water of roasted beetroot, with saccharin in stead of sugar. Vegetable dishes were prepared from bramble and weeds, or potato peels and leftovers. The basic food was bread, and its quality was very poor:

"Externally, this loaf resembles bread, but the dough inside was a secret. It might have contained some flour, but its grey-brown-black colour resembled external mortar. That "something," always tacky always moist, that never dried, was a delicacy for us, despite its repellent appearance and its vile taste. And no one should think that this show-bread was brought to the ghetto on a regular basis. On the contrary. A fortune had to be paid for such a smuggled item (30 Gulden for a 1 kg. loaf)."

Different ailments spread through the ghetto. The fight against any disease was very difficult. There were no hospitals except for a small, temporary medical clinic (all the Jewish medical clinics and hospitals were liquidated during the *Grossaktion* of August 1942) nor were there pharmacy. All medicine had to be smuggled in from the *Aryan* side at inflated prices.

"The typhus epidemic spread and grew, unstoppably. A physician friend of mine who lived in the room with me, told me that he daily counted twenty-five cases of infection. At the time there were still scores of physicians in the ghetto, all of whom were inundated with work. The ghetto inhabitants tried to protect themselves as best they could. They removed their clothes and tried to regularly have a thorough wash despite the terrible overcrowding. There was no bathhouse in the ghetto, and the one outside the ghetto was purely for the militia and could only fit 100 bathers a day."[9]

As an additional problem, it was dangerous to fall ill in the ghetto. Anyone found ill immediately became a victim whom the Germans dispatched for "special treatment" [*Spezialbehandlung*]. As a consequence, the sick walked around with 39°-40° temperatures, in the freezing winter, and pretended to be well. At work they stood, as usual. On their return they had injections, self-administered or by an acquaintance, usually in the toilet so as not to be seen by anyone. The will to live and to overcome all tribulations was so great, that some of those who were wretchedly sick succeeded in recuperating, at least superficially.

[Pages 673-674]

Chapter 15. New *Aktionen* in the Ghetto

On 18th November 1942, the Germans carried out a new roll-call in the ghetto. This time, all the factory workers and those working in the military institutions were given a tin tag that carried the letter "W" (*Wehrmacht* = armed forces) or the letter "R" (*Rüstungsindustrie* = armaments industry), to workers of the munitions factories. About 12,000 men and women received the new tags. The roll-call gave the Germans an opportunity for another "purge," and around 5,000 "unnecessary persons" were murdered. Those surviving the "purge" fell into two categories. Those with the signs "W" or "R," were given the best living accommodations in the ghetto, in stone houses that were turned into barracks, with a sign on each barrack indicating the residents' company and the institution in which they worked, etc. Those with no tags were deemed unnecessary, and were victimised. The cabins and clay shacks were their dwellings and their entire lives became illegal. Every time the Germans searched the ghetto they murdered many of them. The biggest *Grossaktion* took place on 5, 6, 7 January 1943, when around 15,000 people were murdered. This time the Germans also caused havoc among the clerks of the Jewish Council. Before the *Aktion*, an order was issued calling on all the Council members to assemble at the community hall. Once they had gathered, the Germans burst in and removed the clerks, and took them to Bełżec death camp, or to Janowska camp. A short while after that (probably on 4th February 1943), the Germans ordered the members of the Jewish Council (there were still 12 people on the board), to appear for a roll-call. Some of them showed up the others hid. Some of those who did show up, were murdered, including the head of the Jewish Council, Dr. Obersohn and his friends Dr. Marceli Buber, Dr. Kimmelman, Chiger and others. Others were sent to Janowska camp, including Szymon Ulam who was later transferred to Dachau camp, where he perished. Those who managed to hide, were almost all later found and murdered by the Germans. Two board members, Dr. Scherzer and Dr. Leib Landau, hid in *Aryan* neighbourhoods, and their hiding places were uncovered by the Germans (their *Aryan* neighbours probably informed on them). The Germans took them to the Jewish jail in the ghetto, where they were murdered. The physician and board member, Dr. Ginsberg, evaded the murderers, and for a time he masqueraded as a Christian, substantiated by false *Aryan*documents. Later, after the ghetto was emptied of its Jewish residents due to the incessant *Aktionen*, he hid there in caves and among the ruins. Hundreds of men and women hid among those ruins, in those days. As the Germans had condemned them as unemployed, aged, orphaned, homeless and unprotected, they existed in a permanent state of mortal danger. Although the ruins were empty and exposed, still, they encountered Ukrainian detectives or ordinary thieves and extortionists looking for hidden Jews, for valuables left after the massacre, and for the imaginary extreme wealth which according to urban myths had been buried by Jews before their deaths, in basements and in the ground. When the searchers found living Jews –"rats"– hiding among the ruins, they threatened them. To buy their secrecy, they extorted the Jews' remaining possessions. Notwithstanding, on occasion they turned the Jews over to the secret police even after been paid. Such a life grew too much for Dr. Ginsberg, and he committed suicide. Presumably, a large number of suicides were committed under such persecution.

During the *Aktionen* of winter 1942-1943, the Germans employed new "war tactics," to stop Jews from attempting to escape as they had done in the earlier *Aktionen*. Consequently, the Germans removed the clothes from all those they transported, driving them, naked and possessionless to the place of murder. At times the wagons and train carriages (goods wagons) were open, and even in the depths winter the Germans did not alter their tactics. The transports were always closely guarded by German or Ukrainian policemen armed with automatic rifles and assisted by sniffer dogs trained to hunt human-beings. The wagons were closed and bolted (the open carriages were surrounded by barbed wire) and the Jews were not allowed to alight at the stations, even to use the toilet. Despite all the guarding measures, many still escaped. Some managed to break the small openings, some pierced the floor of the wagon and jumped through those during the voyage, and ran. Many of those who jumped, died as they fell, or were murdered by police guns or the hounds' teeth. Many succumbed to the cold and starvation as they roamed naked in the fields and forests. Many of

[Pages 675-676]

those who jumped fell into the hands of the secret police. Very few managed to escape with their lives, and acquire food and some clothes from the farmers who took pity on them. They could return to Lwów. However, not many famers showed any pity for the Jews. The "leapers" (*die Springer*) turned into a household name among the Jewish public. There were experienced experts who had jumped three or four times, and they were noted for being "exemplary people." In general, anyone who had survived a jumping episode was no longer an ordinary person. It was difficult for the "leapers" to adjust to the "ordinary" life of the ghetto. They did not have work certificates, places to live or clothes and personal possessions. Most of them encamped in the hall of the Jewish Council, or in the streets. At the following inspection or *Aktion* they were again sent on the death-transport [*Todestransport*].

From every examination and search through the ghetto jail, the detectives gathered those destined for the death-transports, until they had reached the number required for a transport. To begin with, the jail was at 25 Wierzbiekiego Street in the Kleparów suburb, but after part of the suburb had almost been emptied of people due to the fires and the frequent *Aktionen*, the jail was relocated to 15 Weyssenhofa Street. There was a weekly "clearing" of the jail, and the prisoners were taken to the extermination area in the "Sands" [*piaski* in Polish] near the cemetery on Janowska Street, or to Lesienice [Lysynychi] Forest. The expression "He was taken to the Sands," meant that he was murdered.

[Pages 677-678]

Chapter 16. The Ghetto is made a *Julag*

At the beginning of 1943, the regulations of the ghetto underwent far-reaching changes. By order of Minister Heinrich [Luitpold] Himmler, leader of the Protection Squadron [*Schutzstaffel*] and the SS, the Germans intended to turn the remaining ghettos into labour-camps during 1943. Such an order was issued, for example, to the German Command in Warsaw, in spring of 1943, at Litzmannstadt-Łódź [ghetto], in September 1943, and so on. The change in Lwów took place early, after the *Aktion* of January 1943. At that point, the Jewish area was renamed, from ghetto to *Judenlager* [Jewish camp], abbreviated as *Julag*. The way of life at the *Julag* was different from that in the ghetto. The Germans instituted a strict military discipline. A large part of the old ghetto was liquidated, and all the working Jews were moved to barracks. Other streets, including Żródlana Street and the Kleparów suburb, were placed outside the ghetto parameters. The Jewish Council was totally eliminated (Feil was the last leader of the Council, who had little influence over Jewish public life), and it was not replaced by a single institution that officially represented all the Jews of the ghetto. From now on the Germans assigned so called "Jewish elders" for every work-company, a post which naturally bore no self-governing authority. The Jewish workers were forbidden from leaving the ghetto individually. Only groups could cross the gate at set times on the way to work and back again. The rest of the Jews who did not work, including the workers' families, their parents, wives and children, were a source of plunder for the Germans. The Nazis held the view that the lives of these "unemployed" were superfluous and wanton. A Jew who did not work for the German industry had no right to exist, and inspections were regularly undertaken to catch the "illegal" Jews of whom a few thousands still existed until the Germans managed to reduce the *Julag* residents to 12,000 "legal" workers. And yet, after the *Aktionen*, thousands of "illegals" were still alive until the liquidation of the ghetto.

The SS headquarters also underwent changes. General Katzmann left Lwów at the beginning of 1943. He was superseded by General Jürgen [Josef] Stroop, whom the Germans considered a great expert in the annihilation *Aktionen*. Stroop remained in Lwów for one year, until April 1943, when he was called to Warsaw to organise the war against the ghetto uprisers. SS commanders were appointed leaders of the *Julag*, the first among them was SS Officer Mansfeld, and his deputy Siller. He was followed by the SS Officer (*SS-Hauptscharführer*) Józef Grzymek, and his deputy Heinisch. Grzymek, who took up his position on 19th February 1943, was the cruelest of them all. Even before his arrival in Lwów he excelled as an officer at Jaktorów, the labour-camp for Jews [*Judenlager*] (in east Galicia). It was he who liquidated the camp after murdering all its Jewish prisoners. Later, he managed the Rawa Rusca ghetto. Also this ghetto, which he considered "an exemplar ghetto" because of the iron discipline and the slave labour practised there, was liquidated by himself. Grzymek tortured the Jews in the *Julag* of Lwów, tyrannising them with practical jokes, accessibility, persecution and severe torment, and with his excessive demands for discipline and cleanliness. Demands that bordered on insanity.

"Grzymek undertook the purification of the ghetto," one of the *Julag* inhabitants recounts. "The streets were crammed with litter. The houses were vile and filthy even before the arrival of the Jews. Heaps of waste in every courtyard and corner, and all the houses were like ruins. Grzymek's madness was unstoppable, however. He ordered 24 denouncing placards bearing the slogan "Order must be kept!" ("*Ordnung muss sein*"), to be set in the form of a crescent, and also boards with the saying on the virtue of hygiene: "If your house is clean you will be a healthy person!"

"He particularly harassed the 'cleaners' (Jewish women in charge of the ghetto's cleanliness), and checked their work on a daily basis. He attacked them with cruel anger for the slightest bit of untidiness, and ordered them to hang his boards in the barracks and in all the houses… He wore white gloves as he checked for dust, the holes and cracks. He tortured the gatekeepers to death, if they were unable to repair a broken plumbing, or a blocked sewer. Any gatekeeper considered negligent, received 25 lashings from the whip in Grzymek's hand.["][10]

[Pages 679-680]

Grzymek passed through the entire ghetto in a horse-drawn wagon every morning, for a first inspection. The wagon rushed by and a group of Jewish policemen ran behind at his command. He kept a close watch on the cleanliness in the streets and the houses. When he noticed the slightest spec of dirt on one of the windowpanes, he immediately smashed it to pieces. He entered the houses for inspection, and if he disapproved of anything, he caused a scandal in the house, broke dishes and furniture, spilt and threw out the food. When he found "illegal" individuals wandering in the house, or Jewish workers absent from their work for any reason (ailment, day of rest at the factory where they worked, etc.), he ordered the policemen to put them in jail. He murdered hundreds of Jews in this manner. In addition, Grzymek carried out *Grossaktionen*. In one such *Aktion* on 17th March 1943, around 1,500 people were murdered. In another *Aktion*, 800 individuals were sent to the extermination-camp Auschwitz [Oswięcim].

Grzymek set up a Jewish orchestra that was ordered to play daily, at the entrance to the *Julag*, when the work-companies left for the town. By order of the Germans, the orchestra played dance music, marches (the famous march named after Radetzky, *Radetzky Marsch*) and classical tunes by Mozart or Beethoven (the German soldier Alfred Greiner recalls, for example, hearing this orchestra play Beethoven's Third Symphony, at the gate of the ghetto).

Grzymek remained commander of Lwów's ghetto until the *Julag* was liquidated. After that he was sent to command the Szebnie camp near Jasło in west Galicia, where he also made a name for himself for his cruelty and horrific acts of sadism. Grzymek was caught after the war, and was put on pubic trial in Warsaw, in April 1949. The court sentenced him to death.

[Pages 681-682]

Chapter 17. Statistics of the Crimes perpetrated by the Nazis against Lwów's Jews

The changes in the numbers of Lwów's Jewish population will provide an astonishing description of the Germans' rate of murder. The numbers presented here were given to the author immediately after the liberation of Lwów in August 1944, by Dr. Weiser. Dr. Weiser had been the director of the department for food-cards in the Jewish Council of Lwów, and he still had notes which included the pertinent numbers. These numbers are of course not precise. An office card-index, and food-cards, did not accurately reflect the population numbers for several reasons. On the one hand the number of the population was smaller than that of the listed cards, as many families did not report their dead and murdered, in order to keep the additional food-rations as starvation gripped the Jewish neighbourhood. Many families also believed that their sons, who were taken for "work" or to the camp, would return and therefore kept them on the register. On the other hand, a large number of "illegals," refugees, "criminals," political activists and even ordinary Jews, chose to forgo the substandard food portion because they felt safer when their name was not listed in the open card-index of the Germans. Anyone who planned to hide or to pose as a Christian with the use of fake *Aryan* documents, were not registered. It is difficult to ascertain what percentage needs be added to the number on the register, and what percentage subtracted, but one can surmise that the numbers were closely balanced, and that subsequently the registered numbers closely reflect the truth. The reported numbers were as follows:

In June 1941, according to estimates by the community and by General [Fritz] Katzmann (*see* Pt. IV: Chapter 1), there were between 150,000 and 160,000 Jews in Lwów. Those who registered for food-cards, in subsequent months, numbered as follows:

October 1941	119,000 Jews
November	109,000 Jews
December	106,000 Jews
January 1942	103,000 Jews
February	97,000 Jews
March	96,000 Jews
April	86,000 Jews
May	84,000 Jews
June	82,000 Jews
July	82,000 Jews
August	76,000 Jews
September	36,000 Jews
October	33,000 Jews
November	29,000 Jews
December	24,000 Jews

We do not have official data from this date onwards, since the institutions of the Jewish Council were liquidated at the end of January 1943.

[Pages 683-684]

Chapter 18. Spiritual Life in the Ghetto, the Fate of Writers, Scholars and Artists

It is too early to form a true picture of the cultural life in the ghetto, especially since any cultural life had to be "invisible" and because it operated underground for fear of the Germans' prohibitions and harsh persecutions. The Germans considered even taking part in a private *Minyan*, a grave sin that cost the life of anyone caught (see Pt. IV; Chapter 4). Whereas in some towns, such as Warsaw, Wilno [Vilna; Vilnius], Łódź, and to some extent also at Częstochowa [Chenstochova], Będzin [Bendzin], Sosnowiec [Sosnowitz], Kraków and others, cultural life could develop, Jewish schools, synagogues and Torah-study functioned, it was possible to hold talks and concerts and establish theatres, youth sports associations and even to produce periodicals (such as *Vilner Geto-Yediyes, Litzmannnstadt Getto Zeitung, Gazeta Żydowska*, in Kraków), the Jews of Lwów were prevented from all overt cultural activities. Immediately after the arrival of the Germans, Jewish public activists convened a meeting of all leaders from the different factions and parties, to discuss the establishment of schools, and the 20 participants seriously debated the questions of education and culture (the meeting took place in the summer of 1941). A department of education was formed within the Jewish Council but due to the strict prohibition of the German authorities, not a single school opened. All attempts to obtain permission for any cultural activity, to hold lectures, courses, performances or a Jewish theatre and so on, were futile. The Germans did not manifest such a negative attitude towards cultural expression in any other large Jewish community as they did at Lwów. After a few months of deliberations and unsuccessful lobbying, the Council's department of education and culture abandoned its work. No overt, organised cultural or religious activity took place at Lwów. *Minyanim* and prayer groups convene, children met to study in private houses, and a few authors held meetings, all in great secrecy. Representatives of political parties, youth-movements, etc., met for discussions. On several occasions literary gatherings were held in the offices of the Jewish Council. Such gatherings were also secretly held. These gatherings, initiated by the advocate, Dr. Henryk Graf, who worked in one of the Council offices, were held in different rooms so as not to arouse suspicion (this was during the first months of the German invasion, when the community offices were spread throughout the town). Generally, Abraham Blatt, who had been an editorial board member of *Chwila* (a daily Polish-Jewish newspaper) before the war, opened the gatherings with a short address on current affairs. This was followed by a reading of chapters from the Bible (Prophets, Psalms or the five Scrolls) by the actress, Hoffman. Occasionally, the poet Maurycy Szymel read from his sad-lyric poems. After the literary section, a kind of "live newspaper" was edited with sharp words about the *Judenrat* and so on, (these were usually written by Dr. I. Berman and by the refugees from Kraków, the young writers Elisha Weintraub, Dr. Kornreich and Maksymilian Boruchowicz [later named, Michał Borwicz]). After a while, however, a short mention of these literary gatherings was made in the Kraków newspaper, *Gazeta Żydowska*. The organisers of the literary gatherings ceased holding them, in fear of persecution, but it may have been a false alarm as the Germans paid no attention to the matter.

Only in the fields of music playing and singing, did the Germans permit the Jews, or better said forced them, to undertake public cultural activities. Lwów had many Jewish musicians and singers, some renowned in their field, which the Germans and the anti-Semitic Poles used in their propaganda. A satirical "song" about Lwów's Jewish musicians appeared in the daily newspaper, *Gazeta Lwowska*, which named over forty artists (*see* Appendix VI). The Germans formed two orchestras from among the Jewish musicians, one at the *Julag*, and the second at Janowska camp. The Jewish Orchestra members were forced to play during very tragic moments, during the menacing inspections and the roll-calls at the gate of the ghetto, and in the camp.

In short, all we know about the ghetto's cultural life is that it was not underpinned by progression, and life, but rather, by bitter struggle and the destruction of the Jewish culture and its creators. We were able to assemble a little information about the fate of the intelligentsia during the Holocaust, their works and deaths. We enter this fragmented information here, for eternal memory.

There were in Lwów many Jewish authors who wrote in Yiddish, Hebrew or Polish. During the Russian occupation, these authors formed

[Pages 685-686]

a separate, Jewish section within Lwów's general authors' association. This section was led by the Yiddish writer Dovid Königsberg (who translated the poem *Pan Tadeusz* [by Adam Mickiewicz]) into Yiddish, and the secretary was the young Yiddish poet, Jakób (Jankel) Szudrich [Schudrich]. A small number of the Jewish authors succeeded in escaping from Lwów to reach Russia before the Germans arrived. Those who remained at Lwów were almost all murdered by the Nazis. Among the Yiddish writers were:

Dovid Königsberg was sent to Janowska camp, where he perished. The Yiddish author **Jerachmiel** (Miltche) **Grin** [Grün], author of "The Weavers of Kołomyja" (*Di Veber fun Kolomije*) previously toiled as a porter in one of the departments of the Jewish Council (the department of nutrition, or of transport). Grin continued his literary work while in the camp. He wrote a novel about life in the camp, passages from which he read out loud to his friends at an opportune moment. The text was lost when its author was lost. His wife, the poet **Halina Grin**, was also murdered at Janowska camp. She composed the prisoners' melancholy poem that opens with the words: "We sit on the slopes of the mountain of Sand and drink 'to Life, with Death'," which became known, and soon turned into a kind of hymn of the camp's prisoners. **Jankel Szudrich** wrote poems about the Baal Shem Tov and the Ukrainian outlaw [*Hucuł* in Polish], [Oleksa] Dovbush (according to folk legend, the Baal Shem Tov was on friendly terms with Dovbush), and probably additional poems. In one surviving letter, Szurdich described his mood and his literary work in 1942. "I leave these rough poems, raw and unpolished, without any amendments. I see that the annihilation of my People is a fact. Here, these remaining few poems will, nonetheless, bear witness to the fact that I existed and created while the butcher's knife hovers over my neck… I incessantly dreamt of at least fighting alongside the partisans, somewhere in the forests, even though I have never held a rifle in my hand I would have liked to acquire this craft, and I was prepared to confront the most dangerous. Unfortunately, luck was not on my side…". Despite all the obstacles, eventually Szudrich managed to step in the direction of realising his dream. In February 1943, a group of youths that included Szudrich, got together and tried to break out of the ghetto and join the partisans. They negotiated with some Christians who promised to transport them to the forest, in their cars. It was probably a provocation instigated by the Gestapo, and the youths fell into the trap. The car was surrounded by armed secret police, and all the passengers were murdered.

Some writers disappeared without a trace, including, (Maurycy) **Szymel, Sanie Friedman** who was in Janowska camp. **Debora Vogel-Barenblüth** (who wrote poems and philosophical essays also in Polish). **Berl Schnapper, Daniel Ihr, Esther Schuldenrein**, the young YIVO [Yiddish Scientific Institute] aspirant, etc. It was said that **Izrael Weinlös** was caught during the *Aktion* against the aged (at the end of 1941), and was murdered.

Not everyone who managed to escape before the German invasion, managed to survive. The talented poet and journalist **Samuel Jakób Imber** was obliged to leave Lwów while it was still under Soviet control because it was reported that his poetry was not "Kosher" from the Marxist point of view. He settled in the small town Jezierna, with his parents-in-law. From there he moved to Złoczów, to the house of his brothr-in-law Dr. Hertznik, who was the director of the Jewish hospital. Imber continued his literary work and read out his compositions to the clinic's workers and patients. During the *Aktion* of 3rd November 1942, the poet was caught and taken to Bełżec extermination camp. His friends and acquaintances guarded his literary legacy, until they too were murdered, and with them, Imber's last works were lost.[11]

The renowned Yiddish author, **Alter Kacyzne** [Katzizne], who arrived as a refugee in 1940 and settled at Lwów, had met with a tragic end full of sufferings. During the Soviet period, he was among the spokesmen for the Jewish writers, and was appointed the literary manager of the Yiddish language broadcasts on radio Lwów. The opera *Die Judens Opera* (The Jews'

Opera) which he composed, was accepted for performance by the State Theatre of Kiev. With the outbreak of the Soviet-German war, Kacyzne escaped from Lwów, but when he reached the Tarnopol area, the Ukrainians set upon him and murdered him in a torturous and strange fashion.[12]

Among the lost Hebrew writers were:

Mojżesz Feld, an author and teacher (teacher at the *gymnasium*, 17 Zygmuntowska Street), Dr. **Mozes Waldmann-Goliger**, a researcher in Semitic languages, and lecturer at the Institute of Judaic Studies in Warsaw, was actively involved at the office of the Jewish mutual aid, and assisted authors and scholars. By the end of 1942, he disappeared, probably caught in the *Aktion* of August 1942. **Dr. Israel Ostersetzer**, was a lecturer in the Talmud at the Institute of Judaic Studies in Warsaw, and a renowned scholar in his field. He was caught in the first days after the Germans arrived in July 1941, and he never returned.

[Pages 687-688]

Among the large group of Jewish writers who wrote in Polish, those who were arrested at Janowska camp included:

The poet and literary critic, Dr. **Karol** Dresdner, the poet, **Aleksander Dan**, the satirist, **Zygmunt Schorr**. From amongst them only Zygmunt Schorr continued his writing in the camp. While he wrote notes about camp life, Aleksander Dan and Karol Dresdner fell into depression. The writers **Halina Górska, Rafael Lan** were lost without a trace. Lan's actual name was Lichtenstein (the Bund activist, Israel Lichtenstein, was his son), and he was known as an author of radical-socialist novels. Dr. **Mojżesz Kanfer** and **Chaim Lew**, were both from Kraków. Dr. **Ludwik Roth**, as mentioned, was cruelly murdered by the Germans on 1st September 1942.

A large number of the Jewish victims murdered in Lwów, were scholars. Among the renowned scholars in Judaic Studies, in addition to the above mentioned Dr. Goliger and Dr. Ostersetzer, was the Jewish-Polish historian, Dr. **Jakób Schall**, teacher at the Jewish *gymnasium* at 17 Zygmuntowska Street, who was arrested in the *Aktion* of August 1942. Dr. Schall collected to the very end, the historical details of the tragedy of Lwów's Jews, and he secreted his notes in various places, but they were all lost after his murder. During the occupation, Dr. Schall also prepared an historical study of the Karaites in Poland, at the request of Dr. Leib Landau, head of Lwów's office of Jewish aid. Dr. Landau was ordered by the German authorities to furnish explanatory material on the Karaites and their racial origin. Dr. **Falik Hafner**, a young historian, was one of Prof. Bałaban's students. Hafner, managed the grocery shop on behalf of the Jewish community in the ghetto, and used his position, with the consent of the Jewish Council's financial department, to secretly organise assistance for Jewish writers and scholars, and he was dedicated to his work. During the *Aktion* of August 1942, he hid in a bunker but was found by the Germans. When he tried to escape from among the rows of prisoners led to the gallows, the Germans shot and murdered him. Dr. [Salomon] **Czortkower**, a renowned Jewish anthropologist was murdered during the *Aktion* at the end of 1942. Dr. **Jakób Willer**, a linguist and researcher of the Yiddish language, had been relocated by the Germans to the Zniesienie suburb, where he starved to death. **Isachar Madfes**, the author of "A History of Zionism [*Historia syjonizmu*]" in Polish and Yiddish, was caught by German guards who found him in the street a few minutes after 8 p.m., the curfew hour for Jews (in 1942). Those who disappeared without information about their end, include: the literary critic and Hebrew philologist, **Ozjasz Tillemann**, teacher at the *gymnasium*, 17 Zygmuntowska Street. **Jehuda Kohn**, manager of the Jewish community's library. **Maksymilian Goldstein**, Jewish art collector who owned a large musical collection.

In addition to the teachers mentioned previously among the list of writers and scholars who died, one needs to mention, Dr. **Isachar Reiss**, a founding member of *HaShomer HaTzair* in Vienna and Galicia, headmaster of the Hebrew *gymnasium* "Tarbut" [Culture], at Równe [Rivne; Rovno], died of typhus in the ghetto, at the end of 1942 or the beginning of 1943. Dr. **Barlas**, headmaster of the Hebrew school at Zbaraż and later Hebrew teacher at the Łódź secondary school, also died of typhus. **Abraham Roth**, headmaster of Lwów's commercial secondary-school and manager of the educational department at the ghetto, died during one of the *Aktionen* of 1943. Dr. **Cecylja Klaften**, the educator also renowned for her involvement in training girls for professions, was caught during one of the *Aktionen* and sent to Bełżec death camp (at the end of 1942 or early in 1943). Nothing is known of the fate of [**Benzion**] **Siwek**, the Hebrew teacher and composer of textbooks; about Dr. **Szlome Igel**, psychologist and headmaster of the Hebrew *gymnasium* at 17 Zygmuntowska Street; or about the religion teacher Prof. **Zygmund Sens-Taubes**. All of them disappeared.

There was a large number of Jewish journalists among the Nazis' victims:

Dr. **Marus Sobel**, teacher and active member of *Poale Zion* [Workers of Zion], was murdered at Lwów during the massacre on St. Anna Street. **Benzion Ginsberg** and **Dawid Frenkel** who were at Janowska camp, were both involved with the organisation of Jewish prisoners: Ginsberg, with covert, literary activities, and Frenkel, in the underground and resistance movement. **Henryk Hescheles** was among the first victims of the *Brygidki* slaughter. Lost without trace were: **Meszulem Rettig, Joel Spiegel**, director of the Lwów Bureau of *JTA* [Jewish Telegraphic Agency]. **Zygmunt Reich, Abraham**

Brat among the editors of *Chwila*. **Naftali Hauser**, the administrative director of *Opinia*, **Adolf Krumann, Dr. Henryka Fromowicz-Stiller, Stanisław Salzmann, Henryk Passierman, Isaac Damm, Emil Igel, Leon Dreikurs, Jakób Istner, Maksymiljan Schönfeld, Mojżesz Rabinowicz**, the Yiddish writer **Fischel Witkower**, Dr. **Roller, Józef Markus, Jakób Bodek** and Dr. **Dawid Schreiber**. The last two were, at one time, members of the Polish *Sejm*.

[Pages 689-690]

Those among the scientists whose lives were cut short, were:

The renowned jurist Prof. **Maurycy Allerhand**, the university lecturer Prof. **Szymon Auerbach**, and **Dr. Sternbach**, Prof. of mathematics at the University of Lwów. The physics lecturers, Dr. **Fuchs** and Dr. **Griffel** (murdered at Janowska camp). The psychologist,cl Dr. **Leopold Blaustein**, the philosopher Dr. **Stefan Rudniański**. The classical languages philologists, Prof. **Marian Auerbach**, Dr. **Jakób Hendel** and **Miss Schulbaum**. The Romance languages philologist, **Helena Schlüsser**. The Germanists, Dr. **Izydor Berman**, Dr. **Arnold Spet** and Prof. **Herman Sternbach**, all three of whom wrote extensively about the Jewish problem in German literature and culture. The Polonist, Dr. **Wilhelm Barbasz**. Dr. **Henryk Balk**, who researched the history of Polish literature, committed suicide soon after the German invasion.

We do not yet have full information about the fate of the rabbis and their assistants who were martyred at Lwów. We have data about some of them:

R' **Aaron Lewin**, the renowned rabbi, leader of *Agudas Yisroel* in Poland, and representative at the Polish *Sejm*. His brother, Rabbi Dr. **Jecheskel Lewin** (*see* Pt. IV, Chapter 6, about both of them). The rabbis, R' **Izrael Leib Wolfsberg, R' Mozes Elchanan Alter, R' Schmulka Rappaport** and Dr. **Kalman Chameides**. The *Admor* **Abraham Jakób Friedman** of Boyan, who was a Turkish citizen, was arrested by the Gestapo during one of the *Aktionen*.[13]

There were a great many losses amongst those in the field of Jewish art, especially in music, instrument playing and singing. Amongst the slain artists were:

The orchestra managers, **Jakób Mund**, who was at Janowska camp; **Marceli Horowitz**, and **Alfred Stadler**. The composers, **Leonid Striks** (who was at Janowska camp), **Maks Striks, Józef Frenkel, Skolka** and **Wilhelm Kristal**. The players and pianists, **Leon Zak, Leon Eber**, [Zygmunt] **Schatz** (who was at Janowska camp), **Józef Herman** (who was at Janowska camp), **Hildebrand, Brajer, Edward Steinberger** (was at Janowska camp), Dr. **Aron Dubschitz, Priwes**, committed suicide. The professors at Lwów's conservatoire: **Leopold Münzer, Mark Bauer, Arthur Hermelin** and others. **Pollak**, who was a renowned young prodigy, **Feller, Fiszer, Szrage Buchsbaum** and others, Lwów's opera singers.

During the Soviet occupation, there was a State-Jewish Theatre in Lwów, under the management of Ida Kamińska. Most of the theatre actors and management staff succeeded in escaping Lwów before the arrival of the Germans. Among these who remained and perished in the town, were:

The theatre director, **Mark Katz**, the actors, **Rot** and his wife, **Sonia Altman**, and others. Among the victims of the Nazis were also Jewish actors who performed at Lwów's Polish Theatre: **Roman Grodniewski, Helena Plusner** and the administrative director, Dr. **Axer**.

And among the painters and graphic artists were:

Arno Erb, Marcin Kicz, Henryk Langerman, Julia Acker, Gabriela Frenkel, Stadler, Aleksander Rimmer (died in Paris), the decorator, **Fryc Kleinmann** (perished at Janowska camp), and the graphic artist, **Menkes**.

Among the cultural figures we must also mention the Jewish physicians and the advocates, well known in their fields or for their involvement in public work. There were several hundred Jewish physicians in Lwów before the arrival of the Germans. According to a statistics collected by an anti-Semitic Polish newspaper,[14] in 1937 there were 625 Jewish physicians, and at least 200 in Lwów. Later, especially during 1939-1940, refugee physicians from Germany, Austria and western Poland increased these numbers, and there may have been at least 1,000 physicians in Lwów. Only a few tens of them survived. Some escaped as military physicians with the Russian army, some managed to hide, and others survived the camps. The space is too short to mention them all, and only the names of the best known are listed here:

The stomatologist Dr. **Allerhand**, Prof. Dr. [Adolf] **Gizelt** (veterinarian). The anaesthetists: Dr. [Stanisław] **Ruf**, Dr. [Maksymiljan] **Jurim** and Dr. [Marek] **Gimpel** (who committed suicide), Dr. **Schnitzer**, an internist. Ophthalmologists, the elderly Dr. [Wiktor] **Reiss** and Dr. [Oswald] **Zion**, Dr. **Oxner** (according to rumours, he committed suicide), Dr. [Eugenius] **Wolner**, Dr. **M. Bikeles**, Dr. **Adolf Rosmarin**, Dr. [Mendel] **Brill** and others.

In 1934, there were 365 Jewish advocates in Lwów, and a large number of "applicants" (university graduates awaiting the licence to open a lawyer's bureau)

[Pages 691-692]

Only a fraction of them survived the Nazi destruction, and of these we will mention:

Dr. **Leib Landau** (*see* Pt. IV; Chapter 16), Dr. **E Scherzer** (*see* Pt. IV; Chapter 16), Dr. **Henryk Landesberg** (*see* Pt. IV; Ch. 13), Dr. **M. Achser**, the public activist Dr. **Maks Schaff**, Dr. **Anzelm Lutwak**, Dr. **Leon Chotiner**, Dr. **Henryk Graf**, Dr. **Lauterstein**, and others.

Annihilation of the Jews of Lwów (cont'd)

Translated by Myra Yael Ecker

Edited by Karen Leon

[Pages 693-694]

Chapter 19. Attempts at Defence and Revolt

After the *Aktion* in August 1942 and the news that arrived from other towns, especially from Warsaw, it was clear to everyone that the Germans were plotting to annihilate all of Poland's Jews. Early attempts were then made to organise an uprising from amongst the Jewish population, but there were very great difficulties. Many of the leaders of the Jewish political parties and youth movements were absent, some had fled to Russia and some were murdered by the Germans. Lwów's Polish underground was very weak, because its population was not purely Polish, but was made up of a mixture of Poles and Ukrainians. The massive migration from the villages and the provincial towns during the Soviet rule, greatly increased Lwów's Ukrainian population. With the Ukrainians' memories of being persecuted and accosted under Polish rule, before 1939, the policies of the Germans succeeded in increasing their hatred for the Poles. In addition, the vast majority of the underground in Lwów were members of right wing parties who rejected any association with the Jews. Consequently, the Jews could only negotiate with the democratic or the left wing Polish underground organisations, whose standing, in eastern Galicia, was inconsequential. The Ukrainian underground organised patriotic groups in eastern Galicia, but they were all affiliated with the faction of Stepan Bandera, who simultaneously fought against the Germans, the Poles and the Jews. During 1942-1943, the extreme nationalist Bandera faction (*Banderowcy*) eliminated the rest of the Ukrainian partisan groups that were more liberal or democratic (such as the Bulba group of Wołyń). And from then on, the Wołyń and the Galician forests were under their control.

Due to the difficult circumstances, it was impossible to form an organised, concerted Jewish revolt movement, or a mass exodus to the forests. There were only individual attempts of underground acts, including small groups, mostly from among members of the Jewish youth movements.

At the end of 1942, a group of young officials from the Jewish Council (most were members of Zionist youth movements) organised lessons in military instruction and weapon training. The training was conducted secretly in one of the basements of the community's offices but it did not lead to the formation of a military unit. There were also attempts to escape into the forests, but the youths who fled there, did not find partisan groups they could join. On frequent occasions the Ukrainian peasants turned them in, to the Germans. Bandera's partisans murdered every Jew who came their way. A survivor of Janowska camp, described such a meeting:

"From Janowska camp I fled to the forest. There I met a group of 34 refugees who had fled the camp. The Banderists chased us. (We heard) that in one forest there were some eighty Jews. The Banderists surrounded the forest, blockaded the Jews and slaughtered all of them. Later, they dissected the bodies, and placed their flesh on the trees with the notes, "this is Jewish flesh."[16]

The escaping Jews were often caught even before they left town, and were murdered on their way. Such was the fate of the group which included the poet J[akób] Szudrich. In his report, General [Fritz] Katzmann also accounts about other failed attempts. Most of the Jewish youths who tried to escape to the forests, were armed. Generally they bought all the arms, guns and rifles, from Italian or Hungarian soldiers (the average price of a gun was 2,000 Gulden), who were their principal assistants in organising the escape. Katzmann mentions a group of 20-30 armed young Jews who escaped from Janowska camp, attempting to reach the outskirts of Brody in order to join a group of Jewish partisans operating in the forests. They approached two German drivers and offered them 20,000 Gulden for the drive from Lwów to Brody. The drivers confirmed the reservation, but reported them to the German police, and all the Jews were murdered (the incident took place on 15ᵗʰ May 1943). On 21ˢᵗ May 1943, Katzmann recounted, the Germans destroyed another group of Jews armed with Italian weapons. On the whole,

Katzmann commented, "As the number of Jews in the district (Galicia) decreased, their spirit of rebellion increased. The Jews used all types of weapons, some of which were bought from the Italians." Despite the bitter ending of many attempts, still, some young Jews, on their own or in organised groups, managed to escape to the forests and remain there until the defeat of Germany. Small groups reached even as far the Carpathian mountains (for example, Dr. Borys Pliskin and his group).

[Pages 695-696]

According to one testimony, Goldberg organised a group of youths from among Lwów's Jewish Police officers, which joined a groups of partisans in the town's vicinity. After Lwów's ghetto was declared a *Julag*, the partisan headquarters sent Goldberg to organise the revolt in that *Julag*, but he was caught and murdered by the Nazis.

The Jewish underground of Lwów also produced an illegal newspaper. It was typewritten with a very limited number of duplicates. Six pamphlets in all were issued. Abraham Warmann (Bronek), one of the leaders of *HaShomer HaTzair*, was the newspaper's technical manager, and the person who brought the typewriter into the *Julag* despite the mortal danger. He managed to camouflage the typewriter and pull the wool over the eyes of the policemen at the gate of the ghetto. He used a horse and carriage to deliver it to the "editorial board." The newspaper's editor was M.H. The newspaper disseminated political and military information which was secretly collected from radio broadcasts, or copied from the Polish underground press. It also contained local information about life in Lwów's ghetto, together with announcements and editorial articles calling upon Lwów's Jews to courage, war and uprising. The realisation that the Jewish public would pay in blood for any resistance attempt, was one of the major reasons for delaying any preparation for revolt. The Germans resorted to collective, cruel punishment for any private act of resistance by Jews. The terror incident of 1st September 1942, was previously mentioned (*see above*, Pt. IV; Ch. 13). A similar event occurred on 16th March 1943, in the SS camp at 56 Czwartaków Street. One of the Jewish labourers (the engineer-builder Kutnowski, according to rumours), killed an SS policeman (named Keil according to testimony), who excelled in his cruelty. The following day, the Germans arrived at the Jewish community hall on Łokietka Street, and publicly executed twelve or eleven Jews, including militia officers (the advocate Dr. Mahler and Mendel). But they were not satisfied with that. Grzymek, the commander of the *Julag*, carried out a roll-call that very day. More that a thousand Jews were "chosen" and sent to the "Sands" to be murdered. An eye-witness described that *Aktion*,

"The following day, the orchestra played as usual near the gate, the groups marched out (to work in the town). In front of the gate, along the street, stood physicians who injected an anti-typhoid serum. Behind the gate stood Engels, Pugaszewski and Wöbke (Gestapo officers) who orchestrated the *Aktion*. They jokingly selected men from the groups, be it the blonds, the spectacled, or other characteristics, loaded them onto the vehicle and transported them to the "Sands." Those who marched towards the gate were quite unaware: here they play, there they inject, and just a few steps away death grips them by the neck. That very hour, one thousand, one hundred men were dragged to the gallows!"[17]

Concurrently, the SS police carried out the *Vergeltungsaktion* [retributive *Aktion*] at Janowska camp, where some 200 people were murdered.

[Pages 697-698]

Chapter 20. Liquidation of the Ghetto

The liquidation of Lwów's ghetto started with the blood-*Aktion* of 23rd May 1943. To comprehend the nature of the *Aktion* one needs to describe the structure of the Jewish labour. The Germans split up all the Jewish workers still alive, into two large labour centres, the *Julag*, and Janowska camp. In the camp, the Jews were fully enclosed, while a few "lucky" individuals belonged to the external-brigades (*aussen-Brigaden*) who left every morning for work outside the camp. Most of the Jewish labourers at the *Julag*, who resided in barracks, were organised into labour-brigades that left for work every morning and returned to sleep in the *Julag*. However, the Germans decided to eliminate the external-brigades at the *Julag* and transfer them to the camp. A terrifying slaughter took place at Janowska camp to make room for the new brigades. That was followed by an order calling for all the labour-brigades to come in the evening to the camp, rather than return to the *Julag*, as usual. The brigades were locked up in the camp for several days, with no one coming or going, nor were the camp's external-brigades sent for their work in town. During these days the Germans systematically murdered the tightly crowded masses assembled in the camp, and again thousands of people were murdered.

Those who still remained in the *Julag*, children, women, youths and the internal brigades of the ghetto, now understood the meaning of things, and waited in a state of terror for the horror that still awaited them. They prepared concealed, safe hiding places, and some Jews even obtained weapons. In his report, General Katzmann writes:

"The Jews tried every means to evade the transfer project (!). They did not only try to escape from the ghetto, they also hid in every corner, in ducts, in house chimneys, in the sewers, drains etc. They built batteries in underground passages, they widened basements and turned them into tunnels, excavated underground and created very artfully camouflaged hiding places, in attics, wood stores, huts, in furniture, etc."

In various parts of the ghetto the Germans were greeted with shots, grenades and flammable bottles. The Germans no longer dared enter and petrol Jewish homes, and instead poured gasoline on the houses and set them on fire, thus forcing the Jews to come out. The men and women who resisted or tried to escape were murdered on the spot. The children, in most cases, were murdered with utmost cruelty by throwing them alive into the fire, or shattering babies' sculls against walls or lampposts. The young Nazis also participated in this *Aktion* and they used Jewish children as targets for fire practice.

Some of the men who were caught (nearly 7,000 men) were sent to Janowska camp, where another roll-call took place. The weak ones were sent "to the Sands," and the stronger ones joined labour brigades, but even these brigades were eradicated within a few days.

The project of liquidating the ghetto was conducted with unprecedented excessive cruelty. This is confirmed in the concluding words of Katzmann's report:

"Extraordinary means were required during the liquidation of Lwów's ghetto, where special bunkers were built, as I mentioned before. We were therefore forced to act brutally from the start of the *Aktion*, to ensure we did not suffer a great loss (of men). We had to blow up or burn many houses. This incident exposed a strange thing: instead of the 12,000 officially registered, we succeeded in catching almost 20,000 Jews. We were forced to extract over 3,000 dead Jews from different hiding places: they were the people who had committed suicide by poison."

The two last *Aktionen* were conducted by General [Fritz] Katzmann who returned to Lwów, probably from his activities in the provincial towns of eastern Galicia, where he also headed the annihilation activities. As General [Josef] Stroop was "busy" in Warsaw from 17th April 1943, Katzmann returned to Lwów to complete his activities. After completing his mission, Katzmann prepared "The final report on the Solution of the Jewish Problem in Galicia [*Lösung der Judenfrage in Galizien*]," which he submitted to "the supreme commander of the SS and Secret-Police in the eastern territories, General [Friedrich Wilhelm] Krüger, or his deputy in Kraków." The typewritten report of over 60 pages, including many photographs, was signed by Katzmann on 30th June 1943. After the defeat of Germany, the report was included among the collection of documents of the International Court of Justice in Nürnberg/Nuremberg that in 1946-1947 prosecuted the principal war-criminals. Katzmann had disappeared without a trace. A reporter for the New-York, Jewish-German weekly journal, *Aufbau*,[17a] published the news, the veracity of which is yet to be verified, that Katzmann was in Cairo under the auspices of the mufti [Alhaj Muhammad] Amin al-Husseini.

[Pages 699-700]

Chapter 21. The Jews in the *Aryan* side of town

After the liquidation of the ghetto, the area of the Jews' living quarters turned into a wasteland where only ruins remained, in which gangs of thieves and robbers, beggars and suspicious individuals sought refuge. A very small number of Jews still remained in town, legally housed in barracks on tiny, solitary camps of military factories. A strict guard was set on these survivors. In addition, Janowska camp still existed with thousands of Jews.

A few thousand Jews who had managed to escaped and hide, lived illegally in Lwów. Part of them hid in kinds of "bunkers" and hiding-places of Christian families, and a part resided in *Aryan* neighbourhoods with fake documents as Poles, Ukrainians, Karaites, Muslims, Germans and even Gypsies.

A few, including many converted and assimilated Jews, got along as *Aryans* immediately when the Germans arrived. In 1942, a mass exodus to the *Aryan* neighbourhoods took place. An entire industry was established, faking *Aryan* documents: identity-cards, marriage-certificates, dates-of-birth, registration-cards, work-permits, etc. There were actual certificates (ones that had belonged to *Aryans* who died in the war, or were kidnapped by the Germans and whose certificates remained), and there were essentially forged certificates (documents known by the traders as "Lipa. Those who moved to live on the *Aryan* side, did so with great caution. They concealed their departure from the ghetto from their acquaintances for as far as possible until the last moment. The slow infiltration into *Aryan* neighbourhoods increased in the Spring months of 1942, reaching a peak after the *Aktion* of August 1942.

In 1942-1943, the number of Jews who were hidden by *Aryans* or who masqueraded as *Aryans* based on false certificates, assisted by non-Jewish acquaintances, reached the thousands. The German secret-police who constantly patrolled the homes of citizens and the town's streets, discovered a great many of them. Many were also caught as a result of Christian informants who had been caught assisting secreted Jews, and who faced death. This caused Lwów's special law-court (*Sondergericht*) to be inundated with such cases. In a report of 7th October 1943, the secret-police commander of the *Generalgouvernement*, wrote to the head of Department VII of the SS headquarters in Berlin:

"According to the information from the district of Galicia (for Kraków), the number of pending cases before the Lwów *Sondergericht* regarding the people who shelter Jews, has risen greatly recently. This misdemeanour, carries only the sentence of death, according to law. Under these circumstances, from time to time the *Sondergericht* has to issue frequent death sentences. The judges' circles object to it more or less. The principal objection was that the penalty (death) was best executed by the secret-police. Nevertheless, everyone agrees that the death sentence is absolutely necessary, since the sentence of the Jews who are hiding is the same as that of robbers, under the present circumstances."[18]

This bears witness to the fact that many death sentences were passed on the criminals who hid Jews. If truth be told, during the time this report was written and the proposal to transfer the capital cases from the law-court to the secret police, it happened more than once that the SS and Gestapo personnel did not bother waiting for the trial. Instead, they beat to death the Christians who had concealed Jews. The court's deaths were, however, greatly publicised by the Germans in order to scare the Christians and stop them from helping Jews in any way. A particularly well publicised case was the publicly executed death sentence at the end of 1943, of the butcher Yósefek who concealed several Jews at his apartment in the Kleparów suburb. The execution inspired fear in the Christians and greatly suppressed the rest of the yet concealed slaughter.

Under such an atmosphere, a hiding place within an *Aryan* neighbourhood was not very safe. There were few Christians who concealed Jews for ideological reasons, sheltering or assisting friends from their political party, or work, in bygone days, out of pure pity, or due to their objection to the Nazi regime. But in most cases Jews were sheltered by people who were after material gain. There were those who received from the Jews all their remaining capital in silver, gold, jewels, clothes, paintings etc., and there were those who demanded a monthly payment for the shelter, which was the usual custom. The Jews paid a decent amount as an entry fee, which was in general at least 2,000 Gulden, besides

[Pages 701-702]

a monthly "rent" that ranged between 2,000 and 10,000 Gulden. The prices in this market varied depending on the place and the time. House owners were known to evict the hiding Jews once their funds ran out. There were incidences when blackmailers (*szantażyści*) heard of such a hiding place and demanded large sums or "hush money" on a monthly basis.

Whereas a Jew whose appearance betrayed his origins had no option but to hide among Christians, "good looking (who do not 'resemble')" Jews could seek a different solution. Many among those who "did not resemble," masqueraded as Christians based on *Aryan* documents they had purchased, they lived in *Aryan* neighbourhoods and worked as Christians. In order to avoid any entanglement with the administrative arrangements associated with accommodation, registration with the secret-police, or with the office of food-cards etc., they too required assistance from their Christian acquaintances who knew their secret. The life of such *Aryan* Jews was fraught with danger. Walking down the road they were always exposed to peril. The secret-police representatives, civil agents and specialist spies scoured the streets for masquerading *Aryans*. Extortionists, good-for-nothings and even children who specialised in spotting a masquerading Jew at a glance, be it by his slightly unusual gestures, or expressions loitered in the streets. These hunters invited the suspected individual to the gate of a neighbouring house and ordered him to take down his pants to establish if he was of the Abrahamic faith. Women had an easier time in evading their pursuers. There was however also an "ideological" test in the fundamentals of Christianity, its practices and prayers, by which women were mostly seized. And when all the investigations were unsuccessful, the suspects were taken to the Gestapo's office, for more aggressive methods of searching and examination.

Tens of hiding or masquerading Jews were caught daily in this way. Those who were not murdered immediately upon being uncovered, were taken to a special cell in Janowska camp, known as the "death cell," and from there were taken to be murdered.

Many of those who masqueraded, believed they would find greater safety if they moved to another town, where the danger of being recognised by acquaintances was reduced. Most of them moved to Warsaw and Kraków. Many were caught on their journey, by the secret-police through the many searches undertaken at railway stations or on the trains. Of those who did reach Warsaw, some were caught later, and some were killed during the 1944 Polish Uprising. Few have survived.

[Pages 703-704]

Chapter 22. Places of Extermination in Lwów; Establishment of Janowska Camp

The three main locations of extermination in Lwów were:

1.   The Castle Mound (*Zitadelle*) in the centre of town, between Kopernika and St. Lazarus [św Lazarza] Streets. Thousands of the Russian prisoners of war were murdered in that place.

2.   Lesienice [Lysynychi] Forest, a village on the outskirts of Lwów on the way to Tarnopol, east of the Łyczaków suburb. Between 140,000 and 200,000 people, many among them Jews, were murdered here.

3.   The "Death-valley" or the "Sands [*Piaski*]." A ravine between the hills north-west of Lwów, not far from the foot of Kortumowa Mountain, about half a kilometre from Janowska camp and from the two cemeteries, the Christian and the Jewish cemeteries.

According to the official report published by the "Extraordinary State (Soviet) Commission for the Establishment and Investigation of the Atrocities of the German-Fascist Invaders and their Accomplices,"[19] "Over 200,000 Soviet citizens," practically all of whom were Jews, were murdered at the "Death-valley" near Janowska camp.

One of the main roads leading north-west out of Lwów is Janowska Street, so named due to its vicinity to the small town Janów. The Germans renamed it West Street (*Weststrasse*). At 132-134 Janowska Street stood a factory for grinding-machines, that had belonged to a machine making company, Steinhaus & Company, owned by Jews. During the Soviet rule, following the socialist law, the factory was confiscated and absorbed into the industrial network of the Ministry of Transport, (Factory No. 56 of the Ministry of Transport). Under the German occupation the factory was at first under the municipal administrative government, and a few weeks later, under the management of the SS in Lwów. SS officer Wolfgang von Mohwinkel was appointed manager of the factory, but he was soon replaced by a young man from Berlin, SS officer Fritz [Gotthard] Gebauer, a clerk from the Berlin firm *Siemens-Schuckert*. Gebauer had a pleasant appearance and seemed like a man who was "cherished and polite in words and manners." The workshops on Janowska Street began to produce products for the SS and the German armed forces.

The Jews believed the Janowska workshop work-card was "good," for whoever would dare abduct or manhandle a Jew who had a work-card from the SS itself? Consequently, many tried to find employ at these workshops, in addition to the labourers sent there by the work department. Polish "criminals" were also sent to work there. By the end of September 1941, there were nearly 350 Jewish workers at the workshops. By the end of October 1941, there were 580 Jews and 320 Poles. At the end of September 1941, the perimeter of the entire factory was surrounded by barbed wire, and sheds were erected, but the labourers were still allowed to go home after work. At the beginning of October 1941, a fundamental change took place. Gebauer convened all the Jewish labourers, held a roll-call and informed them: "From today onwards you will remain here!" From that day the factory turned into a labour-camp, known by the name "Janowski camp." Several guard towers were erected, adjacent to the barbed wire, manned by SS men with automatic rifles. The SS guard was headed by the officers Schlippe, Stellwerk and Soernitz. Soernitz was habitually accompanied by his hound "Aza," trained to attack people and devour them alive, at the command of its owner.

From then on, all communication between the Jewish labourers and the world outside, ceased. The camp was split into two parts. The larger part was occupied by the labourers' accommodation huts, the offices, the SS apartments and also by the transit-camp (*Durchgangslager*; *Dulag*) designated for those dispatched to the Bełżec death-camp. A new SS officer, Gustav Willhaus, was appointed commander over that part of the camp. A young man, a printer by trade, Gustav Willhaus was born at Saarbrücken, and according to witness testimony, he took up his job on 2nd March 1942. Soon after, probably on 1st April 1942, his deputy, SS officer Richard [Robert] Rokita, arrived. Around 40 years of age, Rokita was a violinist before the war, and director of a Jazz orchestra in one of west Poland's towns (probably Katowice). Willhaus's second deputy was the SS officer Adolf Kolonko, around 30 years old, who had been an apprentice whitewasher born at Racibórz [Ratibor], Silesia.

The second part of the camp, where the factories

[Pages 705-706]

and workshops were situated, developed into a particular section under the management of Fritz Gebauer, and titled: "German Armament Factories" (*Deutsche Ausrüstungswerke* – D.A.W.). The workshops' labourers had to be sourced from the first part of the camp, from the barracks, but the existing state of mutual jealousy and hatred between the two officers, prevented any cooperation and work coordination. "There were constant conflicts between Willhaus and Gebauer, wrote one of the Jewish women who worked in the camp-office. On occasion, when Willhaus issued an order, Gebauer overturned the order in order to annoy him. The disputes between these two "tough guys," always led to harm for the wretched camp prisoners. After a great dispute, the relations between the two commanders were severed. Willhaus even set-up a separate office for the section of the camp under his supervision."[20]

[Pages 707-708]

Chapter 23. The Hangmen at Janowska Camp

Despite all the differences, disputes and quarrels between Willhaus and Gebauer, they were in agreement over one thing: both excelled in boundless sadism and cruelty towards their Jewish prisoners. Their acts of deception and abuse of the Jews served as a blueprint for all the rest of the German officers at the camp. Much was written about their deeds, in articles, memoirs and witness statements of prisoners at Janowska camp. Rokita, Willhaus's deputy, excelled in a different type of cruelty that was "finer" and more cunning. He was an "aesthete" who enjoyed inventing "refined" tortures for his victims, tortures of body and soul.

"The prisoners remember Rokita," wrote one of the camp survivors, "for murdering tens of people during the roll-call, and during every visit to the bathhouse. He enjoyed speaking with prisoners, even sharing bread with them, saying that he was a 'good' man by nature, who could not bear those who shuddered in his presence. If anyone standing during the command so much as moved, Rokita immediately murdered several people, after which he lit a cigarette, and with a benign smile said: 'I was so good to you and you annoy me. See what you have brought me to'."[21]

Rokita appointed his Jewish friend Kampf, with whom he used to play music in coffee-houses before the war, as the camp-elder (*Lager-eltester*). Kampf's "career" was short-lived, however. It was said in the camp that Kampf was careless with his talk, recounting that Rokita sent large orchestral instruments especially accordions, from the camp to his home. They were not just accordions and instruments. Rokita filled the orchestral instruments with gold and jewels. Rokita heard of it, and murdered Kampf and subsequently, his wife and daughter.

The rest of the SS officers did not fall short of their commanders, in their cruelty. Those who excelled in their wild deeds were, [Adolf] Kolonko, head of the research department; the young (around 20 years old) [Friedrich] Heinen; the Hungarian SS man, Peter Blum, at 17 years old was previously a shoemaker's apprentice; Heinisch, who was Grzymek's deputy at the *Julag*, before arriving at the camp; the SS men, [Martin] Büttner, Grusshaber and Beneke.

There were rumours that the hangmen of the camp included specialists from the *Dirlewanger Brigade*, who trained the rest of the policemen in the practice of murder.[22]

The entire *Dirlewanger Brigade* was made up of criminal felons released from jails and from German concentration-camps, with the proviso that they would volunteer to serve in this brigade. The task of this brigade was to "wipe out" the population in those places where any signs of resistance or revolt were noticed. Members of this brigade specialised in massacring residents, women and children. Consequently, the brigade was also sent to Warsaw during the Polish uprising in August-October 1944.[23] Nevertheless, no explicit evidence has been found, to date, that *Dirlewanger* men were present at Janowska camp.

During summer 1943, a change of management personnel took place in the camp. Rokita was appointed manager of the Jewish labour-camp at Tarnopol. Shortly after, Willhaus was also moved (1st July 1943), and was replaced by Franz Warzog. Changes also took place among the SS officers. Many of them were moved from service in the camp, to military service within the SS companies on the eastern front (*Waffen-SS*). The internal policy of the hangmen at Janowska camp, as in all other camps, oscillated between two opposing targets: the desire to murder, on the one hand, and the preservation of their own lives, on the other. While they were trained to "wipe-out the enemies of Germany" with "total dedication," as the frequent murders led to a shrinking population in the camps, the need for policemen and SS men also decreased, and the superfluous SS men were sent to the front. As the situation on the eastern front worsened, the Germans increased the number of SS men transferred from the camps to the front, and their place was filled by camp policemen

[Pages 709-710]

of non-German origin, SS brigades composed of Hungarians, of men of "Germanic culture" [*Volksdeutsche*], Ukrainian policemen and of Russian men from General [Andrey Andreyevich] Vlasov's companies. They were known by the prisoners as Askaris (a term used for native assistant policemen, in German colonies in pre-1914 Africa.). The Ukrainian and Russian policemen were also termed "black," for the colour of their uniforms.

The non-German policemen served only as regular soldiers or as deputies, in the camp, while the posts of high ranking officers and commanders remained in the hands of the German SS men.

[Pages 711-712]

Chapter 24. The Prisoners at Janowska Camp

Janowska camp was designated for several purposes. Its prime purpose was that of a forced labour-camp for Jews, and for non-Jewish criminals. Secondly, that of an extermination camp for the Jews of Lwów and eastern Galicia. Its third purpose was that of a transit camp. Tens of thousands of Jews passed through it. It was the examination and selection station - who for death and who for labour, who for murder in the camp and who for "transport" to Bełżec death-camp. The transports from the provincial towns began to arrive at Janowska camp in the spring of 1942. At the beginning of April 1942, a large transport arrived from Gródek Jagielloński near Lwów. In May and June 1942, from Przemyśl, in July 1942, from Drohobycz and so on. Concurrently, transports started to arrive from south-east Gaclicia, from Kołomyja, Kosów, Stanisławów, Dolina, Delatyn and so forth.

Small groups of Jews were brought from abroad to Janowska camp, from Czech lands, Slovakia, Hungary, Yugoslavia, Holland, Belgium, Germany, etc. For them, Janowska camp was not a transfer station, but the last stop.

Tens of thousands of Jews passed through Janowska camp. Their number is estimated at between 300,000 and 400,000. At least 200,000 were murdered in the "Sands" and in the Lesienice [Lysynychi] Forest. In relation to such numbers, the number of the camp inmates was small. All of the official, camp statistical records were lost or were destroyed by the Germans before they fled. The only list which was preserved, was part of the statistical survey of Lwów's town minister (*Stadthauptmann*), a report of the roll-call conducted by the Germans in Lwów, on 1st March 1943. The list states that there were no Jews in Lwów, and that there were 15,000 Jews at Janowska camp. (The document [is] kept at the Lwów archives of the Ukrainian Academy of Sciences, economic department). This statement seems exaggerated. According to Jewish witnesses, the number of Jews in the camp did not exceed 10,000, and generally it was less than that. It is possible that on the day of the roll-call, there were a few thousand Jews in Janowska transfer-camp, who were added to the number of the regular prisoners.

Initially, the camp was only intended for men, but after the *Grossaktionen* of 1942, a large number of women was also moved to the camp, and a section was established for them until a specific women's camp was formed separate from that of the men. The women's camp was adjacent to the death-yard (where the murders took place in the camp), where officially there were 30 women in March 1943. The first inmates were 70 women who were brought after the liquidation of the Å»ólkiew ghetto. They worked at the weaving factory (D.A.W.) of the camp. Soon the number of women increased and they were used for other tasks, such as in the kitchen, in cleaning jobs, packing, tailoring, etc. The director of the women's camp was SS Officer Brumbauer.

The social structure of the camp prisoners was divided into different strata. In the upper stratum were the camp axillary clerks. The aristocracy among the labourers, consisted of the labour-elders (*Lager-älteste*), and of the work-divisions' leaders (foremen), the craftsmen, engineers, technicians and mechanics who formed the outside work-companies (the best of them) or the labour-companies inside the camp. Most difficult was the condition of the unskilled labourers. These included most circles of the professional intelligentsia, advocates, clerks, teachers, writers, etc. Only few of the free professionals could work as auxiliary clerks in the camp offices, or as craftsmen. Most had to do hard labour. Generally, they suffered severe beatings. The policemen mocked them, and at times even their "specialist" friends turned them into laughingstocks. They were allocated the worst sleeping places, they were the last to receive their food rations. The new way of life brought down many of them. Rabbi Dr. Dawid Kahane writes that among the rabbis who were brought to the camp together with him, almost all died of hunger, hard-labour, sickness and beatings, after a short period of their arrival.

Original notes:

16.   Testimonial of Moses Erlich. Archive of the Jewish Historical Institute, Warsaw. No. 1247.

17.   Maltiel [-Gerstenfeld, Jacob] *op. cit.* pp. 246-247

   1.   Kurt Juster, correspondence from Zurich. [*Aufbau*] Issue of 22nd February 1950.

18.   From the Archives of The Western Institute of Poznań [*Instytut Zachodni*]. For the full source, (see Pt. IV; Appendix IV).

19.   Pravda, No. 307, 23 December 1944.

20.   "Memoirs of **Irena Szajowicz**", in the book *Machanot* [Camps] edited by N. Blumenthal.

21.   Michał M. Borwicz, *Uniwersytet zbirów* [University of Thugs, 1946]. p. 38.

22.   Vladimir [Pavlovich] Belayev, in his articles "And it Happened in Lwów" that appeared in [the newspaper] *Czerwony Sztandar* No. 54., Lwów 25.10.1944.

23.   Evidence obtained from General and SS commander [Erich Julius Eberhard] von [dem] Bach-Zelewski, at Nürnberg/Nuremberg; document No. 313 of the Russian prosecutor.

[Pages 713-714]

Chapter 25. Life at Janowska Camp

During the years 1942-1943, the area of Janowska camp increased several times, so that it eventually encompassed 2-3 square kilometres. It was first enlarged in March 1942, during the first *Grossaktion* in Lwów. From then onwards, construction continued apace throughout the entire summer until the *Aktion* of August 1942. The construction was overseen by Griffel, a lecturer at Lwów Polytechnic and a distinguished scientist in his field, who was later murdered by the Nazis.

All of the camp huts were constructed in timber, each forming an elongated rectangle that contained four ledges, one above the other. The huts were infected and dirty; they did not have stoves and so were freezing cold during winter. There were no toilets in these huts. In the entire camp there was one toilet with 12 seats (later on, 40 seats), and a single bathing facility. It was only permitted to use these facilities during the morning and evening break-time, which led to an unbearable congestion. The huts where the prisoners slept were locked up from 10 p.m. until 5 a.m., and it was strictly forbidden to leave them even to use the toilet. Some huts did not even contain a chamber-pot, and when they did, it was filled in no time and the air reeked unbearably. Every hut had a shower made up of two troughs connected to a water pipe.

Worse than the housing bane was the hunger bane. The main food was bread. The official daily portion was an eighth of a loaf of bread which amounted to 150-160 gm. daily (1,300 kg. a loaf), however those in charge of the bread distribution knew how to remove slices even from that meagre portion. The bread was fresh and tacky, made of poor ingredients, and when sliced, it crumbled. There were instances when a prisoner received at most 100 gm. bread per day. In the morning the prisoners received a coffee-substitute, the midday meal was a bowl of soup, in fact water in which floated cabbage leaves, some groats, and on rare occasions a bone or a piece of poor quality meat. At times, however, the soup was so bad, that even the hungry prisoners would not eat it. In the winter of 1942, the soup was made of frozen potatoes that were placed on a rubbish heap, where the German police habitually urinated. The soup which was made from these unwashed and unpeeled potatoes had such disgusting odour that most prisoners refused it. On another occasion the soup was made from a horse's carcass, and most of the prisoners who tasted it fell ill and some even died.

The wives, mothers and daughters of the prisoners secretly tried to bring food to their relatives. They stood for hours in front of the camp gates, or near the barbed wire, waiting for an opportunity to hand something to their relative, to an acquaintance or to a bribed policeman. Such standing around the camp was very dangerous, as the police beat the waiting women, rebuffed them and at times even murdered them. in 1943, when every Jew, including women and children, was a candidate for murder, all of the standing near the camp stopped.

The Jewish Council tried to send official deliveries of food rations to the prisoners. In exchange for very costly presents to [Fritz Gotthard] Gebauer and his wife, a permit was eventually granted to send rations to the prisoners, twice a week. This, however, also failed since the rations were not given directly to the prisoners, but rather to the central camp office where the SS men in charge of distributing the deliveries stole the best portions, on the SS confiscated them as punishment for some "misdemeanour," at times throwing them to the dogs in front of the starving prisoners.

A food black-market developed in the camp. The "goods" were supplied by the police and by the labourers in charge of the kitchen, the bread distribution, the storeroom and of the food parcels from the families. The labourers working outside the camp, brought in a considerable quantity of the goods. There were always a number of Polish and Ukrainian prisoners in the camp (the Poles had a red patch on their clothes, the Ukrainians a blue one, to distinguish them from the Jews' yellow patch). They were not life prisoners, and when the period of their incarceration was over, they were free to leave. They were freer than the Jews during their time in the camp . They went out for outside work and were permitted to meet their relatives. The Christian prisoners acted as mediators in the black-market. However many Jews from among the labourers and external-brigades also engaged in this trade. The Jewish work-companies which left for town, worked on the easterly and westerly railway tracks,

[Pages 715-716]

(*Ost* brigade and *West* brigade), at the "Institute for the town's cleanliness" (*Reinigungskommando*), in the factories and at the different military institutions where they negotiated with the town's Christians, and paid in silver, gold, dollars and jewels for food and medicine which they brought back to the camp. The black-market prices were very high. The black-market was particularly active in the toilet, because it was not as strictly supervised by the police as were other areas.

The black-market was a sort of self-preservation for the prisoners, countering the SS's plot to starve the Jews to death. This type of self-protection was also formed in other camps, and throughout all countries which the Nazis had occupied, but it could not breach the overall hunger. The development of this "new economic regime" gave rise to the principle of the bowl turned upside-down. A new "middle-class" thus emerged, opposite to the one which had formed the pre-war Jewish society. The "new social order" in the camp was made up of the black-market traders, the "forceful," expert labourers among the outside work-battalions, and a few "rich men" of days gone by, who had managed to retain their remaining wealth in the form of gold, dollars and jewels. On the other hand, a new proletariat was formed, made up of the people unable to adjust to the new state of affairs, including most of those with free professions, and clerks. Whereas the new middle-class knew how to benefit from every strange situation in the forced labour-camp, the camp's proletariat, that constituted the majority of the prisoners, starved and soon perished.

The sanitary conditions in the camp led to many diseases. Not only were the huts filthy and riddled with lice, but the prisoners' way of life was purposefully structured to deplete their health. At first there was no washhouse in the camp, and once one was constructed, Gebauer forbade its use for a long time, under the pretext that its construction was not finished at the designated time. The use of soap was completely forbidden (a product only available on the black-market), nevertheless, yet Gebauer insisted that the prisoners ensure their bodies were clean, and he conducted inspections from time to time. One day in the depth of winter Gebauer held such an inspection in a temperature of minus 20 degrees Celsius. The prisoners were made to stand naked in the camp yard during the entire inspection. Gebauer eventually picked five prisoners and ordered that they be punished for their lack of cleanliness. The wretched prisoners were drowned in water-filled barrels and they froze to death.

At times, the prisoners were sent to the washhouse on Balonowa Street, which was equipped to remove lice, but it was a small washhouse that could only hold between 100 and 150 people, at a time. Later, battalions of prisoners were fortnightly sent to the washhouse on Szpitalna Street. The wash served as a novel opportunity for the police to abuse the prisoners. They beat the prisoners for the slightest thing that displeased them, and regularly the prisoners left behind in the washhouse, were victims to the beatings and shooting or to broken limbs.

These dreadful conditions led to the spread of different diseases, especially infectious diseases. The highly infectious and endangering typhus, spread in particular during September-November 1942. In those days, according to the testimony of the physician Dr. Edgard Zwilling, typhus claimed some 50 people, daily.[24]

The principal remedy which the Germans provided for the dangerously sick, was to murder them by shooting. Alternatively, the Germans removed the very sick to the area beyond the barbed wire, a no-man's-land, where they were left to starve. The sick consequently tried hard to hide their condition, and they went to work while the fever consumed them. Such patients managed at times, with help from their friends, to hide their condition from the police, and they managed to recover, nevertheless. After great efforts and much bribery, the Jewish Council and the community's assistance committee for camp prisoners managed to get permission, from the camp authorities, to move the seriously sick to the community hospital in the ghetto. The principal physician, Dr. Maksymiljan Kurzrock, organised a separate ward for these patients and tended to them with great devotion. The situation did not last long, however. After the *Grossaktionen* at the end of 1942, the community hospital was liquidated and the Germans organised a "hospital" at the camp. The facilities at the medical clinics were primitive. An unheated hut made of planks and with no medical equipments or sanitary assistance, was allotted to the hospital. Twice a month the SS policemen, Brumbauer, and Birmann, burst into the hospital to conduct a roll-call of the patients. During the check they picked the most severely sick, and murdered them. As far as possible, the sick avoided that dangerous place

[Pages 717-718]

that was termed "the hospital." The medical supervision at the hospital was handled by M. Kurzrock and later by Dr. Z. Rappaport.

To expose the sick and the exhausted who were hiding, the police conducted a weekly check in the form or a race. The prisoners were ordered to run at great speed from gate to gate across the camp, in an orderly fashion, in rows. Whoever stumbled or lagged behind in this death-race, thus indicating his weakness, was sentenced to death. An "advanced" form of the death-race was known as the "vitamins-race," probably an invention of Willhaus. "Vitamins" was a mocking term for three types of heavy loads, logs (*bali* in Polish, known as "vitamin B"), bricks (*cegly* in Polish, known as "vitamin C") and planks (*deski* in Polish, known as "vitamin D"). After a full day's labour of 10-12 hours, the prisoners were ordered to do additional work, to carry on their backs logs, bricks and planks, from Kleparów railway station to the camp. This laborious task had to be performed in running. The menacing race, was deeply imprinted on the heart of the prisoners, and in their memoirs several of the survivors provided horrific descriptions of the "vitamin races."[25]

The following is a description from M[ichal] Borwicz's book:

"The camp's SS police, the *Askaris* and the Jewish policemen created an avenue on both sides of the road that led from the camp's gate to the railway station. The road was highly lit, the prisoners walked in rows in the avenue, one following one another. A five-men row following the next five-men row of prisoners, one brigade after the other, one hundred after a hundred, one thousand after a thousand...

"All of them, after a full day's hard labour. The legs already heavy as lead one had to march swiftly, because the pace of the march was set by the police and the guns in the hands of SS men, and by the riffle butts held by the *Askaris*. When the order rang out "race" (*Laufschritt*), it was not enough to simply run, one had to ensure to maintain the line during the run and the excitement. Behind the railway station, one had to descend the incline to the railway bridge that was a few tens of meter. Here, one quickly had to take the load and return with the freight without delay. The SS men stood above with riffle butts in their hands, ready to shoot, and whips raised in the air, urging us to hurry with their wild shouts, kicks, beatings, shots in the air and shots into the crowded prisoners, thus increasing the confusion with their actions. They loaded the freight without mercy. A weight that under normal situation required at least five men, they loaded at times on two sick, exhausted men. Most of those who fell when transporting the load, never rose again… Those who could bear no more were removed from the line and taken "beyond the barbed wire"… where they were left through the night. In the morning, their half frozen bodies were thrown into the lorries and taken "to the Sands" to be annihilated. On one occasion, after a "vitamins-race" that lasted from 6 p.m. until midnight, 130 men were moved "to the Sands."

The way of life in the camp was configured to hasten the progress of annihilation. To crush any thought of resistance or revolt, and to instil the fear of death in the prisoners, the Germans used cruel terror and spectacle punishments. The punishment at the camp excelled in sadism and savagery. These were mostly carried out in the death-yard. There, the SS men executed all kinds of strange punishments. One of the regular punishments was hanging, but even the hanging was unusual. The "criminal" was hanged with his legs and hands tied by ropes, with his head hanging down. Such hanging led to a protracted death of terrible agony. The women were hanged in the "normal" way, but they were hanged by their hair. Another punishment was one where the stripped naked "criminal" was wrapped in cylinders of barbed-wire, and left outdoors for a few days. For every unfortunate "offence," the Germans beat them 50 to 200 times, and sometimes till death. This punishment was foreseen in cases of escape. The caught escapee was murdered under severe torture, in addition, the rest of the brigade-members were also punished. One Jew escaped from the labour-brigade, and immediately twenty men from the brigade were murdered by shooting.

Among the camp's hangmen were "experts" who excelled at special ways of punishment. One of worst among them was Gebauer. He greatly enjoyed suffocations. With all his force, he tightened the sweater to the victim's neck, until he choked… Another of Gebauer's punishments was the "wash in the barrel of water" as previously mentioned. Another gruesome story about him tells of a man caught stealing a few potatoes. Gebauer made up a special punishment, he ordered to throw the man into a boiling cauldron full of stew, so that the man will be able to enjoy his potatoes straight from the casserole."[26]

[Pages 719-720]

It was said about the young SS man [Friedrich] Heinen, that he had two ways to murder or to punish prisoners. He stabbed them with a sharp stake (a wooden pole or steel rod), and pulled out women's fingernails.

The policemen developed the custom of murdering people into a pleasurable habit, so that eventually they murdered people for no reason at all, purely for the pleasure and sport. According to recollections of prisoners, bizarre sports were particularly practiced by Gustav Willhaus's family. Gustav Willhaus habitually amused himself by shooting at live targets. Without prior warning he used to shoot into the crowd of prisoners queuing near the kitchen or the bathhouse, murdering and wounding many of them. His wife, Otilia, also had a pistol. When the Willhauses happened to have visitors, and they sat on the spacious balcony of their magnificent house, facing the camp, Otilia was in the habit of showing the visitors her prowess as a shot. She aimed at the live targets, and hit some of them to the delight of the visitors. Heineke, the young daughter of the Willhauses, greatly admired her parents' skill and clapped her hands in awe at the sight. This event was also mentioned by some of the writers. They also recalled a Nazi toddler, the son of one of the policemen, who frequently stood at the camp-gate and threw stones at the heads of those leaving for work, badly wounding them.

The policemen abused the prisoners by mockery and jest. Once, two old bearded men with side locks were brought to the camp, one a rabbi the other a slaughterer [*Shochet*]. (There is conflicting information about the origin of the two. They were probably brought from Jaworów after the second *Aktion* which took place there in March 1943). The SS men forced them to daily step onto a raised stage in the camp and dance while holding umbrellas in their hands. (According to the testimonies of Izak Lewin, Farber and of Gerszon Taffet, the policemen held also competitions in murdering Jewish children without any weapons, chopping them in half, crushing their heads, etc.). Every exceptional event triggered novel acts of cruelty by the SS men. On 20th April 1943, Hitler's birthday, Willhaus picked 54 imprisoned Jews and murdered them by shooting, in honour of the *Führer* [leader]. On 25th July 1943, the day Mussolini was forced to give up his position as ruler of Italy, a dreadful event happened in the camp. An SS man blamed a Jew who passed him, for slighting him. The Jew argued that he had greeted the SS man according to the custom and courtesy of the camp, but the policeman insisted that he sensed a covert mockery and gloating at Mussolini, in the Jew's greeting. The policemen decided to take revenge on the Jew. They hanged him upside down, cut off his genitals put it in his mouth and kicked him incessantly leading to haemorrhage in his head and he died suffering gruesomely. This act of cruelty was perpetrated by the policemen Brumbauer and Bermann.[27]

There was at Janowska camp a Jewish orchestra that included such renowned players as Jakub Mund, Józef Herman, Edward Steinberger, Schatz and others, directed by Leon Striks. The orchestra was created on the initiative of SS officer Richard Rokita. This "music fanatic," with an excellent pitch, listened to the playing and when he heard an off note he attacked the orchestra and murdered, by shooting, the player who dared spoil the tonal harmony. On Rokita's initiative a special tune, "Tango of Death," was composed, probably by the composer Schatz. "Tango of Death" was frequently played, especially when work battalions left the camp for work, or when selected groups left "to the Sands."

Besides frequent "selections" and the mentioned methods of murdering, mass slaughters also took place in the camp. One of the last *Grossaktionen* took place in mid-May 1943, when several thousands of prisoners were murdered (eyewitnesses give very conflicting estimates, from 2,000 to 6,000 people).

[Pages 721-722]

Chapter 26. Underground Operations and Uprising Attempts in the camp

All the severe tortures, the physical and mental sufferings which the prisoners underwent in the camp had a single purpose, to eradicate any sense of humanity in them, to reduce them to the level of beasts-for-slaughter (dehumanisation). The SS mens' inequity led however to different outcomes from those they had hoped for. In fact, their impropriety converted the SS men themselves, turning the perpetrators of dehumanisation into wild animals, instead. The target they had set in respect of the prisoners, had not been achieved. There were prisoners in the camp who maintained their human spark, affirmed by the many acts of solidarity, amicable assistance and brotherly love described in accounts of the survivors. Other evidence was the cultural activities and the preparations for armed resistance set up in the camp.

The camp underground operation struggled and was intermittent, as at each attempt many of the leaders died or were murdered. Consequently, no complete depiction of the movement is available, butt only fragments preserved by the few who succeeded in escaping the Valley of Death. We know of a self-help which was organised during 1942, led by: Richard Axer (son of the renowned prosecutor), a young man with a sensitive disposition and spirit, and Jakubowicz. Another group operated at the D.A.W. section of the camp, which was organised by the journalist Dawid Frenkel, a young leader of *HaShomer HaTzair*, Abraham Warmann ("Bronek") and others. The self-help prepared the ground for armed resistance, and meanwhile it assisted individuals to escape from the camp. It provided clothes for the escapees, found them shelters and hiding places in town, false papers, etc. A very important area of operation in the camp was also the assistance to the sick and the hungry, which was mainly led the physicians Dr. Borys Pliskin, Dr. Lust, S. Kohn, M. Osman and H. Birnbaum.

A covert literary activity also took place in the camp. Thus, for instance, a singing party was secretly organised by the author, Schlachter, held on 31st December 1941. This was probably the first party at the camp. During 1942-1943, a string of "literary parties" were organised by members of "the company to clean the town," M. Borwicz (Boruchowicz), Leon Birnbaum, W. Osman, with the participation of Benzion Ginsberg, and Dr. Pliskin. The texts read in these parties were copied in the camp offices by the Jewish clerks, members of the underground, and the copies were distributed among the prisoners. Some writers continued with their literary writings while in the camp. While the writings of Jerachmiel Grin [Grün], Zygmunt Schorr and others were lost, the poem by Halina Grin [Grün] was preserved, as were a few "folk" songs. Many of the camp prisoners kept records and diaries. Most of those were unfortunately lost. Of those that were preserved and published after the war, one need mention M. Borwicz (previously Maksymilian Boruchowicz), who published two books based on his memories of his days at Janowska camp: "University of Thugs" [*Uniwersytet zbirów*] and the "Literature in the camp" [*Literatura w obozie*]. He also wrote poems, two of which were published during the war, in 1944, by the Jewish underground in Warsaw, in the pamphlet *Z otchlani* [From the Abyss], and which later made part of his anthology of poems *Ze smiercia na Ty* ["Face to face with Death"]. Janina Hescheles (the daughter of the editor Henryk Hescheles), wrote a memoir entitled "Through the Eyes of a Twelve-year-old Girl" [*Oczyma dwunastoletniej dziewczyny*]; and Leon Weliczker wrote the book "Death Brigade" [*Brygada Smierci*].

There were different instances of individual resistance in the camp, and besides those recalled by the survivors, there presumably were also those cases that were not written down and are lost forever. The stage is too short to mention all the instances mentioned in the memoirs (compare: memoirs of Borwicz, Szaiawitcz, Farber, Lewin, Maltiel [-Gerstenfeld], Weliczker and others. Many incidents were also mentioned in witnesses' testimonials, kept in archives). Here we have to limit ourselves to three typical images:

Once, for no reason at all, SS man Büttner, cold heartedly and with cruel expression, attacked an elderly Jew in the washhouse, systematically beating him. The Jew fell but did not plead with the murderer who continued to beat him. Instead, the old man raised his head every so often and screamed: "Nevertheless, Hitler will not win!" and with these words on his lips he departed this world.

Rokita stood one day and watched Jews who carried bricks. With the whip in his hand, he hit from time to time.

[Pages 723-724]

His attention and his whip were particularly focused on a rural Jew, who was no longer young but was full-figured and sturdy. Several times Rokita aimed his rifle at him and eventually started to beat him. The Jew stopped his work and began to throw bricks at the SS General. While throwing the bricks he shouted: "Ha, go to the bricks. Let's see how you carry bricks!"

Rokita was so dumbfounded by this sudden reaction that he turned on his heels and began to run. He soon recovered, however, turned to the Jew and shot him dead.

On a different occasion, Willhaus abused a young Jew, Szajowicz, pushing him to the limit of endurance. Szajowicz then verbally abused the SS and eventually jumped on Willhaus and slapped his face. This slap drove Willhaus wild, so that he jumped and shot the Jew, but as soon as he did so, he regretted the easy death he had meted out and started to kick the murdered body.

At the camp there were several attempts to organise armed resistance. On different occasions the prisoners bought weapons, knives and guns in particular, and smuggled them into the camp. In summer 1943, the camp's kitchen turned into a meeting place for the underground. Here it was possible to negotiate –assisted by the kitchen men associated with the underground– with men from the town who supplied food to the camp. In the kitchen, meetings were also very carefully organised between the author Sanie Friedman, who at the time numbered among the camp's Jewish police, and a group of youths who planned a revolt. The meetings and planning did not lead to any action, however. There were occasions when prisoner groups resisted the policemen who led them to "the Sands." Rumours spread in town about an armed revolt near Strzelecki Square, led by prisoners transported in a lorry. Groups of camp-prisoners made several attempts to escape to the forests in the vicinity of the town, and some of them succeeded in implementing their plans with the assistance of the *Askaris*. A lorry once left the camp, filled with Jewish prisoners and their policeman –*Askari*– armed with an automatic gun. There probably was a secret agreement between the *Askari* and the Jews, and the lorry disappeared with all its passengers. Small groups occasionally disappeared, fleeing into the forest where they tried to form partisan units or join the partisans active in the forests. In most cases the runaways died in the forest or fell into the hands of the police or the Ukrainian partisans who murdered them. Nevertheless, such attempts occurred time and again. Among the Jews who escaped to the forest and tried to establish patriotic units there, was a Jew named Czermak, who returned to the camp several times from the forest and smuggled out a few people each time, until he was reported to Nazi police. Czermak was executed together with his assistant, Dr. Zimmet. Still, the underground operation did not stop. The Ukrainian policemen (*Askaris*) who began to track down the secret organisation, were killed by members of the underground (Memoirs of Irena Szajowicz). Other groups attempted also to escape and revolt (recollections of Dr. Dawid Kahane and Michal Borwicz). It seems that there were underground groups that operated in different areas of the camp and at different times, without a joined up, centralised organisation. Many of these attempts were quashed when still in the bud. Significant was the attempt to prepare for the November 1943 revolt. The preparation for this revolt was mentioned by several authors, however the preserved records offer conflicting details and we do not have a full and reliable description of events. From the various versions one can derive that the Germans had uncovered the preparations and decided to precede their execution, by liquidating Janowska camp. The liquidation was set for November 1943. Although the underground was not prepared for the sudden *Aktion*, when it happened it was confronted with an armed resistance and several prisoners successfully escaped to the forests. According to one version, a group of Jewish prisoners reached an agreement with a group of rebelling *Askaris*. A few days before the liquidation of the camp, they murdered a few German policemen and escaped to the forest.

Concurrently, a revolt broke out by a Jewish brigade that operated at Lesienice camp. In mid-June 1943, the Germans assembled a brigade from among Janowska camp prisoners, known as the "Brigade of Death." At the same time, the Germans started to eliminate all trace of the horrific slaughters they had perpetrated. A special German battalion (*Sonderkommando 1005*) was created, tasked with collecting the murdered corpses from all the slaughtering-areas near the ghettos and camps, and burn them without leaving a trace. The officers of the *Sonderkommando 1005* also assembled a "Brigade of Death," in which 150 men from the camp were engaged. The Jewish prisoners plotted revolt, and on 19th November 1943 they suddenly attacked the German policemen, killed some of them and started to escape from the barbed wire surrounded camp. The sudden attack was not wholly successful. In several places the police were not surprised and responded with shots and grenades. Nevertheless, a few tens of prisoners managed to escape and hide in the forests and in the town. Most of them were captured and murdered a short time later. Fewer than ten persons survived.

After all the Jewish camp prisoners were slaughtered,

[Pages 725-726]

Janowska camp still served as a forced-labour camp, and a detention camp for non-Jewish criminals. It held a few hundred Polish, Ukrainian and *Volksdeutsche*. In 1944, the Germans reintroduced a small group of Jewish labourers and craftsmen. They were mostly Jews caught in the *Aryan* side of town, whose death-sentences the Germans altered to incarceration in the camp, because they required tailors, shoemakers, tanners, electricians, gardeners, laundrymen, etc. During the Soviet air attack on Lwów in April 1944, there was a great commotion at the camp, and 15 of the prisoners took advantage of the situation and escaped. The Germans moved the rest to a safer place, but in the turmoil during the transport several Jews managed to escape and hide in the vicinity of Dobromil [Dobrómyl] and Grybów in western Galicia. The Germans continued to burn the victims even after the liquidation of Janowska camp and the "Brigade of Death." They concluded this task in January 1944.

[Pages 727-728]

Chapter 27. The Survivors

During 26-29 July 1944, the Soviet army liberated the town of Lwów from German occupation. Immediately after the liberation a Jewish Committee, housed in a small hall on Jablonowskich Street, was spontaneously formed and it started to register the surviving Jews. Not all Jews dared openly declare their Jewishness. Some of the Christian townspeople did not take kindly to the Jewish survivors. There were even cases of Jews murdered by members of the nationalist Polish or Ukrainian underground. That was the fate of Dr. Bartfeld, the teacher of religion who was murdered after he had come out of hiding.

The Jewish survivors fell into three categories:

a.   The first category was formed by those who had disguised themselves, who had false documents. Many of these never divulged their identity even after the liberation. Among them were also Jewish children who were taken in by Christian families during the Nazi period, and who for several reasons never rejoined the Jewish community and the Jewish faith. At times the Christian families were so attached to the children that they did not wish to part from them, and at times children found out that their parents and families had perished, and that they had no one.

b.   The second category was formed by the "forest people" who emerged from hiding in the forests, or from roaming the land with the partisans, most of whom remained naked destitute.

c.   The third category, colloquially known as "mice," had hidden in caves, ducts, ditches and bunkers, and when they emerged they were weak and exhausted from lack of movement and lack of fresh air in their hiding places. Their legs staggered and their eyesight was faint, their faces were pale and their bodies swollen.

Besides the Jews previously from Lwów, Jewish survivors from provincial towns also chose to settle in Lwów rather than return to their homes, whether because they felt more isolated and lonely in their small towns where everything would remind them of the destruction from which they sought refuge in the large, remote town; or whether because they felt greater personal security in a large community.

Indeed, Lwów remained the only "large" [Jewish] community in eastern Galicia. While Jewish survivors in other towns reached at most a few hundred individuals (as at Boryslaw, Drohobycz, Stanislawów, Tluste), the Jewish population of Lwów numbered a few thousands.

Lwów's Jewish population-count does not truly reflect the number of the Jewish survivors from Lwów proper. Of the survivors who registered with Lwów's Jewish Committee and who settled at Lwów after the liberation, the overwhelming majority were Jews from provincial towns. The Jewish Committee on Jablonowskich Street had no technical means nor experts to undertake a reliable census. Up to 21st September 1944, around 3,400 Jews had registered at the committee office. While the value of this list is questionable, because it was impossible to collect and critically scrutinise all the data in those days, nevertheless, it is the sole source from those days. For this reason, we present here the statistical details (we received the statistics from members of Lwów's Jewish Committee at the end of September 1944). The 3,400 Jews were made up of:

Women aged	20 - 60	2080
Men aged	18 - 55	1215
The aged	over 55	20
Children & youths up to 18	–	85

60% of those who registered, recorded their occupation before the war as craftspeople, traders and clerks. Of these, 15% were professionals, teachers and artists. Among the surviving professional intelligentsia the precise numbers were: 32 physicians, 8 dentists, 42 advocates, 27 engineers, 16 teachers and 9 actors.

The Jewish committee also began to organise assistance for the survivors. The support given by the town authorities, together with the financials means available to the committee (donations of wealthy Jews), were very meagre, and the aid provided up to 21st September 1944, consisted of: 13,000 lunches; 8,000 loafs of bread; 20,000 Rubles in cash, and a small quantity of lightweight clothes.

Subsequently, a new local Jewish committee was formed, managed by experienced public activists (the committee was led by Dr. Dawid Sobel for several months). The town's authorities offered to the new committee the only synagogue still extant after the Nazis' departure. It was the synagogue on

[Pages 729-730]

Weglana Street, which the Germans had tuned into a warehouse and stable, and was not suited for an office. Nevertheless, the temporary offices of the Jewish committee were moved there, where prayers were also held during the Holy days. In November 1944, the [Jewish] committee conducted a new count, and registered 2,571 Jews, including 134 children between the ages of three and sixteen. It appears that many of those who registered at Lwów in the first days after the liberation stayed only temporarily in the town, on their way to Poland. A more thorough investigation by the committee showed that among the survivors only 823 were Jews who were born in Lwów or resided in the town at the time the German invasion. These figures were given to us by Dr. Dawid Sobel, head of the Jewish committee. The Jewish committee was not officially sanctioned by the Soviet authorities who did not want to legitimise a religious community. The authorities only tolerated the committee in the early months, after which the committee resigned. The departure of Jews from Lwów continued. (Following the accord between the Soviet Union and the Polish Republic, the residents of Lwów could choose between a Soviet-Ukrainian citizenship and a Polish citizenship. Lwów was annexed to Soviet Ukraine). The majority of the Jews opted for Polish citizenship and left Lwów. The repatriation to Poland lasted from October 1944 until the end of 1945. Those leaving Lwów practically cleared it of its Jewish residents. Lwów's [Jewish] survivors wandered to various towns in Poland (Warsaw, Lódz, Kraków and others), from there to the displaced-persons camps in Germany, Austria and Italy, and finally to Israel and to countries in the Americas.

Original notes:

24. Archives of the Jewish Historical Institute at Warsaw, No. 858.

25. [Izak] Lewin, [*Aliti MeSpezia*], pp. 139-140;
[Isaac] Farber ["Cronika Shel Ish Lwów…" *Reshumot*], p. 24;
[Michał] Borwicz, *Uniwersytet zbirów* [University of Thugs], Kraków 1946, pp. 34-35

26. Three survivors of Lwów's camp mention this incident in their testimonies:
[Isaac] Farber, *op.cit.* p. 24
[Irene] Szajowicz, p. 44
[Michał] Borwicz, *op.cit.* p. 58.

27. I was told this event by eyewitnesses, a few days after the event (P. F.)

[Pages 731-732]

Chapter 28. References

The author of this article resided at Lwów during the entire Nazi occupation, from 1941 until July 1944, and after the liberation, until November 1944. In addition to the material he personally collected through daily experience and conversation with many people during the period of the Nazis and after their departure from Lwów, he also used the following sources:

1. The daily German Newspaper: *Lemberger Zeitung*, 1941-1944.

2. The daily Polish Newspaper: *Gazeta Lwowska*.

3. The daily Newspapers in Ukrainian: *Ukraïns'ki Shchodenni Visti* from 1941; and Levovski Visti.

5. *Verordnungsblatt für das Generalgouvernement* 1941-1944.

6. *Amtsblatt des Gouverneurs des Distrikts Galizien*, for the years 1941-1944, the official magazine of the German authorities.

7. Official manuscripts of the German authorities:
Die Bevölkerung des Distrikts Galizien am 1. März 1943 (manuscript [about the Population of Distrikt Galicia] in

German and Ukrainian);

Die Landwirtschaft des Distrikts Galizien nach der Lage am 1. Juli 1943 (manuscript in German). (All the manuscripts are kept at the Archives of the Ukrainian Academy of Sciences; Department of Economics; Lwów.

The newspapers and magazines are kept at the Political Archives on Podwale Street; and at the Library of the University of Lwów.)

9. Reports of the Extraordinary State (Soviet) Commission for the Establishment and Investigation of the Atrocities of the German-Fascist Invaders and their Accomplices:
Testimonies of the atrocities perpetrated by the German criminals in the District of Lwów. *Pravda*, and *Izvestia*, 23rd December 1944.

10. Manuscripts of the testimonies and memoirs of 25 Jewish survivors, collected by the Central Jewish Historical Commission in Poland, and by its branches at Łódź, Kraków, Warszawa, Lublin, Przemyśl (The Archive of the Jewish Historical Institute at Warsaw.)

11. Manuscripts of 21 testimonies collected by The Central Historical Commission in Munich (nowadays in Israel).

12. Manuscripts of 24 testimonies by eye-witneses about the Holocaust period in Lwów, kept at archive of YIVO Institute for Jewish Research, New York.

13. Very important documents –amongst them the report by [Fritz] Katzmann – are kept in the protocols of the International Criminal Court of War Criminals. The most complete existing edition is the American edition:

Trial of major War Criminals before the International Military Tribunal Nuremberg, Nov. 14, 1945- Oct. 1, 1946. Nuremberg, Germany, 1947 (Washington D.C. Superintendent of Documents. U.S. Government). 42 Vols.

[Pages 733-734]

Bibliography:

Hebrew and Yiddish:

i.   Unger, Israel [Eliezer]: *Zechor* [Remember] (In the days of Death Wagons). Massada, Tel Aviv (5705) 1944/5.

ii.   Gutwirth, Jisroel: Articles in *Jidisze Cajtung*, Landsberg [am Lech] Nr. 36 (16 Mai 1947); *Ibergang* [Organ fun Pojliszn Jidntum in Dajczland; München], Nr. 16 (30 März 1947).

iii.   Grüss Noé [Gris, Noah]: *Kindermartyrologie* [Zamlung fun Dokumentn Yiddish Bikher-serie dos Poylishe Yidntum], Buenos Aires 1947; pp. 101-102; 141-145; 186-194; 220-221.

iv.   Weissbrod, Abraham [Avrum]: "Ven die Ert kukt mit roiten Oygen [When the World looks on with Red Eyes]" *Oyf di Vanderungen*, München 1947, pp. 51-59.

v.   Zaderecki, Tadeusz: Articles in *Dos Naje Łebn* Łódz Nr. 289; 338 . (1949).

vi.   Yudka: "Beterem Niftecha HaRa'a [Before the Evil broke out]" *MiBifnim*, June 1947, pp. 457-469.

vii.   Lewin, Izak: *Aliti MeSpezia* -Oud Muzal MeGhetto Lwów [I migrated to Israel from Spezia -An Ember retrieved from Lwów's Ghetto]. Translated by Dov Struck from the Polish manuscript. (Sadan) Tel-Aviv, Am Oved, 1947.

viii. Mayer, Szlojme: *Der Untergang fun Zloczów* Munich, 1947.

ix.   Maltiel [-Gerstenfeld], Jacob: *Be'ain Nakam...* [Without Revenge...], Te-Aviv, Am Oved, 1947.

x.   Niger, Schmuel: *Kidush HaShem* [Martyrdom], New York, Cyco, 1948, pp. 317-333.

xi.   Fuks, Tanja: *A Vanderung iber okupierte Gebitn* [(Dos Poylishe Yidntum); A wander over occupied territories]. Buenos Aires, 1947, pp. 49-107.

xii.   Farber, Isaac: "Cronika Shel Ish Lwów- Yesurei Kehila BeYemei Kibush HaNazim" [Chronicle of a Lwów Man- A community's sufferings during the Nazi occupation], *Reshumot*, New Series, Vol.1, [Tel-Aviv] (1946), pp. 33-5.

xiii. "Pletat Sridim [Surviving Remains]." From Lwów via the Ukrainian front to Eretz Israel, *Reshumot*, New Series, Vol.2, pp. 48-59.

xiv. Friedman, Filip: "Megilat Lwów [Lwów's Scroll]" *Tav Shin Hay* [5705; 1945] Tel-Aviv, *Davar*. 1945, pp. 220-233.

xv. Dr. Reifer, Manfred: *Masa HaMavet* [The Death Trek], Tel-Aviv, Am Oved, 1946, pp. 92-105.

xvi. Schnek, Fela: "Ech Hushmedu Yehudei Lwów [How the Jews of Lwów were annihilated]" *Davar* [Newspaper], Tel-Aviv, 5 November, 1946.

Other Languages:

1. Belayev, Vladimir *Czerwony Sztandar* [Red Banner; a Polish language daily newspaper], Lwów, 25.10.1944. *Vilna Ukraina* [Ukrainian language newspaper] Lwów, 28.9.1944. *Ogoniok* [Sparks; Russian Illustrated weekly magazine] Moscow Nos. 14, 15, 17, 1945.

2. Blumental, Nachman *Obozy* (Dokumenty i Materiały [a czasów okupacji niemieckiej w polsce] vol.1).

3. Borwicz, Michał *Uniwersytet zbirów*, [*Rzecz o obozie Janowskim we Lwowie 1941–1944* (wspomnienia)] Kraków, 1946.

4. Borwicz, [Maksymilian] Michał: *Literatura w obozie*, Kraków, 1946.

5. Borwicz, [Maksymilian] Michał: *Ze śmiercią na ty*, Warszawa, 1946.

6. Borwicz, Michał Rost, Nella; Wulf, Józef: *Dokumenty Zbrodni i Męczenstwa* [; Ksiazki Wojewodzkiej Komosji Historycznej W Krakówie Nr 1], Kraków 1946, pp. 122-131; 171-173.

7. Broszkiewicz, Jerzy: *Oczekiwanie*, Warszawa, 1948.

8. Eber-Friedman, Ada: "Z galerii moich Zyciodacow" *Nasza Trybuna*, New York Nos. 109-118; 1945, 1950.

9. Friedman, Filip: *Zagłada Żydów lwowskich*, I ed. Łódz, 1945; II ed. Munich 1947.

10. Heszeles, Janka [Hescheles, Janina]: *Oczyma 12-letniej dziewczyny*, Kraków 1946.

11. Reder, Rudolf: *Bełżec*, Kraków 1946.

12. Silberschein, A[braham] Dr.: *Lwów-Śniatyn-Sandomierz*: L'Extermination des Juifs en Pologne, Serie 5. Genève 1945.

13. Śledziński, Wacław: *Swastyka nad Warszawą*. Edinburgh, 1944, p. 104.

14. Sobieski, Zygmunt: "Reminiscences from Lwów" *Journal of Central European Affairs*, Vol. 6, 1947, pp. 351-374.

15. Szende, Stefan: *Den siste juden från Polen*. Stockholm, 1944; *Der letzte Jude aus Polen*. Zürich, 1945.

16. Taffet, Gerszon: *Zagłada Zydów żółkiewskich*. Łódz, 1946.

17. Weinberg, Józef: *Tam gdzie śmierć była ulgą*. Katowice, 1946.

18. Weliczker, Leon: *Brygada śmierci (Sonderkommando* 1005), Łódz, 1946.

19. Zaderecki, Tadeusz: *Opinia* Łódź-Warszawa No. 11, 12, 13, (1947).

20. *Zvirstva Nimtziv na Lvovshchini* [The atrocities of the Germans in the Lwów region; in Russian]. Lwów, 1945.

[Pages 735-736]

Annihilation of the Jews of Lwów (cont'd)
Appendices

Documents and Certificates

I.

The Song of Janowska camp's Prisoners[*]
[copied here from the original in Polish]

1.
A my chłopcy jacy tacy
Z Janowskiego lagru pracy
Cały swiat nas nie chce znać
Ch… do d…, k… mać
2.
Rano kawa, wieczor kawa
To jest ceła dzienna strawa
Z tego tylko mozna szczać
C…………………………mać
3.
A na obiad jest se zupa
Litra wody, cztery krupy,
Z tego tylko mozna …ć
C…………………………mać
4.
Robić kazą, jesć nie deją,
I codziennie nas strzelają
A że nie masz już czem szczać
C…………………………mać
5.
Akcja w maju, akcja w lutym
Zona, dziecko juz za druiem,
Serce Z bolu chce się rwaća
6.
Nasz Kolanko chłop morowy
Ma karabin maszynowy
Na maszynce umie grać
7.
Kiedy Cię Gebauer dusi
Możesz skarzyć mamusi,
Ze się z tatem Chciała grać

8.
Gdy wyciągną Cię z kolumny,
Nie zobaczysz namei trummy,
I na Piaski pojdziesz spać
9.
A w niedzielę odpoczynek
Na karetce jedzie Grzymek
I na bacznosć trzeba stać

10.
Bo pan Grzymek chłop morowy
Ma karabin maszynowy
Przednim trza na baczosz stać

Version B.
Albosmy to jacy-tacy
dito
Swiat nas kiedys będzie znać
dito
Chochla zupy, cztery krupy
Taka zupa jest do d...
dito
dito

Version C.
My se chłopcy jacy-tacy
dito
Ze nam szafa nie chce grać
dito

Notes:

* When I was in Lwów during the Nazi occupation, and after, I heard and wrote down the different versions of this song, in Polish and in German. The song is not complete, because I was unable to note down the rhymes at the time I heard them. Part of the notes and the German version, are lost. The two last verses concentrate on the living conditions in the ghetto of Lwów under the management of [Józef] Grzymek. P[hilip] F[riedman]

[Pages 737-738]

Translations by Rita Falbel

III.

Lemberg's Jews Relocate: "Lemberger Zeitung (News)" 15.XI.1941

Since the Jews, who until now still roam free in Lemberg, and are taking part very actively in their illicit trade... further ... because they intercept the farmers outside the city and take from them food at high prices, the city government was forced to set up a Jewish residential area. It was thus foreseen that a Ghetto was to be established, since one wants to confirm the supply of an appropriate and useful work force ... The ruling is singularly magnanimous since it is carried out in ways which avoid, as far as possible, all harshness. The Jews must relocate during the time from 16.IX to 14.XII. The Judenrat, the one public agency that employs (supports) up to 500 men is responsible. The Polish and Ukrainian people who live in the Jewish neighborhood will relocate to the city, where they will receive respectable apartments (special offices for assigning apartments, Stadthauptman Peltewna 1). The administrative authority will even make every effort to arrange for appropriate transport. The exclusively Jewish district will be located in the part of the city north of the Lemberg-Tarnopol railroad, with the exception of the core (kernes), through which the Żółkiewskastrasse goes. Poles und Ukrainians have until 14.XII to leave this district. Jews are permitted to take necessary, personal belongings with them to this district. Business supplies, furniture or stock from stores are not permitted to be taken as part of the relocation-action to this Jewish residential district. Any such shops are to be closed and sealed. Entry to the Jewish district after 14. XII is forbidden for anyone except those resident Jews. Exceptions for enforced living in the Jewish district can only be permitted in isolated cases by the Mayor. ... The implementation of the relocation action is to be enforced and directed by the SS- and Chief of Police in the District of Galicia.

[IV. W Sprawie Chrztu Zydow: This section is in Polish]

V.

Administration and Justice

After the initiation of decrees in the district Galicia, the number of cases that came before the special court in Lemberg related to hiding Jews, recently rose quickly and considerably. For this offense the law prescribed the death sentence only. On account of this, the special courts are always expected to decide for the death penalty. Among judges there is a tendency to take a position against this in more or less extreme form. Most criticism points towards the fact that these punishments could only be practical when carried out by the security police. Thus, the necessity of the death penalty is generally agreed upon, because Jews who seek hiding places should, in view of the prevailing circumstances, be viewed as criminals. In taking a position, a judge must not shy away from his responsibility thereby avoiding implementation of this harsh judgment.

As pertains to the "Jewish laws" the judge lacks the consciousness of the political mission. That goes for the law of identity marking of Jews, unauthorized leaving of the district, as well as hiding of Jews. From the judge's point of view, these laws, considering their content and character, are rules that fall purely within the purview of the police. Therefore, the implementation of such laws, or as the case may be, decrees, are to be left exclusively to the police. This also presents the judge with a moral burden, when at the time of judgment, he would disregard following the letter of the law.

[Pages 739-740]

Often enough the facts require a substantially milder judgment from an ethical standpoint. For the judge however, this avenue is blocked from the outset by the law. The judge is only a servant in a rigid preordained sequence of events. Thus, one forces the judge into a situation which is incompatible with his position. An example of this conflict follows: If, for instance, an illiterate Ukrainian farmer would take into his house for a few hours his former Jewish salesman and supplier, by whom he had until now been "looked after," would perhaps even offer him coffee and bread, because he [the Jew], had asked for it, the facts of the case would be fulfilled. Whether the Ukrainian farmer even knew that by taking a Jew into his house he would forfeit his head, would be in question. It is namely thus, that the decree and its punishment have not been distributed widely enough from the larger cities. Besides, it is still a fact, that among individual Ukrainians and Poles on the one hand, and Jews on the other, bonds have already existed from former relationships in this district. Because of this it seems more advantageous to not carry justice to the absurd, if such offenses come before the judge through the duties of the police.

[Paragraphs in Polish]

VI.

Atrocity in Poland!

Written in the year 1943. It was during the months, March, April, May, June, July and August. The general retreat from Russia resulted in my coming to Lemberg with my unit. On. 14. March I arrived in Lemberg. The commander of the [Feldluftparkes] in Lemberg handed me the responsibility of guarding a store in District B4, the news service district. Jews, who had been kept in a ghetto as prisoners in 1942 after the occupation of Poland, were assigned to us to maintain and look after this store. And so it was my daily task to pick up these 25 assigned Jews from the ghetto every morning, and bring them back again in the evening. I had already been told a lot about the inhuman handling of Jews, partly I heard it from the Jews themselves, partly from my Polish friends at that time, but also from my own comrades. Well, I didn't want to believe it, but I was able to convince myself daily, with what bestiality our SS and also the Ukrainian Gestapo that were involved, dealt with these people, only because they held another belief or belonged to another race. It was always my goal, should I be captured by the British or Americans, to give a long detailed account about the inhuman handling of the Jews, to be published in the foreign press.

However, since I wasn't captured, I want this little book, that was basically written at a time when the Hitler dictatorship was still at the helm, to be a legacy to human, thinking mankind, and to those who come after, who will, in the end, have to judge how this series of events, perpetrated by such creatures who stand far below animals, can be justified. I take full responsibility for these notes of mine.

Every morning, when I arrived at the ghetto, I was presented a picture which literally made the blood in my veins freeze. Even at the gate, since I could only enter with a special permit, I heard, quite softly, the wonderful sounds of the 3rd. Beethoven symphony. My readers will wonder how this can be possible, but then it is not different for you as it was for me. I also wondered about it constantly.

[Pages 741-742]

I went in further and there I saw women and children with the men herded together by the SS-hordes and Ukrainian militia, being beaten, and whoever made the slightest movement of resistance was shot down. I heard the whimpering of innocent children and infants, heard the wailing and screaming of women and saw the dumb, but obviously painful witnessing of the men, saw how they were driven in the gutters, how they were tortured, accompanied all the while by the purest tones of the 3rd. Beethoven symphony. So I asked one of these beasts in human form, one of the mindless, drunken SS-men, and they were almost always so, why one would play the most beautiful German music to such behavior. He replied "If you don't like it you can join the rabble." The City Commander [Statdtkommandant] of Lemberg, the SS-Brigadier General Katzmann personally chose the best Jewish musicians to provide the necessary accompanying music for this varied "morning's entertainment." Beethoven and Mozart were thus played to accompany the atrocities of the SS-hordes, sthat the poor tortured people'slow process of dying could be eased.

Now I ask you, my readers, is that not the most disgraceful use of culture? The system that calls itself defenders of the national culture, this system brings it to an end, our purest classical composers degraded by such brutal murder. I was deeply shaken since I love art above everything, but I couldn't dwell on my thoughts for long, but perceived suddenly the meaning of the Jews' word "Aktion". What must I now experience without being able to help. Even the so-called trustees, unfortunately Jews themselves, drove the people together and ordered them to stand neatly in rows, then as soon as the first lieutenant of the SS came, the bloody ceremony could begin. He disclosed the number of lots designated [for the day]. The number 4 was chosen, that means, every 4th male Jew or female Jew with child are chosen for the Aktion. He began to count and every 4th person was taken away. Some, who were already living corpses endured it with quiet stoicism, happy finally, to be relieved of this wasting away; but sometimes one could witness heartbreaking scenes which were played out especially within families. The man had to witness his wife and child being taken away, never to see them again; women had to watch while their men were taken away and if anyone resisted even slightly, how they immediately struck him over the head with the butt of their weapons. I was allowed to witness this tragedy as I had this special permit to enter the camp. Others didn't find out anything, since before every Aktion, the camp was heavily guarded by SS units and anyone who approached the 100 meter boundary outside the camp was shot without warning. I witnessed this tragedy, wanted to, but couldn't help; even though my blood surged inside me, I had to turn away shattered, since when a person sees such things, he loses all belief in the preservation of the most basic laws of humanity, and is then ashamed to be a citizen of a nation from which these SS-hordes spring.

They herded the people onto trucks; each truck held 25. There they had to squat down and at each corner of the vehicle stood an SS-guard with loaded weapon held at the ready. If anyone moved the guard would hit him over the head so that blood would run and [the prisoner] would collapse. Others were transported on the so-called lorries of streetcars, and every ten minutes a streetcar passed one after the other through Lemberg. I know from my own experience, the road went as far as a gravel pit where the Jews were lined up in front of machine guns and row after row were gunned down. Many weren't even shot but keeled over in terror and fell into the gravel pit. Following that, lime was immediately poured onto the dead and living to erase the traces of this treacherous extermination. I found out from many sources that in Lemberg a mass grave of about 500,000 innocent murdered Jews exists.

Every evening as I brought the Jews back to the Ghetto again, they told me that they didn't know if they would see me the next morning.

From these days onward my attitude toward the SS became completely clear and unchangeable. I am of the singular opinion that the whole SS, which perpetrated such atrocities, must be exterminated, especially everyone who committed offenses against the laws of humanity in such a shameful manner.

[Pages 743-744]

I also remember a comment by the notorious SS-General Katzmann, commander of Lemberg, related to me by Captain Guenther, the leader of the B-District of the FLP in Lemberg. The General said to him then: "Katyn, this is only a daily job for us!" So said the man who earned a half million Reichs Marks in cash, only because he called off a planned "Aktion." Whether a planned aktion would take place or not only depended on his mood of the moment. He let his Gestapo men extort sums of up to 100,000 zlotys from the Jews as ransom whom he then accordingly exploited, and he also squandered the money in wild orgies. The conditions in the Ghetto were so unbearable that several of my own Jews even asked me to get them the strongest poisons, cyanide or morphine, at great cost. The poor tortured people only wanted to shorten the time to their certain death when an Aktion was announced. Thus the weeks and months went by, always with my Jews living with the constant terror of "when will it be my turn." The Aktions occurred often during each week, sometimes 3 times. The wehrmacht intervened for the Jews when they could since they could count on them as honest, willing and good workers, until the day when it didn't suit the SS-commander any longer. Such intervention by the Wehrmacht didn't help any more. General Katzmann informed the officers of the wehrmacht (also again as heard by Captain Guenther and Major v. Klenck) that the wehrmacht had no say in the matter, the Jews were his property and he could deal with them as he wished.

On the 10th of July or June 1943 a large Aktion was announced and the aim of this Aktion would be the complete extermination of Jewry. On that day, I was, as usual. in the ghetto in the morning and was able to witness an incomprehensible sorrow. The ghetto was again strongly guarded by the SS, nobody was allowed to approach the camp nearer than 20 meters. In the ghetto itself, the Jews understandably hid themselves in their cellars, some even in the empty sewers. I could see with my own eyes how they took away small children from the women and threw them against the building walls, and how the smashed limbs were scattered on the ground.

I saw one of these young SS-rascals, scarcely 21 years old, showing off with this death work, how he had already "earned" almost a million Reichs Marks. I also saw how they threw sick, fragile Jews of both sexes, naked from the 4th floor of the ghetto's hospital onto a truck and took them away. The air surrounding me was filled with such indescribable lamentation and sorrow, that it was heartbreaking. I then circulated these witnessed events to my Polish friends (Michalina Melnyk, Lemberg, Żółkiewerstrasse 173) and heard also that similar tragedies occurred in the Warsaw ghetto. I often asked myself why the Polish land was selected for this and came to understand that criminal elements in the Polish government of that time collaborated in these atrocities. The outcome of this was that Jews from all Balkan countries were brought to Poland for execution; in my careful estimation, it must have been 3-4,000,000 Jews who were innocently murdered because of the insane idea of Hitler

Again I have to comment, that these writings are not a product of fantasy-induced thinking, but absolutely and completely incontestable, declared under oath from a foreign person, as supplement to reporting of fact. As main witness I submit herewith the name of one of my comrades, who will completely confirm these statements since he also experienced almost all of them with me. His address is: Helmuth Hauck, Chemnitz/Sa. Fichtestrasse

Epilogue:

I didn't write this report after the occupation by the allied forces, but it can be incontestably established that the fundamentals of this report began in Yugoslavia (see other report*).

Note:

* When I was in Munich (Bavaria) in 1946, I was approached by Alfred Greiner, a German who had served in the German army during World War II, and who brought me his typewritten records. From the unpublished records. I present here the one I chose and from which I deleted insignificant issues. Greiner arrived together with Szmuel Reizman, a survivor of the Treblinka death camp, who was in Munich at the time as Secretary of the Central Committee of the surviving Jews.

Greiner Alfred

[Pages 745-746]

VII.

Secret Reichs Matters[*]

The SS-and Police chief   9:30 June 1943
In the Distict Galicia   2 Copy (Ausfertigungen)
Tgb. Nr. 42/43g.R.-Ch/Fr. 1 Copy

Re: Solution of the Jewish Question in Galicia
 Concerning: Enclosed Report
 Encl.: 1 report (3 copies)
        1. Copy (bound)

 To the
 Chief and leader of Police East
 SS-Lt. General and Chief of Police
 Kureger-o.V.i.A.
 Krakau.
 In the enclosed I remit the final report as one copy, regarding the solution to the Jewish question in District Galicia for your attention.

(--) Katzmann
Generalleutnant of the Police
SS-Major General

VIII.

Camp Reports

(Main bureau for Propaganda, weekly report of the Districts).

A. Lemberg, 29. August 1942.

The work force in the district is now stretched to the limit. Additional effects were the radical withdrawal of Jewish workers. The district of Galicia had only a year's time to prepare. Its Arian population is less skilled in craft and trade compared with other districts. Therefore, the war industry is more adversely affected here by the deportation of Jews than the other parts of the General Gouvernements.

The fundamental question, that the removal of the Jews for political purposes is of more importance than war industry, is apparently a decision made at the highest levels that decided in favor of this policy. The decrease of industrial production in the affected areas must be considered. As a precaution, I must point out that these effects in Galicia will have a great impact.

B. Lemberg 16.10.42.

The relocation of the Jews, which, in part, takes forms that are not worthy of a cultured people, promotes the comparison of the methods of the Gestapo with those of the GPU. The trains for transport are reported to be in such bad condition that it is impossible to prevent the escape of Jews. The result of this is that wild shooting and manhunts take place regularly along the way. Also to report is that the corpses of the Jews shot down lie around on the roads for days.

In spite of this, the German citizenry and other folk who live here are convinced of the necessity of liquidating all Jews, though it would be preferable to effect this in a less offensive and provocative way.

Note:

* From the collected documents of the "War Crime Trials," published by the USA Authorities in Germany, Nuremberg/Nürnberg, 1947.

IX.

Ukrainian Daily-News **8.7.1941**

(Translated from Ukrainian)

The Appearance of the New Lwów

...another conspicuous phenomenon for all to see in the New Lwów is the absence of Jews in the streets. And only a few days ago they filled every corner of town... It seemed that during the two years of the Bolshevik occupation Lwów turned into a sort of Tel-Aviv, or at least... the criminals known as "the chosen People" hide in their lairs for fear of the people...

[Pages 747-748]

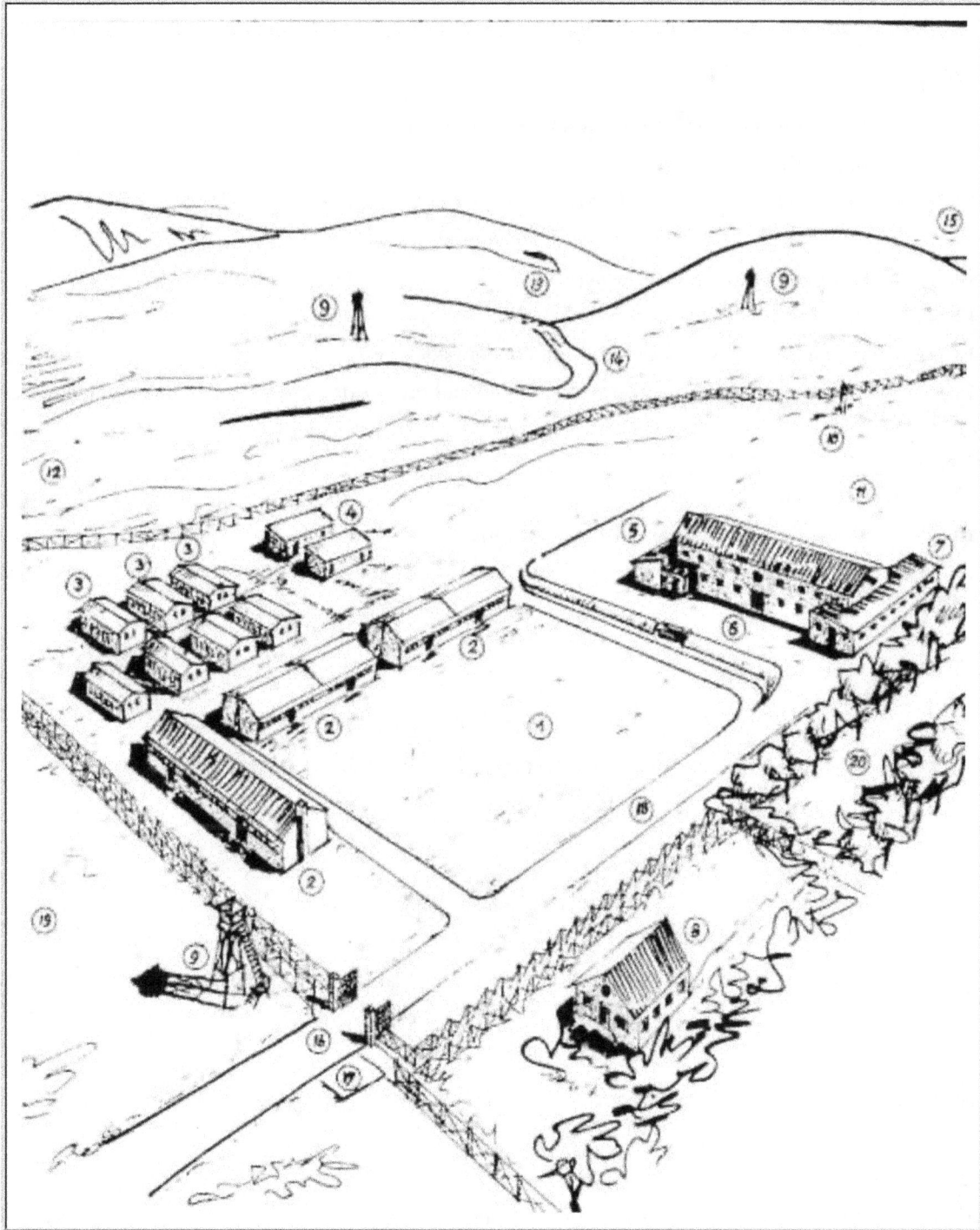

Janowska camp – the living quarters

1.   **The torture and the death yard.**

2.   Living huts of the captives.

3.   Wooden huts.

4.   Latrines

5.   Kitchen-hut, the serving-hatch for dishing out soup and "portions."

6.   The "old" building (earlier, stable and warehouse).

7.   The showers hut.

8.   The shoemakers' hut.

9.   The tower of the *Askaris* (Russians in the service of the SS.)

10.   The hanging yard.

11.   The murder and inspection yard – at the entrance to the camp.

12.   The undressing area for the victims to be murdered.

13.   The "Sands" (*piaski* [in Polish]) where Lwów's victims were buried.

14.   The path that led to the "Sands."

15.   The boundary of the Jewish cemetery on Pilichowska Street.

16.   The main entrance to the camp. (the "selection" and the "death-race" of the condemned, when leaving for work).

17.   The SS men's inspection hut.

18.   Track. paved in tomb-stones from the Jewish cemetery.

19.   First inspection area of those entering the camp.

20.   Vegetable garden next to the accommodation villa of the camp commander (SS officer [Gustav] Willhaus).

[Pages 749-750]

First Day in a Death-camp
From the Diary of a survivor of Janowska camp in Lwów

by Engineer O. Porat (Ochs)

Translated by Myra Yael Ecker

Edited by Karen Leon

16 July 1942

Today, together with a group of eighty Jews, I was brought to the forced-labour camp on Janowska Street in Lwów, which later was made into an extermination camp. At 9 a.m. we entered through the gate of the camp under heavy guard. The camp was surrounded by three-metre-high barbed wire, with an inspection-tower rising from every corner in which German and Ukrainian guards sat, armed with machine guns.

I am beyond the barbed wire… a feeling of horror engulfs me. It seems as if I am led to slaughter. On the way to the camp the thoughts of fleeing rushed through my mind, but the guarding was tight and we were warned that if one person escaped, ten will be murdered. The thought of escaping does not leave me even after entering the camp, but despair takes over. It seems that from here there is no escape…

SS men [Karl] Schubert and Grusshaber received our group from *Scharführer* [Adolf] Kolonko who brought us here.

Now we received an order: "Sit down and do not move. Whoever makes the lightest movement will be killed like a dog…!" I sit down on the grass, stare right in front of me, as it is forbidden to make any move. My eyes search for clues of the deeds that were rumoured about outside, but I don't see anything. The courtyard is clean. Order reigns everywhere. Multicoloured flowers surround us in flowerbeds. It seems to me that the flowers are whispering amongst themselves and mock us. The beauty of nature blooms as ever and takes no pity on us...

So perhaps all I have heard about this camp was exaggerated?... But no. Suddenly I understand that my friends who face me, stare in one direction with great difficulty, and their white faces turn even paler. Endangering my life, I turn my head and steal a glance. Is this a nightmare or reality?... Between the flowerbeds a gallows was displayed. Off the rope hangs the naked cadaver of a young man... I shut my eyes, but the image I have seen is stuck in my mind and will not shift. I am seized by a sense of choking. I want to scream, but I cannot. We all continue sitting, petrified. All of a sudden a wild laugh pierces the silence like a dagger. The German and Ukrainian guards up in the inspection towers are laughing. They pelt us with small stones while the muzzles of the machine guns are pointed at us. We are tense and alert to the extreme. It seems as if a nervous reaction will be triggered at any minute, which will lead to a catastrophe. However the will to live overcomes the torments. The stones also hit our heads, but none of us moves. The provocation did not work...

Silence reigns again. Every minute seems to us like an eternity. The sun is setting and I burn with thirst. The flies seem to sting me stubbornly and viciously, as they arrive buzzing from the hanging corpse: "soon you will also hang there..."

We are sitting for two hours. Eventually, at eleven, the camp kommandant, *Unterstumführer* [Gustav] Willhaus arrives. We saw him frequently in town, when the official ghetto did not yet exist. He spread the fear of death. Tanned, short, stocky and with a sunken forehead, he stands a few metres away from us and receives a report from the SS men. He talks with them and chuckles. He looks like a normal and elegant person with a heart and a soul. When approaching us, however, his face took on the expression of a beast. Cruel flashes sparked in his deeply sunken eyes, and a sadistic, sardonic grin hovered over his lips...

We are ordered to rise. Even though our legs were glued to the ground from the long sitting, we all rose to a man. We were ruled by fear. We faced a man in whose hands lay life and death. Willhaus turned to us:

"Scoundrels, you must remember that the Jews

[Pages 751-752]

are wanderers, people with no pride. You must work loyally and do whatever you are ordered to do. Whoever does not fully comprehend my words will find themselves up there..." and he pointed at the hanging corpse. Finally Willhaus asked each one of us our occupation, and gave instructions to the SS men in regard to the professional workers.

We are led to the reception office. Here we are thoroughly examined. Everything is taken away from us, even the trouser-belts, while we are whipped with crops, are cursed and berated. We are only left with the clothes we wear.

After the registration, we are made to form a line. In the middle of the square stands a Jew whose face is covered in the blood of a half-plucked beard. He holds in his hand a trimming machine and each of us kneels in front of him for a haircut. The Jew who had never been a barber, cuts our hair in a ridiculous fashion, and unwittingly pinches us thoroughly.

A few steps farther stood another old man. He held a pail filled with brown paint, and with the brush in his hand he made a mark on the back of each of us: a Nazi enslavement-mark, and a sign, that will facilitate the capture of whoever tries to escape...

The sun was setting when we were led to our living quarters – a basement, a cement floor with no padding, not even straw. We fell to the floor half-dead with tiredness, fear and hunger. No food passed our mouth throughout the entire day: we had not yet worked today, and had consequently not yet earned our bread...

We are not given long to rest. A long whistle called us to a "roll-call." Following an order, we run to the square where the labour-brigades assembled after a day of toil. I saw among them many of my acquaintances, whom I could hardly recognise. They walked like skeletons dressed in rags. Many dressed their wounds in dirty rags. Many bore on their body, the signs of fresh beatings made during the day's labour. There were also those who could not stand on their feet and were propped up by their friends. Anyone who said that they were unwell, was murdered on the spot...

We were organised - the veterans and the novices - into six rows. Three rows on one side, and the other three rows facing them. *Scharführer* Kolonko gives the order: "Remove the hats." One must remove the hats at once and in one move. Whoever does not remove his hat according to regulations, has his face whipped.

Then comes the order: "Attention !" *Unterstumführer* [Richard Robert] Rokita, deputy of the camp kommandant approaches us. Kolonko goes towards him and reports to him on the progress of work. Four Jews, he announces, escaped on the way to work. Rokita, a type of Prussian *Feldwebel* [sergeant] with a red face and small, cunning eyes, starts screaming like a wounded animal and foam forms on his lips. He gives an order to the SS men to surround us and be ready to open fire. He pulls out his gun, walks between the lines and with his wild look he stares into the eyes of the standing Jews. With a sadistic hint he calls to thirty five Jews in the rows, he organises them in a line in the middle of the square, and orders them to turn around. Then he starts to shoot at the head of each of them, stopping only for reloading his gun. One after the other, thirty five Jews fell, soaked in their own blood…

I stand petrified unable to comprehend what is happening before my eyes. A blow from a gun butt wakes me from my stagnation. We are dismissed back to the basement. A vat of black coffee is brought in and slices of slate bread are distributed among ourselves.

Although we did not eat anything all day, no one touched the bread nor drank the coffee. We lie on the floor, and like a little child, each cuddles up to his friend. From time to time a choked groan or thwarted cry pierces the veil of silence.

I lie with open eyes staring into the darkness. In front of my eyes passes the terrible image about which I can only now, think. I begin to envy them. That they no longer need to wait every minute for their death, that they went to their eternal sleep and no longer need to fear the terrible humiliation that awaits us, who remain alive…

What will be my end?… I shall go mad… Another day like this I will be unable to bear…

I fell asleep for a brief moment, it seemed to me, and dreamt that two spears stick out of Rokita's eyes and very deeply pierce my flesh. I woke up from a panicked scream, all covered in sweat. Dawn has already begun to rise…

This is how I spent my first day in the death-camp…

[Pages 753-754]

The Final Days of the Leaders of Lwów's Jewry

by Yehoshua Shiloni (Shleyen)

Translated by Myra Yael Ecker

Edited by Karen Leon

The published decree of the 14th July 1941, signed by the *Wehrmacht*, stating that every Jew over the age of 14 seen out-of-doors without the "Jewish Tag" on their clothing, irrespective of gender, imposed a total and strict segregation on the entire Jewish population of Lwów. Any contact between the Jews and the non-Jewish population was forbidden unless it was mediated and authorised by the German authorities. The Jewish leadership was thus forced to establish and maintain a complex organisation to take care of the supply, habitation, employment, medical care and hospitalisation, education, social welfare, etc., for a population of 130,000 people, to fulfil the ceaseless demands of the different German authorities. The German machinations of robbery, oppression, exploitation and extortion operated under a satanic order and system, starting with the *Kontribution* payments of millions, and later, extortion-enterprises at every opportunity, aimed to impoverish the Jews and reduce them to ruination. Even the food provision for the labour-camps in the vicinity were partly at the expense of Lwów's [Jewish] community. Everything had to be done in an incessant bloody cauldron, in an atmosphere poisoned by loathing, malicious joy [*schadenfreude*] lust for oppression, with full knowledge of the neighbours, especially the Ukrainians, who considered themselves an active party to the pogroms and that the property, dignity and blood of a Jew was forsaken. Notwithstanding, the Jews of Lwów, especially the older generation brought up on the Viennese version of German culture, believed that one could at last "satiate the viper," and rescue whatever one could, by hard work, great sacrifice, efficient organisation, patience and forbearance. They were surrounded by a wall, with death lurking at every turn beyond the wall. Did they have any other option?

Under these circumstances a huge undertaking of workshops and industry was established, in which 70,000 Jews were engaged. The Germans who supervised these factories used all manner of strategies, including publications in the German press lauding them, in order to extend their existence for as long as possible. However the head of the Gestapo, General [Fritz; Friedrich] Katzmann, and his deputy [Erich] Engels, pressed for the liquidation of these institutions, and they accelerated the annihilation of the Jews of Lwów.

There is scant information about the undertakings, experiences and last days of the leaders, the public activists and the intellectuals who stood watch and were exterminated in Lwów, together with tens of thousands of their People.

May the details here gathered be recorded in their sacred memory:

1. **Imber, Samuel Jakób**. A pioneer of Jewish poetry in Poland. Before the start of the war he returned from America, where he had lived for many years, and settled at Lwów. He focused his very witty and talented writing on the protection of the life and honour of the Jewish community in Poland. His articles and essays which were published in Polish (*Oko w*

Oko ["Eye to Eye"]; *Asy czystej rasy* ["The Purebred Aces"] and others), received great publicity and stormy reactions in the Polish press. He was also a regular contributor to *Haynt* ["Today" a Yiddish newspaper]. In 1937, he received a doctorate for his essay on Oscar Wilde. During the Soviet occupation (1939-1941), he translated into Yiddish, the poems by the Ukrainian-Soviet poet, Pavlo [Hryhorovych] Tychyna. In July 1941, when the Germans entered Lwów, Imber, who was known for his anti-Nazi activities, left Lwów together with his wife and moved to the home of his father-in-law, at Jezierna near Złoczów. From there he moved to Złoczów, his birth place, where he used the false name, Weiss. The Jews of Złoczów looked after their townsman and poet, and they employed him to look after patients in the Jewish hospital where his brother-in-law was the director. Imber wrote a great deal in those days, and read his works out loud to the patients. In November 1942, he was taken to Bełżec, together with 3,000 of Złoczów's Jews, where he was murdered.

2. **Dr. Allerhand, Maurycy**. A well known advocate and jurist, dean of the faculty of Law at Lwów University. Before the [2nd World] War, he was leader of Lwów's Jewish community for a while. He chaired the state committee for examining teachers in Jewish studies. He wrote a book on Jewish laws on marriage and inheritance, amongst other. The German occupation authorities offered him the position as leader of the "Jewish Council" (its official title in Lwów was "The Committee of the Jewish Community" *Jüdische Gemeinde*),

[Pages 755-756]

but due to exhaustion he refused the appointment. He was probably murdered in the early weeks of the German occupation.

3. **Bodek, Jakób**. Publicly active in many enterprises, he continuously extended help and assistance to the poor and the suffering. He was a legendary figure on Lwów's Jewish Street. He remained single his entire life and pursued an austere and frugal life. At one time he was a high official in the country's postal service. In 1922, he was elected to the Polish *Sejm*, by the Jews of Galicia. He was a council member of Galicia's (General) Zionist Party, active on the Council's welfare department. Sick, hungry and neglected at the end of his life, he was seen dragging his feet through Lwów's "Jewish Quarter." He starved to death in the summer of 1942.

4. **Dr. Barlas, Chanoch**. Born at Zbaraż [Zbarazh], he was a teacher of Hebrew, history and Jewish studies at the Jewish *Gymnasium* in Łódź. He was active on the cultural committee of the [Jewish] Council in the Jewish Quarter of Lwów, and later in the Lwów ghetto. He and his only son died of Typhus in the ghetto, at the beginning of 1943.

5. **Brat, Abraham**. An editor of *Chwila*, in Lwów. He was active in Lwów's German workshops for war armaments. He was murdered during the liquidation of the ghetto (which in its last stage was termed *Julag -Juden Lager*) in June 1943.

6. **Grin [Grün], Jerachmiel**. Author, young novelist, born at Deliatyn in the Carpathian Mountains. He published books such as The Weavers of Kołomyja [*Di Veber fun Kolomije*] and others. His talent led critics to foresee his greatness. He laboured in the ghetto of Lwów as a porter, and supported himself, his wife and two daughters with his work. In January 1943, he and his wife, **Halina** née Neuman from Warsaw, were taken to the labour-camp on Janowska Street. In the summer [of 1943], they were murdered together with the last Jews of Lwów, during the liquidation of this terrible bloody-camp.

7. **Ginsberg, Benzion**. Among Lwów's editors of *Tugblat-Morgen*. A talented journalist with a deeply rooted education and a brilliant style. A regular contributor to the Warsaw newspaper *Haynt* [Today] (under the pseudonym B. Cegrowski), and to the New-York [Yiddish newspaper] *Forverts* [Forward] (under the pseudonym B. **Shochet/Schuchat**). He fought hard for his life in the ghetto. His wife and three children were murdered in the ghetto in January 1943. At the same time he was taken to Janowska camp where he was murdered during the liquidation of the camp in summer 1943.

8. **Dr. Gottfried, Schulem**. An advocate, one of the young activists in *HaTzionim HaRadikaliym* group led by Dr. Abraham Insler. He worked at the medical department of the Council in the Jewish Quarter, and later in the ghetto. He was caught during one of the *Aktionen* and was murdered at the beginning of 1943, "in Sand Mountain" [*Piaskowa Góra*], the mass grave of the Jews os Lwów.

9. **Gimpel, Adolf**. A musician, choirmaster, director and owner of the renowned "Gimpel's [Jewish] Theatre" on Jagiełłońska Street in Lwów. This Jewish folk theatre raised and educated an entire generation of Jewish theatre actors, and was a favourite gathering place of Lwów's Jewish folk circles. They flocked there to hear and see song and play, a direct continuation of [Abraham] Goldfaden's tradition, and the Broder singers [*Broderzinger*, from Brody. His son, Bronisław Gimpel, became famous as a talented pianist. Gimpel, the father, made his living as a music teacher in the Jewish Quarter. He was caught in the horrific blood *Aktion* of August 1942, and was moved to Bełżec (at the time around 50,000 Jews from Lwów were murdered, imprisoned in labour-camps or were brought to the Bełżec crematoriums).

10. **Dr. Dromschläger, Mozes**. Teacher at the Jewish *Gymnasium* on Zygmuntowska Street. A historian, one of the true biblical experts. He was an active member on the cultural committee of the [Jewish] Council in the Jewish Quarter. After the bloody-*Aktion* of August 1942, he was lost without a trace.

11. **Dreikurs, Leon (Leibale)**. A journalist, among the editors of Lwów's *Tugblat*. He also contributed to *Unser Express* [Our Express] and to the Warsaw, Polish-Jewish newspaper *Nasz Przegląd* ["Our Review"]. During the Soviet occupation (1939-1941), he was a Yiddish language announcer on [Polish] Radio Lwów. Until the end of 1941, he was with us at Lwów. He moved to the *Aryan* side as a driver, and nothing is known of him since.

12. **Hescheles, Henryk**. The principal editor of the newspaper *Chwila* ["Moment"], organ of Lwów's Zionist Movement. A renowned journalist-writer with a comprehensive education and highly cultured. He had a brilliant Polish style.

After the Germans arrived in Lwów, Gestapo men, following a specific list which had been prepared by certain Ukrainian circles, removed him together with Emil Igel (another of the *Chwila* writers), and he was probably murdered by them.

13. **Hauser, Naftali**. One of writers for *Der Morgen* and for the Polish weekly, *Opinja*, edited by Dr. A[braham] Insler. He had poor health and suffered greatly under the harsh conditions of Lwów's ghetto. He was taken to the labour-camp in Lacki[-Wielie] near Złoczów, where he died at the beginning of 1943.

14. **Hader, Jehuda**. Among the leaders of *Achwa*, the youth association of the general Zionists of Galicia. He was active in the welfare department of the [Jewish] Council. He organised and managed the soup-kitchen for the poor in the ghetto. He was murdered, together with his only son and his wife, during the liquidation of Lwów's ghetto (*Julag*) in June 1943.

14A. **Dr. Hammer, Juda**. Advocate, and activist

[Pages 757-758]

in Lwów's workers' party *Unifiction*. He managed a restaurant in the ghetto, and to his own detriment he assisted the poor with total devotion. He perished from typhus in winter 1943.

15. **Weinstein, Ascher**. Hebrew teacher, school headmaster, one of Lwów's activists of *Tarbut* [Culture]. We was publicly hanged in the ghetto during one of the Gestapo punishment operations, following the killing of a German policeman in March 1943.

16. **Weinlös, Izrael**. Author and historian, scholar of the Jewish Enlightenment in Galicia. He published his work in the newspapers in Poland and also in *Yivo* publications. He was murdered while crossing the Zamarstynow-Żółkiewska railway bridge, the "Death Gate," during the mass robbery and murder (that lasted over a month) when, in December 1941, the Jews of Lwów were moved to the "Jewish Quarter" (which initially was in-between Kazimierzowska-Kleparowska Streets).

17. **Waschitz, Zeb**. A Hebrew teacher, a quintessential scholar in Jewish religion, expert in Mediæval poetry and literature. He was moved to Bełżec in August 1942.

Benzion Ginsberg

18. **Weinstock, Leon**. One of the editors of the newspaper *Chwila*, from its establishment by Dr. Gerszon Zipper. He was arrested by the Soviets (in 1940), together with a group on Lwów Zionist activists. He died in prison.

19. **Willig Jakób**. A multifarious activist, born in Złoczów. A committed Zionist, noble and generous. Together with Samuel Jakób Imber, he treated patients at Złoczów's Jewish hospital. He was murdered in the ghetto of Złoczów during its liquidation at the beginning of 1943.

20. **Dr. Bachmann, Józef**. Among the leaders of *Poale Zion-Jamin* [Workers of Zion-Right] in Galicia. After the Germans had arrived in Lwów, he left for Wołyń, and there is no knowledge about his fate.

21. **Witkower, Fischel**. Born at Krystynopol [Kristianopol], one of the writers for *Tugblat* Lwów, a feuilleton writer with an endearing folk style. One of the veteran Jewish authors and activists in Galicia. Perished of hunger at the end of 1942.

22. **Dr. Chotiner Leon**. A renowned expert advocate in Polish civil law. He was the sole Jewish national elected as dean (president) of the Bar Association of Lwów. He worked in the Law department of the [Jewish] Council. He was moved to Bełżec in August 1942.

23. **Tillemann, Ozjasz**. Teacher and author, historian, mathematician, philologist and philosopher. He spoke 13 languages and published articles, essays, scholarly articles and novels in five languages: Hebrew, Yiddish, Polish, German and Ukrainian. Long suffering from poor health, and modest, he spent days and nights in the study of the Torah for its own sake. In his last years, during the German reign of horror, he diligently studied the Talmud. He was a member of the Zionist Labour Party *Hitachdut*, and held Jewish religious views.

When the Russians took over Lwów in September 1939, all Jewish schools had to teach in the Ukrainian language. Tillemann was appointed as the director responsible for the teaching of the Ukrainian language at the Jewish secondary school [*Gymnasium*] on Zygmuntowska Street. Tillemann, who for years nurtured Jewish children at the institute with warmth and love of the Hebrew language and literature, was forced to teach them "Torah and courtesy" in the language and spirit of the Cossacks… He gave lessons for a slice of bread in the ghetto, but he did not complain nor ask for welfare and assistance. Only his face gave away his fading. When the bloodshed and annihilation that befell us in August 1942 abated for a short while, after the majority of the community of Lwów and its salient members had been massacred, we were informed that Ozjasz Tillemann was no longer with us. The slight and tortured body of this Jewish prodigy went up in flame, together with those of his brethren, to the sacrifice and fate in the crematoria of Bełżec.

24. **Dr. Teichmann, Wolf** [Zeb; Ze'ev]. An advocate, member of the council of *Hitachdut Poale Zion* in east Galicia. Loyal to the Hebrew education movement. He showed exemplary courage and respect during the Nazi rule. He was murdered at Złoczów in January 1943.

25. **Jaeger, Ignacy**. Owner of a printing-house on Lwów's Sykstuska Street. A vigorous entrepreneur active in Lwów's traders' association and in the craftsmen's association *Jad Charuzim*. In 1928, as a delegate of Galicia's Jews, he was elected to the Polish *Sejm* for the *Sanation* faction (Piłsudski [Polish Socialist] Party). According to rumour, he was arrested in July 1941 when the Germans arrived in Lwów. There is no further knowledge about his fate, since.

26. **Kohn, Juda**. Director of Lwów's great [Jewish] community library. A Jewish scholar and a *Maskil*. He specialised in adjudicative literature and responsa, and published scholarly discussions, mainly in Hebrew. According to rumour he died of typhus at the beginning of 1942.

27. **Dr. Landau, Leib**. Advocate, one of the shining figures in Galicia's and Poland's Jewry. Between the two world wars, during the period of an independent Polish state, he was the leader of the Przemyśl community. He made his name through his appearance as defence attorney in the famous trial

[Pages 759-760]

of [Stanisław] Steiger (who was accused in an attempt on the life of Poland's president, [Stanisław] Wojciechowski), and also as defence attorney in the trials of communists (Jews in particular). He received a traditional Jewish education and was cultured. His figure and voice, his acute analysis and rhetorical brilliance struck and convinced the listeners. A champion of Poland's attorneys. One of the country's leading prosecutors who appeared in court opposite Dr. Landau, opened his response to his opponent's question with a phrase from *Pan Tadeusz* by Adam Mickiewicz: "There were many players of the dulcimer, but none of them dared to perform in Jankiel's presence"…[a] And yet, during the Holocaust and the ordeal, none of Mickiewicz's educated countrymen remembered Jankiel, the miraculous musician, and no one hurried to extend to him a helping and relieving hand.

During the twenty months of Soviet occupation (1939-1940) he followed his profession as an advocate. At first, his Polish and Ukrainian colleagues sought his company and strove to shelter in his shade. However his attempts resulted in grave disappointments. In autumn 1941, during the early stage of German rule, he took on the management of the welfare for the needy of Lwów's community, numbering some 130,000 people at the time. Dr. Landau employed teachers, writers, artists and intellectuals to collect funds and goods, and to distribute them among the needy. At the beginning of January 1943, the Nazis began to liquidate Lwów's ghetto. They murdered several of the [Jewish] Council members (Dr. Obersohn, Dr. Kimmelman and others), and reduced the size of the ghetto that was renamed *Julag* (*Judenlager*). Dr. Landau and his wife managed to escape from the ghetto and flee to the *Aryan* side of town, but they were caught by the Gestapo and were taken to the ghetto jail. The following day, a company of Ukrainian policemen took Dr. Landau and his wife from the ghetto jail, led them through the town's main streets, towards "the mound of Sands" - the mass grave of thousands of Lwów's Jews.

28. **Dr. Landesberg, Józef**. Advocate, the third leader of the [Jewish] Council (his predecessors were Dr. Emil Parnas and Dr. Adolf Rothfeld). He was publicly hanged. For three days, his body was hanging off the facade of the house on Łokietka Street in the ghetto, in retaliation for the killing in town of a German policeman by one of the Jewish labourers.

29. **Dr. Leser, Mozes**. President of *Tarbut* in Galicia, an honest businessman, a religious Jew dedicated to Hebrew education. He was elected to the Polish *Sejm* as delegate of Lwów's Jews. He was chief secretary of Galicia's Zionist Organisation. In winter 1939, he was incarcerated together with a group of Zionist activists in Lwów, by the Soviet authorities. He died in prison.

30. **Dr. Lewin, Jecheskel**. Rabbi of the Enlightened [*Maskilim*] [Jewish] congregation of Lwów. Admired and respected by his congregation. Of a distinguished family and a biblical scholar. He published scholarly articles on Jewish history. During the Soviet occupation he was the only one who delivered a sermon to his congregation every Sabbath. The topic of the talks, despite the danger, concentrated on the return to Zion and Eretz Israel.

When the Germans entered Lwów, the town's "underworld" was given the signal to organise the first "spontaneous" pogrom, during which the mob ran wild in the houses of Jews for three whole days. The rabbi, Rabbi J[echeskel] Lewin was then obliged, despite the great danger, to go and see the Ukrainian Archbishop, [Metropolitan] Andrey Szeptycki [Sheptytsky], and ask him to issue a proclamation, or otherwise influence his Ukrainian people to stop the robberies and massacres. On his way back from Metropolitan Szeptycki's Palace, he was caught by the Ukrainian mob and was murdered under severe torture. The Jews taken to the jail on Kazimierzowska Street, in order to remove the murdered for burial, recognised the body of their rabbi who had gone on a mission in their behalf, and did not return.

31. **Meisels-Nachmani, Salomon**. A quintessential biblical scholar and teacher at various schools in Poland and Galicia. Secretary of *Tarbut* centre in Lwów. He suffered hunger and deprivation and was gravely tortured in the ghetto. Died of typhus in summer 1942.

32. **Dr. Maiblum, Zigmunt**. President of the Złoczów community, one of the most prominent activists of the Jewish Cooperative Movement in Galicia. By order of the German authorities he undertook the management of the "Jewish Council's" affairs at Złoczów. Through acts of self-sacrifice, and an equal noble stance towards the German and the Ukrainian murderers, he was martyred. This was attested to by the few remaining survivors of this ancient Jewish community.

33. **Madfes, Isachar**. Publisher and bookseller in Lwów, he was a scion of the first Jewish family of printers in Galicia, an historian and author of the book *History of Zionim*. He was one of the young Zionist activists in Lwów. He was murdered in the street by a Ukrainian policeman in spring 1942.

34. **Siwek, Benzion**. The eldest of the Hebrew teachers and amongst the first who promulgated the Hebrew language in Galicia. A biblical scholar, modest and gentle, he was engaged on the cultural committee of Lwów's "Council." He was moved to Bełżec in August 1942.

[Pages 761-762]

35. **Dr. Parnas, Emil**. Industrialist, chairman of the **national committee** of Galicia's *Keren HaYesod*. Dr. Adolf Rothfeld was the general secretary of the national committee,. The German authorities tasked both of them to organise a system of management for the Jewish community of Lwów. In his undertaking, Dr. Parnas had no misgivings about insisting on improving the situation. At first, the hangmen showed some patience towards the "impudent Jew," Dr. Parnas, who tended to stand erect and exude self-esteem when speaking with them. The Germans seem to have exercised a sort of pretence regarding the matter. However once hangman Engels's "patience had run out," he slapped Dr. Parnas' cheek. From that moment onward Dr. Parnas did not say a word and did not respond to any of the Gestapo's questions. And in this silent and proud fashion he strode toward death, which he willed and wished for since he realised that he had failed in his mission: he wanted to save, but did not save.

36. **Frenkel, Dawid**. Member of the secretariat of Lwów's *Hitachdut Poale Zion* Party. During the German rule he kept in contact with Dr. Abraham Silberschein, who acted on behalf of the "World Jewish Congress," and Jewish organisations in

Geneva. He was a clerk in the supply department of Lwów's [Jewish] "Council." He remained in Lwów until July 1942, and according to rumour, he moved to Kraków. There is no information about his fate.

I[zrael] Weinlös

37. **Dr. Freund, Lewi**. Chief Rabbi of Lwów's congregation of the Enlightened, he was a Biblical scholar [*Talmid Chacham*] and a quintessential man of science. His essay in Polish "O Etyce Talmudu: Odpowiedź 'żydoznawcom'," [On the Ethics of the Talmud: A response to "Jewish scholars"], a research into Jewish wisdom and the history of Israel, was published in *Chwila*, *Opinja* and others. He fell gravely ill and died in 1940.

38. **Dr. Pfeffer**, [Hersch] **Zewi**. Born at Tarnopol, he was a rabbi and preacher at Kraków's congregation of the Enlightened. He received a traditional Jewish education and a general education. He was one of the writers for the [Jewish] newspaper *Nowy Dziennik*, in Kraków. He and his wife worked in the ghetto's kitchen. He contracted typhus and suffered gravely in his last days. He was murdered together with his wife and his son during the liquidation of the ghetto of Lwów in June 1943.

39. **Fuchs, Rojza**. A folk actress at "Gimpel's Theatre," Lwów. Her son, Leon Fuchs, is a renowned Jewish actor in New York. She was moved to Bełżec together with her husband, the actor Roth, in August 1942.

40. **Dr. Kanfer, Mozes**. Born at Buczacz. A journalist, one of the editors of *Nowy Dziennik*, Kraków and a well known literary critic. He headed the group of authors, critics and artists who assisted Dr. Landau in his organisation and management of the welfare for the needy in Lwów's "Jewish Quarter." He was moved to Bełżec in August 1942.

41. **Dr. Kimmelman, Oawald**. An advocate, honest and knowledgeable, member of the presidency of *HaTzionim HaKlaliyim* [General Zionists] Party in east Galicia. He, together with his only son, were murdered in public by the Germans during the murder of the remaining [Jewish] Council members, on 15th January 1943.

42. **Kleinmann, Peretz (Fryc) [Fryderyk]**. Painter-artist, popular among the Jewish Enlightened [*Maskilim*] in Lwów. He worked as a painter at the Jewish theatre in Warsaw and in Lwów. In the Jewish Quarter he was engaged in the medical service of the "Council." He was caught on the *Aryan* side and was shot and murdered on the spot in 1942.

43. **Königsberg, Dovid**. Born at Busk. A poet, he wrote beautiful sonatas in Yiddish. He translated *Pan Tadeusz* into Yiddish. He was murdered by the Ukrainians before the arrival of the Germans in Lwów, at the beginning of July 1941. His body was identified amongst the victims and removed for burial from the jail on Lwów's Kazimierzowska Street.

44. **Dr. Klaften, Cecylja**. She established and managed a network of vocational schools for girls in east Galicia. The New-York Jewish press referred to her, during her visit before the war, as the "Mother of Galicia's Jews," and the description was not a great exaggeration. Hundreds and thousands of Jewish girls acquired a profession and employment through her institutes. She was a noble, highly cultured woman, with virtues and great talents as a pedagogue, and she was trusted and admired by wide circles of the Galician public. During the Germans' rule of horrors in Lwów, she was seen daily in the welfare department for the needy at No. 1 Smocza Street. Among the sea of poverty and suffering, sick and exhausted, she did not abandon her post until almost the last moment. She was murdered in summer 1942. According to rumour, she was shot on the way to the "mound of Sands," while resisting the murderers who led her to the mass grave.

45. **Kupferstein, Abraham Eliezer**. One of the leaders of *HaMisrachi* movement in east Galicia, and a quintessential biblical scholar. At the age of 16 he was granted a qualification to teach. Pure spirited and gregarious, he was a religious Jew who was not embroiled in fanaticism. He took part on the education committee of the "Council." During the dark days, he knew how to encourage

[Pages 763-764]

hearts by shining an honourable light and a fervour of faith. He was caught during the *Aktion* of August 1942, and was taken to Bełżec.

46. **Rappaport, Jakób**. Headmaster of the seminary for Hebrew teachers at Lwów. An author and pedagogue, he published research into the history of the Jewish People. During the Soviet rule, the Hebrew institute under his management turned into a Ukrainian school, which greatly depressed him. He fell gravely ill, and died in the early days of the Nazi occupation.

47. **Reitman, Rona**. Author, pedagogue and activist, editor of the youth section in the *Chwila* newspaper. He was murdered during the first pogrom in July 1941.

48. **Rettig, Meszulem**. Journalist, one of the editors of the *Morgen* at Lwów, was born at Lublin near Gródek Jagielloński. He was a reporter for the Warsaw *Unzer Express*. He suffered with poor health and struggled greatly for his livelihood throughout his life. When the Germans entered Lwów he was caught together with hundreds of Lwów's Jews, and was cruelly tortured at the headquarters of the Gestapo on Łącki [Lantzki] Street. By some miracle he managed to escaped from there, and fled to Gródek Jagielloński, where he was murdered when the ghetto was liquidated at the beginning of 1943.

49. **Dr. Ringel, Michał**. One of the early leaders of Galicia's Jewry and the Zionist movement. Under Gerschon Zipper's leadership after the 1918 pogrom, a new era started in the public-national life of Galician Jewry, that previously under the Austrian rule and the Polish regional rulers, was subject to the influence and authority of the assimilated alliance and the Rebbes' courtyards [*chatzerot Admorim*]. A national education network was established, the newspaper *Chwila* and mutual-aid institutes were founded. Dr. Ringel, together with the Dr. Leon Reich, were among the leading figures in the Zionist movement, that managed to attract many among the Jewish masses in the period between the two [world] wars. He represented Galicia's Jewry among the Jewish delegation that presented its petition to the 1919 Peace-Conference in Paris and Brussels, after World War I. He was an envoy to the Zionist Congress and member of the executive-committee and the congressional tribunal. In 1922, he was elected to the Polish *Sejm* in his home town Stryj. When the Soviets arrived in Lwów in September 1939, and Lwów's Zionist activists were arrested, Dr. Ringel left town and moved to Wołyń. According to rumour, he was near Równe [Rovno], but there is no further information of his whereabouts.

50. **Dr. Fajerman, Debora**. Teacher, headmistress of Lwów's Jewish elementary school, she did much for the foundation of the Jewish elementary school in Galicia. She worked in the welfare department of the "Council" together with Dr. Klaften. She probably perished during the bloodbath of August 1942.

51. **Reiser, Feiwel**. Secretary of the Jewish community of Złoczów [Solotschiw], an active member in the *Hitachdut Poale Tzion* Party. He tried, with great devotion, to alleviate the hardship of those locked up in the ghetto of Złoczów. He was murdered during the *Aktion* at Złoczów, in summer 1942.

52. **Rabinowicz, Mordechaj**. Journalist, writer of the *Morgen* in Lwów. One of the leaders of *Achwa*, the youth association of the General Zionists in Galicia. He was murdered at Janowska camp in summer 1943.

52. **Dr. Rothfeld, Abraham (Adolf)**. Journalist, among the leaders of the General Zionists of Galicia. Chairman of the "Council" after the murder of Dr. Parnas. As representative of the Jews of Lwów, he experienced great difficulties in his dealings with the Nazi authorities. Although his wisdom, energy and talent helped him at times to extract himself from the strait, he knew that his end was nigh. "I am weaving a rope around my neck" he occasionally said, when he returned pale, downhearted and nervous from the frequent "interviews" with the Nazi authorities. In his last days he worked feverishly to assemble books for his library. He died a natural death "with the grace of God." He had a cardiac arrest and died in spring 1942.

Samuel Jakób Imber

53. **Dr. Schreiber, Dawid**. Council president of the General Zionists Party in Galicia. In 1922, he was elected to the Polish *Sejm* as the delegate of the Jews of the Sambor-Przemyśl district. Head of the Eretz-Israel office at Lwów, he was a quintessential public figure with much political experience and authority. He was murdered during the liquidation of the ghetto in June 1943.

54. **Szudrich** [Schudrich], **Jakób**. Poet, labourer. He worked as an expert worker at a hat and fur factory in Lwów. He published lyric poems and prose in Yiddish. His poems also appeared in Soviet publications, in 1940. In winter 1943, he left the ghetto together with a group of youths, armed with some light firearms. The Polish driver who was meant to drive them to the forests around Brody, and who received a good sum of money for this mission, took them directly to the courtyard of the Gestapo headquarters on Łącki Street. According to rumour, Szudrich and his friends resisted the Nazis, and were murdered on the spot.

55. **Szymel Maurycy.** Poet, who initially wrote in Polish, and later composed in Yiddish. A quintessential lyricist. His lyrics were redolent of

[Pages 765-766]

a singularly emotional tune. He was in Lwów until August 1942. He was caught and moved to the labour-camp Lacki[-Wielie] near Złoczów. Sick and exhausted, he did not survive the horrific conditions of that camp.

56. **Dr. Schaff, Maks**. A multifarious activist in the field of Jewish education. He was known at Lwów as "father of the orphans" as the Director of the Jewish orphanage on Janowska Street. He was Dr. Landau's deputy in the welfare department for the needy of the "Jewish Quarter" until August 1942. He fell ill and his powers diminished, still he did not spare himself. In between frequent heart-attacks, he arrived at the office on 14 Bernsteina Street in order to assist a little in the ocean of poverty and hardship. In August 1942, he was moved to Bełżec.

57. **Schnapper, Berl**. A talented tailor, poet and essayist. He published poems, stories and essays in Yiddish. He was part of the delegation of Lwów's Jewish authors that was invited to Moscow in 1940. In August 1942, he was probably moved to one of the labour-camps in the vicinity of Lwów, and there is no further knowledge of him.

58. **Schorr, Zygmunt**. Humorist-writer, composer of feuilletons which as an artist, he read out to his public in the towns and small-towns of Galicia. His wife Kseni, a significant and educated activist, and his talented son, Benjamin, were murdered in November 1942, and he was murdered in the ghetto in January 1943.

59. **Stockman, Mojżesz**. Headmaster of the Jewish elementary school on Zygmuntowska Street, Lwów. He did much for Lwów's Jewish education. During the Soviet rule, he worked as a Yiddish teacher at the school where Ukrainian was the teaching language. Early in the German rule he disappeared, and there is no information about his fate.

60. **Spiegel, Joel**. A veteran Jewish journalist in Lwów. Editor of the [daily newspaper] *Tugblat*, and writer for New-York Jewish newspapers. He died of typhus, at the end of 1942.

61. **Rabbi Hillel Sperber**. The rabbi of the communities of Zbaraż and Złoczów. Among the significant rabbis and leaders of *HaMizrachi* movement in Galicia. He was severely tortured and was martyred at Zbaraż when the Germans arrived there in July 1941.

**

This is not a comprehensive list of the Jewish leaders of Lwów, its rabbis, activists, authors and scholars, and their sufferings and torture during the last days of their lives. A great many names are not mentioned here, and may their memory be bound among the victims who were martyred for God and the Jewish People.

[Pages 767-768]

MAJER BALABAN

ŻYDZI LWOWSCY
NA PRZEŁOMIE
XVI^GO i XVII^GO WIEKU

PRACA ODZNACZONA PIERWSZĄ NAGRODĄ NA KONKURSIE
IMIENIA HIPOLITA WAWELBERGA PRZEZ WYDZIAŁ FILOZOFI-
CZNY C. K. UNIWERSYTETU LWOWSKIEGO

LWÓW 1906
NAKŁADEM FUNDUSZU KONKURSOWEGO IM. H. WAWELBERGA
GŁÓWNY SKŁAD W KSIĘGARNI H. ALTENBERGA WE LWOWIE.

Geschichte der Juden in Lemberg

Geschichte der Juden in Lemberg

von den ältesten Zeiten bis zur Theilung Polens im Jahre 1792

aus Urkunden und archivalischen Quellen

bearbeitet

von

Dr. Jecheskiel Caro

Rabbiner und Gemeinderath in Lemberg

כלילת יופי

מצבת קדש

זכרון צדיקים

חוברת ראשונה

Note:

a.   This quote was taken from Adam Mickiewicz, *Pan Tadeusz*, translated into English by George Rapall Noyes, (1917) p. 322.

NAME INDEX

A

Abele, 79
Ablowicz, 90, 91, 296
Aboab, 231
Abrahamowicz, 27, 55, 83, 90, 323
Abras, 160, 243, 247, 249, 250, 287
Achser, 389
Acker, 388
Adler, 189, 250, 316
Affendyk, 83
Agid, 349, 350
Agis, 195
Ahl, 181
Ahlenberg, 126
Ajalon, 232
Aleksandrowicz, 184, 219
Alembek, 40
Alfasi [al-Fasi, 224, 226, 227, 238
al-Husseini, 391
Alkabetz, 240
Allerhand, 219, 252, 349, 388, 415
Almanzi, 67
Alshech, 311
Alster, 269
Alter, 209, 265, 266, 270, 285, 289, 290, 314, 349, 366, 388
Altman, 388
Altschuler, 311
Altstater, 269
Amsterdamer, 101
Andris, 17
Anschel, 265
Anserinus, 31
Anszel, 314
Appel, 216, 220, 251, 253
Araten, 217
Archduke Ferdinand, 153
Archduke] Karl Ludwig, 217
Arie, 314
Arneth, 113
Aryeh, 311
Asher, 204
Ashkenazi, 226, 236
Ashkenazy, 59
Askenasy, 224
Askenazy, 13, 25, 48, 65, 75, 97, 120, 222, 225, 226, 230, 231, 236
Askenazy [Aszkenazy]-Heilprin [Heilpron], 226
Aszer, 61, 73, 174, 316
Aszkenassy, 48, 120, 236
Aszkenazi, 271, 272, 331
Aszkenazy, 13, 195, 222, 224, 225, 230, 234, 236, 253, 301, 305
Atelmaier, 59
Atlas, 4, 164, 269
Auerbach, 215, 226, 388

Awner, 313
Axer, 388, 399
Ayalon, 232
Azriel, 226
Azrjel, 226
Azulai, 234

B

Baal Shem Tov, 236, 268, 275, 276, 279, 386
Babad, 96, 97, 257, 265, 316
Bacalel, 61
Baceles, 127
Bach, 169, 170, 176, 177, 181, 190, 201
Bachman, 287
Bachmann, 417
Bachner, 97
Bachor, 327
Bachus, 181
Bach-Zelewski, 395
Baczeles, 245
Baczes, 195
Baczewski, 245
Bad, 209
Bader, 122, 252
Bałaban, 15, 16, 17, 18, 36, 46, 52, 54, 57, 68, 69, 80, 81, 83, 90, 91, 92, 93, 101, 102, 108, 111, 122, 125, 127, 136, 151, 166, 167, 168, 173, 189, 190, 191, 209, 217, 219, 247, 252, 257, 258, 263, 275, 280, 296, 297, 299, 308, 309, 311, 315, 317, 319, 320, 321, 322, 323, 324, 325, 327, 340, 387
Balcer, 18
Balk, 388
Ball, 152
Balsambaum, 211
Bandera, 345, 352, 389
Barabasz, 361
Barach, 104, 126, 132, 151, 193, 259
Barach-Rappaport, 144, 148, 158, 172, 173, 178, 245
Barbasz, 388
Barda, 134, 138, 141
Bardach, 311, 349
Bardasch, 188
Barlas, 387, 415
Baron Gautsch, 202, 207
Baron Gautsch [von Frankenthum], 202
Baron Krauss, 169
Baron Leszek Borkowski, 162
Baron Philipp [von] Krauss, 159
Bartfeld, 401
Barwiński, 192
Bass, 315
Batczisz, 315
Batormani, 46
Bauer, 388
Baumann, 289
Baumel, 269

Dubs, 141, 142, 144, 148, 154, 158, 169, 170, 171, 172, 173,
    178, 179, 182, 183, 184, 187, 195, 197, 245, 249
Dubschitz, 388
Dunin–Borkowski, 158
Dups, 87
Duschak, 250
Dylewski, 162, 168
Dzieduszycki, 122
Dzordz, 19

E

Eber, 388
Eber-Friedman, 404
Ebersohn, 349
Ebner, 209, 267
Ecker, 2
Edel, 310, 311
Edelstein, 289
Edil, 310
Efrati, 190, 258
Ehlenberg, 164, 172, 301
Ehrenpreis, 262, 266, 271, 299, 301, 313, 316, 321
Ehrenreich, 320
Ehrlich, 252, 253, 349
Eibenschütz, 80
Eibeschitz, 80
Eiche, 214
Eichel, 174
Eideles, 55, 226, 296
Eilenburg, 55
Eisner, 152
Elimelech, 134, 138, 316
Elowicz, 90
Elster, 272
Emden, 70, 76, 80, 81, 82, 92, 174
Emperor [Kaiser] Franz I, 111
Emperor [Kaiser] Leopold II, 110
Emperor Franz I, 112, 117
Emperor Joseph, 114
Emperor Joseph II, 103, 109, 117
Emperor Leopold, 103
Emperor Leopold II, 109
Emperor Maximilian, 22
Empress Maria–Theresa, 103, 104, 110, 113, 115
Engel, 161
Engels, 372, 377, 390, 414, 418
Enser, 150
Epstein, 100, 116, 140, 141, 165, 195, 199, 225, 245, 279
Erb, 388
Erggelet, 129, 133
Erlich, 395
Ernesti, 249
Erter, 133, 134, 135, 136, 150, 242, 277, 278
Etroger, 182
Ettinga, 207
Ettinga [Ettinger], 207, 238, 239
Ettinger, 140, 146, 173, 187, 197, 199, 201, 218, 238, 243, 244,
    250, 265, 270
Ettinger [Ettinga], 235
Ewen, 210
Eybeschütz, 70, 80, 82, 235, 269

Eybesfeld, 202
Eysinhutel, 17

F

Faibish, 68
Faigels, 108
Fajerman, 420
Falaquera, 151
Falk, 36, 56, 75, 79, 80, 97, 98, 211, 318, 326
Fand, 211
Farber, 349, 362, 398, 399, 402, 403
Fayglis, 90
Fedorowicz, 15, 168
Feierstein, 262
Feigels, 296
Feigenbaum, 209
Feil, 383
Feinberg, 214, 215
Feinsinger, 288
Feinstein, 321
Feiwisz, 291
Feld, 220, 387
Feldkriegs, 145
Feldmann, 18
Feller, 388
Felsing, 117
Fessler, 310
Fest, 80
Festenburg, 148, 156, 249
Filipowicz, 78, 96
Finkel, 113, 319
Finkelstein, 112, 301
Fisch, 266
Fischel, 13, 22, 142, 171
Fischer, 110
Fischler, 126
Fischmann, 134, 136, 150
Fiszer, 312, 388
Flavius, 321
Flecker, 211, 312
Fogt, 56
Fortis, 71, 76
Frank, 77, 83, 84, 144, 235, 294, 296, 352
Franke, 205
Frankfurter, 271
Frankl, 161, 164, 168
Franz I, 110, 138
Franz Joseph I (1830–1916) became·Emperor [Kaiser], 165
Franz Karl, Kaiser Ferdinand's brother, 142
Franz–Joseph I, 216
Fredro, 131
Freimann, 16
Frenkel, 146, 152, 197, 198, 200, 201, 218, 314, 387, 388, 399,
    418
Frenkl, 195
Frensler, 270
Freschel, 105
Freund, 209, 251, 252, 254, 255, 256, 419
Fried, 182, 199, 210, 252
Friedberg, 309, 315
Friedenstein, 321

Friedenthal, 115, 118, 119, 121, 310
Friedl, 314
Friedman, 149, 166, 167, 279, 343, 370, 386, 388, 400, 404
Fromowicz-Stiller, 388
Fruchtmann, 205
Frumkin, 279
Frydman, 297
Fuchs, 388, 419
Fuenn, 321
Führer, 211
Fuks, 403
Fuster, 168
Futernika, 297

G

Gabel, 254, 307
Gaisruck, 112, 114, 132
Gajowski, 32
Galiński, 312
Gall, 157, 179, 250, 262
Gallenberg, 115
Gambai, 46
Gamrat, 27
Ganhovsky, 315
Gans, 222
Gaon, 252
Gardliński, 55
Garfein, 195, 301
Garfinkel, 188
Garwawski, 28
Gawłowski, 51
Gebauer, 393, 394, 396, 397, 398, 405
Gehrzin, 110
Gelber, 1, 3, 191, 258, 292, 316, 317, 341
Gelbhaus, 207
German, 205
Gerschon, 269
Gerstenfeld, 362, 395, 399, 403
Gerstmann, 181
Geshuri, 275, 280
Gezl, 127
Gidzielczyk, 43
Giec, 56, 65, 227, 228
Gimpel, 291, 388, 415, 419
Ginsberg, 349, 382, 387, 399, 415, 416
Gizelt, 388
Glanz, 126, 195
Glanzer, 137, 142, 146, 242, 246, 258, 267, 269
Glaser, 199
Glasgall, 146
Globocnik, 371
Głowacki, 58
Goëss, 132
Goetz, 48, 65, 98, 227, 228, 307
Goldbaum, 142, 158, 170, 175
Goldberg, 18, 125, 141, 165, 179, 220, 269, 285, 312, 390
Goldenberg, 311
Goldenblum, 126
Goldfarb, 212
Goldhaber, 180
Goldman, 193, 198, 200, 202, 205, 207, 209, 210, 306, 309

Goldschmidt,, 151
Goldstaub, 179
Goldstein, 219, 252, 387
Goldstern, 145, 146
Goliger, 387
Goliger-Schapiro, 350
Golski, 19, 31
Gołuchowski, 156, 158, 164, 166, 167, 169, 171, 172, 177, 178, 181, 182, 184, 188, 189, 190, 191, 263, 269, 295, 301
Gombrycht, 43, 53, 55, 56, 297
Górska, 387
Gostmoski, 28
Gottfried, 415
Gottlieb, 138, 148, 182, 191, 197, 198, 199, 200, 201, 204, 208, 269
Grabscheid, 148, 170
Graetz, 318
Graf, 385, 389
Graiding, 119
Granowski, 80
Graupen, 224
Greiner, 373, 384, 409
Greiwer, 370, 371
Grek, 306
Griffel, 271, 388, 396
Grill, 264
Grin, 386, 399, 415
Gris, 403
Grodniewski, 388
Grodzicki, 60
Gross, 166
Grossmann, 311, 312
Grosswajer, 58, 67
Gruder, 148
Gruiński, 217, 218
Grün, 386, 399, 415
Grünbaum, 116, 118
Grünberg, 160, 245, 262, 266, 271, 314
Grüner, 194
Grünes, 146, 152
Grünfeld, 152, 159, 249
Grünspan, 288
Grünstein, 265
Grüss, 403
Grusshaber, 394, 412
Gryziecki, 187
Grzymek, 383, 384, 390, 394, 405, 406
Guardia, 8
Guenther, 408
Gułochowski, 181, 200, 250
Gumplowicz, 182, 184, 192, 322
Gunzenheusen, 117, 118
Gussman, 133, 141, 175
Guszałewycz, 189
Gutmann, 207, 209, 210, 251, 252, 253, 254, 255, 256
Gutwirth, 209, 244, 269, 403

H

Haan, 310
HaAzzati, 66
Haber, 179

Y

Z

Zyskint, 56